AMERICA IN ITALY

.

America in Italy

THE UNITED STATES IN THE POLITICAL THOUGHT AND IMAGINATION OF THE RISORGIMENTO, 1763–1865

Axel Körner

PRINCETON UNIVERSITY PRESS

PRINCETON & OXFORD

Published by Princeton University Press,
41 William Street, Princeton, New Jersey 08540

In the United Kingdom: Princeton University Press,
6 Oxford Street, Woodstock, Oxfordshire OX20 1TR

press.princeton.edu

Jacket art: Giovanni Battista Tiepolo, *Apollo and the Continents*, 1752–53, fresco,
1900 × 3050 cm. Stairwell of the Würzburg Residence © Bayerische Schlösserverwaltung,
Andreas Grindel, Schwarzach.

Library of Congress Cataloging-in-Publication Data

Names: Körner, Axel, 1967– author.
Title: America in Italy : the United States in the political thought and imagination of the
    Risorgimento, 1763–1865 / Axel Körner.
Description: Princeton : Princeton University Press, 2017. | Includes bibliographical
    references and index.
Identifiers: LCCN 2016035758 | ISBN 9780691164854 (hardback : acid-free paper)
Subjects: LCSH: Italy—Relations—United States. | United States—Relations—Italy. | United
    States—Foreign public opinion, Italian. | Italy—Politics and government—1789–1815.
    | Italy—Politics and government—1815–1870. | Political science—Italy—History—18th
    century. | Political science—Italy—History—19th century. | Intellectuals—Italy—
    History—18th century. | Intellectuals—Italy—History—19th century. | Italy—Intellectual
    life. | BISAC: HISTORY / Europe / Italy. | HISTORY / Americas (North, Central, South,
    West Indies). | POLITICAL SCIENCE / History & Theory. | POLITICAL SCIENCE /
    Government / International. | PHILOSOPHY / Political.
Classification: LCC DG499.U5 K67 2017 | DDC 320.94501—dc23
LC record available at https://lccn.loc.gov/2016035758

British Library Cataloging-in-Publication Data is available

This book has been composed in Miller

Printed on acid-free paper. ∞

Printed in the United States of America

10 9 8 7 6 5 4 3 2 1

Den Berliner Freunden

CONTENTS

PREFACE

WHAT DID EUROPEANS KNOW about colonial America and the United States? What role did the emergence of the new nation play in the old continent's political thought and in the cultural imagination that informed the European experience of societal change throughout the eighteenth and nineteenth centuries?

Ever since the Seven Years' War and the American Revolution, Europeans had taken a keen interest in the political and civic institutions that developed across the Atlantic. This widespread curiosity cannot be reduced to blind admiration. Many foreign observers were receptive to American ideas, but rather than being used as blueprints to fashion the political future, these ideas became the sounding board for the assessment of a wide range of political experiences at home. Contrary to views widely held in the United States, Europeans did not necessarily think that the United States had to teach them lessons. They were confident in relating what they observed in America to their own constitutional histories, often to note that things across the Atlantic were not just very different, but sometimes also objectionable. In America, utopia and dystopia seemed to live side by side. As a consequence, references to American political institutions became discursive instruments in complex political and societal debates, where the United States often served as a positive, but not infrequently also as a negative matrix. With reference to the United States, Europeans were able to support progressive as well as reactionary causes.

This is a book on Italian ideas about the United States, but not only. Almost always debates about the United States passed through multiple transnational channels, where information about America arrived from one country and was assessed with reference to a different national school of thought, to then influence political opinion in a third country. Italian authors writing about the American Revolution shaped French political thought during the Napoleonic period; English pamphlets were translated into French and then read in Milan, Florence, or Naples. The American constitution was compared to those of the United Provinces, Switzerland, or the Holy Roman Empire, and assessed against the experience of Italy's own medieval city republics as well as classical authors. Concepts derived from Montesquieu, Rousseau, or Vico served to evaluate what people discovered about the New World. What Europeans heard about the Americans' "domestic manners" was picked up in literature, became the object of operatic plots, or figured in political satire. Analyzing political ideas in relation to Italy's wider cultural imagination is one of this book's objectives.

In Italy awareness of political developments across the Atlantic dramatically increased at the time of the emerging conflict between Britain and its American colonies at the end of the Seven Years' War, coinciding with the spread of political ideas inspired by the European Enlightenment, in which Italian thinkers—Antonio Genovesi, Gaetano Filangieri, Cesare Beccaria, to name but a few—played a prominent (and sometimes underestimated) role. After 1789, and during the years of Napoleonic rule, what Italians knew about the American Republic informed discussions on the political reorganization of the peninsula and was then debated by the different factions of the nascent Italian national movement, as well as its opponents. This long period of engagement with American democracy assumed a very different character with Italy's political unification in 1861, which coincided with the outbreak of the American Civil War. The constitutional parameters of the Italian nation-state were suddenly set; and within the new political climate hitherto pro-American voices could hardly present a nation torn by civil war as a political model.

Until then, American experiences had helped to foster arguments in favor of federal solutions to Italy's national question, but also to assess the potential risks involved in such choices. Democratic Republicans as well as constitutional monarchists used the example of the United States to argue their case. Debates on slavery, and on its implications for the American constitution, resulted in critical reflections on the inner coherence of the Italian nation. Emphasizing the transnational flow of ideas, where references to the United States appear alongside pride in Italian republicanism and a keen interest in the Swiss model of federalism, my book questions concepts of center and periphery in global history, while also connecting cultural and intellectual history in novel ways. Italians' engagement with the United States shows how abstract political ideas were reflected in their cultural imagination during a period most Italians experienced as a dramatic moment of change in historical time.

The origins of this book go back to a collaborative research project at University College London, funded by the United Kingdom's Arts and Humanities Research Council (AHRC), investigating images of the United States in Europe and Latin America during the second half of the nineteenth century. My own research for this project started during a membership at the Institute for Advanced Study in Princeton, New Jersey, during which I became increasingly aware that Italian interest in the United States cannot be reduced to admiration for American modernity in the second half of the nineteenth century and the beginning of Italian mass migration to the United States around 1900. I therefore turned my attention to the eighteenth century, noticing that an increased engagement with the political and societal changes across the Atlantic predated the American Revolution to then accompany political debates in the Italian peninsula throughout the Risorgimento period.

Although this book moved a long way from the original collaborative AHRC project, many of its themes emerged from discussions with other

members of the team. The best sounding board for my work on eighteenth-
and nineteenth-century Italy has been the project's Latin American case study,
conducted by Nicola Miller. Nicola's friendship has been a source of immense
personal and intellectual support that reaches well beyond the work on this
book. The other collaborators on the project, Natalia Bas, Kate Ferris, Adam
Smith, and Maike Thier, made me acutely aware that many of the things I
discovered in Italy were "not normal," did not correspond to how Americans
saw themselves, or differed from perceptions of the United States elsewhere
in the world.

Over the years many academic institutions invited me to present aspects of
my project in seminars and at conferences, including the Max-Planck-Institut
for Human Development in Berlin; the Theater Biel-Solothurn in Switzerland; Brown University in Providence, Rhode Island; the Central European
University in Budapest; the Faculty of Music at the University of Cambridge;
the Institute of Historical Research and King's College London; the Institute
of the Americas at University College London; the Villa Vigoni in Loveno di
Menaggio; the Modern European History seminar at the University of Oxford;
the Arbeitsgemeinschaft Italien and the Universität des Saarlands; and Ca'
Foscari in Venice.

Numerous colleagues used these and other occasions to comment on aspects of my work or read subsequent versions of it: Wendy Bracewell, Lily
Chang, Gabriele Clemens, Michela Coletta, Christof Dipper, the late Christopher Duggan, James Dunkeley, Silvia Evangelisti, Ilaria Favretto, Carlotta Ferrara degli Uberti, Dina Gusejnova, Heinz Gerhard Haupt, Maurizio Isabella,
the late Tony Judt, Reinhard Kannonier, Daniel Laqua, Carl Levy, Adrian
Lyttelton, Maria Malatesta, Julia Mitchell, Sven Oliver Müller, Gilles Pécout,
Marta Petrusewicz, Lucy Riall, Donald Sassoon, Jens Späth, Suzanne Stewart-
Steinberg, Harry Stopes, Miles Taylor, Guy Thomas, and Georgios Varouxakis.

I am immensely grateful that they shared their thoughts with me. I received
many useful comments on my Inaugural Lecture at UCL, which then formed
the basis for chapter 4. David Laven encouraged me over many years, pointed
me to sources I had overlooked, and then read the entire manuscript. John
Davis listened to many of the stories I discovered and offered his journal to
sound some of them out. In order to write this book I had to retrain in both
early modern history as well as in aspects of American history, for which I
received much appreciated help from Christopher Abel, Kathy Burk, Stephen
Conway, Jonathan Israel, Ben Kaplan, and Avi Lifschitz. Richard Bourke
helped me to make sense of Italian responses to the writings of Edmund
Burke. Patrick Chorley introduced me to aspects of the Neapolitan Enlightenment I previously ignored. John North helped to shed light on classical references in my documents, while Antonio Sennis taught me an important lesson
in source criticism during the final stages of drafting the introduction. Amé-
lie Kuhrt and Edoardo Tortarolo offered useful advice on different aspects of

chapter 1. In Lugo di Romagna, Daniele Serafini and Marcello Savini helped me with my work on Giuseppe Compagnoni and with a poem by Carlo Cattaneo. Anne Bruch and Anna Maria Lazzarino Del Grosso shared with me their work on Carlo Cattaneo and Francesco Ferrara. Alessandro de Arcangelis and Simon MacDonald gave me numerous bibliographic references throughout my work on this book.

Invaluable was the encouragement I received from Anselm Gerhard and Roger Parker during my work on various operas discussed in my book, especially Giuseppe Verdi's *Un ballo in maschera*. I am particularly grateful for the information Anselm Gerhard provided on Verdi's library, reflected in chapters 3, 4, and 5. An important context of debate for my work on these chapters became an international network entitled "Re-imagining Italianità: Opera and Musical Culture in Transnational Perspective," sponsored by the Leverhulme Trust and hosted by the UCL Centre for Transnational History. To complete my work on the book's musical sections I relied on friendly support from Laura Basini, Marco Beghelli, Matilda Ann Butkas Ertz, Harriet Boyd, Fabrizio della Seta, Richard Erkens, Sarah Hibberd, Andrew Holden, Paulo Kühl, Valeria Lucentini, Vincenzina Ottomano, Laura Protano-Biggs, Susan Rutherford, Emilio Sala, Arman Schwartz, Emanuele Senici, Mary Ann Smart, Carlotta Sorba, Anna Tedesco, Jutta Toelle, Francesca Vella, Ben Walton, René Weis, Alexandra Wilson, and Flora Wilson. During the early stages of this project I was fortunate to get help from a number of very able research assistants: Daniel Cassidy, Federico Mazzini, Nicola Pizzolato, and Katharina Rietzler. At many stages my daughter Elsa stepped in with research and IT support. David Laven, Ivan Polancec, and Martin Thom did much to improve my prose.

Much of this book was written at the British Library, where I benefitted in particular from advice offered by curator Susan Reed. The friendly professionalism of the staff in the Manuscripts Room and in particular in Rare Books and Music made a real difference to my work. I am equally grateful to colleagues who helped my research at the Biblioteca dell'Archiginnasio and at the Archivio Storico Comunale in Bologna, the Biblioteca Malatestiana in Cesena, the Biblioteca Centrale in Florence, and Biblioteca Comunale "Aurelio Saffi" in Forlì; to Raffaella Ponte and Liliana Bertuzzi from the Istituto Mazziniani in Genoa; to Archivio storico della Città di Lugano; to staff at the New York Public Library of the Arts, the Remarque Centre and the Library of New York University, the library of the École Normale Supérieure in Paris, the Istituzione Casa della Musica in Parma, the Šternberský palác of the Národní gallerie in Prague, the Institute for Advanced Study and the Firestone Library at Princeton University, the Biblioteca Nazionale Centrale in Rome, the Hartley Library at the University of Southampton, and the Österreichische Nationalbibliothek and the Allgemeine Verwaltungsarchiv of the Österreichische Staatsarchiv in Vienna.

During the work on this book I was able to benefit from two periods of sabbatical leave granted by my department at University College London. I did some of my writing up in the peaceful surroundings of Perinaldo, a small town in the Ligurian mountains that enjoys its own very special outlook on the wider world. I am grateful to the *Journal of Modern History* and the *Journal of Modern Italian Studies* for allowing me to use material from previously published articles for chapters 4 and 5. Two anonymous reader reports from Princeton University Press did much to improve the final manuscript. Ever since Princeton University Press took an interest in this project, Ben Tate has been an immense source of advice and encouragement. When we started working together I was completely unaware that editors of his kind still exist in the modern world. I shall add my thanks to the team at Princeton University Press, where Kathleen Kageff, Sara Lerner, Hannah Paul, and other colleagues greatly impressed me with their professionalism and their friendly interest in my book.

It seems quite appropriate acknowledging Ben Tate just next to an expression of gratitude to my family for the enjoyment of doing much of my work surrounded by Lenka and Elsa, as well as Kaspar and Fridolin, who joined us halfway through the project. Figure 2 of this book, in the introduction, shows Giovanni Battista Tiepolo's ceiling fresco depicting the New World in the Residenz Würzburg. Shortly after arriving in the West, my parents celebrated their recently acquired freedom with a motor-scooter trip through southern Germany, during which they visited the Residenz, then severely damaged by the war. They got married shortly after. Lenka and I took a different approach, visiting the Residenz on the way back from our marriage in Prague, but with several children on the backbench of our car, to join my grandmother for her one-hundredth birthday. As the introduction will reveal, Tiepolo can tell readers much about my project, but his fresco also presents a link between four generations of my family.

The book is dedicated to all the friends I once left behind in Berlin and who kept supporting us for the past quarter of a century.

London, May 2016

A NOTE ON REFERENCES AND BIBLIOGRAPHY

ENDNOTES PROVIDE FULL REFERENCES for primary sources appearing for the first time. Thereafter I use an abbreviated form. Modern editions of primary sources and secondary sources appear in abbreviated form, with full references listed in the bibliography. Electronic publications appear in the notes only, with the exception of electronic journals. Full details of pamphlets and broadsheets appear in the notes only, with the relevant collections listed at the start of the bibliography.

Material from chapters 4 and 5 was previously published in "Uncle Tom on the Ballet Stage: Italy's Barbarous America, 1850–1900," *Journal of Modern History*, 83, 4 (December 2011), 721–52; and "Masked Faces: Verdi, Uncle Tom and the Unification of Italy," *Journal of Modern Italian Studies*, 18, 2, (March 2013), 176–89; as well as in different sections of *America Imagined: Explaining the United States in Nineteenth-Century Europe and Latin America* (Körner, Miller, and Smith, eds.), New York: Palgrave Macmillan, 2012.

AMERICA IN ITALY

Introduction

In order to have news the American only has to tell what he sees around himself.

—CARLO CATTANEO, 1855[1]

A White Canvas

Commenting on an allegorical drawing by Jan van der Straet depicting Amerigo Vespucci's arrival in the New World (1587), the philosopher Michel de Certeau explained how Europeans treated America as "a white (savage) canvas on which to inscribe Western desire."[2] Europeans wrote the New World and saw in it what they wanted to see in order to make sense of their own changing world.

For several centuries after the discovery of the Americas philosophers and artists continued to be inspired by the societal myths associated with the New World's natural otherness.[3] Many thinkers of the Enlightenment used the little they knew about America in ways similar to those suggested by de Certeau: the Marquis de Condorcet, Hector Saint Jean de Crèvecœur, Jacques-Pierre Brissot, or the Baron La Hontan. Robert Darnton called this phenomenon "Americanized Rousseauism," where America became the stage for societal experiments inspired by the ideas of Jean-Jacques Rousseau, as a land far from corrupting civilization, where equal people in woollen dress invent brilliant laws.[4]

In addition to animating philosophical treatises and academic works on human geography, the societal myths associated with the New World were also discussed in periodicals and encyclopedias, which were more widely accessible. They often featured in poems, opera libretti, and choreographies (*libretti da ballo*), where they reached nonscholarly audiences. While many of these sources reflect sympathetic curiosity toward the New World, they also pay

FIG. 1. Jan van der Straet, called Stradanus (Netherlandish, Bruges 1523–1605 Florence), *Discovery of America: Vespucci Landing in America* (1587). Metropolitan Museum of Art, New York (Gift of Estate of James Hazen Hyde, 1959). www.metmuseum.org.

witness to a sharp distinction between civilization and the absence thereof. In the case of the Italian sources explored in this book, they demonstrate that the New World did not necessarily appeal to the self-conscious bearers of the Mediterranean's millenary civilizations.[5]

In 1784 King Gustav III of Sweden visited Italy, an episode to which I will briefly return in chapter 4. On the occasion of this official state visit, the Venetian Republic honored the Swedish monarch with the organization of an international regatta. A boat representing "gl'americani" featured "savages" with feathers and skirts, a mixture of Incas and Aztecs.[6] The Venetians' picturesque representation of the New World hardly differed from the far more famous one by another Venetian, the painter Giovanni Battista Tiepolo. Working with two of his sons and a small colony of Italian artisans, in the early 1750s Tiepolo had produced the world's largest continuous ceiling fresco for the Residence of the Prince-Elector of Würzburg, one of the greatest examples of eighteenth-century art. Representing the world in four continents, the painting's architectural frame is such that it can never be seen as a whole, in the same way as the globe can never be seen as a whole.[7] Any visitor ascending the palace's monumental staircase is first confronted with Tiepolo's depiction of America, the only continent visible already from the foot of the stairs.

Portrayed within a picturesque tropical setting, the continent's human species looks as exotic as the wild animals at their side.[8] Tiepolo's America is

FIG. 2. Giovanni Battista Tiepolo, ceiling fresco, Residenz Würzburg,
Treppenhaus (1753). Image courtesy Schloss- und Gartenverwaltung
Würzburg / Bayerische Schlösserverwaltung. Picture reference:
Bayerische Schlösserverwaltung, Andreas Grindel, Schwarzach.

characterized by the absence of the most basic markers of civilization. There
are no buildings, only basic signs of industry or the art of writing. The severed
human heads in the foreground of Tiepolo's fresco pay witness to the continent's alleged habit of living on human flesh, only rendered more gruesome
by the scene to the right, which shows four men roasting a large piece of meat
on a spit. This idea can be traced back to the early sixteenth-century prints
illustrating editions of Amerigo Vespucci's letters, which were unashamed in
depicting naked savages chopping up human limbs and urinating in public.[9]

Tiepolo's emphasis on the New World's savage otherness was not the idea
of an artist removed from the academic debates of his day. Writing in 1757,
the Neapolitan economist and philosopher Antonio Genovesi was convinced
that Native Americans were unable to "count to three," despite the fact that
by that time Native tribeshad been trading with European settlers for several
centuries.[10] The widely read *Relationi Universali* by the Piedmontese geog-
rapher Giovanni Botero, first published in Rome in the 1590s and still used
as a source by Italian writers in the late eighteenth century, summed up the
fundamental differences between the humans of both hemispheres: "Not verie
well favoured, but of savage and brutish behaviours, excellent footmen and
swimmers, cleanly in their bodies, naked, libidinous, and men eaters. Some
worship the divell, some Idols, some the Sunne, and some the Stars."[11]

These widely read comments notwithstanding, by choosing to accentuate
the "man eaters," Tiepolo's America goes beyond what most authors during
the mid-eighteenth century were writing about the New World: a painting
can express thoughts most commentators at the time would hesitate to put
into words.

Tiepolo composed the painting so that the American continent never receives much natural light—less than any of the other continents depicted;
and a huge black cloud hangs over the scene. Art historians have compared
Tiepolo's fresco to a stage set, which plays on popular representations of the

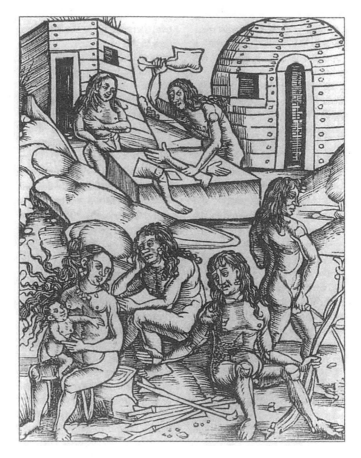

FIG. 3. Illustration from Vespucci's letter to Soderini (Strassburg, 1509). Image from https://commons.wikimedia.org/wiki /File:Cannibalism_in_the_New_World_(1509).jpg.

New World in contemporary theater.[12] Contrasting with de Certeau's reference to America as almost completely invented by European men of letters, Tiepolo evokes empirical authenticity. A European dressed in a long coat and with Cracow shoes, fashionable in the fifteenth century, is creeping toward the cannibals, hiding behind his canvas to observe the scene, as if intending to capture what he sees in a painting. Empirical observation became an important new feature of eighteenth-century representations of the New World.

The images of America discussed in the preceding paragraphs demonstrate the extent to which Europeans, shortly before the American Revolution, still thought of the New World in terms of the absence of civilization.[13] Deciding to stage these strong images in the palace of a prince-bishop, in Italy's magnificent theaters, or in front of the panorama of the Grand Canal in Venice, the contrast between civilization and its absence could not be more striking.

The practice of representing Native Americans as savages (often equipped with considerable erotic appeal) and placed in a wild, empty environment, survived even into the early nineteenth century, when steamships and railways started to connect most states of the northern Republic. They still influenced a thinker like Carlo Cattaneo, protagonist of Milan's 1848 revolution and one of Italy's foremost contemporary experts on the US constitution. In an erotic poem of the early 1830s, he compares the body of a female Native American to the classical image of Venus rising from the sea:

Americana

Venìa leggiera come piuma; il braccio
Ritonda e il petto e il fianco, e dolcemente
Sottile al mobil collo e alla cintura.
Nera il crin, nera gli occhi. E come sorge
Nella sale de' re di fulvo bronzo
Nuda Venere antica; o come appare
Allo sposo che immoto alla finestra
Miro' la smorta luna e sazio alfine
Si volse indietro, in la secreta stanza
Al greve lume d'una fioca lampa
La vaga sposa che dal casto letto
Nuda il petto s'eleva e sulla culla
Del sorridente bambolo s'incurva
Tutta suffusa di rosso chiarore:
Tale un color su quelle lisce forme
Il cielo americano indotto avea.[14]

Cattaneo's poem refers to a style of poetic allegories of America common in the late eighteenth century.[15] Still playing with ideas evoking Tiepolo's fresco, in the early 1840s Cattaneo described the "unexplored lands, which bear only the first indicators of civic life among scattered tribes, who live in perpetual cruelty, possibly still feeding themselves on human flesh. . . . What an immense void to fill, those lands!"[16] America was largely empty, populated by cannibals, and poor. Similar images still appear in Italian debates about slavery and the American Civil War, discussed in the book's final chapter. A history of political thought investigating the Risorgimento's relationship to the United States has to take account of this wider cultural context of references and associations.

This initial discussion of Italian images of America sets the scene for a long introduction. Owing to the specific thematic structure of the following five chapters, the introduction will present the main source materials used throughout the book. These range from early Italian histories of the American Republic to philosophical and political writings, from parliamentary documents to memoirs and correspondence, including literature and representations of America on stage. Roughly organized along chronological lines, the following chapters cover the period between the end of the Seven Years' War in the early 1760s and the American Civil War a century later, which coincided with the Unification of Italy under the crown of Savoy.

Chapter 1, on early Italian histories of the American War of Independence, compares the context in which these works were created to the changing responses they generated during the later course of the Risorgimento. The works of Botta, Londonio, and Compagnoni offer examples of three different historiographical approaches to the early history of the United States. With a focus on concepts such as constitutional government, representation, and federalism, chapter 2 analyzes references to the United States in the Risorgimento's political language. The works of Giuseppe Mazzini, as well as those of a wide range of other prominent political thinkers including Cesare Balbo, Vincenzo Gioberti, Gian Domenico Romagnosi, and Antonio Rosmini, used the United States as a matrix to discuss Italy's present and future political institutions. Based on case studies of Lombardy, Tuscany, and Sicily, chapter 3 examines the ways in which protagonists of the Italian Revolutions of 1848 engaged with American political institutions. Because historical and constitutional experiences varied greatly across the peninsula in 1848, they discussed the United States with very different emphasis, illustrating how references to the United States could serve very different ideological purposes. Moreover, chapter 3 demonstrates how wrong it would be to assume that European revolutionaries necessarily had to look across the Atlantic to conduct their constitutional debates. The short-lived republic in Florence is point in case. Despite Tuscany's long history of engagement with the United States, we find far fewer references to American political institutions than for instance in Sicily, where the revolutionaries adopted a monarchical constitution.

The book's final two chapters move the focus of analysis into a different direction, looking at resonances of engagement with American political institutions in the cultural imagination of Italians around the time of their nation's unification. This analysis will start from an examination of contemporary debates around two hugely influential stage works. Chapter 4 analyzes the creation of Giuseppe Verdi's American opera *Un ballo in maschera*, first performed around the time of Italy's Second War of Independence, in 1859. After a number of works dating back to the eighteenth century, Verdi's new work was the first modern Italian opera set across the Atlantic. The history of the work's creation and the subsequent debate around *Un ballo in maschera* demonstrate that the New World still served to negotiate perceptions of otherness. Closely related to chapter 4, the book's fifth and final chapter examines the Italian reception of Giuseppe Rota's ballet *Bianchi e Neri*, based on Harriet Beecher Stowe's celebrated novel *Uncle Tom's Cabin*. Among the most frequently performed ballets in nineteenth-century Italy—and often staged in connection with Verdi's *Un ballo*—the work inspired comments that reveal the passion with which Italians engaged with issues such as race and slavery across the Atlantic. The debate on the ballet had an important impact on Italian responses to the unfolding American Civil War, which coincided with Italy's own civil war in the South.

The book's main argument holds that Italian ideas of the United States during the period of the Risorgimento cannot be reduced to blind admiration for America's political experiments. Contrary to widely held views among American observers of the Risorgimento, which still inform a good deal of transatlantic historiography today, Italians largely abstained from treating recent American history as a blueprint for their own struggle for independence. Instead, Italians engaged with what they knew about the early Republic in relation to their own constitutional history, as well as to a whole range of different European experiences. During that process, different ideological factions of Italy's national movement, as well as its opponents, used references to the United States to achieve a variety of political objectives. Emphasizing the transnational flow of ideas, my book questions concepts of center and periphery in global history, while also connecting cultural and intellectual history in novel ways, thus demonstrating how abstract political ideas were reflected in Italians' wider cultural imagination.[17]

Where, When, and What Was America?

In 1814 two of Italy's most influential publicists, the Italianized Genevan historian Jean-Charles Léonard de Sismondi and the publisher Giovan Pietro Vieusseux, also of Genevan origin, lamented "un pays où l'on ne lit pas," a country where people don't read.[18] Likewise Ugo Foscolo, writing in 1824, complained that "compared to other European peoples, the Italians do not take the same pleasure from reading."[19] While complaints such as these might explain Italians' often rather unrealistic views of the United States, they cannot be taken as statements of facts. It is more likely that they express a deeply felt need for more public debate, debate to take account of the epochal changes associated with the American and French Revolutions. Although the Napoleonic regime and the Restoration period imposed limitations on the availability of certain books, geographical and philosophical works (as well as periodicals with reviews of such works) circulated widely among the educated elites and frequently crossed the peninsula's internal borders. That Italians knew relatively little about the North American Republic had more to do with the fact that—compared to Britain, France, and Spain—the transatlantic world mattered far less to Italians, whose economic and intellectual connections were tied to the Habsburg monarchy and the German states, the Adriatic, France, and to some extent England.

While Italian navigators and explorers played a crucial part in the discovery of the New World, they left the systematic colonization of the continent

to the powerful monarchies of Spain, France, and England. The governments
of the Italian states frequently intervened to hinder their subjects from emi-
grating to America.[20] Only a small number of Italians achieved significant
roles in transatlantic trade or in missionary activity during the seventeenth
and eighteenth centuries. The formation of a Catholic Church in the British
colonies remained mainly the work of Irish immigrants. "In the vast territories
of that New World, discovered by an Italian, among all the nations of Europe
only the Italians have no settlements, and at no point did a sizable number
of Italians decide to move there," the Italian translator of the *History of the
European Settlements in America* complained in 1762, a book by Edmund and
William Burke.[21] Even basic geographical information continued to be rather
sketchy. Were one to believe Niccolò Piccini's immensely popular opera *I napoletani in America* (1768), the libretto's action took place "between Florida
and Virginia, where the immense deserts of Canada are located."[22] Judging
from a comparison of geographical studies and maps circulating in Italy during the seventeenth and eighteenth centuries, Piero del Negro comes to the
conclusion that America was the continent about which Italians knew the
least, and certainly less than about Asia and Africa.[23] In many geographical
surveys there is no mention at all of the English colonies, or they are listed as
part of French Canada. According to Giorgio Spini, an important reason for
the lack of knowledge about North America was the "Iron Curtain" that the
Counterreformation had erected between Catholic Italy and the Protestant
world, along with the decline of the peninsula's role in global trade.[24] As a
consequence, Italians were more likely to read works about Latin America. In
the case of the seafaring Italians from the Venetian Republic, their interest in
Latin America was often motivated by polemical confrontation between their
republican pride and the Spanish monarchy.[25]

Patterns of migration also explain Italians' limited knowledge about North
America. Instead of debating migration from the perspective of American
domestic politics, Donna Gabaccia has argued for an emphasis on "transnational linkages" between America and different parts of the world, created
"from below" by immigrants.[26] Within such a perspective, chronology is key
to a better understanding of connections. Italians increasingly had "foreign
relations" (to employ Gabaccia's use of the term), but before the end of the
nineteenth century relatively few of them resided in the United States. Even
at the time of Unification, Italians were still more likely to emigrate to other
European countries or to Latin America than to chose the United States. New
Jersey was among the states of the Union Italians knew best, but according to
the census of 1860 it counted only 106 residents born in Italy (among a rapidly
growing population of over 672,000).[27] Between 1820 and 1860 not more than
13,792 people had left the Italian peninsula for the United States, of whom
many returned after relatively short spells in the New World. During the following decade (1861–70) 99,272 Italians migrated within Europe, compared to

21,768 choosing a non-European country, still predominantly Latin America. The huge wave of Italian emigration to the United States started only during the first decade of the twentieth century, when numbers reached 232,945.[28] Meanwhile, very few Americans traveled to Italy as part of a Grand Tour or decided to settle there on a permanent basis.[29]

Despite this relative lack of direct contact, what fascinated Italians about the early American Republic was the idea of the country as a metaphor for the rapid transformation of the modern age. The motto by Cattaneo, quoted at the start of this introduction, pays witness to this idea: in America everything was new; and the new was the closest one could get to the future.[30] Writing in Vieusseux's influential *Antologia*, Michele Leoni claimed in 1822 that Americans operated with a different mode of time, where social relations "every day take a different outlook."[31] Carlo Giuseppe Londonio, discussed in more detail in chapter 1, argued that the speed with which the former colonies reached prosperity "is enough to turn their history into an interesting topic for the philosopher."[32] Meanwhile, he also mentions Americans' widespread "timore delle future," the fear of futures (in the plural), suggesting an undetermined openness of future time.[33] According to Londonio, when Americans broke with their mother country, they decided to step out of their own present and left their history behind, but their future remained unknown, a frequent source of anxiety. While as a matter of fact relatively few immigrants left their histories behind completely, Londonio's understanding of a semantic shift in time is reflective of Italians' perceptions of transcontinental experiences.

Commenting on the perceived change in the semantic of historical time across the Atlantic helped Italians to negotiate their own experience of change after the French Revolution. In doing so, they took reassurance from the fact that they perceived their own future as less open. Most Italians saw their nation as the descendant of an ancient civilization—a term discussed in more detail in chapters 2 and 4. They were proud of their nation's past, whatever had gone wrong with it as a result of adverse circumstances. As a consequence, they had little reason to blindly endorse the uncertain future of a foreign country across the ocean. Italians were fully aware of modernity's accelerated pace of time, reflected in the political turmoil associated with the French Revolution and their own nation's Risorgimento; but they negotiated their present and future in relation to a proud past as well as foreign experiences.

European Exchanges

An important step toward greater appreciation of the New World was the bestseller of 1770 *Histoire philosophique et politique des deux Indes* by the Abbé Guillaume Thomas de Raynal. Coauthored by Diderot and immediately placed on the register, the book circulated widely in various French and

FIG. 4. Guillaume Thomas Raynal, frontispiece from his *Histoire philosophique et politique des établissements et du commerce des Européens dans les deux Indes*. Geneva: Pellet, 1780.

Italian editions; extracts and reviews appeared in numerous periodicals. As the following chapters will show, it is one of the books most frequently quoted in Italian debates on America, though mostly in terms of general references, without attempts at a more detailed discussion of Raynal's theses. Commenting on Raynal's depiction of European atrocities and the "barbarism of the 'civilized,'" Jonathan Israel described the work as "the Radical Enlightenment's—indeed the whole Enlightenment's—most devastating single blow to the existing order."[34] While making commendable exceptions for Pennsylvania, Raynal presented the North American colonies—puritanical, hierarchical, with an economy largely based on slavery—in a remarkably critical light.

A revised extract of Raynal's book appeared in 1781 as *The Revolution of America*.[35] Its political potential was world shattering: "Forget not that . . . the power of those who govern is in reality but the power of those who suffer government," Raynal claimed in the introduction.[36] Like its prequel, *The Revolution of America* immediately generated much sympathy for the rebels, while also urging them to establish a more equal and humane society: "fear the affluence of gold, which brings with luxury the corruption of manners, the contempt of laws. Fear a too unequal distribution of riches, which exhibits a small number of citizens in opulence, and a great multitude of citizens in extreme poverty; whence springs the insolence of the former, and the debasement of the latter. Secure yourselves against the spirit of conquest. The tranquillity of an Empire diminishes in proportion to its extension. Have arms for your defence; have none for offence."[37] Raynal's warnings about the Americans' materialism and their expansionist ambition was to become a major theme for Italian commentators on the United States, most prominently among them Mazzini.

Many of the *philosophes* Italians read during the second half of the eighteenth century had met Americans in Paris, but few of them ever set foot in the New World. Written ten years after the Declaration of Independence, Condorcet's *De l'influence de la révolution d'Amérique sur l'Europe* has often been read as praise for a model of society that embodied the Enlightenment principles of liberty and progress, allowing natural man to achieve material prosperity alongside political freedom and equality. These claims notwithstanding, *De l'influence* remains surprisingly abstract; and Robert Darnton has characterized it as a "fantasy," bearing little relation to the new nation across the Atlantic.[38] While Condorcet had met several revolutionaries in person, including Benjamin Franklin, Thomas Jefferson, and Thomas Paine, he never traveled much beyond Paris nor did he visit America. He was made an honorary citizen of New Haven, Connecticut, but John Adams considered him "ignorant, totally ignorant of all Writings on the Science of Government, with very little knowledge of the Human Heart and still less of the World."[39]

In his better-known work on human progress Condorcet's main objective was to explain the temporal dynamic of the American Revolution, how it occurred in response to Britain's denial of Americans' natural rights. As for the Revolution's "influence" on Europe, Condorcet largely reduced it to its impact on French trade.[40] Thus a note of caution seems necessary before employing Condorcet's *De l'influence* for arguments on the American Revolution's wider repercussions. Moreover, important aspects of American democracy contradicted Condorcet's own political principles. He was profoundly hostile to any form of organized religion, and, like Lafayette, he was an outspoken opponent of slavery, prohibited at the time only in New England and in Pennsylvania. Despite Condorcet's immense role as architect of the constitution of 1793, his political thought hardly survived his death.[41] He knew Beccaria; and with the help of his wife he had translated Filippo Mazzei's important manuscript on the United States into French. But few Italians were aware of Condorcet's philosophical works.

While some of the early French books on America mentioned above included credible ethnographies and reliable accounts of political events, Europeans had to wait for authors such as Filippo Mazzei, an advisor to the Grand Duke of Tuscany, Pietro Leopoldo, to receive a less idealistic, more rational and also more useable account of life in the American Republic.[42] In addition to purely descriptive ethnographies, knowledge of American agriculture and its relevance for Europe became more widely available shortly before the American Revolution; and more French and English books appeared in Italian translation.[43] The French legal scholar Jacques-Vincent de la Croix (1743–1832) was more specific on American political institutions than Condorcet, adding two chapters on the American War of Independence and the United States' early constitutional development to his work on comparative constitutional history.[44] First published in 1791, his book included a *Catéchisme patriotique à l'usage de tous le citoyens français*, meant to be of particular pedagogical value for the French legislators of the revolutionary period.[45] Although Italian authors rarely mentioned the work, it appeared in several editions and translations and was well known beyond academic readers.

The following chapters take account of French and British debates about the North American colonies, of authors like Diderot and Edmund Burke, where they directly shaped Italian political thought. For instance, Italian authors frequently referred to the Abbé Raynal; and Rousseau's ideas were brought up in discussions about American freedom, although the *citoyen de Genève* was so famous that he did not need to be named, let alone be discussed in any great detail.[46] Meanwhile, Louis-Sébastien Mercier was well known in England and the Netherlands, but rarely mentioned in Italy. Similarly, Mary Wollstonecraft's ideas were deeply influenced by debates about American freedom and by her acquaintance with Thomas Paine; but very few Italians seemed to have been aware of her writings.[47] The same is true for the two volumes on American society by Harriet Martineau, despite her contacts with Italian exiles.[48] Many of the authors discussed in the following chapters knew William Robertson's *History of America*, which informed their thinking on the relationship between barbarism and civilization, but because his narrative was then interrupted by the Anglo-American war, his main arguments were less relevant to their interest in North American political institutions. Some Italian political thinkers, including Mazzei and Botta, commented on American developments from the perspective of their involvement in French political events, as a consequence of the peninsula's political turmoil in the wake of 1792.

While Guizot and Tocqueville generated ample interest among Italian commentators, Michel Chevalier, who published his *Lettres sur l'Amérique du Nord* in 1836, influenced the Sicilian economist Francesco Ferrara but was less well known among the other Italian commentators on the United States.[49] One of the reasons for this selective approach to foreign books on America is the fact that as the nineteenth century progressed educated Italians were able to rely on a much wider range of Italian authors and Italian-language texts, as well as on ideas derived from American literature and literature about the North American Republic.

Transatlantic Connections

There exists no nation, as long as it has a fleet, that is so far from any other nation of this world that it is not at the same time also always close to this nation.

—ANTONIO GENOVESI, 1757[50]

Italians' awareness of the Western Hemisphere increased considerably during the Seven Years' War, which took place between 1756 and 1763, involving most of the world's great powers and affecting Europe, the Americas, and parts of Africa and Asia. The Italian states stayed out of this conflict and enjoyed an unusually long period of peace, which lasted from the Treaty of Aachen in 1748 to the French Revolution.[51] Commercial and diplomatic relations benefitted from this "mezzo secolo di pace," as Franco Venturi described the period.[52] For instance, in his pioneering study of the eighteenth-century Neapolitan economy Patrick Chorley demonstrated how growing foreign demand provided the impulse for the economic revival of the southern kingdom's coastal areas; in particular the demand for olives, mulberries (for silk), almonds, and vines.[53] This renewed economic activity was also a response to Naples's terrible famine of 1764, which led Antonio Genovesi to dedicate most of his subsequent writings to the revival of commerce.[54] The result was a new outlook on the world, which now included the Americas.

The end of the American War of Independence led to diplomatic relations with the new Republic and facilitated trade, followed by a new wave of cultural exchanges. Franklin's work on electricity constitutes a particularly prominent example of transnational exchange, picked up in Italy by Beccaria as well as by the world's first female university professor, Laura Bassi, in Bologna, and by the Italian physicist Giuseppe Toaldo.[55] As early as 1784 the United States sought to sign commercial treaties with the Kingdom of Naples. After early negotiations remained inconclusive, a first American consul was accredited in Naples in 1796, although it took until 1825 for Naples to send a consul to the United States. Since 1802 the US government had exchanged consuls with Sicily, then under British protection, and by 1805 it had consuls in several of the island's cities.[56] The Kingdom of Piedmont-Sardinia opened its first representation in the United States in 1817, in Savannah, Georgia, followed two years later by a consulate in Philadelphia. After the acquisition of the former Republic of Genoa, with its important international trading ports, the state's diplomatic relations were strongly driven by economic motives. A rare and detailed report of 1822 by the kingdom's consul in Philadelphia offers ample insights into this commercial relationship, from the American interest in wine and silk to Piedmont's need for cotton and tobacco, also signaling potential for future mercantile expansion.[57] Although American periodicals sympathized with the beginnings of the Italian national movement, official relations between the governments of Piedmont-Sardinia and the United States remained friendly throughout the period of the Risorgimento. The Monroe Doctrine of 1823 meant that the United States would not interfere in Italy's internal affairs.[58] Yet, there were exceptions. After the execution of the patriotic priest Ugo Bassi in August 1849, the pontiff's legate to the United States was expelled.[59] American diplomats increasingly encouraged the Department of State to adopt an "Italian policy," recognizing the role the Sabaudian monarchy would play in the process of Unification.[60] For Americans, an important source of information on political developments in Italy up to 1849 was Margaret Fuller, the Boston journalist reporting from Italy for the *New York Tribune*. Meanwhile, Fuller impressed Italians with her image of the new nation's professional women.

American interest in the Risorgimento not only served altruistic purposes: Young America, modeled on Mazzini's Young Italy, was founded in 1845 to propagate an aggressive expansionist nationalism, reflecting the United States' "manifest destiny." Mazzini's concept of a nation's "mission" was applied here to justify the United States' aspiring hegemony on a global scale, "democratizing" and "civilizing" other people according to the United States' own ideals.[61] The movement was later absorbed into the Democratic Party and sometimes described as the party's "radical fringe."[62] Americans' interest in the peninsula's political developments not only provoked sour reactions in Vienna; in turn it led many protagonists in the Risorgimento to take a more pronounced interest in American history, its politics, and its constitutional development. Early on the Italian national movement recognized in the United States a potential ally, but also a profoundly different country. As further discussed in chapter 5, the United States was among the first states to recognize the Kingdom of Italy. By 1864, American history had become sufficiently important for the Italian Ministry of Foreign Affairs to introduce it into the program for the exams of future diplomats.[63]

An important example of exchange across the Atlantic were contacts between American and Italian Protestants. A miniscule grouping forced into a largely sectarian existence, the Valdesi (Waldensians) were mostly found in parts of Piedmont. Although brutally persecuted by the dukes of Savoy and the kings of France during most of the early modern period, at specific junctures they served their governments as a political and military ally, granting them a position to exercise a certain degree of influence on Italian diplomacy.[64] Italian Protestants maintained close connections with Protestant communities and established churches abroad. A small community of them had settled in Delaware during the seventeenth century, where American Puritans saw them as martyrs, comparing their destiny to that of the people of Israel. Among the first Italian books translated in the United States was a Protestant hagiography, Niccolò Balbani's *Istoria della vita di Galeazzo Caracciolo* (1751), published under the title *The Italian Convert*. The first American book about Italy was Joseph Sansom's *Letters from Europe during a Tour through Switzerland and Italy* (Philadelphia, 1805), which gave an important impetus to American *filovaldismo*.[65]

In turn, for many Italian Protestants, Calvinist tradition and Enlightenment became almost synonymous, explaining the prominent role of Geneva in the development of Italian liberal thought, exemplified by the circle around Madame de Staël, by Sismondi, Pestalozzi, and Vieusseux.[66] Vieusseux's *Antologia* became an important forum of discussion about the American Republic, while continuing to represent a moderate voice in Risorgimento debates, which kept a clear distance from radical republican ideas.[67] The publisher's *Gabinetto di lettura* in Florence was a meeting place for intellectuals from both sides of the Atlantic. These transnational contacts played a significant role in challenging the idealized legacies of eighteenth-century images of America. For instance, since 1813 the Franco-American Quaker Etienne de Grellet had used a Waldensian hostel in Geneva to propagate his pacifist-abolitionist ideas, pointing his listeners—among them many Italian Protestants—to the persisting contradictions within the American constitution.[68]

In contrast to Vieusseux's cautious approach, the Risorgimento's engagement with American Protestantism also gave birth to more radical forms of political thought. Through the American section of Young Italy Mazzini established connections with American Protestants who shared his hostility toward the papacy.[69] Quirico Filopanti, secretary general of Mazzini's Roman Republic in 1849 and a prominent member of the Italian exile community in London, developed a theory of theocratic dominion, where the protestant nations progressed, while the Papal States in Italy and Latin America fell behind, owing to the negative impact of Catholicism on education and science in those regions.[70] Observers in the United States often described Giuseppe Garibaldi as a man of Protestant virtue, with some going so far as to convince themselves that Italy was turning into a Protestant nation.[71] Theodore Dwight, of the American Philo-Italian Society, had met Garibaldi during his exile in New York. Seeing him as "both a theologian and statesman," he was convinced that divine providence had chosen Italians to play a leading part in the prophesies of the Bible.[72] Like the American and Foreign Bible Society and the Foreign Evangelical Society, Dwight's organization actively pursued the evangelization of Italy. After 1849 the American Embassy in Rome continued to hold Episcopalian services. When the papal government prohibited these in 1851, Protestant organizations in the United States requested a break in diplomatic relations with the Papal States.[73]

While drawing on their financial and moral support, Mazzini was aware that open contact with American Protestant organizations risked compromising his movement in the eyes of many Italians, making his insurgencies appear to be driven by foreign interests.[74] Maintaining a strong aversion to Protestantism throughout his life, Mazzini realized that organizations such as the Christian Alliance were politically too conservative to meet his own political agenda. Moreover, by that time nativist American Protestants resented the influx and influence of Catholic Europeans, seen as poisoning transatlantic relationships.[75]

America's Place on the Risorgimento's Map

Italians related debates about their country's future not only to the American present, but also to a much wider context of political, historical, and cultural comparisons. Nineteenth-century periodicals devoted a great deal of space to travel and the discussion of foreign countries. Any analysis of Italian ideas about America has to take account of the fact that interest in the United States always went with a much broader trend of curiosity about foreign cultures. For instance, the American Revolution was often discussed in connection with the French. Cattaneo's federal thought made frequent references to Switzerland and to the constitutions of the Holy Roman and Austrian Empires. Giuseppe Compagnoni, one of Italy's major historians of America, who is discussed in chapter 1, also wrote multivolume scholarly works on Russia, on the Ottoman Empire, and on the Tatars. Furthermore, there are many places where the historian would expect discussion of American political institutions but is struck by the absence of the United States.

John H. Elliot has warned that "any examination of European history in the light of an external influence upon it, carries with it the temptation to see traces of this influence everywhere. But the absence of influence is often at least as revealing as its presence."[76] Consequently, the main reason for writing this book is not that Italians, during the Risorgimento period, constantly referred to the United States. Where they reflected on American experiences, their assessment of what these experiences meant tends to vary according to specific political circumstances. Usually, these references are used as discursive instruments within a wide range of political debates. Disregard for the United States was also the consequence of the Atlantic World's still rather peripheral role in intellectual debate compared to the rich cultural heritage on which Italians could draw at home. This peripheral role is also underlined by Christopher Bayly's *The Birth of the Modern World*, in which the American Revolution plays an almost insignificant role.[77] Bayly's view puts the Atlantic history project into global perspective; but it also suggests that the more Eurocentric approach informing Hobsbawm's idea of a "dual revolution," one "industrial" the other "French," retains a place in explaining the modern world.[78]

It makes little sense to separate Italian debates about the American Revolution from those about the French Revolution. For instance, Paine and Brissot emphasized the two revolutions' common roots and purpose, prompting a historiographical tradition, perhaps most famously represented by R. R. Palmer's *Age of Democratic Revolution*, which speaks of one big revolutionary tide reaching both sides of the Atlantic.[79] Challenging historiographical conventions associated with this tradition, Richard Whatmore has argued that an important strand of political thought welcomed the North American colonies' struggle for independence, while condemning the French Revolution's radical republicanism, which had resulted in a war on monarchy and religion. Most famously among these thinkers was Edmund Burke, who distinguished "between the events in America he had supported, and those in France he had condemned."[80] In most of these comparisons, the American Revolution's defining principle was in effect not its republicanism. Identifying differences between both revolutions—as they emerge for instance from a comparison between Botta's *History of the American War of Independence* (1809) and his *History of Italy, 1789–1814* (1824)—frequently resulted in a condemnation of democratic republicanism, which in the case of North America was reduced to the natural consequence of the country's independence from Britain, with no ideological roots in the Old World's political development.

To make things more complicated, condemnation of the French Revolution did not automatically mean endorsement of the American. While demonstrating a great deal of interest in the American experiment, many Italians were conscious of the fact that the conditions under which democratic republicanism had emerged in the United States would never apply to their situation at home. As a consequence, the Milanese patriot Giorgio Pallavicini, who had been involved in the Revolutions of 1820 and subsequently spent many years in Austrian prisons, recommended to Italians the constitutional monarchies of Belgium and Greece as alternatives to French republicanism.[81] Owing to widespread Italian disillusionment with the results of the French Revolution, few accepted Thomas Paine's analysis that presented American and French republicanism as almost identical. Moreover, originally positive assessments of the American Revolution, still prevailing during the earlier years of the Risorgimento, were increasingly tainted by the idea that certain aspects of American democracy, such as its federalism, would not provide a solution to Italy's own constitutional problems. Perceived cultural differences reinforced doubts about the American Republic. For instance, the thought of the Savoyard philosopher Joseph de Maistre displays strong prejudice against America. Although his attitude to the United States was certainly not representative of North Italian intellectuals as a whole, he held that "America is often cited by us: I know nothing so provoking as the praise showered on this babe-in-arms: let it grow. . . . Weakness and decay could not be better combined."[82]

Emiliana P. Noether, who in an edited collection of essays celebrates the impact of the American constitution on Italy, concedes that only a small intellectual elite of Italians seriously considered the United States when discussing the future of Italy.[83] They read about the federal constitution, but knew very little about the constitutions of individual states. While the United States offered important points of reference in political debates, Italians did not look for blueprints abroad and were far from considering the implementation of foreign models when discussing their liberal and constitutional demands.

The idea of a division of the world in two parts—dividing progressive, modern countries from retrograde, oppressive regimes—was far from political realities. Any such model, where one part of the world has to implement the lessons learned from the other, seems to aim at reconciling antithetically defined norms of development, explaining the past in terms of a predefined philosophy of history. Instead, eighteenth- and nineteenth-century political thought draws on a broad range of cultural legacies and civic traditions, which are revealed according to specific historic conditions and set in complex sets of relationships with each other, where "foreign" experiences are constantly translated and assimilated into local vocabularies.

Questioning the one-dimensional flow of ideas across the Atlantic raises the more general issue of to what extent political models can be imported or exported from one specific historical-political context to another. To what extent do such schemes merely reflect the wishful thinking of the "export nation," hoping to assert its international role, while in turn confirming a hegemonic relationship that relegates the "import nation" to the status of an underdeveloped client in need of foreign aid? Paola Gemme, in *Domesticating Foreign Struggles*, argues that the idea of America as a model for the Italian Risorgimento was at least partly an American projection, where "the discourse on Italy contributed to the articulation of America's own national identity."[84] Gemme's analysis shows how the United States' patronizing attitude toward Risorgimento Italy went hand in hand with the idea that Italians were not ready for freedom, mirroring Americans' attitude to their black population at home, who they deemed unfit for democracy.[85] Though mainly investigating an American phenomenon—the nationalistic and self-congratulatory intent informing American narratives about the Italian Risorgimento—Gemme's analysis is crucially important to the objective of this book, which examines the complexity of Italian engagement with American democracy.

Daniele Fiorentino has demonstrated how during the Revolutions of 1848 President James Polk and a good part of the United States' political establishment considered Europe in need of guidance toward a democratic and republican future, despite the United States' official policy of nonintervention in European affairs.[86] Very similar was the attitude of James A. Hamilton, acting secretary of state to President Andrew Jackson, who was convinced that the political changes taking place in Italy around 1848 were "due to our example," where the spirit of 1776 became "the pillar of light by day and of fire by night to all mankind."[87] A lot of Italo-American history has traditionally been written in this perspective. For instance, Howard Marraro opened his book of 1932 with the self-consciously heroic statement that "during the middle decades of the nineteenth century America heard her battle cry of 1776 . . . raised by subject peoples throughout the length and breadth of Europe."[88]

David Armitage and Sanjay Subrahmanyam have mocked such simplifications, noting that "the democratic revolution was thus a gift from the North Atlantic world to other peoples who had apparently contributed nothing to its original emancipatory potential."[89] Claudia dell'Osso, in *Voglia d'America*, also remarks that Europe's *americanismo* was often "prefabricated" by the American elites themselves.[90] Few voices expressed a different view. In 1911 the Oxford historian Herbert A. L. Fisher argued in *The Republican Tradition in Europe* that European admiration for the American Republic, its political institutions, and its constitution did not necessarily mean that the same Europeans considered it a viable model for the old continent.[91] Although Europeans certainly demonstrated a great deal of interest in the social, political, and cultural development of the United States, it was to a large extent the Americans who liked to think of themselves as a model for the rest of the world.

David Armitage recently reaffirmed the global symbolic power of the American Declaration of Independence, providing "the model for similar documents around the world."[92] While his assessment is undoubtedly true, establishing the exact nature of the relationship between the model and its followers is a complicated task. The Declaration's uncertain legal status—neither statute nor constitution—is reflected in the ways Italians engaged with it, or not. While in mid-September 1776 its text appeared in a Florentine newspaper, two months after the original pronunciation, later references to the Declaration, to the Bill of Rights, or other constitutional documents were often used interchangeably. More specific comments remained rare.[93] Moreover, the context of dependence (resulting in independence) often differs dramatically from one country to another. Usually a wide range of other constitutional histories was discussed in connection with the American Declaration of Independence: regional or even local traditions, as the example of Sicily, discussed in chapter 3, suggests.

Like Armitage, George Athan Billias stressed the global influence of American constitutionalism over the past two centuries: its principles and practices, defined in terms of constitutional documents, procedures, and institutions that came into being. Billias concludes that "the world was never the same, constitutionally speaking, after 1776."[94] However, the fact that European patriots were in correspondence with men like Franklin and Jefferson, or that at certain junctures assemblies circulated translations of American legal texts, does not give license to the assumption that political developments in Europe were sparked off by the events of 1776. Instead, it is in the nature of legal practice that constitutionalists make themselves familiar with legal and political theory on an international scale. It was in this spirit that the fathers of the American constitution traveled to Göttingen to study the constitution of the Holy Roman Empire, or read Beccaria and Filangieri.

Moreover, if European constitutional documents adopted a structure or language similar to that of the American documents, the political intentions of those referring to the American model could be dramatically different from the political ideas of the American founding fathers. As the example of the Italian states shows, constitutional monarchists as well as Democrats and Republicans were able to draw on the United States. Billias himself points to the example of the Belgian constitution of 1831, which featured radical elements of the American federal constitution, but resulted in the establishment of a constitutional monarchy with extremely restrictive suffrage.[95] The Frankfurt Assembly of 1848–49 borrowed (rather freely) from the American constitution, but the document was never implemented.[96] The impact of the American model on French and Swiss debates around 1848 is well documented. In the French case there remained important differences, while Switzerland was able to draw on its own constitutional history.

The argument for the United States' case as a model for Italy is often made on the basis of their supposedly parallel histories. In his book on Franklin and Italy, Antonio Pace explained how "the American Revolution itself became a complete paradigm of the Risorgimento." As he argues, "the parallels were obvious. Both the United States and Italy began as agglomerations of separate states dominated by foreign powers and weakened by internal dissent. The condition of victory seemed the same in both instances: indomitable patriotic zeal, brilliant, though necessarily limited, military action against the oppressor, and an astute international diplomacy to neutralize the opposition and enlist the support of friendly powers."[97] Within Pace's logic, Garibaldi and Camillo Cavour came to reenact the roles of George Washington and Franklin, as if world history had been waiting for the two to appear on the political stage, ideally after having read and rehearsed the American script. Pace goes so far as to speak of America's "palingenetic role" in explaining the Italian Risorgimento.

While there are obvious parallels between the historical development of the two countries, historians should avoid explaining the past by falling into the trap of two frequently made mistakes. First, history does not lend itself to analogical conclusions: similar conditions can lead to different outcomes; and despite some striking similarities, there remain vast differences between the two countries. Second, teleological reasoning takes the formation of a unified nation-state for granted and reads the history of Italian Unification back into a period of the peninsula's past, when the formation of a unified Italian nation-state was simply not on the political agenda, at least not for the majority of political thinkers and not in the form that emerged in the aftermath of

1848. The similarity of conditions at the outset cannot be constructed on the basis of hypothetical references to later developments.

Americans' overestimation of their role in teaching the rest of the world was not a new phenomenon at the time when Italians started thinking about their own political future. Janet Polasky begins her recent book *Revolutions without Borders* with an episode about the young Bostonian Elkanah Watson, who set off for Europe to witness in 1780 the beginnings of the Dutch Patriot Revolution, only to learn that his European brothers in arms, like Americans before them, considered themselves God's chosen people for the achievements in their recent political struggle.[98] In this case their pride was nourished by a tradition of fighting for freedom that reached back to the Dutch Revolt of the sixteenth century, long before America's struggle for independence. Transnational experience put American national pride into perspective. American travelers to Italy often came to the conclusion that "the United States could teach more than it could learn."[99] While this might be a common view among Americans even today, Italians had reasons to reject these perceptions confidently.

The moderate political thinker Pellegrino Rossi serves as an example to illustrate this point. During the first half of the nineteenth century he was one of Italy's most influential voices on an international scale. A naturalized citizen of Geneva and a professor at the Collège de France, Rossi's political and legal thought draws on a wide range of non-Italian experiences without translating into a sense of inferiority toward supposedly more advanced countries, a position almost unthinkable for a graduate of the University of Bologna, where the study of Roman law dates back to the eleventh century. Throughout the modern period Italy had produced a number of legal theorists whose works were discussed all over Europe and across the Atlantic. Meanwhile, the very notion of national schools and hierarchies of thought must have seemed strange to the protagonists of the Risorgimento, who were typically polyglot and often extremely well traveled. Owing to his long periods of exile, Rossi mostly wrote in French; and along with references to the classics, he develops his political and legal thought in response to a great number of thinkers from Condillac, Kant, and Hume to Bentham and Lamennais, making a distinction between national schools almost impossible. His ideas on legal reform reflected revolutionary events in Latin America and experiences within the British Empire.

Meanwhile, these examples do not serve him as models for the reform of a supposedly less advanced society back home, but as spaces of experience from which to draw general empirical evidence for the analysis of social and political change.[100] For instance, Rossi rejects English criminal law as "a chaos where every useful word is drowned in a mass of useless words."[101] Likewise, North America was only one of many places from where he drew ideas, despite the large volume of writings on the subject that had appeared in the aftermath of the American Revolution. The first version of his *Droit pénal* was published in 1829, two years before Gustave de Beaumont and Alexis de Tocqueville embarked on their famous trip to investigate the United States' penitentiary system. Although Rossi's book is full of detailed references to examples from England, France, and the German states, among others, the United States played practically no role in his extremely well-informed multivolume investigation. Despite ignoring the United States, it became one of the internationally most influential works in the field of criminal law.[102] Rossi serves as a powerful example to relativize the role of the United States in Risorgimento political thought. In the event that he ever had the intention of integrating American experiences into his legal thought, he was denied the chance to do so: in November 1848 Radical Republicans assassinated him in front of the recently inaugurated Rome town hall, symbol of the pope's new constitutional government.[103]

Rossi's work, similar to that of many other Italian political and legal thinkers at the time, is exemplary of the wide philosophical, chronological, and geographical horizon beneath which their ideas evolved. What some historians have described as "American" ideas owed profoundly to European traditions of political thought, a fact the Old World was acutely aware of. John Pocock offers a useful key to this way of thinking, which was never one directional. In the *Machiavellian Moment* he describes "the product of the ideas and conceptual vocabularies" that were widely available to political thinkers of the early modern and modern periods, constituting an Atlantic tradition of thought that traveled to and fro between the Old and the New Worlds.[104] A postwar classic on American relations with Italy by H. Stuart Hughes introduced its subject with a chapter called "Terra Incognita," explaining how little Americans knew about Italy.[105] While this certainly applies to ordinary Americans, an exception has to be made for the intellectual elites, where classical studies and an admiration for the Italian Renaissance often generated an interest in Italy's current affairs and the Risorgimento in particular. By the late eighteenth century Americans were able to look back on a long tradition of American knowledge on Italy, testified by the many Italian books in the libraries of the Pilgrim Fathers.[106] John Adams's *Defence of the Constitutions of Government of the United States of America* contained long passages on Italy's medieval republics, although they presented Italians in a rather dark light.[107] The writings of Beccaria and Filangieri had a profound impact on American constitutional history. As one recent historian, Karl Bessler, has written, "Italians were obsessed with liberty and America's independence as much as Americans were enthralled by the Italian Enlightenment itself."[108]

According to Pocock, since the fifteenth century the Aristotelian polis had reemerged in Europe's civic humanist thought and became a political reality that existed in many different forms and historical guises. For educated Italians this civic tradition resonated in a vast canon of literature from the classical tradition to Dante, Machiavelli, and Francesco Guicciardini. Here, republican thought was not an abstract modus operandi of long-forgotten states, but a way of thinking that, over centuries, informed Italians' search for meaning in the secular world. As Pocock has shown, the thinking of the "Revolutionary generation in America" was "anchored" in this Aristotelian and Machiavellian tradition, mediated through the experience of an Anglicized republic.[109] These connections would make it absurd to think about transatlantic intellectual exchange as being one directional. Once the American Republic had been established, ideas continued to flow in both directions. In the same way as Europeans continued to study antiquity as a way of thinking about modern political institutions, they also looked at developments across the Atlantic. Vincenzo Gioberti, among the most prominent thinkers discussed in this book, has argued that "America emerged from Europe, in the same way as Europe today leans toward America."[110] Tocqueville's concern with the despotism of opinion in a society where everybody ought to be alike refers back to problems Aristotle had discussed in his *Politics*.[111] As Lucien Jaume has argued, when Tocqueville wrote about America, he indirectly addressed the problems of French society.[112] Italian readers of Tocqueville were fully aware of these references.

What we study, then, is the traveling back and forth across the Atlantic of ideas that had informed political thought for centuries. In each new historical and geographical context these ideas had to be domiciled anew. Modern political concepts cannot be divorced from this tradition. Palmer defined the Age of Democratic Revolution as "a new feeling for a kind of equality, or at least a discomfort with older forms of social stratification and formal rank."[113] Meanwhile, Palmer admits that democracy also represented an aspect of the new age that many European observers found repulsive, especially when relying on secondhand accounts, without knowing much about it. A methodologically thorough analysis of Italian debates about the United States will be able to identify a rather cautious assessment of the American model, which takes into consideration the role of different political traditions and geopolitical conditions. Moreover, historiographical arguments on the apparent appeal of the United States to Italians are often based on the historians' rather limited chronological scope of research. A vast literature on early Italian responses to the American War of Independence and the American constitution during the first decades of the Risorgimento should not lead to the assumption that these ideas about the United States remained unchallenged throughout the Risorgimento. The frenzied fascination with the modernity of American lifestyle starts only toward the end of the nineteenth century, when larger numbers of Italians arrived in the United States not just as emigrants, but also as travelers, with the specific aim of experiencing the New World's modernity.

Reassessing the transatlantic flow of ideas, then, inserts itself into new ways of thinking about the history of the Italian Risorgimento. For most of the postwar period, in the aftermath of the publication of Gramsci's historical writings, historians of Italy understood the Italian Risorgimento as a passive revolution, which lacked the support of the popular classes and was largely the product of the socioeconomic interests of the Italian elites.[114] This perspective was called into question with the publication of Alberto Banti's *La nazione del Risorgimento* in 2001, which pointed to the role of ideology, language, and literature in transforming Italian nationalism into a mass movement. Defining the nation through a language of kinship, honor, and sanctity, Italian nationalism developed an appeal, Banti argued, that reached well beyond the narrow circles of intellectual elites. With its emphasis on language and literature, Banti's approach sought to establish a dialogue between the history of political ideas and cultural history.

The transnational context from which these political ideas emerged is of pivotal importance to our understanding of Italian patriotism and liberalism, concepts of independence and nationality, or constitutional expectations. Although the Risorgimento was a national movement, it had its roots in Italy's *secolo dei lumi*, which according to Pietro Verri's Milanese periodical *Il caffè* had turned Romans, Florentines, and Lombards into Europeans.[115] Despite the Italian Enlightenment's awareness of forming part of a larger European movement, over the past two decades a number of innovative studies on Italian nationalism, some of them inspired by postcolonial approaches, have demonstrated the extent to which Italians internalized the northern European discourse about Italy as a beautiful but in all other respects backward nation, the product of long-declined civilizations.[116]

Other historians have demonstrated how Italian patriots were capable of questioning these stereotypes. Rather than passively accepting ideas coming from abroad, transnational historiography has emphasized the extent to which this exchange of ideas worked in both directions. An important work exemplifying this approach has been Maurizio Isabella's *Risorgimento in Exile*, which demonstrates how transnational experiences shaped Italian national identity.[117] Returning to their homeland in 1848, the exiles celebrated the experience of their transnational encounters, as reflected for instance in Italian broadsheets praising the Princess Belgiojoso, whose salon's hospitality many of the Italian exiles had enjoyed during their time in Paris.[118] What the new cultural and intellectual history of the Risorgimento has shown is that ideas are not passively received but translated into a new context, where the final product often bears little similarity to the original. Likewise, recent work on travel writing has demonstrated that "orientalizing" discourse worked both ways, leading travelers from the so-called periphery to confirm self-confidently their native values and their own understanding of modern change.[119] In the Italian case, Vincenzo Gioberti offers a persuasive example. Arguably the Risorgimento's most prominent political theorist before 1848, and briefly prime minister of Piedmont during the revolutionary turmoil, he explained in his hugely influential *Del rinnovamento civile d'Italia* of 1851 that

England was an oceanic island in the periphery of Europe. America (its republican version) was even further away. According to Gioberti, England was to Europe what Sicily was to Italy.[120] Reversing the stereotypes with which European travelers described the Mediterranean, Gioberti was not unsympathetic to the United States, comparing the Americans' pride to the "fierezza dei popoli antichi"; but his federalism did not need an American model.[121]

The often peripheral place of the American Revolution in Italian political thought was further affected by the ways in which Italian commentators tended to lump England and the United States together as two versions of the same Anglo-Saxon tribe, with similar constitutions, one monarchical and the other republican. Giuseppe Pecchio is among the few Italian commentators who emphasized persisting differences and tensions between Britain and the United States.[122] For Mazzini Americans belonged "to the English race," as was the case for Bettino Ricasoli, an early prime minister of unified Italy, who spoke of the "glory of the *razza Anglo-Sassone* in the two hemispheres."[123] As Leonardo Buonomo has pointed out, American "citizens were commonly called *inglesi* [English], a frequent cause of irritation for US travelers and an actual disadvantage: among all foreign visitors of Italy, the least popular were precisely those from England."[124] American newspapers were also often summed up as "*giornali inglesi*."[125] Cattaneo referred to the *britanni d'America*,[126] asserting that "it does not matter if this tribe organises itself under one or more governments; it does not matter that one part calls itself the United Kingdom and the other the United States. The particular mix and temperament of this tribe remain the same, as is the case for their language, the same religious traditions, their urge for expansion."[127] If many Italians did not distinguish between Americans and the English, the distinction between the United States and South America was also far from obvious. Frequently one notices confusion about which territories of the New World formed part of the northern Republic.

Literary Tropes

Among the most effective means to overcome the lack of familiarity with the American continent was literature. The works of James Fenimore Cooper became an especially important source of information for Italians. The first translation of *The Last of the Mohicans* had appeared in 1828, the year Cooper spent with his family in Italy, only two years after it was first published in the United States.[128] The Italian subtitle—*Romanzo storico relativo ai tempi delle guerre americane*—illustrates that the novel was presented as a source for America's role in the Seven Years' War. (The English-language editions used the subtitle "A Narrative of 1757.")[129] Cooper's earlier novel of 1821, *The Spy*, set during the American Revolution and glorifying George Washington as an almost godlike character, not dissimilar from the general's portrait in the early

Italian histories of the War of Independence, was also particularly popular. Like the Italian edition of *The Last of the Mohicans*, the Italian version of *The Spy* also used the subtitle *Romanzo storico relativo ai tempi della guerra americana*, reinforcing the novel's documentary character.[130]

An important aspect of *The Last of the Mohicans* is the encounter between British, French, and Native American populations. The relationship between Colonel Munro's daughters Alice and Cora and the Mohican members of the caravan, Chingachgook and his son Uncas, animated the readers' imagination regarding the New World's racial composition, representing an important aspect of Italian dramatizations of the New World, discussed in chapters 4 and 5.

Many more editions followed the first translation of *The Last of the Mohicans*, and abbreviated versions were included in the author's collected works. Educated Italians frequently read Cooper's French translations. In France scenes from the novel became a popular topic for paintings exhibited at the Paris Salon, and stage adaptations made it to several theaters as well as to the *Opéra*. The frenzy for Cooper's novels went hand in hand with the French fashion of "exhibiting" Native American tribes, long before the famous Buffalo Bill Shows came to the Continent.[131] In 1835 the catalogue of Vieusseux's lending library in Florence listed twenty works by the American author.[132] In 1852 the *North American Review* proudly claimed that "no American writer has been so extensively read as James Fenimore Cooper"; and that "in Naples and Milan, the bookstalls bear witness that *L'Ultimo dei Mohicani* is still a popular work."[133]

Following Cattaneo's reviews of American literature for various periodicals during the mid-nineteenth century, Enrico Nencioni became Italy's most influential commentator on American fiction and poetry. A close friend of the celebrated poet Giosuè Carducci, he started reviewing American literature during the 1860s, mostly for *Nuova antologia*. His love of American poetry influenced an entire generation of Italian authors, including Giovanni Pascoli, Gabriele D'Annunzio, and Giovanni Papini.[134] For Nencioni "true American poetry" corresponded to the myth of America's natural world, characterized by an absence of civilization that he had similarly found in Cooper's novels: "the true echoes of Mississippi and Missouri, of Virginia and Maryland have something rude and primitive about them, a natural and mesmerizing music like that of the vast lakes and the winds among the lianas, impulsive and violent, similar to the sounds of those deafening floodgates."[135]

These impressions are easily reconciled with images in Walt Whitman's *Leaves of Grass* (1855), though Nencioni also admired American authors such as Edgar Allan Poe and Ralph Waldo Emerson. A first Italian essay on Emerson had appeared in 1855. Poe was initially translated in 1858; and Italians were deeply taken by what they knew of his life. Henry Wadsworth Longfellow, among the first American translators of Dante Alighieri and author of a poem

"To Italy," long remained America's best-known poet in Italy, though Nencioni criticized him for imitating English or German models: "too many ballads, too many idylls, too many elegies, too many album verses."[136] Mentioning Bret Harte among the better-known American poets in Italy, Nencioni did most to popularize Whitman, celebrated as the poet of "cosmopolitan democracy" and of humanity's future.[137] Mark Twain had visited Italy in the 1860s, around the time of his first literary success, but in order to read his works in translation Italians had to wait until the turn of the century. Herman Melville visited Italy in 1857, and his work shows frequent references to the country's culture and its history, but also in this case Italians became aware of the author only later in the century. Chapter 4 will briefly return to Cooper and Melville.[138]

Despite Italy's increasing familiarity with books from the New World, Mazzini found American literature "sickening."[139] His idea seems to reflect the impression that Cooper himself gained when traveling in Italy in the late 1820s. While forming himself a most favorable opinion of Habsburg rule in Tuscany, Cooper observed that the only thing Europeans could praise about America was their fine ships: Europeans considered America to be a nation of traders and not much else.[140]

Mazzini's judgement might have been informed by what returning exiles had to say about the United States. They often made a living of publishing their accounts, but what they wrote about rarely made their life enviable.[141] They admired the United States' republican constitution but found it difficult to make a living across the Atlantic.[142] As for the American pull factor, Mazzini was convinced that the times were gone when immigrants could easily make a fortune across the Atlantic.[143] One of the first Italian novels on emigration, published by the Mazzinian Antonio Caccia just after 1848, presented the unpleasant image of an American nativist who resented "the daily arrival of hungry Europeans."[144]

Garibaldi's arrival in the United States had been greeted with a great deal of anticipation, but widely read accounts of his life did not present a rosy picture of his experiences in the United States.[145] Because the general can hardly be described as a political thinker, he deserves less of a place in this book than for instance Mazzini. Moreover, despite his short (mostly negative) experience in New York, he hardly ever mentioned the United States and contributed little to what Italians knew about the country. His experiences in Latin America were certainly more formative for his political career than the disappointing months spent on Staten Island.[146]

On his accession to the Austrian throne in 1835, Ferdinand I had issued an imperial rescript granting Italian prisoners a commutation of sentence on condition that they agreed to be deported to America. While some accepted the condition, others preferred to serve out their sentences in prison in order to avoid crossing the Atlantic.[147] European revolutionaries knew that public opinion in the United States was not unanimous in its support for their uprisings, and that many Americans resented their alleged radical socialism and its potential impact on business relations with the old continent.[148] While American Protestants feared a new wave of Catholic immigration as a consequence of the European turmoil, Catholic Americans condemned Italian patriots for their treatment of the pope.[149] During the Second War of Independence, in 1859, the US State Department's major worry was that the war might affect free trade between neutral countries.

The 1860s were the years when novels about emigration as well as travel accounts became increasingly popular and more foreign works were translated into Italian. They often transmitted the idea of a primitive lifestyle and corrupt manners, as demonstrated in the works of Friedrich Gerstäcker. The son of opera singers, he emigrated to America in 1837, where personal experience formed the basis of his colorful descriptions of life among the settlers, a life deeply marked by moral corruption and religious fanaticism, an impression only superficially smoothed by a good deal of schmaltz in the description of personal relationships and praise for virtuous Natives. The very first sentence of his popular novel *Die Regulatoren des Arkansas* (1846) remarked on the absence of culture in the wide woods of the American South. Many of his stories appeared in the international periodical press, including *L'Universo Illustrato*.[150] His descriptions of American landscape and characters became an important model for Karl May's popular novels.

Italians did not have to resort to fiction to engage with this world: travel writing also offered a good deal of picturesque entertainment. Although certainly not prejudiced against Americans, Giovanni Capellini, a geologist and future rector of the University of Bologna, included in his travel account numerous episodes illustrating the unfamiliar manners of the New World. Hotels especially did not offer what Capellini expected. He was tortured by the feeling that he had to keep a colt under his pillow; and during the nights mice danced on his blanket and happily passed over his face.[151] A man who had traveled through many of the most remote regions of Italy remained deeply impressed by the United States' combination of ambition and backwardness.

A realistic and most brutal account of daily life in the United States appeared in 1852 and was immediately translated into Italian. Harriet Beecher Stowe's novel *Uncle Tom's Cabin*, discussed in detail in chapter 5, became one of the most widely read novels of nineteenth-century Italy, reaching many more people of different classes through various stage adaptations, most prominently in the form of a ballet. In Italy the story of Uncle Tom was soon read in conjunction with the unfolding of the American Civil War, contemporary to the beginnings of Italy's own civil war in the South. Henceforth Italian periodicals also started writing in much more detail about events and political developments across the Atlantic, presenting their readers with the shocking image of life in a war-torn society.

An important element of Stowe's international success was her claim that the novel's fictional account was based on historical facts, which she had researched and then documented in a separate volume, which also appeared in Italian translation. The early Italian histories of America, discussed in chapter 1, took credibility for granted. Contrary to Stowe, many of the aforementioned autobiographical accounts shifted freely between fiction and fact. These narratives demonstrate how events are manipulated by later acts of remembering; and how they are read in constantly shifting historical contexts.[152] Lorenzo da Ponte's memories of New York present a particularly pertinent example of the creative mixture of fiction and fact, while also demonstrating how the meanings of a text changed during different stages of its life. Mozart's famous librettist published his memoirs in multiple editions and volumes between 1823 and 1830, dedicating two chapters to his experiences of life in the New World and living on the commercial success of his book for the remaining years of his life.[153]

Many years earlier, in 1776, the year of the American Revolution, da Ponte had written a Latin poem entitled "Americano in Europa," which he recited in a public meeting at the seminary in Treviso:

Nempe illic nemo est, qui sceptra potentia dextra,
Gemmea qui claro serta gerat capiti.
Nemo est qui certo componet foedere leges,
Qui teneat propria sub ditione solum.

Non domus aggestas messes, non terminus agros,
Nec sortita gravis dividit arva lapis.[154]

There certainly is nobody who, the sceptre of power in his right hand,
Is crowned with twinkling gems.
Nobody writes fixed laws
Nobody holds all land in his power.

No home divides the harvest; there are no boundaries to the fields,
No stone divides the ploughed land.

The poem's egalitarian message cost Da Ponte his position as a teacher at the seminary. From his time in Venice and Vienna, Da Ponte was familiar with several operatic works that treated life in the New World as a fictional utopia, a genre that flourished in Italy and the Habsburg monarchy during the second half of the eighteenth century. One such work was Joseph Haydn's *Il mondo della luna* (1777), based on a popular play by Goldoni, where men on the moon became a metaphor for life in the New World. Another example of this genre was Alessandro Guglielmi's *La quakera spiritosa*, discussed briefly in chapter 4, which Da Ponte staged for Joseph II's court theater in Vienna. Idealized images of American life—still rooted in Enlightenment discourse—were increasingly replaced by accounts of real-life experiences in a country that brought material wealth to some, but lacked the culture that distinguished the lives of educated Europeans. Many of these operas linked democratic experiments to economic prosperity, a theme echoed in Mozart's *Le nozze di Figaro*. Rather than the common (and absurd) suggestion that these works "anticipated" the French Revolution, according to Pierpaolo Polzonetti *Figaro* was a critique of the ancien régime's social hierarchies as much as a commentary on the changing social realities exemplified by the North American Republic. Reading da Ponte's libretti in this light also makes sense if one considers that Beaumarchais, the play's original author, had been an active supporter of the American insurrection.[155] The political significance behind these plays is perhaps less radical than might appear at first sight: Europe's enlightened rulers often shared their critique of the aristocracy; and often they followed American events not unsympathetically. Joseph II, who had abolished many feudal privileges, intervened against the performance of Beaumarchais's all too explicit plays, but on moral rather than on political grounds. He personally approved the project for Mozart's *Le nozze di Figaro* and took a keen interest in its original staging.[156]

Da Ponte left for the United States in 1805 to escape his creditors after filing for bankruptcy. His memoirs offer a firsthand account of daily life in the North American Republic, very different from the philosophical speculations that circulated among educated Italian readers during the earlier parts of the eighteenth century. Published in three volumes and taking the popular memoirs of his friend Giacomo Casanova as a model, they were soon reviewed in the Florentine *Antologia*, an influential forum for debate on the early American Republic. Suppressed in several Italian states, they remained freely available under the Habsburgs in Tuscany. In 1858, shortly before Italian Unification, Lamartine rediscovered da Ponte's work, leading to first French and then German translations. Widely discussed in literary circles, the Mozart renaissance of the nineteenth century further increased interest in the book.[157] As a consequence, da Ponte's colorful account of life in the United States influenced several generations of Italians.

The main message behind da Ponte's account of American life is easily summarized. In the New World "Italian language and literature were . . . about as well known as Turkish or Chinese."[158] For da Ponte this was less of a comment on his own difficulties when arriving in New York than a statement that Americans were deprived of Europe's classical tradition and its cultural heritage. For years da Ponte spent his time in America fighting against swindlers, corrupt lawyers, and mean creditors, telling his readers that Americans were never to be trusted. Materialism caused their lack of appreciation for culture, with which he had hoped to contribute to the New World's prosperity. Instead of showing an interest in his collection of Italian books, they preferred shopping next door for cheap Italian sweets and fat sausages from Bologna. As he summarized in one of his many poems,

All sciences are cultivated,
The numerical especially,
For it America is well known.
But it is not as distinguished
In the study of languages.[159]

Da Ponte played an important role in laying the foundations of opera in America, but financially most of his projects turned out to be disastrous. While his image of America was largely a reflection of his own life, the popularity of his account did little to change Italians' prejudice against a country that offered freedom but no culture.

Explaining America

While chapters 4 and 5 of this book examine the United States in the Italian cultural imagination, where literature and the stage played pivotal roles, the bulk of this book concerns the role of the United States in Risorgimento political thought. Which were the books that helped Italians to articulate their ideas about American political institutions?

The first Italian translation of an English book about America appeared in 1763, *An Account of the European Settlements in America*, published in Venice and attributed to the coauthorship of Edmund Burke and his distant cousin William.[160] While it seems unusual to relate the Risorgimento back to the 1760s, global political events such as the Seven Years' War, combined with the profound transformation taking place in Italy as a consequence of Enlightenment reforms, started off debates about the peninsula's political future, which would leave a profound legacy for the Risorgimento. These debates were marked by a pertinent awareness that Europe was entering a new epoch, and they became the breeding ground for Italy's brief period of republican government at the time of the Napoleonic conquest, the *triennio repubblicano* (1796–99).[161] First published anonymously in 1757, the Italian translation of *The Account of the European Settlements in America* also omits the authors of the work. Richard Bourke explains this omission mainly through the Burkes' positive assessment of French colonization in the New World, an inappropriate argument during times of a major British war against France.[162] Along with their praise for French *Colbertisme* in international trade, the Burkes' critique of the British slave economy directly attacked the interests of Britain's colonial establishment, explaining why the Burkes decided to conceal their authorship.[163]

For Italian readers the book represented a watershed in factual knowledge about the Americas, now readily available in Italian translation. The book outlines the original discovery of the continent, its natural history, and the customs of its Native population, to then account for its colonization and its economic relevance in global trade. For readers with an interest in North America, the most relevant sections were to be found in the second part, dealing with the Native populations, as well as in the almost three hundred pages on the English colonies, exposing the settlers' free and republican spirit.[164] The same ideas would play a significant role in Edmund Burke's analysis of the colonies' conflict with the motherland two decades later. At the time of writing, Burke so admired the new continent that he even considered emigration.[165] Analysis of the continent's commercial potential is one of the book's main objectives, making it a distinct contribution to the emerging science of comparative political economy.[166] The work's anonymous publication contrasts with its remarkable popularity, resulting in six English editions before 1777 as well as French and German translations.

With the Seven Years' War's unfolding, the American colonies became an independent agent on the international stage, helping Europeans to appreciate the significance of the New World for their own future. Coinciding with the end of the war in 1763, the same year as the Italian translation of the Burkes' book, a three-volume geographical encyclopedia on the New World appeared in the Tuscan port city of Livorno. In numerous monographic articles *Il Gazzettiere Americano* gives a detailed overview of the continent's geography and its flora and fauna, as well as its cities and their economic development, all lavishly illustrated with maps and plates by prominent graphic artists from Tuscany.[167] Also included are vignettes showcasing the customs of local populations, or innovative technologies applied to the continent's commercial activities. Based on an English publication of the previous year, the Italian edition is considerably more elegant than the original. According to the publisher's own preface, the scarcity of books on America written in Italian is the main motive for producing this altogether rather extravagant work.[168]

The *Gazzettiere*'s entries on North American cities gave Italian readers insight into institutions of self-rule and the emerging democratic culture of the British colonies. Its article on Boston emphasizes that there were many well-furnished bookshops and five publishing houses.[169] The description of New York points out that "in 1754, a set of gentlemen undertook to carry about a subscription towards raising a public library, and in a few days collected near 600 Lire Sterling, which were laid out in purchasing about 700 volumes of new, well chosen books. Every subscriber, upon payment of 5 Lire principal and the annual sum of 10 shillings is entitled to the use of these books. . . . This is the beginning of a library, which in process of time will probably become vastly rich and voluminous." Meanwhile, the article argued, the city's schools "are in the lowest orders; the instructors want instruction, and through a long shameful neglect of all the arts and sciences, the common speech is extremely corrupt; and the evidences of bad taste, both as to thought and language, are visible in their proceedings, publick and private."[170] These entries show that the survey was not limited to praising the wonders of the New World. In much detail the same article reports the local population's concern over the mother country's habit of exporting its prisoners to the colonies: "can agriculture be promoted, when the 'wild boar of the forest' breaks down our hedges, and pulls up our vines?"[171]

Although the edition's print run is unknown (the British Library alone holds six original copies of the Italian translation), Marco Coltellini's decision to undergo the commercial risk of this expensive publication bears witness to growing Italian interest in *Americana*. Coltellini was a visionary publisher, who would print Cesare Beccaria's *Dei delitti e delle pene* the following year, taking advantage of the relaxed attitude of Tuscany's Habsburg rulers to censorship.

Another example of Tuscany's early interest in North America is the *Storia del governo d'Inghilterra e delle sue colonie* by the literary scholar Vincenzo Martinelli. After having spent several decades in London, Martinelli returned to Tuscany in 1776 and published his book at exactly the time when conflict broke out.[172] Well timed to catch his readers' interest, it was mostly based on his understanding of English politics and appeared too early to foresee the outcome of the American Revolution.

Compared to the intensity of debates in Tuscany, the Lombard Enlightenment remained largely indifferent to political developments in the New World.[173] The above-mentioned periodical *Il Caffè*, published between 1764 and 1766, first in Brescia and then Milan, rarely mentioned America; and Pietro Verri's first article for the periodical, "Storia naturale del caffè," concludes with the less than reassuring remark that "worse than any other coffee is the American."[174] (It is unclear if by that time he has had a chance to taste English coffee.) In his later writings he followed current events in the colonies, but his admiration for England led him to believe that the fanaticism of the revolutionaries would not prevail.[175] Giuseppe Pecchio, another *lombardo* who frequently quoted Verri, displayed similar views. The eye-opening travels of Verri's brother Alessandro to London and Paris, where he met Franklin and other American revolutionaries, happened after his experience at the Milanese periodical.

Regarding the Lombards' relative lack of interest in the New World, exception needs to be made for the Milanese scientist Count Luigi Castiglioni, who traveled the thirteen states during the 1780s, witnessing the very beginnings of the Republic.[176] One of the first Italians to publish a major book about the United States, the main objective of his travels was to collect specimens of plants and seeds that could be of economic interest to Europe. Castiglioni also stayed in Monticello, studying in Jefferson's library. Back in Italy he regularly opened his house to American visitors.[177] His book is of interest not only for its commentaries on the early Republic's political institutions, but also for its independent ethnographic observations, which no longer simply relied on

French or British accounts from the earlier eighteenth century. A reflection Castiglioni found worth commenting on was the fact that in America people from many different national backgrounds formed a population in its own right, a phenomenon many Italians observed.[178] While he admired William Penn and the democratic constitution of Pennsylvania, Castiglioni was aware of continuing social inequality among the new Republic's inhabitants; and he strongly condemned the treatment of Native Americans and the brutality and exploitation that underpinned the institution of slavery in the southern plantations.[179] In doing so, he related Italian debates on America to the big themes of Voltaire's historiography and of the Enlightenment.[180]

Contrary to the comparative indifference in Lombardy toward America, intellectual elites in the Kingdom of Naples voiced their interest in the American colonies and the United States early.[181] These contacts led to a number of immediate legacies. When, in 1783, the Calabrian city of Castelmonardo was destroyed by an earthquake, the local authorities copied William Penn's plan for the Pennsylvanian capital to rebuild their city as Filadelfia. The project for the new city was the idea of Filangieri's friend Giovanni Andrea Serrao, bishop of Potenza and himself a native of Castelmonardo. Filangieri corresponded with Franklin, an admirer of his *Scienza della Legislazione*, which had been published in Naples between 1780 and 1785.[182] It was Franklin who sent Filangieri an early copy of the American constitution.[183] In 1782, Filangieri begged Franklin for help with his project of moving permanently to America as a solution to his financial difficulties in Naples and to overcoming obstacles to his marriage to a Hungarian noblewoman, Charlotte Frendel, whom he described as "a Lady whose virtues would lend her distinction even in Pennsylvania."[184]Advocating social reform through legislation, Filangieri was, in the words of John Robertson, a Neapolitan heir to Montesquieu.[185] Education and a free press were key to his aims. This is what he hoped to find in the United States.

While Filangieri's work made for a great comment on classical thought, frequently expanding on examples of British legal practice, references to American political institutions remained rare. Where Filangieri's mentions the American Revolution, these references remained abstract, presented alongside those to Athens and Sparta.[186] Filangieri's interest in the American experiment reflects an often rather patronizing attitude of a knowing teacher, for instance when commenting on excesses during the War of Independence: "free citizens of America, you are too virtuous and too enlightened to ignore that having acquired the right to self-government you have in front of the Universe the rare obligation to be more moderate, wiser and luckier than any other people. In front of the tribunal of humankind you have to account for any sophistry that your errors could infringe upon liberty. Do not embarrass its defenders, do not make common cause with its enemies."[187]

Filangieri's example of offering Americans advice illustrates an argument made at the start of this introduction: that intellectual flows were never one directional and that in many cases they formed complex networks of debate. Several years after completing his *Scienza della Legislazione*, and still stuck in Naples, Filangieri befriended Johann Wolfgang von Goethe, an encounter documented in the German's *Italienische Reise* and leading to a short reference in his novel *Wilhelm Meisters Wanderjahre*. It was Filangieri who introduced Goethe to Giambattista Vico's philosophy.[188] Almost two decades later, when Madame de Staël first visited Weimar, Goethe hosted Benjamin Constant. Introduced by Goethe to what he knew of the Neapolitan Enlightenment, Constant became Filangieri's most influential commentator. He published his two volumes of annotations on Filangieri's legal theory in 1822 and 1824.[189] It was this commentary that integrated postrevolutionary (including American) experiences into Filangieri's debate on legal and economic concepts. The impact of Filangieri's work on Risorgimento political thought rests firmly on the Italian reception of Constant's commentary. Instrumental to its initial reception was a substantial review of Constant in Vieusseux's *Antologia*, followed shortly after by several Italian translations, signaling a continued interest in the work as late as the 1850s. Introducing the creative force of civil society into Filangieri's state-centered concepts of reform, one of Constant's main contributions was to translate the language of the Neapolitan Enlightenment into liberal concepts of postrevolutionary Europe.

One very specific aspect of American society Filangieri discussed regards its demographic development, used as a matrix to point to societal issues at home. Reflecting on the noxious consequences of legally imposed celibacy in much of Europe, Filangieri praised the American right of any citizen to marry as an instrument in support for the nation's economic development, while at the same time reducing the vices associated with crime and prostitution.[190] An important condition of this demographic development, Filangieri explains, was the equal distribution of land among settlers. Consequently, there seemed to be an economic and a political foundation to the culture that emerged in the new society across the Atlantic.

Castiglioni, who, unlike Filangieri, knew the United States through personal experience, gave a rather different account of the United States' demographic foundations. Describing Connecticut's laws on adultery, Castiglioni almost despaired at the Presbyterians' interference in private lives, describing the different forms of corporal punishment, where the culprit "and his accomplice are brutally whipped on the bare body, then branded on the front head with a hot iron marking the letter A. Both then have to wear a rope around their neck and above their cloths, to be always visible."[191] Severe punishments notwithstanding, Castiglioni heard of surprising levels of *libertinaggio* in Connecticut, "which can only surprise the ears of a European," noting in particular the ease with which "one gets familiar with young ladies, but also spend the night with them. . . . I was in doubt whether these tales were not exaggerated until I had the opportunity to see incontestable proofs."[192] Introducing his

Italian readers to the English term "bundling," he explains that these opportunities offered him only limited pleasures. "Love in the United States, and in particular in the Northern states, is less lively, less refined than in most parts of Europe. Repulsive vices diminish in ladies the potency of amorous passion. The young pay on a daily basis for the satisfaction of their appetites. As a consequence, behind the search for more delicate proofs of love there is either complete indifference or brutish avidity. Women become quasi insensible, presenting themselves like statues in front of cupid's tribunal. They compromise any modesty and make it a virtue to receive with indifference the most passionate declarations of love."[193] Olwen Hufton has suggested that characters as they appear in Castiglioni's narrative "are part of male fantasy, all of them bigger and stronger than the men who enjoy them"; but they also serve as a striking contrast to another male fantasy: that of the chaste woman representing the virtuous nation as it had emerged in European literature from the mid-eighteenth century, from Rousseau's Julie to Vittorio Alfieri's Virginia.[194] Incapable of explaining the customs he observed, or his attitude toward the women he met, Castiglioni moves on quickly to discuss Connecticut's commerce in horses and sweet corn.

Despite these hands-on debates, idealist visions and abstract philosophical references remained the more important aspect of Italian *Americana* before 1800. Alfieri's five odes *L'America libera* (1781)—celebrating the Marquis de Lafayette, Franklin, and Washington, and bemoaning the tyranny still reigning Italy—became the most famous expression of pro-American sentiments in Italy. Meanwhile, Alfieri's expression of sympathy was still far from suggesting the application of American constitutional principles to Italy's own political future. His support for the American Revolution went hand in hand with his increasing hostility toward the outcomes of the French Revolution at home.

While the aforementioned examples of Italian works on America demonstrate how Italian attitudes toward the New World had changed during the years of the American Revolution, for a surprisingly large number of Italians the United States remained insignificant, also after the War of Independence. For instance, despite its author's academic and political background as an economic advisor to the Habsburgs, Count Gian Rinaldo Carli's widely read ethnographic account, *Delle lettere americane*, published between 1780 and 1785, was still concerned with debates over the state of nature and the question whether the New and the Old Worlds had been connected via the sunken island of Atlantis.[195] Carli, who had published his famous essay "Della patria degli Italiani" in Verri's *Il Caffè*, offers a wide-ranging panorama of the Native populations' physiology, of the continent's climate and nature, and of social and political structures, as well as of religion, mores, and cultural practices, but in doing so his main source of information remains the continent's very first descriptions of the sixteenth and seventeenth centuries. Carli's myth-loaded book seems to have had a more profound impact on Italy's literary and philosophical debates than, for instance, the Burkes' study of the colonies' political economy.[196] Rejecting Cornelius de Pauw's thesis of the inability of America's Native population to reach a state of civilization, Carli saw the Mexican and Peruvian civilizations as closely related to those of Egypt and China, a view for which he was praised by Franklin.[197]

Emphasizing these connections, as well as the comparability of ancient civilizations, had been an important theme since the publication of *Religious Ceremonies of the World* by Bernard Picart and Jean Frédéric Bernard (1723), which included rich material on Native Americans.[198] Meanwhile, an important purpose of Carli's argument was philosophical, a justification of absolute power, directed against the fashionable political theories associated with Rousseau's *Social Contract*. Twelve years after his *Lettere americane*, in 1792, Carli published a *Ragionamento sulla disuguaglianza*, also directed against the doctrines associated with Rousseau and the French Revolution.[199] Despite the fact that their main focus was on South American civilizations, the *Lettere americane* are indirectly relevant to the purposes of this book, exactly because it sparked wider debates on political principles.

Similarly to Carli, Giacomo Leopardi's perspective on the New World also remained largely Iberocentric. While little of his thought on the topic reached the outside world, Leopardi shows the extent to which even highly educated Italians, writing in the early decades of the nineteenth century, perpetuated the anthropological concerns of eighteenth-century philosophers. He was convinced that only thanks to Incas and Mexicans the rest of America's Native population abolished its alleged cannibalistic practices.[200] Leopardi knew about the *californii* that they had no proper language and that they lived in a "pure savage state," representing "the last traces of primordial humanity." Many of his ideas were based on William Robertson's *History of America*, of which several Italian translations had been in circulation since the 1780s.[201] The savage from California could not think; indeed he "does not know of thinking."[202] Rather than being a negative reflection on the savages, for the depressingly pessimistic Leopardi this was a celebration of a state of development that ignored the burdens of civilization. His view of the Natives' character as determined by geographical conditions closely mirrored his ideas about Italian national character.[203]

Pamphlets, Not Muskets

Books played an important, but not exclusive role in expressing Italian political thought on the United States during the Risorgimento. The brochures and pamphlets used throughout the different chapters of this book can be found in libraries and specialized collections throughout Italy and abroad. Huge numbers ended up in the British Library, often donated by Italian exiles and collected in hefty folders or as individual items. Some were published anonymously, with incomplete or no bibliographic information. In many of these pamphlets the United States appeared only briefly, in the form of a passing reference used as a discursive instrument in a specific political context.

America also became a motive in political satire. For instance, in February 1848 the Genovese printer Luigi Banzoli published an *aerostatic correspondence* entitled "Nero's travel to the Moon."[204] Printed on a single leaflet, this short play described the Roman emperor's travels from America to the moon, represented as an allegorical satire on Ferdinando II of Naples. Nero knows that Americans see themselves as the proud defenders of liberalism and that they have formed an alliance with the constitutional movement in Italy. As a consequence, he fears not being welcome on their shores, which are richly populated by the Italian exiles of 1821. Forced to move on, Nero briefly descends on Venus, where the aged seducer becomes the object of much hilarity among the local women. Reprimanded for his tyrannical rule over Naples, his only option is to settle on the moon. Without engaging in any complex debate about American political institutions, the play pays witness to a widely held belief that the American Republic was a natural ally of Italy's constitutional movement.

In a city like Genoa, a principal center of transatlantic trade and home of Christopher Columbus, local populations easily understood the sense behind references to America. Sicily, with its international trade connections and a constitutional tradition bound to British experiences, had similar reasons to evoke the example of the United States. In other parts of the peninsula, for instance the Papal Legations, the situation could be different. Chapter 3, which deals with the Revolutions of 1848 in Lombardy, Tuscany, and Sicily, examines pamphlets and documents of the parliamentary assemblies in conjunction with published accounts of the Revolution's protagonists. A particular feature of satirical pamphlets and broadsheets published in Genoa was the playing with foreign accents, again typical for a port city. A short scene featuring a fictional dialogue between Radetzky and Metternich after the field marshal's defeat in Lombardy transcribes the Bohemian's Germanic sounding Italian, turning all the soft sounding into hard consonants:

RADESCHI: Fieni Metternich, fieni!
METTERNICH: Attio Radeschi, mi afer saputo che ti star qui assediato, afer sapute tue tiscrazie e afer a to portato soccorso.
RADESCHI: Si afer tante discrazie, non afer mangiar, ti portato mangiar?[205]

Throughout the Risorgimento, censorship permitting, Italy's learned journals engaged with international debates on a wide range of intellectual and political issues. Reviews of Italian and foreign books about America were a major source of information on the North American Republic. In particular, Vieusseux's Florentine *Antologia* discussed social and economic developments in the

FIG. 5. "Soccorso di Metternich a Radeschi." Illustration from a flyer. Milan and Genoa: Dagnino [1848].BL: Miscellanee politiche genovesi. 804.k.13.320. British Library.

United States, helped by direct exchange agreements with the *North American Review*. An important role in communicating global political events on a wider scale was played by Giuseppe Compagnoni, whose *History of America* will be discussed in chapter 1. Assuming the editorship of the Venetian periodical *Notizie del Mondo*, the future inventor of the Italian *tricolore* set a new standard in Italian political journalism.[206] With his publication Compagnoni helped Italians to realize that social and political change at home was linked to world affairs, drawing on connections between the American and French Revolutions as well as on the experience of Napoleon's rule in Italy.

Occasionally newspapers produced by the small community of Italian exiles in the United States, among them the Mazzinians Giuseppe Avezzana and Eleuterio Felice Foresti, offered insights into Italian views on American political institutions, but their influence on Italian debates remained extremely limited, with many of these papers never crossing the Atlantic.[207] In this respect they differed, for example, from Marx's and Engels's American journalism; also, they mostly wrote about the political situation in Europe, with information on the United States remaining scarce. Articles on America in the Italian press were frequently based on extracts from official documents and speeches, often translations from newspapers such as the *New York Tribune* and the *New York Herald*, and dispatches from Reuters or the *National Intelligencer*. As a consequence, the reading public in Italy was increasingly well informed about American affairs. Because much of this information appeared without further commentary, some of it is of limited interest for an assessment of Italian ideas about the American Republic. The beginnings of the American Civil War, coinciding with the Unification of Italy, marked the moment when newspapers started reporting in much more detail, and often on a daily basis, on American events. As chapter 5 will show, Italians experienced the American Civil War as a truly unsettling event.

Relying on a vast network of contributors with connections around the globe, Italy's Catholic press played a particularly prominent role in shaping Italian ideas about the New World. In this context it is interesting to note that Italy's most important (and most detailed) commentator on Tocqueville's *Democracy in America* was the Roman Catholic priest Antonio Rosmini, whose critique of American political institutions will be discussed in chapter 2. The Jesuit *Civiltà cattolica* was among Italy's best-informed periodicals, regularly reporting on social and political developments in the United States. While fighting an ideological battle against the liberal nation-state at home, it hoped that the young Republic across the ocean would one day be cured by conversion to Catholicism.[208] Despite its status as an antigovernmental publication, *Civiltà cattolica* was among the peninsula's most influential periodicals, claiming that even in Piedmont it had more subscribers than all the liberal papers taken together.[209]

Singing and Dancing America

Within the context of this book, representations of the New World in literature, opera, or dance serve to relate the role of the United States in Italian political thought to Italians' wider cultural imagination, attempting to bridge the gap between abstract political ideas and more widely held views about the New World. The uses of these forms of fictional narratives (and their reception in changing historical contexts) offer different keys to views on the American Republic. The new quality of debate on the United States in the Italian press of the 1850s and 1860s is reflected in the programming of Italian theaters during the period of Unification. Writers of libretti picked up on the fashion for American themes in literature, but also on political news now readily available.

During the course of the nineteenth century the emergence of a transcontinental opera industry—as a means of exchange between the Old and the New World—was an important factor in this process.[210] Singers and musicians increasingly worked on both sides of the Atlantic. As a consequence, not only traveling opera companies, but also publishers and impresari, sought to appeal to audiences in both worlds. Italian musicians were behind the New York–based Mazzinian periodical *Il Proscritto*, fiercely opposed to the politics assumed by the Piedmontese government after 1848.[211] While they formed part of a still small group of people at home in both hemispheres, chapters 4 and 5 will show that their experience contributed significantly to giving authenticity to plots about America.

How socially relevant were images of the New World on stage? In Italy, theater was at the center of municipal structures of sociability; and more than anywhere else in Europe, theater helped Italians to identify themselves as a *Kulturnation*, an idea that was crucial to the project of Unification. The repercussions of this art form reached well beyond the social elites, who owned or rented private boxes in the peninsula's famous opera houses, the Teatro alla Scala in Milan, the Teatro Comunale in Bologna, the principal Roman theaters or the Teatro San Carlo in Naples. The *loggione* in the upper floors of these theaters was usually populated by an audience that was more mixed socially, to include members of the lower middle classes and students. Barrel-organ players and municipal bands carried the most important tunes from the current program into the piazza, where they were also appreciated by those sections of society who would not be able to afford to go to the theater. For many Italians these potpourris of popular tunes were the only music they ever heard performed.[212]

Italian society in the nineteenth century was fractured not only along social divisions, but also regionally, where inhabitants of the Papal States had little in common with people from Tuscany or Piedmont, and where the majority of Sicilians or Calabresi knew little about people from Lombardy or Venetia. Thanks to the activities of impresari and the geographical mobility of their industry, productions of opera and ballet toured the entire peninsula, spreading from some of the world's finest theaters to countless venues in smaller cities and performances at markets and trade fairs.[213] Responses may have differed regionally, but the same art was shared across the peninsula. In this sense theater fulfilled a role comparable to that of periodicals, which circulated between *gabinetti di lettura* across Italy.

Owing to the limited availability of sources, analyzing the reception of an opera or ballet across different sections of Italian society raises methodological challenges.[214] Meanwhile, the fact that the same works were usually performed all over Italy, from North to South and including the islands, makes theater a particularly interesting source for research into nineteenth-century Italian culture. The musical press, with its network of correspondents covering some of the most remote theaters in Italy (and abroad), spread news about performances and their reception all over the peninsula.[215] Newspapers and learned journals too reported on the current season, with the effect that even those readers who did not go to the theater knew what was happening on stage. Historians usually leave those articles in the periodicals to the few opera scholars interested in reception studies. What they miss are the heated debates over life in the United States—debates on slavery, the Civil War, and even the American constitution, all triggered by the experience of Verdi's *Un ballo in maschera* or Rota's ballet *Uncle Tom*. Including these sources in my analysis stands for an approach to intellectual history that attempts to bridge the gap between political thought and culture.

CHAPTER ONE

America as History

Fratricide and Civil War

"'Kill him! Kill him!' . . . The maledictions, the imprecations, the execrations of the multitude, were horrible. . . . The cries, the howling, the menaces, the violent din of bells, still sounding the alarm, increased the confusion and the horrors of these moments."[1] With these words the Italian historian Carlo Botta re-created the Boston massacre of 5 March 1770. The passage forms part of his monumental *History of the War of Independence of the United States of America*, first published in France in 1809. Most probably a piece of fictional writing, the quote describing the scene was frequently picked up by later Italian historians of the United States. For Italian readers the episode came to symbolize the brutality associated with the North American colonies' noble quest for independence. Although Botta never set foot in the United States, his book became one of the most successful histories of the American War in any language, followed by numerous reprints, translations, and new editions. It was the first book on the country's history to be widely read among educated Italians, a standard work on the war on both sides of the Atlantic, held in high regard even by surviving protagonists of the conflict itself.[2]

Most Italians writing about the American War of Independence found the brutality of a war dividing spouses, brothers, and entire families deeply unsettling.[3] Making full use of the emotional register that characterized the literary as well as the political language of the Risorgimento, these authors described the War of Independence and the American Revolution as a "civil war," a term used by William Robertson in his 1777 *History of America*, by that time widely available also in Italian translation. The use of the term contrasts dramatically with the enthusiasm for America's struggle for independence among many of the French philosophes, who considered American freedom the political realization of Enlightenment ideals.[4]

The Wyoming massacre of July 1778 (*Viomino* in Italian) is reported in almost all Italian accounts of the American War of Independence and serves to illustrate the Italians' emphasis on factional violence.[5] In an effort to gain control over the Hudson River, British troops recruited American Loyalists as well as Native Iroquois to seize a stronghold of revolutionaries in the fertile Wyoming Valley in Pennsylvania. In Botta's words, "this little country presented in reality the image of those fabulous times which the poets have described under the name of the *Golden Age*."[6] During its seizure several hundred revolutionaries were killed in combat; and many dozens more, including women and children, were massacred after the battle was over, their houses set on fire, their fields devastated, and their cattle killed. While many English-language accounts of the war do not mention these events at all, Italian descriptions of the massacre go into almost unbearable detail. Botta describes how a Loyalist, "whose mother had married a second husband, butchered her with his own hand, and afterwards massacred his father-in-law, his own sisters, and their infants in the cradle. Another killed his own father, and exterminated all his family. A third imbued his hands in the blood of his brothers, his sisters, his brother-in-law, and his father-in-law."[7] The description of these scenes contrasts dramatically with Mazzini's idea of the nation as a community of blood, when he described the family as "the *patria* of the heart."[8] For any reader the images evoked by Botta's accounts are deeply disturbing. The fact that the family occupied such a prominent role in allegories of the Italian nation added a further semantic dimension to the horror. Another Italian historian, Carlo Giuseppe Londonio, writing a few years after Botta, explains that "not barbarians or foreigners, but brothers against brothers, sons against their parents, all turned to iron parricide."[9] Similar the emphasis of Giuseppe Compagnoni, writing in the early 1820s: "warriors, old or young, women, everybody . . . perished, some tortured in horrendous carnage, others burned alive. They were colonists and fellow citizens, who in such manner treated their own fellow citizens and colonists who were their equals."[10]

In most accounts the depiction of the bloodshed continues over several pages. Botta concludes his account with an apocalyptic image of total devastation: "They cut out the tongues of the horses and cattle, and left them to wander in the midst of those fields lately so luxuriant and now in desolation, seeming to enjoy the torments of their lingering death."[11] As the first Italian to describe the Wyoming massacre, Botta, in his own words, "long hesitated whether we ought to relate particular instances of this demonic cruelty; the bare remembrance of them makes us shudder. But on reflecting that these examples may deter good princes from war, and citizens from civil discord, we have deemed it useful to record them."[12] Botta makes it obvious that no people should follow the Americans suit. Trying to overcome the mental barrier that distances his Italian readers from this almost inconceivable barbarity, Londonio offers a psychological explanation for the unfolding levels of violence. Describing the descent of a once happy community from paradise to hell, he resorts to an almost poetic register of language to expound what happened: "The contest with England brought about two parties unequal in strength, but equal in obstinacy." Those made to leave returned with the British troops. "[Their] thirst for revenge, for a long time repressed by a feeling of impotence, became ever more ferocious, comparable to a river, which, long restrained by its banks, suddenly breaks over the borders and releases itself with full strength over the planes, destroying woods, fields, cattle and villages. As a consequence, the revenge of these exiles came late but ever more sinisterly and frighteningly."[13]

While Italian historiography about the American War of Independence cannot be reduced to a phantasmagoria of devastation and fratricide, its emphasis on the conflict as civil war (rather than the aspect of a war against British oppression), and the stress on brutal bloodshed and uncontrolled passion, has been largely overlooked by later generations of historians. The war's violent impact on civil society, as depicted in these accounts, seems to make it crucially different from traditional military conflicts, such as the recently ended Seven Years' War.[14] The experience of war in these accounts also appears strongly gendered, presenting men enacting the historical change associated with the War of Independence on the back of women as victims. These gender divisions contrast dramatically with female allegories of the nation in mid-nineteenth-century Italy, which tended to represent the nation's strength and purity, or alternatively, the nation in dignified gestures of mourning.[15] Although recent historiography on women in the American War of Independence challenges the conventional distinction between male agents and female victims, early Italian attempts to historicize the events employ these gender roles as an idiosyncratic aspect of the war.[16] For comparable images of civil ruin Europeans had to turn to the Greek War of Independence. For instance, Eugène Delacroix's *Scène des massacres de Scio*, painted for the Paris Salon of 1824, depicted the hopeless suffering of victims, rounded up for enslavement. The scene is set in a landscape of complete desolation.[17]

In Delacroix's painting the contrast between aggressor and victim opposes Ottomans and Greeks, Orient and Occident, understood as the contrast between civilization and barbarity. In the case of the Italian descriptions of the American War of Independence the authors are perplexed by a war between brothers, dividing one nation. The brutal destruction of the American paradise in Wyoming Valley becomes a metaphor for American men entering historical consciousness, a process that contrasts most strikingly with the innocence of prewar life in the colonies' natural world. Meanwhile, the Italian narratives confront us with a sharp distinction between the process of American nation building and Italians' idea of their own nation as it emerged in literary tropes during the period of the Risorgimento—an image of kinship, honor, and sanctity, analyzed by Alberto Banti in *La nazione del Risorgimento*.[18] While

FIG. 6. Eugène Delacroix, *Scène des massacres de Scio* (1824). Paris, musée du Louvre, D.A.G. Photo © RMN-Grand Palais (musée du Louvre) / Thierry Le Mage.

Italy's struggle for independence freed the nation from an ethnic foreigner, the American War of Independence was a war between brothers. In his *Theory of Moral Sentiments* Adam Smith distinguishes between the "animosity of hostile factions" and "that of nations."[19] It is the emphasis on this distinction with which Italians explain the American Civil War's atrocious nature.

This chapter examines how Italians have written the history of the American War of Independence, frequently in contrast to ideas of their own nation. With references to a wider range of Italian authors, at the forefront of this analysis are three substantial historical accounts of the war—Botta, Londonio, and Compagnoni—written during the first few decades of the nineteenth century, when Italians were attracted to the subject by its novelty, but also by the confrontation with experiences of political and social change at home, in the aftermath of the French Revolution. Furthermore, this chapter will demonstrate how subsequent commentators on these works, during later stages of the Risorgimento, have occasionally used this body of historiography to provide empirical evidence to support a different political agenda.[20] Despite the abhorrent brutality of the saga depicted by Italy's early historians of the United States, within the changing political context of the Risorgimento American experiences helped some Italian political thinkers to outline an Italian path toward Unification. In teleological fashion, those thinkers read their own political ideas back into earlier histories of the American War of Independence. It was this process that suddenly allowed the later protagonists of the Italian Risorgimento to turn these histories into blueprints for Italy's road to independent statehood. While this reading of American history became influential during the later course of the Risorgimento, my chapter argues that it had little in common with the authors' original intentions. Moreover, their views always represented only part of the political spectrum.

Histories and the Politics of Reception: Carlo Botta

Carlo Botta was born in San Giorgio Canavese, north of Turin, in 1766 and died in Paris in 1837.[21] Initially trained as a medical doctor, in the early 1790s he became involved in anti-Sabaudian and republican activity, was briefly arrested, and then spent some time in Switzerland, before joining the French army as a medical officer. After moving to Lombardy, he started a career as political commentator and collaborator on various periodicals. Following an expedition to Corfu (then still part of the Venetian Republic) he published *Storia naturale e medica dell'isola di Corfù* in 1798. That year he briefly joined the provisional government of the short-lived Piedmontese Republic, before it was absorbed by France. Like other Italian Republicans, Botta grew increasingly hostile toward the French administration and was among the first signatories of a petition in favor of Italian unification (*Consiglio dei cinquecento*, July 1799). After various positions in the French administration in Piedmont, he became a member of the French legislative assembly (1802 to 1809) and settled permanently in Paris. During those years, with easy access to France's best research libraries, he wrote most of his *History of the American War of Independence*.[22] Following Napoleon's defeat, he was appointed rector of the Academy of Rouen (1817–22) and later lived from his writings. Readmitted to the *Académie* in Paris, he was made a *Chevalier de la legion d'honneur* in 1834.[23]

History, and in particular the history and geography of the New World, fascinated more than one generation of the Bottas. During a short stay as doctor in Grenoble, still in the 1790s, Botta had married Antonietta Viervil, with whom he had three sons. The eldest, Paul-Émile, originally followed his

FIG. 7. Francesco [Carlo] Giuseppe Guglielmo Botta, in F. Morghen, *L'omnibus pittoresco* (1839). Lithograph by Focosi. Image courtesy Wellcome Library, London.

father's career as a doctor but then became an explorer and archaeologist, and later a diplomat in the Middle East. Admired by the young Benjamin Disraeli, he worked closely with the diplomat and fellow archaeologist Austen Henry Layard, who was well connected to the Italian exile community in London.[24] Unlike his father, Paul-Émile visited the New World and then wrote up his impressions, but he is mostly associated with discoveries concerning the Assyrian civilization and the first excavations of Khorsabad and Nineveh.[25] Carlo translated his son's book of travels to the New World into Italian.

Carlo Botta was the best-known Italian historian of his generation, a household name even among intellectuals outside Italy.[26] His weighty *History of the American War of Independence* is divided into four volumes and fourteen books. The original Italian edition was printed in France in 1809, followed by editions published in Parma between 1817 and 1819, and a Milanese edition in 1819. There are four more Italian editions printed before 1856. The first French translation appeared in 1812, the first American translation in 1820–21. In addition to the *History of the American War of Independence*, Botta's major historical works were a *Storia d'Italia dal 1789 al 1814*, published in 1824, and *Storia d'Italia continuata da Guicciardini fino al 1789*, originally published in 1832. Within the Risorgimento's political debates, after his early republicanism, Botta emerged as a moderate Liberal, who was disillusioned with the French experiences in Northern Italy and perceived Napoleonic rule as a form of despotism. He shared his feelings about the French occupation with famous writers such as Count Vittorio Alfieri and Ugo Foscoli. Botta's interest in American history served as a contrast to these European experiences. As he explains in the first chapter of his book, the American concept of national independence was rooted in a social model that favored the notion of civil liberty: "Everything . . . in English America was based on an unusually broad context of social life; tended to favour and develop civil liberty; everything appeared to lead towards national independence."[27] For Botta "the intellects of the Americans" were "perfectly free," not just in matters of religion, but "especially upon the affairs of the government," contrasting with the situation he had experienced prior to the Revolution in Piedmont.[28] It was on this basis that in America "the republican maxims became a common doctrine"[29] and that social hierarchies disappeared: "The composition of society in the English colonies rendered the inhabitants averse to every species of superiority, and inclined them to liberty. Here was but one class of men; . . . opulence, and hereditary honours, were unknown amongst them."[30] What he explains to his readers is not an abstract concept of political liberty, but one that had developed out of the very specific conditions of the historical relationship between Britain and its American colonies, out of its religious, political, and economic context. "Finding all his enjoyments in rural life, [the American] saw spring up, grow, prosper, and arrive at maturity, under his own eyes, and often by the labour of his own hands, all things necessary to the life of man; he felt himself free from all subjection, from all dependence; and individual liberty is a powerful incentive to civil liberty."[31]

The circumstances under which this very specific notion of American liberty emerged could not be more different from those in Botta's home country, where social, economic, and political life had been based on the division of labor and social hierarchies for centuries. Rather than presenting a critique of social conditions at home, what he explains here are the specific circumstances of life in the New World. This image of American life was not free of romanticized idealizations: "As they lived dispersed in the country, mutual affection was increased between members of the same family, and finding happiness in the domestic circle they had no temptation to seek diversion in the resorts of

idleness, where men too often contract the vices which terminate in dependence and habits of servility. . . . It is therefore evident that in America the
climate, the soil, the civil and religious institutions, even the interest of families, all concurred to people it with robust and virtuous fathers, with swarms
of vigorous and spirited sons."[32]

Botta's emphasis on the connection between climatic and social conditions suggests a debt to eighteenth-century reports on America as exemplified
in the writings of Constantin-François Volney.[33] Long sections of Botta's book
deal with descriptions of land and people and the political and economic relations between the colonies and the mother country, as well as with detailed
accounts of political and military developments. Botta's view of American
life is easily read in the context of recent European events. For instance, his
description of George Washington's virtuous character serves as a contrast to
Napoleon Bonaparte, without needing to mention the latter. Similarly, the
principles behind the American Revolution are described in opposition to
the recent experience of the French Revolution. Without becoming more explicit, Botta's outline of these entanglements starts from French motives for
supporting the American Revolution, a "desire for vengeance, the hope of
retrieving its losses, the remembrance of ancient splendour, the anguish of
recent wounds."[34] Although Botta admits that love of liberty also played a role
in stimulating the French to side with the Americans, hatred of the British
was their main motive.

While recent European events constitute an important background to
Botta's narrative, many of his later Italian commentators went beyond these
transatlantic entanglements, reading his book as a direct reflection on Italy's
struggle for independence. According to their account, Botta presented the
American War of Independence as a blueprint for Italy's own political future,
for an Italian War of Independence against Austria. Considering that Botta
wrote his book during the Risorgimento's very early stages, long before Napoleon's defeat and prior to the reorganization of Italy's political map at the Congress of Vienna, drawing this connection seems far-fetched, even if Botta had
grown disillusioned with Napoleon and wished to see the end of foreign domination within the peninsula. Such interpretations mostly reflect the idealistic
intentions of later commentators and a teleological approach to Italian history that became fashionable during the later stages of the Risorgimento and
after Unification. Writing several decades after Botta, those commentators
took the view that "he undoubtedly thought about his fatherland. . . . Unable
to talk about his people, he chose the Americans": so for instance his early
biographer Paolo Pavesio, writing in 1874.[35] Because for Pavesio the historical
context of the book's creation is obvious, he sees no need to declare his evidence. Based on his experience of four Italian wars of independence, a book
on the American War had to be intended as a recipe for Italy's own struggle
for independence. Pavesio's reading stands for a much wider Italian debate on

Botta's book, before and after Italian Unification, which will be examined in later sections of this chapter.

The point of examining the nineteenth-century use of Botta in political debate is not to criticize the author's Italian reception. Instead, Pavesio's version of the political and intellectual context in which Botta was allegedly writing points to the interest of historiographical debate for a history of Italian political thought. John Pocock speaks of a plurality of languages contributing to political thought, including law, but also historical writing.[36] Applied to the nineteenth-century debate on Botta, this means to carefully distinguish between the political and intellectual context in which the author himself wrote, and subsequent readings by different audiences acting within a variety of political contexts. Instead of making assumptions about what constitutes the political and intellectual context of the book's creation, the historian has to reconstruct its exact nature, using available sources and texts as evidence, and confront these findings with the context of later historiographical debates. When Botta wrote about the early history of the United States, the idea of the Italian nation's political resurgence was taking hold among intellectuals and political activists, but it was far from obvious that the Risorgimento would fulfill itself through a series of wars of independence against Habsburg and Bourbon rule. What then constitutes the political and intellectual context in which Botta wrote his *History of the American War of Independence*? And how does this context relate to the role the book played in later political debates, at different stages of its life?

Botta developed the idea for his book in Paris, after he had become a member of the French legislative assembly. During this period the salon of his compatriot Giulia Beccaria became an important intellectual context for his writings. Giulia Beccaria was the daughter of Cesare Beccaria (1738–94), a leading figure of the Lombard Enlightenment, and the mother of Alessandro Manzoni, future author of the *Promessi sposi* (1827), the most important work of literature associated with the early Risorgimento.[37] Years later Manzoni would play a significant role in publicizing Botta's writings. Cesare Beccaria's work on penal reform *Dei delitti e delle pene* (1764) had enjoyed considerable influence among the founding fathers of the American Republic, with some historians arguing that it stood at the origin of American law.[38] Beccaria, for his part, had shown little interest in the life of the American colonies; and his series of lectures *Elementi di economia pubblica* (published posthumously in 1804) did not refer to the colonial question at all. As explained in the introduction, many among the thinkers of the Lombard Enlightenment based their ideas on wider European experiences—political debates in France, and in particular reforms within the Habsburg domains.

Botta decided to take a different approach, relating the emergence of the American Republic to European events, in particular the French Revolution. One of the reasons for this new focus was simply that he belonged to a new generation. Beccaria's contemporaries observed the unfolding of the Seven Years' War prior to the emerging conflict between Britain and its American colonies. Botta, who was born in 1766, started his career as a writer once the American Revolution had led to the establishment of the American Republic. Despite this changing world-historical context, Botta's interest in the American Revolution still seems remarkable, considering that he never crossed the Atlantic—unlike several other Italian commentators on the early Republic and, a further generation ahead, the Frenchman Tocqueville.[39] Despite his detailed descriptions of the war's cruelty, Botta presented an altogether enthusiastic account of the American struggle for independence. The tone of his account might explain the book's popularity as well as subsequent attempts to read it in relation to Italy's own liberation from foreign domination.

Of the many editions of Botta's work, the most influential in terms of its reception was the 1856 edition by one of Italy's principal publishers, the Florentine Felice Le Monnier. Relying on an effective distribution system, Le Monnier made good use of advertising across the different states of the peninsula, with lists of his books appearing in most of Italy's major periodicals. Published almost half a century after Botta's original edition, the 1856 version contained a detailed and very accessible introduction by the respected historian and protagonist of the Risorgimento in Sicily, Michele Amari. Unlike the original edition in four parts, Le Monnier produced a handy work in just two volumes, offering Amari a convincing platform to set out Botta's alleged intentions for a wider readership.

In his introduction to Botta's book, Amari described the emergence of the North American Republic as a model for an Italian war of independence. The focus of his account is not the political institutions, which interested most of the early commentators, but the idea of a country that had liberated itself from foreign oppression.[40] Like Botta, Amari also had no particular expertise in modern American history. A former civil servant of the Neapolitan government in Palermo, and a specialist in Sicilian and Arabic medieval history, he wrote his introduction to Botta from the perspective of a Risorgimento activist, shortly before Italy's Second War of Independence. During the years of his exile in Paris, Amari had frequented the salon of the Principessa Belgiojoso, where he made the acquaintance of numerous Italian patriots.[41] Amari's exile was directly linked to his activity as a scholar. In 1842 he had published the influential history of another revolt against foreign oppression, the thirteenth-century Sicilian Vespers; even today this is regarded as an authoritative account of the island's struggle against French rule.[42] Giuseppe Montanelli, who will be discussed in more detail in chapter 3, recounts in his memoires how the book had been immediately banned and its author removed from his government post in Palermo. Called back to Naples, Amari preferred to go into French exile.[43]

Since the 1820s the Sicilian Vespers had been a popular topic for historical paintings, poems, and drama, including operas by Giuseppe Poniatowski

(1838) and later Verdi (1855).[44] Amari's book built on this tradition, becoming an important source of inspiration for the Risorgimento. In 1848 patriotic songs celebrating the Sicilian Revolution circulated widely throughout the peninsula and frequently referred to the events: "In te del Vespro memore."[45] Amari had written his account of thirteenth-century Sicily as a political allegory of the island's modern quest for independence from Naples. In addition to offending the Bourbon rulers in Naples, the book's strong anti-Catholic bias could be read as a critique of the neo-Guelph project for Italy's Unification under papal leadership, based on the peninsula's existing states. Although censored in several Italian states, new editions of Amari's *Sicilian Vespers* as well as translations circulated widely in Italy, and among exiles abroad. Amari's role during the Sicilian Revolution of 1848 further increased interest in his book.[46]

References to the Sicilian Vespers remained controversial throughout the Risorgimento, not only in Naples. In 1855, at the time of the French premiere of Verdi's *Les Vêpres Siciliennes*, Eugène Scribe, the libretto's author, published a program note claiming that the massacres that provided the background to his plot were a historical invention and had never happened. In this way the most successful French dramatist of all times hoped to avoid offending the French emperor Napoleon III, who attended the opera's premiere in company of the king of Portugal. The influential periodical *L'Italia musicale* replied to Scribe's statement with a detailed summary of Amari's main arguments, demonstrating how far his historiographical agenda reached beyond scholarly debate.[47]

The furore caused by Verdi's new opera happened just a year before Amari published his new edition of Botta's *History of the American War of Independence*. After the defeat of the Revolutions in 1848–49, an armed uprising against foreign rule in the peninsula had become an even more pressing issue. Given this context, and Amari's own political experiences, it comes as no surprise that Amari read and presented Botta's American history as a narrative closely related to the topic of his own *History of the Sicilian Vespers*, as well as to Italy's contemporary struggle for independence. Since the publication of his *Sicilian Vespers*, more than a decade earlier, the Risorgimento's political circumstances had changed. Amari no longer had to fight neo-Guelphism; and his radical democratic beliefs had given way to a more pragmatic approach to Italian Unification. Shortly after publishing the long introduction to his edition of Botta, Amari started to play a crucial role in gathering Sicilian support for the island's annexation by Piedmont. Although he still hoped to achieve some degree of autonomy for his native island, he worked closely with Cavour and then served as Italy's first minister of public education.

How did Amari present Botta's *History of the American War of Independence* to a new generation of Italian readers? Exploring the rhetorical skills for which he had been known since 1848, Amari's introduction starts by claiming that Botta's book had transformed generations of patriotic readers into a mnemonic community: "Who among us, having studied Botta's works during the happy years of thriving youth, was not inspired by the experience of this book, truly Italian not just in words but in its heart?"[48] Given the reception Botta's book had enjoyed, there is no reason to doubt Amari's account of its impact on subsequent generations of readers, offering convincing evidence for Banti's concept of a literary canon shaping the ideas of Risorgimento patriots.[49] Meanwhile, Amari's statement says little about Botta's original intentions, the intellectual context of the book's conception, or its reception during the Napoleonic period. For Amari, the idea behind Botta's *History* was no longer the exposure of a foreign argument, "argomento straniero," but a way to address contemporary Italian concerns: "General considerations about the virtues of America's English colonists . . . served the author to discuss the vices which he opposed, . . . the double yoke of absolutist power and foreign domination under which Italy had fallen."[50] While Amari abstains from offering evidence for his interpretation of Botta's intentions, or further insight into the alleged parallels between American past and Italian future, the bulk of his fifty-seven pages of introduction constitutes an essay on those aspects of American history that Botta had covered only briefly or not at all. After an ethnographic description of Native Americans, Amari accounts for the discovery and early colonization of the continent, followed by an overview of its different states, and culminating in a discussion of the United States' constitutional development after independence. Amari's stated intention was to synthesize works of history and descriptions of the American continent, which had been unavailable to Botta, assuming that these represent areas that Botta himself would have added, if he were to rewrite the book.[51]

While Botta concentrates his narrative on the heroic fight of the war's leaders, Amari aims to discredit England, offering moral grounds for the liberation from foreign occupation: "By England we mean here some of the merchants; the stubborn and proud George III, incited by his courtesans; an aristocratic parliament of hereditary peers and a House of Commons based on the narrowest suffrage; and more than anything a pedantic, choleric and inflexible bureaucracy, short-sighted, but with deep pockets."[52] Thus Amari's treatment of the mother country differs considerably from Botta's altogether positive evaluation of England's constitutional history, an assessment that was widely shared by different strands of Risorgimento political thought. Contrasting with Italy's tradition of praise for England's political system, Amari emphasizes the policies of a country from which any colony might legitimately seek independence. His immediate political aim here is not to discard England in favor of any other constitutional model, but to incentivize disobedience against foreign rule. In doing so Amari avoids differentiating between England's imperial ambition and the situation of Europe after 1815: the return to a system of international law, recognizing the post-Westphalian order of legitimate rule.[53]

For Amari, Botta's *History of the American War of Independence* had become an instrument to explain and justify Italy's struggle for national independence. But how widespread were references to Botta in accounts of the Risorgimento's political events? Is there evidence that Botta's book served this purpose? The republican campaigner and nurse to Garibaldi's troops Jessie White Mario suggested in her memoires that the Milanese boycott of tobacco and of the Austrian lottery prior to 1848 was directly inspired by Botta's account of the Boston Tea Party, but she fails to provide evidence for this connection.[54] While pamphlets in favor of the boycott and distributed at the time in Milan made reference to "i cittadini di Washington" (despite that fact that no city of that name existed in 1773), White's insistence that the campaign had been directly inspired by Botta's book is not shared by other accounts of the events.[55] References to the American War of Independence were common during the Italian Risorgimento, but there are no hints that Botta was instrumental in inspiring those connections between the American and the Italian Revolutions.[56] For instance, in the Sicilian assembly of 1848 the writer Fuccio Lionardo Vigo quotes a phrase by Franklin to tell Sicilians that "the war of emancipation is there; now follows that of independence." While Botta does indeed recount the same episode, we do not know that Vigo got his idea from Botta. Franklin's ideas circulated widely in Italy, independent from the alleged political impact of Botta's book.[57] Educated Italians were aware of Botta's book, and conscious of the role its author had played during the years of the French occupation, but drawing connections between American and Italian events does not mean that these were directly informed by the reading of Botta's book. Giuseppe Montanelli acknowledged Botta's interest in America's democratic revolution but made it clear that this fact alone should not cause one to credit Botta with democratic convictions or the belief that the American events constituted a model for the future of Italy.[58] Instead, it was on the basis of Botta's moderate inclination that the Russian tsar Alexander I expressed his appreciation for the *History of the American War of Independence*.[59] Botta's *History of Italy*, first published in 1824, confirms the Piedmontese's strong antidemocratic credentials: "in Europe the chimera of political equality has damaged liberty more than all of its enemies together"; this is a statement that makes Botta an unlikely advocate of American democracy.[60]

Within Italian political thought references to the American War of Independence often appeared within a wider context of European events, and not in connection with a specific course of action in Italy. For instance, speaking in the Sicilian Commons in April 1848, Gaetano La Rosa compared America's vindication of liberty to the ousting of the French kings Louis XVI, Charles X, and more recently Louis-Philippe and then used this analogy to justify the deposition of the Bourbon rulers by the Sicilian assembly. The broad connection he draws between these events served La Rosa as a rhetorical tool in an animated debate, but not as a blueprint for action at home.[61] While the *History of the American War of Independence* makes no direct reference to the future of Italy, Botta's *History of Italy* is one of the first accounts of the transatlantic entanglements between the French and the American Revolutions, arguing that awareness of American events fueled the discontent of the French nobility prior to 1789. However, Botta sees the subsequent impact of the French Revolution on Italy as almost entirely negative, in line with his *American History*, which had presented the American Revolution as an antipode to the more recent events of the French Revolution. In contrast with his account of American events, he describes the French Revolution's export in an almost apocalyptic language: "Europe turned upside down, confronted with the terror of an unrestrained licence in the name of liberty."[62] Finally, Botta's *History of Italy* underlines the author's doubts concerning the applicability of foreign political recipes at home, questioning "that an American plant can grow good fruits in European soil."[63] Reading both of these works together obliges us to question the extent to which Botta intended his *History of the American War of Independence* as a model of action for Italy.

As the following two chapters will demonstrate, Italians associated the United States with specific notions of freedom and independence but rarely adopted foreign models to define their course of action at home. Even Amari, drawing on his experience of 1848, stops short of presenting the outcomes of the American Revolution as a model for Italy. Here American federalism was his main concern. Amari details the persisting conflicts between individual states and the United States' federal institutions, where "each place lives with the difficulties of the present and the uncertainty of the future; industry did not recover, capital did not move; trade could not be revived without a system of common customs. It almost seemed as if America, freed from English tutelage, did not get back onto its feet." If ultimately the constitution saved the United States from anarchy, conflicts between Federalists and Democrats presented a constant risk of civil war, leading Amari to compare the situation to the formation of the Swiss *Sonderbund in 1847*.[64] For Amari these experiences taught the Italians lessons that were directly relevant to the insights they had gained during the Revolutions of 1848. From being an advocate of Sicilian independence, Amari had turned to endorsing the political program of the Piedmontese moderates, the Unification of Italy under the crown of Savoy. What he retained from his reading of Botta was the idea of a war of liberation fought under the guidance of a virtuous leader. Amari therefore warns, "the future history of Italy should never add synonyms of foreign vocabulary to our dictionary! More than any other example, America shows the danger this involves." He ends his introduction with the affirmation that, applied to the old continent, the American constitution "would not live for long."[65] Despite these warnings over foreign influences, by reading Botta's *American War of Independence* as a prequel to Italy's own liberation, Amari projected onto Botta political aspirations that had more in common with the script for his

Sicilian Vespers than with Botta's original intentions. Botta had written his book within a dramatically different geopolitical context.

Later historians often endorsed Amari's idea that Botta was thinking about Italy when writing about American independence. Even before Pavesio, discussed earlier in this chapter, Carlo Dionisotti had suggested in 1867 that Botta's principal aim had been "to show Italians the means that were needed to free themselves from the yoke of foreign despotism and to regain their national independence."[66] Although Dionisotti was closely familiar with Botta's writings—he played a leading role in publishing documents and correspondence Botta had left behind after his death—he does not provide proofs to support a direct link between Botta's American history and Italy's political ambition. Lack of evidence notwithstanding, Dionisotti's reading of Botta became canonical.[67] When Stefania Buccini, writing in 1997, explains that Botta wanted to show Italians "which means they should utilize to remove themselves from the yoke of despotism and regain national independence," her evidence is not a quote from Botta, but from Dionisotti.[68]

Recent commentaries on Carlo Cattaneo's Americanism are based on similar assumptions regarding Botta's influence. Based on a comment in which Cattaneo relates the American War of Independence to Italy's situation in 1860, Daniele Fiorentino assumes that Cattaneo was directly inspired by Botta, reading his objectives as to show "Italians what means were needed to free themselves of the yoke of despotism and to regain their national independence."[69] But the passage of Cattaneo Fiorentino references makes no mention of Botta; and the reader is given no clues about how Cattaneo understood Botta's political intentions or whether he related the book to Italy's own political circumstances.[70] As in Buccini's case, Fiorentino's wording comes directly from Dionisotti. Cattaneo was extremely well-read in the history of the United States and his library included most of Botta's works, among them his *Storia della guerra Americana dell'indipendenza* in the four-volume edition of 1819.[71] But this fact alone tells us little about Cattaneo's understanding of Botta. Instead, considering the clear ideological differences between Botta's and Cattaneo's political thought—as well as Cattaneo's disdain for the role of Piedmont in the process of Italian Unification—his reluctance to refer to Botta in this context might be understood as a deliberate strategy.

History, Literature, and the "Erotics of Art"

Given the extent to which the events of the Risorgimento impacted Botta's reception—and the extent to which later comments have distorted our idea of the book's intentions—what do we know about the original context in which Botta wrote and published his book? The book's genesis from discussions in Giulia Beccaria's *salotto* seems directly relevant to a reconstruction of the author's literary motivations. At the time of Botta's acquaintance with Beccaria, her circle debated whether events in modern history still lend themselves to the writing of heroic poems in the classical tradition. As a test case, the salotto chose the American War of Independence.[72] If the topic was good for a poem, Botta decided it should suffice for classical history as well and started to write a book fashioned in the tradition of the Italian humanists—based on detailed descriptions of battles, while seeking the moral truth behind the great deeds of the historical actors.[73] In doing so Botta followed an Enlightenment model of history writing according to which, in the words of Pocock, the narrative of "exemplary actions of leading figures," together with erudition and philosophy, became essential components of a "historiographic package."[74] This approach necessitated a certain level of manufacturing. As Botta explains in his preface, in order to enliven his characters he put words into their mouths that they could plausibly have uttered, a technique referred to as *prosopopoeia* and a reference to the historians of antiquity, Thucydides, Tacitus, or Livy. As Carlotta Sorba has argued, the modern use of this technique stood for a general ambition to experiment with new narrative forms in the reconstruction of the past.[75] A closely related aim of Botta was to exemplify with his book the good use of correct Italian language, again more a literary than a political motive.[76] Inspired by classical models, he explicitly rejected the methodology of the new German school of historiography, of Niebuhr, Ranke, and the men behind the *Monumenta Germaniae Historica*.[77] As Benedetto Croce pointed out, Botta was not interested in a philological-analytical approach to archival material, which at that time started taking hold in Italy, exemplified by the Neapolitan scholar Vincenzo Cuoco.[78] Instead, in a letter to Count Tommaso Littardi, Botta commented: "I certainly will not reduce myself to the role of a simple narrator, following the historians of today: a different, higher duty calls the historian. If they do not exalt virtue and struck vices, they had better stay silent, underserving of the title historian. If they expect newssheets from me, I do not know how to do those. I want to write as I can, like Tacitus, not like a modern scribe."[79]

The dichotomy of virtue and vice became key to Botta's style. Already Friedrich von Schiller, in his famous inaugural lecture on universal history at Jena, had expressed his contempt for the mere "craftsmen of history."[80] Botta followed a similar path. Representing the American events in terms of their moral virtue, he responded to a genre of heroic writing, popular at the time, which was more poetry than history. Even those commentators who later read a political program into Botta's work had to admit that "he cultivated prose as well as poetry," as Pavesio wrote in 1874.[81] John Burrow called this style of history "a highly literary form of composition, written by amateur men of letters."[82] Taking Botta's formal intentions into account means recognizing what Susan Sontag has called "the erotics of art," in many respects a more promising undertaking than speculation over Botta's political ambition.[83] "Metahistory" did not need discovery: nineteenth-century historical writers were frank about their methods and intentions.[84]

Botta's narrative strategy makes it difficult to apply insights gained from American events to Italy's own circumstances.[85] In this respect Botta's history was very different from Cattaneo's or Tocqueville's thoughts on American democracy.[86] Many of Botta's earlier writings showed clear signs of political convictions, in particular of his critical engagement with the ideas of Rousseau.[87] Botta's volumes on the American War, however, stick closely to chronology and contain little in terms of abstract political thought or constitutional debate. Not even the introduction seems to offer hints to contemporary European debates on national freedom, as they emerged during the Napoleonic period. Its focus on the colonial economy and on religious practice seems almost unrelated to Italy's contemporary circumstances. Rather than being an ovation for the principle of national independence, Botta's book explains the very specific process of an early example of decolonization. Comparing it to historical scholarship reviewed at the time in the Italian periodical press, there existed a general fascination with detailed descriptions of past military events, a genre popular among Italian readers independent from Italy's own historical and political developments. Botta's book responded to this fashion.

Long before the commentaries of Amari, Dionisotti, and Pavesio created connections between Botta's American War of Independence and Italy's own political future, Alessandro Manzoni had tried to help Botta finding a publisher for his work. Writing to Nicolò Bettoni in 1808, a year before the work's first edition was published in France, Manzoni praised Botta's skill in describing "the almost ancient and classical nature of some of his heroes, and of the entire American nation."[88] The same emphasis on the book's portrait of personalities still resonated many years later in an obituary for Botta by the secretary of the Accademia della Crusca, Fruttuoso Becchi, describing Botta's aim as creating better men, "uomini migliori."[89] Manzoni made no attempt to link Botta's American Revolution to the past or present condition of Italy. The Risorgimento idea of the Italian nation was in fact rather different from Botta's understanding of the American nation. Referring to the American War of Independence as the very "foundation of a people," Botta draws on a fundamental difference between the American and Italian nations. Through links of blood, the Italian people had existed for centuries; that they did not form a political union was due only to adverse political circumstances.[90] Unlike Americans, their nation had ancient origins. Thus, while praising the book and drawing literary inspiration from Botta, Manzoni must have been fully aware of America's otherness.

Botta's aesthetic preference for classical heroism responded to the tastes of his time but was not unproblematic in the context of Risorgimento literary debates. During the early decades of the nineteenth century, the reliance on predefined genres in contemporary literature—epic heroism, classicism, romanticism—was frequently criticized by Italian commentators. For instance, Giandomenico Romagnosi, writing in the *Conciliatore* in 1818, rejected the classification of literature according to artificial schemes of romanticism versus classicism, demanding instead a literature "adapted to our times and the needs of reason, taste and morals."[91] His views still reflect the controversies sparked by the Italian response to Madame de Staël several decades earlier. If Manzoni saw Botta as a writer in the classical, heroic tradition, not everybody appreciated his efforts as a positive contribution to the nation's resurgence. It was for these reasons that Mazzini, writing in 1830, despised the influence of "Manzoni in literature and Botta in history" as "injurious."[92] Botta was proud of Italy's classical tradition and denounced the romantics as "unpatriotic traitors," as "immature boys, vile slaves of foreign ideas."[93] These thoughts make it less likely that Botta intended to apply insights gained from the American Revolution to his homeland. Manzoni's attempt to interest Bettoni in Botta's book remained unsuccessful, and Botta had to wait another decade to find an Italian publisher for his work. By then, the sudden change in Italy's political circumstances created completely new conditions for Botta's reception at home.

Botta's Federalism of Nation-States

Throughout the Risorgimento, Botta's *History of the War of Independence* was read in connection with his other historical writings, not only the *Storia d'Italia dal 1789 al 1814* published in 1824, but also political pamphlets, like his *Proposizione ai Lombardi di una maniera di governo libero*, originally published in 1797 and reprinted as a book in 1840, three years after his death.[94] Despite gratitude toward France for having freed Lombardy from what he considered to be "foreign" rule, Botta—*il giacobino pentito* or repentant Jacobin—became highly critical of the experiences and legacies of the French Revolution in Italy.[95] As mentioned earlier, his appreciation of the American Revolution, referred to as a liberating revolution, was his response to the experience of the French Revolution and of Jacobinism in particular, often employing a language not dissimilar to that of Edmund Burke in his *Reflections on the French Revolution*.[96] Botta's fascination with George Washington serves foremost to present his readers with an *antinapoleone*, a man of virtue who contrasts with the *usurpatore* Bonaparte, reflecting Botta's growing disillusionment with Italy's French period after 1796.[97] A similar strain of thought can be detected almost a decade before he published his *History of the American War of Independence*. In his essay of 1797 he insisted that France should not oblige Lombardy to accept a constitution analogous to its own.[98] It has been debated whether Botta wrote this treatise as part of an official essay competition. While the famous competition of 1796 referred explicitly to the future of Italy, it is worth noting that Botta uses the concept of nation only in terms of the "nazione lombarda."[99] Meanwhile, even at that time his political thought shows awareness of the US constitution, where he rejects federalism on the basis that it was applicable only to a great nation.[100]

Another work, until recently unpublished, provides further insights in his views on federalism: *L'Equilibre du Pouvoir en Europe*.[101] Although written after his American history, and most probably after the Congress of Vienna, his pamphlet makes no mention of the US constitution, proposing instead a supranational federalism as an alternative to a Europe of independent nation-states. The work combines historical analysis with an assessment of contemporary issues. While the first three sections of his essay cover the period from the fall of the Western Roman Empire to the Peace of Utrecht of 1713, the fourth section takes him to the second partition of Poland in 1793, followed by a conclusion based on the most recent events since the French Revolution. His only references to the United States regard the expansion of its territory, emphasizing a major difference with the European state system.[102] His plans for the federalization of Europe develop out of the continent's own history and the emergence of international law since the Treaty of Westphalia. Rather than suggesting a radical break with the past, he looks at Europe's long periods of peace until the Seven Years' War, reminding his readers that "the different States almost formed just one nation, where the term foreigner was applied only to the inhabitants of Asia."[103]

Botta's *Equilibre du Pouvoir en Europe* suggests that the historian of the United States saw Europe's future not in the New World, but in its own past. Meanwhile, the same Botta whom the Risorgimento remembers as the herald of American freedom justifies the division and foreign domination of Poland as the best way to protect the country from its own faults, "a vicious system of government, the corruption of administrative power . . . , the plots of ambitious pretenders and the arrogant privileges of the high nobility."[104] Praise for American freedom did not exclude the justification for a policy that Botta's own patriotic readers widely regarded as despotic.

Transatlantic Botta

Probably the most influential reaction to Botta's *History of the American War of Independence* was a thirty-two-page review in Vieusseux's *Antologia*, published more than a decade after its first edition in 1822, at a time when Botta's book became more widely known in Italy. The piece is the direct translation of another review published the previous year in the *North American Review*, a periodical greatly admired by Vieusseux.[105] Although no author is mentioned, it is attributed to Edward Everett, a future secretary of state and president of Harvard University, who was in close contact with several Italian exiles.[106] The Italian version of the original review is the work of one of the *Antologia*'s regular contributors, the poet Michele Leoni. A collaborator of Ugo Foscolo and an early translator of Shakespeare, Ossian, Lamartine, and Byron, Leoni also wrote several historical works and occasional music criticism.[107] His contemporaries have sometimes called his political reliability into question, but it was one of Leoni's articles that caused the censors to suspend the famous periodical in 1833.[108]

The *Antologia*'s editors offered only scant information about the original source of Botta's review, reflecting common practice regarding the publication of foreign articles. As demonstrated later in this chapter, reprinting American reviews of Italian works became an important feature of Italian publishing, not restricted to the *Antologia*. It helped educated Italians to recognize the appreciation their scholarship enjoyed abroad. According to the American review of Botta's book, one reason for the remarkable public interest in American independence was the fact that the experience could be imitated elsewhere.[109] While this suggestion corresponds to the ways in which Botta's work has usually been read, it was written more than a decade after he first published the work, and during the wave of revolutions and uprisings that shook the Mediterranean in 1820–21. More importantly, this interpretation originates from an American periodical, the *North American Review*, in which the idea that the American Revolution had taught the world lessons in democracy was an orthodoxy. In this sense the review offers further evidence for Paola Gemme's view that the idea of America as a model for the Italian Risorgimento was at least partly an American projection.[110] Rather than being the view of Italian liberals, the article expresses the opinion of an American academic and aspiring politician. Meanwhile, by reprinting the American article, the editors of *Antologia* make themselves complicit in suggesting that America could (and should) serve as a model for national movements elsewhere in the world. Moreover, the review distances itself from the ill-considered uprisings that shook Europe at the time and contrasts them with the well-measured approach of the American colonists.[111]

Everett is full of praise for Botta's literary achievement, but he also raises a number of criticisms on factual grounds. In particular, the reviewer claims that Botta underestimated the colonists' strong affection for the motherland, arguing that Americans embraced the prospect of independence late and mostly with great reluctance.[112] Around the time when the review was published, John Adams confessed that he "always dreaded Revolution." He would have given everything he "ever possessed for a restoration to the state of things before the contest began."[113] Translated into its Italian context, the review suggests that a war of independence should be a means of last resort, certainly not an aim in itself. American independence was the consequence of a complicated process of deterioration in the colonies' relationship with the motherland after the end of the Seven Years' War. According to the *North American Review*, Botta underestimated this aspect. In the context of Vieusseux's *Antologia*, the emphasis on revolution as a last resource reads like a note of caution and criticism toward Italy's revolutionaries. Emphasizing the revolutionaries' loyalty to the crown was in line with the periodical's own moderate position, which understood the American Revolution as an alternative to the excesses of the French Revolution, without wanting to instigate another revolution in Europe, thus closely matching Botta's own views.

The article's Italian translator and coauthor Michele Leoni stood for a similar position. A native of Fidenza, in the duchy of Parma, Leoni saw himself as a devoted subject of the Duchesse of Parma, Marie Louise of Habsburg-Lothringen, daughter of Franz II and second wife of Napoleon Bonaparte, who throughout her reign (and after) remained extremely popular in Parma. After accepting a chair at his local university, Leoni's proximity to the throne even led to the discontinuation of his collaboration with Vieusseux.[114] In printing the American review of Botta's book, rather than instigating revolution at home, the journal cautioned its readers against searching for their future in another country's past. Unlike later readings of Botta, this was perfectly in line with the author, whose aim it had been to "deter good princes from war, and citizens from civil discord."[115]

Independently of continental debates, most Americans, including Thomas Jefferson, were highly appreciative of Botta's *History of the American War of Independence*. In 1821 the American Academy of Language and Belles Lettres chose Botta's book for its first public award.[116]

Carlo Giuseppe Londonio and the American Revolution

According to a later issue of the *North American Review*, published in 1828, Italians—owing to language, character, and culture—had a special disposition for the writing of history, and of American history in particular.[117] They also had the legitimacy to do so. Having abstained from establishing colonies in the New World, the Italians had won the American periodical's recognition and praise for the profound impact they had had on the discovery, exploration, and description of the new continent.

A famous Italian following in Botta's footsteps was Carlo Giuseppe Londonio. While some passages of his work closely followed Botta's narrative, taken as a whole his project assumed a different scope. Published only three years after Botta, in 1812–13, his three-volume *Storia delle colonie inglesi* starts at the end of the fifteenth century and goes on to the Constitutional Convention at the end of the 1780s. Its main emphasis, therefore, is on colonial America. Like Botta, in addition to printed documents, Londonio uses secondary sources in several languages, including histories of the major European powers involved in the project of colonial expansion.[118] Although his history is a largely chronological account of events, one of Londonio's main interests is in understanding the driving forces behind the exploration of new territories and the encounter between different civilizations. There is a theoretical and philosophical dimension to Londonio's work, although not in a narrow political sense. Londonio belonged to moderate liberal circles in Milan, working for the Napoleonic and then for the returning Austrian administrations, mostly in the field of public education, where the young Carlo Cattaneo was among his collaborators.[119] A translator of Gotthold Ephraim Lessing, as a literary critic Londonio played a prominent role in the Italian debates provoked by Madame de Staël; like Botta, he positioned himself against the Romantics and the group of the *Conciliatore*. Highly decorated for public service to the Austrian monarchy, he was an unlikely candidate to pursue revolutionary intentions with his *History of America*.[120]

Despite a certain number of similarities, Londonio's book is a far cry from Botta's heroic account of the American nation's origins and independence. His detailed analysis of the early settlements in volume 1, of religious fanaticism, and of Britain's colonial and commercial administration expresses little admiration for the project of establishing new civilizations across the Atlantic. He refers to religious minorities' looking for a home in the New World as "bande di dissidenti," expressing disdain for a culture that seems to be lacking any degree of cohesion in the most fundamental questions of cultural values.[121] His self-confidently distant description of Britain's seventeenth-century constitutional turmoil and its wars with France and Spain throughout much of the eighteenth century make for a bad start for the emerging nation across the Atlantic. In Londonio's account neither do the big powers of the Old World nor does the New World offer the historical nations of the Mediterranean models to emulate. In his aloof assessment of life in the American colonies, the only exception he cautiously makes regards the early history of Pennsylvania, described as a "rare example of virtue," to be admired by the "most civilized nations of the Old Continent.[122] Otherwise colonial America appears as a space of constant warfare, marked by massacres at the hands of Native populations, the destruction of settlements, exhausted by disease, the constant struggle for survival, and the oddities of an exploitative colonial administration.

In his description of fights between settlers and Natives—throughout the book referred to as *selvaggi* or "barbari rapaci e crudeli"—Londonio emphasizes violence on both sides, in marked contrast to many of the French eighteenth-century accounts, but similar to other early nineteenth-century Italian descriptions of life in the New World.[123] The constant contestation of space, as well as the harsh confrontation between civilization and its absence, deeply troubled Italian commentators, often expressing itself in the use of pejorative language when referring to Native populations, while at the same time expressing horror at attempts at their extermination. The description of the American colonies in the Italian translation of the Burkes' book, published almost half a century before Londonio's account, was not entirely sympathetic toward Native cultures but mostly spoke of "americani" and "gente d'America" as well as "aborigines" and "indiani," suggesting that a different use of language was not unthinkable at the time.[124] While European fascination with the otherness of Native Americans is reflected in most Italian accounts of the War of Independence, Giuseppe Compagnoni was one of the few commentators to realize that the American Revolution became the final blow to the populations' territorial integrity and political independence.[125] Others uncritically echoed the revolutionaries' view that the Natives' alleged savagery justified their extinction. For instance, Botta explained the Indians' participation in the war with "their natural thirst for blood and pillage."[126] Recognizing that the Iroquois nations had long been allied to the British in their wars against France, it was George Washington—admired by all Italian accounts of the war—who ordered that their territory should not "merely be overrun but destroyed."[127] Their villages and orchards were burnt down, even women and children massacred. Despite their relative indifference toward the Natives' fate, for most Italian commentators this situation did not present a healthy start for a new civilization: "history has taken note of it; and the fame of this horrible sacrilege will be eternally remembered," Compagnoni concluded his *History of America*.[128]

In Londonio's account, the settlers offer little scope for the colonies' moral or material improvement: "Rarely do you find a good family man or citizen. They are people of limited faculties and disorderly behaviour, pushed by their whim to seek fortune in these settlements. Without the means to put these vast and raw lands to profitable use, they often end up ruining everything they have."[129] Like most Italian commentators, Londonio also considered the institution of slavery utterly repulsive.[130] One of the few praiseworthy points about the colonies is the principle of religious toleration, but he sees its merits overshadowed by sectarianism and fanaticism, describing the Shakers as "gente idiota" and the Quakers as "hypocrites."[131]

With his emphasis on military conflict and struggle between great powers, Londonio produced a global history of colonial America in an age of international warfare, with events such as the Austrian War of Succession and the Seven Years' War forming the context for the emergence of the American nation. Viewed from this perspective, Italy appears as a haven of civilization, contrasting with the constant turmoil and bloodshed of the transatlantic world. Without even mentioning his homeland, he writes as a self-conscious and proud Italian, describing an exotic and deeply unsettling polity. Medieval hostility between the Italian city-republics constitutes a long-forgotten past, with the modern Italian states presenting the world with a superior form of international relations. Concluding the first volume of his history with the British conquest of Canada in 1763, Londonio offers a rather demoralizing picture of the merits of victory: "The efforts made to support this war in America, Europe and other parts of the world exhausted [Britain] of men and money. In the midst of victory's splendour taxes doubled, public deficit exploded, and while repeated triumphs provided the State with an illusion of increased power, its strength diminished and the difficulties of proceeding with the war became greater every day."[132] From the Americans' point of view, the motherland's circumstances after this global war were the start of their fiscal exploitation and their submission to the English parliament's dictates. According to Londonio, the notion of American freedom, "la libertà dell'America," had become irreconcilable with a colonial regime.[133] Londonio's description of colonial exploitation in the New World contrasts dramatically with the author's proud consciousness as a Milanese patrician, who reconciles the notion of shared Italian culture with a local sense of civic duty and loyalty toward Lombardy's changing rulers.

For Londonio, the American nation developed its political identity in response to the colonies' conflict with the English parliament. He uses events such as the Boston massacre to describe with unfailing realism the brutality of this process—"ammazzalo, ammazzalo!," "kill him, kill him!"—quoting directly from Botta's description of the scene mentioned at the start of this chapter.[134] However, opposition to the imposition of taxes not only united Americans but also created ideological divisions between them, adding to the cultural and religious heterogeneity, which was the source of consternation throughout Londonio's work. Despite his sympathy for the Americans' economic and political concerns, his description of the Revolution as a "civil war" between settlers and mother country has a particular resonance with Italian readers, evoking images otherwise associated with Petrarch and the medieval author's description of the wars between Italy's city-republics, where every community was divided along ideological lines.[135] In America, the rebellion resulted in despotism: "new men, without any sense of public responsibility, directed the people according to their own beliefs, who obeyed as if they followed the despotic will of a single man."[136] Londonio concedes an exception for George Washington, but later developments also showed how "the almost dictatorial authority conferred on Washington by Congress created jealousy among many rigid republicans who viewed America's nascent liberty abandoned to his discretion. . . . The wicked, the envious, all those who were opposed to his authority, or abused his virtue, moved openly against him."[137] Londonio's emphasis on violence and political and social disintegration contrasts remarkably with the classical account of America as a frontier society, where the shared experience of freedom united the pioneers into one nation.[138]

What follows is a detailed description of numerous battlefields, not dissimilar from Botta, but exposing with unfailing clarity the determination on both sides. Commenting on the destruction of Norfolk in 1776, Londonio concludes that "the fury led men on both sides to the most ferocious excesses against their fellow citizens, well beyond the anger of any foreign enemy."[139] The price America paid for its freedom was immense, leading to a people deeply marked by "massacres and devastation."[140] Despite the troops' courage and determination, their condition was miserable and the wider populations' attitude toward them indifferent. Summarizing their fate during the winter of 1777 he shares the following episode: "in a climate where the winter is so cold that even the biggest rivers freeze, the American soldiers, some without clothes, others with no shoes, were forced to walk over the ice and to sleep under open sky. Their feet were so torn that one could have followed them along the bloody footsteps they left behind. . . . Even harder was it to procure provisions. The farmers, more likely to look after their own interests than those of the Republic, preferred to offer their cattle and their corn to the enemy, returning with a full bag of coins, instead of selling them to the agents of the national army, who gave them a paper receipt of no value."[141]

Londonio's description of the American War is not a heroic tale of liberation from foreign oppression. It remains a narrative of a callous civil war, where the English mother country holds its own subjects at knifepoint and where solidarity between settlers has broken down. While recent historiography abstains from reducing the American Revolution to a fight between Englishmen, this view informed much of the Italian imagination.[142] The narrative of fratricide destroys the Italian readers' American dream. For Londonio not even victory brought relief: "with no money left, a huge debt, torn by internal divisions, without industry or trade, [America] was in no position to enjoy the independence it had gained through such toil and bloodshed. . . . Unhappy in its condition, worried about its future, its people gave itself up to darkest speculation about the Republic's future."[143] An Italian reader was not to envy Americans for the fruits of a war of independence.

America and Universal History: Giuseppe Compagnoni

In 1823, after a long career in politics and journalism, Giuseppe Compagnoni (1754–1833) completed his *Storia dell'America* in twenty-nine volumes, conceived as an Italian-language sequence ("in continuazione di") to the "compendium of universal history" by Louis-Philippe Comte de Ségur.[144] A history of both Americas, written in the Hispanocentric tradition typical of many Italian authors, only the last volumes of this monumental work are dedicated to the British colonies and their development since the American War of Independence. According to Compagnoni, this history became relevant only at the end of the seventeenth century, but then it offered great promise. "If internal discord doesn't produce a violent breakup, [the United States] will without exception become the biggest empire on earth, created not by chance or force, but by human industry."[145] Similar to other works written after Botta, Compagnoni's chapters on the war closely follow the Piedmontese's account of events, albeit with different intentions, as the following section of this chapter will show.

Compagnoni is the third Italian historian of America discussed in this chapter who never set foot in the United States. For Botta, chronicling the heroism of a modern war, his task was mainly a literary challenge. Londonio wrote as a scholar, but also to deter Italians from the prospect of a violent war of independence at home. Also Compagnoni composed his work for pedagogical purposes, though following a more abstract agenda.[146] While Ségur simply intended to inform the younger generation of past events, Compagnoni had a philosophical ambition—"to compare the history of the New World with that of the Old World."[147] Not only did he claim to be the first author to give the New World equal importance to the Old; he also wished to get beyond the ideological debates, which divided supporters of the Catholic Church's mission from those influenced by the Enlightenment.[148] Despite his appreciation of America's achievement, Compagnoni's account offers no incentive to model the Old World after the New.

Compagnoni was born into a once wealthy family of Lugo di Romagna, a provincial city in the Papal States, not far from Bologna and Ravenna.[149] Originally studying theology with the intention of becoming a priest, he then decided on a career in journalism and was soon drawn into politics. His first literary journal was the *Memorie enciclopediche*, published in Bologna.[150] He started reading widely in the field of legal studies, including the works of Samuel von Pufendorf, Montesquieu, Beccaria, and Filangieri. Although an early admirer of the American rebels, in his writings Compagnoni expressed almost equal appreciation for the ideas of Joseph II, Friedrich the Great, and the Grand Duke of Tuscany, Pietro Leopoldo.[151] The large number of historical works Compagnoni reviewed for various journals formed a central element of his training as a historian. Philosophy of history became an important aspect of his political journalism, "to organise the facts and to try to give them meaning, integrating them into their wider context."[152] Traces of this approach are easily detected in his comparisons of the Old and the New Worlds. In 1787 Compagnoni moved to Venice, where he became director of the fortnightly *Notizie del Mondo*, chronicling the events that transformed Europe during the years of the French Revolution.[153] Under his editorship the periodical played a crucial role in connecting Venetians (and increasingly Italians from other parts of the peninsula) with the rest of the world.[154] In Venice he also published his remarkable *Saggio sugli Ebrei*, arguing for the emancipation of Jews.[155]

In 1796, the beginning of Italy's *triennio jacobino*, Compagnoni founded his own monthly periodical, *Mercurio d'Italia*. In the agitated political debates of this period he championed the rights of women and opposed municipal autonomy in favor of constitutional unity.[156] In addition to his career as *deputato* of the Cispadanian Republic, he obtained a chair in constitutional law at the University of Ferrara. An important legal work of those years, *Elementi di diritto costituzionale democratico ossia principi di giuspubblico universale*, pays witness to his Jacobin convictions: "freedom is the people's right and its duty," his title page states.[157] In the constitutional debates of those years he passionately opposed the concept of a state religion, perceived as a violation of democratic principles. Protecting one religion, even his own, undermined the freedom of religion. The Cispadanian constitution largely ignored his views on the issue.[158] While religious freedom in the United States informed his thinking, many years later he perceived the fragmentation of its religious life as one of the American Republic's major weaknesses.[159]

Compagnoni's major claim to fame is often said to be his "invention" of the *tricolore* as symbol of the Cispadanian Republic, later adopted by the Italian national movement. After the unification of the Cisalpine and Cispadanian Republics, he was elected to the parliament in Milan. In 1797 he created another newspaper, the *Monitore Cisalpino*. The same year he published in Venice his *Elementi di diritto costituzionale democratico*, but several hundred pages contain only one passing reference to the United States.[160] During the years of the Republic and the Regno d'Italia he occupied several influential positions in politics and the judiciary and received a number of distinguished honors. Contrary to Botta and many other former Italian Jacobines, on the eve of Napoleon's coronation as king of Italy he saw the emperor as "a man who will surpass Alexander and Caesar," burying most of his earlier republican convictions.[161] After Napoleon's fall he lost all political office but continued to write for a living, including works on philosophy and Italian language and literature.[162]

Compagnoni's *History of America* evolves from a detailed description of the natural world—flora and fauna, landscape, and the indigenous population within this world—into a history of the Spanish, French, and English colonies, culminating in the independence of the United States. Alexander von Humboldt's scientific observations constitute an important source of information for Compagnoni, offering him empirical evidence to move beyond the debates of the early Enlightenment, which still informed Italian authors such as Carli as late as the 1780s.[163] Compagnoni involves his readers in a direct confrontation between two worlds, Old and New, explaining the work's universal ambition in the tradition of Ségur. Compagnoni presents the transition from a state of nature to civilization, and subsequently the overcoming of the (old) colonial order for independent statehood, as an outline of humanity's future, which directly reflects the reader's own experience of temporal change. Moreover, using his anthropological observations of native cultures as key to our own prehistoric past, he argues that studying the New World will reveal the origins of the Old: "The history of America clearly shows us what once was true for the entire planet. The philosophers have tried through speculation to guess at the world's beginnings; but the historian presents evidence based on the truth of facts."[164] As late as the 1820s John Locke's idea that "in the beginning, all the world was America" still offered orientation. The noble savage populated the European imagination still at a time when philosophers had passed their sceptre on to modern ethnographers.[165]

In 1828 the American diplomat and politician Caleb Cushing, writing in the *North American Review*, praised Compagnoni's history as a work "no other nation but Italy possesses, a full and methodical account of events in America, from the first discovery of the New World by Columbus down to the present day."[166] As in Botta's case, instead of commissioning its own review, Vieusseux's *Antologia* featured an Italian version of Cushing's piece the following year, which in turn was also picked up by *Il nuovo ricoglitore*.[167] A Neapolitan edition of Compagnoni's work from 1842 also reprinted Cushing's review.[168] In Cushing's view Compagnoni's American history contributed to the anthropological, philosophical, and psychological understanding of mankind as a whole; and its monumental scope made Compagnoni's work even more interesting to American readers than Botta's earlier survey of the Revolution. Perhaps surprisingly for an American commentator, Cushing pays particular attention to Compagnoni's description of the continent's indigenous populations, despite its depiction of the settlers' cruel methods of colonization. As Compagnoni demonstrates, the eradication of the Indians continued with equal brutality after the War of Independence.[169] The horror of those events notwithstanding, Compagnoni supports the United States' ambition on the basis of its civilizing mission: "barbarous people" will discover "their taste for civilisation through the excitement of industry, the attractions of commodities, the insinuation of religious principles. Time will show the fruits of this policy; and the day will come when Missouri will see its races changed to the extent that they will not remember what they had been like."[170]

Similarly to Botta and Londonio, Compagnoni's *History of America* includes astonishingly detailed descriptions of political and military events, despite the work's universal and philosophical ambition. Whereas Botta's account concentrates on the battlefields, in Compagnoni's case the accent is more on constitutional developments and political structures. Meanwhile, Compagnoni also largely abstains from discussing the war's potential impact on developments in Europe, surprising for an author so deeply involved in the Risorgimento. There is little to suggest that he conceived of his book as a model for Italy's own future; and there is no evidence that it was read with such ideas in mind. In Compagnoni's view, Italy had a rich constitutional and political history on which to draw for its future.

Compagnoni's decision to lend his name to the completion of Ségur's monumental history might seem an odd editorial decision. Undoubtedly, his multivolume work would have offered enough material to present itself as a major editorial enterprise in its own right. Why then did Compagnoni decide to write "in continuation" of the Comte de Ségur? And what does the reference to Ségur stand for? Born into the distinguished nobility of the court of Versailles, Ségur had been a high-ranking officer in the French army and an ambassador to Russia during the final years of the ancien régime. His father had been a commander of the French army as well as a minister of war under Louis XV. Through his mother's salon the young Ségur had met many of France's philosophes firsthand; and he was among the early supporters of American independence. When the crisis in Britain's American colonies emerged, Ségur's initial motive for supporting the Americans was deep-seated Anglophobia, similar

to the attitude of many French aristocrats and reflecting a century of warfare between Britain and France. During the Revolution Ségur's mood soon
shifted from anti-British to positive pro-American feelings.[171] Together with
the Marquis de Lafayette and the Vicomte de Noailles, he decided to support
the American war effort, but his departure was delayed until 1782, well after
France had opened hostilities against England.[172] He became friends with
Washington, Jefferson, and Franklin and at some point considered settling
permanently in America with his family. For Ségur, America was a country
associated with freedom and youth: "Everyone lives for himself and dresses as
he pleases, not as it pleases fashion. People here think, say, and do what they
like; nothing compels them to submit to the caprices of fortune and power. . . .
I shall be told that America will not always preserve such simple virtues and
such purity of morals, but were she to retain them no longer than a century,
is a century of happiness so inconsiderable a blessing?"[173] Although for much
of his life Ségur had been a moderate Royalist, after the French Revolution he
turned to supporting Napoleon, and, in 1805, he was appointed to the office
of the emperor's grand master of ceremonies, a position allowing him to make
full use of his artistic inclination and his talent as a poet and playwright.[174]

Compagnoni's book reflects Ségur's enthusiasm for the young country only
in some sections toward the end; but he shared the Frenchman's intellectual
ambition and his affinity for liberal and egalitarian values. In their admiration
for Napoleon, Ségur and Compagnoni contrasted with Botta, and many other
Italian admirers of the United States, who had become disillusioned with the
French Empire. For both men Napoleon's fall meant that they lost their previous position in society and had to earn their living as writers. By the time
Ségur set out to publish his history of the world in 1817, he was exasperated
by the course of events. The perfection he found in the past became an escape
and saved him from personal despair after Napoleon's fall.[175] Many nostal-
gists for the empire shared his feelings, a mood that affected many in France
as well as in other parts of the former empire. With the exception of a critical
article in the *Journal des débats*, Ségur's pessimistic outline of world history
was favorably reviewed by most of France's major periodicals.

Despite Ségur's firsthand experience of the American Revolution and his
enthusiasm for the young Republic, he never completed his ambitious literary
journey around the world. Compagnoni accepted the task of completing Ségur's work a decade before the count's death in 1830, but almost half a century
after the count had left the United States. Speculation as to whether Ségur
might add his own version of American events continued even after Compagnoni had published his sequence.[176] Despite the caveat of an all too famous
predecessor, continuing in Ségur's footsteps gave Compagnoni's project much
needed authority to undertake this task; it also added a certain noble flair to
the enterprise. For his publisher, establishing this connection was mostly a
sales strategy. As a monumental multivolume series, Compagnoni's American

history was sold by subscription, which guaranteed the publisher the amortization of a minimum number of copies. While it became one of Italy's most influential and certainly its most wide-ranging survey of American history, in Compagnoni's own judgement, publishing the *Storia dell'America* as a supplement to Ségur was a serious impediment to his own recognition as a scholar.[177]

Notwithstanding their biographical affinities, in many sections of his work Compagnoni decided to ignore Ségur's positive evaluation of the American Revolution. If one accepts the account given in his autobiography, Compagnoni was psychologically less affected by the changing world-historical circumstances. Compared to Ségur, Compagnoni felt more at ease rebuilding his life after Napoleon's fall, and there is no indication that he used the past as an escape from a depressing present. He was surrounded by a close circle of friends and intellectuals, including Vincenzo Monti and Giacomo Leopardi.[178] While recognizing the opportunities offered by the American Republic, Compagnoni abstained from seeking a better world across the Atlantic.

As for the American Revolution, perhaps surprisingly for a former Jacobin, Compagnoni saw first of all the huge and regrettable bloodshed of the war. Despite expressing his admiration for George Washington, the final chapters of volume 27 speak at length about the fragility of the early Republic and the frustration of the soldiers, the poor state of public finance, and the popular revolts against taxation. He sympathizes with the anxieties of the population after a long and exhausting war. At the moment of victory, the Republic's survival was far from guaranteed. Volume 28 starts with the "quadro funesto," the sinister picture the United States represented four years after the end of the war. Compagnoni discusses the weakness of the government and the urgent need to reform the federation.[179] Despite this dire outlook, of all the early Italian historians Compagnoni offers the most detailed and the best-informed discussion of the United States' early constitutional development.[180] Providing a largely descriptive account, the reader is reminded of the author's earlier career as a constitutional theorist, who during Italy's republican period had established the subject as an academic discipline at Italian universities.

As in Botta's case, Compagnoni's work is closely related to his previous writings. The *History of America* echoes an assessment of the American Revolution he had produced thirty years earlier, in an article for his Venetian journal *Notizie del Mondo*. Writing in 1791, he had positioned himself against the ministers of George III, who wished to "suppress a people by the use of force"; but he also lamented the quantity of blood Europe was paying for America's freedom: "the seas of the two hemispheres absorb the blood and the dead bodies of Europe." Dramatically, he asserts that he mentions "this fatal record only briefly, but already the pen slides from the pacifist writer's trembling hand."[181]

As with other Italian historians before him, Compagnoni also demonstrates a remarkable sensitivity toward basic humanitarian concerns, easily overlooked by the military historians of his day and the modernist philosophies of history that reduce human beings to fuel for the slaughterhouse of history. The tone of this passage is surprisingly similar to those quoted at the beginning of this chapter, penned many years later, in the early 1820s, and describing the Wyoming massacre. In 1791 Compagnoni came to the conclusion that America was profoundly different from Europe, still marked by the same absence of civilization that early modern authors noticed when confronting the New World: "In Europe we no longer have the cruel epidemics, which pass from one country to the next, leaving behind mountains of infected cadavers and cities emptied of inhabitants. Oh, gracious God! Is war less fatal than the plague?"[182] Although in the 1820s he is aware of the astonishing growth of the United States' population, he concludes the last volume of his *Storia dell'America* with a long passage on medical conditions affecting the United States, plagues that the Old World no longer knew—ferocious fevers, terrible spells of rheumatism affecting entire populations, and scurvy causing "the loss of all teeth at the earliest age," a condition that, according to Compagnoni, affected more than 90 percent of the United States' population under the age of thirty.[183] Robert Darnton was not the first historian to write about Americans' dental health, it having been a preoccupation of Italian observers since the times of the American Revolution. Castiglioni maintained in 1790 that the women of New England "suffer from losing their teeth early on and often die at a young age from resulting complications."[184]

Despite the constant struggle against the natural world and the nation's persisting political fragility, the war and the republican constitution, according to Compagnoni, had created conditions that allowed Americans to exploit the continent's immense riches: he lists the opportunities for agriculture generated by a favorable climate and seemingly endless space; the limitless availability of primary resources for the growth of industry; the inventive spirit of the population, which designed tools and machinery Europeans could only dream of.[185] Here Compagnoni does not simply rehearse established stereotypes. Instead, in the tradition of Italian authors like Castiglioni, he offers his readers a rich and evidence-based account, full of statistical information and based on a thorough understanding of America's political economy. Frequently he enlivens these passages with up-to-date curiosities to animate the reader's imagination: a four-year-old pig slaughtered in Georgia in 1819 produced the extraordinary weight of 698 pounds; the first Merino sheep introduced into the United States were sold at a price of up to $1,500, but they reproduced so rapidly that their cost was now less than $30.[186] In this respect Compagnoni offers more practical information on the United States than Botta and Londonio. However, his excitement is always balanced by reference to the country's very specific natural conditions as well as historical circumstances, which remain profoundly different from the situation of his home country. Like Botta and Londonio, Compagnoni's *History of America* was also not written to serve political debates back home in any immediate sense—and it could hardly be read as such. Conceived as a philosophical work to help its readers to reflect on their own experience of historical time, it was not a political pamphlet instigating Italians to follow the American rebels on their path to national independence.

The *Storia dell'America* became Compagnoni's most successful work, published alongside several other volumes on European history. Most of the countries he wrote about he never visited; and he had no access to their archives. Nevertheless, all his works were thoroughly researched in the libraries of northern Italy, to which reputation and political office granted him almost unrestricted access. The result was a philosophical reflection on historical time, about differences between peoples and cultures, but not a political theory that could be universally employed. Although later commentators occasionally criticized Compagnoni for having written too much, largely for economic purposes, his scholarly recognition is evidenced by the fact that even in 1831, two years before his death, Gian Pietro Vieusseux still invited him to contribute to the *Antologia*, then the most respected periodical published in the Italian language.[187] At his death in 1833, Tullio Dandolo remembered Compagnoni's *History of America* as a beautifully written, great scholarly achievement.[188] Despite this reputation at the time of his death, as a historian and protagonist of the Risorgimento he was quickly forgotten. Over the next few decades the role of the United States within the changing political context of the Risorgimento assumed very different meanings, which made Compagnoni's philosophical and anthropological approach less relevant to Italian readers.

Historiography as Political Thought

As mentioned at the start of this chapter, John Pocock reads historiography as political thought, a form of writing capable of introducing new political concepts. Most Italian historians writing about the American Revolution presented the United States as a political reality far removed from European experiences. Many commentators expressed their unease at the cruelty of colonization and the subsequent path to independence. As this chapter has demonstrated, not even the Italian Jacobins necessarily championed the American Revolution, including those who later distanced themselves from their experience of French rule. Meanwhile, subsequent commentators on the early Italian histories of the American Revolution frequently read these texts in teleological fashion, as intellectual contributions to the political project of the Italian national movement, most obviously in the case of the reception of Botta. While these teleological readings constitute an integral part of the later lives of these histories, we need to differentiate between the texts' original meaning—including their authors' intentions—and their later usage in a changing political and historical context.

Independently of their changing historiographical contextualization, these early Italian histories of the American Revolution posed questions about political and constitutional developments that their contemporaries sought to answer. In this respect Piedmont's first constitutional prime minister, the moderate Count Cesare Balbo, is of particular interest.[189] Like Botta, Balbo occupied several functions in the French imperial administration before embarking on a career as a publicist. He was also an influential historian, initially inspired by the critical-philological methods of German *Rechtsgeschichte*.[190] Historical and historiographical references constitute an integral part of his political thought, providing him with an analytical framework and points of comparison for the study of Europe's political present and future. It might seem surprising to see a moderate politician from Piedmont, a man who stood firm against any democratic or republican tendencies during Italy's Risorgimento, drawing on experiences from revolutionary America. However, while Balbo's political principles denied the right of resistance to legitimate government, he allowed for a number of historical exceptions from that rule, citing among other examples Wilhelm Tell, the Dutch Revolt, and the American War of Independence.[191] More importantly, to him references to America served as a contrast to the revolutionary experiences of France and Italy, to the republican experiments of the 1790s, and to the Revolution of 1848.

Balbo's concept of "independence" is of particular relevance here. In an essay published posthumously in 1857, but written during the Revolution of 1848–49, Balbo described "independence" as the principal aspect of "unità di nazione."[192] In his *Sommario della storia d'Italia* he described the twelfth-century conflicts of the Italian city-republics against Barbarossa as "guerra d'indipendenza."[193] The understanding of unity in terms of independence from foreign rule was key to the Moderates' political project during the Risorgimento. This project did not start from a positive definition of the nation, its inner coherence and cultural homogeneity: national unity did not necessarily mean that the members of a nation were "united by blood, custom, language and religion"—characteristics that only partly applied to the Italian nation. Nor did it require the existence of a single unitary state. For Balbo, the principal issue defining the unity of a nation was independence from foreign power. These characteristics made the United States an interesting point of comparison: emerging from a struggle for independent statehood, while being constituted by "very different peoples and tribes."[194]

While Balbo seems to justify Italy's lack of homogeneity with reference to the United States, the American people's "diversity" persistently troubled Italian commentators, to the point that some denied Americans recognition as a nation. As Compagnoni pointed out, the population of the colonies "might think of itself merely as an artificial union of men, consistent only thanks to chance and not due to harmony of blood, language, principles, of providence, as would be the case for other civilised societies, who by their right cannot be denied the title of nation."[195] What troubled Italians when confronted with Americans was the fact that conventional ideas of nationhood did not seem to apply. Meanwhile, Italians knew that they themselves lacked inner coherence as a nation. If Americans had been able to overcome their diversity to form a nation, Italians should be able to do the same. While such considerations illustrate the role of American experiences in the Risorgimento's political language, they did not mean that the United States offered Italians strategic or constitutional recipes to resolve their own future.

Balbo was intimately familiar with the work of Carlo Botta and repeatedly referred to him in his autobiography.[196] Yet in his discussion of the terms "independence" and "national unity" Balbo makes no mention of Botta's American history. This absence seems particularly striking given that Balbo used the American example to prove that liberation from foreign domination constituted a natural and positive process of historical development. In his *Meditazioni storiche* he argued that "as soon as the great experiment of America's English colonies was completed, their great transformation from the conditions of colonies to that of former dependencies [*nazioni figliuole*], a new fact emerged, which in the future might be recognized as a historical law, that former dependencies as well as the mother country benefit from their separation."[197]

Balbo made it clear that the American experience did not constitute a blueprint for radical change at home. He contrasts American independence to the Italian events of 1848, which aimed for independence, unity, and freedom "all at once," a project that would have required "a whole generation or a century" to be put into practice.[198] Trying to deter his Italian readers from radical ambitions, Balbo saw the American Revolution as a successful example of "moderate change," a conception of politics Antonio Rosmini had defined in a letter to Balbo as "improvement without offending the law."[199] What characterized the emergence of the United States, according to Balbo, was not the revolutionary break-up from the mother country, but the "moderation" of its founding fathers, who had abstained from a radical overthrow of the preexisting order, a constraint mirrored in the fact that the thirteen colonies of the British crown became the thirteen republics of the new federation, without trying to establish a unitary state, which would have had no historical precedent. The institution of the governors, dating back to the monarchy, was maintained. The monarchy became a republic, but the representative system remained. Any new territory joining the federation accepted these premises.[200] Emphasizing these continuities, Balbo's portrait of the revolutionaries' qualities takes up a theme previously treated by Guizot in an essay of 1839: *Washington: Fondation de la république des Etats-Unis d'Amérique*. For Guizot, as for King Louis-Philippe, Washington was a man of the *juste-milieu*, who had little sympathy for the "laisser-aller démocratique," a portrait of the nation's founder that was widely appreciated even in the United States. The notion of the *juste-milieu* became a crucial point of reference for both Balbo and Cavour.[201]

Balbo's emphasis on constitutional continuity between monarchy and republic closely echoes Botta's assessment. While making no direct reference to Botta, Balbo's outline of the American experiences contrasts less with the ideas of his Piedmontese fellow historian than with the use some of Botta's later commentators made of his American history. Amari's introduction to Botta, discussed above and published just a year before Balbo's essay appeared in print, took a very different approach, going so far as to criticize Botta for undermining the revolutionaries' intentions. Amari quotes Botta: "happy at having left behind reality, they retained the old order"; but then contends that Botta "misrepresents the historical facts and puts on record an idea that would in fact diminish the Americans' glory."[202] As the passage shows, Amari rejects Botta's emphasis on continuity and differs substantially from Balbo's idea of the American Revolution as an example of moderate change. Within the context of Risorgimento debate on Botta, Balbo offered an early critique of the radical readings of Botta, putting the experience of the American Revolution to a very different use at home.

Even half a century after the Declaration of Independence, Italian references to the United States did not necessarily mean an open endorsement of popular sovereignty, an idea Piedmontese Moderates clearly rejected. Instead, Balbo's interest in the history of the United States was in step with his awareness of the French and English constitutions, and his expertise in Roman and Italian history. His example shows that American history contributed to a much larger European debate on the early United States, which inspired aristocratic Liberals as well as democratic Radicals, and had much to offer to an Enlightened absolutist ruler such as the Grand Duke Pietro Leopoldo (as discussed in the following chapter). Foreign constitutions helped Italians to develop a set of political and legal concepts that gave direction to their own constitutional debate, without simply copying experiences that would not fit their nation's historical realities.

Especially the experience of 1848 led many among the Risorgimento's protagonists to reconsider their priorities; and the Moderates' emphasis on independence from foreign rule was not the only lesson to be learned from events. For instance, the Sicilian patriot Gioacchino Ventura, active mostly in Rome and supporting Gioberti's concept of a federation of Italian states, considered Sicilian independence from Naples to be of equal importance as the end of Austrian rule. It was in this context that he compared the Sicilian to the American and Belgian Revolutions.[203] Moreover, for many political thinkers, including Giuseppe Montanelli, Giuseppe Ferrari, and Carlo Cattaneo, national independence was not the main and only goal of their political struggle. As discussed in more detail in the following two chapters, their understanding of democracy forced them to reconsider political freedom beyond the abstract notion of national independence, seeking political conditions that would guarantee individual freedom as a true reflection of humanity's natural condition. Too narrow a focus on the nation risked loosing sight of the other important legacy of the Enlightenment, which was individual liberty.[204]

As regards the connection between American experiences and Italian notions of national independence, a different set of lessons could be learned. The Moderates were prepared to sacrifice liberty in the name of the nation, at least temporarily. After the Second War of Independence in 1859, Camillo Cavour wrote to Giuseppe La Farina, president of the Società Nazionale, that celebrations should be based more on "ideas of nationality and independence" than on "principles of liberty."[205] However, for Montanelli and Ferrari independence as such did not merit a revolution.[206] Instead, their main priority was the creation of political conditions that would guarantee individual freedom. For Montanelli the Italian Revolution was more than "a border conflict" (1851);[207] and for Ferrari, the aftermath of 1848 had reduced the notion of independence "to the ambition of the King of Sardinia." Instead, the Revolution had to be "the work of every single state: unification is an external political issue, revolution an internal social issue."[208]

There was no obvious connection between independence from foreign rule and freedom. For Montanelli and Ferrari, it was the correlation between revolution and democracy that mattered. While the United States served as one possible model of democracy, from 1848 the concept of democracy was increasingly tightly bound up with the idea of a social revolution as propagated in France.[209] Within the context of this debate, studying the transatlantic military conflict between 1775 and 1783 lost much of its earlier appeal. A wider range of political concepts associated with the United States became relevant to Italian political thought, but these were almost always discussed in relation to Europe's and Italy's own experiences. The following two chapters will engage with a number of different political concepts drawn on transatlantic experiences. The Revolutions of 1848 will serve as a case study to investigate the ways in which Italians evaluated the insights they gained from looking across the Atlantic.

CHAPTER TWO

Concepts in the
Language of Politics

When the American people declared its independence and the French
people proclaimed the rights of men, they were giving to all peoples a
lesson in philosophy.

—THE EDITORS OF THE *POLITECNICO* (MILANO), 1860[1]

Political Ideas and National Character

The introduction to this book questioned some of the assumptions behind
R. R. Palmer's concept of a transatlantic Age of Democratic Revolution, the
idea that the world needed America for instruction in constitutional rights and
popular sovereignty. The opening statement to this chapter, however, seems
to support just those views, that the American and French peoples taught the
rest of the world lessons in democracy. Two issues stand in the way of simple
conclusions based on this statement from the editors of *Politecnico*. First, they
talk about a lesson in philosophy, not in applied politics. On a philosophical level Italians always discussed American freedom; but this did not mean
that their own intellectual tradition had nothing to contribute to the nation's
future. Second, and more importantly, the editors made their statement in
1860, at a time when Italy reached the fulfillment of its Risorgimento and
constituted itself as an independent nation-state, in the months between the
French-Sardinian victory in Italy's so-called Second War of Liberation and the
proclamation of the Kingdom of Italy. Carlo Cattaneo had created *Politecnico*
in 1839 and revived it in 1859. He was a stern critic of Italy's Unification under
the House of Savoy. Therefore, rather than stating a fact, the editors wished
to remind Italians of a tradition of popular sovereignty that went well beyond
the limitations of the Piedmontese constitutional framework. Cattaneo aimed

for democratic republicanism; and he never returned from Swiss exile to live under Piedmontese rule.

The previous chapter argued that Italians were far from simply admiring the path Americans had chosen to reach independent statehood; that independence was not the only concept Italians discussed in relation to recent American experiences; and that they were aware that these experiences could not easily be applied to their own political circumstances. While events leading to American independence animated debates among educated Italians, the idea of humbly looking up to the United States' political institutions is misleading. Moreover, despite widespread sympathy with the revolutionaries, for some early Italian observers of revolutionary America, including for instance Filippo Mazzei, the constitutional development of the former colonies had remained below their expectations.[2] Others were even more critical, taking the view that there was something fundamentally wrong with the American understanding of freedom. Their assessment was not necessarily directed against America as such, but against those who thought that the United States provided blueprints for Europe's own political future. For instance, with reference to the so-called American School of French liberalism, Mazzini criticized Americans for their individualism, and the Republic for its institutionalized selfishness. America "suffocates the principle of association under the omnipotence of the self," he concluded in 1835.[3] Mazzini differed from those Italian Radicals who admired the American notion of freedom, although even they often refrained from choosing the United States as a model for the future of Italy.[4] Mazzini's critique of America echoes the views of an earlier generation of English Radicals. For instance, Mary Wollstonecraft held that America was "a head enthusiastically enterprising, with cold selfishness of heart." She described America as "the land of liberty and vulgar aristocracy, seated on her bags of dollars."[5] Because the Risorgimento's leading Republican was also one of the most critical commentators on American institutions, I will return to Mazzini throughout this chapter.

Perhaps surprisingly, some of the thinkers most profoundly inspired by American institutions were Mazzini's political opponents. Different groups of Moderates used America's constitutional development as a contrast to Europe's experience of the French Revolution. However, even among the relatively small elite of aristocratic Liberals, admiration for American moderation did not go uncontested. The letters of the Piedmontese nobleman Carlo Vidua, published after his death in 1834, described Americans as "devoid of imagination, incapable of generous passions, the coldest, most calculating people the earth has ever seen."[6] Count Federico Confalonieri, who went to America in 1836 and was received by President Martin van Buren in Washington, judged the speculative nature of the American economy harshly and voiced doubts that the Union would hold together. Although he had experienced one of the Habsburg's most notorious prisons, the Spielberg in Brünn/Brno, he confessed that he preferred it to a life in the United States.[7] The idea of Americans' lack of cultural sophistication further aggravated political disillusionment with American democracy. A powerful Franco-Italian image of the United States appears in Stendhal's novel *La Charteuse de Parme*, when Fabrizio del Dongo speaks of his plans to emigrate to New York, but is warned by his aunt of a sad life without elegance, music, theater, or love, dominated by the cult of the dollar.[8] The example closely mirrors Lorenzo da Ponte's impressions of American society discussed in the introduction, but also what Italians knew about Frances Trollope's *Domestic Manners of the Americans* and her novel *The Refugee in America*, both published in 1832.[9]

The examples quoted above bear witness to the proximity of political thought and cultural prejudice. Italian attempts to draw such connections reveal their ideas as to the social character of the American people, while also reflecting on their own national character. Pocock encourages us to view political ideas as an aspect of social behavior, reflecting social experiences.[10] This approach brings the analysis of political ideas closer to Koselleck's *Begriffsgeschichte*, which seeks to explain historical change through the analysis of social and political language, and understands itself as a form of social history.[11] Instead of taking the impact of American institutions on Italian political thought for granted, this chapter examines the complex process in which Italians engaged with American ideas when considering their own political future.

Similar to the mixing of ethnographic observation and political analysis in the early Italian histories of the United States, most Italian commentators on America wrote about political ideas within their wider social and cultural context. While Paola Gemme's work discusses how Americans "domesticated" what was happening in Risorgimento Italy for their own project of nation building, this chapter investigates how Italians domesticated American ideas—reading them according to their own terms of reference, or, at times, deciding to leave them to what they still considered an uncivilized Other.[12] This examination of the ways in which Italians assimilated and translated American ideas into the historical context of their experiences is centered on a number of key concepts as they appear in the writings of different political thinkers. While the previous chapter discussed concepts of independence generated by the Italian response to the American Revolution, the main themes discussed in this chapter are constitutional government, political representation, and federalism in the context of the more general Italian assessment of American political institutions. In discussing political thinkers including Gioberti, Romagnosi, Rosmini, and Mazzini, the chapter combines a thematic overview with a chronological one.

Natural Rights and Constitutional Government

Ever since the American Revolution Europeans connected the concept of representation with that of constitutional government.[13] Many understood the traditional diets, or the consultative representations of eighteenth-century enlightened despots, as detrimental to civil progress. For instance, a short pamphlet, published in Palermo in 1848, identified four principles of constitutional government: personal liberty and the writ of habeas corpus in the context of the rule of law; the separation of powers, with an independent legislator, a reference to Montesquieu's concept of representation; national guards; and freedom of the press.[14] These four elements combined would have the power to make an essential contribution to the civil progress of any people. The link between modern political institutions and civil progress was one of the points that authors like Filippo Mazzei had admired about the United States as early as the 1770s.[15] Nothing is known about the context of the pamphlet from Palermo, but its author quotes the United States alongside France, England, and Switzerland. In addition to foreign references, these debates always also pointed to the proud tradition of Italy's northern cities and the political institutions created during the medieval conflicts between empire and papacy.

Italian debates over the American constitution started long before the Revolutions of 1848. The plans by Tuscany's Habsburg ruler Grand Duke Pietro Leopoldo for a constitution (against strong local opposition) made direct reference to the Virginia Declaration of Rights of 1776, to the point that the draft included straight translations of entire passages from the American document.[16] Pietro Leopoldo, son of Maria Theresia and brother of Joseph II, was the most advanced ruler on the Italian peninsula and closely involved with the philosophes in Paris. In accepting the dedication of the *Encyclopédie*'s Livorono edition, he was instrumental in the diffusion of Enlightenment ideas south of the Alps at a time when kings, censors, and clerical authorities all over Europe agreed on denouncing Diderot's project as an expression of godless human hubris.[17] Pietro Leopoldo's project for a Tuscan constitution formed part of a larger package of legal reforms that gained considerable international praise, including the approval of Jeremy Bentham.[18] Following an early draft by Pompeo Neri, president of the Tuscan Council of State, Francesco Maria Gianni, another leading civil servant and future prime minister, wrote most of the final text.[19] The grand duke's progressive stance during discussions on the project usually outdid that of his advisors.[20] An important source of legal information in these discussions was Filippo Mazzei, with whom the grand duke maintained a close intellectual exchange, resulting in regular reports on Mazzei's experiences in the New World.

Born in Poggio a Caiano near Florence, but a naturalized citizen of both the United States and, later, Poland, Filippo Mazzei had moved to America from London in 1773.[21] Living in Virginia as a neighbor and close friend of Thomas Jefferson, his original plan had been to start large-scale wine production in the United States, but he soon became involved in politics and diplomatic missions. Having previously worked as a tradesman in London (where he taught Edward Gibbon Italian), Mazzei was intimately familiar with British and American constitutional history. A self-confessed cosmopolitan, his works played an important role in defending the New World's colonization and American institutions against their European critics, despite his later disappointment with political developments in the United States. For Grand Duke Pietro Leopoldo he wrote a report about Americans' political concerns prior to independence, published in 1775 in the *Gazzetta Universale*.[22] As he was an experienced tradesman, his analysis of the conflict concentrated almost exclusively on commercial and economic aspects. Subsequently he threw himself into the movement for independence, writing for American newspapers and representing his Virginia county on revolutionary committees. He was briefly imprisoned by the English, before returning to Europe in 1779, from where he continued gathering support for the American cause, although he did not officially represent the American government. In 1788 Mazzei published his *Recherches historiques et politiques sur les États-Uni*, defending the country against European accusations of anarchy and confusion, and pointing instead to a civic tradition of education and public debate that would support the process of American nation building.[23] His *Recherches* was specifically designed as a response to French debates, in particular the influential interpretations of two very different authors, Raynal and Mably. Originally written in Italian, the work was translated for publication in French by the Marquis and the Marquise de Condorcet.

Mazzei was convinced that Europe could learn from developments across the Atlantic, although this did not mean blindly copying its political institutions. It was in a similar spirit that Mazzei had translated the Virginia Bill of Rights and advised the Grand Duke of Tuscany on his constitutional project: "Any human being has to show an interest in the existence of a good government, in whatever part of the globe this government might be located," he wrote in his *Recherches historiques*.[24] But this did not mean to simply emulate American institutions. Moreover, emphasizing the American Revolution's moderate nature, he presents its causes not in terms of abstract rights, but as a long-term consequence of Britain's own constitutional development since the English Civil War. The Virginia Bill of Rights was merely the consequence of the colonies' separation from the mother country.[25] When advising the Grand Duke of Tuscany, rather than suggesting the transformation of his lands into a democratic republic, he translated the Virginia Bill of Rights into the monarchical context of the duchy's historical circumstances. As a safeguard against revolutionary appetite in his Italian homeland, and unlike some of the early European commentators on the American War of Independence, Mazzei's *Recherches* clearly emphasized the colonies' reluctance to break off their relationship with the motherland.[26]

Mazzei's *Recherches* demonstrates that Italians were able to conceptualize the American Revolution independently of the idea of a transatlantic democratic movement, distinct from the prospect of democratic revolution back home. Mazzei's ideas were far from contemplating a war of independence uniting the peninsula; and he saw the recognition of natural and civic rights as independent of the state's constitutional form. Rights could be applied to a republic as well as to a monarchy. Viewed from this perspective, the Virginia Bill of Rights served for Italians as a concrete example of how natural rights could be translated into legal language. Despite his involvement in Tuscan constitutional debates, nowhere in the four volumes of his *Recherches* did he refer to the political situation in his native Italy.[27] Meanwhile, the exchange of constitutional ideas between Virginia and Tuscany facilitated the United States' diplomatic recognition abroad. In the United States political observers were aware of the impact the bill had on constitutional debates in Europe, and on Gianni's concept of the *monarchia temperata* in particular.[28] It was in this context of constitutional exchanges that Franklin thanked Mazzei for contributing American ideas to political debates in the Old World. Later, as a consequence of tensions between the administration of Virginia and Franklin, their relationship cooled down.[29]

Mazzei was not the duke's only source of information on the American Revolution. At the time, long before the first histories of the American War of Independence appeared, Italian periodicals such as the *Gazzetta Universale* and the *Notizie del Mondo* followed the conflict between England and its colonies in unusual detail, frequently including references to the pro-American views of Edmund Burke.[30] Awareness of constitutional developments across the Atlantic has to be seen in the context of a much wider tradition of legal debates sparked off by the Enlightenment. Political interest in North America was reflected also in a more general fashion for all sorts of *Americana*. For instance, Piccini's short opera *L'Americano* of 1772 was premiered in Rome and then performed in Florence as well as in Pietro Leopoldo's country residence, before traveling on to Vienna.[31] An intermezzo for four voices, the libretto ridicules the gap between social conventions among the European aristocracy and the Americans' cultural inaptitude. If in the end Pietro Leopoldo's constitutional project was not translated into law, this was largely because of his legal advisors in Vienna and Florence.[32] After the death of his brother Joseph II, he became Holy Roman emperor and moved to Vienna. Uprisings after his departure prevented the constitution's implementation.

The previous chapter concluded that interest in the American constitution among Piedmont's liberal aristocracy was not to be read as an endorsement of republicanism. Likewise, despite its recognition of natural rights, the Tuscan constitutional project never questioned the divine right of dynastic sovereignty.[33] What is more, the main architect of the constitutional project, Gianni, strongly opposed the idea of Italian national unity. When in 1853 Giuseppe Montanelli, protagonist of the Tuscan Revolution of 1848, reviewed Pietro Leopoldo's achievements, he acknowledged his good intentions as a reformer; but for his constitutional project he did not have a single word.[34] The political agenda had completely changed.

While Mazzei is usually considered to be among the most influential early defenders of the United States in Europe, during the 1790s he also realized that political developments across the Atlantic lost much of their initial appeal, largely owing to the early Republic's internal political conflicts. Further complicating this assessment, many Italians started to become disillusioned with their experience of French policies at home. Thomas Jefferson, one of Mazzei's closest American friends, had been disheartened at political developments in the American Republic ever since his return from France in 1789, where he had served as American ambassador.[35] According to Jefferson, America had become monarchical, its citizens too aristocratic. Corruption had taken root, and many of the Revolutions' original achievements had been lost.[36] In April 1796 Jefferson claimed in a letter to Mazzei that over the past two decades the Republic's political system had been dramatically transformed, undermining the principles of republican freedom established during the War of Independence. This, he argued, was mainly the work of a new Anglican-monarchical party of aristocrats, intending to impose on the United States the British form of government. The executive power, the judiciary, and the central administration, supported by the interests of English and American finance, were acting despotically against the republican interests of the majority of citizens.[37] On his return from France, Jefferson had initially intended to retire from active politics, which explains why he expressed his views in such open language. In order to help Italians understand America's perceived political crisis, Mazzei had Jefferson's letter translated and published in Italian, with further versions appearing in a French newspaper and then, translated back into English, in the English press.[38] "This corrupted translation of a translation of a translation" was picked up by several newspapers in the United States, where it caused a major scandal.[39] The letter was read out in Congress, and Jefferson was accused of targeting his criticism directly at George Washington, putting the Federalists in a position that allowed them to use Jefferson's expression of unease about America's political development as an effective weapon against their main political opponent, who at the time was considered the de facto leader of the Republicans. Several years later, in 1801, this affair still seriously undermined Jefferson's election to the presidency.

For two reasons this feud within the early Republic is of significance for this chapter. First, many continental commentators understood the American system of government as a republican variation of the English system. While in their view this resemblance presented an asset, Jefferson was appalled by it. Second, the fact that Mazzei decided to publicize Jefferson's critical assessment in Italy, provoking a political scandal of considerable dimensions, sheds doubt on the extent to which Mazzei still advocated the American model at home. The America he knew was no longer that of the Virginia Bill of Rights. Mazzei himself had decided to leave the United States for good, despite the fact that he was offered compensation for his service to the country. Mazzei, who had lived in London long enough to understand the English system of government, always spoke of the English monarchy with great contempt, making it clear that the comparison between the United States and England was not intended as a compliment. While moderate forces in France and Italy praised America for being modeled on the English system, Democrats often condemned this legacy. One of Italy's first witnesses to American democracy, Mazzei quickly caught up with the political and social realities of the country he had once admired as the accomplishment of his political ideals.

Luigi Angeloni and Jacobin Americanism

During his exile in Paris Carlo Botta had briefly befriended Luigi Angeloni, a Jacobin from the Papal States and an early admirer of his book on America. Although a shared hostility toward Napoleon initially united the men, they subsequently fell out. Unlike Angeloni, Botta still considered the Napoleonic regime a force of moderation after the oxoooooo of the republican regime. In 1832 Angeloni went so far as to publish a pamphlet entitled *Schifezze politiche proposte dal dottor Carlo Botta*, condemning Botta's antirepublican attitudes.[40]

The 1790s had added an important layer of meaning to the classical republicanism of Machiavelli and Montesquieu, but these experiences were soon superseded by the imposition of the Napoleonic regime, eliminating any political freedom.[41] From around 1800, disillusionment at French rule turned into widespread odium for Bonaparte, encouraging some Italian patriots and Jacobins to look for alternative models of republican freedom across the Atlantic, where the utopia of the New World was progressively being transformed into a political reality. Drawbacks such as those outlined by Jefferson and Mazzei served to illustrate differences between democratic and aristocratic forms of republicanism, but they did not challenge the general appeal of the American model as a modern form of political organization. Described by one of his political opponents as the "Nestor of Italian Jacobins,"[42] Angeloni became a leading figure among those Italian exiles whose admiration for America—for Washington, Jefferson, and Bolivar—was largely fueled by anti-Napoleonic sentiment.

After the fall of the Roman Republic in 1799 Angeloni went into French exile, where he befriended Napoleon's infamous police minister Joseph Fouché as well as General Lafayette and joined the sect of the *Philadelphes*. In 1800 he played an active role in the first attempt on Napoleon's life; and in 1812 he took part in the republican coup organized by Claude François de Malet, after which he was arrested.[43] Thanks to Fouché's intervention he was saved from execution, but as one of Malet's close collaborators he remained under arrest for two years.[44] After his release, Angeloni developed a number of specific projects for Italy's political future. In 1814 he proposed a federal solution based on the restoration of the ancient republics of Genoa, Venice, and Lucca, and the strengthening of Piedmont and Modena as barriers against future French or Austrian aggression. Within this scheme the Papal States were to be maintained. Published in Paris, the pamphlet ended up on the Index but was secretly distributed through a publisher in Milan. According to Angeloni's own account, it also circulated among diplomats and was received with interest by the king of Prussia and his chancellor, Hardenberg.[45]

Although his 1814 pamphlet makes no specific reference to the United States, his plans for the federalization of Italy reflect his interest in American institutions. Meanwhile, his booklet also includes long elegies praising the "magnificent and immortal" Russian emperor Alexander I as the only European monarch capable of bringing Napoleon to a halt.[46] Within the context of the Napoleonic wars many European patriots had hoped that Alexander would support their national ambitions. However, his autocratic rule in Russia was well known; and in the case of Angeloni it shows that admiration for Washington and Jefferson did not stand in the way of seeking an alliance with Russia. Likewise, Angeloni's admiration for American freedom went hand in hand with suggestions to strengthen Prussia at the expense of Poland. Austria was allowed to expand into Ottoman territory, similar to later plans of Cesare Balbo.[47] All this shows the passion, but also the diplomatic *calcule*, with which Italian Jacobins turned against the threat of French hegemony.

Before the Congress of Aachen in 1818 and the formation of the Holy Alliance, Piedmont actively sought Russian help in forming an Italian federation under Piedmontese leadership. It was in this context that Russian diplomats pointed the Prince of Carignano, the future king Carlo Alberto, toward Angeloni's work.[48] Hoping that Carlo Alberto would form an Italian federation, Angeloni set aside his own republican convictions in support of Piedmont's diplomatic initiative. Angeloni entered into direct contact with the court, where his writings, though still on the Index, were favorably received. Until the outbreak of the Sicilian Revolution of 1820, Angeloni maintained a frequent and almost personal correspondence with several members of the court, including the later king Carlo Alberto. While the American constitution continued to present an important pillar of Jacobin federalism, Angeloni did not hesitate to take advantage of monarchical solutions and of diplomatic constellations to achieve his goal of political unification. Other democrats at the time regarded these solutions as the utmost examples of princely despotism, contradicting the principle of popular sovereignty. In a footnote to the second volume of his *Della forza nelle cose politiche*, published in 1826, Angeloni became more cautious in seeking Russian assistance, but a decade later, in 1837, he repeated once more his praise for Alexander, the liberator of Europe from Napoleonic tyranny.[49]

Angeloni's 1818 pamphlet on Italy's international position after the Congress of Vienna explicitly recommends following "the free and beautiful government of the United States," whose success was based on the principle of "uniting in a federation the different parts of a great country through different levels of legislation."[50] Like other Italian admirers of the US constitution, he discussed Italy's current condition in the context of a wide range of European models, including England, considered the "probably the freest monarchical state of all time."[51] Meanwhile, he insisted that "American freedom, as much as it is the beautiful product of English freedom, now offers much more [freedom] than its mother country."[52] He opined that American federalism was perfectly applicable to the conditions of Italy, meaning "to connect, without confounding them completely, the different parts of our beautiful peninsula."[53] In this context he also praised Switzerland, "an equally free country, the consequence of its confederate government."[54] American federalism remained Angeloni's answer to the experience of Napoleonic despotism. Years after the emperor's defeat he still held him responsible for Italy's misery after 1815. Only "a new Washington" could free Italy from the situation in which it had been locked since the Congress of Vienna.[55] When General Lafayette, in 1830, decided to support Louis Philippe, Angeloni broke with one of his last Franco-American connections. The former Jacobin found himself increasingly isolated, incapable of building bridges with the new generation of exiles now gathering in the British capital. At a time when Mazzini proselytized among the Italian exiles in London, Angeloni's own pragmatism and his materialist convictions made it difficult to associate himself with the rector of spiritualist nationalism. He occasionally collaborated with the periodical *Esule*, but Mazzini never invited him to join *Giovine Italia*.[56] Forgotten by most of his compatriots, he died in 1842 in a workhouse in Cleveland Street. By then Italian Jacobinism had been declared dead many times.[57] Angeloni was the last example of the species.

Representation in Transnational Perspective: Romagnosi and Balbo

During his visit to Genoa in January 1847, Richard Cobden spoke at a dinner hosted in his honor by Massimo d'Azeglio and attended by about fifty people, including the consuls of France, Spain, Belgium, and Tuscany as well as many local nobles and merchants. In his diary Cobden later remarked: "my speech was intended for the ministers at Turin rather than my hearers. In this country, where there is no representative system, public opinion has no mode of influencing the policy of the state, & therefore I used such arguments as were calculated to have weight with the government."[58] Although some observers, including Cavour, were not impressed by Cobden's command of French, many agreed with his concern for the need of some form of political representation, a topic that generated a good deal of interest in foreign political institutions.[59]

An important contribution to Italian debates on representation had been Constant's essay of 1819 *The Liberty of the Ancients Compared with That of the*

Moderns, which argued that representation was a modern concept, very different from the ancients' forms of direct political involvement.[60] Modern forms of political representation were closely linked to the development of commercial society and to notions of civil progress. The language of representation also served as a defense against the excesses of democracy associated with the period after 1789.[61] However, during the years since the French Revolution representation had gained little ground in Italy. While the sovereigns of the Italian states were generally prepared to grant their subjects the rule of law, growing sections of society wished to play a part in public affairs through representative institutions.[62] Restrictions imposed on economic life and public debate, along with fiscal pressures, caused discontent, especially among the middle classes. Representation was meant to address these issues. Meanwhile, even debating representative government could have negative consequences in Restoration Italy: Jessie White Mario, for example, recorded that Cobden's lectures were frequently followed by arrests and imprisonments.[63]

One of the first Italian thinkers to translate French and English ideas of representation into the Italian political language of the post-Napoleonic age was Gian Domenico Romagnosi, whose *Della costituzione di una monarchia nazionale rappresentativa* of 1814–15 sought an alternative to both models. Although he used England to explain the rule of law, he considered the English constitution a relict of medieval feudalism.[64] Instead of trying to implement English political institutions in the Mediterranean, as the Sicilians had done in 1812, Romagnosi aimed for a constitutional development of the Napoleonic State that Italy had experienced prior to 1814, not dissimilar from Cuoco's efforts to push Murat toward conceding a constitution.[65]

The writings of Francesco Mario Pagano were an important source of Romagnosi's concept of constitutional monarchy. Pagano had presided over the Neapolitan Republic's *Comitato di Legislazione* in 1799, which owed much to the spirit of 1789 and 1795. Meanwhile, Pagano was also familiar with the American constitution. Contrary to the abstract theoretical debates of the ancients, for Pagano the American constitution took account of mankind's civil progress and its modern institutions of economic exchange. Although in the reports of the Neapolitan Legislative Committee passing references to the American constitution remained mostly unspecific, they speak to a deep-seated fear of modern politics leading to despotism and arbitrary power.[66] Based on his experience of Napoleonic rule, Romagnosi shared these fears. In these debates the question of monarchy versus republic remained secondary, because a balanced constitutional government would always result in a republic, independent of its form. Constitutional monarchy was nothing more than a republic with just "one" head.[67]

Also Romagnosi had worked for the French administration in Italy, at the same time as pursuing an academic career as a jurist, philosopher, and economist. Although the returning Austrian authorities suspended him from teaching, his influence continued to grow after 1814, partly helped by the journalistic writings of his most famous pupil, Carlo Cattaneo. During the two decades following the Congress of Vienna Romagnosi developed his constitutional thought in constant dialogue with an idiosyncratic and in some ways crudely positivist concept of civic philosophy (*civile filosofia*), which was grounded in the recognition of natural rights and the historical study of societal development.[68] His concept of *incivilmento* relates to the ideas of Giambattista Vico's *Scienza Nova*, albeit with important departures from the Neapolitan's understanding of history. As a universal law regulating the lives of nations, Vico's philosophy of history had influenced numerous Italian, French, and Latin American thinkers. Romagnosi's concept of *incivilmento* differs from that of other Vicchiani in its emphasis on the perfection of society by means of good government, based on a positivist notion of progress developed partly in response to what he knew of Kant and Hegel.[69]

Despite his often polemical tone against various schools of thought, Romagnosi's insistence on perfectibility and on the law of progress, and his attempts to present the history of humankind as a reasonable process, undoubtedly bear out connections to a wide range of Italian, French, and German thinkers.[70] An important source of this concept of incivilmento was his study of the ancient civilizations in America, largely based on the work of Scottish historian William Robertson. Moreover, like Cattaneo later on, Romagnosi reviewed countless volumes on foreign travel, history, and geography for the *Annali di Statistica*, *Biblioteca Italiana*, and a range of similar periodicals. His conceptual writings on the process of incivilmento are full of cross-cultural comparisons derived from these works.[71] Meanwhile, references to modern America and its constitution and political institutions remain rare. For instance, his *Introduzione allo studio del diritto pubblico universale* (1805/1825) is mostly a theoretical work, offering few specific examples of legal practice. His posthumous *Constitutional Theory* briefly refers to the American War of Independence, but without discussing its constitutional implications.[72] Meanwhile, Romagnosi's method of cross-cultural comparison laid the foundations for the interest in American political institutions among a later generation of Italian political thinkers, most famously represented by Cattaneo and Francesco Ferrara.

In the course of his life Romagnosi was several times arrested for his involvement in subversive activity, but he did not join the Carbonari and never translated his philosophy into a political program of action. This is one of the reasons why Mazzini, in 1838, denounced "Romagnosi's slavishly exaggerated fame," a view shared by Sismondi, who confessed to the Piedmontese revolutionary Santorre di Santarosa that "it is rare that I could push myself to read something by Romagnosi. I have an extreme antipathy, not only for his style, which hides his thinking, but even more so for the efforts of a man who aims to get with his thinking beyond anything he himself or I could achieve."[73]

Despite these verdicts, Romagnosi remained a constant point of reference for any constitutional thinker in Italy well beyond Unification.[74]

Luigi Angeloni, in 1818, had offered a very basic definition of representative government, as the system that guarantees "every citizen those rights, freedoms and advantages that any country that is not completely barbarous should enjoy."[75] His emphasis on "every citizen" was certainly not acceptable to moderate Liberals, who for a long time dominated Italian debates on representation and tended to define the concept in merely consultative terms and as a privilege of the aristocracy. Within the wide spectrum of debate around the concept, the United States offered one among several examples, usually discussed alongside those of Britain and of various French political regimes. Given the fact that many Democrats still struggled to reconcile Italy's own Jacobin tradition with more recent political and ideological developments encountered during periods of exile abroad, it was in moderate political thought that references to the United States first assumed an important role. Viewed as a particular application of English constitutional principles, references to the United States were used to underline claims about the progressive nature of their own political concepts.

In debates on representation, one of the Risorgimento's most outspoken admirers of the United States in the moderate camp was again Cesare Balbo, who dedicated several sections of his late work *Dalla Monarchia Rappresentativa* to the history and the constitution of the United States. As the spearhead of Piedmontese aristocratic liberalism, esteemed by some of the most conservative forces in European politics, his enthusiasm for the United States might come as a surprise.[76] However, by the mid-nineteenth century there was a long-standing tradition that saw the United States as the example of a mixed constitution rather than as a democratic republic, an idea associated with the president's strong executive powers. Already in 1781, the progressively minded Abbé Raynal, discussed in the introduction, had written that the United States "joined all the power of monarchy with the internal advantages of republican government."[77] The concept of an aristocratic republic was not news to political thinkers at the time, invoking the examples of Poland, the Netherlands, Venice, or Genoa.

For Balbo, the United States' geopolitical position in the world constituted a significant difference to the conditions of any European country.[78] This difference allowed him to treat the United States as a laboratory for political institutions, without suggesting that these should be narrowly applied to the old continent. Moreover, in Balbo's view the American revolutionaries' pragmatism contrasted dramatically with the utopian ideals of European Republicans, who sought their future in "inapproriate and antiquated models, Greek or Roman, or even worse, in models never seen, purely theoretical or, as they pretend, rational and philosophical, though they seem rather poetic or fictional."[79] While moderate pragmatists studied the real world, according to Balbo, Radicals gave themselves up to theoretical speculation. As his evaluation of the European events of 1848 reveal, in Balbo's case it is certainly not positive political freedom that he admired about the United States. Not since 1138, he argues, had Italy had a better opportunity to liberate itself from foreign dominion, if the revolutionaries "had not been distracted, disturbed, incapacitated and fooled by the insults and the slanders of newspapers, of political associations and parliaments, that is, by foolish abuses of freedom."[80] Contrasting American with European experiences of revolution, for Balbo it is "a miracle to have . . . here nearby the splendid and glorious example of that American Republic, so well adapted to our present state of civilisation."[81]

Beyond the comparison of specific historical circumstances, Balbo's principal motivation for looking across the Atlantic was to develop a concept of constitutional monarchy in the sense of a "limited monarchy," equipped with some form of representation.[82] An important clue to this design was to be his understanding of the American constitution's separation of powers, which for Balbo serves to underline the continuities between the British monarchy and the American Republic.[83] What distinguished the American Republic from the forms of democracy Europe had experienced during the revolutionary period was the separation of legislative and executive powers. The fathers of the American constitution "knew that the centuries have worked towards that goal, and that civilisation had reached that stage, of separating, and of keeping in separation, those two powers; and that the combination of the two, either in one man or in one assembly, is exactly what was and still is called tyranny."[84] For Balbo the American Revolution was everything the French Revolution was not.

As Lucien Jaume has argued with reference to Tocqueville's understanding of American political institutions, equality meant "equality in front of the law . . . , civil, not political equality."[85] Likewise for Balbo, civil equality did not mean equal participation in the formation of the political will. For Balbo the distinction between legal equality and political equality served to speak out against democracy at home, blaming an excess of political freedom for the lost opportunity of achieving national independence in 1848.

As a Moderate he identified freedom of the press and of public opinion as a threat to *civiltà*, a civiltà understood as *"moderazione sociale,"* protected by God, presenting himself as diametrically opposed to views that had taken root in Italy since the eighteenth century, articulated in particular by Filangieri.[86] For Balbo, the United States' variation on England's constitutional tradition did not signal a new political model that fits all. Instead, these variations were to be explained by the particular circumstances in which the country emerged, which were different from the present conditions of any European nation. At present, Italy and Europe simply lacked the civic virtues to be able to adopt a representative republican system. With reference to the relationship between political ideas and national character discussed at the start of this chapter, Balbo considered the American system inapplicable to the conditions of Italy:

"our peoples have never known how to assume this spirit of legality that is synonymous with the spirit of freedom. . . . Only the British tribe, in Europe and in America, had the prudence, the wisdom, the fortune, the divine grace to keep this spirit of legality; and therefore this spirit is still unique in Europe and in America, and exists under two forms of representative freedom, as a representative monarchy or as a representative republic."[87] Rather than making assumptions about the future of Europe, Balbo's interest in the United States reflects the Moderates' self-image as a political force for reform. England represented a venerable past, America a different temporal point of reference. The discussion of constitutional differences aimed to explain the principles of political representation, independently of republican or monarchical forms of government.

Many of the conclusions Balbo drew on the United States mirrored François Guizot's views on British political institutions. During the Restoration period Guizot had given his famous lectures *Histoire des origines du gouvernement représentatif en Europe* at the Sorbonne, first published in the early 1820s, followed in 1838 by his essay *Democracy in Modern Communities*.[88] The fact that the work appeared in English, before being translated into several other languages, offers an indication of Guizot's standing in European political debates throughout the mid-nineteenth century.[89] Based on his belief in a specific Anglo-Saxon approach to political institutions, what mattered to Guizot was not the question of sovereignty but the principle of political representation. Representation meant to make use of the best of society in terms of reason, justice, and truth, and to apply their insights to the art of government.[90] Rejecting Rousseau's concept of the "general will," Guizot maintained that democracy would lead to the oppression of the minority by the majority.

Although Guizot understood his historical writing as being informed by contemporary concerns, his works on the origins of representative government mostly abstain from direct references to the United States. Even Tocqueville, when discussing the principles of representation, rather than looking at the United States, compared ancien régime France with England, echoing the approaches of Benjamin Constant and Madame de Staël.[91] In turn, Tocqueville's critique of American democracy was influenced, at least partly, by Guizot's praise for the British constitution. Given that throughout the late eighteenth century France had been almost the only country where a deeper debate on the American constitution had taken place, this shift in focus from American to English institutions of representation can be explained only by the profound impact of the French Revolution and Europeans' need to discuss constitutional concerns on the basis of their most immediate political experiences. While Palmer asserts that "many people first came to sympathize with the Americans because of their dislike of England" (and Filangieri seems to fit this assessment), distinctions between the two countries remained often blurred.[92] In this context an argument discussed in the introduction to this book becomes relevant: European ideas about the United States were frequently almost indistinguishable from references to Britain. Even Cattaneo regarded England and America as "a single nation under two governments."[93]

Although Balbo and Guizot both stressed political representation as the defining marker of the English and American political system, there were also distinctive differences between the assessment of the Italian and the Frenchman. For Balbo the main issue in debates on sovereignty remained *indipendenza* from foreign domination. For Guizot it was *liberté* understood as a positive concept, which made a nation free: "If England had conceded America to be free, America wouldn't have declared itself independent," wrote Guizot in the opening passages of his 1816 essay *Du Gouvernement représentatif*.[94] Freedom, not independence, was at the core of Guizot's understanding of the United States' political achievement. For Balbo, the United States worked as a model precisely because he did not think of freedom as its most significant characteristic.

Democratic Challenges and the Limits of Italian Anglophilia

Guizot's and Balbo's understanding of political representation did not go unchallenged in Italian political debates. One of the most powerful articles in favor of universal suffrage and democratic principles of representation in Italian political thought was published in 1839 by Giuseppe Mazzini.[95] Mazzini's essay offers a detailed critique of census democracy, targeting directly those Piedmontese Moderates who were influenced by Guizot. While many of Balbo's references to Guizot were implicit, Mazzini's essay was written as a direct reply to the Frenchman's *Democracy in Modern Communities*, and to the Moderates' attempts to domesticate his ideas.

Like many other Italian exiles, Mazzini had initially been influenced by Guizot's and Cousin's philosophies of progress.[96] Mazzini's understanding of the European tradition of political thought was in large part filtered through French channels, in particular Michelet's work on Vico and Quinet's translation of Herder. Rather than seeing his studies as an Italian attempt to catch up with European philosophy, he was convinced that French concepts of progress owed much to the study of Vico. Meanwhile, responding to specific political debates in Italy, Mazzini turned to a far more critical evaluation of French political thought, targeting in particular Guizot's aristocratic principle of census representation. Here, for Mazzini the example of the United States serves to point to the profound limitations of Europe's constitutional monarchies: "have not the Americans relied on these two fundamental principles of every association—liberty and equality—to build something that, though far from being faultless in our eyes, nevertheless lives, proceeds, and prospers?"[97] Given Mazzini's reservations about American political institutions, it is not surprising that his essay contains only one short reference to the United States. His misgivings about the United States notwithstanding, Mazzini's essay sparked off a debate among French and Italian political thinkers that directly influenced the formation of the different political camps in Italy prior to 1848. Against Guizot's idea of a bourgeois revolution, Mazzini defended democratic representation based on popular sovereignty, a concept that England and the France of Louis-Philippe denied to their respective nations. He firmly scorned Guizot's claim that Democrats "only reject, overthrow, and destroy," that they were driven by a "desire to arrest progress."[98] The United States offered a different model, to which Mazzini (reluctantly) referred.

While Guizot became the *padrino* of the Italian Moderates, Mazzini's polemic against Guizot helped Italy's *partito d'azione* to sharpen its ideological profile. In his 1847 essay "Thoughts on Democracy in Europe," Mazzini insisted that "representative government," as discussed by the Moderates, had nothing to do with "representative democracy," which he saw as the future: "they have nothing but the word in common; the thing is radically different."[99] On the basis of this differentiation various factions of Democrats were able to set themselves apart from the aristocratic principles of the English monarchy and to unite behind the egalitarianism of the United States. Frequently, they connected their critique of aristocratic principles to Britain's social question and the condemnation of British imperialism. Giuseppe Montanelli went so far as to rank Palmerston below Metternich in his list of evil European statesmen, taking the view that Britain's imperialism contradicted any true concept of liberalism.[100] The aristocratic foundations of British liberalism, according to Montanelli, constituted a stark contrast to the democratic principles that informed the European revolutions, leading him to conclude that England no longer had a role to play as mediator of the Continent's uprisings.[101]

This critical attitude toward Britain increasingly overshadowed Italian admiration for the rule of law that prevailed in the British Isles and helped to raise the democratic profile of the American constitution. Returning once more to Angeloni, his experience of exile only increased his hatred of the English economic mentality and the extent to which structures of power were determined by land ownership.[102] Angeloni's assessment of structural inequalities mirrors that of Benjamin Constant, who described British society as "a permanent conspiracy of the rich ruling class against the poor working class."[103] These divisions also had a negative impact on exile communities in London. For instance, Count Carlo Pepoli, married to a rich Scotswoman, was frequently criticized for a standard of living few Italian exiles could reach.[104] Although in no way critical of all aspects of British society, Filangieri too noticed the deep-rooted materialism of the English and wrote of their educational system that "no other country in Europe makes the acquisition of knowledge so expensive; in no other country [do] you need to be so rich to become learned."[105]

Regarding the argument that British imperialism contradicted liberal principles, Ugo Foscolo's passionate critique of British policies toward the Ionian Islands had set an important precedent, which contrasted with his appreciation of English polite society expressed in the *Lettere scritte dall'Inghilterra*.[106] Foscolo was a native of the Ionian island of Zante/Zakynthos, then part of the Venetian Republic, before moving to London after the Napoleonic period. For many followers of Italy's national movement he became the "modern heir to Dante, the first and greatest of Italian exiles."[107] Recognized as "The United States of the Ionian Islands" by the Congress of Vienna, Foscolo's homeland was subsequently integrated into Britain's Mediterranean empire under conditions that many among the local population perceived as more despotic than those of the previous political regimes. When in 1817 Britain granted Parga to the Ottoman Empire, there was a mass exodus of locals from the city to Corfu.[108] Owing to the region's Venetian past, Italian *letterati* were at the forefront of international protests against Britain's Mediterranean policies, inviting direct comparisons with British attitudes toward its American colonies a few decades earlier. Although Foscolo was far from idealizing the relationship between the islands' rather heterogeneous populations, the very name "United States of the Ionian Islands" evoked this connection. Opting for a confederation of the islands, Foscolo calls on the example of the United States, where the constitution had emerged from their shared experience of fighting for independence.[109]

Public outrage at Britain's imperial appetite, combined with the debate on the social cost of Britain's industrialization, became important motifs of Italian democratic thought during the 1840s. The Sicilian patriot Gioacchino Ventura condemned English rule over the Irish in the harshest terms, putting it on equal terms with Bourbon rule over Sicily, and describing it in terms of a slave economy: "it never was and will never be advisable, fair or generous. . . . This unhappy people asks for bread and they reply with guns."[110] Moving beyond the colonial question, Carlo Pisacane opined that England's "appearance of grandeur only hides the cancerous sores of that society."[111] Even a Moderate like the future prime minister Marco Minghetti, a close ally of Count Cavour, described in 1841 "these most unhappy people" of the English working class, the "ignorance" and "immorality" that reigned in England's factories.[112] Returning to the Italian reception of Guizot, Mazzini's polemic was directed exactly against those voices who used Guizot's political thought to impose the English model on Italy. But it was not only Radical Democrats who rejected this form of Italian Anglophilia. Writing in 1851, Vincenzo Gioberti described Guizot as "an Englishman of the past century rather than a Frenchman and a European of our century."[113] For Gioberti the "imitation of foreign things" was one of Italy's most damaging vices, contributing significantly to what he considered the nation's effeminate weakness, a stereotype frequently evoked by British and American commentators, only to then be internalized by the Italians themselves.[114]

These critical voices notwithstanding, negative attitudes toward Britain never completely dominated Italian debates. Foscolo's early biographer, the economist Giuseppe Pecchio, opined in an 1826 essay on the British electoral system that "in practice freedom is even sweeter and more seductive than in theory."[115] He recognized the rule of law as a founding principle of public life: "the King of England can scare many kings all over the globe, but he cannot scare one of his own subjects."[116] Pecchio's idealization of British society went so far as to completely reject his compatriots' focus on the social costs of industrial capitalism and to criticize those measures that tried to address these concerns: "the poor along with the institution of poor relief represent two of England's sores. Poor relief encourages dissipation, imprudence and marriages between proletarians. The poor represent a human species that looses any sense of modesty, they depend on the parishes like ancient slaves on the glebe, improvident, procreators of an offspring to be handed over to the parishes."[117] His *Half-Serious Observations on England by an Exile*, published slightly later in 1831, was translated into several languages. Anglophilia notwithstanding, even Pecchio had to admit that "the moon in Naples feels warmer than the sun in London."[118]

With regard to Britain's Mediterranean empire, some Italians shared British concerns over apparent Greek backwardness; and its attempts to modernize the Ionian Islands also evoked approval, for instance when Minghetti, shortly before Unification, met the then high commissioner William Gladstone on Corfu.[119] Here Britain's Mediterranean policy helped the emerging Italian nation-state to formulate its own policy toward the *mezzogiorno*. The same liberal elites also found much to admire in the United States, despite the country's growing role as a panacea for the Democrats' political expectations. There are only a few references to the United States in the writings of Count Camillo Cavour, but he had known Tocqueville in Paris and London and read *Democracy in America* early on.[120] His concept of "a free Church in a free state" was influenced by Tocqueville, though he also read Alexandre Vinet and the Count Montalembert on the subject.[121] While for some anticlericals, including Ferdinando Petruccelli della Gattina, Cavour's formula still granted the church too much freedom, Cavour's supporters were in a position to evoke the example of the United States, "paese della libertà per eccellenza," to defend their position.[122]

Not surprisingly, the Catholic press questioned the whole issue of religious freedom in the United States. Although for a long time it had followed a strategy of ignoring the Protestant nation, *Civiltà cattolica* now argued that America's civil life and its institutions were profoundly marked by organized religion.[123] Reviewing Claude Jannet's *Les Etats-Unis contemporains* (1876), the Catholic periodical pointed out Christian oaths, religious services in Congress, and religious state holidays to undermine the nation's claims to religious freedom. The US government's intervention against the Mormons in Utah served as another example that threw into doubt the promise of religious freedom.

Of immediate political concern during the process of Unification was the dispute over the title of Italy's head of state. Early in 1861 parts of the political Left attempted to push Cavour's government to introduce the title "King of the Italians," or "Re degli Italiani," following the model established during the French and Belgian Revolutions of 1830. Cavour firmly rejected the idea, insisting that the monarch had to be "King of Italy" (Re d'Italia). Not only did the people themselves refer to Vittorio Emanuele as "Re d'Italia," he argued, but also across the Atlantic the president of the United States was not president of the Americans. Instead, his title conveyed the idea of a "magistrate representing the entire nation."[124] The same question had excited Italians ten years earlier, during debates over the Statuto in 1848, in this case regarding the king of Sardinia.[125] A further example of Moderate Liberals' evocation of the United States was Minghetti's reference to General Washington in an attempt to defend government restrictions imposed on political associations. "In his political testament George Washington said . . . that associations whose objective it is to counter and to inhibit the Government in its actions are contrary to freedom. They only serve to organise factions and provide them with extraordinary and artificial strength. Rather than the nation's will, as expressed through its legitimate representatives, they impose the will of an astute and bold minority."[126] These examples show how references to the United States served to allow Moderates to fight Democrats with their own weapons.

From liberal admiration for the American Revolution's "moderation," Italian Democrats had turned America into a powerful argument against the aristocratic privilege of representation. Democratic views contrasting English and American forms of representation made it increasingly difficult for the Moderates to discuss the United States in positive terms without at the same time lending unwanted support to their political opponents. Meanwhile, democratic endorsement of the United States and critique of the Moderates' Angophilia did not denote a monopoly on references to American politics. Instead, the debate shifted from the big issue of representation to more specific aspects of American political life.

Federalism

Cesare Beccaria's *Dei delitti e delle pene* was published in 1764, two years after Rousseau's *Contrat Social*. In the work, Beccaria pronounced himself in favor of a federal organization of smaller states. Although this is by no means his main argument, he might have been thinking about Rousseau's small-community-based democracy. Small states help to foster republican sentiment against the dangers of despotism; and a confederation protects them from foreign intervention.[127] In Beccaria's words, "as a society grows larger, the significance of each member becomes less and the republican sentiment is diminished if the citizen is not protected by the laws. . . . A republic that is too large cannot save citizens from despotism unless it subdivides itself and then reunifies as numerous federal republics."[128] Writing before the outbreak of conflict in the American colonies, Beccaria made his argument independent of America's constitutional experiences, at a time when federalism (with the exception of the Holy Roman Empire, the United Provinces, and Switzerland) was largely posed as a theoretical problem.

The situation changed considerably during the Napoleonic period and after the Congress of Vienna, when the political map of Italy was suddenly back on the international agenda and Italy's future constitution was at the center of debates between the different factions of the national movement. In these debates federalism was understood as a concept that could bridge the gap between the political reality of Italy's existing states and the ambition of national unification. Confronted with this scenario, the experience of the Americas combined national freedom, liberalism, and federalism, offering Italian patriots concrete models of how to approach the problem of Unification while remaining respectful of historically grown traditions of individual statehood. As Maurizio Isabella has shown, Italian exiles understood American federalism, both in North and in South America, as a constitutional framework that combined liberal citizenship and respect for individual rights, with modern forms of administration.[129] While opponents of federalism tended to point to the external vulnerability of federal states, the Americas' success in fighting off their former mother countries seemed to offer proof of the opposite. Sismondi contributed to this debate by exploring the same argument as part of his theoretical study of free constitutions.[130] The prominent role of federal models in Risorgimento political thought seems to suggest that there existed alternatives to those ethnic or cultural concepts of Italian nationhood that denied differentiation between the peninsula's historical states. A federation of independent states offered the opportunity of accommodating Italians on the basis of very different and largely separate histories, including regions such as Sardinia, Sicily, and the Kingdom of Naples.

The previous chapter briefly discussed Carlo Botta's *Quale dei governi liberi meglio convenga alla felicità dell'Italia*, a contribution to an essay competition organized by the Amministrazione generale of Lombardy in 1796, during the period of the French occupation. One of the respondents to the competition was Giovanni Antonio Ranza, who proposed a federation of free states based on the Swiss or American models. His preference for federalism was in line with the majority of respondents to the competition.[131] A priest and then a professor of literature, Ranza was an early supporter of the Revolutions in northern Italy, became a Jacobin, and was involved with several influential, but mostly short-lived periodicals. His argument in favor of federation was simple:

As Italy has been for many centuries divided into dominions, cultures and dialects, each with different interests, it is now impossible to give it a form of government that is the same for all. Therefore we shall adopt the unity of the federal government of the United States and the Swiss cantons, . . . organised into eleven federated Republics under the name of Free Federal States of Italy.[132]

The example demonstrates that federalism was on the political agenda long before Piedmontese Moderates developed plans for the unification of Italy on the basis of a federation of existing states. Ranza mentions the United States only briefly, without further discussion of how American federalism worked in practice. His main argument was developed on the basis of Italy's own history of political and cultural diversity. Unlike America, Italy had a history.

As Vittorio Criscuolo has pointed out, it is not clear whether the essay competition was meant to discuss proposals for the administration of Italy as a whole, or if it was intended for the region then occupied by the French armies.[133] For Ranza, as for many other commentators at the time, federalism served not so much as a positive reference to the United States, but as a critical reflection on the experience of French centralized administration.[134] Meanwhile, comparisons also helped to highlight potential risks behind American developments. For instance, a subsequent edition of Ranza's pamphlet compared the position of the American president with that of the Dutch stadhouder and warned against "the Washingtons, with their immense wealth and their omnipotent influence, so that they do not blindly undermine the new edifice of our democracy."[135] Ranza seems to mirror some of the same concerns revealed in the exchanges between Mazzei and Jefferson. Furthermore, the United States represented only one among a number of systems discussed by contributors to the competition. Not only Switzerland and the United States, but also the Holy Roman Empire and Italy's own experience of alliances between city-republics, competed against the model of a centralized unitary state. The limited role of American federalism in the political debates of Italy's revolutionary *triennio* seems to suggest that commentators were able to differentiate between spontaneous federal arrangements and historically grown federations.[136]

The revolutionary experiments of the 1820s were short-lived and mainly aimed at the constitutional transformation of existing monarchies. While the transnational dimension of the events renewed the focus on federal solutions, the following decades also show that for many political thinkers federalism remained a largely abstract concept. Balbo's *Delle speranze d'Italia* of 1844 offers no insights regarding how Italian federalism would work in practice. The same is true for his *Della monarchia rappresentativa*, which discussed in much detail the administrative and constitutional particularities of representative monarchy, but painted with a broad brush when praising American federalism.[137] Influenced by Gioberti (although they disagreed on the future role of the pope), Balbo, instead of making a juridical or theoretical argument, explained his endorsement of neo-Guelphism with tribal experiences: chased by Barbarossa from the Republic of Chieri, his family had allegedly joined the Lombard League to fight on the side of the pope, as he says, "per l'indipendenza d'Italia."[138] Balbo's reluctance to consider the practical implications of federalism makes Vincenzo Gioberti Italy's most influential federalist prior to the Revolutions of 1848–49.

Gioberti's Federalism, or "Britain, the Sicily of Europe"

The roots of Gioberti's federalism are easily misunderstood if one reduces his role to the ideas outlined in *Del primato morale e civile degli Italiani*, published in 1843 during his exile in Brussels. Instead, there is a close connection between his political thought of the 1840s and his earlier philosophical writings in the fields of metaphysics, aesthetics, and moral theory. Produced at a time when he was an influential figure in the salons of Italian exiles in Paris, it is here that he integrated ideas of progress, religion, and civilization into an almost deterministic philosophy of history.[139] Although there are significant differences with Romagnosi, Gioberti's approach stands for another facet of the early nineteenth-century *Vicchiani*, a loose group of political thinkers profoundly marked by their study of Vico. First outlined as part of his *Teorica del sovranaturale* of 1838, Gioberti explains Italy's historical mission from the perspective of a specific experience of temporal change affecting Europe as a whole. Influenced by Hegel's dialectic and his philosophy of history, Gioberti sees religion as forming the basis of civil progress, which differs from Romagnosi's emphasis on good government.[140] Translated into political thought, for Gioberti Italy presents the center of Europe's religious life and therefore "the mother nation of the human species." Italy's *primato* within a wider teleology of European nations is the logical consequence of Rome's position as "the religious metropolis of the world." "Italy, due to its universalist ideal, is the synthesis and the mirror of Europe."[141] Hence Gioberti's philosophy of history is at the same time universalist, Eurocentric, and Italocentric.[142] As a consequence, the history of the church and that of Italy became inseparable and indispensible ingredients of the progress of humanity as a whole. It comes as no surprise that American or any non-European experiences played little or no role in Gioberti's thought, signaling another major difference with Romagnosi.[143]

Despite its religious and metaphysical foundations, Gioberti's program recognized the importance public opinion gave to closer economic integration of the peninsula. His thinking on Italy's political unification started with the four monarchies—Piedmont-Sardinia, Tuscany, Rome, and Naples—which, linked in a confederation, would have the strength to chase the Austrians from the North and undertake a program of administrative reform. The sovereigns would retain authority within their respective states, while common affairs were to be decided by a diet presided over by the pope, as Italy's civil head

FIG. 8. Vincenzo Gioberti, from *Illustrazione del libro La Italia - Storia di due anni 1848-1849*, by Candido Augusto Vecchi. Claudio Perrin: Torino, 1851. Image courtesy https://en.wikipedia .org/wiki/Vincenzo_Gioberti#/media/File:La_Italia-309.jpg.

of state. In the words of Giorgio Candeloro, synthesizing several decades of liberal-catholic debate, Gioberti's version of neo-Guelphism transfomed a cultural movement into a political one.[144]

Understood as a political concept, neo-Guelphism emerged as a consequence of a specific constellation of time that put Italy in a position to fulfill its historical mission. In this sense Gioberti's federalism is not a theoretical concept, but a historical necessity, rooted not in a foreign but in Italy's own past: "the Italians' federal Union is not based on probability, because it seems clear that God had devised Italy for this form of regimen, already containing all the elements it needs for this outcome."[145] Echoing Vico's and Cuoco's idea of the ancients' knowledge of Italy, Gioberti's view was that the nation was federalist by nature of its ethnic and historical origins.[146] Gioberti fostered his federalism with awareness for Italy's municipal tradition, combining a message of national pride with an emphasis on local identity.[147] This juxtaposition was a major theme of his propaganda tour in 1848, and this municipal identity added an important new aspect to Risorgimento political thought, which finds similar resonance only in Cattaneo's political writings.

In 1851 Gioberti published *Del rinnovamento civile d'Italia*, another major book on Italy's political future. His sudden turn toward a unitary and centralized program for the Unification of Italy reflects the experiences of 1848 and a transformed, but equally teleological understanding of history.[148] During his short spell as Piedmontese prime minister (December 1848 to February 1849), Gioberti had moved toward a cautious endorsement of democratic republicanism, away from the ideas of mainstream Moderates, eventually leading to his return to Paris.[149] Despite his ideological mutation, there remained a considerable difference between Gioberti's plans and the position of other 1848 Democrats. Unlike Mazzini and Cattaneo, the author of *Del rinnovamento* endorsed Piedmont's hegemony over the rest of the peninsula. What is more, while many Democrats increasingly looked to American experiences, his long chapter on democracy again makes only one short reference to the United States, concentrating instead on a detailed survey of European political developments between the Revolutions of 1789 and 1848.[150] While he follows the canon of Italian political thinkers in describing the United States as a variant of the English system, at the same time he reiterates his dislike of the Anglophiles and describes Britain as "the Sicily of Europe," a peripheral island in the northern seas that could not possibly teach Europe lessons.[151] By implication, this also turned the United States into an "Other," located outside the realms of history and civilization, occupying only a marginal place on Gioberti's map of civil teleology. One of the first political thinkers to explicitly use the term "modernity" (as a noun) to describe the temporal transformation affecting his nation, he asserts that "Italy cannot come back to life if it doesn't look for its own origins; its modernity has to take stock of its antiquity, true to itself and to its nation."[152] He had no doubts that the eternal city of Rome, not the New World, represented the future of mankind; and the civiltà of any other people would derive from there.[153] It would take another generation before Giosuè Carducci, in the 1870s, referred to the Third Rome as the New Byzantium, a symbol of decline that had lost the promise of the nation's resurgence.[154]

Despite the idiosyncrasies of his work, Gioberti's influence resonated well beyond the core of liberal Catholicism. For instance, in the early 1840s Giuseppe Montanelli criticized many of Gioberti's spiritual and political concepts but recognized the importance of his early philosophical writings, calling him "a philosopher who had understood his time," "founder of a new philosophical school in Italy, with the aim of reconciling philosophy and catholicism."[155] Based on the argument that Italy's economic structures no longer corresponded to the conditions of the medieval city-states, Cattaneo rejected unification based on a medieval papal alliance.[156] Nonetheless, Gioberti remained an important reference point for Cattaneo's federalism, which will be discussed in more detail in the following chapter.

Rosmini and the Limits of American Democracy

Gioberti's argument in favor of federalism shared important elements with Antonio Rosmini-Serbati's political thought, despite the fact that the two Catholic philosophers had substantial ideological differences. If not the most influential, Rosmini was certainly one of Italy's most effusive Catholic thinkers; and he was a federalist.[157] Unlike Gioberti, Rosmini read widely on US history, and in his political writings he frequently referred to its constitutional development. Of old imperial nobility and founder of a powerful religious order, Rosmini in 1848 suddenly became a protagonist of the political turmoil in Piedmont and in the Papal States.

Despite his knowledge of the United States, Rosmini also developed his federalism principally on the basis of Italy's own historical experience. Unlike Gioberti, he engaged critically with the United States' institutions, mostly as the antithesis of an imaginary Italian future. The other antipode to his idea of Italy was France. According to Rosmini, a centralized unitary state was incompatible with Italy's "fourteen centuries of foreign invasions, of dissolution, individual action, partial organisation and internal divisions. This is not about organising an imaginary Italy, but the real Italy, divided along its back by the Apennines, with its marshes, in the form of a boot, reckoning the variety of its tribes not fused yet into one, with its differences of climate, customs and experiences, its governments, the true representatives of our social condition."[158] In Rosmini's view, after Unification these differences would gradually disappear, thanks to the country's prospective economic and social development: "the railways will shorten Italy; marriages will mix the blood, and opinions will fuse as well."[159] A cautious level of uniformity in governance would do the rest; and not all of Italy's historical states had to survive: smaller states could merge with bigger ones in order to create a more powerful confederation, perhaps even creating a single state north of the Apennines.[160] Assimilation notwithstanding, the key to Unification remained federalism.

While Gioberti's early philosophical writings are today largely forgotten, Rosmini still attracts the interest of philosophers and theologians, reflected in several modern editions of his work and series of commentaries. In addition to identifying in Gioberti's ontological concepts a dangerous pantheism, Rosmini was critical of the democratic tendencies behind his constitutional concepts. Ironically, he charges Gioberti—a man with clear Italocentric convictions and certainly no friend of foreign models—with being dependent on unduly foreign influences.[161] The polemic emerging around their disagreements created a noticeable ideological divide among Italy's Catholic patriots prior to 1848. Their differences notwithstanding, in 1848 both philosophers had a cordial encounter in Rome, expressing mutual respect.

Within the vast body of Risorgimento political thought, Rosmini left us with what is possibly the most detailed Italian commentary on Tocqueville's *Démocratie en Amérique*.[162] Although restricted to volume 1, his reflections on the Frenchman reached beyond the academic ivory tower, as demonstrated by an article for Cavour's newspaper *Il Risorgimento* from July 1848.[163] Throughout his *Filosofia della Politica*, published shortly after the first edition of Tocqueville's work, Rosmini discusses (and dismisses) democracy, using the United States as his main point of reference. Along with his reflections on democratic despotism, he uses Tocqueville as an anthropological source on the life of Native Americans, their languages, customs, and religious practices, to further develop his own understanding of natural law in relation to the different stages of civilization. Whereas most Italian commentators based their assessment of the New World's natural life on writings from the period around the American Revolution, or predating this event, Rosmini introduced a new empirical dimension into Italian debates. His many references to American democracy support the idea that Italian interest in the United States was almost more widespread among moderate political thinkers and critics of the American Revolution than among its progressive and radical supporters. Meanwhile, Rosmini's own constitutional project for Italy, developed in 1848, is mostly about what America and France were not.

In 1848 Rosmini represented the Piedmontese government on a mission to Rome, which aimed at convincing the pope to lend support to Piedmont's efforts to end Austrian rule in the peninsula and to set up a confederation of Italian states under his presidency.[164] At the end of March, shortly after the Milanese Revolution and just before his departure, Rosmini published his essay *La Costituzione secondo la giustizia sociale*, furnished with a passionate appendix, *Sull'unità d'Italia*: "The Unity of Italy! This is a universal cry, and there is not a single Italian between the Alps and the toe of the boot whose heart is not moved by it. Therefore it is useless trying to prove its utility or necessity: where everyone agrees there is no question."[165] The opening to his constitutional essay demonstrates that combining Catholicism with a critique of democracy did not undermine patriotic credentials. For Rosmini, a treaty between the existing princes as the sole source of legitimate power was the only way of proceeding toward political unification. He explicitly rejects unitary models in the tradition of the French Revolution: "they would level out all the municipalities, all the Italian provinces, smoothen differences and qualities to the point where only one eminent centre would be left, that of the capital city."[166]

While his constitutional project reflects a wide range of European political thought, including debates on the separation of powers, his main reference to the American constitution was his support for a strong executive in the form of a president or constitutional monarch. While the republic seemed an appropriate form of government for a new country recently conquered by a bunch of adventurers, he considered monarchy a more civilized form of rule, which avoids "the bloody and incurable sore" of electoral proceedings.[167] As a purely legislative power, the parliament should stay away from day-to-day politics, reflecting Rosmini's disdain for parliamentary democracy. Recognition of individual rights, guaranteed by the rule of law, is at the heart of Rosmini's political philosophy and forms the basis of his constitutional project. The first of his constitution's "fundamental principles" proclaims that "every person's natural rights and reasoning are inviolable."[168] Rosmini understands individual rights as natural rights, not as positive rights conceded by a legislator, monarch, or representatives of the people. Although influenced by Rousseau, his conception of rights differed from the tradition of the French Revolution. "All nations that imitated [the French Revolution] suffered from the same political diseases, the same painful experiences," Rosmini writes of the French type of constitution. Born "out of the demagogues' passions, the fury of parties, the terror and uproar of national and foreign armies," these constitutions never last and offer little political stability.[169] His fear of democratic despotism and tyranny of the majority refers explicitly to Tocqueville's critique of American democracy.

Roughly a decade prior to the Revolution of 1848, between 1836 and 1839, Rosmini had established his reputation as a major political thinker with a weighty *Filosofia della Politica*, in which he set out the basic structures and aims of society.[170] In Rosmini's view democracy and popular sovereignty did not represent aims in themselves. Instead, he investigates the extent to which these concepts serve individual freedom and natural rights. Tocqueville analyzed American democracy as an alternative to the French concept of revolutionary democracy, but without presenting the United States as a universal template for government. Similar to Cattaneo's interest in the United States, Rosmini accepted Tocqueville's book for what it was—an empirical study of democratic practice. But he then proceeds by dissecting the critical elements of Tocqueville's study in order to advance his own argument against democratic rule.

Quoting at length from volume 1 of *Démocratie en Amérique*, Rosmini rejects the idea that universal suffrage generates leaders who deserve public trust. As demonstrated by the United States, where the more respectable members of the public rarely hold public office, democratic systems struggle to identify competent political leaders.[171] His constitutional essay of 1848 reiterates this idea, warning Italians that the democratic principles of most modern constitutions lead to corruption.[172] According to Rosmini, in a democratic system people's vices combine with their ignorance to unfold in a scenario that makes societal collapse almost unavoidable: democracy results in the "tyranny of the majority," in anarchy, and in the loss of liberty.[173] Despotism starts where governments use the common good to suppress individual freedom, an idea Rosmini clearly associates with Rousseau, with revolutionary France, and in particular with Napoleon's rule. While he acknowledges that in the United States no similar tyrant has yet emerged, he is aware that Hamilton, Jefferson, Madison, and *The Federalist* had all warned of the danger of such deteriorations of the democratic system.[174]

Instead, he argues, Christianity and the teachings of the church condemn any form of despotism. A renewed Christian order is the only safeguard against this state of decadence. While, for Rosmini, Tocqueville's study of American democracy serves to set out how majority rule undermines individual freedom, the two authors clearly disagree about what they see as the basis of freedom. Where in Tocqueville's secular theory the will of the majority is limited by the principle of justice, which in itself is determined by majorities, for Rosmini justice is eternal, revealed only by God.[175] Rosmini's engagement with modern political philosophy stops there. Constructing his arguments on the basis of empirical evidence, Rosmini situates his political philosophy clearly within the tradition of the European Enlightenment, consistent with his intention of reconciling reason and religion. The fact that throughout his work he derives his evidence from Tocqueville, a secular theorist, becomes a powerful tool in making his theoretical work relevant to the political debates of his day.

Beyond the specific constitutional order he outlined in his essay of 1848, Rosmini's principal political concern was to secure guarantees for the privileged position of the papacy within the system of Italian states, a position that for him remained nonnegotiable. Resembling Gioberti's view of Italy's primato, Rosmini argues that the civilized nations of Europe are the daughters (*figlie*) of the Christian religion; and it is for this reason that Christ's vicar will continue to guide (*annoverar*) the nations of Europe, first among them the Italian people.[176] Although Rosmini recognized the equality of all citizens before the law, he was critical of civil society's modern development. Crediting Christianity with the reconstruction of civil society after the fall of the Roman Empire, he recognized the importance of open debate and the free circulation of information.[177] However, having lost its religious foundations, modern society was doomed to also lose its moral compass. Rosmini's project, therefore, was about the renewal of society's religious foundations. Because of its despotic tendencies, modern civil society needed to be framed and controlled by the autonomous institutions of the family and by "theocratic society," the only agents of a truthful relationship between man and God.[178]

Rosmini's understanding of the social order meant that Italy's constitutional future had to be based on the independence of the Papal State within the Italian confederation. Papal influence within this system of states needed to be strengthened through agreement on certain legal standards such as the replacement of Austrian family law with canon law.[179] His whole approach to modern democracy shows that for an important strand of debate within Italy's constitutional thought the United States constituted a negative model. This conclusion should not distract from the fact that Rosmini recognized the benefits of the American understanding of religious freedom. As mentioned earlier, Cavour's idea of a free church within a free state was also partly inspired by Tocqueville's writings on the United States. In *Delle Cinque Piaghe della Santa Chiesa*, written in 1832 and published in 1848, Rosmini acknowledged that the United States offered the church more freedom than some Catholic nations, at that time an almost heretical position to take for any Catholic. He regarded the movement toward national churches as one of the principal challenges of the modern age, another negative consequence of a civil society not restricted by the authority of the church.[180] Soon placed on the Index, no work caused Rosmini more difficulties within his own institution than *Delle Cinque Piaghe*.[181] Dogmatic quarrels notwithstanding, Rosmini's main concern was the role of the church as a state within the future Italian federation, underlining the extent to which he believed that any future Italian civilization was still to be conceived as a theocratic state.[182] Any such idea was diametrically opposed to the very idea of American democracy. Within this worldview the American concept of civil society had nothing to contribute to the future of the Italian peninsula, despite the fundamental role it played as an antipode.

Rosmini probably offers the best example that a keen interest in the societal developments of the United States did not necessarily mean admiration for or endorsement of its political system. His constitutional essay of 1848 seems to reject the most basic assumptions of American democracy, including social mobility ("an unfashionable ambition to continuously move up to higher grades of society.")[183] Like many constitutional theorists at the time, Rosmini expressed pride in Italy's own political traditions. Where he agreed with Gioberti was that Italians were in no need of copying the ideas of any other country: "Italians! Do not demean yourself by imitating foreign models without first examining and discussing them, without prejudice, using your own sense of reason and applying your own splendid intelligence!"[184] His attempts to reconcile reason and religion (including a project for a Christian encyclopedia to counter the French secular model) offered liberal Catholicism important philosophical and theological foundations. Meanwhile, he never represented the mainstream of political neo-Guelphism; and his ultramontanism prevented him from breaking with papal authority. Constantly attacking the modernist semantic of time behind the progressive constitutional theories of his day, for many of the protagonists of 1848 it became impossible to build bridges with Rosmini's political thought. In this context it is not surprising that for Carlo Cattaneo Rosmini's writings represented a form of obscurantism for which there was no place in the modern world.

Even for the moderate Cesare Balbo there was too much religion in Rosmini's political philosophy.[185]

Despite these predictable tensions with the more advanced positions of political liberalism, the principal attacks against Rosmini's work were theological in nature and came from the Jesuits. While strongly opposing the European revolutions in 1848, they could claim expertise on the United States, owing to the orders' strong presence across the Atlantic.[186] Giovanni Antonio Grassi from Bergamo left for the United States in 1810, where he spent seven years and became president of the country's first Catholic university, Georgetown College in Washington. Although Grassi discouraged Italians from leaving their home country and condemned an excess of democracy, the account of his time in the United States recognizes the Americans' sense of freedom, their keen interest in education, and the constitution's respect for the freedom of religion, which he identified as a long-term advantage for Catholicism.[187] I shall return to Grassi in the last chapter. Unlike Grassi's book, several of Rosmini's works were placed on the Index.[188] Although Rosmini was rehabilitated in the 1870s, it was not until 2007 that Pope Benedict XVI beatified him.

Mazzini's Challenge: Democracy beyond the American Way

In 1847 Mazzini wrote to Giuseppe Montanelli that "the democratic republican future" would not follow "the example of the United States."[189] Italy's most famous Democratic Republican was also the Risorgimento's most outspoken critic of the United States, an opponent of any attempts to export this model from across the Atlantic. Meanwhile, as Enrico dal Lago has demonstrated, Mazzini was greatly admired in the United States and also had close friends there, among them the country's most prominent abolitionist, William Lloyd Garrison. What connected the two men was not admiration for American republicanism, but their shared hostility to tyranny and any form of racial discrimination. Garrison was so critical of his own country that in 1854, on the occasion of a spectacular forced return of a fugitive slave from Boston to the South by federal authorities, he publically burned copies of the Fugitive Slave Act and the US constitution, calling them "a covenant with death, an agreement with hell"—all this accompanied by Bible readings.[190]

In order to understand Mazzini's own critical attitude to the United States we have to go back to the early years of his political activity. The revolutions in the Americas were a major point of reference for the Italian Carbonari; and Mazzini was adamant that he had to distance himself from the sect's strategies and political concepts. More importantly, Mazzini's attacks on the US model were a response to the influence of the "American School" in France, briefly mentioned in the introduction, which in turn also left its imprint on the Italian exiles. After his release from prison in Savona, in 1831, Mazzini had gone to France to escape restrictions imposed on him by the Piedmontese

FIG. 9. Giuseppe Mazzini, 1860. Image courtesy
https://commons.wikimedia.org/wiki/File:Giuseppe_Mazzini.jpg.

police. During those early years of the July Monarchy, General Lafayette, Édouard Laboulaye, and Armand Carrel, editor of *Le National*, praised the American constitution for the exclusive role it assigned to individual rights, while opposing those French Radicals who advocated social reform based on a more extensive understanding of equality.[191] Having recently returned from a tour of the United States, Lafayette was idealized by Italian exiles, among them Guglielmo Pepe; but Mazzini called him a man "mediocre intellect."[192] Based on his social and religious convictions, Mazzini's idea of democracy went beyond political rights. As he explained in *Thoughts on Democracy in Europe*, a government should be "acting for all," making people equal in social and economic terms—a vision of society dramatically different from his understanding of the United States' individualized democracy. "America is the embodiment, if compared to our own ideal, of the philosophy of mere rights: collective thought is forgotten: the educational mission of the State overlooked. It is the negative, individualistic, materialist school," he instructed Jessie White Mario, who was then writing on the United States for periodicals associated with Mazzini's movement.[193] For similar reasons he contested the idea of a national economy based on low taxation.[194]

Referring to US federalism, Mazzini confessed in 1838 to his friend Luigi Amedeo Melegari, one of the founders of Young Italy: "Be so good not to talk to me about America: I have a cordial antipathy to the very name of that country" (*ho un'antipatia cordiale al solo nome del paese*).[195] Considering the federal model a great risk to the future of his movement, he favored the republican centralism of the French revolutionary tradition. Although in other respects he was critical of French political thought, this principle of republican centralism drove him into an antagonistic position toward many of the Risorgimento's main political thinkers, including Gioberti, Rosmini and Cattaneo.[196] In the 1830s Mazzini made every effort to recruit Gioberti for his movement; and he shared with Gioberti the idea of Rome's civilizing mission in the world. But he was convinced that the Catholic Church was destined to give place to a new form of religious life.[197] Referring to his democratic rivals, he described Cattaneo's federalism simply as "madness."[198] Increasingly polemical in his judgements, in 1853 he considered "federalism, after foreign dominion, the greatest plague that might befall Italy: foreign dominion just about grants us a life; federalism would render [the nation] impotent and condemn it to a slow and inglorious death from the moment of its emergence."[199] The strong language he used made any reconciliation with the American model impossible.

Calling for new insurrections after the failed uprising of February 1853 in Milan, Mazzini's republican pamphlet *Agli Italiani* was written in Switzerland, and printed copies were secretly distributed under the most difficult of circumstances. While reiterating his argument that under a federal constitution Italy would be under constant threat of external enemies, he described federalism as an expression of self-centered materialism, incapable of appreciating collectivist notions of life. He denies Italian federalism any historical legitimacy, claiming that the medieval leagues constituted only temporary and largely unsuccessful alliances, restricted to the North of the country.[200] Mazzini also held that the leagues had principally served the interests of local aristocracies, holding back any socially more progressive development. Taking account of American experiences, federalism applied to Italy would produce a new aristocracy, constituted by the governors of the different states, undermining the egalitarian principles of popular sovereignty. In line with this assessment, he deprecated the American Senate as an "an open asylum for aristocrats."[201]

Mazzini always rejected the whole idea of comparing Italy to the United States, or of modeling one on the other. Many years earlier, and two years before the publication of the first volume of Tocqueville's famous study, Mazzini had outlined the reasons for the incompatibility between the two countries—geographically, in matters of religion, in its economic structures, and regarding its historical experience.[202] While the United States was characterized by a strong degree of internal heterogeneity, he saw Italy, perhaps surprisingly, as a basically homogeneous country. Contrary to many of the political thinkers quoted above, he thought that Italians were all "beset by the same vicissitudes, educated during the golden centuries to common glories and common liberties, then to common servitude, oppressed—no province excepted—by the same tyranny, subject to similar needs."[203] Mazzini warned constantly of the danger of granting Italy "a French or an American constitution, rather than an Italian one."[204] As he explained in a letter to Montanelli, Italy's future was democratic and republican for providential reasons, not because it had to follow America.[205]

While Sismondi was convinced that federations stood for a natural form of political organization, following the laws of history, for Mazzini Italy's future had to be unitary.[206] Regarding his views on Tocqueville, Mazzini conceded in 1862 that he "was certainly a man of acute insight, foreseeing the triumph of democracy, but looking at it gloomily as on a fatality: a man of cold intellect, without wider views and no aspiring element."[207] After the American Civil War, Mazzini proclaimed America's duty and mission to teach the world republicanism, but this did not mean that the United States constituted a model that had to be adopted throughout the world.[208]

Many progressive Italian thinkers—their democratic and republican principles notwithstanding—shared Mazzini's critical attitude toward the United States.[209] The Neapolitan aristocrat Carlo Pisacane, an early Socialist and the first to present a materialist reading of the Revolutions of 1848, opined that US federalism worked only because of the country's isolated geopolitical position, preventing the different states from forming alliances with third forces.[210] Others were less hostile to the United States but shared Mazzini's view that its federal constitution was not applicable to Italy. Filippo Buonarroti, despite his break with Mazzini, argued that federalism was not compatible with popular sovereignty.[211] A veteran of Babeuf's Conspiracy of the Equals of 1796 and a leader of the Giunta liberatrice italiana, Buonarotti considered federalism a project that suited the interests of the nobility and the better-off. The situation of Italy, with its many external enemies, could not be compared to that of the United States, where "a vast sea separates it from all those powers that might challenge it."[212] Also Botta had pointed to risks involved in federalism, where a Civil War could tear apart the allies of a federation.[213] Cesare Agostino made a similar point when speaking to the Constituent Assembly of the Roman Republic in 1849: American federalism was not suited to the situation in Italy, where communes and municipalities would dominate a federation with their particularist interests. A point frequently raised by Mazzini, America simply did not have a municipal tradition like that of Italy.[214]

As this chapter has shown, critical attitudes toward American society and its political institutions were common in Risorgimento political thought. Mazzini's stance influenced broad strata of Italians at a time when political ideas started circulating more widely in the public arena. What makes Mazzini stand out from many of the thinkers discussed in this book is the fact that he created a political organization, which from the early 1830s counted up to sixty thousand members, according to his own (possibly exaggerated) esti- mate. More than any other political activist of his time, Mazzini believed in the role of the press in the dissemination of ideas, one of the few instances where he was directly influenced by the example of the United States.[215] Ironically, many Italian commentators understood the importance of the press for mod- ern politics by learning from the United States.[216] Contrasting with Mazzini's movement, neo-Guelphism never translated into a political organization, de- spite the remarkable impact of Gioberti's *Primato* on Italian political thought. As for the Moderates' aristocratic liberalism, they wrote books for educated elites, but forming mass organizations contradicted their very idea of poli- tics.[217] Given Mazzini's reservations about the United States, it might seem surprising that New York, in 1878, honored the Italian patriot with a monu- ment in Central Park.

Democratic Diversions from Mazzini

After the failed revolutions of 1848, Mazzini became increasingly isolated, even among Italian democrats, explaining why after Unification and after his death in 1872 his name was for a long time sidelined by official Risorgimento hagiography.[218] In addition to his conflict with Cavour's Società Nazionale, which attracted many former Democrats, the divisions between Mazzini and the Socialist International were particularly pronounced.[219] Many Demo- crats and Republicans disagreed specifically with Mazzini's strong views on the United States and with his stern opposition to federalism.[220] Cattaneo endorsed the concepts "Stati Uniti" or "l'unione Americana," exactly because they expressed an "intimate and spontaneous form of unity."[221] Many Italian Americans too supported a federal solution to the Italian question, signaling differences with Mazzini's political thought.[222]

Meanwhile, the French model of republicanism, previously so influential, had demonstrated many weaknesses. The collapse of the Second Republic and Louis-Bonaparte's coup d'état led to a reexamination of republican traditions and principles in Italy, reviving the idea that democracy might be achieved through nonrepublican forms of government.[223] Rather than understanding the French coup d'état as the end of democracy, republicans like Cattaneo and Mauro Macchi believed that Napoleon III had eliminated the threat posed by the conservative majority in the Assembly and the various fractions of French legitimists. While Cattaneo remained a stern opponent of the Savoy monarchy, some Republicans were prepared to advance the cause of national liberation and democracy within the framework of a monarchy: for Mazzini, using an expres- sion of Thomas Carlyle, this was "a philosophy of sorrow and renunciation."[224]

The nation's political unification in 1861 obliged Italian Democrats to articulate their relationship to the new nation-state. Many of them read John Stuart Mill's *Considerations on Representative Government*, published that same year, in 1861. Appearing only a few years after Balbo's *Monarchia rappresentativa*, the international context of political debate had changed considerably, with the outbreak of the American Civil War calling the Union's survival into question.[225] Mill seemed to suggest that Italy did not present the level of internal diversity that required federalism, using a comparison with England and Scotland, which coexisted "under one united legislature." Rooted in the classical tradition of political language, federalism for Mill described a mixed government, "ruling a large territory through representation," as opposed to democracy, where "small republics are ruled directly by the people who kept all state functions in their own hands."[226] His main emphasis here was on the control of government, whether advocating a federal or a unitary constitution. Mill's arguments were directly relevant to debates in Italy, where the new Italian parliament rejected a project for regional autonomy designed by Cavour's minister of interior Marco Minghetti.[227] Some Moderates opposed the idea of regional autonomy but tended to support Minghetti on the issue of municipal and provincial self-government. Others criticized the plans for administrative decentralization, believing that Italians lacked the necessary sense of responsibility for self-government.[228] In the early years after Unification, at a time when the government still feared losing the mezzogiorno, any challenge to centralized control seemed out of place.

Or not? Federalist challenges to the existing constitution never totally disappeared from Italy's political agenda, which continued to call on the American example for years after Unification. Alberto Mario described Mazzini as "a saint" but always retained his belief in federalism as an essential condition of democratic government.[229] In the 1870s he still proposed federal self-government, a system where every region makes its own laws, as the only way of tackling Italy's regional diversity.[230] Without referring to Mill directly, Mario used the term "self-government" in English as a reference to his own international experiences. Self-government and federalism remained at the core of Italian republicanism.[231]

CHAPTER THREE

A Model Republic?
The United States in the
Italian Revolutions of 1848

The past we talk about throbs side by side with the future we fear or hope for. Memories mix with trepidation and hopes.

—GIUSEPPE MONTANELLI, *INTRODUZIONE AD ALCUNI APPUNTI STORICI SULLA RIVOLUZIONE D'ITALIA*, 1851[1]

An Age of Constitutions: From 1820 to 1848

1848 was a year of triumph for the North American Republic. At the end of the Mexican-American War the United States acquired huge territories from the Texan border all the way to California, as well as land previously contested by Britain in the Northeast. Some Italian Americans, like Alessandro Luigi Bargani, were eager to recommend American blueprints for solving Italy's constitutional question.[2] In March 1848, Daniele Manin's provisional government of the Republic of Venice sent an address to the United States of America, proclaiming that

> the ocean divides us, but we are not divided by the bonds of sympathy; and liberty, like the electric current traversing the seas, will bring us your examples, and maintain the communion of thought and feeling, which is far more precious than that of interest. We have much to learn from you; and, though your elders in civilization, we blush not to acknowledge it.[3]

Meanwhile, the fact that the United States assumed an official policy of strict neutrality toward Italy during the years 1848–49 also created disillusionment among the revolutionaries as well as among those Americans who had taken an active interest in the events, like the journalist Margaret Fuller or the American chargé d'affaires in Rome, Lewis Cass Jr.[4]

Before assessing the role played by the United States in Italian political thought of 1848, the Italian experience of the Revolutions of 1820–21 and 1830–31 also needs to be taken into account, both marking a watershed for the peninsula's national movement. During the Revolution of 1820–21 Piedmont and Naples adopted versions of the Spanish constitution of 1812, the so-called Constitution of Cadiz, whereas Sicily returned to its own constitution of the same year, 1812, which had emerged during the British occupation. The Spanish constitution enjoyed an almost mythical reputation among Italian patriots and retained its symbolic value long after it was revoked.[5] Drafted during the Spanish Peninsula War, it combined liberal, federal, and nationalist elements in an anti-Napoleonic spirit. While American constitutional documents influenced Spanish debates in 1812, Kate Ferris has demonstrated that Spanish Liberals had conceived their constitution mostly as an alternative to the American documents.[6] It granted near universal male suffrage but entrusted sovereignty to the more abstract notion of the nation, not the people itself, thus emphasizing representative elements and the state's exercise of power. Establishing a moderate constitutional monarchy, the Cadiz Constitution was the outcome of close intellectual exchange between Italian and Spanish political theorists throughout much of the eighteenth century.[7]

As a consequence of its strong monarchical elements, some Italians, including Mazzini, were highly critical of the Cadiz document. For instance, the Calabrian patriot General Guglielmo Pepe criticized the constitution for granting the king the position of military commander.[8] A protagonist of the Napoleonic Wars and the Revolution of 1820–21, Pepe would still play an important role in the Venetian Revolution of 1848, drawing heavily on the insights gained during several of the peninsula's recent revolutions. Although he was friends with Frances Trollope, the very outspoken critic of America, Pepe admired the US constitution and set his hopes on the United States' support for Italy's political struggle.[9] Pepe's detailed analysis of the Cadiz Constitution was certainly not representative of the usually rather unspecific or passing references to a variety of constitutional documents during the Revolutions of 1821 and 1848. Details of the Spanish constitution of 1812 were not necessarily well known in Italy, even among those who endorsed it, and its adaptability to the conditions of the Italian mezzogiorno was not obvious. Only after the failure of the Revolutions of 1848 were the 1812 documents slowly erased from political memory.[10]

Unlike the Constitution of Cadiz, adopted in Piedmont and Naples, the Sicilian constitution of 1812 was almost homemade. It had been forced on the Bourbon king Ferdinando III, now residing in Palermo, by the British representative in Sicily Lord William Bentinck.[11] Endorsed by parts of the anti-Bourbon Sicilian aristocracy, the constitution's supporters made claims as to

the supposedly shared Norman heritage of the English and the Sicilian constitutional traditions. According to Pepe "it was but a reform of the old Constitution modified according to the new social exigencies."[12] This logic, however,
was not universally followed. According to Foscolo it was a terrible document,
"because it was too similar to the English [constitution], ignoring the fact
that the Mediterranean is not the Atlantic."[13] Botta presented the same argument, describing the document as the importation of a foreign model.[14] The
journalist and Bourbon civil servant Ferdinando Malvica simply called it "the
English constitution," complaining that Sicily found itself "con un vestito non
suo," undermining Sicily's own constitutional tradition.[15]

Based on a bicameral system, the document was adopted under conditions that had turned Sicily into a part of Britain's informal empire. Instead of
citing altruistic motives, according to John Rosselli the main motive behind
Britain's engagement in Sicily was its alliance with the Bourbons against the
French.[16] Meanwhile, the document abolished feudalism and separated the
powers of king and parliament. More importantly, it represented a constitutional alternative to the authoritarian centralism established by Napoleon
and Murat on the mainland.[17] In 1820, the Sicilian parliament briefly revived
the constitution's main articles, keen to reestablish Sicily's separation from
Naples. As a consequence, English constitutionalism retained its place in the
political thought of the South. In 1848, Moderate Liberals such as Giacinto
Galanti presented England as a model that, unlike so many other experiments, had passed the test of history.[18] The Sicilian revolutionaries referred
to their 1812 constitution as a modern and—in the words of Marino Stabile,
secretary of the revolutionary committee—a "reformed version" of its historical rights.[19]

Compared to the period of Napoleonic rule, constitutional debates in 1820
arose under very different circumstances—during a relatively short-lived
period of revolutions. Unlike elsewhere in the peninsula, in Palermo the Revolution of 1820 was of a mostly popular character and driven by urban violence,
despite the fact that Cardinal Pietro Gravina headed its provisional government, made of representatives of the local aristocracy. As would be the case in
1848, for Palermo independence from Naples was one of the Revolution's principal objectives, whereas other parts of the island were in favor of keeping the
union with Naples, accepting the recently granted constitution of the Bourbon
rulers.[20] Rather than seeing these divisions as signs of southern backwardness, they reflected the many forms of political mobilization witnessed in the
Italian South since the late eighteenth century.[21]

The conflicts leading to revolution in 1820–21 were largely homegrown,
concerned with local traditions and legal circumstances, which did not neces-
sitate the importation of foreign ideas from across the Atlantic. They left little
space for the discussion of American ideas. While the Spanish constitution of
1869 would reproduce the US constitutional preamble almost word for word,

its predecessor of 1812 and the various constitutions modeled after it were not especially influenced by the experiences of the American Revolution.[22]

The other moments of unrest Italian revolutionaries looked back to in 1848 were the Revolutions of 1830–31 in Modena, Parma, and the Papal States. To some extent these events were a response to developments in France, where many Italian exiles had resided since 1821, while also reflecting the political program of the Carbonari that operated without much support from the population at large.[23] Only in parts of the Papal States was repression felt such that wider sections of the local aristocracy and the middle class supported those revolutions. At the time, the protagonists of these movements felt little need to look abroad or across the Atlantic for political models. In some cases, most prominently that of Count Carlo Pepoli from Bologna, only the experience of exile, once the revolutions had been defeated, led to a closer engagement with Anglo-Saxon constitutional thought. Although the revolutionaries respected the territorial integrity of Italy's existing states, there is nothing to suggest that the federal structure behind the United Provinces of the Papal States took their cue from the American Revolution.[24] Moreover, in response to the failure of these revolutions, Filippo Buonarroti abandoned the project of a federalist republic in favor of a unitary one. It was around this time that he started his correspondence with Mazzini, Italy's most famous democratic opponent of federalism.[25] Many of Buonarroti's arguments against federalism—the potential exposure to external threats, the need to establish a central authority— remained similar to those of Mazzini.

In July 1831 Mazzini created La Giovine Italia, adopting the antifederalist motto, "without Unity there is no real nation."[26] With reference to the previous chapter, it needs no further explanation that American democracy did not play a positive role in Mazzini's political project. Equality between the members of one nation was understood as a God-given quality of humanity, which did not need foreign models. Recently assumed antifederalism notwithstanding, Buonarroti differed from Mazzini on several strategic questions, and (as mentioned in the previous chapter) the two revolutionaries soon fell out with each other. While Mazzini rejected Buonarroti's concept of communism, his experiences were directly relevant to Mazzini's analysis of the social question, which during those years assumed an entirely new dimension and would make a substantial contribution to the political agenda of 1848. The uprisings of the Canuts in Lyon in 1831 and 1834 and the republican agitation in Paris in 1832, as well as the growing influence of Saint-Simonism all influenced the Italian exiles. This wider European context of debates helped radical Italian exiles to formulate alternatives to the moderate liberalism of the Piedmontese aristocracy. Meanwhile, their strong belief in Italy's own destiny, rooted in a philosophy of progress going back to Vico, and recently renewed by Gioberti and Romagnosi, pushed the discussion of foreign models into second place. These facts challenge those historians, discussed in the introduction, who assume that Italians were bound to look across the Atlantic in order to form their own constitutional nation-state.

Despite the role of Italy's own revolutionary and constitutional experiences throughout the 1820s and 1830s, references to American political institutions started to play a more significant role during the Revolutions of 1848. Moreover, the national movement had begun to inspire much wider sections of the population, and, as a consequence of the prospect of revolution, the national question was more frequently discussed in relation to the entire peninsula rather than in terms of isolated uprisings against local rulers. Especially toward the end of 1848, when disillusionment with the recently granted constitutions became more widespread, the United States gained a new prominence in political debates. Also, the pope's decision to distance himself from the national movement, and fears over the failure to establish an Italian League, contributed to renewed interest in the American constitution.

As a consequence, 1848 was the moment when American constitutional experiences played their most relevant role in the history of the Risorgimento. This, however, was not the case from the start, and it did not apply to the entire peninsula. The huge number of surviving leaflets and broadsheets publicizing the songs and patriotic poems of 1848 bears witness to the revolutions' initial hopes for the constitutional development of the peninsula's hitherto existing states and the formation of an Italian League between them. Instead of foreign models, a hymn from Liguria simply evokes Italy's own constitutional rulers: "Long live the magnificent Pio, long live the *Re riformatori*," the "reforming Kings."[27] A *Canto popolare* from Genoa celebrating "Italy and the League" lists "Pio IX," "Leopoldo II," and "Carlo Alberto" along with the "Sicilian heroes," without foreign references.[28] Another song, published by a different printer in Genoa and which also praised the Italian League, evokes the same constitutional rulers as well as pride in Italy's own power to free itself from foreign rule:

> Viva Alberto, Pio Nono, Leopoldo,
> Prenci caldi d'Italico zelo:
> Le Falangi vendute ad un soldo
> Presto, presto sconfitte cadran.
> Sì, tremate, tremate, o tiranni,
> Al cospetto d'un popol, che sorge
> Sù quel capo esecrato gli affanni
> Della Patria piombare dovran.[29]

A "Song of Italian Women" expressed similar patriotic pride in Italian values:

> Accorrete, accorrete, fratelli,
> Accorrete al bramato cimento,
> E mostrate che ancor non è spento
> Nel'Italici petti il valor.[30]

Huge numbers of similar odes and chants, printed as leaflets or published in newspapers, circulated across the peninsula, many of them written by women, or praising the role taken by women during the Revolution. The origin of the songs from Genoa, which had been under Savoyard rule since 1815, explains their often monarchical emphasis. Police control over the print industry stifled any republican voices. Repression notwithstanding, many Genoese still resented the fact that the Congress of Vienna had not restored an independent Ligurian Republic or the ancient Republic of Genoa. When they rose against Piedmontese rule in 1849, the rebellion was ruthlessly crushed by the army under the command of Alfonso La Marmora and with support of the British navy.

As the following sections of this chapter will show, republicanism was often a reluctant reaction to the failures of the new constitutional monarchies. Meanwhile, American assumptions that the peninsula was in eager need of lessons in American constitutionalism seem a long shot from the patriots' confidence in their own political traditions. The references to specific rulers, including the Habsburgs in Tuscany, demonstrate the extent to which the most obvious response to the Italian question remained a federal solution on the basis of its existing states: "that Kingdoms and Pepoles will fuse into one," as another song proclaimed.[31]

While the following sections of this chapter examine references to the United States during the Revolutions in Lombardy, Tuscany, and Sicily, a number of existing studies have investigated connections between the Roman Republic and the United States. The Roman Republic emerged late in the period of revolutions, in February 1849, and never spread to the wider territory of the Papal States. It was defeated by three months of French siege, in July 1849.[32] These circumstances explain why, compared to the other Italian states, the Roman Republic is less relevant to an analysis of American references during the Italian Revolutions of 1848–49. Moreover, owing to the eminent international role of the papacy, connections between the American and Roman Republics in 1849 are of greater interest to diplomatic historians and offer less material to historians of political thought. Finally, with Mazzini as the main protagonist of the Roman Republic, the previous chapter has already offered important insights in his evaluation of American institutions.

Instead of adopting a Roman focus, this chapter compares references to American political institutions during the Revolutions in Lombardy, Tuscany, and Sicily. In all these states the United States had informed societal and constitutional debates for several decades, along with references to developments elsewhere in Europe. The chapter will start with Carlo Cattaneo's reflections on the defeat of the Revolution in Lombardy. Italy's most influential political thinker during the period after Mazzini dedicated a considerable amount of his work to American political institutions. His analysis of the events of 1848 is closely linked to his federal thought, which integrates the discussion of the American example with a much wider range of federal traditions in Europe.

MAP. The Italian peninsula between the Congress of Vienna and the
Unification of Italy. The map lists the major cities mentioned in the book.

Another Federalist Republican, Giuseppe Monatenelli, reflected on his experience as a minister in the provisional government of Tuscany, which had a
strong tradition of debating aspects of the US constitution, already referred
to in previous chapters. Despite this important historical connection with political thought across the Atlantic, and despite the fact that later during the
Revolution the grand duchy became a republic, there was less need in Tuscany to discuss its emerging political institutions with reference to the United
States. The section shows that Italians were able to discuss republicanism
without looking across the Atlantic. Finally, different political factions within
the Sicilian constitutional assembly made frequent references to the United
States, relating American experiences to Sicily's own constitutional tradition,

in particular its constitution of 1812. Sicily offers a perfect example to illustrate how opposing political camps make their ideological case with the help of references to American examples.

These three case studies are integrated with a discussion of several political thinkers who shared an interest in federalism and American democracy and were actively involved in the Revolutions of 1848. They include among others Giuseppe Ferrari, Carlo Pisacane, and Giovanni Battista Tuveri. Throughout the chapter, pamphlets and broadsheets serve to draw connections between the revolutions in different parts of the peninsula. In order to show how references to the United States were used to elucidate local political experiences, all three case studies start with a summary of local events. A systematic comparison of constitutional documents emerging in Italy during the Revolution of 1848–49 would go beyond the scope of this chapter.[33]

Carlo Cattaneo and the Revolution in Lombardy

The rhetoric used during Milan's famous tobacco boycott, which started on New Years Day 1848, illustrates the connections anti-Austrian protesters drew between their grievances and what they knew about the beginnings of the American Revolution:

> When the citizens of Washington, oppressed by English tyranny, formed the famous league refusing paying the stinging taxes imposed by England, they gave a great example of concord and of the indomitable values that ultimately triumphed undefeated in the great struggle for independence. Youths! Like America hitherto, our fatherland now finds itself in difficult conditions. But along with the taxes that burden us stand those that depend on our free will. Franklin's fellow citizens abstained from tea; as of today you ought to refuse tobacco.[34]

The reference to the "citizens of Washington" to describe the events of the Boston Tea Party in 1773—long before the general had assumed a leading role in the Revolution, at a time when there was no city called Washington—shows how little it mattered what protesters in Milan actually knew about American independence, how history had turned into myth. The point here is not to expose their ignorance, but to illustrate how rhetorical devices work in political discourse, how Italian revolutionaries used Americanisms for the purpose of their struggle against Austrian rule. An initiative of the brothers Giovanni and Gaetano Cantoni and Giovanni Pezzotti, anecdotal evidence suggests that many among the Italian populations of urban centers observed the tobacco boycott, although supporters frequently felt compelled to discipline members of the public who continued smoking, including officers and common soldiers of the Austrian army, many of whom were Italians.[35] Cattaneo, alongside other *letterati* in Milan, was critical of the boycott, fearing an escalation of the confrontation to a point where the conflict could no longer be won. In Cattaneo's view it was this escalation that led to the militarization of the conflict and pushed the movement into submission under Piedmont, ultimately causing the Revolution's collapse.[36]

A leading Milanese publicist and protagonist of the Revolution in Lombardy, Cattaneo was well acquainted with recent political developments in the United States. Although the Austrian government regarded him with suspicion, his relationship with the Italian national movement was never unambiguous, both prior to the Revolution and after it. He opposed a violent overthrow of Habsburg rule, a position that led to tensions with the more radical sections of the national movement. Once revolution broke out, Cattaneo became one of its major strategists but was not prepared to sacrifice the ideals of liberty and self-government for new forms of external domination. It was on this basis that he opposed Lombardy's submission under the Savoy monarchy, a political conviction he stood by even after the Second War of Independence in 1859 and the creation of the Kingdom of Italy.[37]

The day-to-day practicalities of American political institutions constituted an important source of empirical information for Cattaneo's understanding of modern societies. Though he was not uncritical of all aspects of American democracy, for Cattaneo the United States stood for the most advanced form of humanity's political organization, which helped him to critically assess Italy's own progress toward political nationhood and more specifically to analyze the country's situation at the crossroads of 1848. Vice versa, Cattaneo's hostile position toward Carlo Alberto's campaign to "free" and annex Lombardy was shared by a good number of American observers, who questioned the king's disinterestedness and who hoped that Italy would come to a different arrangement for its political future.[38]

Cattaneo's understanding of 1848 helps the historian to question the reduction of these events to the issue of national revolution erupting from a desire to constitute independent national states. Although since the 1840s the national idea had gained considerable support among wider strata of the population, at the time relatively few protagonists of the revolutions were in a position to imagine a political nation beyond the relatively loose concept of a confederate league between existing states. Many of those participating in the events leading to revolution, Cattaneo first among them, fought for the recognition of constitutional rights and hoped to create new channels of political and economic participation for the rising middle classes. These demands were further fueled by economic grievances and tensions with the state authorities. Their main focus was the framework of Italy's existing states.

In the case of Lombardy, despite the advance of the national idea, it is not necessarily helpful to approach the analysis of the uprisings from the teleological perspective of a then nonexistent Italian nation-state.[39] Instead, taking the viewpoint of Lombardy's position within the Habsburg monarchy, it appears

that most of the empire's constituent parts—kingdoms, duchies, and princi-
palities, as well as many of its nationalities—voiced their growing discontent
at the Restoration regime in terms of demands for political representation
and recognition within a reformed empire. David Laven's work on Venetia
constitutes a formidable example of the opposition's emphasis on representation.[40] For some political thinkers and publicists, like Cattaneo, these debates within the Habsburgs' Italian provinces took the novel form of federal
arrangements.[41] Most of the national movements emerging within the empire
during the Restoration period considered independent national statehood a
last resort that came to form part of their political program only once the revolutions had been defeated. In Lombardy, the reluctance of many revolutionaries to ask for complete independence from the empire reflects their experience
of participation in local administration and reform prior to 1848, as well as a
strong sense of regional identity they did not wish to sacrifice for an uncertain
future under the Savoy dynasty. Critical reflection on these experiences formed
the background to Cattaneo's involvement in the Revolution.

In order to assess references to American experiences in the Milanese Revolution a short survey of developments leading to the events is needed. In his
groundbreaking study of Lombardy during the Restoration period, Kent R.
Greenfield analyzed the dynamics of the region's agricultural and commercial
development after 1814 (including the more modest beginnings of its industrial production), arguing that this was sustained over several decades through
educational and administrative reforms.[42] Although much of this program
was enacted under Austrian rule, local elites closely cooperated with this process and saw in the region's economic progress a potential source of future
self-government. While the constitutional concept behind the Habsburgs'
Lombardo-Venetian kingdom remained unconvincing, compared to other
Italian states before Unification it offered an exceptional level of local participation in public life.[43] Despite the political activities of patriots such as Silvio
Pellico and Federico Confalonieri, during the 1820s and 1830s the Austrian
monarchy's Italian territories were marked by a noticeable absence of unrest,
almost unlike anywhere else in Europe, which cannot be explained by political
suppression alone.[44] According to David Laven, "'the black legend' of oppressive Austrian rule was the invention of patriotic propagandists who paid scant
regard to reality."[45]

The situation changed during the second half of the 1840s, when government failure to respond to harvest shortages resulted in famine, the collapse of
trade and industry, unemployment, and violent protests in urban centers. Publicists in Lombardy, among them Cattaneo, were calling for further economic
reforms and progressive educational policies, including greater autonomy
from Vienna. However, despite frustration at Ferdinand's rule, this criticism
was rarely translated into open challenges to authority. The proposed federal
solutions to the Italian question did not necessarily mean the end of Habsburg

rule. Meanwhile, there was genuine enthusiasm at the election of Pio IX, his program of reforms, and the appointment of an Italian archbishop in Milan. In the autumn of 1847 the relationship between the Milanese population and the government turned into open hostility. Women were increasingly involved in these activities. But in January 1848 there were still serious attempts at reconciliation between the citizenship and the Austrian viceroy. *Albertismo* (that is, the movement in favor of Lombardy's union with Piedmont) gained ground, especially among the local nobility and the municipal authorities, but remained a minority position.[46]

When over the coming months several Italian states granted their subjects constitutions, Austria responded with new levels of repression, arrests, and increased military presence. While the Milanese celebrated the Revolution in Palermo and praised the Neapolitan constitution, the upper classes expressed concern at what they heard about a "Red Republic" in Paris.[47] Then Milan got its own revolution, which after only five days resulted in the departure of Radetzky's troops, Milan's famous *cinque giornate*.[48] Most major cities in Lombardy followed the same course. Milan remained divided between Gabrio Casati's *Albertisti*, who aimed for Piedmontese intervention, and the War Council under Carlo Cattaneo, who was vehemently opposed to submission under Piedmont.[49] The situation in the countryside, where at least parts of the peasant population remained pro-Austrian, was rather different. Though it was mostly a sign of antiseigniorial attitudes, as late as June 1848 peasants were said to greet Austrian troops passing through their villages with "Viva Radetzky."[50] These examples again reflect attitudes that can be observed more widely throughout the Habsburg monarchy.

The proclamations and decrees of the Revolution in Lombardy refrained from any explicit reference to the United States.[51] The commission in charge of calling a national assembly frequently referred to the legal traditions of France, Piedmont, and Spain, or the newly established Venetian Republic, but made no reference to the American Republic.[52] When the provisional government organized the plebiscite for Union with Piedmont, Republicans (including Mazzini) protested with an open letter to the *Giornale ufficiale*, but without evoking American concepts of freedom and sovereignty.[53] Contrasting with the European references in some of the Revolution's official documents, local legacies of reform and civic participation formed the background to Cattaneo's political thought and to his understanding of 1848—not as a national revolution, but primarily within its local and regional dimension. Meanwhile, his emphasis on progress through self-government reflects his interest in American democracy. Before analyzing his understanding of American political institutions, the following section will briefly account for Cattaneo's role in the Milanese Revolution.

Cattaneo was proud of his Lombard roots, considering his native region among the culturally most advanced in Europe.[54] Until the first days of the

IL TRIONFO DI CARLO ALBERTO
CONTRO RADESCHI

FIG. 10. Illustration from "Il trionfo di Carlo Alberto contro Radeschi," Genoa: Dagnino [1848]. BL: Miscellanee politiche genovesi. 804.k.13.54. British Library.

Milanese uprising in March 1848, Italian nationalism was less of a driving force behind Cattaneo's political thought than was his keen interest in forms of representation and constitutional rights. National unification did not occur to him as a primary political objective, and he concentrated his journalistic and political activity on the rights of an independent Lombardy within the Habsburg Empire.[55] In this respect his views bear similarity to those of the Florentine publisher Giovan Pietro Vieusseux, who believed in the possibility of Austria's assuming a liberal and modernizing role in northern Italy[56] As Norberto Bobbio argued, despite being a prominent representative of Italy's Radical Left, "from necessity Cattaneo was an anti-revolutionary writer and a reformer."[57] Through his legal studies at the University of Pavia, which included Austrian civil law, he was intimately familiar with the Habsburg administrative system. When writing for Francesco Lampati's *Annali* in the 1830s, Cattaneo's journalistic activity was not directed against the Austrian government, concentrating instead on the "rationalisation of Lombardy's system of government as it stood, without posing the problem of leaving it altogether."[58] His aim in those years was to enable Lombardy to catch up with the most advanced regions in Europe. Self-government was what he added to the Moderates' concept of representative government. What this might entail could be learned from the United States. National unity, or a common language, played only a secondary role in his thought on empire and federalism.[59]

As for the prospects for Lombardy's convergence with the other states of the peninsula, Cattaneo was pessimistic—unlike some of the thinkers discussed in

CARLO CATTANEO.
Disegno del sig. Barchetta, incisione del prof. Salvioni

FIG. 11. Carlo Cattaneo, from the illustrated magazine
L'Universo illustrato, 27 June 1869. Image courtsey Casa
Cattaneo, Historical Archives of the City of Lugano.

the previous chapter, for instance Rosmini. He emphasized Naples's remarkable prosperity during the reign of Ferdinando II but insisted that the South lacked the features of bourgeois civilization, which Lombardy shared with most of central and northern Europe. In particular, he points to cultural differences resulting from "an arbitrary and prohibitive system" of government, which had the effect that the people of the South "are extremely inclined to trust in fortune more than to their own assiduous labours and savings."[60] In contrast, notwithstanding his discontent at specific features of the Habsburg administration, Cattaneo held that Lombardy enjoyed all the benefits of infrastructure and civil society that lead to continuous progress. Mazzini, writing in the 1840s, seems to have partly shared Cattaneo's assessment of the Austrian provinces' advancement compared to the rest of the peninsula: "the provinces of the Lombard-Venetian Kingdom are less unhappy and better run than any of the other Italian states. You see some signs of progress that you simply cannot find in the Papal States or elsewhere."[61] "Elsewhere," for Mazzini, included Piedmont.

Cattaneo's concept of cultural progress was close to Romagnosi's idea of *incivilmento*, discussed in the previous chapter, and important to his understanding of the political nation, which reflects what he knew about the United States' political institutions. The prospect of progress was key to the constitution of any political nation. Writing in the *Rivista europea* in 1845, Cattaneo argued that the Italian South was far from catching up with the North. Contrasting it with Milan's civic culture, he offers a dire and almost hopeless picture of life in the South, in line with the Risorgimento's narrative of Bourbon *malgoverno*.[62] He describes an entirely foreign country, which contrasts dramatically with the cosmopolitan spirit connecting the middle classes of the northern countries across national boundaries. In Cattaneo's view Lombardy's Habsburg administration prior to 1848 appears as an unfortunate context for the conduct of public affairs, but it will not stop its striving liberal middle classes. In light of his comparative assessment of North and South, any social, economic, or cultural integration between those parts seemed unlikely.

Even in 1848, when Cattaneo openly turned to denounce the Viennese system of government, he identified local problems as a temporary moment of crisis, insisting on the difference between the current political climate and the Habsburgs' tradition of imperial rule. Describing Austria as "a cosmopolitan entity," he noted that its peoples were allowed to live within the empire "according to their own traditions."[63] His evaluation of the Austrian principles of multinational rule looks surprisingly similar to those of the Sicilian patriot Gioacchino Ventura. Often considered a federalist influenced by the American model, Ventura in 1848 still praised the legal tradition of Habsburg rule:

What forms the Austrian Empire's strength? Perhaps the fact that it counts some twenty million inhabitants? No. It is the fact that these are organised into five or six separate peoples with different Kingdoms, their own institutions, laws, their own governments, that they are united under one sceptre only in a political sense.[64]

In the context of the Italian Revolutions of 1848 it seems remarkable to find some of Italy's most prolific supporters of the Revolution praising the Austrian model of government. The liberal economist and statesman Stefano Jacini went so far as to call Maria Theresia's 1755 reform of the local administration Lombardy's "Magna Carta."[65] After the French period, Franz I revived the same framework of administration almost without changes. Cattaneo's disillusionment with Habsburg rule notwithstanding, it was a reflection on this tradition that in a letter to Italian exiles of 1 May 1859 he questioned whether Piedmont would grant the peoples of Italy the democratic freedom they expected:

Let's take it that Austria is threatened again in the East by Hungary, assaulted by its people in Vienna, under the shock once more of insurrections in the capitals of all kingdoms; and it is then confronted with proper and decisive will by Piedmont, and pushed back over the Alps. Do you really believe that the victorious monarchy, expecting to lead the entire force of the nation, would put down the sword and the crest of triumph to turn to voting? Once it has succeeded in liberating and unifying Italy?[66]

Cattaneo's hostile position toward the prospect of Piedmontese rule was mirrored by Carlo Pisacane. Discussing the fate of the Roman Republic, he argued that Piedmont and the Kingdom of the Two Sicilies should be considered on equal terms with Austria.[67] Genoa's *Corriere mercantile*, in May 1848, went beyond this assessment, describing the Neapolitan regime as "molto peggiore" than the Austrians'.[68] Cattaneo's friend Giuseppe Ferrari took a similar stance, arguing in an article for the *Revue indépendante* of January 1848 that Piedmont was far more reactionary than Austrian-ruled Lombardy.[69] Gioberti allegedly responded to the charges by reporting his fellow countryman to the French clerical authorities. Gioberti's intervention demonstrates how misleading it is to consider the Italian exiles as one big political family. Although he had recently moved from moderate to more democratic positions, the same Gioberti did not hesitate to describe Mazzini as Italy's greatest enemy.[70]

When seeking possibilities to reform the Austrian system of government according to federal principles, Cattaneo rediscovered the constitution of the Holy Roman Empire:

The Holy Roman Empire was not a Germanic but a Papal institution, imposed upon the divided pagan peoples of Germany by the sword of Christianity. Within its borders all Christian peoples counted as equal, as they did within the Church and within the heraldic brotherhood of the Crussades. The Emperor was King in Italy as well as in Germany.[71]

By evoking the example of the Holy Roman Empire, Cattaneo found himself in good American company. Inspired by Montesquieu's praise for this early federation of states, Franklin, in 1766, had traveled to Göttingen to discuss the constitution of the Holy Roman Empire with Johann Stephan Püttner and Gottfried Achenwall, both leading authorities on German imperial as well as comparative constitutional law.[72] During this trip Franklin also went to Bad Pyrmont (where he met the Hanoverian prime minister Baron Gerlach Adolph von Münchhausen), and to Cassel, Marburg, Frankfurt, Mainz, Trier, and Cologne, cities that offered the American traveler an extraordinary opportunity to discuss the history and practice of German federalism from a range of different perspectives. Püttner had described the empire as a "state composed of states," the "only body politic of its kind."[73] Unlike the cantons of Switzerland or the United Provinces of the Netherlands, the states making up the Holy Roman Empire had a common sovereign or overlord, while at the same time enjoying a great measure of freedom and independence. All members had their own state parliaments. In the event of conflict, the Imperial Diet or the Supreme Court were able to overrule decisions of individual states. Franklin took several of Püttner's publications back to London.

As Jürgen Overhoff has argued, the "Holy Roman Empire figured largely in the debates of the American Federalists": James Madison referred to the federal organization of the United States as a variant of the federal constitution of the Holy Roman Empire.[74] Jacques-Vincent de la Croix, an early commentator on the American constitution, described the German constitution as "the most essential example to follow in every one of its aspects, because it is the centre around which the interests of all the principal states of Europe gravitate."[75] Therefore, when Cattaneo looked at the Holy Roman Empire as a federal model for the reorganization of Lombardy's relationship to Austria (and later as a model for Italy), he consulted the same sources that had influenced the fathers of the American constitution. Like Cattaneo, also Francesco Saverio Salfi, in 1821, had taken the German Confederation as a model for the federalization of Italy. In Salfi's view, by preserving its present sovereigns the imperial model presented the advantage of a much looser structure compared to the United States or the Swiss constitutions.[76]

Upon receiving news of the uprisings in Vienna, on 17 March 1848, just a day before revolution broke out in Milan, Cattaneo still set his hopes on a federal transformation of the empire, writing an article—never published—advocating a free Lombardy within the structures of a federal Austria.[77] Only after experiencing the events of the following days did Cattaneo reconsider the future of Lombardy as part of an Italian federal republic. The course the Italian Revolutions quickly took was diametrically opposed to Cattaneo's own hopes and ideas. He was not prepared to follow the Milanese *Albertini* in seeking an alliance with Piedmont, but he also refused to lend support to the insurrection in Livorno; he declined nominations to the Piedmontese parliament and the constituent assembly in Tuscany; and he rejected an offer to become minister of finance in Mazzini's Roman Republic. Rather than reading his attitude as individual stubbornness and an inability to compromise, according to his deep-seated federalist conviction political office had to emerge out of local civic engagement.[78] He simply did not see the point why a Milanese intellectual should lead uprisings in Tuscany or represent the Roman people. As an analysis of his writings on American political institutions will show, this thinking echoed what he knew about the United States.

After the defeat of the Italian Revolutions Cattaneo devoted much of his time to the collection of documents for his project of an archive documenting the events between 1846 and 1849, the *Archivio triennale*. It is not surprising that Cattaneo's analysis of those events took a critical view of Mazzini, mostly on federalist grounds, but also questioning the authoritarian structure of his organization *Giovine Italia*. Cattaneo admired Garibaldi but rejected the idea of "unity at any cost."[79] After the Second War of Independence, in 1859 he refused to play a role in setting up a new administration in Lombardy and turned down a seat in the Italian parliament. When Italy was unified as a centralized nation-state under the Savoy, Cattaneo decided not to return *in patria*.

Cattaneo's Understanding of American Democracy

Like other Italian political thinkers, Cattaneo approached American democracy via England's constitutional tradition. Considering Britain an aristocratic dictatorship, which prevented the masses from taking their share in parliamentary liberty, the United States offered a democratic version of the same constitution.[80] Cattaneo's comparative assessment echoed Tocqueville's belief in the relationship between political institutions and cultural-historical traditions. Where Botta had considered the republic an inappropriate form of government for any country in Europe, Cattaneo took the view that republicanism reflected Italy's own civic legacy. While Italians recognized that their country lacked a modern constitutional tradition, they also thought that for them republicanism was not a foreign form of government. This did not mean that foreign experiences were irrelevant to the development of modern political structures. Italian constitutional thought often included diachronic or transnational comparisons. For instance, Adrian Lyttelton has demonstrated how Sismondi explored English constitutional debates to present Italians with a "usable past" in the form of their own medieval and early modern republics. Questioning the role of those legacies, Anna Maria Rao has argued that these republics were frequently associated with civic discord, and that they contributed to the peninsula's international weakness.[81] In Rao's view this legacy made ancient and pre-Roman models more attractive. Meanwhile, these classical political forms were also frequently discussed with reference to American and French developments since the late eighteenth century, practically as a mirror image of the Machiavellian moment described by John Pocock.

In 1848, faced with the prospect of Lombardy's annexation by Piedmont, Cattaneo emphasized the extent to which a monarchical option contradicted Italy's own historical experiences: "Every institution in Italy has had republican roots for three thousand years. Crowns never brought any glory. Rome, Etruria, Magna Grecia, the League of Pontida, Venice, Genoa, Amalfi, Pisa, Florence acquired all glory and power on the basis of Republican rule."[82] Piedmont's expansionist ambition became the main target of Cattaneo's republicanism, he blaming the war against Austria for the fact that Liberals abandoned their constitutional principles: "The war seemed to dominate all their thinking. They saw reactionaries and barbarians only in Austria, without noticing reactionaries and barbarians here in Italy; because each country has its own."[83] While the House of Savoy constituted Europe's longest reigning dynasty, it represented an exception within the pensinsula's history, leading

Cattaneo to suggest that a federal Italy did not need Piedmont: "without Piedmont it will still count 20 million people. There is no need for Piedmont."[84] In 1860, after joining Garibaldi in Naples, he is said to have joked that "Italy should cede Piedmont to France and separate it by a Chinese Wall."[85]

The role of Italy's republican legacy, in Cattaneo's view, was even more important than France's recent republicanism: "while in France the term Republic still sounds foreign, in Italy it represents splendour on every page of its history. It is interlaced with the memories of the patricians and that of the Church. It belongs to the tradition of the most established people."[86] His comparison also targets the contrast between France's model of centralized republicanism and Italy's federal republican tradition, which he developed in his pamphlet *Militarism and Centralism in France*.[87] This difference is also about a liberalism reduced to representative government as opposed to American-style self-government. For Cattaneo, self-government extended the concept of personal autonomy to levels of local, provincial, and national government, a distinction that was central to Tocqueville's analysis of American democracy.[88]

Cattaneo's emphasis on shared civic traditions (rather than nationality or a common language) directly reflects the insights he had gained from studying the United States. The United States had to split from Britain (with which it shared a language) owing to different visions of public affairs. Americans formed a federation between the secessionist states on the basis of their common understanding of economic and political values. Why should the English-speaking peoples of the British Isles, Pennsylvania, California, Canada, Australia, and Jamaica all share the same legislator? "Whatever the commonality of thoughts and feelings a language creates between families and communities, a parliament united in London will never satisfy America. . . . Laws discussed in Naples will never resuscitate neighbouring Sicily. . . . This is the reason why there is a federal law, or the law of peoples, which stands alongside the laws of the nation and the laws of mankind."[89] Reading these ideas within the wider context of his writings on Lombardy and the Habsburgs, Cattaneo makes an argument for federalized (as opposed to centralized) empires. In an attempt to connect his Italian experiences and his understanding of American political institutions, he notes that Lombardy had more to share with the civilizations of central and northern Europe than with most Italian states. While this argument evokes northern stereotypes of the South, it also reflects his profound appreciation of civic traditions in Lombardy.

Contrary to other nineteenth-century federalists, Cattaneo retains the idea of diversity among members of the same federation, leading Giuseppe Armani to describe Cattaneo's federalism as "policentrismo culturale," rooted in a concept of progress based on the diversity of experiences, which in turn generate innovation in culture, science, technology, and social organization.[90] As Cattaneo concluded in a philosophical essay of 1844 for *Politecnico*, "a people is more civilised the more numerous the principles it incorporates. . . . Its history is the eternal contrast between diverse principles, which the nation tends to absorbc and unify."[91]

The events of 1848 removed the idea of a reformed Austrian Empire from the table and obliged Cattaneo to reconsider federalism as a structure for the Italian states. As outlined in the *Corollarii* of his book on 1848, the future freedom of Italy was to depend on a federation of independent states, each of which had to guarantee civic rights to its citizens. The years under French domination had demonstrated that unification and centralization undermined freedom, in Cattaneo's case defined as more than freedom from foreign interference. The sovereignty and freedom of Italy's individual states, understood as "political families," were now to form the basis of national independence.[92]

Despite his very clear emphasis on the "native" character of Italian federalism, rooted in the nation's civic traditions, Cattaneo's writings show that he was far from idealizing the prospects of federalism; and it is here that he draws on adverse examples derived from recent developments in US history. In 1833, in an article for the *Annali universali di statistica*, Cattaneo had discussed the tariff conflict between the US federal government and South Carolina. The so-called Nullification Crisis had been caused by diverging economic interests between the manufacturing states of the North and those of the largely agricultural South.[93] In 1828 federal authorities had introduced a new tariff to protect manufacturing in the North, while also helping the federal government to repay public debt at a time when its income relied almost exclusively on tariffs. Since Europe was likely to react to this policy by raising its own tariffs on agricultural commodities (cotton, rice, tobacco), politicians in South Carolina argued that the policy was detrimental to its economic interests. The state government responded by nullifying the tariff, risking a federal military intervention to protect the United States' legal integrity.

Cattaneo was fully aware of the conflict's wider implications, especially the relationship between slavery in the South and the economic interests of the federation as a whole. Therefore, Cattaneo's piece had lost little of its interest when in 1860, almost thirty years later and shortly before the outbreak of the American Civil War, he decided to republish it as part of his collection *Memorie di economia pubblica*. Warning of the risks of civil war almost thirty years before it broke out, Cattaneo had concluded his essay by remarking, "he whose heart beats with a sense of justice and humanity must almost feel tempted to invoke the terrible but transitory scourge of war if it carries with it the hope to finally end this infamy of trafficking of people."[94]

Meanwhile, in reissuing the article exactly at the moment of Italian Unification, many of the same issues were also relevant to debates at home. During the 1860s, conflicts over taxation—the *dazio*—and its impact on local economic development animated the political life of the young nation-state, turning Cattaneo's study of the American tariff crisis into a contribution to domestic politics. While Cattaneo sides with the federal government, his awareness of the implications for the organization of any federal system demonstrates that he was far from idealizing the political and economic realities of the United States. In light of his insistence on differences between the Italian North and South, it is difficult not to read his essay as a warning about federal solutions for countries characterized by diverging economic interests. Using highly dramatic language to describe the scenario of an armed confrontation between federal and local troops, the father of Italian federalism was fully aware of the complications of implementing federal democracy.[95]

Cattaneo's comments on specific aspects of American economic and political life remained exceptions within the huge bibliography of his writings. His essays on the United States allowed him to outline his idea of federalism as a condition of political liberty, but without offering much further detail about the United States' political institutions. Passing references to the United States in his analysis of Italy's experience of 1848 illustrate this point:

> Each Italian state has to remain sovereign and free in its own right The painful example of the French peoples, who won their freedom three times, but never retained it, proves right the dictum of our ancient sage Machiavelli, that freedom cannot be preserved if the people do not keep their hands on it. Yes, every people in its own home, under the protection and observation of all other peoples. This is what the wisdom of America teaches us. Each political family needs to have its separate patrimony, its magistrates, its weapons. Meanwhile, whatever it is due, it has to comply with common needs and reflect common greatness. In the fraternal congress of the whole nation it has to take its seat in sovereign and free representation, deliberating together the laws that guarantee . . . the indestructible unity and cohesion of the whole.[96]

A positive, but very vague mention of the United States makes up this conclusion to his memories of 1848, a lesson learned from defeat. Rather than reflecting insights into the American constitution, his reference to the United States is based on his assessment of the recent war against Austria, in which Lombardy handed itself over to the king of Piedmont, who in Cattaneo's words "had a stronger intention to suppress peoples than to free them."[97] Fearful of republican radicalization and popular sovereignty, the Revolution in Milan had surrendered to monarchical absolutism only to then be crushed by Austrian troops.[98]

The examples mentioned above all allude to specific historic events. Norberto Bobbio has argued that Cattaneo was not a theorist of federalism, a fact that is reflected in the ways in which he writes about the United States.[99] According to Filippo Sabetti the main aim of Cattaneo's references to the United States was to show that there existed an alternative to the European model of the unitary state; to provide empirical evidence that society can govern itself;

to propagate a new political science focussed on society's institutions of self-government, a *Gesellschaftswissenschaft* (science of society), as opposed to a *Staatswissenschaft* (science of state).[100] In 1859, in a letter to Agostino Bertani, Cattaneo wrote "of the example and the experience of eighty years" since the foundation of the North American Confederation, on which the "United States of Italy" could rely.[101] Although he followed many English-language periodicals and regularly reviewed books on the United States, he never studied the US constitution in any great detail.[102]

Cattaneo's idea of the United States as a federal experiment stood in the tradition of late eighteenth-century Italian debates on the American Revolution. Nevertheless, within its Lombard context Cattaneo's interest in the United States represented something of a novelty. The local legacy of enlightened absolutism as well as the Austrian approach to administration after 1815 had meant that political thinkers in Lombardy were able to discuss economic and legal progress without making references to foreign places such as the United States of America. Cobden, who met Cattaneo in Milan, commented on some of the Habsburgs' progressive policies in Italy.[103] Romagnosi, discussed in the previous chapter, was an important influence on Cattaneo but rarely referred to the United States.[104] Cattaneo's critique of present conditions in Lombardy emerged as a local discourse on reform and legal theory, with references to the United States remaining largely abstract.

Commentators often take it for granted that Cattaneo's federalism was directly influenced by Tocqueville's *Démocratie en Amérique*.[105] While his interest in the United States is undeniable, Cattaneo's federalism had multiple roots. In his voluminous writings he cites *Democracy in America* only once, with a few more references to Tocqueville's coauthored report on the American penitentiary system, most of which was written by Gustave de Beaumont.[106] Cattaneo's library contained the first volume of the 1836 French edition of *La démocratie en Amérique*, but not volume 2, the more conceptual and politically abstract part of the work.[107] There is no evidence that he ever read volume 2. Considering that the large majority of Cattaneo's writing (and of his journalistic activity in particular) consists of reviews and discussions of existing works, the relatively limited role played by Tocqueville in Cattaneo's political thought is worth noting. This fact seems especially striking if compared to the importance Rosmini accorded to Tocqueville.

Cattaneo's relative indifference toward Tocqueville not only points to misconceptions in recent historiography; it also underlines the fact that some of Italy's most progressive political thinkers were by no means reliant on the United States to develop their political concepts; and that ideas about the United States did not always arrive via third countries. This is not to say that Tocqueville played no role in Italian political thought. While an Italian translation of *Démocratie en Amérique* appeared only in 1884, a large majority of intellectuals in northern Italy during the first half of the nineteenth century was perfectly francophone and often had better French than Italian.[108] Visiting Paris in 1835, Cavour remained deeply impressed by the young Tocqueville as well as by his recently published first volume of *Démocratie en Amérique*. In Cavour's words, the book revealed the future: "jette plus de lumière qu'aucun autre sûr les questions politiques de l'avenir."[109] Among the Italian democratic thinkers influenced by Tocqueville's study, Gabriele Rosa deserves mentioning, as does Alberto Mario, who had himself lived for many years in the United States.[110] Yet, the fact that Tocqueville became the French foreign minister responsible for the suppression of the Roman Republic in 1849 impacted on his Italian reception, in particular the political Left.

Considering the wider international context of the French intervention against the Roman Republic, the United States gave Italian patriots little reason to set their hopes on transnational republican solidarity. In spring 1848 Mazzini and his followers had besieged the American representatives in Rome, hoping that their government would grant the Roman Republic official recognition. Despite the fact that parts of the press and some politicians in the United States expressed themselves favorably, the State Department followed the course of European chancelleries, excluding any establishment of diplomatic relations, thus contradicting its stated policy of granting recognition to any government enjoying popular support. Lewis Cass Jr., American chargé d'affaires in Rome, not only declined invitations to official dinners; he even felt unable to accept seats at the opera offered to him by the revolutionaries. Mazzini concluded that Cass behaved "very badly," although the American later issued him and his allies passports, allowing them to leave Rome. When Washington eventually changed course it was too late: before the American representative received new instructions, the French army had reestablished papal rule in Rome.[111] For Italian Republicans, Tocqueville, the French foreign minister, had lost any credibility to act as a spokesman for the American model.

An eager observer of political and societal developments in the United States, Cattaneo did not need foreign guidance to make sense of what he read. Instead of trying to trace the extent to which he was influenced by *Démocratie en Amérique*, it seems more relevant to assess how he arrived at his understanding of American democracy on the basis of a much wider range of sources. Cattaneo found in the United States' federalism and republicanism the conditions for a society of free and entrepreneurial citizens, reflecting his ambition for his native Lombardy. Rather than wishing to emulate the American model, or French readings thereof, he looked in the United States for what he recognized as a modern version of Italy's own civic traditions, adapted to democratic conditions.

It is not the United States, but Switzerland that is the country most frequently referred to in Cattaneo's writings, a more immediate model for Italy's federal future. His interest in Switzerland went back to the years when he frequented the Liceo in Milan and he visited the country for the first time aged twenty. He also translated a German history of Switzerland into Italian.[112] Although Swiss public opinion was divided over this issue, there was a widespread view that Switzerland had to support other peoples' fight for freedom. Cattaneo's critical stance toward Piedmont was reciprocated in the cantons since 1834, when European refugees in Geneva, supported by the local population, had attempted to cross the border into Savoy to start a European revolution.[113] Later, as a consequence of his long exile in Lugano, Cattaneo acquired excellent insights into Switzerland's civic institutions and the country's constitution.[114] What he gained from these insights was the idea of self-governing independent cities, quite different from a federalism of regions or territorial states.[115]

Meanwhile, in the eyes of many, and especially from a Piedmontese perspective, it was Cattaneo's belief in Switzerland as a model for Italy that delegitimized his federalism: "If anybody was seriously to come forward asking whether Switzerland is a nation, and whether as a nation it enjoyed a sovereign existence, the right to independence and equal respect similar to any other state in Europe, this person would provoke nothing but laughter," wrote the Genoa-based newspaper *La lega italiana* in February 1848.[116] What the journalist seemed to ignore is the fact that even the United States was interested in the Swiss federal constitution. An early expression of the United States' fascination with the Swiss was the first American opera of which the music has survived, Benjamin Carr's *The Archers, or The Mountaineers of Switzerland* of 1796. It was an early version of *Wilhelm Tell*, a work that subsequently, in Schiller's and Rossini's versions, aroused great interest in Italy.[117] Particularly popular was the second act of Rossini's *grand opéra*. It contained the wonderful duet of the lovers Arnold and Mathilde, but also the gathering of the delegates from the different cantons and their passionate oath "Jurons, jurons par nos dangers."

In addition to being influenced by Constant and Sismondi, both closely acquainted with the Swiss model, Cattaneo's federalism also reflects his reading of the French historian Auguste Thierry, whose work he reviewed. As Martin Thom has pointed out, for Thierry France's ancient Gallo-Roman cities, rebelling against the feudal structures around them, became the heroic ancestors of the Third Estate during the beginnings of the French Revolution.[118] Similar ideas were reflected in the works of Alessandro Manzoni, who had met Thierry in Paris and applied some of his theories to his own writings on the relationship between Lombard and Italian history. Botta also favored political representation based on small administrative units. It was not the United States that served him as a model, but Italy's own history. Cautioning his readers that Lombardy would be too big to form a centralized political unit, Botta offered the historic examples of Lucca or San Marino to argue that the unit of government had to be small. Following the same logic, even Lombardy had to be divided "into lots of parts, each nominating its own delegates."[119] For Cattaneo, small units of free cities, not unlike Rousseau's small-community democracy, were to form the basis of federal self-government. A Piedmontese invasion, as favored by the Lombard aristocracy in 1848, would destroy any such hopes.

An early example of Cattaneo's capacity to distinguish between the social conditions of the United States and the historical realities that marked the Italian peninsula is a debate on railways in the second half of the 1830s. Deeply involved in plans for a railway connecting the two major centers of Austria's Italian possessions, Milan and Venice, Cattaneo knew that Italy was different from the "vast and deserted" territory of America.[120] The point of projecting railways, for Cattaneo, was not to build the most direct connections, but to take account of Italy's historical development and environmental circumstances, marked by the high density of its population in the North and the numerous urban centers with their significant economic activity. Instead of direct tracks between Milan and Venice, following the more economical American model of railway development, according to Cattaneo the project had to connect the historical centers of Brescia, Verona, Vicenza, and Padua. Passengers moving between these urban centers were to constitute the basis for securing revenue. The United States had no comparable networks of cities. For Cattaneo the aim of railway development was not to build prestigious fast lines, but to serve civil society by creating benefits for the majority of its population. Contrary to the conventional argument whereby the Habsburgs' retrograde Italian provinces had to copy lessons from more progressive nations, Cattaneo describes a historically constituted civilization in its own right, which, owing to specific cultural experiences, articulated more complex answers to the challenges of the modern age.

Among Cattaneo's most detailed discussions of life in the United States is his essay "Di alcuni stati moderni," published in 1842 in *Il politecnico*.[121] While full of admiration for the phenomenal economic and technological development of the United States, he underlines the extent to which much of its progress relied on the continuous growth of its population. Huge public deficit—the consequence of the War of Independence and of subsequent investment in infrastructure—is constantly reduced and balanced by way of a growing number of consumers and producers, who colonize and develop hitherto deserted or underpopulated territories. Cattaneo understood that a constant influx of migrants offers opportunities for economic expansion. For Cattaneo, the United States represented a fabulous example of development, at a time when economic progress at home was at the forefront of his mind.

Meanwhile, this progress had come at a price that abhorred many European observers. Extending the territories populated by the "stirpe britannica" had meant extinguishing entire populations from their legitimate place on earth.[122] Cattaneo expressed this concern in a long review of Henry Wadsworth Longfellow's poem "Evangeline," describing in passionate detail the consequences of the British conquest of the Canadian maritime provinces.[123]

While he might have underestimated the importance of Longfellow's aesthetic intentions in writing this poem, Cattaneo's articles show that he was far from blindly admiring the British expansion in the New World and that he continued to regard the United States as a very special set of experiences. Critical distance notwithstanding, as a political laboratory the United States served to test practices of self-government and federalism, which were at the core of Cattaneo's plans for Italy's political future.

Cattaneo's interest in federalism and the United States continued to animate debate among Italian Democrats for decades. One of his most influential early commentators, Alberto Mario, disagreed with Cattaneo's supposedly narrow understanding of federalism. Quoting the American example, Mario opined that federalism was not antithetical to political unity: "everything that is federal in Switzerland and America constitutes political unity."[124] Contrary to Cattaneo, for Mario federalism did not mean "the federation of governments, as in ancient Germany," but "the federation of peoples."[125] It was Mario's attempt to reconcile Cattaneo's legacy with Mazzini's political thought.[126] Writing several decades after the events of 1848 and more than a decade after the end of the American Civil War, Mario's principal aim here was to overcome a conflict that still divided the Italian Left. Within this scheme, he saw the United States as a model for the "Stati Uniti d'Italia."[127] Although Mario made his remarks on the American constitution in a piece dedicated to Cattaneo, for the theoretical section of his paper he mostly quoted from John Stuart Mill. As the man who kept Cattaneo's memory alive after his death in 1869, Mario was largely responsible for reading Cattaneo's idea of Italian federalism in terms of the American constitution, representing the views of Italy's Radical Democrats a generation after the Unification of Italy.

Giuseppe Montanelli and Federal Democracy in Tuscany

In November 1848 the two democratic leaders of the Revolution in Tuscany, Giuseppe Montanelli and Francesco Domenico Guerrazzi, asked voters for the parliamentary assembly to elect "simple men of ancient virtue," men like Washington, "the Virginia farmer."[128] Keen to return a constitutional majority, the two democratic leaders wished to tame the influence of Radical Republicans on the Revolution.

As had been the case with Lombardy's tobacco boycott, in Tuscany too rhetorical references to the American Revolution helped to amplify the grandeur of the events unfolding, building on a long-standing tradition of Tuscan interest in the United States.[129] Those occasional references to America do not stand for an ambition to emulate the events of 1776. Municipal reform and local autonomy were at the forefront of critical demands in Tuscany, prior to and during the Revolutions of 1848. Although the grand duke's government was frequently blamed for its failure to acknowledge the need for reform, the principal issues in question were not linked to the fact that Tuscany was ruled by the Habsburgs. On the contrary, comparing their state to other parts of the Italian peninsula, the social and cultural elites were aware of the Duchy's remarkable economic progress over the past decades and of the prestige their rulers' enlightened absolutism carried in Europe.[130] As for the grand duke's commitment to the national cause, the patriotic songs of the Revolution frequently referred to "leal Leopoldo," the "loyal Leopold."[131] A "National Anthem" distributed in Liguria intoned:

> Giuriam, giuriam giuriam
> Per Pio Nono e Carlo Alberto
> Giuriam giuriam giuriam
> Per Leopoldo Tosco Re.[132]

Similar to most Italian states prior to 1848, Tuscany's social and economic elites asked for increased local autonomy, or forms of *autogoverno*, a concept that had marked the peninsula's political debates for centuries.[133] This context of debate explains the widespread disappointment when Unification under the crown of Savoy eventually resulted in a far more severe curtailment of local rights compared to any of the duchy's previous political regimes.

During the 1840s Tuscany's local discourse of reform started to engage with wider Italian debates on the peninsula's resurgence. Progress was defined in economic as well as political terms. Reflecting on the state of the region's commerce and industry, Luigi Calamai, in June 1848, used a talk at the Accademia dei Georgofili to complain about the duchy's "secular decline."[134] On the other side of the argument were those who defended the state's reliance on agriculture and its moderate approach to technological innovation as the only way to avoid the lamentable process of the population's pauperization and the proletarization witnessed in modern industrial societies.[135] Beyond the discourse of local constitutional reform, Gioberti's neo-Guelphism fell on fruitful ground in Tuscany as well, though with reservations as to the pontiff's temporal power within a federalized Italy.[136] Both concepts—autogoverno and federalism—lent themselves to the discussion of American political institutions.

Tuscany's last Habsburg ruler, Leopoldo II, shared the interest in the United States of his predecessor Grand Duke Pietro Leopoldo, discussed in the previous chapter. Early on in his reign, in 1828–29, he twice received James Fenimore Cooper to learn more about the American people and the general conditions of his country, impressing the American traveler with his "simplicity and justness of his mind."[137] Leopoldo also met the American politician and historian Edward Everett, mentioned in connection with the American reception of Botta's *History of the American War of Independence*, offering him access to the Florentine archives.[138] As explained in chapter 1, the transnational exchange of ideas between journalists, their readers, and their publishers was a significant characteristic of the publishing industry in Tuscany. Ideas continued to circulate widely despite Leopoldo II's efforts to keep publishing under control.[139] A proud local tradition of political thought resonated with a widespread interest in American and British political institutions. Democrats in particular formulated their ideas in relation to what they knew about American political institutions. For instance, the democratic federalist Giuseppe Mazzoni, along with Montanelli and Guerrazzi a member of the Tuscan Republic's triumvirate in 1849, had the works of Jefferson and Tocqueville in his library, along with the writings of Romagnosi, Botta, and Comte.[140]

Since the beginning of 1847 different parts of Tuscany had witnessed rising levels of social protest, caused by shortages of foodstuffs and by inflated prices.[141] The Revolutions in Palermo and Milan set loose a mobilization of workers and sections of the middle classes, whose aims no longer coincided with the liberal aristocracy's demands.[142] The national question also led to tensions. As Thomas Kroll was able to demonstrate, the response to neo-Guelphism among the Tuscan nobility retained elements of an eighteenth-century understanding of the nation that remained behind the modern concepts of the Risorgimento's national movement as it had emerged since the 1830s. Like the grand duke himself, large sections of the liberal aristocracy hesitated to get involved in the national movement for the peninsula's liberation from foreign domination. Confronted with the crisis in the Austrian possessions, Tuscany's political elite cautiously endorsed plans for an Italian confederation to be based on military cooperation and a customs union, without touching the sovereignty of its members. Safeguards against centralization were to be part of this program. Contrary to Lombardy, Albertismo enjoyed little or no support; and even those few who were attracted to Piedmont opposed a unitary state under the House of Savoy. Most Tuscan Moderates had strong doubts over the role to be played by the Savoy dynasty within an Italian federation. Tuscany's moderate prime minister Marquis Cosimo Ridolfi, one of the *Antologia*'s original founders, considered Carlo Alberto among the peninsula's most reactionary monarchs, even after he granted the *Statuto*.[143] His regime would destroy all the achievements liberal reformers in Tuscany had been fighting for over decades.

In February 1848, after some hesitation and the rejection of various drafts, the grand duke granted a constitution, largely following the Neapolitan model and welcomed with great enthusiasm by wide sections of the population. While recognizing the Duke's executive powers, the legislature was divided between a senate, nominated by the duke, and an elected chamber based on census. Catholicism was recognized as the sole religion of the state, with concessions made for other cults.[144] What destabilised the political situation in Tuscany was not the granting of the constitution, but Italy's First War of Independence and the question of the state's relationship to Piedmont. Representing the peninsula's weakest military power, until April the Tuscan government hesitated to send troops into Lombardy, despite strong popular support for the campaign. Meanwhile, Tuscan volunteers succeeded in making considerable territorial gains in the northern duchies, although these were considered recaptures of Tuscan territories that the Austrians had given to the northern duchies as recently as 1847.[145] Foreign policy initiatives to form a league with Naples, Rome, and Turin failed, largely owing to Piedmont's subordination of Italian interests under its own sovereign ambition. The pope's hesitant reaction to the plans accelerated their failure. The combination of war and revolution in the rest of the peninsula aggravated the economic and financial crisis at home.

During the summer of 1848, after the defeat of Piedmont at Custoza, Ridolfi was forced to resign in response to popular discontent at his government's separate peace with Austria. Democratic circles had played a key role in his resignation. His successor, Marquis Gino Capponi, another Moderate, continued his cousin's federalist policies, while also trying to curb the influence of democratic associations. In October 1848 he too was forced to step back in response to popular and increasingly violent pressure over the failure of his national policies. Capponi was replaced by a new ministry under the Democrat Giuseppe Montanelli, representing the end of the aristocracy's liberal governments in Tuscany. Protests in the port city of Livorno, fueled by the economic crisis and violent workers' unrest, contributed significantly to this political watershed. With its magnificent ships arriving from America, and as one of Italy's main ports of departure to the New World, Livorno was like no other city in Tuscany in having been so widely exposed to dreams of the New World.

A professor of law in Pisa, a musician, and a successful poet, Giuseppe Montanelli had been wounded and arrested during the volunteers' campaigns in northern Italy and was the first Tuscan prime minister of the revolutionary period to enjoy great popular support.[146] In this sense he was comparable to Mazzini, and Montanelli's contribution to setting up the newspaper *L'Italia* in 1847 demonstrates a shrewd awareness of the role of the press in modern political communication. Not least through his collaboration with Vieusseux's *Antologia*, he was well known beyond the Tuscan borders.[147] Meanwhile, his government was strongly opposed, to the point of a complete boycott of any collaboration, by the hitherto governing moderate aristocracy in Tuscany, making any compromise over the democratic legitimation of the constitutional monarchy almost impossible.

Montanelli's answer to the political crisis in Italy, and to the failure of the powers' diplomatic efforts, was the formation of a *Costituente nazionale*, a constituent assembly elected by universal male suffrage, understood as a new democratic approach to the formation of an Italian federation. It also represented a significant step toward catching up with recent developments in the German lands, where the Frankfurt parliament had been in session since May. Reluctantly tolerated by moderate patricians, but opposed by the exiled pope, for Montanelli the *Costituente* represented a fundamental move away from

MONTANELLI, DÉPUTÉ AU PARLEMENT ITALIEN.

FIG. 12. Giuseppe Montanelli, 1862.
Photo: akg-images / De Agostini Picture Library.

the neo-Guelphs' federalism of states toward a new concept of national federalism based on a democratically elected constituent assembly.[148]

Apart from his initiative for the *Costituente*, Montanelli's program of government remained substantially in line with that of the Moderates. Only after
the grand duke abandoned Florence for Siena and then Gaeta, early in 1849,
Guerrazzi and Montanelli reconstituted their ministry as a provisional government, still trying to tame republican ambitions, which they feared they were
unable to control.[149] In the subsequent elections for a Tuscan Constituent
Assembly, based for the first time on universal male suffrage, the Democrats
secured a majority of over 80 percent. The large majority of those elected represented various strata of the middle classes, from lawyers and doctors to civil
servants, and a small representation of rich merchants and landowners.[150] A
few months earlier, still under the monarchy's electoral law, Montanelli had

proposed elections following the American model. He got what he had hoped for during Tuscany's short democratic moment, in March 1849. While artisans and workers took part in the election, the group Montanelli failed to mobilize in favor of democratic government were the large numbers of rural workers and sharecroppers.

Despite the recognition of popular sovereignty, attempts to form a federation between Italy's existing states remained the basis of Tuscan political experiments during those months. When Mazzini suggested a union between the Roman and Tuscan Republics, it was Guerrazzi who stood firm, asserting instead Tuscany's independence within an Italian federation. Some observers read Guerrazzi's insistence on Tuscan independence in the context of his popular novel of 1836 *L'assedio di Firenze*, narrating Florence's sixteenth-century fight for independence from Spain. During the Revolution Guerrazzi himself alluded frequently to these historical events.[151] In less than a month the provisional government collapsed under renewed pressure from moderate patricians, who were able to mobilize rural discontent and legitimist sentiment. The coup, organized by the moderate aristocracy, brought Tuscany's democratic experiment to a premature end. Austria's defeat of Piedmont and the French subjugation of the Roman Republic sealed the fate of the revolutions in the Italian peninsula. Austrian troops occupied Florence on 25 May.

Rather than directly mirroring his experiences of 1848, Montanelli's recollections of these events reflected subsequent insights he gained during his exile in France, combined with a good portion of nostalgia for his homeland. An analysis of Montanelli's political thought reveals how local Italian traditions were related to American experiences, but also how the former overshadowed the latter. Among Montanelli's acquaintances in Paris was Giuseppe Verdi, whom he assisted with the libretto for *Simon Boccanegra* (1857), set in fourteenth-century Genoa and steeped in references to local traditions and awareness of Italy's internal historical diversity.[152] It was also an opera about Genoa's first plebeian doge. Although opinions as to the artistic value of the verses Montanelli contributed to *Simon Boccanegra* are divided, there are at least six important passages of the opera that he drafted; and the highly technical requirements for the work on any opera libretto demonstrate Montanelli's skills as a poet. Verdi's appreciation for Montanelli's poetic works is documented in several editions the composer kept in his library in Busseto.[153] He was in a position to compete directly with an established expert in this field like Francesco Maria Piave, who had been unable to join Verdi in Paris.

Montanelli's take on the plot was influenced by his admiration for Schiller, whose tragedy *Die Verschwörung des Fiesko zu Genua* is only indirectly related to the plot of *Simon Boccanegra*, but offers very similar references to local political culture.[154] The example shows how an Italian plot could be the outcome of a complex transnational web of intertextual references. After *Die Räuber* and *Kabale und Liebe, Fiesko* was one of Schiller's first plays to be staged in Italy: one version loosely based on Schiller as early as 1806, followed by several more stagings after 1815 and in 1847–48. Verdi's library contains an undated German edition of *Fiesko* by Philipp Reclam from Leipzig.[155] Translations had circulated in Italy since 1819.[156] In 1853 Verdi's former friend and collaborator Andrea Maffei published another translation, a work Montanelli was likely to have known. Montanelli was exposed to Schiller not only through the poet's Italian reception (prompted by Madame de Stael's travels and Giovanni Gherardini's translation of Schlegel's lectures as well as Manzoni's interest in the German poet), but also through the prominent role Schiller played in French literary debates.[157]

In addition to reminiscences of Schiller, Julian Budden has pointed to the parallel between Fiesco's appearance as the prophet of doom toward the end of *Simon Boccanegra* and the final scenes of Guerrazzi's above-mentioned drama *L'assedio di Firenze*, which played a huge role in the national movement's literary imagination, almost becoming the archetype of a Risorgimento drama.[158] In 1848 Verdi had considered turning Guerrazzi's play into an opera, exactly at the time when Montanelli and Guerrazzi were forming Tuscany's short-lived democratic government. While the historical events of the two plots have once again little in common, the parallels lie in the dramatic exploration of the connections between political institutions and interpersonal relations. Montanelli's contribution to acts 1 and 3 of *Simon Boccanegra* was an open reference to the civic context in which both works were set, including a celebration of the Ligurian people, but also a reflection on his understanding of the political institutions he had hoped to shape during his short spell as a leader of the Revolution in Tuscany.[159]

Montanelli's federalism was rooted in local political traditions, as they featured in Schiller's play and Verdi's opera, while also showing signs of engagement with American practices of democracy. In many respects close to Cattaneo in political thinking, Montanelli questioned the extent to which the peninsula's existing political map represented cultural identities. While Cattaneo largely accepted Italy's existing states as historically grown and culturally homogenous, for Montanelli they were based on conquest and treaties. They did not reflect the nation's true natural diversity, the "varietà subnazionali della Gente Italiana."[160]

Seeking to establish a new notion of organically grown communities, Montanelli's federalism was to be founded on a constituent assembly elected by universal (male) suffrage, understood as the highest form of popular sovereignty.[161] His belief in popular sovereignty as a legitimate source of political power shows the extent to which his ideas had moved beyond the conservative paternalism represented by the *Antologia*. During those years at the periodical Montanelli was first in contact with Protestantism, which played an important role in his appreciation of American civil society. He partly blamed the Revolution's failure on Italy's *clerocrazia*.[162] While his two volumes of memoires hardly mention the United States, it figures prominently in a number of his theoretical reflections on the revolutionary experience in Tuscany.[163] These transnational comparisons were in line with his previous approach to the teaching of law in Pisa. Based on a conceptual framework derived from Kant and Savigny, his discussions regularly featured examples of foreign countries as well as different Italian states.[164] More explicitly than in Cattaneo's case, Montanelli's idea of the United States was influenced by his reading of Tocqueville, whom he might have met in Paris in 1849.[165] While Tocqueville's analysis of American democracy provided Montanelli with the historical-theoretical foundations for his own vision of politics, he offers no detailed analysis of the Frenchman's political theories. More interesting are Montanelli's general comments on the development of American society, which seem to draw on a wider range of reading, including Guizot as well as original American documents.[166]

Contrasting the United States with Italy's and Europe's intellectual development since the end of the eighteenth century, Montanelli's *Introduzione ad alcuni appunti storici sulla rivoluzione d'Italia* (1851) emphasizes the degree to which the American understanding of freedom was rooted in "libertà di coscienza," or freedom of thought, which Americans made the basis of their civil society.[167] Montanelli explains the failure of the Italian revolution with reference to this concept of "libertà di coscienza," the incompatibility between national unity and the pope's temporal power, which corresponded to a general estrangement between politics and society in Italy. Contrary to the situation at home, American democracy had been able to bridge this gap.[168] For Montanelli, a new "sapienza civile" had to replace the role traditionally occupied in Italy by the Roman Church. This was to become the key to Italy's political future.[169]

Applying the insights gained from reading Tocqueville to the situation at home, Montanelli created a link between the American form of locally rooted government and the Italian concept of the *comune*, understood as a widely conceived organic community going beyond the municipality's administrative structure. Territorially, his concept linked city and hinterland in a functional system of exchange. Like Cattaneo, Montanelli considered the comune to be deeply rooted in Italian political culture, tracing the concept back to Etruscan origins.[170] As for his analogy between Italian and American political institutions, he claimed that the comune had disappeared from the political structures of the Old World, only to reemerge within the "puritan colonies of New England," forming the "beginnings of American democracy." He described the American states as "natural agglomerations, sons of liberty" and as a "family of free citizens," an idea used to bridge the gap between politics and society.[171] Adding semantic content to his concept, Montanelli gendered the Italian comune as "maschio" (male), standing for independence and contrasting with the French model, where "la commune" was feminine and "subjected" to a superior power, explaining an allegedly typical French connection between democracy and monarchy.[172]

A decade after the failed Revolutions of 1848 these concepts gained new political significance during the process of Unification. Protesting against the imposition of preconceived administrative structures, Montanelli opposed Tuscany's annexation by Piedmont in 1859, and after Unification he was among the few members of the Italian parliament who advocated the creation of regions as a new approach to the nation's territorial organization. Understood as a response to Marco Minghetti's failed project of provincial autonomy, Montanelli's concept of regions reflects his interest in American democracy, insisting that in unitary federations (*federazioni-unitarie*) the constitution makes specific provisions for maintaining a sense of unity.[173]

Despite these examples of constitutional borrowing marking his political thought, Montanelli abstained from idealizing American democracy. He was well aware that conditions in the United States were very different from those back home.[174] Moreover, it is telling that in his two volumes of political memoires the only specific reference to political life in the United States concerned the slave trade. A few years later, in November 1859, he described the fight between democratic and oligarchic principles in the United States as a "true battle of civilisation," where protestant humanism "assaults the feudal institution of colour."[175] The American Civil War was not far off. Like Cattaneo, rather than a prophet of American democracy, Montanelli had become the advocate of a "comune europeo."[176]

Independence and Constitutional Models in Sicily

The European revolutions of 1848 started not in Paris or Berlin, and not in Milan, but on 12 January 1848, on the streets of Palermo, in the words of Rosario Romeo the local expression of "a European consciousness," a new form of awareness of the island's historical rights.[177]

Sicilians perceived their revolution first and foremost as a fight against Naples, considered by many of the Risorgimento's protagonists to be the most tyrannical of the peninsula's political regimes, in every respect comparable to Sicily's medieval period of French oppression. In the words of Gaetano Somma: "Sicily, left on its own, the very last part of Italy, but always the first when it comes to great action, broke the chains and intoned the cry of war. Sicily, more oppressed than any other kingdom on this beautiful peninsula, the slave of a thousand tyrants, recalled in the unhappy facts of the present the even unhappier facts of domination under the Angevins."[178] A future Italian League had to include an independent Sicily. In order to give this independent Sicily a constitution of its own making, politicians from all factions looked at the United States.

Led by Giuseppe La Masa, a veteran Republican recently returned from exile, the uprising in Palermo spread rapidly into the surrounding countryside and then into the region around Salerno on the kingdom's mainland. Armed squads and brigand bands were quick to expand the initial unrest. For several months economic hardship and growing unemployment had fueled unrest in the region, accelerated by news of conspiracies in Messina and Reggio Calabria. The Bourbon dynasty was the target of much discontent among popular classes as well as among members of the educated elite. At the end of January Ferdinando II felt compelled to grant a liberal constitution, leaving Sicily unaffected, but provoking a brief moment of enthusiasm on the mainland.[179] Remarkably, given his reputation, he became the first of the Italian sovereigns to grant a constitution.[180] In Sicily requests for independence led by the Moderate Ruggiero Settimo dominated political debates. They were increasingly focussed on the restitution of the island's constitution of 1812.[181]

The first section of this chapter, on the Revolution in Lombardy, briefly discussed Cattaneo's pessimistic analysis of the possible convergence of the different parts of the Italian peninsula. According to Marta Petrusewicz, North and South existed in a relationship of *alterità*, where self-perceptions of the North depended largely on the image of an Other in the South.[182] Cattaneo's view of the South bears witness to this argument. It would be misleading to conclude from Cattaneo's argument that the South was completely cut off from intellectual and constitutional debates elsewhere in Italy or indeed Europe. For instance, the introduction has argued that the Neapolitan Enlightenment showed a much more explicit interest than Lombardy in political developments across the Atlantic. After the watershed of the Neapolitan Revolution in 1799, the years of Napoleonic rule under Joseph Bonaparte and then Murat turned Naples into an object of France's modernizing mission.[183] Since 1830, under Ferdinando II, a new and prosperous middle class had benefitted from economic as well as political reforms and had become increasingly involved in public affairs. Periodicals started playing a more important role in public debate, even in Sicily: first in Palermo, then in Messina and Catania.[184] Owing to the exchange between intellectuals from Sicily and Tuscany, periodicals closely reflected debates in other parts of Italy, in particular the *Antologia*.[185] Sicily's cultural heritage constituted another important focus of these periodicals, forming the literary and academic background to the resurgence of the island's identity.

On 8 December 1816 the Kingdom of the Two Sicilies had become a single kingdom under Ferdinando I. The island was again governed from Naples, eradicating any form of autonomy gained during the years of the Napoleonic wars. This included the loss of the nobility's privileges, making them prone to mounting another revolution. A modernized form of absolutism divided the territory into identical administrative units, ruled by intendants of central government. Because of its reluctance to introduce constitutional and representative forms of government, Naples struggled to construct an alliance with the liberal elements of the Sicilian middle class, which opposed traditional baronial privileges as much as despotic rule from Naples.[186] Turbulence in the market for wheat throughout much of the Restoration period further accelerated discontent, all this contributing to the crisis of January 1848.[187]

Because of the earliness of its Revolution, Sicily enjoyed an exceptional reputation among Italian 1848ers reflected in leaflets and pamphlets all over the peninsula. Although Cattaneo's above-mentioned depiction of the Bourbon Kingdom demonstrates how stereotypes of the South were used to justify the divided nature of the Italian nation, Sicily's prominent role in 1848 seems to confirm Marta Petrusewicz's argument that the Southern Question was largely constructed after Unification.[188]

The recognition Sicily gained for its Revolution contrasts with its allegedly peripheral position, geographically as well as vis-à-vis the state of its political development. Viewed from a Sicilian perspective, the island was far better connected with the wider world than is usually thought. As Jane and Peter Schneider have argued, Sicily has always played a role in world trade, questioning common assumptions about so-called traditional societies.[189] Already before 1848 utopian socialism, in particular Fourier, had left traces among Sicilian thinkers.[190] During the Napoleonic years, along with Sardinia, Sicily had been the only part of Italy that remained independent from the French Empire. British protection during those years and the transfer of the court to Palermo brought much cosmopolitan flair to the island. Although not all Sicilians appreciated these connections, they were still ruled by a prestigious European dynasty with multiple links to the major capitals of Europe. A surprising number of wealthy Americans included Sicily on their itinerary of Italy.[191] Shortly before the Revolution the people of Palermo still rejoiced in an extended visit by the Russian imperial family, which spent the entire winter of 1845–46 on the island, considered by many to be the most exciting event of the decade, inspiring poets, painters, and musicians to celebrate the occasion in their works. In their own ways both the vast local aristocracy as well as the popular masses took part in these events, which were commented on throughout the European press.[192] What might be seen as a minor episode in the island's diplomatic and cultural history demonstrates the problematic nature of a mental map narrowly based on a static system of centers and peripheries. In 1848 the palace that had housed the Russian court became one of the Revolution's most sinister *lieux de mémoire*, where hundreds of citizens fell victim to the city's bombardment by the Bourbon army.[193] In leaflets and broadsheets distributed all over Italy the king became known as "Bomber Ferdinand," *Ferdinando il bombardatore*.[194]

But what was the view of the island from the kingdom's mainland? And what role did Sicily occupy in the game of the great powers? In March 1847 Richard Cobden reported that "the Neapolitans call Sicily their Ireland."

Granted an audience with Ferdinando II, Cobden found that the monarch showed particular interest in "the future solution of the Irish difficulty—a question which seems to be uppermost in the minds of all statesmen & public minds on the Continent," Cobden's diary reveals.[195] Given this parallel, it can be read only as a bold sense of imperial entitlement that Britain had long championed Sicilian independence, forcing the Neapolitan government to seek support in Vienna to keep the post-1815 settlement in place, while at the same time resisting Irish demands for repeal of the Union.

Constitutionally, the Kingdom of the Two Sicilies had consisted of two separate crowns, Naples and Sicily, reflecting a long history of separate laws and constitutions and independent jurisdictions, joined only in the person of its Bourbon ruler. Meanwhile, speaking of mainland and island as "Two Sicilies" referred to a medieval tradition when the Norman Kingdom of Sicily had governed Naples. The widespread comparison between the Sicilian and the Irish question, on the one hand, and the perceived threat of a British intervention in favor of an independent Sicily on the other, reveals the extent to which at least the mainland saw British foreign policy as being driven by self-interest. Since the late eighteenth century, for commercial as well as military reasons, Britain had actively sought access to new ports in the Mediterranean. As Nello Rosselli has argued, after the Congress of Vienna Sicily was increasingly transformed "in una mezza dipendenza inglese," keeping commercial, mineralogical, and industrial agencies firmly in British hands, without any real concern for the local situation.[196] In 1847 Lord Palmerston sent Lord Minto to Italy and began to offer open support to the Italian national movement. Initially the British government showed little interest in Sicily, but when revolution broke out, attitudes to Sicily and Naples changed immediately. Britain's diplomatic intervention in the affairs of the kingdom was mostly at the expense of Austria, arguably in violation of the Vienna settlement. Bourbon monarchists and legitimists considered Britain largely responsible for the Sicilian crisis of 1848.[197]

Unlike the concepts of nationality discussed elsewhere in Italy, the break-up of the Bourbon Kingdom and the prospect of an independent Sicily had a concrete meaning to most Sicilians, suddenly catapulting the question of the island's future into the center of international politics. Under the impression of the abrupt breakdown of government, accompanied by the escape of up to twelve thousand prisoners as well as bonfires of title deeds, there is a risk of overlooking the dedicated efforts of middle-class Liberals, patricians, and nobles to come up with specific proposals for the island's constitutional future.[198] Meanwhile, the popular masses—employed (or exploited) by the nobility in their fight against Neapolitan rule—had little to do with the constitutional debates of the *signori*. Usually they failed to realize that the same local landlords whose revolution they now supported had caused their own social misery.[199] Instead, the pamphlets circulating at the time tended to blame the Bourbons in Naples for everything that was wrong: "the only cause of our ills is the government, and the head of the government is King Ferdinando II," as the literary critique Luigi Settembrini summarized the situation in his 1847 *Protesta del popolo delle Due Sicilie*.[200]

Sicily has often been singled out for its privileged relationship to the United States and the strong interest of Sicilian patriots in constitutional developments across the Atlantic.[201] Early in 1848 Sicilian feelings for the United States were reciprocated when, joined by other foreign representatives, the American consul protested wholeheartedly against the Neapolitan bombardment of Palermo. In July 1848 the US government recognized the island's independence from Naples, before similar moves by England and France, and contrasting with its later attitude toward the Roman Republic. After the Revolution's failure and throughout the 1850s, Americans clandestinely supported Sicilian revolutionaries.[202]

Returning exiles took part in the Revolution and were elected to the new parliament, helping Sicilians to engage with international political thought. The federalism of Francesco Paolo Perez and Filippo Cordova, or the republicanism of Giuseppe La Farina and Pasquale Calvi, was at least partly inspired by Swiss and American models, presenting tensions with the neo-Guelph version of federalism that still prevailed elsewhere in Italy, but also with the policies of the Sicilian Moderates.[203] Among the most famous documents of the Sicilian Revolution that made explicit reference to US federalism is the *Catechismo politico siciliano*, written by Michele Amari in 1839, but reprinted in 1848 as part of an influential pamphlet collection, where it was erroneously attributed to Niccolò Palmieri:

> The same kind of relationship, that now appears to establish itself as the only way forward for the other Italian states, also seems suitable for Sicily. That is a federation, in which each state would have its own independent government, with exception being made for the right to declare war and peace as well as regarding political treaties with foreign nations. The advantage of this system would be obtaining a strong power without suffering the disadvantages of being dominated by a foreign and faraway ruler. Without mentioning ancient examples, this is the path followed by the United States of America, the Swiss Confederation and up to a point also of the German Confederation.[204]

Not surprisingly, Mazzini was particularly concerned at Sicilian interests in federalism; and even Gioberti feared that Sicily's separation from Naples might lead to dangerous divisions within the nation.[205] As a consequence, Sicilian Moderates around Gioacchino Ventura remained firmly behind Gioberti's idea of a confederation of the existing Italian states, understood as a safeguard against Sicilian separatism and against some of the more radical inclinations behind other forms of federalism.[206] Once the Revolution started, it soon became clear that the aim of references to the United States was not to replicate America's political institutions in Sicily. Most Sicilian Federalists saw the United States simply as a state that stood against the despotism of European congress diplomacy.

Behind these debates was a deeply rooted desire that the island's fate should no longer be determined by international powers. While the years under Ferdinando I and Francesco I were characterized by tensions with Austria, Ferdinando II, for most of his early reign, relied heavily on support from Vienna, delivered through one of Metternich's most distinguished diplomats, Felix von Schwarzenberg, Austrian minister in Naples before himself becoming the empire's minister-president in November 1848. While Schwarzenberg was keen to keep the Vienna settlement in place, he also pushed Naples to respond to its internal crisis, actively working against corruption and neutralizing revolutionary tendencies, in particular in Sicily.[207] However, both Schwarzenberg and the king became increasingly aware that in the event of a revolution Vienna would not have the means to intervene in support of the Bourbon monarchy. Once the insurrection had started Ferdinando II hoped that the granting of the constitution (conceded against Schwarzenberg's advice) and support for a League of Italian States would keep his kingdom together.[208] For the Sicilians the Neapolitan constitution was not enough. Their expectation was of entering a federation of Italian states as an independent Sicily.

Based on the French model of 1830 and proposing a single parliament for the two kingdoms, the Neapolitan constitution demonstrated the extent to which the Bourbon dynasty still ignored the situation in Sicily. For most Sicilians—including the liberal middle class as well as nobles keen to guard their privileges—the Neapolitan proposals were unacceptable, and they insisted instead on the revival of their own constitution of 1812. Keen to prevent Sicily from turning to radical republicanism, British diplomats supported negotiations with Naples to recognize the 1812 arrangements.[209] Mediating between Naples and the island's revolutionaries, Palmerston's special envoy Lord Minto suggested an autonomous parliament for the island's internal affairs and a mixed commission in charge of relations between the two parts of the kingdom. Pressed by Lord Minto, the king offered de facto self-government as long as Sicily accepted Bourbon sovereignty. The proposal was rejected by both parties and negotiations collapsed on 7 March. Sicily would now follow its own independent path. Suddenly, American political institutions should play a more prominent role than ever; but for most Sicilians it was not democratic republicanism that attracted them to the American constitution.

Sicilians elected their new parliament on the basis of a relatively progressive suffrage, which nevertheless excluded the illiterate population and, therefore, almost all the island's peasants. The parliament met on 25 March and appointed a government presided over by Ruggiero Settimo as "President of the Kingdom," or *Presidente del Regno*. Settimo was a former rear admiral of the Bourbon navy, a veteran of 1820, and owner of one of Sicily's largest estates. In

January he had been among the early organizers of the revolutionary committees. Reflecting the parliament's moderate majority, the government included
only a few Democrats, among them the Michele Amari as minister of finance.
Rather than radical change, the ideological orientation of the island's new political elite reflected, in the words of Rosario Romeo, the "continuity between
the politics of the old feudal class and the new liberalism."[210] According to the
early socialist patriot Carlo Pisacane, "the government of Sicily was the least
revolutionary of all Italian governments emerging from the insurgency."[211] Access to large rural properties had transformed the upper strata of the middle
classes into a conservative force, associated with the interests of the island's
traditional *classe dirigente*. They presented their economic interests in the
language of local autonomy, claiming legitimacy for their project through discursive references to the political institutions of the United States. Polemiciz-
ing against the French imperial tradition of the centralized state, Prince Lanza
di Scordia had argued in 1841 that Americans considered the subordination of
private property to public interest a form of "civic heresy" (*eresia civile*). In the
United States, thanks to self-government and free competition, a handful of
immigrants had transformed themselves into "the leading people of the Universe."[212] He now was a member of the revolutionary government.

Rejecting any demands for Sicilian independence, Gioberti had described
Naples as Sicily's link to the rest of Italy. In his view Sicily had to enter a federation of Italian states as an integral part of the Kingdom of the Two Sicilies,
that is governed from Naples.[213] As a consequence, and contrasting with the
almost frantic cult around Gioberti in other parts of Italy, in Sicily there was
no place for the mainland's understanding of neo-Guelphism. In addition to
the marked differences between Sicilian moderate liberalism and moderate
politics elsewhere in Italy, the island's Democrats also differentiated themselves from Democrats elsewhere, despite individual connections between
some of the movement's protagonists, as in the case of Amari and Mazzini.
Sicilian democracy remained a movement of the *borghesia*, without much following among the lower classes; and the island's separatist tradition was difficult to reconcile with Mazzini's aims.[214] Although Italy's national movement
shared a strong sense of resentment at the Bourbon dynasty, a conspicuous
gap separated the mainland's genuine enthusiasm for the Sicilian Revolution from its indifference (or straightforward opposition) toward its quest for
independence.

Despite this noticeable lack of support for its project of independence,
on 13 April the Sicilian parliament unanimously declared the Bourbon monarchy to have ceased, with the intention of offering the Sicilian crown to a
different Italian prince. While many Sicilians considered the Duke of Genoa,
the younger son of Carlo Alberto of Piedmont-Sardinia, a suitable contender
for the throne of Sicily, others suggested a prince of the Tuscan line of the
Habsburgs, an option supported at the time even by Republicans such as

Giuseppe La Farina. These preferences demonstrate once more that resentment of Austrian hegemony in Italy was not necessarily directed against the Habsburg dynasty.[215] During Sicily's constitutional debates no mention was made of a unitary Italian state; and public attitudes toward Piedmont remained largely indifferent. The quest for independence from Naples was translated into autonomy within a future Italian federation, discussed with frequent references to the US constitution. These references notwithstanding, the Revolution's emphasis on the revived constitution of 1812 could hardly be classified as progressive.[216] It is therefore all the more striking that during the Revolution, under the threat of seemingly uncontrollable democratic forces, aristocracy and borghesia returned power to the hands of the Bourbons, mirroring not only the Tuscan experiences discussed in the previous section, but also developments elsewhere in Europe.[217] When Italy was eventually unified, after its Second War of Independence, instead of insisting on the island's autonomy, many among the Sicilian moderate forces adhered to the idea of Unification under the crown of the Savoy, preventing once more the release of the island's revolutionary potential.[218]

With the middle classes still underrepresented, the liberal nobility played a crucial role not only in Sicily's constitutional debates, but also in articulating concern for order and in containing the popular element of the Revolution. It was the nobility that found much to be admired about the American constitution. Although a majority of Sicilians saw the island's future as a monarchy, the parliament represented a wide and in some respects incoherent spectrum of ideas, from Bourbon reformers to supporters of Sicilian independence and from monarchists to Democrats, Republicans, and early Socialists. During the inaugural session of parliament on 25 March 1848, Ruggero Settimo evoked Sicily's ancient tradition of freedom, which had been revived in 1812 only to be suppressed once more in 1815.[219] Making reference to Britain's historic influence on Sicily's constitutional debates, he thanked Lord Minto for his assistance in the ultimately unsuccessful negotiations with Naples.

Although the commentators who considered the 1812 constitution a foreign document remained few, in 1848 the same anxieties reemerged: "we fought to be Italian, to have an Italian Prince; it is for this reason that we need our own, an Italian Charter," observed the ecclesiatical peer Filippo Evola during the constitutional debates of the summer.[220] As a matter of fact, the 1812 constitution had done little to resolve Sicily's problems regarding the ownership and distribution of land. What the Bourbon rulers had tried to address, Napoleon was able to at least partially resolve on the mainland; but for the reasons mentioned above, land reform was not a priority for Sicily's revolutionaries. Meanwhile, English constitutional history continued to enjoy great prestige among the Sicilian landowners who supported the Revolution. Moreover, constitutional rights and political representation, so long denied by Naples and Vienna, were at the core of demands in both parts of the kingdom.

For Sicilians they were a way of translating ancient rights, long contested under a succession of foreign rulers, into modern political concepts. Here the American constitution, widely regarded as a republican form of the English model, could serve as a point of reference. It was not American republicanism specifically but Anglo-Saxon constitutional tradition that inspired the revolutionaries.

The Sicilian constitution of 1812 had followed exactly this model, based on a two-chamber parliament and proclaiming the end of feudal privilege, but with limited effects on land ownership and the redistribution of political power.[221] While recognizing the island's autonomy, the constitution was progressive only in its Sicilian context. The aristocracy gained more from the abolition of feudalism than it lost; and rather than leading to the distribution of land to the poor, the process created a new "gentry" class.[222] According to Lucy Riall, "estates now assumed the status of 'unfettered private property,' which the owner could use and dispose of as he saw fit."[223] All this had a devastating effect on the peasants' economic position and on the rural poor. In 1848 protests against the enclosure of common lands played an important role in the escalation of rural violence, directed less against Naples than against local landlords. Meanwhile, the abolition of feudalism had offered little to the democratic middle class. Nevertheless, it was this constitution of 1812— as a symbol of the island's independence—that was to be adapted "a' tempi" and became the revolutionaries' main point of reference.[224] The Revolution sparked off an intense interest in Sicily's recent constitutional past, including for instance the publication in 1848 of Paolo Balsano's *Memorie segrete*. Balsano had been among the principal authors of the 1812 constitution, and his work had been suppressed after his death in 1816, but now it appeared in print for the first time.[225] Copies of the constitution itself were quickly reprinted and widely distributed.[226]

The fact that in 1848 Sicily had a constitutional tradition to rely on became a source of great pride. Conscious of its history, Sicily found itself positioned to teach the rest of Europe lessons. Gioacchino Ventura, plenipotentiary of the independent Sicilian government at the Holy See, maintained that "Sicily is the most ancient constitutional country. One could even say that Sicily invented the institution of free government for the rest of Europe, similar to the ways in which Sicily gave birth to Italian language and literature."[227] Statements such as these force us to reconsider our mental map of Europe, to rethink the relationship between centers and peripheries, with direct implications for the ways in which we understand the impact of foreign ideas on Italian and Sicilian traditions. According to Maurizio Isabella's understanding of transnational intellectual exchange during the Risorgimento period, political thought emerged in a "dialogue between foreign economic and political models . . . and the cultural heritage of Italy, whose particularity Italian patriots continued to value and defend."[228] Within Sicily's constitutional debates of 1848, it was mainly members of the Lower House who considered Sicily's recent political experiences within a wider international context and who as part of this discourse referred to the example of the United States. In comparison, the Chamber of Peers was generally more inward looking; but when a specific occasion occurred, the members of the Upper House also referred with sympathy to the "star-spangled banner" of the "globe's freest nation."[229]

As these examples illustrate, references to the United States often served abstract or idealist purposes, rarely influencing details of legislation. On other occasions the absence of references to the United States seems worth noting, for instance when Vincenzo Di Marco declared in the Sicilian Commons that "the two greatest revolutions are Cromwell's English and Robespierre's French," without mentioning American events, and possibly aware of the more conservative elements driving the events of 1776.[230] When the assembly discussed the state of secondary education in Sicily, speakers referred to the *Gymnasien* (Grammar Schools) of the German States, to France, and to England, without looking across the Atlantic.[231] Likewise, in the debate over the National Guard, which continued over the entire revolutionary period, the United States never came up.[232] In the four thousand pages of minutes from the parliamentary assemblies very few American politicians or protagonists of their revolution are named. Gian Domenico Romagnosi is among the legal theorists most frequently quoted in parliamentary minutes, coming before Bentham and Montesquieu; at some point a member of the Sicilian parliament compared Romagnosi to Washington.[233]

Some members of parliament remained explicitly adverse to the discussion of foreign models, but it is significant in itself that on those occasions they evoked the United States. "Why reach out all the way to North America to find what is amalgamated with reason in each of us?" asks Giuseppe Tedaldi in a debate on the new government's diplomatic conventions.[234] "Neither France, nor Naples or England or the United States of America—Sicily, only Sicily, Sicily and always Sicily in 1848," Stefano Napolitano exclaimed in a debate on civic rights. "We are reunited here to look after the necessities of our country; and we therefore examine our country, and we do so in our time."[235] Michele Bertolami, in the debate on the electoral law: "silence, gentlemen, over the well known history of the European and Amerian constitutions; they have been referred to too many times."[236] Similarly, Giuseppe Natoli, a patrician from Messina and a future foreign minister of unified Italy: "gentlemen, does America perhaps represent the benchmark of humanity's law, so that no improvement could be made to its constitution?"[237] Yet ten days later, when seeking to convince his colleagues that parliament should be elected every two years, the same member of the assembly called America "a beautiful example."[238] These passages of parliamentary debate show that references to the United States were used as discursive instruments no matter what direction the debate took. For most members of parliament America remained an ideal, but one that was far from the historical realities that the fathers of the Sicilian constitution had to confront.

Few are the examples where references to American political institutions served a specific purpose, as in the debate on executive powers. Filippo Cordova pointed out that the American president was unable to call early elections in moments of crisis. He used the example of President Jackson's conflict with Congress to illustrate how this configuration might lead to major political tribulations.[239] Painting the picture of a situation close to civil war, what he described did not seem a model to follow. Peers were more cautious about giving the head of state the right to dissolve parliament, warning that even the most liberal politician might be tempted to follow Napoleon rather than Washington, or even Nikolai of Russia.[240] Safeguards against a renewed "prepotenza napoleonica" remained an important element of political debate throughout the Italian peninsula.[241] While Prince Lanza di Scordia praised the egalitarian principles behind the election of the North American president,[242] Baron Francesco Ventura used the United States to argue exactly the opposite, pointing out that in order to vote, or to be elected, citizens had to pay taxes. Describing universal suffrage as a form of "comunismo," he opines that it "would reduce Sicily to anarchy."[243]

At that stage of the debate even the question of the form of state was yet undecided, with Giuseppe Natoli taking the view that, instead of an American-style president, Sicily needed a monarch who would function as "the first servant of the State."[244] The incident suggests that the United States could be used for whatever argument served a particular point in the constitutional debate. Once again it was Giuseppe Natoli who considered references to foreign laws unworthy of Sicily's proud tradition: "the Commission found this electoral law in America and wants to transplant it into Sicily. But how very different are its two peoples?"[245] Another member of the assembly reminded his colleagues that the United States excluded the black population from suffrage.[246] With similar emphasis, Gaetano La Rosa questioned the basis of the comparison between the United States and Sicily: "it seems against all reason to compare a federal Republic in virgin territory, based on a simple and patriarchal culture, with the old and corrupted continent of Europe."[247] The fact that some members of parliament felt compelled to defend local traditions against the evocation of transatlantic examples would suggest that America inspired the Sicilian debates in 1848—and it did so more than elsewhere in Italy.

Similar issues regarding the validity of direct comparisons emerged in debates over the freedom of the press. While Democrats like the economist Francesco Ferrara used the United States as a positive example, the Moderates argued that Sicily first had to create public opinion before adopting the same level of freedom as the United States, "God's blessed country."[248] References to French and British press laws served a similar purpose.²⁴⁹ Should the constitution talk of religion? While Ferrara evoked the United States as an example for the separation of church and state, Vito D'Ondes criticized the Pilgrim Fathers' fanaticism, "religiosissimi di religione."²⁵⁰ With similar intent, Ignazio Romeo mentions the police in Massachusetts or New York State controlling the observation of church holidays, an excess of religious intervention in the private sphere.²⁵¹ As for the issue of a state religion, La Rosa used a comparison with the Anglican Church to argue that "if Sicily is Catholic it can only be governed by a Catholic King. If you don't recognise this condition, it means that a Muslim or a Protestant could also take the Sicilian throne. . . . Nobody here would advise the Turks to choose a Catholic Emperor."²⁵²

Allusions to French constitutional history serve as warnings against the excesses of the French Revolution, tracing them back to its philosophical origins in the eighteenth century, or to a tradition of a centralized state as it had emerged during the seventeenth century:

> Rousseau's doctrine of the Social Contract led to the form of despotism that enabled Napoleon to declare: *I am France*. According to Rousseau, man enchained by the general will is freer than the man without chains, because the whole of society guarantees his freedom. This is the consequence of a convention to which he freely adheres. This sophistry allowed to destorte liberty, independence, life, everything.²⁵³

Such fears are remarkably different from the reading of Rousseau by Giuseppe Ferrari, whose *Philosophy of Revolution* would praise the *Citoyen de Génève* for his egalitarian concept of distributive justice, which subsequently inspired Robespierre.²⁵⁴ It is in the context of these debates on France that moderate Sicilian commentators recognized the advantages of the American constitution. Giuseppe Natoli, who on other occasions rejected the temptation of direct comparison, applauded "the caution of Philadelphia's legislators," inviting his colleagues to imitate "an example that produced beautiful results, given to us by the world's freest nation."²⁵⁵

The aforementioned Giuseppe La Farina, a Republican whose interest in the right to work had been noted by Marx, was secretary of the Commons and occupied several ministerial positions in the Sicilian government.²⁵⁶ His history of the Sicilian Revolution confirms what many members of the two chambers repeated throughout the session of parliament, that the constitution of 1812 had to undergo serious revisions to respond to the new conditions of 1848. While the first draft of the new constitution maintained a Chamber of Peers as he recalled, "without mentioning the example of the American Model Republic"²⁵⁷—the new constitution replaced it with a senate, largely based on elected membership. The commission reporting on the convocation of parliament, presided over by Pasquale Calvi, described bicameralism as a constitutional principle of any free nation, "including the Model Republic of America."²⁵⁸ The main reason for replacing the hereditary chamber was the experience of January 1848. A surprisingly large faction of peers considered hereditary principles outdated after the recent political events. As Lorenzo Cottù Marsiani Marchese di Roccaforte maintained: "the Constitution of 1812 was not the aim of our glorious revolution. . . . Do we now pretend that we shed all that blood in Sicily, that we achieved so much only to be ruled for ever by the Constitution of 1812? Anybody who dares to repeat today that hereditary peers have to be maintained, because it's a right based on this Constitution? . . . Gentlemen, I never would have believed such words could be professed in Sicily, in 1848, after a revolution so beautiful that it served as a model half of Europe."[259]

Instead of discussing foreign examples, Roccaforte considered the recognition of popular sovereignty to be the principal outcome of Sicily's glorious revolution, describing the moment when the people of Palermo rose to invoke its rights. But not everybody shared this revolutionary furore. Speaking against an elected chamber, Francesco Marletta argued that "since Norman times Parliament had always been composed by nobles and bishops." Reformed in 1812, "it was agreed that the Chamber of Peers was to be composed of bishops and nobles, whereas the Commons were to be made of representatives. Who now can take from Peers this right acquired over the centuries?"[260] A professor of the University of Catania and an elected member of the Upper House, without noble title, Marletta reminded his colleagues that in England the peers "have always protected the rights of the aristocracy." Meanwhile, Marchese Vincenzo Mortillaro knew many examples of "modern constitutions" that had abolished a purely hereditary chamber. But the list he used to prove his statement excluded the United States.[261]

Not surprisingly, references to the US Senate appeared more frequently in discussions of the Commons. For Bertolami it was exactly what a Sicilian upper house should look like: "The American Senate is more than a legislative chamber. It also serves as advisor to the executive power. . . . In America the Senate represents a true aristocracy, not a feudal, territorial or noble aristocracy, as in Old Europe, but a new kind of aristocracy, whose power is grounded in the superiority of wealth, of talent and social position."[262] Moreover, the American bicameral system compared favorably with the French revolutionary experience, which served to recall "the damage a single assembly had inflicted upon the French Republic."[263] Few of these references to the United States were supported by a more detailed analysis of what American bicameralism meant in practice. In the end both chambers voted in favor of an elected senate without hereditary peers. Rather than seeing this move as the importation of a foreign model, it represented the adaptation of the 1812 constitution to the sprit of 1848.

The main issue the Commons discussed with close reference to the United States was that of "federazione o unità," which started out from the Sicilian debate over the convocation of an Italian Diet. "Italy will constitute itself as a single nation of united states, like Switzerland, like North America, like Germany," Cordova insisted in May 1848.[264] While federalism served to underline the distinctiveness of the Sicilian people within the Italian nation, references to the United States also made the island close ranks with the most advanced country on earth:

> A variety of people shape a great nation. These people, however, are free and independent, have their own political administration. This is the people we want to be, that's us. . . . Heaven help that we, that all peoples who descend from the great mother *Italia* follow the eternally glorious United States of America! [Applause!] Confederation and merger are certainly not the same thing, are two very different things. You in fact confederate peoples who are not the same, who are not as one.[265]

There was a broad consensus to reject "the despotic centralisation" of the French tradition.[266] In comparison, America was seen as a loose federation of independent states and therefore a model for Italy: "Each state will have its own Constitution, as the whole nation will have its federal Constitution, which will regulate common affairs, commerce, the navy, the army, customs and so forth." In marked contrast to Italy's neo-Guelph tradition, this understanding of federalism emerged as a democratic form of popular sovereignty: "in the American Congress, the Swiss diet, the Frankfurt diet, the representatives of the different *peoples* meet, not those of the American, Swiss or German *governments*."[267] In many of these debates, America served to deliver empirical evidence: "Without America humanity had no practical confirmation of its theories of freedom," Baron Canalotti maintained in the Upper House.[268] Meanwhile, comparisons with the German federation led to questions over how Prussia and Bavaria relate to the German nation, whether "Sicily is a nation or the nation is indeed Italy?"[269] These examples demonstrate that in discussions over Sicily's future relationship with the mainland the United States was by no means the only point of reference.

Once the constitution was proclaimed, in July 1848, opportunities to discuss American political institutions became rare. In debates on tariffs the main points of reference were France and England.[270] From constitutional ideals the debate moved on to the day-to-day business of a small state in revolutionary turmoil, partly under siege and engaged in a war with Naples. Pensions for revolutionaries' widows or mutilated soldiers were discussed alongside provisions for local libraries.[271] As events progressed, Europe and the Italian states became a more important reference point than the United States.[272] National pride informed the rhetoric. "Soldiers with a courage similar to that of Sicilians are rare in Europe," the minister of war Giuseppe Poulet exclaimed in the House of Peers during the dramatic days of February 1849.[273] The first histories of the Revolution too were written with the intent of revealing to "any people or government" the "most unusual example of all the world's revolutions."[274]

Drawing on parallels between the Revolution of 1848 and the Sicilian Vespers of 1282, an anonymous citizen of Palermo rejoiced, "Palermo, my homeland, you were always beautiful; now you are also enlightened and great!"[275] Even when defeat was in sight, the fact that the European revolutions of 1848 had started in Palermo remained a source of pride. Michele Bertolami, a friend of Vincenzo Bellini and Giacomo Leopardi, and a member of the moderate majority in the Commons reminded his colleagues that "the Sicilian revolution raised the people's banner to replace the banner of absolutism, it demonstrated to the Italian people and soon to peoples all over Europe that rights give force and that this force is a thousand times superior to the force of power."[276]

From Defeat to Annexation

While Cattaneo fought against Lombardy's subordination to Piedmont, and Sicily dismantled its union with Naples, the government in Turin had ended Sardinia's constitutional autonomy and merged the island with the Piedmontese provinces of the mainland. This process had started in 1847 and was completed in 1849. The federalist republicanism of the Sardinian legal theorist Giovan Battista Tuveri (1815–87) developed in direct response to this process, rooted in a strong tradition of regional autonomy, where popular sovereignty formed the basis of democratic legitimacy.[277] Making explicit references to American and Swiss federalism, Tuveri's political thought bears remarkable similarities to Cattaneo's ideas.[278] His federalism was homegrown but strengthened its legitimacy through reference to existing federal constitutions. As Paolo Bagnoli has argued, for Tuveri a sovereign democratic state had to be based on the "the people's right to constitute itself autonomously according to its own history and culture."[279] Sardinia's difficult relationship with Piedmont shared a great deal with the collapse of the union between Sicily and Naples in 1848. In his later political writings Tuveri continued to praise the United States' egalitarian principles: "It doesn't matter from whom you are born, but who you are. In the succession of American presidents we see a Lincoln, a Johnson, a Garfield, who had spent their adolescence in factories."[280]

For the philosopher Giuseppe Ferrari, another Republican and Italy's most influential Federalist after Cattaneo, the experience of the failed Revolution of 1848 led to an important ideological reorientation, at the center of which stood the concept of individual liberty. As with Montanelli and Cattaneo, Ferrari distanced himself from Mazzini.[281] For Ferrari popular sovereignty had to be based on "sovranità umana," guaranteed by a declaration of the Rights of Man. He considered the unity of the nation a purely "literary" or intellectual concept, far from the country's political realities. Italians existed only as Romans, Toscani, Piedmontesi, the idea that formed the basis of Ferrari's federalism.[282] "The states' historical division represents a reality in Italy. It is the right of every state to live freely on its own. Reality and rights therefore lead to the Italian confederation."[283]

In the early 1840s Ferrari had taught briefly at the University of Strasbourg, where opposition to the role of the Roman Catholic Church in the modern world became a central motif of his political thought.[284] The experience of his growing opposition to the church later influenced his critique of Cavour's formula of "a free Church in a free state." As mentioned in the previous chapter, Cavour's thinking on the relationship between church and state had also been influenced by the example of the United States, but Ferrari understood this American experience differently: North America was the only "free state," one that "does not pay the clergy, that does not confiscate the property of any church, that does not request Te Deums, or religious funerals, or blessings from the clergy of the various religions."[285] After the French coup d'état Ferrari could no longer hope for an academic position in France, and many of his former political friends were imprisoned or exiled. Nevertheless, he cautiously identified the emperor as a force against legitimism and as a social reformer after the failed upheaval of the weak Second Republic. Cattaneo was unable to agree with this assessment, asserting that the Second Empire would produce a social revolution without liberty, an imperial dictatorship.[286]

Despite these and other differences, what united Ferrari and Cattaneo was their opposition to Mazzini's *programma unitario*, their ideal of federal republicanism, which found expression in the constitution of the *Comitato latino* of 1851.[287] An initiative by Félicité de Lamennais, Enrico Cernuschi, and Giuseppe Montanelli, its aim was to offer a federalist alternative to Mazzini's *Comitato centrale democratico europeo*. Only in federal states, they argued, could democratic and republican principles prevent specific groups from seizing power.[288] For Ferrari Italy's transformation had to start from revolutionary initiatives in the different Italian states, leading to a federation of constitutional states able to oppose Austria.

While Mazzini remained opposed to federalism, his hostility toward American political institutions changed under the impression of the defeat of the revolutions. He now assigned to the United States the role of democratic leadership for the progress of humanity. As he explained in an address, "To Our Friends in the United States," Mazzini claimed that the United States had a moral duty toward Republicans all over the world to form an alliance that would determine the new world order.[289] For Cattaneo and Ferrari, however, the main focus of their international thought remained European *Realpolitik* and the immediacy of the problems posed by the relationship between the Italian states and their neighbours, France and Austria. Shortly after his *Filosofia della rivoluzione*, Ferrari completed *La federazione repubblicana*, both published in 1851.[290] Defending the work against Mazzini's critique, a benevolent Cattaneo suggested that Ferrari's ideas were inspired by Swiss and American models, but as a model of federalism Ferrari needed America even less than Cattaneo. Despite its topic and title, it is a book entirely conceived on the basis of Europe's and Italy's own political and constitutional experience, at the center of which were the Revolutions of 1848. Unlike Cattaneo, Ferrari entered into an active political career after Unification. Although he was largely isolated within parliament, he remained a deputy for sixteen years and represented an important voice of the radical opposition and the country's poor. During the years of his career in parliament there were many occasions when Ferrari demonstrated that being a Federalist and a Republican did not mean blind devotion to American democracy. Discussing economic inequalities between states, Ferrari opposed the free trade treaty of 1863, citing the example of Native Americans who under the aegis of free trade sold virgin forest for gunpowder and cheap alcohol.[291]

The experience of 1848 had destroyed many hopes for a federal solution to the Italian question. The previously influential French model of republicanism also became less attractive. The collapse of the Second Republic and Louis-Bonaparte's coup d'état led to a reexamination of republican principles, supporting the idea that democracy might be achieved with nonrepublican forms of government.[292] Rather than understanding the French coup d'état as the end of democracy, Republicans like Cattaneo and Mauro Macchi believed that Napoleon III had eliminated the threat posed by the conservative majority in the Assembly. As a consequence, some Mazzinian Republicans turned themselves into radical Democrats, prepared to "[fight] alongside the Savoy dynasty to complete the national revolution," and to advance the democratic cause within the framework of a monarchy.[293] Following Tocqueville's and Laboulaye's admiration for American civil society and associational culture, they recognized that the same political culture could be achieved under a liberal monarchy like that of England.

This process of ideological repositioning did not mean that Italian patriots lost sight of the ideals they associated with American political institutions. In 1860, Francesco Ferrara, who had been a member of the Sicilian Commons in 1848, still proposed following "the American model" to help integrating Sicily into the Kingdom of Italy. Federal principles, he thought, would secure the consent of the Sicilian people for the project of nation building.[294] Ferrara went on to become a member of the Italian parliament, minister of finance, and finally senator, without ever being in a position to impose his federal thought on the country's political realities.[295] Agostino Bertani, a deputy for the extreme Left who had played a leading role in Garibaldi's Expedition of the Thousand, likened the Piedmontese system of government in Sicily to the "metodo anglo-indiano," passionately criticizing the extent to which Piedmont misread the Sicilians' understanding of liberty.[296]

CHAPTER FOUR

Unveiling Modernity: Verdi's America and the Unification of Italy

Addio diletta America . . . addio miei figli per sempre!

—GIUSEPPE VERDI—ANTONIO SOMMA,

UN BALLO IN MASCHERA, ACT 3, 75[1]

Murder in Boston, Parma, and Paris

On 17 February 1859, Giuseppe Verdi's opera *Un ballo in maschera* was premiered at the Apollo Theater in Rome, at the time the city's principal theater.[2] A *melodramma* in three acts, the opera is set in New England during the seventeenth century and deals with the love affair between the governor of Boston, Riccardo, and Amelia, the wife of his secretary and intimate friend, Renato.[3] Although the relationship was never consummated, when Renato discovers the affair he joins a group of conspirators and assassinates the governor at a masked ball.

While Italian stage works about the New World were by no means new, Verdi's American opera counts among the most famous of its kind. Although a fictional plot borrowed from a different national context, contemporary reactions show that it was a work that audiences related to political ideas they had received about the New World, at a time when Italians were becoming increasingly aware that their nation's own Risorgimento had reached a decisive turning point. The opera was first performed under the electrifying climate of the international crisis that led to Italy's Second War of Independence and the foundation of the Kingdom of Italy, an event that directly impacted on several of the work's early productions.[4]

FIG. 13. Frontispiece to the 1860 vocal score, Roberto Focosi / Francesco Corbetta, "E tu ricevi il mio!," in Giuseppe Verdi, *Un ballo in maschera: Melodramma tragico in tre atti.* Riduzione per canto e pianoforte di Luigi ed Alessandro Truzzi. Milan: Ricordi [1860]. Image courtesy https://en.wikipedia.org/wiki/Un_ballo_in_maschera#/media/File: Giuseppe_Verdi,_Un_Ballo_in_maschera,_Vocal_score_frontispiece_-_restoration.jpg.

This chapter, as well as the following final chapter, will move my book's focus of analysis from an examination of political thought to resonances of en-gagement with the New World in the cultural imagination of Italians around the time of their nation's political unification. Based on a close reading of two specific cultural forms of representation—opera and ballet, as well as sur-rounding debates—I hope to show that ideas about the New World mattered to Italians beyond the level of debate on political institutions.

Like any successful opera or ballet, *Un ballo in maschera* reached huge numbers of Italians. While in nineteenth-century Italy even the most popular American-set novels by James Fenimore Cooper rarely had a readership in the tens of thousands, a single performance of a popular opera or ballet at one of Italy's big theaters, like Milan's Teatro alla Scala, was attended by an audience of up to three thousand people every night. A popular work was usually scheduled for twenty or more evenings in a single season and then restaged in subsequent years, along with productions elsewhere in Italy. While some patrons in the private boxes saw the same work evening after evening, in the upper balconies and the stalls audiences changed more frequently between performances. They were socially more diverse, and as a consequence productions reached a wider strata of the population than the social profile of the private box owners would suggest.[5] For those who did not go to the theater, premieres generated reviews in newspapers all over Italy as well as in the musical press. Even subsequent stagings were regularly discussed in newspapers. Piano reductions of popular operas and extracts were widely available, in the case of *Un ballo* as early as 1859.[6] Municipal bands brought the most popular tunes from the work into the piazza; and frequently barrel organ players picked up tunes from local opera houses and carried them into the poorest neighbourhoods.

Hence, Verdi's American opera could hardly be missed. In this respect the opera had a far more important impact on the spread of ideas about America than novels, academic works, or travel writing. Moreover, debates over stage works featuring life in America were directly related to the discussions of American democracy analyzed in the previous chapters. In the context of this book, the debate over Verdi's American opera serves as a perfect example of the cultural imagination surrounding life in the New World, and of the wider social impact of political ideas in nineteenth-century Italy.

As already intimated, to political observers, as well as to followers of European opera and literature, the plot of *Un ballo* would have sounded familiar. In 1792, the Swedish king Gustav III had been assassinated at a masked ball, a scandal that inspired the famous playwright Eugène Scribe to write a libretto entitled *Gustave III, ou Le bal masqué*, in which he presented a love affair between the king and his secretary's wife as the cause of the king's otherwise rather mysterious assassination. Scribe's main source was a French version of John Brown's sensationalist book *The Northern Courts*, originally published in 1818.[7] Scribe's libretto was first set to music as a grand opéra by Daniel Auber in 1833. In 1841 Vincenzo Gabussi picked up the plot, using a version of the libretto by Gaetano Rossi for his opera *Clemenza di Valois*. In 1843 Saverio Mercadante composed a further version of the story using a libretto by Salvadore Cammarano. Under the title *Il Reggente*, he shifted the plot to sixteenth-century Scotland.[8] The examples show that Verdi was not the first to use Scribe's story for a range of different settings. Mercadante's opera in particular was popular and remained in the repertoire for several decades. Bellini too had at one point considered setting Scribe's libretto to music.[9] A number of dramatic adaptations of Scribe's work toured European theaters during the 1850s, including several Italian stages. In Rome, the Dondini company produced a *Gustavo III* by Gherardi del Testa.[10]

For years presenting these works on political assassinations went largely unnoticed until it suddenly became more problematic to present an opera featuring regicide, with not uncertain consequences for Verdi's decision to move the plot of his new opera from Sweden to America. In 1858 the Italian patriot Felice Orsini attempted to assassinate Napoleon III on his way to the opera in Paris. Orsini was well connected to a number of key political players of the Italian national movement, including Marco Minghetti, a former member of the Papal Council of State as well as close collaborator of Count Camillo Cavour (and a future Italian prime minister).[11] He was also a friend of Mazzini and had personal connections with the Democrats in the United States. In 1854 he had been among the guests at a reception at the American Embassy in London to celebrate the anniversary of George Washington's birthday. The event was organized by the American consul George Sanders, leader of Young America and representative of the Democratic Party's radical wing.[12] Other guests at the reception included numerous American dignitaries, as well as the revolutionaries Lajos Kossuth, Alexander Herzen, Aurelio Saffi, Mazzini, and Garibaldi. In 1857 Orsini had also taken tea with William Gladstone.[13] Like Mazzini, Orsini regarded the Risorgimento as part of an international struggle for freedom, in which the United States was supposed to play a prominent role. Starting with the overthrow of the Roman Republic in 1849, Orsini saw the policies of Louis-Bonaparte as a major obstacle to Italian Unification, symbolizing Europe's antiliberal reaction to the 1848 revolutions. While the emperor survived Orsini's attempt on his life, several other people were killed and many wounded.

The incident had major implications for the further course of the Risorgimento, causing Napoleon III to rethink French policies toward Italy, ultimately leading to the Second War of Independence and Piedmont's annexation of Lombardy. In addition to the parallel between the political events and the plot of Verdi's opera, the war and the impending fulfillment of the Risorgimento's political ambition form the background to the first performance of *Un ballo in maschera*. Meanwhile, political assassinations were not uncommon during the 1850s. For Verdi, of greater significance than the attempt on the life of Napoleon III would have been the assassination in 1854 of the Duke of Parma Carlo III by the anarchist Antonio Carra. Also relevant to the context of the opera's premiere in Rome was the assassination of the Roman prime minister Pellegrino Rossi a decade earlier, in November 1848.[14] While these events made the Italian states more wary of nationalist revolutionaries, the censors had long been cautious about works that might inspire regicide, although without banning the topos completely from the stage.[15] In Paris too political censorship had become stricter since the days of the early July monarchy or the Second Republic. While a relationship between the Orsini affair and Verdi's decision to change the original plot seems likely, it would be hazardous to overstate the connection, or to treat it as grounds for claiming that here there was a particularly severe regime of censorship in the Italian peninsula. In contrast to Scribe's original plot, all in all staging a political murder in a fictional New England seemed to be more acceptable.

Much has been written about the transformation of *Gustavo III* into *Un ballo* and on the impact of censorship on the content of the final version of the opera.[16] What these debates have overlooked is the fact that moving the opera's plot across the Atlantic was also significant in the context of political debates over Italy's constitutional future at the time of its transition to political nationhood. Given the political context of the opera's performance— the collapse of Italy's ancient system of states and the formation of an Italian nation-state—a work set in America made sense to Italians. Although Verdi paints an altogether rather dark image of America, the move was consistent with Italians' curiosity about the New World and their close engagement with political ideas arriving from across the Atlantic. The claim that the censors' intervention led to a completely arbitrary change of locale is therefore open to question. Unlike the old story about Gustav III, which had been adapted for the stage and set to music many times, the American background of *Un ballo* was of considerable cultural and political significance to Italians in 1859. Future events—news about the American Civil War spreading—consolidated its interest as an opera set in America. I will return to the impact of censorship on the plot of *Un ballo* toward the end of this chapter.

Un ballo *and the Unification of Italy*

Since the 1840s, any new opera by Verdi was considered a major event. Although there are a number of eighteenth- and early nineteenth-century works of opera and ballet set in the New World, the American plot of *Un ballo in maschera* stands out for the opera's close connection to the Unification of Italy. The work's premiere in Rome coincides almost exactly with the collapse of the peninsula's old state system, which led to the creation of the Kingdom of Italy under the crown of Piedmont-Sardinia. The relationship between the staging of an American opera by Verdi and the historical context of the performance— the fulfillment of the nation's political aspiration—certainly deserves historiographical attention.

At the time of *Un ballo*'s premiere, Verdi was widely considered Italy's *compositore nazionale*, the nation's foremost composer, and the leading representative of a musical genre—opera—that since the seventeenth century had played a central role in defining Italy as a *Kulturnation*, a nation constituted on the basis of a shared aesthetic and intellectual culture, and common cultural practices.[17] The association made at the time between Verdi's new work and current political events seems even more relevant. An early review of *Un ballo* in the *Gazzetta musicale di Milano* explicitly connected the premiere with the political upheaval that shook the nation in those days, the "grande commozione in cui s'agita inquieto il nostro paese."[18] Although in February 1859 the political unity of Italy was not yet a fact, the time seemed ripe for the next step in the nation's Risorgimento. The majority of the national movement now expected Piedmont to lead the way toward Unification. France and Piedmont had agreed on a second war against Austria, which would result in Piedmont's annexation of Lombardy and precipitate the collapse of the existing system of states on the peninsula. Both Italians and the whole of the European continent were acutely aware of this context. While the idea of Italian opera houses as the stage for political manifestations during the Risorgimento are often exaggerated, since January 1859 performances in Milan's Teatro alla Scala were marked by political unrest, especially the performances of Bellini's *Norma*, with its famous chorus "Guerra, Guerra!" At about the same time graffiti associating Verdi with the future King of Italy ("Viva V.E.R.D.I.," Vittorio Emanule Re d'Italia) had appeared for the first time in the streets of Milan.[19]

While historians and musicologists have convincingly dismissed many of the myths concerning the supposedly patriotic meaning of Verdi's early works, it seems safe to argue that from the late 1840s onward Verdi himself identified with the aims of Italy's national movement.[20] By the time of *Un ballo*, in 1859, he was generally considered among Italy's most famous patriots, soon to be elected to the new kingdom's constituent assembly and the Italian national parliament. Although it is difficult to read any particular national agenda into the libretto of *Un ballo*—Verdi never made such claims—the libretto's author, Antonio Somma, was an outspoken opponent of the Habsburgs' role in Italy. Originally trained as a lawyer, during his time as director of the theater in Trieste he had been among the founders of the Risorgimento newspaper *La favilla*. In February 1849 he was elected to the assembly of the Venetian Republic and then became the head of its administration. In 1852 his tragedy *La figlia dell'Apennino* had been performed in Milan, Padua, and Venice. Although it passed the Austrian censors, at the time his dramatic work was read as being closely connected to the political agitation in Venice and elsewhere in Italy.[21]

As in the case of his collaboration with Montanelli on *Simon Boccanegra*, Verdi was not concerned by associating himself with a prominent member of the nation's patriotic intelligentsia. For various reasons Somma himself wanted his name to be omitted from the program and from the printed versions of the opera, but his role as author was known to insiders and *melomanes*. It was not discontent with the transfer of the opera's original plot to America that led Somma to dissociate himself from the project, but rather the fear of being haunted by his own revolutionary past.[22] Anonymity did not shield Somma from the blame directed at the weaker aspects of the libretto, although almost any librettist at the time faced some criticism of that sort. After the opera's premiere the musical periodical *L'Armonia* recommended that he look for a new occupation.[23]

Staging the New World

At the very moment when the Risorgimento finally seemed to fulfill its promise, the nation's leading composer proposed an opera set not in Italy, but in America. His decision needs to be examined within the wider context of Italy's dramatic engagement with the New World. Goldoni's "American" tragicomedies of the mid-eighteenth century looked at the New World through commentaries on typical aspects of the "savage world," based on the works of Prévost and Voltaire.[24] The same topics were frequently explored in Italian ballet, like Raimondo Fidanza's *Colombo, ossia La Scoperta del Nuovo Mondo* (Genoa, 1802) or Antonio Monticini's *Colombo all'isola di Cuba* (Milan, 1832).[25] Here America was not just a New, but a different World, treated in a rather undifferentiated fashion and usually emphasizing its natural otherness. As suggested in the introduction, the enlightened humanism of Western civilization contrasts with the noncivilized peoples of the New World. Depending on the author's position within the philosophical debates of the day, lack of civilization could be described as an advantage or a disadvantage. What most authors seemed to agree on was that savages constituted "different" subjects, and that therefore they did not enjoy the same rights as Europeans. As in Tiepolo's ceiling painting discussed in the introduction, in most of these stage works the American continent became a canvas on which a contrast with the civilized genius of the Italian people might be drawn.[26]

During the second half of the eighteenth century the emphasis of American topoi in stage works changed. Eighteenth-century enthusiasm for the noble savage vanished. Attention progressively shifted from Latin America to the British colonies, and then to the emerging Republic in the North. As Pierpaolo Polzonetti has demonstrated, many Italian composers of the late eighteenth and early nineteenth century made direct or indirect references to the social and cultural transformation taking place across the Atlantic, either by making life in the New World their topic or by composing operas on an imaginary utopia inspired by the revolutionary social realities of the North American Republic, as with Haydn's *Il mondo della luna*.[27] Often these works took the form of *opera buffa*, which offered a wide spectrum of emotional and rhetorical expression, tolerating political commentary to a greater extent than *opera seria*. Mozart, Haydn, Piccini, and Pasiello—along with many today less well known composers of the late eighteenth century—made direct or indirect references to the social and cultural transformation taking place in North

America, forming part of the wider cultural commentary on political ideas crossing the Atlantic. Performances of Piccini's *I napoletani in America* coincided exactly with the first Italian reports on American uprisings against the British tax regime. Many of these works no longer presented the New World as exotic and foreign, but rather as a modern place of trading and business, as the "new frontier of Western civilisation."[28] There are aspects of this emphasis on economic life also in Verdi's opera, especially in the character of the soothsayer Ulrica, who runs her shop as a modern business.

Pennsylvanian Quakers were a particularly popular topic of early Italian stage works on the New World, allowing composers and librettists to express a certain ironic distance from the political ideas that informed America's social realities. In Pietro Alessandro Guglielmi's opera *La quakera spiritosa* (Naples, 1783), based on a librettto by Giuseppe Palomba, an American Quaker girl rejects an arranged marriage and proposes instead to a Neapolitan vineyard worker, not bothered by the fact that he himself feels more attracted to men.[29] Although Piero del Negro has argued that eighteenth-century Italians knew little about the Quakers, they frequently featured in fantastic or comical accounts of life in the New World and became one way to discuss American life in terms of alternative models of society.[30] Voltaire's letter about the Quakers had been translated into Italian in 1760, circulating in various editions throughout the nineteenth century. Pecchio's widely read *Osservazioni* contained a chapter on the Quakers with some references to the United States.[31] Franklin's Italian contacts also helped to familiarize intellectual circles with the life of the Quaker colonies. Franklin was also at the origin of a significant musical connection between the American continent and Italy. As he explained in a letter to Beccaria, it was to honor Italy's musical tradition that he gave his recently invented glass-armonica its Italian name, an instrument soon explored by Mozart, Beethoven, and Gluck, and later by Donizetti in the famous "mad scene" of *Lucia di Lammermoor*.[32]

Also the playing with sexual identity, as in the case of Guglielmi's *Quakera spirtosa*, was common in opera around 1800. For instance, in Rossini's first full-length opera, *L'equivoco stravagante* (1811), the principal tenor is made to believe that his lover Ernestina is indeed Ernesto, castrated by her father to be sent to the theater and then hidden in female dress.[33] Guglielmi's opera is to be read in this context of debate about challenges to social and cultural practices, in which America and in particular the Quakers played an important role. Opera was one medium to discuss these challenges. As the chapter's following sections will demonstrate, aspects of Verdi's *Un ballo* refer back to this tradition.

These examples serve to justify the role of cultural imagination within a book on political ideas. Guglielmi's opera seems to suggest that Americans did not want their role to be defined by external factors such as gender or status. While Guglielmi discussed these facts from a position of ironic distance,

S.d'A.   T.45.

S.Marçeau dis.   G. Carattoni inc.

Quakeri e Quakeressa che predica.

FIG. 14. Giuseppe Compagnoni, "Quakeri e quakeressa
che predica," *Storia dell'America* (1822), vol. 25, 104–5
(insert). Biblioteca Malatestiana, Cesena.

attitudes toward sexuality in a free country such as the American colonies gave
Italian political thinkers much stuff for debate. The accounts of Filangieri and
Count Castiglioni, presented in the introduction, illustrate this point. Composers and librettists used operas on the New World to reflect ideas that
animated Italian and European debates at the time. While many of these
individual works were later forgotten, they left an important imprint on its
composers as well as on contemporary society as a whole.

When Verdi and Somma wrote *Un ballo in maschera*, more recent musical representations of America included among the then more famous works
Donizetti's cantata *Cristoforo Colombo o sia la scoperta dell'America*.[34] Paolo
Giorza, composer of the ballet discussed in the following chapter, established
himself as an expert on the theme of America: in addition to his Uncle Tom
ballet *Bianchi e Neri* he composed the music for Monplaisir's ballet *Colombo*,

which became a real hit on the Italian stages.[35] Works on Christopher Columbus became particularly popular with Italian audiences, reaching a new zenith later in the century in connection with celebrations for the four-hundredth anniversary of his discoveries. The most famous of these works was Alberto Franchetti's *Cristoforo Colombo*, commissioned by the city of Genoa, with a libretto by Luigi Illica.[36]

Un ballo, *from Rome to the World*

Verdi's contribution to American-themed stage works needs to be seen in the context of Italy's ambition of fostering the country's international recognition in producing great works of opera. As far as Italian commentators were concerned, this is what Verdi stood for during those years when Italy finally became a player in international politics. After the remarkable success of *Nabucco* in 1842, his *Rigoletto, Il trovatore*, and *La traviata* were considered works of maturity and helped to consolidate the composer's fame abroad. Verdi conquered not only Italian theaters, but also international stages—Paris, Vienna, and London, where the still relatively new genre of grand opéra had established the highest standards for the performance of opera. In 1843 Donizetti directed *Nabucco* in Vienna. *I masnadieri* of 1847 was first performed at Her Majesty's Theatre in London. His French opera *Jérusalem* of the same year, based on *I Lombardi*, was premiered at the Académie Royale de Musique in Paris. Chapter 1 briefly discussed the 1855 premiere of his *Les vêpres siciliennes*, also written for Paris and attended (despite the plot's alleged anti-French undertones) by the emperor Napoleon III. *Le Trouvère*, a revised version of *Il trovatore*, was first performed at the Paris Opéra in 1857. Several operas were premiered in Milan, Venice, and Trieste, among the Habsburgs' greatest theaters. Verdi's reputation among the Austrian imperial family would grow to the point that Emperor Franz Joseph considered Verdi among his favorite composers, notwithstanding the fact that some opera scholars credit his work with having contributed to Italy's liberation from Habsburg rule.[37] Germans took note of his interest in Schiller and Shakespeare. There can be no doubt that Verdi's international position helped to bolster Italy's prestige among the more advanced nations of the world.

Although the Italian response to Verdi was often more mixed than myths about Italy's compositore nazionale would have us believe, the Roman premiere of *Un ballo in maschera*, prepared as was usual by Verdi himself, was an immediate success. The work's extraordinary popularity with audiences and critics alike is a further reason why Verdi's American opera deserves special attention in a book about the United States in the Italian imagination. The Teatro Apollo was sold out evening after evening. Verdi frequently received more than thirty curtain calls.[38] Although Rome was at that time still under papal government, the municipality did not hesitate to exploit the composer's success for their own purposes, honoring Verdi with a crown of golden laurels, presented to him after the opera's third evening.[39] Ticket prices rose to almost unprecedented levels. As the *Gazzetta musicale di Milano* commented, rarely had "the public been more excited," though this might have been a deliberate sales strategy, owing to the fact that the journal was owned by Verdi's publisher Ricordi has to be taken into account.[40]

The opera's immediate success was helped by the premiere's spectacular cast—carefully negotiated between Verdi and the theater—and always an important factor in the success of the composer's works. It included Gaetano Fraschini in the role of Riccardo, an international star and famous for his appearances in *Trovatore* and Donizetti's *Lucia*. Devotees were later to remember his voice as "un diamant," an "organe naturellement sombre, énergique, viril, dont le timbre, d'une douceur exquise."[41] Verdi himself was a great fan, stating, "I take enormous pleasure in Fraschini's success, as if it were my own personal triumph or something even greater."[42] The original Renato was Leone Giraldoni, who had starred as the first *Simon Boccanegra*. The French soprano Eugénie Julienne-Dejean created the role of Amelia. Although she disappointed Verdi, audiences and critics took to her and recognized in her the star of the London and Paris stages, where she had sung Donizetti, Halévy, and Meyerbeer as well as Verdi's *La traviata* and *Jérusalem*.[43] Not slow to exploit the opera's enormous success, within days of the first performance Ricordi took out newspaper advertisements for sheet music featuring extracts from the opera.[44] Pougin's famous "anecdotal biography" of 1881 (published before the completion of Verdi's last works, *Otello* and *Falstaff*) remembers *Un ballo* as "one of the greatest triumphs of his career."[45] The initial difficulties with the censors do not seem to have impinged in the slightest on the opera's acceptance.

The opera's first Italian staging after the premiere in Rome took place at Bologna's Teatro Comunale on 4 October 1860, then one of the peninsula's most prestigious theaters. Within the city's changing political context—the former Papal Legations had just voted for the annexation to the Kingdom of Piedmont—the excellent performance was considered a very special event, attended by the local public with an almost "religious" attitude. Its musical director was Angelo Mariani, considered Italy's greatest conductor at the time.[46] Part of the opera's success in Bologna was due to the superb performance by tenor Ludovico Graziani, who in 1853 had created the role of Alfredo Germont in the premiere of *La traviata*. Since Bologna had previously been exposed to Verdi less than other major Italian cities, the production allowed its inhabitants to feel part of the narrative that linked Verdi to the Italian nation. Turin, now the capital of unified Italy, presented the opera in December 1860. Venice—still under the Habsburgs—Genoa, and Florence scheduled it in 1861; la Scala in Milan and the San Carlo in Naples followed in 1862.[47] *Un ballo* belonged to the relatively few works by Verdi that remained in the repertoire for decades.[48] Genoa, Verdi's second home town after Sant'Agata, staged the work twenty-four times up to the composer's death in 1901.[49]

Every new work by Verdi was regarded a major event in the life of the young nation-state and as a source of considerable prestige for any city able to mount such a performance. The new plot about the assassination of the governor in Boston was brought to many of the more provincial locations of Italian theater life, offering local populations an opportunity to engage directly in debates about the New World. Ancona, Alessandria, Catania, Cremona, Genoa, Pesaro, Piacenza, Reggio Emilia, and the Fiera in Senigaglia all presented the opera before it was staged in Milan and Naples, thereby demonstrating that scheduling a new opera by Verdi was not the exclusive privilege of a few famous theaters in the peninsula's former capital cities. Italians in their tens of thousands saw the opera within the first few years of its existence.

Likewise, Verdi's American opera attracted considerable interest outside Italy, including many of the international centers of nineteenth-century music theater, but also places where the performance of opera was still fairly rare or where opera depended on financial support from colonial administrators.[50] Even before the Bologna staging, Lisbon put the work on in April 1860. In 1861 alone it was performed in Paris and Nice, at the Hofoper in Berlin, in London and Dublin, St. Petersburg, Barcelona, and Madrid, but also in Cuba, then under Spanish rule. Although this was certainly not the main reason for the opera's success, its admission into the international repertoire coincided with greater interest in American affairs and the escalating conflict between the northern and the southern states of the Republic, which newspapers around the world reported in great detail. In 1862 Hamburg and Stuttgart, Constantinople, Malta and Corfu, Buenos Aires and Rio de Janeiro, Moscow and Odessa scheduled the opera, followed in 1863 by performances in Budapest, Amsterdam, Lima, and several North American opera houses. In 1864 *Un ballo* was presented in Australia, Egypt, and Vienna, in 1866 in Calcutta and Prague. Prague's German premiere was followed by a performance in Czech in 1869. That year also saw productions in Bogota and in Indonesia. Rarely had an opera conquered the stages of the world in such a short period of time. For all these cities it was not only an opera by Italy's, and probably the world's most famous living composer, but also an opera about life during North America's colonial period.

While audiences generally appreciated Verdi's new opera, press reaction was more uneven, including the review in the periodical *Il trovatore*, in competition with Verdi's own publisher.[51] Often these voices disliked Verdi's departures from the tradition of *bel canto*, which until recently had marked the repertoire of a majority of Italian theaters, before they embarked on an internationalization of their programs. After the opera's *prima* in Milan, *La Fama* criticized Verdi for "leaving behind the Italian style, approaching more and more the foreign school represented by Meyerbeer."[52] The Prussian composer Giacomo

Meyerbeer stood here for the emergence of French-style grand opéra. Arguably, in order to gain international recognition, Verdi had to write in a more cosmopolitan idiom, but not everybody in Italy responded well to these changes. Bologna presents a case in point, with the city's principal newspaper considering *Un ballo* "difficult music": the opera was well performed, but based on "abstruse harmonic and melodic combinations."[53] These views were shared by one of Bologna's most respected commentators on the life of the Teatro Comunale, Enrico Bottrigari, who opined that the work "lacks vigour and imagination. The first act is poor, the others contain effective moments, but altogether hardly anything is new, it is a mosaic made up from various other scores."[54]

Most Italians who heard the work not only took a different view, but their comments also went beyond purely aesthetic considerations, focussing instead on the plot's content. The opera's success was based on more than the composer's personal reputation or the influence of his publisher Ricordi. Its place in the repertoire facilitated a continuous debate about a powerful depiction of life in the New World, at a time when news items about America started to become a general feature of Italian periodicals. The fact that *Un ballo* presented a work of fiction was not an obstacle to the impact its image of America had on audiences. Here the opera's American reception is of particular interest. Since the mid-1840s operas by Verdi were regularly staged in the Western hemisphere, starting with a production of *I Lombardi* at the Teatro Tacón in Havanna in 1846. Over the following years Verdi's early works were regularly staged in New York City, Boston, and New Orleans, as well as in Buenos Aires, Lima, and Rio de Janeiro. *Ernani* in particular proved popular, resulting in numerous productions in the United States, Cuba, Mexico, and Canada, though not always praised by the critics.[55]

American performances of *Un ballo* started in 1861 with productions in New York, Boston, and Philadelphia. If some commentators mentioned the plot's lack of authenticity—and one certainly might wonder about Verdi's depiction of sexual adventures in Puritan New England—this particular aspect did not seem to disturb American audiences, who should by rights have been most affected by Verdi's characterization of their ancestors. This chapter will return to the opera's American reception.

Reading Un ballo in maschera

Arguably, the meaning of Verdi's opera—including details of its image of colonial America—is not necessarily borne by the libretto or the score themselves, but rather by its reception. Historians have to find sources to establish how the work was read and understood within the specific historical context of its performance. Where these sources of reception are missing, or where they leave an incomplete picture, we must endeavour to reconstruct the meaning of references and images with the help of other sources.

Along with the numerous reviews of Verdi's new opera in musical peri-odicals and major newspapers—including shorter comments on individual performances—there is one major contemporary analysis of *Un ballo*, a de-tailed article and description of the opera by Filippo Filippi in the *Gazzetta musicale di Milano*, first published at the time of its Roman premiere in 1859 and reprinted at full length three years later for the opera's first performance in Milan. Together with Francesco d'Arcais, Filippi was Italy's most influential music critic at the time. While we know little about most of the correspon-dents who wrote about the first performances of *Un ballo*, Filippi's biography is closely interwoven with contemporary political events in Italy. Trained as a lawyer, pianist, and composer, he published his analysis of *Un ballo* when he was working as a correspondent for the influential *Gazzetta musicale di Milano*, shortly before becoming its main editor. Meanwhile, he also wrote for the moderate Milanese newspaper *La Perseveranza*, founded in November 1859 and widely read among Italian Liberals, despite its elevated price. Its sec-tion on the arts was respected well beyond the political circles of Lombardy's conservative-monarchical establishment.

What makes Filippi's early analysis of *Un ballo* interesting is the fact that he had received little in terms of formal philosophical-aesthetic education, and that therefore his judgement was largely based on intuition. Unlike other professional critics at the time Filippi is prone to express views that were simi-lar to those Italians who were passionate about opera without grounding their judgement in philosophical principles. He also shared the wider audience's general passion for Verdi, at a time when parts of the musical press criticized the composer for his departures from Italian tradition. In this sense Filippi displayed a rather unusual openness toward recent international develop-ments (and he enjoyed a certain recognition in Bayreuth), convinced that Italian opera had to follow new paths if it was to retain its preeminent role in Europe.

While the *Gazzetta* was owned by Verdi's publisher Ricordi, who for com-mercial reasons was certainly not impartial, many Italians who saw *Un ballo* for the first time would have read Filippi's analysis (or references to his article in other musical periodicals), a reading that in turn had an impact on their own response to the opera. His interpretation of *Un ballo* was probably the "saggio" or essay that received most attention at the time, forming an impor-tant basis for subsequent debates on Verdi's new work.[56] Another important contemporary commentary on Verdi, Abramo Basevi's *Studio sulle opere di Giuseppe Verdi*, was not only more technical and academic in its approach to its subject but was also completed shortly before the prima of *Un ballo*.[57] Contemporary commentary, rather than our own reading of the libretto and the score, should form the basis of an analysis of nineteenth-century opera.[58]

Along with press reviews, historians interested in a work's reception can consult the opera's *disposizione scenica*, which, in the case of *Un ballo*, is preserved and published, offering hints about the ways in which the opera's Boston setting and the work's main characters were presented to audiences. While we can assume that the *disposizione* for *Un ballo* was based on Verdi's own staging ideas, the book itself was composed by Giuseppe Cencetti, who came from a family of musicians and music publishers, and who himself wrote several successful operas and libretti, mostly for the Teatro Apollo in Rome, where *Un ballo* was premiered. Since the early 1850s he had worked as stage director for several Roman theaters and counts as one of the most innovative professionals in the field.[59]

Verdi's America

Verdi and his wife were avid readers; and their library, in addition to general works of geography and on travel writing, was rich in Americana, including several editions of Botta, William Robertson, and Alexander von Humboldt.[60] How did Verdi depict America? And how does his depiction relate to Italian debates about America at the time? Since the 1840s, set and costume designs, with descriptions of locales and characters, had become increasingly important in Verdi's operas; and not infrequently, reviewers paid more attention to those details of the production than to the music itself.[61] Traditionally, although this changed during the nineteenth century, the libretto—in the sense of a literary-dramatic text—was the main feature of any operatic production, while the music was mostly considered an aspect of staging, symbolized by the fact that the composer's name often figured less prominently on printed materials than the name of the opera and the author of the libretto.[62] Verdi carefully chose the subjects of his operas and weighed up their dramatic potential. By the time he wrote *Un ballo*, he tended to be in control of all aspects of the work, the distribution of the different parts and their performance. According to Fabrizio della Seta, he was "the real author of his libretti."[63] Therefore, the fact that *Un ballo* became an opera set in America constitutes an aspect of the work that greatly matters and therefore cannot be ignored.

Un ballo is not a work that celebrates life in the New World. The opera's dramatic language, the strong contrasts between its different scenes, and the constant interplay of light and darkness, often described as chiaroscuro, deserve particular attention. Many of Verdi's contemporaries as well as later musicologists have commented on this particular aspect of *Un ballo*.[64] Through its mix of musical styles the opera is hard to grasp: French versus Italian elements; aspects of opera seria as well as of grand opéra; episodes characteristic of Jacques Offenbach as well as the role of buffo characters like the "saucy" page Oscar.[65] The phenomenon described as chiaroscuro is also to be found in the opera's modal contrasts: frequent shifts in harmonic color, between major and minor, making it difficult to come to terms with the opera's emotional content, but at the same time supporting the drama's semantic structure. Finally there are the contrasts in the plot as a whole: elements of comedy and tragedy; masking and unmasking; love and hatred; friendship and betrayal; guilt and purity; gaiety and despair.[66] This almost excessive playing on contrasts marks the opera's originality but also creates a general sense of confusion, which in itself is an important aspect of the drama's unfolding tragedy.

Verdi's description of colonial America certainly does not correspond to a historically informed idea of Puritan New England. There is simply too much worldly life at the palace of the governor, culminating with the masked ball in the opera's final act. The role of the page Oscar is interesting here, his antics creating a rather Gallic comedy atmosphere throughout the opera. The main characters seem to further undermine the libretto's adaptation to the American setting. The governor of Boston, Riccardo, lacks any sense of responsibility toward his associates and the people of New England, or indeed any regard for his own safety. His sole preoccupation throughout the opera is to seduce Amelia, which means betraying his closest ally and "piu' fido amico" (act 1) Renato. His feelings unfold uncontrolled by reason, and his only thought is to see his lover "nell'estasi, raggiante di pallore" (act 1, 2).[67]

Regarding *Un ballo*'s emphasis on issues of sexuality, the continuous masking and unmasking in the libretto can also be read metaphorically. To complicate things further, it could be argued that for well-informed members of the audience homoerotic feelings were associated with the original character of the historical Gustav III, presumably in conflict with preconceived ideas about early modern British colonies, and certainly with the image of New England's frugality, temperance, and chastity Botta had diffused among his Italian readers.[68] Although same-sex desire largely disappeared from the libretto during its journey across the Atlantic, elements of it survived in the interpersonal dynamic between Riccardo and Oscar. In this respect the disposizione scenica is more explicit than the score itself, especially when it comes to the depiction of Oscar's reaction to Riccardo's adventures.[69] Interpretations of the opera's internal gender dynamic depend on the audience's engagement with Verdi's and Somma's literary sources, as well as its awareness of opera as a genre, which throughout its history has frequently redrawn gender divisions. Some of the sources for Scribe's libretto, first among them Brown's very popular and openly gossipy *The Northern Court*, are explicit about these sexual complexities: "This prince did not pay homage at the shrine of Venus," Brown explained, and his entourage at the court was made of nobles "whose vices were at once a stain to manhood, and a scourge to their country."[70] The sources of reception for *Un ballo*—as far as we know them—seem more discrete about this background, but these intertextual references certainly made the plot more interesting.

In other ways too Riccardo does not represent the role of an enlightened ruler usually associated with politics in the New World. He refuses to engage with reality or to hear about the conspiracy mounting against him, convinced, as he exclaims in act 1, that his protection comes from the love of his people (*del popolo mio—l'amor mi guardi—e mi protegga Iddio*). The same attitude is underlined later on, when he ridicules Ulrica's prophecy with the famous aria "è scherzo od e follia." While Riccardo's reaction can be read as the refusal of a modern-minded man to engage with the manipulated reality of a witch, in the context of the opera's overall plot the scene seems to suggest that Riccardo is incapable of grasping the situation evolving around him. Within the plot's narrative, Ulrica has the role of publicly revealing truth—she foretells the unfolding tragedy. Taking note of the conspirators' devious conduct and their contempt for the cheering crowd, she demonstrates that she is not simply a charlatan. She rightly concludes that treachery is in play and that she has a genuine reason to repeat her warnings. Riccardo, however, is driven by feelings rather than reason, rejecting her advice.[71] Toward the end of the opera the same scenario repeats itself: unable to heed Amelia's warnings, he falls on his murderer's knife. To the horror of the onlookers, he makes his private affairs public. It is not the drama of a political assassination, a historical tableau from the tradition of grand opéra, as in Verdi's *Les vêpres siciliennes*, but a contemporary display of human passions similar to *La traviata* or *Rigoletto*.

How are we to explain the opera's apparent contrast between the historical New England and Verdi's fictional canvas? And what did audiences make of it? Italian opera often ignored historical authenticity for the sake of a less specific "romantic colouring" associated with an imagined past.[72] For Verdi, opera was no longer meant to portray historical realities; or at least this was not its main purpose, especially if the work engaged with a foreign setting. Compared to Scribe's original play, Verdi stripped his version of all the political content that still formed the background to Auber's opera. If in Scribe's libretto the conspirators acted with clear political motives, in Verdi's version references to politics remain extremely vague. As for Riccardo, Verdi is solely interested in the man's feelings and psychology. According to Sarah Hibberd, the interest of Auber's *Gustave III* lies in the fact that it presented history "as a synchronic moment" or as a "kaleidoscopic fashion," where "conflicting personal actions" gesture both backward and forward in time.[73] Verdi went a step further: *Un ballo in maschera* marks the end of history in opera. In this respect Verdi seems to have learned from his engagement with Shakespeare, who in Barbara Everett's words "was never anything like a 'realist' . . . caring for the merely factual, sociological or politico-historical."[74] In this context it should be remembered that it was Shakespeare who set one of his most famous plays on the seacoast of Bohemia.

The dehistoricization of music theater in favor of the display of mentalities and emotions marks a crucial change in nineteenth-century opera. Historians of literature have made similar arguments for late eighteenth-century drama, where, according to Norbert Oellers, the historical became a timeless foil to display human character.[75] It is, therefore, misleading to start the analysis of Verdi's opera with the plot's historical credentials. It distracts from what the opera is principally about: in this case an argument about a particular psychological disposition and interpersonal situation. Verdi shifted the action to America exactly because for most Italians the New World constituted a white canvas, an unknown other, enabling Verdi to depict a social-psychological drama without specific historical restrictions. This is the role America played in cultural discourse, in many respects consistent with the ways in which opposing political factions, during the Revolutions of 1848, used the same references to the United States for very different purposes.

Verdi's strategy was facilitated by the fact that Italians did not have a clear idea about what life in the early modern English colonies was like. British readers associated the ports and whaling centers of Massachusetts with the hard, seafaring people they encountered in the works of Herman Melville. His pacific bestseller *Typee* was published in London in 1846, the less successful *Moby Dick* following in 1851. Italians had to wait another century to read Melville in translation.[76] Readers of Castiglioni, Botta, and Londonio knew about Boston through these authors' colorful descriptions of the growing conflict between Americans and the mother country, discussed in chapter 1. In these early Italian histories of the American Revolution, the Boston massacre of 1770 and local opposition to the imposition of taxes on tea played a particularly evocative role in describing life in Massachusetts, fitting the image of civic unrest that forms the background to Verdi's opera.

As the author of one of the most widely read Italian books on America, Botta had informed his readers that most English settlers in the New World had arrived at the time of the late Stuarts.[77] Therefore, for educated Italians Restoration England served as a possible source of information about colonial America. Walter Scott's historical novels also played an important role here. Italian translations had appeared since the early 1820s, often published simultaneously in different editions.[78] His longest novel, *Peveril of the Peak*, discussed a Jesuit attempt to assassinate Charles II. The memoirs of the Count de Grammont about life at Charles's court were also read in Italy. All these works reached a far more restricted audience than nineteenth-century opera.[79] Versions of *Maria Stuarda* by Carlo Cocca and Rossini, and the latter's *Elisabetta* and *La donna del Lago* (and his pasticcio of 1826, *Ivanhoe*), were all directly based on or influenced by the writings of Walter Scott. The same is true for the ballets and several operas by Pacini and similar works by Donizetti.[80] Many Italians would have been familiar with Carlo Pepoli's libretto for Vincenzo Bellini's last opera, *I puritani*, set during the English Civil War and featuring another complicated love story, this time between a Puritan and a Royalist.[81] Images derived from these works helped audiences to explain the relative grandeur of the first and last acts of Verdi's opera, which were relics of the original Swedish setting.

Referring to the opera's first scene, Filippo Filippi described the governor's residence: "a hall in the palace of Boston's English governor: sumptuous rooms with representatives, officers and commoners who are in attendance upon him, and sing his praises."[82] The scene did not seem to clash with the critic's own imaginings. To the Italian mind there was no particular reason to dissociate puritan New England from passionate and ill-starred love relationships. Nineteenth-century Italy associated political ideas from across the Atlantic with what they knew about England. Comparison—assimilating foreign facts into local knowledge—was a way to make sense of news from America. Commenting on act 2, Filippi likened the choruses in which the people praise the governor to "canti patriotici," similar to what Italian patriots were chanting at the time of Unification. Audiences interpreted what they saw through their own terms of reference.

Un ballo's only image of American landscape is a "field outside Boston" in act 2, the scene of the encounter between Riccardo and Amelia, with the later arrival of Renato and the conspirators. The fifth book of Carlo Botta's *History of the American War of Independence* had started with a description of Boston's beautiful geographical position in 1775, followed later on with an account of the popular exaltation in and around Boston after independence had been declared in 1776.[83] The widely read 1856 edition of Botta includes the introduction by Michele Amari, which adds to Botta's description a short section on Massachusetts in the seventeenth century, mainly focussing on the role of the Puritans, the state's constitution, and its bicameral system. Colonial Boston is praised for its civic institutions, which formed the basis for the city's role in the War of Independence.[84] In Amari's brief synthesis, colonial Massachusetts appears as an early version of the United States.

Verdi's field outside Boston retains nothing of Botta's idealized depiction of the American landscape and its people. Instead, the opera's *disposizione scenica* describes a truly gruesome setting of horror and desperation, with symbolic references to death and the decline of civilization. While classical elements in American architecture usually stand for ancient political virtues, Verdi's scene shows only the ruins thereof. The positioning of the gallows on the hill evokes images of the site of Golgotha. Arriving at the scene, Amelia (in Filippo Filippi's words) is terrorized, "invasa da superstizioso terrore." If we think about the New World as a place free of oppression, Mary Ann Smart's reading of act 2 has argued that Amelia's kneeling pose shows the subordination of her body to a higher force of spirit. One of the rare scenes where Verdi allows his characters to sing their love together, Amelia's kneeling scene represents the denial of the impulse of love, the sublimation of her whole persona. If she cannot overcome her adulterous love for Riccardo she hopes that her heart will finish "di batter e muor,'" to stop beating and die.[85]

Despite the apparent discrepancy between existing Italian descriptions of New England and Verdi's libretto, *Un ballo* was understood as an opera in which Verdi proved his capacity to speak a language of authenticity, for which the love scene in act 2 is a good example. For commentators the apparent lack of historical accuracy did not seem to undermine this impression. Filippi argued in his review of the prima that "no composer was so adept at swiftly varying local colour and sentiment, at identifying himself with each topic so as to transform at every turn its colour and style."[86]

What Verdi's America retains from early modern depictions of the New World is the exoticism of place and people, still present in the work of Leopardi.[87] References in the libretto and disposizione scenica to Creoles and people of different races served to exoticize the setting. It was exactly this quality that in the view of contemporary audiences and critics made Verdi's work authentic. According to the disposizione scenica the chorus includes people of black and white skin, mulattos as well as Creoles, united in praising the governor. During the final ballroom scene "the waiting is done by negroes, and everything breathes magnificence and hilarity."[88] The ethnic mix was an important aspect of Verdi's representation of America, one for which there would have been no place in the original Swedish setting. Despite the libretto's emphasis on magnificence and hilarity, from the drama's very beginning it becomes obvious that in Verdi's view America's ethnic diversity and cultural mix does not lead to a stable political community. A deciphering of the meaning associated with the different ethnic groups appearing in the opera reveals an important aspect of Italian perceptions of difference between the New and the Old Worlds.

It is difficult to assess what Verdi and Somma meant when they described Renato and members of the chorus as Creoles. Renato assumes a key role in Verdi's plot, with particular significance for the image of American political institutions that the opera creates and transmits. The nineteenth-century meaning of the term "Creole" differed according to time, space, and cultural context. While in colonial language the term was often used as a juridical category to create legal distinctions between groups of populations, in Europe it formed part of the repertoire that made the New World a different, exotic place. The usage of the term also reveals how in the Italian cultural imagination the distinction between North and South America, and its populations, remained blurred until well into the nineteenth century. Many Italians still knew more about South America, where more Italian migrants went, than about the Northern Republic. What they knew about South America was then read into their image of North America.

In most cases the term "Creole" was employed for people of European heritage who were born in the Americas. As both Spaniards and Creoles were usually white, the distinction was not an ethnic one; and it did not necessarily have economic or social significance, because Creoles often accumulated more wealth than the royal officials who were sent across the Atlantic; and frequently they were of nobler origin than the Spaniards who arrived later.

The main characteristic of the distinction was a spatial-political one, based on a negative *jus soli* applied to men born in the Indies.[89] The fact that they had lived for several generations in the New World left a suspicion of racial mixing, resulting in different shades of whiteness, which was one of the reasons why Creoles were not simply described as Europeans.[90] This included the possibility of sexual contact with "Indians," another category invented by Europeans, to describe "Native" people in an ethnic sense of the term. In Spanish America the term *criollo* also described the offspring of people from Africa who were born in the New World.[91] In New England, where Verdi's opera was set, the term "Creole" was often used for Europeans from the West Indies.[92] Of British, European, or mixed descent, they came into contact with people from New England through the slave economy and the administration of the British colonies. This might explain why Verdi's Creole Renato works in the service of the governor of Boston.[93] Creoles were rare in New England but formed part of the picturesque cultural and ethnic mix Italians associated with life in the New World.

Personally Verdi was not entirely unfamiliar with the category. The wife of his friend and collaborator Giuseppe Montanelli, discussed in the previous chapter as one of the protagonist's of the Revolution in Tuscany, was a Creole; and Verdi was probably aware of the Creole composer and pianist Louis Moreau Gottschalk (1829–69) from New Orleans, who impressed Berlioz, Chopin, and Bizet by integrating Afro-American and Latin American music into his work.[94] Personal contacts did not mean that Italians viewed Creoles without prejudice. In a review for the *Rivista Europea*, published in 1845, Cattaneo revealed what racial mixing involved, describing the *stirpe Messicana* as "lazy, superstitious, rather lustful, given to strong liquors. The remaining inhabitants are Zambos, a mixture of Indian and Negro, more industrious and active, but turbulent and heavy drinking as well."[95] Before Cattaneo, Claudio Linati, a patriot from Parma, had studied and described the Mexican population.[96] Carlo Botta in his *War of American Independence* mentioned "a certain Brandt, born of mixed blood, the most ferocious being ever produced by human nature, often too prodigal of similar monsters." A well-known figure, Joseph Brant was not mixed race but a Mohawk chief elevated by the British. Compagnoni described him as a "lion dressed up as a man."[97] These Italian descriptions of *mestizos* contrast sharply with the ways in which they were incorporated into the independent Latin American nations.[98] While many Italian exiles took part in the constitutional development of these countries, ethnic kinship was fundamental to the concept of their own nation.[99] This tension might explain Cattaneo's worry that "the Spanish blood diminishes" in the American colonies and will eventually disappear."[100]

A concept of cultural identity rooted in ethnicity and kinship made any mixed heritage suspicious. In the unfolding of Verdi's drama Renato serves to paint a particularly dark picture of life at the governor's court in Boston.

Once he discovers the affair between Riccardo and his wife, Renato offers the conspirators his own son as hostage in order to prove his commitment to the dark cause. Despite his intentions, the opera's final scene reveals that the relationship between Riccardo and Amelia had never been consummated, that Amelia had in fact remained pure. As a consequence, Renato turns out to be the opera's most tragic and perhaps its most disgraceful character, burdened with a double-edged guilt. Blindly devoted to his master Riccardo, Renato simultaneously distrusts his beloved and ultimately innocent wife. Cutting her prayers short—"sangue vuolsi e tu morrai" ("blood must flow, and you must die") is his only reply to her plea—he denies her the chance of exonerating herself. His distrust leads him to the betrayal and murder of his friend.

For the audience Renato plays an utterly discomforting role in the opera, revealing a deep sense of almost slavish loyalty, but also uncontrolled passion. His personality is shattered by profound dilemmas of human existence. Verdi's Creole certainly does not stand for the regenerative human force of life in the New World, which some of Latin America's national movements associated with their heritage of ethnic mixing. Breaking with the Enlightenment paradigm of the New World as an untouched and therefore better place—along the lines of Goethe's *Amerika, Du hast es besser*—the opera and its libretto do not convey a happy idea of America as a prelapsarian paradise or as the locus of mankind's new beginning.[101]

The depiction of magic forms another defining feature of Verdi's idea of American folklore, magic placed in the context of the supposedly modern reality of America. The description of the fortune-teller's dwelling (act 1, 6) offers a powerful example:

> On the left a hearth; the fire is lit, and the magic cauldron is steaming over a tripod; on the same side the opening of a dark recess. On the right a twisting stairway loses itself under the vault; at its end to the fore a small secret door. . . . In the centre a round table, from the roof and on the walls instruments and furnishings appropriate to the place are hung.

For Milan's *Gazetta musicale* "siamo nel regno del sovranaturale," in a "supernatural realm," an atmosphere reflected also in the music: "long and groaning notes of the bass clarinet, fanciful tremoli, the gloomy voice of a woman who talks amidst these noises."[102] The key to the sombre opening scene eludes the listener. Evoking her magical powers, Ulrica uses the voice of the *ùpupa*, the hoopoe, a topos of the then fashionable sepulchral literature, known to the informed reader or listener from Ugo Foscolo's poem *Dei sepolcri (On Tombs)* of 1807.[103] Previously, Verdi had used the bird's magical voice for the witches' scene in *Macbeth*.

The opera's commentators praise the effectiveness of the scene, and there is little to suggest that it disturbed the audience's preconceived ideas of life in the American colonies. Since the early nineteenth century the display of fantasy and the miraculous in opera and ballet constituted an important element of Italian *romantismo*. Associated with the foreign, it was a stylistic element audiences had no reason to question.[104] Therefore, what educated Italians saw on stage met their aesthetic expectations and resonated with what they read about in literary journals. In 1830 a translation of Walter Scott's essay "On the Supernatural in the Fictitious Composition" had appeared in the periodical *Indicatore lombardo* and as an appendix to his historical novel *Ufficiale di fortuna (A Legend of Montrose)*.[105] Verdi's play with magic responded to these debates.

It is the witch scene where composer and librettist remain closest to the narrative presented in Scribe's principal source, John Brown's *The Northern Courts*. Brown did not treat Ulrica as belonging to the natural world, offering instead a rational explanation of her skills: "Her calculations being founded upon practical knowledge of human weakness and folly, they were fully verified."[106] In Brown's account, the fortune-teller's insight into social relations and her use of informers explain the prediction of the king's assassination. Although Somma and Verdi closely followed the sequence of Brown's account (or Scribe's version thereof), there is no sense that any of the actors in the opera's plot are the subjects of their own history.[107] Linking Verdi's version of the narrative to the historical context of his opera's performance, *Un ballo in maschera* seems to raise profound questions over the reality of the modern age at the very moment when Italy entered this stage of its societal development.

Turning Gustavo into Riccardo

Although audiences and critics accepted Verdi's music as an authentic description of "creoles," "negroes," and the colonial administration of New England, the history of the plot's evolution from *Gustavo* to the masked ball in Boston needs further explanation, not least because the changes to the composer's original plan are frequently used to present Verdi as the political and aesthetic victim of his vicious censors. As mentioned earlier, Verdi's opera was based on Scribe's French libretto about the assassination of Gustaf III, to be performed at the San Carlo in Naples. When negotiations with the censors reached an impasse and Verdi was no longer prepared to make further compromises on the libretto, the composer set out to seek a new home for his work. In the meantime Verdi had also realized that the Kingdom of the Two Sicilies, where his new opera was meant to be premiered, did not yet apply the recent international conventions on authorship. Writing an opera for Naples therefore might have resulted in an important loss of royalty payments. Rome and its social and political elites were particularly keen on spectacular works of opera. The Apollo's powerful impresario Vincenzo Jacovacci promised Verdi to get his libretto accepted in no time at all. But the papal authorities likewise demanded changes to the work, prompting the decision to move the location of the drama across the Atlantic, to Massachusetts.[108]

Scribe had called his work on Gustav III an *opéra historique*, with the aim of putting on stage a historical event in as much detail as possible. This was exactly what Verdi did not want to do. As he explained in a letter to Vincenzo Torelli, he considered such an approach "too conventional."[109] After *I Lombardi, Giovanna d'Arco*, and *La battaglia di Legnano*, or most recently *Les vêpres siciliennes*, Verdi was not much interested in writing another opera on a specific historical-political event. Investigating human relationships, depicting personal character and psychology with the help of music, was what had interested Verdi since the 1850s. There were clear traces of this in *Macbeth*, but with *Il trovatore* and *La traviata* the psychology of his main characters and the relationship between them became the main aspect of his work. Through extracts in Carlo Rusconi's translation of Shakespeare, Verdi knew about August Wilhelm Schlegel's *Lectures on Dramatic Art and Literature*. We also know that he read Madame de Staël's *De l'Allemagne*, which discussed the same themes treated in the works of the Schlegel brothers, albeit in more accessible form. These readings helped Verdi to develop his own concept of dramatic unity and theatrical effect.[110] While he continued to write operas set in the past, history itself disappeared into the background, a change of emphasis for which he was severely criticized by some contemporary observers.[111] Meanwhile, a dehistoricized plot seemed appropriate for an opera set in America. As demonstrated in chapter 1, many Italians thought of the United States as a country untainted by history, living the experience of modern time without the constrictions of the past.

Verdi, however, is far from depicting life without history as a liberating experience. In the case of *Un ballo*, the use of masks throughout the opera—not just for the ball at the end but also during Riccardo's encounter with Ulrica and for Amelia's secret meeting with Riccardo—was more than a reference to specific courtly forms of entertainment. Instead, the masks stood for the alienating behavioral forms of modern individualized society, which had lost its organic origins.[112] Verdi presents himself as a critic of the modern human condition, which he associated with the dehistoricized society he imagined across the Atlantic. The change of locale allowed Verdi to fully focus his attention on the unfolding of the psychological drama between his main characters.

For those Italians who followed debates on America and the United States, the change of locale still worked: as chapters 2 and 3 have demonstrated, most Italians engaged with America in a more critical fashion than traditional historiography suggests; and they viewed American democracy as an experiment tied to the very specific conditions of a young and inexperienced country. A reading of *Un ballo* as an American opera, which actually met Verdi's particular dramatic needs, suggests that the narrative of Verdi as a victim of his censors—reflecting the claims of those commentators who are keen to politicize his patriotic role as bard of the Risorgimento—has been exaggerated. They overlook the extent to which the plot's move to America served the composer's own dramatic ambition. Verdi did not particularly mind the change of scene; and once it had been done, he recognized the advantage of moving the plot to America.

In addition to Verdi's own dramatic intentions, which other factors influenced the move to America? As a libretto based on the historical events in Sweden was unlikely to pass the censors, Verdi and Somma first had proposed to move the plot to Pomerania. However, since 1648 much of Pomerania had belonged to Sweden and was therefore far too close to the original plot. The Pomeranian House of Greifen was not a fairy-tale dynasty; they had been the rulers of a duchy residing in Stettin, which since the Middle Ages had supplied Scandinavia and the Holy Roman Empire with several kings and queens. But was regicide—and the opera's possible connection to the political situation in Italy—the censors' main concern? Politics merely form the background to the actual psychological drama between the protagonists, with the conspirators Samuel and Tom playing at best a marginal role in the opera. Arguably, moving the plot to colonial America allowed for an even more significant political reading of the libretto. From Carlo Botta and other sources Italians knew that discontent with governors and the tightening grip of the imperial administration on the North American colonies were closely linked to the outbreak of the American War of Independence.[113] Increasingly, the emergent American nation perceived the system of imperial administration and the imposition of governors as a form of foreign rule. This certainly was a topic that sounded familiar to Italians, who were engaged in fighting foreign rule in their own homeland. Moving the plot to America potentially increased the opera's political significance for Italian audiences. This would suggest that there must have been other, nonpolitical motives why an American opera was more acceptable to the censors than a plot set in Europe.

The opera's moral (or rather amoral) content was certainly bound to preoccupy the censors—a story revolving around adultery and guilty love, where the king (in the final version turned governor) desires and assaults the wife of his best friend and dedicated servant. This said, censorship was rarely applied consistently throughout the different Italian states; and Verdi's work was frequently criticized for its political as well as its moral content.[114] One of the demands of the Neapolitan censors was indeed for Amelia to become Renato's sister, destroying the adulterous triangle between Riccardo, Renato, and Amelia. While Verdi resisted the intervention of the Bourbon censors, the version devised for the Apollo in Rome was itself heavily trimmed, but in this case Verdi accepted a compromise. Rome did not object to the triangular love relationship as such but considered it inappropriate for such a relationship to take place in the Old World, in which the Catholic Church still claimed to determine moral conduct. They simply insisted on having this unseemly relationship moved across the Atlantic, where they considered Protestantism to undermine moral norms anyway. The work's depiction of immorality could not be tolerated within a European setting, but it seemed to fit with the censor's idea of a foreign American context. Turning Gustavo into an American governor might even have been a direct suggestion from Rome.[115]

Along with questions of morality, good taste, and religion, diplomatic relations often determined the decisions of the censors.[116] As Franco Venturi has demonstrated, since the late eighteenth century not only the United States but, perhaps surprisingly, the Kingdom of Sweden had also played a non negligible role in Italy's political imagination.[117] The social reforms of Gustav III and his response to the country's economic crisis went hand in hand with a curbing of the power of the estates, which in their turn started sympathizing with the ideas of the French Revolution.[118] It was on this basis that Gustav's assassin, Jacob Johan Anckarström, defended his act of tyrannicide. More relevant to the potential diplomatic implications of Verdi's opera were Gustav's religious reforms. Although Voltaire had praised Sweden as "the freest kingdom on earth," it did not recognize freedom of worship. Only under Gustav III were religious affairs relaxed. An ordinance of 1781 allowed foreign denominations (including Roman Catholicism) to have an organized religious life, as long as they did not proselytize.[119] These changes did not go unnoticed in Rome, a city that Gustav, as a great patron of the arts, was keen to visit. For the sake of political prestige, during his travels he also wished to be received by as many foreign rulers as possible, including the pope.

In 1783 Gustav made his journey to Italy and met Pope Pio VI in Rome, becoming the first Protestant monarch to be received by a pope: an event of considerable diplomatic significance. Pio treated Gustav with great respect and generosity and made him a Knight of the Golden Spur. On Christmas Day, together with Holy Roman emperor Joseph II, Gustav attended Mass at Saint Peter's, officiated by the pope. Gustav later commissioned a painting from Louis Jean Desprez featuring the moment of the Holy Communion in which the pope elevates the sacramental bread in front of the monarchs, depicting Joseph and Gustav as equals. A few days later, on New Year's Day, the pope guided Gustav through the new museum, the Pio-Clementino, arguably the world's greatest collection of antiquities, offering the king of Sweden personal advice on how to build his own collection in Stockholm.[120] Together with the Mass in Saint Peter's, the two princes' educated conversation on ancient art was among the most memorable events of Gustav's Italian journey.

To acknowledge its significance Gustav commissioned another painting, this time by the French neoclassical painter Bénigne Gagneraux (1756–95). A work of remarkable grandeur, the painting's composition was inspired by Raphael's School of Athens, showing a benevolent pope entering the Vatican galleries with his Swedish guest, surrounded by the highest dignitaries of both courts. Before the painting was shipped to Stockholm, a private viewing at

FIG. 15. Bénigne Gagneraux, *Pope Pio VI and Gustav III in the Vatican Museum*. National Gallery, Sternberg Palace, Prague. Photograph © National Gallery in Prague 2016.

the Vatican was arranged for the pope. Subsequently exhibited in the palace of the Cardinal de Bernis, the painting attracted considerable attention among the Roman nobility. Among many others, Goethe praised the work in his *Italienische Reise*. The pope made no secret of his admiration and decided to commission a copy for his own collection.[121] Gustav's visit to Rome was a diplomatic event of considerable historical significance, as important to the Swedish king as it was to the papal court. It was this privileged role of the Swedish king in the Vatican's diplomatic *annali* that caused Rome's decision to avoid any possible offense. Even half a century after the encounter between the two rulers the Vatican was keen not to spoil the carefully guarded image of its diplomatic tradition.

Although Somma and Verdi transposed Scribe's play into a completely new context, the Italian periodical *Il Trovatore* reported in 1860 that Scribe tried to oppose the representation of *Un ballo* in Paris on the basis that his rights as author had been violated.[122] Verdi's American version still featured many elements from its original Swedish model. What is more, Cencetti's *disposizione scenica* for *Un ballo* was clearly influenced by Auber's opera based on Scribe, even if it is unlikely that Verdi had seen the opera performed.[123] Considering that Verdi and Somma had invested a lot of time in earlier versions of the opera, the question has to be asked why they themselves never considered returning to the plot's original Swedish version, as modern stage directors (and musicologists from Dent to Gossett) frequently do. As the examples of *I Lombardi, Rigoletto, La traviata, Stiffelio,* and *Les vêpres siciliennes* demonstrate, Verdi often reworked existing operas, changing their setting or producing new versions of earlier works in order to meet specific requirements of production.[124] He usually did not hesitate to return to the original plot if there was a particular rationale for it. He never did so for *Un ballo*; he never adapted the American version to the original Swedish setting. At the time of *Un ballo*'s premiere, Rome was still under papal administration, but shortly afterward the political situation in Italy had changed, leading to a relaxation of censorship. In 1860, when the opera was first performed in Bologna, some critics even suggested returning the plot to the court of Gustav III.[125] Verdi and Riccordi refused. Why did they resist the temptation?

Initially, Verdi regretted the pressures to change the plot: "A pity! To have to renounce the pomp of a court like that of Gustavo III; and it will be difficult to find a Duke to compare with that Gustavo!! Poor poets and poor composers!"[126] But when the censors wanted the plot to be moved outside Europe, it was Verdi himself who suggested America. The only alternative he briefly considered was the Caucasus (where social relations between lovers, friends, and their spouses were presumably as terrible as they were in New England).[127] Nevertheless, he quickly settled on the American locale, without considering other options.

There were other factors too that made *Un ballo*'s return to Sweden difficult. Despite setting the American version in the seventeenth century, Verdi definitely wanted the opera to be a "modern" drama, rejecting the idea of changing the time frame to the Middle Ages: his censors suggested that the *strega* Ulrica would easily fit into a medieval drama, "when people still believed in witches" (although Scribe's sources had specified that Gustav III as well as the queen consulted "their" fortune-teller, Madame Arvedsen, as recently as 1792).[128] Instead, Verdi and Somma decided to make their witch part of the ethnic exoticism associated with their imagined America. Ulrica became a witch "dell'immondo sangue dei negri" (of the foul blood of the Negroes) (act 1, 1, 18).[129] The Burkes' *Account of the European Settlements in America,* which had been published in Somma's Venice in 1763, included a detailed section on witches in New England and their persecution by the colonial administration.[130] Having worked with representations of witches before, Verdi had a clear idea of their function in the unfolding of the drama. Already in *Macbeth,* rather than representing historical reality, the witches fulfilled a specific psychological function: giving voice to the destructive elements in the depths of the human soul, in this case the dark forces governing the protagonist Lady Macbeth.[131] Early commentators on *Un ballo* recognized the similarity in the dramatic function of Ulrica and Lady Macbeth.[132] Meanwhile, compared to Verdi's earlier work, Ulrica plays a more active role in the opera and offers the audience a key to the psychological disposition of both Riccardo and Amelia. Verdi had no problem using this dramatic device in a modern American setting. Returning it to Sweden would have required very substantial adaptations.

Virgil in America

Ulrica's role in the American drama requires a further step of analysis. Acting as a fortune-teller, she is presented by Verdi and Somma as a modern Sibyl, negotiating between mortals and superhuman powers. As Anselm Gerhard has pointed out, for the educated listener or reader, Riccardo's "Tu, sibilla, che tutto sai" (act 1, 2, 61) was a direct allusion to a classical context and possibly to Virgil's *Aeneid*, the great epic about the fall of Troy and the origins of Rome.[133] As the following section will show, references to Virgil are instrumental in creating a direct connection between the opera's American plot and the future of the Italian nation.

Although Auber's and Mercadante's versions of the drama also called the fortune-teller a Sibyl, in Verdi's opera the use of the term is a far more conscious reference to classical literature and to narratives about the fall and rise of civilizations.[134] While drafting the libretto for *Un ballo*, Somma was also working on his tragedy *Cassandra*, concerned precisely with the theme of prophecy and with the consequences of the fall of Troy, perhaps the single most important topos in Europe's literary tradition. Verdi held a copy of the play's first edition, with dedication from Somma, in his library.[135] Unlike Aeschylus, Somma did not call his piece *Agamemnon* but decided to focus specifically on Agamemnon's captive and lover, the daughter of King Priam. The most significant connection between Somma's two pieces is the importance awarded to the gift of prophecy.[136] Cassandra's prophecies, like those of Ulrica, were fatefully met with disbelief. The astonishing parallels between Somma's libretto and Virgil's *Aeneid* suggest that Somma introduced them in full awareness of their resonance among educated Italians. The petrifying atmosphere evoked by the sets and the music of Verdi's second act bears startling similarities to Virgil's description of the underworld, when in book 6 of the *Aeneid* the hero descends into Hades to meet his former lover Dido, the queen of Carthage. Somma, like Virgil, tells us a story about the impossibility of love. Meanwhile, Aeneas's descent into the underworld is also the passage in which the hero most clearly expresses his patriotic vision for Rome's future mission, a theme Virgil picks up in his much-quoted *Fourth Eclogue*.[137] Verdi's opera concludes with a somewhat similar patriotic outburst, in which the last words of the dying Riccardo praise the future of the American nation: "Addio, diletta America . . . addio miei figli per sempre!" (act 3, 75).

Relating Virgil's idiosyncratic *Eclogues*, or Pastorals, to Somma's craftsmanship might seem farfetched but appears to be crucial if Verdi's depiction of America is meant to be understood as a philosophical reflection on the relationship between Italy's past and its future. Moreover, these references were entirely consistent with Europe's Neoplatonic tradition, which believed in the Christian fulfillment of ancient prophecies. Exploring Virgil's founding myth, Julius Caesar claimed Aeneas as his direct ancestor, a theme that is then carried through the classical tradition, via Dante's *Divina comedia* and the Renaissance into the Risorgimento. Throughout the eighteenth and nineteenth centuries references to Virgil remained commonplace in academic as well as in less specialized literature, including Carli's *Lettere americane*, Rosmini theological writings, and the political thought of Filangieri and Romagnosi.[138] The Victorians compared the collapse of the Roman Republic in 1849 to the triumph of Augustus, the historical context that motivated Virgil to write the *Aeneid*. In 1820 the British radical poet William Blake, who greatly admired the American Revolution and was a friend of Thomas Paine, had produced engravings for Robert Thornton's commentary on *The Eclogues*, which were read as subversive of the existing social and political order. Finally, Thomas Carlyle's writings on the French Revolution made ample reference to Virgil's Rome, a tradition that directly influenced the thought of Italian exiles including Pepoli, Galenga, and Mazzini.[139] Ferdinand Lassalle opened his book in support of the Italian War of 1859 with a quote from Virgil.[140]

These examples demonstrate that drawing connections between Virgil and modern politics was by no means exceptional in nineteenth-century Europe. In light of this tradition the parallel between the literary context of Verdi's libretto and the political context of the opera's performance seems striking. Like Virgil's epic, *Un ballo* deals with the complexity of interpersonal relations as well as with the rise and fall of a polity. Somma and Verdi chose to use these contextual references for an opera whose premiere was to coincide with the fulfillment of the Risorgimento's political ambition, nurtured over generations with the help of the nation's literary imagination, in which Virgil had played a most prominent role. In this context the allusion to Virgil's *Fourth Eclogue* seems particularly relevant. Beyond its messianic message, it offered a design of world history—*magnus ab integro saeclorum nascitur ordo*—that deeply marked ideas of Italy's mission in the world, picked up among other Risorgimento political thinkers by Gioberti in his *Primato*.[141] Since 1782 the same passage from Virgil had been quoted on the Great Seal of the United States, used to authenticate official documents.

Verdi and Somma built on these intertextual references. Beneath the unfolding of the dramatic action itself, Verdi's opera creates a connection between three key moments of different civilizations: the legendary origins of ancient Rome; the beginnings of modern America; and the future of the Italian nation. Verdi and his librettist use their work to rethink the relationship between past and present, ancient and modern. Read in this context, *Un ballo in maschera* works only as an American opera and as a reflection on Italy's primato, Italians'

preoccupation with their place in world history. If the opera describes the colonization of the New World as the troublesome transition toward a new age, it
invites the audience to speculate about Italy's own path into the modern world.

Verdi and "il suo tempo"

The opera's American setting came to form a crucial aspect of its worldwide
success. For Verdi, the changes to the plot constituted less of a problem than
later historians would have us believe. Early on, Verdi wrote to Vincenzo Torelli, secretary of the San Carlo in Naples, that he did not think "there should
be any difficulty in moving the scene elsewhere."[142] Once the Roman version
had been completed, he even informed Somma that the libretto had gained by
moving the plot to America.[143]

What is more, *Gustavo III* had never been an ideal scenario. Originally,
Verdi had planned to finally write his opera based on King Lear, an idea that
he ultimately dismissed.[144] The alternative could not possibly be *Gustavo III*.
As Julian Budden argued, "a plot fifty years old, already set by at least three
composers of note."[145] While a generation earlier Europe's frenzy for Scribe
had reached almost epidemic dimensions, from the late 1850s the French
playwright was increasingly considered a man of the past, his oeuvre of over
four hundred *pièces de théâtre* in all possible genres perceived as a commod-
ity, produced by a collective of up to 130 professional coauthors.[146] Of the
more famous composers only Offenbach, with his *Barkouf* of 1860, produced
another work based on Scribe. Instead, a modern opera set in Boston was
something completely new. Verdi wrote an opera that related to his audiences'
own preoccupation with modern change.[147] The fact that the opera was set
in America, depicting unfamiliar social forms and human relations, became
part of this story; and Verdi himself knew that *Un ballo* was different from
anything he had written before.

Aware of the composer's original plans, the *Gazzetta musicale di Napoli*
ventured the opinion that a "governor of Boston doesn't present the same interest as the original topic of the drama by Scribe"; but the reviewer admitted
that "situations of great effect and of continuously growing interest make the
argument one of the best works of popular-lyric poetry."[148] The critic of *La
Fama* accused the work of being "troppo popolare e quasi volgare";[149] but the
opera's essentialist account of interpersonal relations does not require a royal
court. As Milan's *Gazetta musicale* told its readers:

> The end of King Gustav is a story purely of passionate love, framed by the
> luxury of a court: the plotting, the viciousness, all the dark and brilliant
> colours only serve the purpose, the variation and the inner harmony of
> the plot, which simply by changing proportions adapts itself to common
> citizens as well as to royalty, in no matter what latitudes. We say this

beforehand in order to respond to any objections by anybody alarmed by the need to shift the scene from one hemisphere to the other.[150]

A plot set in America seemed more real and relevant to modern society than a drama set at a royal court. Filippi claimed that the drama and its effects are enhanced by the fact that it is no longer based on historical facts, that America indeed had no history.[151] The opera's nonhistorical setting and its emphasis on the human drama evolving between its main characters was clearly reflected in Verdi's musical style, a music that easily adapted to the context in which it was performed. The great Italian music of the first half of the century had been superseded by a new style that better fitted modern times, "a brilliant reflex of the present civilisation, an eloquent and ideal commentary of our history," according to Filippi.[152] It was psychological and dramatic realism that made Verdi's music modern. Filippi concludes that with *Un ballo* "Verdi ha compreso il suo tempo."[153] Verdi understood his own time.

Returning for one last time to possible political interpretations of the censors' intervention, there is further reason to reassess arguments over the alleged political content of Verdi's original plans.[154] The libretto proposed by the Neapolitan censors was in some respects more explicitly political than the original version proposed by Somma and Verdi: an opera on the conflicts between Guelphs and Ghibellines, and still indeed a libretto about the assassination of a political leader. In the context of the Italian Risorgimento this version would have seemed extremely timely, engaging directly with the highly politicized debates on Italy's medieval past.[155] This choice of the censors would suggest that their main concern was not politics, but questions over the moral implications of Verdi's plot. Moreover, Verdi had just completed an opera that took place against the background of a Guelph rebellion: *Simon Boccanegra*. This context made the Neapolitan suggestion unattractive for Verdi. The fact that the author of the version suggested by Naples, Domenico Bolognese, was an official poet of the Bourbon's Teatro San Carlo, and could therefore be considered to be politically more loyal, means little: shortly after, in 1860, he wrote the text for an anthem by Erico Petrella celebrating Vittorio Emanuele as the new king of Italy.[156] Previously, Verdi had worked with Salvadore Cammarano, another poet officially assigned to the San Carlo, who wrote the libretti for *Alzira*, *La battaglia di Legnano*, *Luisa Miller*, and *Il trovatore*.[157] On the whole it seems most likely that Verdi rejected the Neapolitan suggestions because it would have required him to overhaul the opera from start to finish. Although the San Carlo remained unsuccessful in its attempt to impose Bolognese's libretto, they did not object to the version Verdi and Somma produced for Rome. Already before the Roman premiere, Naples asked Verdi's publisher Ricordi for a staging of the work in Naples.[158] Contrary to claims made by some of the national-romantic literature on Verdi, the assassination of the ruler was not the main concern of the censors. A political reading of the different versions of the libretto, which tries to present Verdi as the censors' patriotic victim, is misleading and only contributes to the political myths created around the composer during his lifetime and ever since.

Rome seemed unconcerned with adorning its cultural life with a new work by Italy's compositore nazionale.[159] In 1844 Rome had accepted the performance of Verdi's *I due Foscari*, a political plot featuring a forced abdication. Considering that just a year before the opera's premiere Mazzinians had tried to stage an uprising in the Papal Legations, it seems remarkable that Rome had not been more fretful of the opera's content. In 1848 the papal regime in Rome permitted the performance of *La battaglia di Legnano*—before the Republic, at a time when the political and ecclesiastical censors of the papal regime were still in place.[160] Either the work's political message was more blurred than later commentators suggest, or the censors turned a blind eye to a libretto that, in the context of the Italian Risorgimento, could be understood as promoting the idea of an independent Italy. For the performance of *Il trovatore*, also premiered in Rome, most references to religion had to be omitted, but other controversial scenes survived, despite the fact that the periodical *Civiltà cattolica* regarded the work as one of the most decadent plots in the entire history of opera.[161]

In the case of *Un ballo*, the pope personally granted permission for the production. Rules on censorship were fluid; and the performance of great works of opera was regarded as important enough for the city to compromise on content.[162]

Lincoln's Un ballo

What turns the early performances of *Un ballo* into a political event is not so much the libretto, but the changing political landscape in Italy and abroad. During the spring of 1859, shortly after the opera's premiere in Rome, the Second War of Independence ran its course, with the consequence that the Habsburgs' military bastions in the peninsula collapsed. *Un ballo* became the opera most closely connected with the events of Italian Unification, an opera composed by the nation's most celebrated composer, a man of sufficient patriotic credentials to give political meaning to the fact that *Un ballo* coincided with Italy's Unification. Verdi's celebrity—much more than the political content of his libretti—made him compositore nazionale. *Un ballo* became the work used to celebrate the Unification of Italy.

The world stage was itself marked by political changes that created an important context for the opera's impact on audiences. One of the first Americans to see the new opera was president-elect Abraham Lincoln. As the *New York Times* reported,

The party occupied a large prosecution box on the right-hand side of the house, and entered shortly after the performance had commenced. There was no demonstration until after the first act, when the President elect's presence having been discovered by a few persons familiar with his appearance, (there was nothing whatever to distinguish the box in which he sat, or attract the public attention,) a round of applause brought him to his feet.[163]

The fact that the opera by the famous Italian composer was set in America contributed to its immense success across the Atlantic.[164] According to the *Brooklyn Eagle* "a good deal of fun" was made of Verdi's depiction of "manners and customs of the old Boston Puritans," but hardly any opera had ever attracted so much excitement among New York audiences.[165] The New York performances of this "latest novelty in the operatic world" were seen as a symbiosis of Old and New World culture.[166] When the company finally recognized the president-elect in his box "the artists sang the "Star Spangled Banner"—at least Mesdames PHILLIPS and HINCKLEY did, for the Italians, although they have been here for many years, have not yet mastered the difficulties of the language, and could not, of course, condescend to sing it. Entrusted to two American girls, the anthem received the best of treatment, and was vehemently applauded."[167]

Despite the joy of these moments, contrasting with the tense political climate in the weeks leading up to the Civil War, the libretto alarmed the security forces. As the *New York Herald* reported, the police received notice of a plot to kill Lincoln, to coincide with the onstage murder of the governor. Lincoln and his wife were safely escorted away before the final scene.[168] In light of later events, Lincoln's decision to leave early certainly seems significant. Did Americans remember the incident when Lincoln was shot in a theater four years later? Through the connection with its New York premiere *Un ballo* also became part of the history of the American Civil War.

The international resonance of Verdi's operas invariably played a role in the appreciation of his works at home. In this case the fact that the opera was set in America became significant in itself. Shortly after the New York premiere the American Civil War broke out, adding a further semantic dimension to the work's reception: for the first time political events from across the Atlantic were discussed on the front pages of Italian newspapers. The break-up of the American union was seen in close connection with Italy's own unification, its unfolding Civil War in the South, and the deposition of the pontiff, perceived by many Italians as a symbolic patricide. The trauma associated with Unification seemed to echo the reference to sin and fraternal war on the way to freedom in Virgil's *Fourth Eclogue*: *sceleris uestigia nostri*.[169] Was the Italian union going to survive after the nation's founder Camillo Cavour unexpectedly died, just weeks after the Kingdom of Italy had been declared?[170] As discussed in more detail in the following chapter, both supporters and opponents of Unification drew close connections between events at home and the outbreak of the Civil War across the Atlantic. Verdi's opera helped to negotiate this relationship.

Compared to Verdi's understanding of "tinte locali," the music written to negotiate this relationshipe between the New and the Old World would soon assume a very different tone. Jack Sullivan has argued that most "New World Symphonists," from Dvořák to Stravinsky, were driven by a direct engagement with American culture.[171] Where personal experience of the United States was limited, writers such as Cooper, Longfellow, and Henry James, and later T. S. Eliot and Melville, supplied the scripts for this exercise. In the case of Verdi we know that his library contained early editions of Cooper's *The Pathfinder*, a sequel to the hugely popular *Last of the Mohicans*, and *The Spy*, both English-language editions, published in Paris and Leipzig respectively.[172] Verdi's wife at least was said to read English well.

There is one further hint as to the couple's direct engagement with contemporary events in the United States. At the height of the success of Verdi's new opera the composer's wife, Giuseppina Strepponi, passed on a book from her library to a moderate member of the new Italian parliament, the writer Giovanni Minghelli Vaini. It was a copy of Harriet Beecher Stowe's famous novel of 1852, *Uncle Tom's Cabin*, of which the Verdis had several copies in French as well as in English with Italian notes.[173] The novel circulated widely in Italy and was not unrelated to the performance history of *Un ballo in maschera*: the opera's Roman prima coincided with a staging of Giuseppe Rota's *Bianchi e neri*, a hugely successful ballet adaptation of Stowe's novel, premiered at La Scala in 1853 and then repeatedly touring the entire peninsula.[174] Florence in 1861 and Naples in 1862 likewise staged Verdi's *Un ballo* in combination with *Bianchi e neri*, both works presented during the same night.

The enormous success of *Bianchi e neri*, first in Milan and then all over Italy, and the Italian debates on Stowe's novel, in which Verdi's wife took part, suggest that it was *Uncle Tom* rather than romantic poetry that influenced the composer's invention of an American setting for his new work. What exactly *Uncle Tom* meant to Italians will be discussed in the next chapter, but the combination of *Un ballo* with *Bianchi e neri* transformed the audiences' theatrical experience into an evening on an American theme, cementing the significance of *Un ballo* as an American opera. The America these two works depicted was not a happy place. Race played only a secondary role in Verdi's opera, but as a consequence of the opera's combination with Rota's ballet it clearly marked the work's reception.

Most Italians at the time of Unification did not have the means to approach Verdi's opera with a clear idea of what North America stood for, despite the role the United States had played in Risorgimento political thought. The relative ignorance of audiences made the impact of Verdi's and Stowe's images of America still more compelling. Risorgimento political thought never wholly transcended the idea of America as a savage other, a New World without civilization, profoundly different from the Old World. Theater played an important role in transmitting this image of a New World characterized by the absence of civilization. The following chapter investigates an even more powerful and also a more brutal image of America, which offered a kind of authenticity Verdi's operatic America lacked.

CHAPTER FIVE

A War for Uncle Tom: Slavery and the American Civil War in Italy

For some years already, Americans embarrass the friends of freedom every day. To the crime of keeping up slavery they added another crime of denying the black race any form of education, as well as the crime of denying the free slaves any guaranties, who are always exposed to the threat of being picked up and thrown back into slavery.

—J.C.L. SIMONDE DE SISMONDI, 1836[1]

The principle in the name of which Garibaldi has sent a salute to Lincoln—the principle that God has imposed as the aim of the American battles . . .—is the most sacred of all. . . . It is the principle of humanity, the principle which claims that wherever there exists a capacity for learning, for progress, for association, there is the finger of God.

—G. MAZZINI, 1863[2]

"Of the Foul Blood of Negroes"

In Verdi's opera *Un ballo in maschera*, the only black character to assume a leading role was the fortune-teller Ulrica. Although the opera's plot is not explicitly centered on issues of race or racial prejudice, the judge makes an overtly pejorative comment on Ulrica, describing her as "dell'immondo sangue de' negri" (act 1, 1), "of the foul blood of negroes."[3] Contemporary commentators noticed the wording of this phrase—it is one of the very few instances where Filippo Filippi, in his review for the *Gazzetta musicale di Milano*, quotes directly from the libretto, highlighting the sentence in italics. The incidence is followed by a controversial discussion of Ulrica's alleged racketeering, during which Oscar launches into a spirited defense of the fortune-teller ("Diffenderla vogl'io!"). Although the incident presents a relatively short moment in the opera, Filippi's review suggests a certain sensibility toward the race issue in Italy. Depictions of the New World's racial diversity were by no means new for the Italian stages. But during the 1850s, the representation of race had moved from picturesque descriptions of America's black and Native populations as "good" but "savage," to a much more politicized discussion of race, and of slavery in particular.

This final chapter will take us from the 1850s to the Unification of Italy and the American Civil War. Abraham Lincoln became president of the United States just ten days before the king of Piedmont-Sardinia Vittorio Emanuele II was proclaimed king of Italy; and the United States was the first country to recognize the Kingdom of Italy. As the chapter will show, many Italians developed a better understanding of the events that shook their own lives by looking at the turmoil across the Atlantic. Despite the fact that in the Italian South Unification produced a Civil War in its own right, for many Italian observers slavery and the excesses of the US Civil War served to draw a line between barbarism and civilization.

Slavery in Italian Political Thought

In 1853 Milan's Teatro alla Scala premiered the ballet *Bianchi e neri (Whites and Blacks)*, a spectacular adaptation of Harriet Beecher Stowe's novel *Uncle Tom's Cabin* by the star of Italian choreography, Giuseppe Rota. The ballet became one of the greatest success stories in the history of Italian dance.[4] Although a rather free adaptation of the novel in not more than six or seven scenes, depending on the version, Rota's ballet presents the dehumanizing brutality of a slaveholding society with unfailing clarity. While touring most of the peninsula's major theaters, *Bianchi e neri* became a crucial point of reference in Italians' critical assessment of life in the United States, presented in stark contrast to the focus of earlier representations of America as a land of liberty and enlightened principles. What is more, educated Italians could read the ballet's title as a reference to Italy's own sanguineous divisions between the medieval Guelfs, the supporters of the papacy (often described as *bianchi* or Whites) and the Ghibellines, supporters of the Empire (described as *neri* or Blacks). As these conflicts of the twelfth and thirteenth centuries were often described in terms of civil war, the reference made the ballet's American context directly relevant to Italian spectators. *Bianchi e neri* transformed the ways in which Italians discussed and imagined the New World.

How did slavery affect Italians' view of the United States during the mid-1850s, before the outbreak of the American Civil War? The periodicals of the Risorgimento period occasionally referred to slavery in the New World, but their focus was often on Latin America.[5] This does not mean that Italians were unaware of the extent to which the United States' rapid rise in the world economy was dependent on slave labor. This chapter opened with a quote by Simonde de Sismondi, at the time still immensely influential among educated Italians, pointing to the perverse contradiction between American notions of freedom and the maintenance of institutionalized slavery. For Sismondi slavery was the first thing to come to mind when mentioning the United States in his book on the constitutions of free peoples, published in 1836. In his view, the existence of slavery overshadowed any other aspect of America's democratic republicanism, explaining why the United States played only a very minor role in his study of modern constitutions. Although at that time Sismondi had already read Tocqueville, a nation whose economy was based on slavery simply could not count as being free.[6]

Unlike the British and the French, who had participated in debates over abolition for several decades, Italians had no direct experience of colonization and the slave economy. During the Middle Ages cities like Venice and Genoa had been important centers of the slave trade, as briefly referred to in Verdi's abovementioned opera *Simon Boccanegra*, but in the late eighteenth and early nineteenth centuries debates on abolition did not receive the same attention as in Spain, Cuba, or Brazil, where the issue was at the center of political debate. The famous and widely referenced autobiography of the freed slave Olaudah Equiano, first published in 1789, was translated in the United Provinces, Russia, and Germany, but not in Italy.[7] A certain Italian distance from the debates on abolition does not mean that slavery was not recognized as a defining feature of the colonial expansion of other European powers. Rather, Italians were in a position to contrast their humanitarian tradition to attitudes of other countries and their involvement in European expansion. The Burkes' *Account of the European Settlements in America*, translated into Italian in 1763 and discussed in the introduction to this book, included three chapters on the fate of the slaves in the British colonies of the New World. They describe the British approach to the exploitation of slave labor as possibly the most complete system of forced labor existing anywhere in the world, leading to an especially deplorable situation for the black populations of the colonies.[8]

Among the papers Ugo Foscolo took into his London exile in 1815 was the manuscript *Della servitù dell'Italia*, in which the poet replied to some of the criticism he had received for his ideas of a post-Napoleonic order in northern Italy. Rejecting any unfavorable comparison between Italy and England, he points specifically to the moral corruption he associates with the British role in the slave trade: "I looked for fairness among the English, famous for the robustness of their laws, the impartiality of their courts, for the prosperity of their arts and the freedom of their citizens; and I found ships full of black men in chains, scourged, and brought from their hovels in Africa to the glebe of America."[9] By the time he was writing, Britain had abolished the slave trade, though not the institution of slavery itself. Although this section of Foscolo's work remained unpublished, it documents Italians' awareness of the darker aspects of Britain's role in the world economy. Sharing similar concerns, Pellegrino Rossi concludes the second volume of his political economy with a detailed and powerful condemnation of slavery, putting the main emphasis on the British slave economy and mentioning the United States only briefly. In addition to citing moral grounds for abolition, he points to the economic disadvantages of an economy based on slavery, similar to the arguments made by the Burkes.[10] A rather brief mention of the slave economy in Filangieri motivated Benjamin Constant to discuss the slave trade in his commentary on the Italian's *Scienza della Legislazione*, turning an Italian debate into an international one.[11] Finally, Giuseppe Ferrari's *Filosofia della Rivoluzione* includes an important chapter on slavery but does not mention the United States.[12]

As for the early Italian histories of the United States, discussed at the beginning of this book, Botta includes a short paragraph on slavery in his introductory chapter. According to the Piedmontese historian, observing on a daily basis the fate of their own slaves had taught Americans to cherish their freedom.[13] While from a modern perspective this argument seems morally corrupt, it reflects a widely held view of individual freedom in the Ancient World, where the experience of free citizens living alongside slaves informed the political concept of *libertas*, referring directly "to the status of non-slavery."[14] Writing in the early 1820s, Botta expects the institution of slavery to disappear for economic reasons, when the mechanization of agriculture would increasingly narrow the slave owners' economic advantage.

Although he was a great admirer of American freedom, for Count Castiglione slavery contradicted the most basic laws of humanity. Without engaging in complex debates on natural rights, Castiglioni's analysis largely ignores eighteenth-century philosophical discourse, describing slavery simply as the United States' "deadly scourge."[15] Meanwhile, his sympathy with the American political experiment led him to compare the condition of American slaves favorably with those working on British Caribbean sugar plantations. Taking a related view, Compagnoni argued that the lives of slaves in Virginia did not differ much from those of the settlers themselves.[16]

The assessment of Botta, Compagnoni, and Castiglione notwithstanding, for a majority of Italian commentators the institution of slavery raised serious questions about the economic and moral conditions on which the project of European expansion had been built. Thinkers more openly hostile to the American Revolution rejected the hypocrisy of those patriots who signed "with one hand the Declaration of Independence, while holding in their other hand the cane over the heads of their fearful slaves," as the Venetian traveler and Jacobine Francesco Apostoli put it.[17] The aforementioned Antonio Rosmini concludes his critique of modern democracy with a detailed comment on the institution of slavery in the United States, largely based on his reading of Tocqueville.[18] For a less academic readership the 1835 Italian translation of George Hamilton's travel account offered a most depressing description of American slaves in Cincinnati, depicting the sadistic brutality of their masters in disturbing detail.[19] As these sources show, even before the publication of Harriet Beecher Stowe's best seller these arguments were not confined to debates in philosophical circles.

As one of the best-informed Italian commentators in the field of political economy, Carlo Cattaneo held views on slavery that deserve a special mention. In 1833 he discussed in the Milanese *Bollettino di notizie statistiche ed economiche*, the House of Commons' decision to compensate British slave owners for the abolition of slavery in the British colonies. That year the government set up the Slave Compensation Commission, which over the following decade would pay out £20 million to (mostly absentee) British slave owners, whereas the enslaved received nothing. Many of those awarded compensation were members of the empire's metropolitan elites, including many MPs, but there also were considerable numbers of clergymen as well as small-scale slave owners. In the West Indies alone, over thirty thousand British slave owners received compensation for more than 655,000 slaves.[20]

While Pellegrino Rossi had been full of praise for the British Empire's determination to end slavery, Cattaneo made no secret of his repulsion at the decision to compensate slave owners with taxpayers' money for something they had no right to own, especially at a time of increased economic hardship for England's lower classes.[21] For Cattaneo, Britain's slave economy was able to survive for so long only owing to the empire's protectionism, barring other producers of similar goods from access to the British market, resulting in hugely inflated prices for colonial goods. While in the context of his article no mention is made of slavery in the United States, another piece, also published in 1833 and discussing US tariffs, describes the institution of slavery in South Carolina as an "offence against the laws of humanity."[22] Again, Cattaneo links the moral to an economic argument, explaining the negative effects of slavery on the South's economic development, where

> idleness became a sign of freedom and status, it was corrupt, but more profitable than a plentiful industry. The white man who lowered himself to the level of himself undertaking servile labour was looked down upon, as if he risked contaminating his own rank; he was persecuted and expelled. This is the reason why both ship-building as well as heavy industry became so prosperous in the Northern states, the so-called New England, while they did not take off at all in the Southern territories, among the masters of the slaves.[23]

In Cattaneo's view it was largely a consequence of the slave economy that the South depended on imports, on which the federal government wished to levy taxes. He was appalled at the idea that the rebels from South Carolina invoked the name of God and humanity to claim their rights and to protest against the alleged federal oppression, while "their representatives sanctioned a law which forbids to teach negroes how to read," thus "declaring war against the alphabet."[24] Sismondi, quoted at the start to this chapter, produced exactly the same argument. Cattaneo welcomed the constitution of Liberia, where former slaves were able to govern themselves free from European interference.[25] Only later did he realize the levels of mortality among those former slaves and their alleged involvement in a new slave trade among the black populations of Africa.[26] Like other Italian commentators before him, for instance Genovesi, in the 1840s Cattaneo still expected the mechanization of agriculture to resolve the problem of American slavery: machines would replace those "countless arms," ignoring the fact that at precisely that time the American South developed plans for using slaves in mining and for building new railroads.[27]

Despite these occasional references to slavery in writings about the United States, among a majority of Italians there was little awareness of the fact that slaves constituted America's largest financial asset, more important than the value of its banks, factories, or railroads. Until relatively late, when the conflict between North and South became part of international political debates, slavery was not recognized as an inherent aspect of American modernity and its economic expansion. Instead, most Italians associated slavery with ancient Rome or with orientalizing images of non-European societies. Italians were aware of Voltaire's denunciation of slavery in *Candide* but read his famous satire as a contribution to philosophical debates, without direct implications for the political economy in other societies. Consequently, political commentators frequently used the term "slavery" in a more abstract sense, for instance when Cattaneo referred to the rule of the Habsburgs in 1848 as a form of enslavement.[28]

During the years leading up to the American Civil War, with more information on American politics becoming available, Italian awareness of slavery as a distinctive feature of life in the New World changed dramatically, with striking effects on how Italians imagined life in the United States. Referring to abolition in two writings of 1860 as his "santa causa," his "holy cause," Mazzini reminded his readers that "Negro slavery" still contaminated America's republican institutions.[29] In 1846 he had written a poem expressing his hopes that the American Republic would put an end to the evil of slavery. He regularly contributed to the American abolitionist periodical *Liberator*, which considered Italian independence and the liberation of American slaves as connected issues.[30] But consternation at American slavery reached beyond Mazzini's revolutionary republicanism. Shortly before Italian Unification, in November 1860, a report on the US presidential elections in the Florentine liberal newspaper *La Nazione* simply referred to "la vergognosa piaga della schiavitù."[31] The combination of the words *vergognoso* (shameful) and *piaga* (plague) had become a standardized form of speaking about slavery in Italy.

In line with these political debates, representations of slavery onstage were revived; and their reception demonstrates that they directly reflected society's concern over this issue. In addition to his *Uncle Tom* ballet, Giuseppe Rota treated slavery in his *Elda e Dielma*, produced at the Roman Apollo Theatre during the Carnival of 1861.[32] During the carnival of 1867 the famous choreographer Paolo Taglioni presented at Milan's La Scala the ballet *Thea o la fata dei fiori*, which included representations of "Oriental" and African slaves. The Regio in Turin and again La Scala scheduled Pasquale Borri's *Nephte o il figliol prodigo*, including a huge number of black slaves. *Bianchi e neri* has to be seen in the context of these representations and of an increasingly politicized debate on slavery. As an early review of *Bianchi e neri* in the literary periodical *La Fama* argued, "slavery is a sin and a crime of remote countries, and has nothing to do with us, where everybody is the same before the law."[33] The reviewer reversed a well-established mental map of civil progress, which had habitually presented Italy as trailing behind the more advanced nations. In this sense the review echoed Cattaneo's earlier comparison between slavery in the American South and Asiatic types of feudalism.[34]

The idea of slavery as an aspect of America's "otherness" relates to arguments made in the previous chapters, which demonstrate that Italians, instead of blindly relying on foreign political recipes, frequently pointed to their own civic and constitutional traditions. Based on a similar argument, in an essay of 1858 Cattaneo recalled how in 1236 Bologna had freed its serfs, six hundred years before the end of slave ownership in the British Empire. In the thirteenth century the city had announced death sentences for anybody still keeping slaves.[35] Debates about Rota's *Bianchi e neri* resulted in an open rejection of what Italians detected as a defining aspect of American political institutions. For *La Fama* the painful representation of human barbarity in Rota's ballet made it almost impossible to enjoy the performance.[36] *L'Italia musicale* speaks of "ferocious" scenes demonstrating the "degradation of human nature," "the more disgusting the closer they are to the truth."[37]

References to Rota's ballet in newspaper articles and the periodical press demonstrate that *Bianchi e neri*, along with the wider Italian debate on Stowe's novel, prepared the ground for a dramatic change in perception with which Italians discussed political and social realities across the Atlantic. In light of these debates on American slavery Cattaneo changed his otherwise largely positive assessment of the United States. In 1842 he had explained how in America two thousand *liberissimi* newspapers shaped the political opinions of a country marked by violent political and religious divisions. While speculating that an inexperienced foreigner must read these divisions as signs of the imminent "outbreak of civil war between these countless sects, between federates and unionists, . . . between those states that still maintained slavery and the true supporters of emancipation," he reassures his readers that "these private disagreements would never turn into civic conflict." America's federal institutions and free expression of opinion would make civil war impossible.[38]

Over the following two decades awareness of the slave economy and of its impact on social and political relations in the United States made the prospect of civil war increasingly plausible to Italians, a change of awareness toward which Stowe contributed a great deal, very much along the lines of Lincoln's allegedly apocryphal dictum that the Civil War was indeed Mrs. Stowe's war.[39] In 1862 Cattaneo too realized the extent to which slavery had corrupted the whole of American society. In an article on "human typology" he denounced the ways in which slavery had stained scientific research in America. Some of the most important works of human anthropology and modern phrenology originated from the United States, but racial prejudice, as Cattaneo pointed out, profoundly compromised the work of scientists from the American South, who in order to justify the institution of slavery went so far as to assimilate the physiological appearance of people of African origin to that of monkeys.[40]

Cattaneo's article for the Milanese periodical *Il Politecnico* pays tribute to the ways in which Italians engaged with the subject of American slavery, debates that thanks to Rota's ballet and the wider reception of Stowe's novel increasingly reached beyond the audience of specialized debates in economic and political affairs. For the *Gazzetta musicale di Napoli* Rota's work was in fact more than a ballet: "you could easily call it a *drama without words*." Naples had revived the work that year, in 1862. At the height of the American Civil War one could hardly imagine a timelier program for the theater.[41] The fact that the ballet was often staged in combination with Verdi's *Un ballo in maschera* underlines the sombre picture of the United States that had emerged in Italy during those decades, decades that led Italy to Unification and the United States to Civil War.

Slavery on Stage

Bianchi e neri was certainly more than an entertaining dance show. Regarding its specific theatrical genre, *Bianchi e neri* was what Italians referred to as *ballo storico* or *eroico*, usually performed at the leading theaters in conjunction with (and during the same evening as) opera seria, financed, in addition to regular ticket sales, through subscription by the theaters' box owners and by public subsidies.[42] Therefore it would be misleading to compare *Bianchi e neri* with, for instance, the popular Uncle Tom shows staged all over Europe and America during the second half of the nineteenth century. For nineteenth-century Italian audiences, this particular genre of ballet was as important as opera itself; and the two genres, opera and ballet, often influenced one other. For example, in 1838 the Teatro alla Scala had staged Antonio Cortesi's ballo storico *Nabuccodonosor*, which became the model for Verdi's first great success, his *Nabucco* of 1842.[43] Early stagings of *Bianchi e neri* at La Scala coincided with the premieres of some of the greatest works in the history of Italian opera, notably Verdi's trilogy *Rigoletto, Il trovatore*, and *La traviata*. This notwithstanding, *Bianchi e neri* was often more successful than the opera with which it was staged together. When in 1862 Naples scheduled *Bianchi e neri* together with *Un ballo*, Verdi's opera was widely criticized, while Rota's ballet was received with great enthusiasm.[44]

Rota's ballet was able to build on the immense success of Stowe's novel in Italy. The first Italian translation of *Uncle Tom* appeared in the year of the original American publication, 1852, only a year before Rota's ballet.[45] Both *Il Mediterraneo* in Genoa and Cavour's *Il Risorgimento* in Turin serialized the novel.[46] Within a few months various cheap editions of the novel were available in all the peninsula's capital cities, with the noticeable exception of Rome, where the papal censors were concerned about the book's positive depiction of Quakers and Methodists, and the popularity of Harriet Beecher Stowe as a Protestant hero.[47] Another Italian translation of the novel was published the following year in Switzerland, and a further version appeared in 1898.[48] As mentioned in the previous chapter in connection with Verdi's interest in the novel, foreign-language versions also circulated in Italy, and as early as 1854 translations into many "minor" languages were available, including Armenian, Slovenian, and Welsh. Probably its most important impact outside the United States was that the novel had in Spain, where generous calculations estimate that it reached over 780,000 readers as early as 1853, or up to 20 percent of the literate population.[49] In this case the novel's popularity seemed to be connected to the Spanish debate on abolition in the country's colonies. The fact that in some Italian cities Rota's ballet adopted the title *La capanna di Tom*, making direct reference to the novel, suggests that the book was by then widely known. When in 1858 *Bianchi e neri* was performed in Turin, the reviewer for *L'Italia musicale* simply informed readers that "the ballet is nothing other than *La papanna dello zio Tom*," with no need for further explanation.[50]

The success of *Uncle Tom* made Harriet Beecher Stowe "the most internationally visible American writer of her time,"[51] and arguably her novel had a more important impact on images of the United States than Tocqueville's writings, for instance, or even those of James Fenimore Cooper discussed in the introduction. The novel was the focus of a general critique of American society. *Uncle Tom* became a household name, regularly referred to in Italy's illustrated magazines, in academic treatises on slavery, and in more general writings on the United States.[52] In a review of the poetic works of H. W. Longfellow, published in *Crepuscolo* in 1855, Carlo Cattaneo was able to refer to Stowe without even mentioning her name, simply citing "a female writer," who "revealed to us the painful mysteries of slavery among the black settlers."[53] The Italian reception of the novel set the scene for subsequent coverage of the Civil War. Along with general consternation at the brutality of this bloodshed, in the context of Italy's recent unification the excesses of

FIG. 16. Harriet Beecher Stowe, c. 1870. Image courtesy
https://commons.wikimedia.org/wiki/File:Beecher-Stowe.jpg.

the Civil War seemed to confirm both the impracticality of federalism, which for a long time had been considered the most probable solution to Italy's own constitutional problems, and the need to control a disparate country from the center through military force.

Soon, a variety of stage adaptations of *Uncle Tom's Cabin* started to appear. Although one needs to be careful in granting Stowe authorship of the numerous dramatizations of the novel,[54] these adaptations are almost as old as the novel itself and represent a well-studied aspect of the international Stowe phenomenon throughout the nineteenth century.[55] Often presenting white actors with black faces in a mix of comical and sentimental emotions, stage adaptations of *Uncle Tom's Cabin* can be read in many different ways; and not all of them were necessarily understood as antiabolitionist, with some of them even taking a proslavery position.[56] American newspapers referred to the traveling shows economically as "U.T.C. companies" (*Uncle Tom's Cabin* companies).[57] They were generally regarded as mediocre but often attracted even more spectators than the later Buffalo Bill shows. Surprisingly, in Europe, and in Italy in particular, stage adaptations proved almost equally popular. In Naples alone three theaters presented different adaptations of the novel in May 1853, including a version in local dialect.[58] As Henry James noted, "the fate of Mrs Stowe's picture was conclusive: it simply sat down wherever it lighted and made itself at home."[59]

Rota's Italian ballet, however, was in many respects different from other stage adaptations; and it certainly represents more than a casual attempt to make money from the success of a literary model. In historical ballets the choreographer was usually his own librettist.[60] While most stage adaptations were the products of authors we know little or nothing about, usually local theater directors, La Scala commissioned its ballet from one of the most celebrated stars of Italian ballet of all time, the young dancer and choreographer Giuseppe Rota (b. Venice, 1823; d. Turin, 1865), described by the influential literary magazine *Il trovatore* as "il Verdi della coreografia."[61] In the history of Italian dance Giuseppe Rota is remembered for his own virtuosity as a *ballerino*, but also as the choreographer who revived the Italian tradition of dramatic pantomime.[62] Rota knew how to enliven the action of his plots through the skillful addition of ensemble scenes and brilliant pas de deux, performed by outstanding dancers. In the case of *Bianchi e neri* this included Augusta Maywood (b. New York, 1825; d. Lemberg/Lviv, 1876), the first American dancer to win a place among the top-ranking ballerinas of Europe, a fact perceived as giving the plot additional authenticity. She had begun her career as a child prodigy in the United States and then spent many years in Italy, where she was the first ballerina to found her own touring company, complete with managers, soloists, and a fully equipped corps de ballet.[63]

The ballet's music also proved popular with audiences and critics. The bulk of it was written by the celebrated theater composer Paolo Giorza, whose score was distributed by one of Europe's leading publishers, Lucca in Milan.[64] The beauty of the ballet's genre-specific standard elements—the multisectional grand waltz early on or the gallop at the end of the piece—increased its popularity with audiences. The sets of *Bianchi e neri* were usually of matching splendor. Turin used the same sets as for Meyerbeer's grand opéra *Le prophète*, giving us an idea of the staging's grandeur. Meanwhile, for the local authorities as well as for some critics, the Turin staging appeared to have been rather too advanced in its natural exhibition of the female slaves, causing the police to suspend a number of ballerinas. The famous theater critic Francesco d'Arcais complained about a stage resembling the "whore of Babylon."[65] Notwithstanding similar moments of crisis, the success of *Bianchi e neri* lasted for several decades.

After its premiere in Milan, the ballet had thirty-five performances at Genoa's Carlo Felice in 1856, followed by another fifteen performances there in 1857 and a further twenty-two in 1861, becoming one of Genoa's most successful ballets of the whole nineteenth century.[66] As mentioned earlier, the great port city and hometown of Christopher Columbus always had an explicit interest in American themes. In 1858 *Bianchi e neri* was produced in Rome, Turin, and Bologna. Naples's San Carlo gave a total of thirty-seven performances in 1862–63, before the ballet returned to Milan in 1863, and to Turin's Teatro Regio in 1873 and 1875, after the choreographer's death.[67] Within a decade the ballet had been staged in all of Italy's major theaters. The extraordinary success of *Bianchi e neri* established Rota as one of the leading choreographers of his time and as an important innovator in the genre. His productions dominated Italian stages for more than a generation, and many of his original works were regularly revived by other choregraphers, even during the years when ballet became too expensive for many Italian theaters and when developments within the opera genre left little space for separate ballet productions.[68]

Reading Uncle Tom

The splendor of the ballet's choreography and of its music was not the main reason for its success. Reviews focussed primarily on the plot's allegorical content and its literary source.[69] At the time, Italian choreographers often chose the victory of virtue and of true love as their topic, and an emphasis on social justice was a common theme.[70] Hence Italians associated certain expectations with this genre, which the choreographer had to take into consideration when proposing a *libro da ballo*, the libretto with the synopsis of the work.

The reception of *Bianchi e neri* changed with the specific context of its productions. During the second round of performances in 1863, at the height of the American Civil War, the ballet made a significant impact on Milanese audiences, because it was read as a direct commentary on an issue of international politics that was closely covered in contemporary newspapers. The performance had also been a success ten years earlier, but then the piece was presented in rather a different context, that of the Italian Risorgimento, as a story about liberation. As a matter of fact, for the scene of the slave rebellion Rota had asked the composer to introduce four bars of the Marseillaise into the score. When the audience exploded into applause during this scene, the Austrian police suspended the performance.[71] While the work's reception changed with the context of its performance history, its success was more than just the consequence of the choreographer's own popularity or of his tearjerking subject. From the very beginning *Bianchi e neri* was read politically.

Loosely based on selected scenes of the novel, Rota's ballet underlines the story's *terra incognita* aspect through the introduction of allegorical scenes, which are typical for the genre, but not to be found in the original novel.[72] During the prelude nature deposits on earth two children, one white, one black, reminding both of them that they are brothers. The white boy suppresses the black boy and then makes him his slave. In the ballet's original version (1853), the first scene (1) that follows features a party at the house of Thompson, the English envoy to Washington, who is a member of the society for the emancipation of Negroes. Unexpectedly, the fugitive slave George enters the room. He had been freed by Thompson and now hopes to liberate those who still share his former fate as slaves. Humanity offers George guidance and presents him with a book, the *Code of Truth*. In scene 2 George starts his mission on Legrey's plantation, offering himself to the master as a new supervisor for his slaves. Legrey makes indecent approaches to the slave Dellay but is interrupted by the arrival of his daughter Angelina. In order to break Dellay's resistance and isolate her from her family, Legrey decides to sell her father (Uncle Tom), her husband (Sab), and their young son (Henry) to the slave trader Christie. Angelina promises to protect the family from her father's evil intentions. In scene 3 Legrey discovers Sab with a book and punishes him for intending to instruct himself. When Legrey makes another attempt to conquer Dellay, her husband, Sab, intervenes, and Legrey orders George to beat him. George refuses, and Legrey orders him to leave. Legrey sells Tom, Sab, and Henry to Christie. While Tom obeys, the rest of the family decide to escape. Scene 4 takes place at the home of the merchant Gordon, whose life Sab had once saved and where his family is now hiding. However, Gordon reveals the hiding place to Christie for a sum of money. While George helps Dellay and Henry to escape, Sab is caught in a fight. He shoots Gordon and is subsequently arrested. In scene 5 George enters Sab's prison and convinces the incarcerated slaves to pray for God's help. When Legrey enters the prison to retrieve his slaves they suddenly find the strength to oppose him. The ballet concludes with another allegorical scene, set in the Temple of Truth, where the Genius of Humanity ends centuries of racial division and unites black and white for ever more.

The apparatus of the Italian translation of *Uncle Tom*—as well as the debates both the novel and the ballet generated at the time—facilitated a political reading of the ballet.[73] The preface to the novel's first Italian edition includes a detailed commentary by the French critic Jean Lemoine, which discusses the problem of slavery and points readers to the role that women like Harriet Beecher Stowe played in public debates on this issue. Stowe was building on a significant tradition of women writers using their medium as a critique of society.[74] As with the American and English editions of *Uncle Tom*, the Italian edition also presents the story as more than just a piece of compassionate literature. Its apparatus offered background information on the plot to which the press often referred, including in reviews of the ballet. A two-volume commentary on *Uncle Tom* was also published in Italy in 1853, the so-called *chiave* to the novel, a translation of Stowe's own "key." Its aim was to reconstruct the facts on which the novel was based and to help Italians to contextualize the work within wider political developments of the United States.[75] For Italians the "key" opened a window on a largely foreign society, which was perceived to be profoundly different from anything known on the Italian peninsula. While we have no figures to show how many Italians read the "key," literary critics who wrote about Stowe's novel regularly referred to the factual information it offered and used it in reviews not only of the novel, but also of the ballet. The detailed and well-documented volumes of the "key" offered Italians proof that the novel was more than a piece of fiction, and that it delivered an authentic image of American society. With its "oral histories" and its rich quotations from original documents, correspondence, legislation, and newspapers, the *Chiave* differed from the many books on America published in Italy since the eighteenth century. After the early histories of America and the books on po-litical institutions, the *Chiave* became one of the first social-anthropological studies of modern life in the American Republic accessible to Italian readers in their own language.

The novel itself also made it sufficiently clear that the story constituted an authentic account of life in America. In the last chapter of the final volume, Stowe explains the background to the plot, which was based on a careful char-acter study of people living in a slaveholder society either as victims or as per-petrators. Referring to the original description of the person who became the model for the slave trader Legrée, Stowe's postscript underlined once more the barbarity of the slave economy: "he actually made me feel his fist, which was like a blacksmith's hammer, or a nodule of iron, telling me that it was *calloused with knocking down niggers*." Situating the narrative in a realistic account of life in the United States, she continued that "this injustice is an inherent one in the slave system,—it cannot exist without it."[76] For anybody not used to debates over the experience of slavery, as would be the case for the majority of Italian readers, the consequences of the slave trade for the individuals in-volved were almost inconceivable.

As Stowe explains to her readers, "the writer has given only a faint shadow, a dim picture, of the anguish and despair that are, at this very moment, riving thousands of hearts, shattering thousands of families, and driving a helpless and sensitive race to frenzy and despair. There are those living who know the mothers whom this accursed traffic has driven to the murder of their chil-dren; and themselves seeking in death a shelter from woes more dreaded than death. Nothing of tragedy can be written, can be spoken, can be conceived, that equals the frightful reality of scenes daily and hourly acting on our shores, beneath the shadow of American law, and the shadow of the cross of Christ."[77]

The fact that these passages are included in foreign translations of the novel is important, because it suggests that *Uncle Tom* could not be read as mere fiction, not even in countries that were at the time largely unaffected by political or religious debates over slavery. The documentary passages of the novel had an especially important impact on the construction of an image of America in Italy, because compared to Britain or France relations with the

United States still played only a minor role. While other countries enjoyed a closer relationship, with a wider range of information about the United States readily available, in Italy *Uncle Tom* played a comparatively more important role in the construction of an image of the United States, because of the book's detailed factual information.

Every libretto is no more than a loose adaptation of its literary source. While ballet as a genre makes it almost impossible to represent the narrative structure of a novel closely, Rota's allegorical scenes at the start and the end of the ballet serve the purpose of integrating the humanist intentions and religious motives of Stowe's novel. The fact that some of the ballet's first reviews criticized Rota for these additions to the novel's narrative demonstrates how closely audiences and critics associated the ballet with the novel.[78] In his libretto da ballo, Rota decided to conflate scenes from the two main narratives of Stowe's novel: the story of Eliza (becoming Dellay in the ballet), heading north for freedom; and the story of Tom, sold south and dying under even more terrible conditions. There are also variations between the different productions of the ballet. In the 1858 version Angelina becomes Erichetta, a name read as an Italian version of Harriet. The "Book of Truth" in the 1853 version later becomes simply the Bible. In the ballet, Uncle Tom himself plays a secondary role, but the novel also refers to him only in some sections. Despite these alterations to the plot, the choreography takes up many central elements of the novel, on which Stowe had commented in her "key": the destruction of family structures as a consequence of the slave trade; the sexual implications of the relationship between the master and his female slaves; the physical brutality of slaveholders and traders; the role of education and religion in the life of slaves. In addition to commenting on the general issues of the adaptation and on the choreography itself, most reviews go into some detail in describing the ballet's sad and brutal content.[79]

Stowe became a star in Italy and was well known beyond circles of educated Italians. Visiting Rome in 1857, she would have disturbed those of her fellow countrymen residing at the time in Rome who held southern sympathies, but she found many admirers among the Italian people. Visiting the workshop of the sculptors Castellani and observing one of the two brothers carving the head of an Egyptian slave in onyx, she was recognized and allegedly addressed with the words: "Madam, we know what you have been to the poor slave. We ourselves are but poor slaves still in Italy; you feel for us; will you keep this gem as a slight recognition for what you have done?"[80] As inappropriate as the comparison between American slaves and Italians in the Papal States might seem, one of the reasons for *Uncle Tom*'s popularity was the fact that Italians were able to assimilate their own fate to that of the oppressed slaves. In 1858 the then very popular poet Giuseppe Regaldi drew a similar relationship between emancipation and the Italian struggle for independence in a preface to a poem on African slaves, which he had dedicated to Stowe.[81] Stowe herself compared the fugitive slaves in her book to the patriots fighting "Austrian tyranny."[82] A few years later, in an editorial on the American Civil War of March 1862, the Florentine liberal newspaper *La Nazione* drew the same comparison between the Roman Question and the emancipation of the American slaves.[83] Likewise the republican almanac *L'amico di casa* of 1863 saw no difference "between Jews in the Papal States and Negroes in America."[84] The American journalist Margaret Fuller, who had visited Europe during the Revolutions of 1848, had also drawn similar comparisons.[85]

These references show that Stowe was read and discussed in the context of general humanitarian concerns, but also in connection with ideas about national liberation. During Italy's Second War of Independence, which led to the country's Unification, Henri Dunant visited the battlefield of Solferino and mounted his legendary campaign for the relief of wounded soldiers. In doing so, the founder of the International Red Cross was inspired by his reading of *Uncle Tom*. He hoped that his devastating account of the war, published as *Un Souvenir de Solferino*, would, similar to Stowe's novel, shape his contemporaries' understanding of modern warfare and influence the actions of future generations.[86] His book became the most widely read account of the war. Stowe herself contributed to making connections between her work and the political events of the Risorgimento. In 1859, on her second visit to Italy, she attended the meeting of the Tuscan Assembly at which the adherence of Tuscany to Piedmont was declared, a decisive step on the way to Unification.[87] Apart from her admiration for the Catholic Church's symbolism and its authentic spirituality, Stowe echoed the condemnations by Italian patriots of the church's tyranny and made the pope's "perverted religion" the topic of another, lesser-known novel, *Agnes of Sorrento*.[88] Later, Italian anticlericals found a willing supporter in the first American minister to the Kingdom of Italy, George Perkins Marsh, who "indulged in anti-Papal diatribes" and regarded the Catholic Church as an institutionalization of "tyranny, reaction and superstition."[89] Meanwhile, *Uncle Tom* could also be read as a narrative of a "racialized Christ-like passion,"[90] with the devout Uncle Tom being beaten to death by his master. In this reading the novel responded to religious sentiments, which were shared by many Italian anticlericals. All this facilitated the Italian response to Stowe.

Despite the novel's role in Italian debates on America, one should not reduce the impact of Rota's ballet to this one specific aspect of its reception. In many respects the production fitted in with Rota's general interest in foreign and exotic topics, which in turn belonged to a more general thematic genre of historical ballets. As mentioned earlier in this chapter, slavery often served to depict oriental despotism and cruelty within cultures described as uncivilized or nonenlightened.[91] The common association between slavery and *oscurantismo* reflected Montesquieu's belief that Christianity had led

to the abolition of slavery in Europe, a view strongly contested by a number
of other enlightened philosophers, in particular Raynal, who unmistakably
linked the discovery of the New World to the beginning of the transatlantic
slave trade.[92] Meanwhile, the fact that Italian audiences knew representations of slavery on stage mostly from descriptions of non-European, so-called
oriental societies makes the connection between Rota's American ballet and
this particular genre also more meaningful, seriously undermining the ideals
conventionally associated with the North American Republic. By the time
Rota presented *Bianchi e neri* at La Scala, even most countries of the New
World had abolished slavery, with the notable exceptions of Cuba, Brazil—
and the United States.

What Stowe's America seemed to represent was a particularly crude form
of what in the view of most Italians usually characterized non-European
societies. It is exactly this aspect—slavery contradicting the ideals of civilization and progress—that references to the United States in the reviews of
Bianchi e neri underline. On the occasion of the ballet's 1863 revival, the
Milanese literary journal *La Fama* discussed William Wilberforce's early
nineteenth-century movement against the transatlantic slave trade. It had
been widely assumed, the periodical argues, that the "trade in human flesh"
would disappear from the globe as a consequence of the movement's success:

> Unfortunately, one did not consider the indomitable tenacity of the
> Anglo-Saxon race in the Southern United States. They are united
> around an anti-social principle, based on the pure reason of force: that
> the white man owns the black, a principle sanctioned by laws, which
> treat these men as simple objects, to be exploited and commercialised
> like wild beasts.[93]

Not only is it remarkable that the review of a ballet engages in debates
about this wider historical and social context of slavery; the author also presents his readers with a most condemnatory judgement on American society.
The article goes on to outline the implications of slavery for the United States'
constitutional system, explaining the causes of the current Civil War, "the most
horrible massacre in the history of humankind," as the reviewer points out.[94]
The fact that it was the federal character of the constitution that gave American slaveholders the ability to oppose abolition seemed to confirm Mazzini's
fears concerning the risks a federal solution posed to Italy's Unification.

Italian Unification and the American Civil War

Despite the recent secession of the Confederacy, Americans continued to
closely follow the events in Italy that led to the country's unification. In January 1861 *La Nazione* reported a meeting in New York bringing together more
than three thousand people in support of Garibaldi.[95] Likewise, while Italians

had reason enough to concentrate on their own Civil War in the South, they closely followed the news about the escalating conflict across the Atlantic. When the Italian prime minister Ricasoli voiced his support for the constitutional authorities of the North, he did this also in the awareness of the secessionist ambitions of papal and southern legitimists in Italy.[96] The government of the new Kingdom of Italy soon lost control of the south, with large areas placed under a state of siege and governed by special laws. The authorities were forced to rely on military coercion to enforce conscription, collect taxes, and repress insurrection and brigandage.[97] These difficulties notwithstanding, many Americans understood the "liberation" of the Italian South as closely connected to the aims of their own battle against slavery.[98]

The Italian response to the American Civil War, however, went beyond a shared concern for the integrity of the nation-state. Owing to their close engagement with Stowe's novel, and with Rota's ballet in particular, Italians were able to engage with the American conflict on a much more personal and emotional basis; and references to *Uncle Tom* in general debates about American politics and the country's constitution suggest that the reception of the novel played an important part in making the consequences of slavery an issue of public concern in Italy.

As Enrico dal Lago has argued, many Italian patriots saw their nation's political unification and the abolition of slavery in America as "one single cause": a struggle for the good of humankind as a whole.[99] However, arriving at this insight was not straightforward. Historically, the Italian Democrats had close relations with the Democratic Party in the United States; and at first they were hesitant in declaring themselves in favor of Abraham Lincoln. Their attitude changed relatively late, only after the Emancipation Proclamation of January 1863. Meanwhile, as an international champion of freedom Mazzini was popular in American antislavery circles; and his concern at the dangers of the federal system shared common ground with the political aims of American Republicans.[100] American dailies such as the *Tribune*, the *Herald*, and the *Times*, as well as periodicals including the *Democratic Review*, the *International Monthly Magazine*, and the *Boston Weekly Museum* all regularly wrote about Mazzini in favorable terms, at least until the early 1850s, when his reputation briefly suffered owing to his alleged implication in Orsini's attempt on the life of Napoleon III. Mazzini knew Stowe's family, including her husband, long before the publication of *Uncle Tom's Cabin*. Lyman Beecher first contacted Mazzini through the Christian Alliance back in 1842 and then met him in London in 1846. It was through him that Mazzini got to know Margaret Fuller, who then became one of the American protagonists of the Roman Republic of 1849. Henry Ward Beecher, the most famous Congregationalist preacher of his time, supported Italian Republicans in exile, as well as Jessie White Mario, who in 1858 toured the United States to appeal for American help with the unification of Italy.[101]

Mazzini's revolutionary tactics also directly influenced the antislavery conspiracies of the American abolitionist John Brown. During the American Civil War, Lincoln offered Garibaldi a commission as major general in the Union Army, an idea Mazzini was highly critical of, as he thought the general was needed at home.[102] A Garibaldi Brigade of 350 men, of which no more than about fifty were Italians, fought for the North. Moreover, many individual units included experienced Italian officers, among them the later director of the Metropolitan Museum, Luigi Palma di Cesnola. However, there were also about five hundred Italians fighting for the South, including former soldiers from the Bourbon army. The American administration itself saw the Italian Redshirts largely as a wild bunch of adventurers seeking American-paid transportation to the New World.[103] Garibaldi sympathized with the abolitionists and the North but was rather indifferent to the preservation of the Union. As for Mazzini, even after the Civil War he repeated his view that in a society based almost exclusively on individual rights—an aspect of American democracy he loathed—a large section of society could not be denied the right to secede.[104] In the long term this particular evaluation of the Civil War alienated Mazzini (and at least some of his Italian followers) from the American republican experience.

At home in Italy, the decision not to recognize the Confederacy, despite the fact that Italian cotton mills depended on raw material from the South, was one of the few issues on which Italian Democrats and Moderates were able to agree.[105] In this respect the policy of the Holy See was less clear; and the American South even tried to capitalize on the fact that the pope maintained correspondence with the Confederate president Jefferson Davis. While the Catholic Church called for an end to hostilities, it abstained from open condemnation of the institution of slavery.[106] According to *Civiltà cattolica*, "under any circumstances man is always under the order of a higher authority; therefore, the slave is never completely under the order of his master, as the master himself always remains a subject."[107] In this respect the periodical differed from earlier Catholic commentators writing about the United States. In 1818 Giovanni Antonio Grassi, head of the Jesuit College at Georgetown and mentioned in chapter 2, had condemned the institution of slavery for being "in open contradiction with one of the first articles of the general Constitution of the Republic, which declares that freedom is an inherent and inalienable right of man."[108]

Since the early nineteenth century, and as a direct consequence of Italy's national movement for unification, Catholics' perspective on the United States had changed. As was the case with most Italian comment on life in the United States, the Catholic periodicals' main objective when writing about America was to support its ideological battles at home.[109] Thus, the church questioned the legitimacy of the United States on the same basis as it questioned the Kingdom of Italy: "while Italy constitutes itself as one, which it has never been, . . . in the United States they dissolve their union, because for some of them unity is such an unbearable condition that a war seems justified."[110] But even the church was unable to defend the slave economy in the South and presented it as one of the contradictions behind the modern ideologies of liberalism and democracy. Although not against slavery in principle, it took the view that under the paternal protection of the church "the master becomes father, and the slave almost a son. But in America things are different: there slavery results in tyranny, a monstrosity."[111] According to the Catholic paper, this constituted the difference between slavery in the United States and slavery as practiced in Catholic countries like Brazil.

Along with widespread enthusiasm for the North's cause, what Italians followed most closely, and with growing consternation, was the unimaginable cruelty of the American Civil War, echoing a theme discussed in chapter 1 in connection with Italian responses to the American War of Independence. Italian newspapers were filled with detail describing how the bloodshed penetrated every corner of American society. From the presidential elections of 1860 onward, not only widely read newspapers such as *La Nazione*, but also smaller regional publications such as the *Giornale di Sicilia* wrote about the events leading to the war and in particular about the military strategies adopted by both sides in preparation for the conflict. What soon becomes obvious from these articles is the belief that it is the federal structure of the Union and of the armed forces that makes a civil war of such gigantic dimensions possible.[112] As for the lessons Italy could learn from the American events, there is a growing sense that once the Italian South was to be defeated and conquered, true federalism of independent states, as imagined by Cattaneo or the Sicilian revolutionaries of 1848, would no longer be practicable.[113]

While early on during the war, some Italian newspapers expect that "the great nation, *figliata della civiltà*, will rise greater and more united" from this conflict, many commentators abandoned this hope while the conflict continued.[114] The aforementioned Giovanni Capellini, future rector of the University of Bologna, who traveled the United States during the Civil War, described the conflict as the "devil's war." Cities devastated by the guerrillas made a big impression on him, and he showed particular concern at the circulation of weapons among the civil population.[115] The railways he used were frequently destroyed in order to stop the trains of enemy forces, or simply to rob and kill civilian passengers. Conflicts between the troops of the Union and the Sioux further aggravated the situation. Capellini's impressions did little to reassure Italians about Americans' ability to handle the conflict. At St. Joseph, in Missouri, his train was going no further, and Capellini had the chance to meet the commander, who "kept company with a bottle of whiskey" at his desk, using the upper part of a human scull as a cup.[116] Meeting a young Union officer, who had become an abolitionist during a journey to Europe, but whose family from the South fought for the Confederates, Capellini experienced in person how the war had destroyed not just a nation, but cities, villages, and even families. Wherever he came close to the battlefields Capellini noticed how the war destroyed even the nation's few signposts of culture: museums, noteworthy buildings, galleries.[117]

If America was usually unable to impress Europeans with its collections of artefacts, *Civiltà cattolica* lists the number of railway carriages and steam engines deliberately destroyed during the conflict.[118] According to the Catholic paper the fact that on both sides black people were enlisted further increased the level of violence in combat. Some newspapers adopted sensationalist or ironic undertones when reporting the excesses of the conflict, for instance comparing the deployment of female soldiers to the role of Amazons in ancient warfare. Commenting on female regiments and the role assumed by the wives of officers, *La Nazione* opined that "wherever there existed military corps of women the male population has been in part eliminated, in part reduced to slavery."[119]

La Nazione used the term "terrorism" to describe the policies of the South but did not hesitate to shed doubts on Lincoln's personal integrity: "for him the negroes are just a means to go to war against the whites," the liberal newspaper writes.[120] Here, the paper from Florence ignored the extent to which abolitionism had become a religiously and politically motivated mass movement in the United States. Although this sort of attack on the president was rare, the paper seemed to echo the personalized campaigns of prosouthern members of the British parliament around the *Saturday Review*, which caricatured Lincoln as a rude frontiersman, the opposite of Jefferson Davis's image of "an able administrator and calm statesman."[121] For the Catholic press, the North's regime during the civil war was "a kind of military dictatorship," likened to the political situation of "occupied" Sicily, which the church openly condemned. Suddenly discovering a concern for the treatment of prisoners and for the freedom of the press, the Catholic paper also noted that Lincoln's regime no longer respected the law of habeas corpus. It reported how numerous newspapers were banned, "following exactly the same practice as the Neapolitan Garibaldini in the service of Piedmont."[122] Here too Italy interpreted the events of the American Civil War within its own terms of reference. While Catholic papers questioned the motives of the Union, the liberal press pointed to the desperate actions of the Confederates, "burning their own cities, devastating their fields, prepared to suffer privations of any kind."[123] Apart from their respective political sympathies, Liberals and Catholics in Italy seemed to agree that "a lot of blood and violence could be spared. A war pursued with such levels of obstinacy [*accanimento*] has to have the most horrific consequences," the *Gazzetta delle Romagne* wrote.[124]

Confronted with the cruelty of the American Civil War and the political realities of the United States, for those who still regarded American institutions as a model, such a model lost much of its appeal. As Raymond Grew has argued with regard to plans for the federalization of the peninsula, "a nation torn by civil war was an awkward model of federalism," with the newspaper of the Italian National Society warning that the federal constitution had proved to be the American Union's "germ of death."[125] Retrospective assessments of the Civil War echoed many of the earlier arguments that had contrasted slavery in the United States with the values of the civilized world.[126] Mazzini, writing from London in 1865, described the end of the Civil War as the completion of the process in which America had constituted itself as a nation: "your nation's vitality and force have lately been clarified beyond any doubt."[127] But at the same time he was shocked that even some abolitionists still doubted whether African Americans should be given the right to vote.[128]

For many Italian commentators the Civil War had left wounds that could never be healed. As the liberal *Nuova antologia* maintained in 1867, political life in the United States "had become extremely corrupted and violent. If one would implement this model of society and government in one of our states, it would collapse within a week."[129] The moderate Minghetti also came to associate American democracy primarily with corruption, reminding his readers that already Tocqueville had pointed to this problem. He identifies the formation of political parties as the main source of this evil, having created a political class, "classe dei politicianti [politicians]" depending on lobbies or "rings," which increasingly "resemble what in Italy we would call Camorra or Mafia."[130] According to Minghetti, these developments clearly started during the Civil War, under the administration of Lincoln, who despite his great merits "had to make concessions to violence and to pressure from his party."[131]

Furthermore, for *Nuova antologia* the example of the United States seemed to confirm the views of those who feared the negative consequences of democratic advances without the progress of political education.

> [In the American South], the honest, virtuous and well-off classes retire from political life, feeling unable to give direction or to influence decisions. They leave matters to the country's least educated and least distinguished strata. Thus, democracy seems ochlocracy, where the government of the people becomes the government of the plebs. The Congress of the United States has today the reputation of being the most corrupted assembly in the entire world.[132]

In assessing the views of this influential periodical it is interesting to note that, originally, the journal's predecessor *Antologia* had always advocated the federalization of Italy. While completing his law degree in Milan, Cattaneo had published his first article in Vieusseux's periodical.[133] Experience taught Italy's former supporters of the American constitution a different lesson. With the observation of political developments across the Atlantic, republicanism in general lost its appeal. While Mazzinians and Radical Democrats continued to see a link between prosperity and republicanism, Italian Liberals compared developments in the United States with those in Britain, coming to the conclusion that progress did not depend on the form of government.[134] What a country this was, where elections were won "by means of tumultuous meetings and the use of colts?," commented liberal as well as Catholic papers.[135] News about Andrew Johnson's conflict with Congress seemed to confirm that the American constitution simply did not provide the stability that was needed to steer the country out of its self-incurred crisis.[136]

Italian debates demonstrate a great degree of awareness of the profound crisis affecting the United States during the period of reconstruction, in particular debates over the status of Afro-Americans, the future role of the former Confederate elites, and the recruitment of new Unionist leaders in the South.[137] The North had serious doubts over the southern states' readmission to the Union, urging President Johnson to impose strict conditions.[138] These were problems that sounded familiar to political observers in post-Unification Italy, still involved in a battle to submit its own South to Piedmontese rule. Resistance to nation building in the Italian South had much in common with the situation that had brought the United States to Civil War.[139]

From Subject Nation to International Arbitrator

Despite their own traumatic experience of nation building in the South, as well as in other regions of the peninsula, many in post-Unification Italy thought that their nation had no reason to feel inferior to any of the allegedly more advanced nations. The experience of the American Civil War helped Italians to argue this case. Not only were Italians able to invoke the example of the Civil War to point to the absence of civilization in a nation that some continued to view as a democratic model; Italy also gained international recognition as an arbiter in the conflict. The *Alabama*, one of several warships built in England and that subsequently participated in the Civil War on the side of the Confederates, was at the center of American claims for compensation against England. Count Federico Paolo Sclopis di Salerano, an internationally respected legal historian, member of the Italian parliament, and one of the authors of the Piedmontese civil code, was appointed head of the international tribunal set up in Geneva to resolve this conflict, at the end of which England had to pay the United States 15.5 million dollars for damages inflicted on the nation by the *Alabama* and other warships.[140] This spectacular case helped to establish the principle of international arbitration and the codification of international law, a process in which Italian legal experts played a crucial role. International arbitration as a means to global peace became one of the keys to Mazzini's cosmopolitanism of nations.[141] Likewise, in 1864 Count Sclopis di Salerano had played a leading role at the Congress of Geneva, which resulted in an international convention on the treatment of prisoners of war.

Italy's role in efforts to find an international solution to the internal problems of the United States brought considerable prestige to the young Italian nation-state. In the debates on these new legal institutions, Italy was able to point to expertise stemming from centuries of legal studies, enshrined by Europe's oldest university, Bologna, which had its origins in the rediscovery of the Roman law books in the eleventh century.[142] One of the Italian experts in the international debates on arbitration was Pasquale Stanislao Mancini, who had become famous as a penal reformer opposed to the death penalty.[143] It was with specific reference to "the titanic war of secession between the North and the South of the American Republic" that the Italian parliament stressed the need to lead the world's most advanced nations in propagating international arbitration as a means to avoid future military conflicts.[144] In the words of Foreign Minister Emilio Marquis Visconti-Venosta, "we wish that justice and the reason of the law will play an ever growing role in international affairs. It is our greatest ambition that a policy of equity, reason and *civiltà* will determine the fate of our country. . . . For Italy it was an honour to associate its name with these facts, which ultimately allowed us to demonstrate that international arbitration is more than a benign utopia of certain academics or judges, that it was sanctioned in practical application. Italy prides itself . . . on not sitting back and of marking the beginnings of a great tradition."[145]

While during the first half of the nineteenth century abolitionism had played a less prominent role in Italy compared to debates in France, England, or Spain, *antischiavismo* became an important cause for internationalist activism in Italy. From 1867 Italy's Società antischiavista published a regular periodical. With American slavery having finally come to an end, its main focus was on the African slave trade.[146] While during the Civil War Italian Catholic opinion had maintained an ambiguous position toward abolition, the new antislavery movement was partly supported by the church, despite its deep implication in the colonial exploitation of Africa.[147] Raised sensitivity over these issues came to form the basis of Italy's strong anticolonial movement, when toward the end of the century Crispi's colonial ambition—the idea of completing the Risorgimento through territorial aggrandizement in Africa—came under attack from the Italian Left.

If the outcome of the American Civil War solved the problem of slavery in the United States,[148] this did not mean that Stowe's novel and its Italian dramatizations became a matter of the past. They related directly to the continuing debates about slavery: "Isn't it that this novel about Uncle Tom might serve a purpose in the African cause?" asks the Italian author of a volume on the international movement against slavery in 1893, forty years after the novel first appeared in Italy.[149] By that time Italians' historical reflections on the Civil War were increasingly marked by the reception of Walt Whitman, discussed at the start of this book and celebrated by Nencioni as "il poeta della gran Guerra Americana." In this capacity Whitman left a profound imprint on the poetic language of the Italian avant-garde around the turn of the century, especially through his collection of war poetry *Drum Taps*.[150] Whitman's realist descriptions of dying underaged soldiers, of amputations and the wounded's feverish delirium constituted a hitherto unknown poetic genre for Italians, which spoke to a country that had reached its political unification via several bloody wars of liberation. Nencioni's *saggio* on Whitman counts among the most powerful Italian descriptions of America's titanic war:

> Never was a war fought within more limitless territories. Military genius constantly created new means of destruction used in the fields as well as at sea. The war was fought on snowy mountains, in the marshes, on lakes and at sea, in underground caves and above dizzying heights. . . . Fifteen-year old boys moved fearlessly, gun in hand, side-by-side with the veterans of Potomac. For entire nights they fought through burning woods or under torrential, glacial rains. They suffered starvation like in Jerusalem or Saragossa, while frantic fevers and dysentery decimated entire army battalions.[151]

The poor treatment of black Americans, as depicted by Harriet Beecher Stowe, or by Walt Whitman a few years later, still resonated in the reports of labor migrants returning to Italy, in American news items in the Italian press and in more substantial articles for illustrated magazines, with lynching becoming a particularly disturbing topic of debate on the realities of American life. The fact that many of these articles traced America's race problems back to the trauma of the Civil War suggests that the conflict had left Americans in a state of moral decline, which affected an entire society—men, women, and children. This at least is the view coming across in Italian comments.

The fact that Italy's own civil war in the South had been fought with similar levels of brutality, albeit on a much smaller scale, is largely blended out of such observations. The treatment of South Italian rebels fighting against the submission under the Savoy and the application of martial law in the recently "liberated" kingdom of the South had much in common with the political situation across the Atlantic, but as the analysis of the Catholic press has demonstrated, these kinds of comparison remained rare. If the story started in this chapter was to be written on into the concluding decades of the century, similar comparisons could be made to Italy's growing colonial appetite and the racial hierarchies informing Italian attempts to create an empire across the Mediterranean. Drawing parallels between Italian depictions of the American Civil War and the ruthlessness with which Italy pursued its imperial adventures later in the century would go beyond the scope of this book and are better treated as a topic of Italy's new colonial history.[152]

Looking back at those years when Italians for the first time engaged on a broader scale with racial tensions in the United States, the great liberal philosopher and historian Benedetto Croce listed Stowe's novel among the key works of nineteenth-century literature; but he spoke unsympathetically about the United States. For Croce, the North American Republic had once been "the typical country of democracy." It then remained paralyzed by "the conflict between advocates and opponents of slavery," an issue Europe had overcome "a millennium and a half ago" and that it was now "rooting out in her colonies." Immersed in what was basically a conflict of economic interests, for Croce, the United States fell out of step with the great struggle between liberalism and democracy, which characterized the progressive countries of Europe.[153]

While Italy's conflict in the South was often described as a civil war in its own right, the idea of a war between brothers that cost the lives of six hundred thousand men remained incomprehensible for a nation that had constructed the idea of its own national resurgence on the concepts of brotherhood and kinship.[154]

Conclusions

IN APRIL 2011 the cover of the American magazine *Time* featured the picture of a weeping Abraham Lincoln, asking why "we're still fighting the Civil War." After 150 years the Civil War continues to provoke contentious debate in the United States, focussing in particular on the question whether the extension of slavery into western territories was its real cause.[1] Europeans were in no doubt about the issue; and transnationalizing US history—looking at this debate from a transatlantic perspective—might help to shed additional light on a past that will not pass until societies replace empty pride in their nation with collective responsibility for their histories.[2]

Many Italians learned about the horrors of American slavery from the stages of their gorgeous theaters. In order to become widely respected arbitrators in international conflicts, they had to travel a long way. The self-confidence with which Italians referred to the troubles of the North American Republic also served to deter attention from their own problems of nation building after Unification. Linked to this short moment of glamour on the stage of international politics, their self-confidence was perfectly in line with the views of a nation that, throughout its Risorgimento, had rejected the temptation of looking for its own future in the past of foreign nations. Pride in their own past notwithstanding, Italians continued to explore the United States as a laboratory of political practice also after Unification, similar to the ways in which America had served an earlier generation of political thinkers like Romagnosi or Cattaneo in coming to terms with the experience of social, political, and constitutional change during the Risorgimento period. A final example of cross-Atlantic exchange will serve to illustrate how Italians explored what they knew about the United States for their own purposes, without simply imitating foreign prescriptions.

The assassination of Abraham Lincoln provoked an outcry of grief all over the world, including in Italy, with commentators praising the "courageous defender of the sacred principles of civilisation and progress."[3] As "popolo fratello," but also as a country with its own tradition "of violent and bloodthirsty passions," Italy felt particularly touched by the American president's murder.[4] As these quotations show, even provincial newspapers went into detailed analysis not only to explain the magnitude of these events to its readers, but also to explore Italy's and the United States' parallel histories. Countless Italian institutions felt the need to send their condolences to the American nation, usually via American consuls. As Mary Philip Trauth summarized in her book on George Perkins Marsh, "the diplomatic volumes of 1865 are thick with testimonials to the memory of Lincoln. From royal palace to hamlet; from masonic lodges mourning the death of a brother, to charitable associations sympathizing for the untimely passing of the Emancipator."[5] Cardinal Antonelli, the pope's secretary of state, used a meeting with the American plenipotentiary Marsh to express the pontiff's horror at the assassination and to affirm the church's solidarity with the American people. Given Antonelli's reputation among Americans in Rome as wicked and untrustworthy, it is not clear whether his condolences were well received, but in view of the church's previously rather ambiguous position vis-à-vis the American Civil War it was a not insignificant gesture.[6] In private Italians expressed their grief too: "the whole world cries for the cruel loss of the new Washington," the historian and legal scholar Enrico Bottrigari recorded in his private chronicle of Bologna.[7]

The experience of Lincoln's death profoundly transformed the United States' political culture. Italy was one of the many nations that recognized early on the event's impact on America's process of nation building. In turn, the rituals invented to turn the great statesman's death into a founding moment for the new American Republic also informed the symbolic language of Italy's political life. As Sergio Luzzatto has shown, Lincoln's "railway obsequies" and the preservation of the dead president's body became the model for staging Giuseppe Mazzini's funeral in March 1872, offering a new model for cleberating republican rituals of death.[8] Embalming had become popular during the American Civil War in order to allow the relatives of fallen soldiers to receive the remains of their beloved ones in decent physical condition. Lincoln's widow had made a request for her husband to be buried in Springfield, Illinois, rather than in Washington, DC. As a consequence, Congress decided to have the body embalmed so as to prevent its deterioration during the two-week journey to Illinois. Following Lincoln's martyrdom, the railway journey formed the backdrop for his canonization. Countless Americans saw their president lying in state. Along the way, from Baltimore via Philadelphia, New York, Buffalo, Cleveland, Cincinnati, and Indianapolis to Chicago, people staged commemorations for their president; and even in small towns and villages, where the train did not stop, farmers stood with hat in hand along the tracks, accompanied by mourning mothers with children in their arms, to give their president a last salute.[9] In the words of Henry Ward Beecher, Harriet's brother, "cities and states are [the president's] pallbearer's" and "the nation rises up at every stage of his coming."[10]

Mazzini died in Pisa, having recently returned from decades of exile spent in Switzerland, France, and England. His body had to be transferred to Genoa, his birthplace and one of the centers of Italy's republican movement. Mazzini's death coincided with the celebrations for the name day of King Vittorio Emanuele II; and as a consequence the journey had to be delayed in order to avoid clashes between Mazzinian sympathizers and the authorities.[11] Following the example of Lincoln's railway obsequies, instead of taking a direct train from Pisa to Genoa, Mazzini was sent through the lands of his most fervent republican supporters. With the train traveling through Emilia and the Romagna, via Pistoia, Bologna, and Piacenza, the government feared that the passage of the exile's body might provoke political manifestations. On the contrary, there was no need to be concerned. The commemorations remained peaceful throughout the long journey, marked by an almost religious piety.[12] Once more following the model of Lincoln's obsequies, Genoa's republican leaders decided Mazzini's body was to be immortalized. Although Mazzini had pronounced himself explicitly against the practice of embalming, within the traditional language of Catholic symbolism immortalization would turn the prophet of democratic nationalism into a saint, marking an important transition from his position as revolutionary leader to spiritual icon.[13]

The American Civil War provided Italian Republicans with the symbolic tools to transform a revolutionary movement into a political religion that could be accommodated within the existing framework of the Savoy monarchy. Along with the movement's institutional accommodation within the liberal nation-state, the implicit comparison between the Unionist cause and Italian republicanism also helped to establish claims that the Mazzinians' sacrifice for the national cause throughout the long struggle for independence had played an equally important role in the history of the Risorgimento as Lincoln's crusade had done in the history of the United States.[14]

As demonstrated in chapter 5, the American Civil War and the Unification of Italy were connected events, which we understand differently if we look at them in transnational perspective. Transnationalizing US history involves understanding events in American history through their perception and their impact abroad, which informs the ways in which the world reacts to the United States. Meanwhile, the Italian experience of the American Civil War helped Italians to make the experience of their own Unification meaningful. The American Civil War provided possible readings for the events that were evolving at home, especially in the South. While some Italians assimilated their own fate to that of Uncle Tom, others found in Harriet Beecher Stowe's novel a way to understand the political events in their moral dimension. Stowe also offered a model for a Christian understanding of political change, one that was different from religion understood as an official doctrine. Many Italians had had similar experiences during the earlier period of the Risorgimento, when radical priests, especially after 1846, had joined the national movement and propagated the ideas of Mazzini from the altar.

At the same time these connected histories also helped Italians to draw distinctions between Italian and American experiences. The idea of a war between brothers seemed to prove the inexplicability of the United States as a country that remained incompatible with the political and social developments of the old continent, and of Italy in particular. The Civil War seemed to underline once more the absence of civilization that marked the American continent, a fact Italians had discussed since their first encounters with the American War of Independence. Confronted with social and cultural realities across the Atlantic, Italy was able to step out of its own alleged backwardness and affirm its historically and culturally informed identity. Although chapters 2 and 3 have demonstrated Italians' emphasis on the New World's otherness, this did not mean that political thinkers—as different from one another as Rosmini and Cattaneo—could not explore the United States as a laboratory of modernity. Especially during the periods of unpredictable political developments, in 1848–49 or during the Second War of Independence in 1859, Italians sought the United States as a constant point of reference to discuss their own experiences of historical change.

Within the perspective of the long nineteenth century Italians' predominantly distant and critical approach to American experiences also serves to contrast the sudden change in Italian attitudes toward American modernity during the *finesecolo*, which coincided with the start of Italian mass migration to the United States. During the first decade of the twentieth century Italian migration to the United States for the first time outnumbered other destinations, with 232,945 Italians immigrating to the United States.[15] As Emilio Franzina has demonstrated, "la febbre o la smania di andarsene" became a contaminating folly.[16] In 1901 the mayor of the small town of Moliterno in Lucania, better known from Carlo Levi's novel *Christ Stopped at Eboli*, presented the Italian prime minister Zanardelli with "the greetings of 8000 citizens, 3000 of which are in America, soon to be followed by the remaining 5000."[17]Not all of them made it on the other side of the Atlantic. As a proverb from Basilicata says, "L'America a ci acconza e a ci uasta" (America accommodates some and ruins others); similarly popular was the simple phrase "Managgia l'America!" (Damn America!).[18] An enquiry among working-class readers of the *Società Bibliografica Italiana* of 1906 revealed that at least forty-nine out of 459 had read Edmondo De Amicis' classic emigration novel *Sull'Oceano*, which depicted the fate of migrants with a grim realism.[19]

Bad feelings toward the host country notwithstanding, tales of Italy's American dream reflected growing disillusionment with the outcomes of Italy's Unification as a nation-state. These changing attitudes toward the United States should not be read in teleological fashion to obscure a long prehistory of Italy's self-confident distance toward a country that seemed to lack anything comparable to the proud history and culture of the Mediterranean world. For too long Italian evaluations of the new continent seemed to have echoed what Tacitus had written about Germany seventeen hundred years earlier: "to say nothing of the perils of a wild and unknown sea, who would leave Asia, Africa or Italy to visit Germany, with its unlovely scenery, its bitter climate, its general dreariness to sense and eye?"[20] Following Pocock's categories, the people inhabiting those spaces were "barbarians" in senses exceeding the original, classical meaning of the term as peoples who did not speak Greek or Latin. These people lived in "encampments among forests or open plains; they were 'uncivilised,' whatever the meaning of the term thus negated."[21] For a long time Americans stood for this absence of civilization. To argue such a case was not prejudice, but statement of a fact.

Too often debates about America's role in the political and cultural imagination of other countries have been reduced to questions of pro- or anti-Americanism, the idea of a blueprint for future political developments or blind admiration for material progress in a land of unlimited opportunities. Such ideas are always based on concepts of hierarchy and on static mental maps. Yes, America nurtured Europe's ambition, and in John Elliot's words "it also kept its dreams alive. And perhaps dreams were always more important than realities in the relationship of the Old World and the New."[22] But there also was a different, more philosophical dimension to Europe's relationship to America, which went beyond political and material progress. Therefore thinking about America was foremost a way of coming to terms with the changing semantic of time. The experience of modernity was the anthropological dimension of a philosophical problem that preoccupied Italians throughout the eighteenth and nineteenth centuries.

Since the second half of the eighteenth century, reflecting on their experience of change, commentators increasingly have attempted to give a secular philosophical meaning to time, widely reflected in social commentary and historical writing. Carlo Botta, one of the early protagonists of this book, prefaced the new edition of his constitutional pamphlet on the future of Lombardy with a detailed reflection on what "a man of the future might have to tell us."[23] For Botta, the historical future was not necessarily a rosy one: "Your ancestors could at least imagine themselves happy; your decendents will not."[24] Carlo Cattaneo was less pessimistic but noted in 1836 that "humanity's progress is tiresome, slow and gradual."[25] Both men used the United States as a way to reflect on the future, but without turning this future into prescriptive blueprints. Thinking about America represented a particular mode of articulating the changing semantic of time, the experience of a changing world at home.

A thinker who exerted considerable influence on the protagonists of the Risorgimento and Italian Unification—on Carlo Cattaneo, Giuseppe Ferrari, Gaetano Filangieri—was the early eighteenth-century

philosopher Giambattista Vico, who enjoyed a remarkable renaissance during the Risorgimento period.[26] Vico's theory of history offered them tools to
explain the New World in the making, as for Vico the facts of history, language,
and customs were man-made and therefore key to human nature.[27] The fact
that also "nations were made by men," and that they emerged from barbarism,
sets them apart from the sacred history of the divinely guided Hebrews.[28]
Thus, contrary to the history of Hebrews, profane nations are constituted by
the tension between barbarism and civilization (*mondo civile* in Vico's words).
Moreover, like Plato, Vico rejected the idea of humankind's perpetual progress,
propagating instead a cyclical idea of history and a form of idealism where the
idea constitutes a guiding principle rather than an attainable fact.

While Vico's cyclical concept of history creates tension with the belief in
progress that informed thinkers like Romagnosi and Cattaneo,[29] his concept
of human development was easily reconciled with the facts Italians observed
across the Atlantic during the second half of the nineteenth century: a history marked by the constant relapse into a state of barbarity. As Joseph Mali
has observed, for Vico "the fact that modern society was technically more advanced in its manners, laws, arts and sciences did not necessarily imply that
modern people have become more civil in their religious, moral, and aesthetic
disposition."[30] In the conclusions to his *Scienza Nuova* Vico observed that toward the later part of the new age of men the barbarism that had marked
the first stages of civil society returns as a "civil disease" to corrupt the body
politic from within. Writing from a European perspective, Vico associated this
"second barbarism" with the Middle Ages. America's classical age had been
the period of independence and the writing of its constitution. Ever since, the
United States had descended into a period of deep turmoil, in almost every
sense comparable to the "obstinate factions and desperate civil wars" Vico had
described in the concluding pages of his *Second Scienza Nuova*. Here humankind had started to turn "their cities into forests and the forests into dens and
lairs of men . . . , beasts made more inhuman by the barbarism of reflection
than the first men had been made by the barbarism of sense," words echoed in
the Italian descriptions of the American Civil War.[31] In line with providence
Vico also predicted that a new civic life would emerge from these ruins, a life
which in the Old World had begun several centuries ago.

For John Pocock the barbarism Edward Gibbon's *Decline and Fall of the
Roman Empire* associated with the fall of classical civilization also constituted the seeds of liberty; and in this context it is important to remember that
Gibbon wrote as a member of Parliament during the crisis of the American
Revolution.[32] The dying Riccardo in Verdi's *Un ballo in maschera* pursues a
similar idea, when he evokes the future of his "beloved America," an idea Verdi
and Somma applied to the situation of Italy in 1859, when the nation was
about to finally reach the fulfillment of its Risorgimento. What Cattaneo said
about humanity's future applied to America as well as Italy, that "misfortune

regenerates itself across the globe. Travelling shepherds pass over the ruins of marble cities. But an inextinguishable principle always survives and receives new strength after each convulsion, globally. Incorporating nation after nation, this principle condenses as a treasure of successive ages, the achievements of centuries and even the most remote labours of the human species."[33] There was every reason to believe that America would catch up with the Old World, in the same way as Italy would catch up with the most advanced nations of Europe. For Cattaneo, there was nothing to stop human progress.

Considering the many different experiences on which Italians were able to draw when they discussed their political future, why then does the United States still play a relatively prominent role in Risorgimento political thought? For many Italians—intellectuals and political activists in particular—America simply became a metaphor for a wide range of possible futures. A young country, still in a rough state of societal development and seemingly without history, America appeared nevertheless to be ahead of the present. As a possible future civilization (but one that was not quite there yet), comparisons with America allowed Italians to negotiate their own perception of change in historical time. Despite their lack of historical statehood, Italians were conscious of their past; but they also shared the common experience of being unsure about their present and future. It is in this sense that, following the suggestion by Michel de Certeau, America became a white canvas onto which Italians projected their own idea of a utopian, or indeed a dystopian future.

Reading Italy's relationship with the United States within this framework of debates on the changing semantics of historical time, it seems that Italians did not look to the United States as a political, social, or constitutional model; and if in the eyes of many Italians the United States became an epitome of modernity later in the nineteenth century, they did not necessarily identify with the particular model of modernity America stood for. Instead, rather than constituting a blueprint for their own future, America offered Italians an outlook on a wider range of possible futures. Most of these were set in conditions that were profoundly different from Italy's own experiences, making it in every respect unlikely that Italy would follow the same path.

NOTES

Introduction

1. Cattaneo, "Il poeta americano Longfellow" (1855), *Scritti letterari*, vol. 1, 461–73, 461

2. de Certeau, *L'écriture de l'histoire*, 9f. Van der Straet was a Flemish-born artist active in Florence, where he worked for the famous Giorgio Vasari.

3. On early European responses to the discovery of the New World, see Todorov, *La Conquête de Amérique*. Chiapelli, ed., *First images of America*. Bitterli, *Die "Wilden" und die "Zivilisierten."* Madsen, ed., *Visions of America since 1492*. Also Turgeon, Delâge, Ouellet, eds., *Transferts culturels et métissages*. For Italian reactions, see Buccini, *The Americas in Italian Literature and Culture*. del Negro, *Il mito Americano nella Venezia del Settecento*. Franzina, "L'America." For the transnational dimension of those debates, see Gerbi, *The Dispute of the New World*. For further bibliography, see Körner, "Introduction."

4. Darnton, "The Craze for America: Condorcet and Brissot," in *George Washington's False Teeth*, 119–36, 126, 123. On related readings of Rousseau, see also Taylor, *Mary Wollstonecraft*, 223. On Crèvecœur, see Gabaccia, *Foreign Relations*, 34ff.

5. See, in particular, Pocock, *Barbarism and Religion*, vol. 4. For a short introduction to this debate, see Philippe Roger, "Aufklärer gegen Amerika." Further to the works mentioned above, see O'Gorman, *The Invention of America*. Pagden, *The Fall of Natural Man*. Pagden, *European Encounters with the New World*. Greenblatt, *Marvelous Possessions*. Brading, *The First America*. Caesar, *Reconstructing America*. Canizares-Esguerra, *How to Write the History of the New World*. Fernández Armesto, *The Americas*. Craiutu and Isaacs, eds., *America through European Eyes*.

6. For an analysis of the available sources, see Del Negro, *Il mito Americano*, 466.

7. Alpers and Baxandall, *Tiepolo and the pictorial intelligence*, 115. In the context of this discussion on Giovanni Battista Tiepolo's *America*, see also Karol Berger's analysis of the work of Tiepolo's son Giandomenico, *Il Mondo Nuovo: Bach's Cycle, Mozart's Arrow*, 1–5.

8. The idea to rest the female allegory of America on an enormous alligator was not new when Tiepolo started the decorations in Würzburg: Jean Dumont had used the same image only a decade earlier, in 1742. Tableware and glassware, as produced at the time in Meissen, featured similar allegories. See, for instance, the reproductions in Honour, *The New Golden Land*, 108ff.

9. See, for instance, the illustrations for Vespucci's letter to Soderini, printed in 1509 in Strasburg. Italian images were similar, for instance Paolo Farinati's "America" (1595), in Honour, *The New Golden Land*, 10f., 97. References to cannibalism in the New World were common throughout the sixteenth century.

10. Genovesi, "Da *Delle Lezioni di commercio o sia d'economia civile*," *Scritti*, 133–207, 183. On Genovesi also Venturi, *Settecento riformatore: Da Muratori a Beccaria*, 523ff.

11. Quoted from an early English translation: Giovanni Botero, *Relations, of the Most Famous Kingdoms and Commonweales thorough the World* (London: Iohn Iaggard, 1616), 425. This is a strongly abbreviated edition. For one of the more widely used Italian editions, see Giovanni Botero, *Relationi universali di G. B. divise in quattro parti* (Venice: Bertani, 1659). The point of discussing these early representations here is to underline the remarkable continuities of certain features.

12. Krückmann, *Heaven on Earth*, 53. On the use of light, see Alpers and Baxandall, *Tiepolo and the Pictorial Intelligence*, 118. For a detailed description of the scene, see

Helmberger and Staschull, *Tiepolo's World*, 29–35. With the end of the Spanish War of Succession, and Venice in political and economic decline, Venetian artists happily accepted well-paid commissions from the princes North of the Alps.

13. Del Negro, *Il mito Americano*, 498.

14. Cattaneo, "Americana," *Scritti letterari*, vol. 2, 358–59.

15. A better-known example would be the erotic cantata by Johann Christoph Friedrich Bach, "Die Amerikanerin" (1773), on a text by Heinrich Wilhelm von Gerstenberg.

16. Cattaneo, "Di alcuni stati moderni" (1842), *Scritti storici e geografici*, vol. 1, 255–301, 255. (The piece was first published as an anonymous review of a book by Cristoforo Negri in *Politecnico*.)

17. Maurizio Isabella's book has set the agenda for transnational approaches to the intellectual history of the Risorgimento: Isabella, *Risorgimento in Exile*. On the idea of the United States as "a working model" for republicans abroad see Doyle, *The Cause of all Nations*, 7f.

18. Quoted in Galante Garrone, *La stampa periodica italiana dal 1815 al 1847*, 116. On the general situation of the press during the first half of the Risorgimento, see Galante Garrone, "I Giornali della Restaurazione 1815–1847." See also Capra, "Il giornalismo nell'eta rivoluzionaria e napoleonica," in Castronovo and Tranfaglia, eds., *Storia della Stampa italiana*, vol. 1, 373–540.

19. Quoted in Galante Garrone, "I Giornali della Restaurazione," 14.

20. Del Negro, *Il mito Americano*, 458. Porcella, "Premesse dell'emigrazione di massa in età prestatistica (1800–1850)," 31.

21. [Burke], *Storia degli stabilimenti europei in America divisa in sei parti* (Venice: Antonio Graziosi, 1763), vol. 2, iii.

22. Polzonetti, *Italian Opera in the Age of the American Revolution*, 139.

23. Del Negro, *Il mito Americano*, 464. On this late encounter also Spini, "Prefazione," in Spini et al., *Italia e America dal settecento all'età dell'imperialismo*, 9–24, 11f., and Spini, "I puritani della Nuova Inghilterra e la cultura italiana," in *Atti del I Congresso Internazionale di Storia Americana*, 23–31, 23.

24. Spini, "I puritani della Nuova Inghilterra e la cultura italiana."

25. Del Negro, *Il mito Americano*, 458. Palmer, *The Age of Democratic Revolution*, vol. 1, 241.

26. Gabaccia, *Foreign Relations*. During the nineteenth century up to 80 percent of immigrants returned to Europe at least once to visit their countries of birth: ibid., 26.

27. Connell, "Darker Aspects of Italian American Prehistory," 12.

28. In the decade from 1881 to 1890, 24,487 immigrated to the United States, but more than twice as many still preferred Argentina or Brazil as their country of destination: *Sommario di Statistiche Storiche dell'Italia, 1861–1975*, 34f. See also Marraro, *American Opinion on the Unification of Italy*, ix, and Martellone, "Italian Mass Emigration to the United States, 1876–1930: A Historical Survey." Golini and Amato, "Uno sguardo a un secolo e mezzo di emigrazione italiana," 47. On the profile of later waves of immigrants, see *Gli Italiani negli Stati Uniti*. On the preference for other countries than the United States, see Pierattini, *"Vien via, si va in America, si parte,"* 59. For a critical debate of these issues, see Friedman, "Beyond 'Voting with their Feet': Toward a Conceptual History of 'America' in European Migrant Sending Communities, 1860s to 1914." For a cultural perspective, see Franzina, *Dall'Arcadia in America*, and Franzina, *L'immaginario degli emigranti*.

29. Del Negro, *Il mito Americano*, 453. Fiorentino, *Gli Stati Uniti e il Risorgimento d'Italia*, 28. For Italy and Rome in American cultural imagination, see Vance, *America's Rome*, vol. 2.

30. Cattaneo, "Il poeta americano Longfellow."

31. Michele Leoni, "Viaggio agli stati uniti d'America: Od osservazioni su la società, i costumi e' il governo di quella contrada; Di Miss Wright: Londra 1821," in *Antologia*, 7, July–September 1822, 390–410, 391.

32. Carlo Giuseppe Londonio, *Storia delle colonie inglesi in America dalla loro fondazione, fino allo stabilmento della loro indipendenza* (Milan: Destefanis, 1812–13), t. 1, 1.

33. Ibid., t. 2, 87. On uncertainty associated with independence, see Burk, *Old World, New World*, 161.

34. Jonathan Israel, *Democratic Enlightenment*, 413ff., quote 414f.

35. Guillaume Thomas François Raynal, *The Revolution of America* (London: Lockyer Davis, 1781). The same publisher also printed the French edition.

36. Ibid., 8.

37. Ibid., 180.

38. Darnton, "The Craze for America: Condorcet and Brissot," 122. On the biographical context, see Badinter and Badinter, *Condorcet: Un intellectuel en politique* (Paris: Fayard, 1988), 201ff.

39. Quoted in Lukes and Urbinati, "Editors Introduction," in Condorcet, *Political Writings*, xv–xlii, xxxix.

40. Condorcet, "The Sketch," in *Political Writings*, 1–147, 104f. On the limits of Condorcet's claims as for the Revolution's influence in Europe, see Williams, *Condorcet and Modernity*, 251. His 1788 *Lettres d'un citoyen des États-Unis à un Français* specifically identified Franco-American parallels.

41. On Condorcet's role in drafting the constitution of 1793, see Israel, *Revolutionary Ideas*, chpt. 13.

42. On Mazzei, see, in particular, Tortarolo, *Illuminismo e rivoluzioni*.

43. For instance, the references to America in Claudio Todeschi, *Saggi di agricoltura, manifatture, e commercio, coll' applicazione di essi al vantaggio del dominio pontificio* (Rome: Stamperia di A. Casaletti, 1770). Louis de Beausobre, *Introduzione generale allo studio della politica, delle finanze, e del commercio: Opera riveduta dall' autore, ed accresciuta e corretta in più luoghi dal traduttore* (Yverdon, 1771). Domenico Grimaldi, *Saggio di economia campestre per la Calabria ultra* (Naples: Orsini, 1770), 100, 185, 209, 316. Jacques Savary des Brûlons, *Dizionario di commercio, accresciuto di vari importantissimi articoli, tratti dall' enciclopedia e dalle memorie dell' accuratissimo Mr. Carcin, ec. Ed. prima italiana* (Venice: G. Pasquale, 1770–71).

44. Jacques-Vincent de la Croix [Delacroix], *Constitutions des principaux des États de l'Europe et des États-Unis de l'Amérique* (Paris: Buisson, 1791). De la Croix also translated John Adams into French. For his political role, see Michel Gilot, "Jacques-Vincent de la Croix," in *Édition électronique revue, corrigée et augmentée du Dictionnaire des journalistes* (1600–1789) (eds., Anne-Marie Mercier-Faivre et Denis Reynaud), http://dictionnaire-journalistes.gazettes18e.fr/journaliste/214-jacques-delacroix (accessed 25/8/2015), and Borré, *Un rivoluzionario durante l'antico regime*. (Throughout documentation, dates will be given day/month/year.)

45. De la Croix, *Constitutions des principaux États de l'Europe et des États-Unis de l'Amérique*, vol. 2, 341. For direct comparisons with the situation in France, see ibid., 355f.

46. See, for instance, Foscolo, *Lettere scritte dall'Inghilterra*, 19.

47. On Wollstonecraft's attitude toward the American Revolution, see Chris Jones, "Mary Wollstonecraft's *Vindications* and Their Political Tradition," in Johnson, ed., *The Cambridge Companion to Mary Wollstonecraft*, 42–58. Taylor described Wollstonecraft's *Vindication of the Rights of Men* as the first "general onslaught on Burke": *Mary Wollstonecraft*, 7.

48. An exception is the economist Francesco Ferrara, who acknowledged Martineau: Anna Maria Lazzarino Del Grosso, "Gli Stati Uniti d'America nell'opera di Francesco Ferrara," in *Francesco Ferrara e il suo tempo*, 551–72, 553. On Martineau's general impact, see Burk, *Old World, New World*, 290f.

49. Lazzarino Del Grosso, "Gli Stati Uniti d'America nell'opera di Francesco Ferrara," 557, 567.

50. Genovesi, "Dall'Edizione della *Storia del Commercio della Gran Brettagna* scritta da John Cary," *Scritti*, 88–119, 112.

51. The Treaty of Aachen concluded the War of the Austrian Succession over Maria Theresia's succession to the realms of the Habsburgs.

52. Venturi, *Settecento riformatore: Da Muratori a Beccaria*, 411.

53. Chorley, *Oil, Silk and Enlightenment*, 11.

54. Franco Venturi, "Introduzione," in Genovesi, *Scritti*, 287–97, 292. See also Venturi, *Settecento riformatore: Da Muratori a Beccaria*, 571ff.

55. Tortarolo, *Illuminismo e rivoluzioni*, 42. See also "Laura Bassi," in *Encyclopedia of World Biography*, 2004, http://www.encyclopedia.com/doc/1G2-3404707527.html (accessed 14/10/2015).

56. Giura, *Russia, Stati Uniti d'America e Regno di Napoli*, 23f., 68. Howard R. Marraro, "Il Risorgimento in Sicilia visto dagli Americani," in *La Sicilia e l'unità d'Italia*, vol. 2, 444–61, 444. On the role of these bilateral treaties and hesitance establishing them, see Gabaccia, *Foreign Relations*, 13, 42ff. Emphasizing the reciprocal nature of these relationships also helps to transnationalize US history: Tyrrell, *Transnational Nation*. Bender, *A Nation among Nations*.

57. Istituto Mazziniano, Genoa. Cart. 101, 23685: G. Deabbate, Filadelfia, *Relazione sul commercio tra America e Stati Sardi*. Americans produced similar lists of imports and exports to specific Italian cities, in this case linked to the American project of mercantile expansion in the Mediterranean: Gemme, *Domesticating Foreign Struggles*, 61. For an overview of the kingdom's relationship with the United States, see Mariano, "Da Genova a New York?"

58. Ducci, Luconi, Pretelli, *Le relazioni tra Italia e Stati Uniti*, 19–23. For a full overview of diplomatic relations, see Marraro, ed., *L'unificazione italiana vista dai diplomatici statunitensi*.

59. Sarti, "La democrazia radicale: Uno sguardo reciproco tra Stati Uniti e Italia," 137, 144f.

60. Fiorentino, "La politica estera degli Stati Uniti e l'unità d'Italia," 47f., 52f. Fiorentino, *Gli Stati Uniti e il Risorgimento d'Italia*, 21ff., 44f. See also Pécout, "Cavour visto dagli Stati Uniti," 128.

61. Monsagrati, "Gli intellettuali americani e il processo di unificazione italiana," 26. Fiorentino points to ideological differences between the movement's Italian and American wings: *Gli Stati Uniti e il Risorgimento d'Italia*, 41.

62. Gemme, *Domesticating Foreign Struggles*, 72.

63. *Monitore di Bologna (MdB)*, 20/12/1864.

64. Kaplan, *Divided by Faith*, 339. Spini, *Risorgimento e protestanti*, 10f. On Italian protestants' transnational connections, see also Vangelista and Reginato, "L'emigrazione valdese."

65. Spini, *Risorgimento e protestanti*, 218.

66. Ibid., 41, 74ff., 83f. Sestan, *La Firenze di Vieusseux e di Caponi*, 4.

67. On Vieusseux and his circle, also see Bagnoli, *La politica delle idee*. See also Kroll, *Die Revolte des Patriziats*. On Vieusseux's international circle, see Pacini, "Ospiti stranieri di casa Vieusseux nella Firenze di metà ottocento." Ciampini, *Gian Pietro Vieusseux*, offers

a rather idealized account of the group. For the wider editorial context of *Antologia*, see Coppini, *Il Granducato di Toscana*, 223ff.

68. Spini, *Risorgimento e Protestanti*, 88f.

69. As Eugenio Biagini has pointed out, Mazzini's thought included important elements not just of Saint-Simonism and Janseism, but also of Protestantism: "Mazzini and Anticlericalism: The English in Exile."

70. Quoted in Tarozzi, "Filopanti professore universitario e insegnante popolare," 112.

71. Riall, *Garibaldi*, 146f., 299.

72. Theodore Dwight later published *The Roman Republic of 1849, with accounts of the Inquisition and the Siege of Rome* (1851). Spini, *Risorgimento e protestanti*, 324.

73. Ibid., 223f.

74. Rossi, *The Image of America in Mazzini's Writings*, 31ff.

75. Marraro, *American Opinion on the Unification of Italy*, chpt. 2.

76. Elliott, *The Old World and the New*, 7.

77. Bayly, *The Birth of the Modern World*.

78. For a critical assessment of the "dual revolution" approach associated with Hobsbawm, see Jones and Wahrman, "Introduction: An Age of Cultural Revolutions?"

79. R. R. Palmer, *The Age of Democratic Revolution*. For a recent critique, see Nash, "Sparks from the Altar of '76: International Repercussions and Reconsiderations of the American Revolution." Polasky argues that "the call to liberty resonated with different accents across the Atlantic world." Polasky, *Revolutions without Borders*, 5. With regard to the Italian Risorgimento, Fiorentino takes a similar approach: *Gli Stati Uniti e il Risorgimento d'Italia*, 9.

80. Whatmore, "The French and North American Revolutions in Comparative Perspective," 223.

81. Giorgio Pallavicini, "Discorso ai Repubblicani" (Genoa: Dagnino, [1848]), British Library (BL): Miscellanee politiche genovesi. 804.k.13.16.

82. de Maistre, "Considerations on France," in *The Works of Joseph de Maistre*, 47–91, 67, 84. During the Revolution Savoy was taken by France. De Maistre then worked in the service of the king of Sardinia. On de Maistre's attitudes, see Roger, *The American Enemy*, 45.

83. Noether, "Introduction," vii.

84. Gemme, *Domesticating Foreign Struggles*, 3. The reference to Gemme is not necessarily meant to endorse her description of the peninsula in terms of "foreign" occupation and "colonial bonds."

85. Ibid., 108.

86. Fiorentino, "Il governo degli Stati Uniti e la Repubblica Romana del 1849," 94.

87. Quoted in Gemme, *Domesticating Foreign Struggles*, 16. Gemme discusses numerous similar examples.

88. Marraro, *American Opinion on the Unification of Italy*, ix. He also stands for a romantic vision of the Risorgimento rooted in the Roman Empire and a sentiment that could be traced back to the thirteenth century.

89. Armitage and Subrahmanyam, "Introduction: The Age of Revolutions, c. 1760–1840—Global Causation, Connection, and Comparison," xvii. For a more balanced account of the United States as a model Republic, see Ferris, "A Model Republic."

90. Dall'Osso, *Voglia D'America*, 13.

91. Fisher, *The Republican Tradition in Europe*, 167f., 270ff.

92. Armitage, *The Declaration of Independence*, 3.

93. On the Declaration's legal status, see Armitage, *Foundations of Modern Political Thought*, 193, 202.

94. Billias, "American Constitutionalism and Europe, 1776–1848," 13f. As for the Declaration of Independence, Billias's chapter provides little evidence of direct influence in Europe apart from the Low Countries. Regarding other documents, Billias points out that "extreme care must be taken, however, in attributing these general European developments to direct American influence" (25). Even during the period of direct American intervention in Italy's political future after World War II, Italy "did not feel the need to turn to American political culture and believed the intellectual instruments their own tradition provided were enough." See Bonazzi, "Tradurre/Tradire: The Declaration of Independence in the Italian Context," 1355.

95. Billias, "American Constitutionalism and Europe," 28.

96. Lerg, *Amerika als Argument*.

97. Pace, *Benjamin Franklin and Italy*, 169.

98. Polasky, *Revolutions without Borders*, 1, 51ff.

99. Baker, *The Fortunate Pilgrims*, 186.

100. See, for instance, Pellegrino Rossi, *Traité de droit pénal* (troisième édition), Faustin Hélie, ed. (Paris: Guillaumin, 1863), t. 1, 13f.

101. Rossi, *Traité de droit pénal*, t. 2, 366, also 377.

102. An exception is a passing reference to Franklin: Rossi, *Traité de droit pénal*, t. 1, 203. Based on his lectures at the Collège de France, this course was originally written in the second half of the 1830s. Also his four-volume *Constitutional History*, while drawing on numerous English comparisons, hardly mentions the United States: Pellegrino Rossi, *Cours de droit constitutionnel* (Paris: Guillaumin, 1866), t. 1, 283ff. (These lectures were first delivered between 1835 and 1845.) The situation is similar for his lectures on political economy, which rarely refer to the United States: Pellegrino Rossi, *Cours d'économie politique*, 4th ed. (Paris: Guillaumin, 1865), t. 3, 254 and t. 4, 318ff.

103. Isnenghi, *L'Italia in piazza*, 57. For the effects of Rossi's assassination on the development of Mazzini's political thought, see Biagini, "Mazzini and Anticlericalism," 150f.

104. Pocock, *The Machiavellian Moment*.

105. Hughes, *The United States and Italy*, 3.

106. Giorgio Spini, "I puritani della Nuova Inghilterra," 24.

107. Connell, "Darker Aspects of Italian American Prehistory," 16.

108. Bessler, *The Birth of American Law*, 119. See also Tortarolo, *Illuminismo e rivoluzioni*, 42.

109. Pocock, *The Machiavellian Moment*, 506.

110. Vincenzo Gioberti, *Del rinnovamento civile d'Italia* (Paris and Turin: Giuseppe Bocca, 1851), vol. 2, 119.

111. Ibid., 538.

112. Jaume, *Tocqueville*, 9, 13f.

113. Palmer, *The Age of Democratic Revolution*, vol. 1, 4. For a more recent French perspective, see Solé, *Les révolutions de la fin du XVIIIe siècle aux Amériques et en Europe*.

114. For a critique of this historiographical convention, see Isabella, "Nationality before liberty? Risorgimento Political Thought in Transnational Context."

115. Venturi, *Settecento riformatore: Da Muratori a Beccaria*, 727.

116. See, for instance, O'Connor, *The Romance of Italy and the English Imagination*. Petrusewicz, *Come il Meridione divenne una Questione*. Moe, *The View from Vesuvius*.

117. Isabella, *Risorgimento in Exile*.

118. Istituto Mazziniano, Genoa: 001410, "Cristina Belgiojoso," Milan 29 aprile 1848; 00245, "La Principessa Belgiojoso," Tip. Faziola, [1848].

119. See, for instance, Bracewell and Drace-Francis, eds., *Under Eastern Eyes*

120. Gioberti, *Del rinnovamento Civile d'Italia*, vol. 1, 201.

121. Gioberti, *Del rinnovamento Civile d'Italia*, vol. 2, 765, 122.

122. Pecchio, "L'anno mille ottocento ventisei dell'Inghilterra" (1827), *Scritti politici*, 277–354, 332f.

123. Rossi, *The Image of America*, 78. For Ricasoli, see *La Nazione*, 29/3/1862. On the idea of an Anglo-Saxon race uniting the peoples of Britain and America, see Thier, "A World Apart, a Race Apart?" On the image of Britain and London among the early Italian exiles, see Morelli, "Gli esuli italiani e la società inglese nella prima metà dell'ottocento." For an analysis of their ideas about Britain, see Isabella, *Risorgimento in Exile*, chpts. 6 and 7.

124. Buonomo, *Backward Glances*, 18.

125. See for instence *La Nazione*, 5/5/1861.

126. Cattaneo, "Le origini della civiltà in Europa" (1863), *Scritti storici e geografici*, vol. 3, 280–91, 290.

127. Cattaneo, "Di alcuni stati moderni" (1842), *Scritti storici e geografici*, vol. 1, 255–301, 272f. See also Ridolfi, "La *Démocratie en Amérique* di Tocqueville e la sua ricezione nell'Italia del Risorgimento," 136.

128. James Fenimore Cooper, *L'ultimo dei mohicani: Romanzo storico relativo ai tempi delle guerre americane* (Livorno: Vignozzi, 1828).

129. James Fenimore Cooper, *The Last of the Mohicans: A Narrative of 1757 by the Author of The Spy* (London: J. Miller, 1826).

130. James Fenimore Cooper, *La spia: Romanzo storico relativo ai tempi della guerra americana* (Livorno: Sardi e Bertani, 1828).

131. Honour, *The New Golden Land*, 229ff. On Buffalo Bill Shows, see Körner, "Barbarous America."

132. Chiavistelli, *Dallo stato alla nazione*, 158.

133. N.A., "The works of James Fenimore Cooper," in *North American Review*, 74 (1852), 147–61. I am grateful to David Laven for this reference. On Cooper's impact among Italians, see Rolle, *The Immigrant Upraised*, 26, 59.

134. Lombardo, *La ricerca del vero*, 14, 21f. For the imapact of American literature on the later generation of Italian writers, see also Gustavo Strafforello, *Letteratura americana* (Manuali Hoepli; Milan: Hoepli, 1884). Strafforello uses the term "letteratura' in a large sense, to include academic, scientific, and philosophical works as well as travel writers and journalists.

135. Enrico Nencioni, "I poeti americani" (1885), in Nencioni, *Saggi critici di letteratura inglese* (Florence, 1897), 99–126, 100f. Edited with an introduction by Carducci in 1897, the volume collects a selection of articles published by Nencioni over the past thirty years.

136. Nencioni, "I poeti americani," 100, 113. For Longfellow's poem, see Marraro, *American Opinion on the Unification of Italy*, xv.

137. Gustavo Tirinelli, "Edgardo Allan Poe," *Nuova antologia*, April 1877, 731–62. Nencioni, "I poeti americani," 109. Bizzarely, Strafforello lists Whitman under "Umoristi," at the very end of his small volume of 1884: *Letteratura americana*, 144ff. On Whitman, see also Nencioni, "Il poeta della guerra americana" (1891), in Nencioni, *Saggi critici di letteratura inglese*, 204–30. Lombardo, *La ricerca del vero*, 25–29.

138. On Twain's visit to Naples, see Macry, "The Southern Metropolis: Redistributive Circuits in Nineteenth-Century Naples," 59. For Melville and Italy, see Berthold, *American Risorgmento*.

139. Rossi, *The Image of America*, 2f. Mazzini to Emilie A. Hawkes, 12/12/1857, *Edizione nazionale*, vol. 60, 180–82, 182.

140. Cooper, *Gleanings in Europe*, 33, 80, 245, 167.

141. Franzina, *Dall'Arcadia in America*, 76. On the concept of the "professional exile," see Tóth, *An Exiled Generation*, 114.

142. Sioli, "Se non c'è il conquibus si muore come cani: Luigi Tinelli a New York (1851–1873)." Tinelli spent two periods of exile in the United States, first from 1836 to 1840 and then from 1851 to 1873. See also Liburdi, "Le Memorie Autobiografiche di Pasqule Papiri e i suoi viaggi in America," 392.

143. Mazzini to his mother, 22/3/1839. *Edizione nazionale*, vol. 15, 428–34, 431.

144. Antonio Caccia, *Europa ed America: Scene della vita dal 1848 al 1850*. Monaco, 1850. The two protagonists of the novel were surprised how little interest Americans had in their revolution: Franzina, *Dall'Arcadia in America*, 43. On criminalizing southern Italians in America, see Margavio, "The Reaction of the Press to the Italian-American in New Orleans, 1880–1920." On the difficult integration of Italian migrants, see Schneider and Schneider, "Gli Stati Uniti e la Sicilia: Ripercussioni di un rapport nord-sud," 206ff.

145. Giuseppe Garibaldi, *Memorie autobiografiche* (Florence: Barbèra, 1888), 264ff. Jessie White Mario, *Garibaldi e i suoi tempi* (Milan: Treves, 1884), 364f. See also Riall, *Garibaldi*, 107ff. Scirocco, *Garibaldi*, 192, 93. For comparisons between Garibaldi and Washington, see Francesco Bertolini, *Garibaldi e la nuova Italia* (Naples: Detken, 1882, 6, 9). For further examples, see also MackSmith, *Garibaldi*, 69. On General Avezzana's reception in New York, see Marraro, *American Opinion on the Unification of Italy*, 166.

146. Marcella Pellegrino Suttcliffe has argued that in international political debates Garibaldi's role was often subordinate to that of Mazzini: *Victorian Radicals and Italian Democrats*, 6.

147. Stefani, *I prigionieri dello Spielberg sulla via dell'esilio*, 9ff., 37f. Sioli, "Se non c'è il conquibus si muore come cani: Luigi Tinelli a New York (1851–1873)," 141. On those who made their way to America, see Montini, "Vita Americana di Pietro Borsieri." Mentioned also by Giuseppe Ferrari, "La Rivoluzione e le riforme in Italia" (January 1848), *Scritti Politici*, 3–55, 49f.

148. Fiorentino, "La politica estera degli Stati Uniti e l'unità d'Italia." See also Riall, *Garibaldi*, 113, 166. When Americans supported the Risorgimento it was often not out of idealism but anticipating future economic benefits from a potential market for American products. See Gemme, *Domesticating Foreign Struggles*, 6.

149. Monsagrati, "Gli intellettuali americani e il processo di unificazione italiana," 18. Vance, *America's Rome*, vol. 2, 122ff., 129. Gemme, *Domesticating Foreign Struggles*, 131ff. See also Buonomo, *Backward Glances*; as well as the essays in Martin and Person, eds., *Roman Holidays*. For a general overview on anti-Italian sentiment, though within a different chronological framework, see Connell and Gardaphé, eds., *Anti-Italianism*. (The ethnocentric agenda of some of the volume's contributions is not unproblematic.)

150. See, for instance, *L'Universo illustrato* 1, 8 (November 1866), 122ff.

151. Giovanni Capellini, *Ricordi di un viaggio scientifico nell'America settentrionale nel 1863* (Bologna: Vitali, 1867), 20f.

152. When differentiating between the text and its reception, I do not claim to uncover the original meaning of a text. Instead, my emphasis is on recovering the historical consciousness with which texts were read in changing historical contexts. An important basis for this approach is Gadamer, *Wahrheit und Methode*. The relationship between event and memory describes a different problem. See for instance W. G. Sebald, "Beyle, or Love Is a Madness Most Discreet," *Vertigo*, 1–30. Sebald's piece analyzes Stendhal's Italian experiences during the Napoleonic period, which are directly relevant to this book.

153. For the Italian edition, see Lorenzo Da Ponte, *Memorie di Lorenzo da Ponte da Ceneda in tre volumi scritti da esso* (2nd. ampl. ed.; New York: Gray and Bunce, 1829–30). I am grateful to Antonio Sennis for his help with the translation.

154. For the full text and the reading in Treviso, see Marchesan, *Della vita e delle opere di Lorenzo da Ponte*, 365, 372ff. Hodges, *Lorenzo Da Ponte*, 227. See also Del Negro, *Il mito Americano*, 645.

155. Polzonetti, *Italian Opera in the Age of the American Revolution*, 309. Fohlen, *Benjamin Franklin*, 276ff. On the popularity of American-themed theater, see also Darnton, "The Craze for America: Condorcet and Brissot," in *George Washington's False Teeth*, 119–36.

156. Hodges, *Lorenzo Da Ponte*, 66f. Beales, *Joseph II*, vol. 2, 467, also 656–62.

157. Hodges, *Lorenzo Da Ponte*, 202. Livingstone, "Introduction." On the work's reception, see Boni, "Studi danteschi in America." Also Buccini, *The Americas in Italian Literature and Culture*, 161ff. Further Italian editions appeared in 1871 and 1900.

158. Quoted after the American edition Da Ponte, *Memoirs*, 345.

159. Si coltiva ogni scienza,
  Sopratutto la numerica,
  In cui celebre è l'America.
  Ma ne' studi le lingue
  Un po' meno si distingue.
Quoted in Buccini, *The Americas in Italian Literature and Culture*, 169.

160. [Burke], *Storia degli stabilimenti europei in America*. For the English original, see [Burke], *An Account of the European Settlements in America: In Six Parts* (London: Dodsley, 1757). On the question of authorship, see Bourke, *Empire and Revolution*, 162. (I am grateful to the author for his help with the contextualization of the work.) On the Italian edition's impact, see Del Negro, *Il mito Americano*, 475f.

161. On these chronological issues, see Banti, *Il Risorgimento italiano*, v–xii.

162. Bourke, *Empire and Revolution*, 174f. The work also served as a warning to France against colonial expansion: Lock, *Edmund Burke*, vol. 1, 131.

163. [Burke], *Storia degli stabilimenti europei in America*, vol. 2, 145ff.

164. Ibid., vol. 2, 68.

165. Maciag, *Edmund Burke in America*, 10. See also Lock, *Edmund Burke*, vol. 1, 126.

166. Whatmore, "Burke on Political Economy," 85.

167. *Il Gazzettiere americano contenente un distinto ragguaglio di tutte le parti del Nuovo Mondo*. 3 vols. (Livorno: Marco Coltellini, 1763). For a modern facsimile and a series of excellent articles on the edition, see *Il Gazzettiere americano* (Silvia Di Batte, ed.; Livorno: Debatte Editore, 2003). The Italian edition is based on *The American Gazetteer Containing a Distinct Account of All the Parts of the New World* (London: Millar and Tonson, 1762).

168. *Gazzettiere Americano*, vol. 1, v.

169. Ibid., vol. 1, 43.

170. Ibid., vol. 3, 235f., 241. Quoted from the English original, vol. 3, unpaginated.

171. Ibid., vol. 3, 237. Quoted from the English original, vol. 3, unpaginated.

172. Vincenzo Martinelli, *Storia del governo d'Inghilterra e delle sue colonie* (London, 1776).

173. Venturi, *Settecento riformatore: La caduta dell'antico regime*, vol. 4, i, 46.

174. P. [Pietro Verri], "Storia naturale del caffè," in *Il Caffè: 1764–1766*, 14–17, 17. For the periodical's intellectual context, see Venturi, *Settecento riformatore: Da Muratori a Beccaria*, 681ff.

175. Grab, "The Italian Enlightenment and the American Revolution," 38.

176. Luigi Castiglioni, *Viaggio negli Stati Uniti dell'America settentrionale fatto negli anni 1758, 1786, e 1787* (Milan: Marelli, 1790), vol. 1, vif.

177. Bessler, *The Birth of American Law*, 105. For a summary of Castiglioni's description of the United States, see ibid., 109ff.

178. Castiglioni mentions this fact in the preface of his first volume: Castiglioni, *Viaggio negli Stati Uniti*, vol. 1, v. For similar observations, see, for instance, the anonymous article Em. R., "Ricerche sui progressi dell'instruzione, sulle invenzioni meccaniche e su

i costumi, negli Stati Uniti dell'America Settentrionale," in *Antologia*, vol. 5, *January–March 1822*, 420–30, 420.

179. Grab, "The Italian Enlightenment and the American Revolution," 42.

180. For this context, see Pocock, *Barbarism and Religion*. vol. 2, 155.

181. Venturi, "Introduzione," 295.

182. Frosini, "Introduzone." On Filangieri's international impact, see Trampus, "Verfassung und Recht: Filangieri und die europäische Rezeption der Scienza della legislazione." See also Bessler, *The Birth of American Law*, 132f.

183. de Pascale, *Filosofia e politica nel pensiero italiano fra sette e ottocento*, 72.

184. Pace, *Benjamin Franklin and Italy*, 155. The episode shows surprising parallels to the experience of Beccaria and of Pietro and Alessandro Verri: Israel, *Democratic Enlightenment*, 338.

185. Robertson, *The Case for the Enlightenment*, 385f.

186. See, for instance, his discussion of desertion, which briefly mentions the United Provinces of America, although he develops his main argument with reference to ancient authors: Filangieri, *La Scienza della Legislazione*/Constant, *Comento sulla Scienza della Legislazione* (Vittorio Frosini, ed.), t. 2, 54f.

187. Ibid., t. 2, 56.

188. Goethe first met Filangieri in March 1787. For a short account, see Goethe, *Italienische Reise*, in *Goethes Werke*, vol. 10, 197f., 209. In *Wilhelm Meisters Wanderjahre* Juliette mentions Filangieri to Wilhelm: *Goethes Werke*, vol. 7, 68.

189. Frosini, "Introduzone," xviff.

190. Filangieri, *La Scienza della Legislazione*/Constant, *Comento sulla Scienza della Legislazione* (Vittorio Frosini, ed.), t. 1, 197.

191. Castiglioni, *Viaggio negli Stati Uniti*, vol. 2, 92f. On changing cultural attitudes to fornication and adultery in the early modern period, see Hufton, *The Prospect before Her*, vol. 1, 299ff., and for the Puritan context ibid., 306f. For a transnational perspective on the domestication of politics, see Soldani, "Il Risorgimento delle donne," 187f.

192. Castiglioni, *Viaggio negli Stati Uniti*, vol. 2, 92f.

193. Ibid., vol. 2, 93.

194. Hufton, *The Prospect before Her*, vol. 1, 308. On the sexual conventions to which Castiglioni compared his American experiences, see Bizzocchi, "Una nuova morale per la donna e la famiglia," in Banti and Ginsborg, eds., *Storia d'Italia*, 76ff. On the representation of virtuous women in national discourse, see Banti, *L'onore della nazione*, 47ff. For the changing image of American women, see Miller, "Liberty, Lipstick, and Lobsters," in particular 93ff.

195. [Gianrinaldo Carli], *Delle lettere americane*, 2 vols. ([Florence]: Cosmopoli, 1780), vol. 2, 66ff. Carli was originally from Capodistria (Koper) and wrote on a wide range of historical, economic, and literary topics, while also working as an economic advisor to the Habsburgs. See also Sergio Romagnoli, "Il Caffè tra Milano e l'Europa," in *Il Caffè: 1764–1766*, lxiv. On Carli's significance for the Risorgimento, see also Beales and Biagini, *The Risorgimento and the Unification of Italy*, 69.

196. In addition to two eighteenth-century Italian editions, French and German translations were published shortly after the Italian original. The volume was included in Carlo Cattaneo's library: Lacaita, Gobbo, and Turiel, eds., *La biblioteca di Carlo Cattaneo*, 173.

197. Carli states in his preface that his main motive in writing these letters is to respond to the thesis put forward by de Pauw, to whom he refers as Pavv or Paw. [Carli], *Delle lettere americane*, vol. 1, 3ff., 8. De Pauw's theories were also rejected by Castiglioni, *Viaggio negli Stati Uniti*, vol. 2, 155. For the origin of de Pauw's argument and his impact on Robertson and Raynal, see Pocock, *Barbarism and Religion*, vol. 4, 175–79.

198. Hunt, Jacob, Mijnhardt, *The Book That Changed Europe*.

199. Elio Apih, "CARLI, Gian Rinaldo," in*Dizionario Biografico degli Italiani*, v. 20 (1977), http://www.treccani.it/enciclopedia/gian-rinaldo-carli_(Dizionario-Biografico)/ (accessed 3/2/2015). Carli's confrontation with Rousseau's *Second Discourse* and *The Social Contract* becomes obvious from letter 17, vol. 1, 158ff.

200. On cannibalism and the role of Incas, see Leopardi, *Zibaldone*, 3797, 3801, 3833.

201. Leopardi, *Zibaldone*, 3801. For a summary of Leopardi's understanding of the Californians, see Buccini, *The Americas in Italian Literature and Culture*, 196, 199. William Robertson, *The History of America* (Dublin: Whitestone, etc., 1777). For a contextual reading of Robertson's history, see Pocock, *Barbarism and Religion*, vol. 4, 181ff.

202. Leopardi, *Zibaldone*, 2712. For the philosophical background of Leopardi's assertion, see Pocock, *Barbarism and Religion*, vol. 4, 170.

203. Thom, "The 'hermite des Apennins': Leopardi and the *Antologia* in 1824–26," 538ff. On the Californians' "cheerfulness" as a consequence of their lack of civilizations, see Leopardi, *Zibaldone*, 3660.

204. Istituto Mazziniano, Genoa: 001534, "Il Folletto Scimamu, Viaggio alla Luna di Nerone Secondo Corrispondenza Aerostatica. Lettera II (Dall'America al Mondo di Venere)." Tip. Luigi Banzoli, 25 February 1848.

205. "Soccorso di Metternich a Radeschi" (Milan and Genoa: Dagnino, [1848]) (BL: Miscellanee politiche genovesi. 804.k.13.320).

206. Infelise, "Gazzette e lettori nella Repubblica Veneta dopo l'ottantanove," 311f.

207. Deschamps, "Dal ficle al miele: La stampa esule italiana di New York e il Regno di Sardegna (1849–1861)."

208. Gennaro Lerda, "La schiavitù e la guerra civile nelle pagine della Civiltà cattolica," 234.

209. See "La stampa cattolica in Italia," in *Civiltà cattolica* (sixth series), 16, 1, *January 1865*, 43–59, 44.

210. On the globalization of Italian opera, see also Toelle, "Der Duft der großen weiten Welt: Ideen zum weltweiten Siegeszug der italienischen Oper im 19. Jahrhundert"; Walton, "Operatic fantasies in Latin America"; Rosselli, "The Opera Business and the Italian Immigrant Community in Latin America 1820–1930." On Italian dancers in the United States, see Lo Iacono, "Manzotti e Marenco: Il diritto di due autori," 443.

211. Deschamps, "Dal fiele al miele," 89ff.

212. For an analysis of how opera reached beyond the confines of theaters, see the contributions in Carlini, ed., *Fuori dal teatro*. On theater and sociability, see Sorba, *Teatri*. Körner, *Politics of Culture*, chpt. 2. On the development of theater in the South, see Zingarelli, "Teatri nuovi e nuova domanda."

213. For an overview, see Rosselli, *The Opera Industry in Italy from Cimarosa to Verdi*. Rosselli, *Music and Musicians in 19th Century Italy*. De Angelis, *Le carte dell'impresario*.

214. On methodological issues, see Körner, "The Risorgimento's Literary Canon and the Aesthetics of Reception: Some Methodological Considerations."

215. The main musical periodicals used throughout the book are *L'Arpa* (Bologna); *La Fama: Rassegna di scienze, lettere, arti, industria e teatri* (Milan); *Gazzetta musicale di Milano* (Milan); *Gazzetta musicale di Napoli* (Naples); *L'Italia musicale* (Milan); *Il Trovatore: Giornale letterario, artistico, teatrale con illustrazioni* (Turin).

Chapter One. America as History

1. Carlo Botta, *History of the War of Independence of the United States of America by Charles Botta* [1809], translated from the Italian by George Alexander Otis (New Haven, CT: Brainard, 1840), vol. 1, 113. Throughout this chapter, I make use of different editions and translations of the book, depending on context and argument. Where the English

translations do not match the Italian original, I translate from the original myself. Otis's translation doesn't always read well but was many times reprinted and became a hugely influential text.

2. Several Italian authors writing about the American War of Independence simply summarized Botta and acknowledged their dept. See, for instance, Tullio Dandolo, *Il settentrione dell'Europa e dell'America nel secolo passato sin 1789: L'Inghilterra e l'America* (Milan: Boniardi-Pogliani, 1853).

3. The emphasis on human suffering as an integral part of Italians' perception of the American War of independence also raises questions about the alleged connection between humanitarian sentiment and claims of human or natural rights. For a discussion of this problem, see Moyn, *Human Rights and the Uses of History*, 5f.

4. Contrary to modern conventions, many Italians used American Revolution and American War of Independence interchangeably. On Robertson's use of the term "civil war," see Pocock, *Barbarism and Religion*, vol. 4, 182f. On the American Revolution as civil war, see Burk, *Old World, New World*, 109. Armitage, *Foundations of Modern International Thought*, 192. On the "emotional amplification" of literature, see Sorba, *Il melodramma della nazione*, x. On the *philosophes'* view, see Thom, *Republics, Nations and Tribes*, 126f.

5. Mancall, *Valley of Opportunity*, 135–38.

6. Botta, *History of the War of Independence* (transl. Otis 1820), vol. 2, 554. On the British use of Native populations, see Shannon, "The Native American Way of War in the Age of Revolution."

7. Botta, *History of the War of Independence* (transl. Otis 1820), vol. 2, 561.

8. For the quote and similar references, see Banti, *L'onore della nazione*, 229.

9. Londonio, *Storia delle colonie inglesi in America*, t. 3, 130.

10. Giuseppe Compagnoni, *Storia dell'America in continuazione del compendio della storia universale del sig. Conte di Segur opera originale italiana* (vol. 27; Milan: Tipografia di commercio, 1822), 123.

11. Botta, *History of the War of Independence* (transl. Otis 1820), vol. 2, 561.

12. Ibid., vol. 2, 561.

13. Londonio, *Storia delle colonie inglesi*, t. 3, 125.

14. On growing violence between rebels and loyalists, see Burk, *Old World, New World*, 146, 173. On warfare's markers of modernity, see Chickering, "Introduction: A Tale of Two Tales; Grand Narratives of War in the Age of Revolution."

15. Banti, *L'onore della nazione*, 3ff., 229ff. See also Smart, "'Proud, Indomitable, Irascible': Allegories of Nation in *Attila* and *Les Vêpres siciliennes*."

16. For an introduction to the connection between modernity, gender, and war, see Hagemann, Mettele, and Rendall, eds., *Gender, War and Politics*. For the role of women in the war, see Mayer, "Bearing Arms, Bearing Burdens: Women Warriors, Camp Followers and Home-Front Heroines of the American Revolution."

17. For a short analysis of the painting in historical perspective, see Banti, *L'onore della nazione*, 263f.

18. Banti, *La nazione del Risorgimento*. See also Banti, *L'onore della nazione*, 112ff.

19. Smith, *The Theory of Moral Sentiments*, 155.

20. On the democratic admiration of the American model, see Sarti, "La democrazia radicale," 137.

21. Giuseppe Talamo, "Botta, Carlo," in *Dizionario Biografico degli Italiani*, vol. 13 (1971), http://www.treccani.it/enciclopedia/carlo-botta_(Dizionario-Biografico)/.

22. Botta gives a precise overview of the main materials used for his work: Carlo Botta, *Storia della guerra dell'indipendenza degli Stati Uniti d'America scritta da Carlo Botta*. 4 vols (Paris: D. Colas, 1809), vol. 1, vii–xi.

23. Archives Nationales (AN), LH/302/49 (Botta, Charles).

24. See, in particular, Carlo Pepoli to Austen Henry Layard, 11/2/1860, BL: Layard Papers, vol. 38. Italian papers on Cavour etc. Bequeathed by Lady Layard. BM Add. MS.39068, f.76.

25. On Carlo and Paul-Emile, see Bergamini, "*Spoliis Orientis onustus*: Paul-Émile Botta et la découverte de la civilisation assyrienne." Also Larsen, *The Conquest of Assyria*, 14ff.

26. During his travels in the Middle East, Paul-Émile is regularly introduced as son of the famous historian Carlo Botta: Larsen, *The Conquest of Assyria*, 16, 29

27. Botta, *Storia della Guerra dell'Indipendenza* (1809), vol. 1, 6. The English version of this paragraph makes some significant cuts: *History of the War of Independence* (transl. Otis), vol. 1, 15.

28. Botta, *History of the War of Independence* (transl. Otis 1820), vol. 1, 15.

29. Ibid., vol. 1, 16. Botta, *Storia della Guerra dell'Indipendenza* (1809), vol. 1, 8.

30. Botta, *History of the War of Independence* (transl. Otis 1820), vol. 1, 18. Botta, *Storia della Guerra dell'Indipendenza* (1809), vol. 1, 11.

31. Botta, *Storia della Guerra dell'Indipendenza* (1809), vol. 1, 12. The English translation includes again some minor differences: Botta, *History of the War of Independence* (transl. Otis 1820), vol. 1, 19.

32. Botta, *History of the War of Independence* (transl. Otis 1820), vol. 1, 20, 25.

33. On Volney's use of climate as an analytical category, see Thom, *Republics, Nations and Tribes*, 142f.

34. Botta, *History of the War of Independence* (transl. Otis 1820), vol. 1, 215.

35. Paolo Pavesio, *Carlo Botta e le sue opere storiche* (Florence: Tipografia dell'Associazione, 1874), 70.

36. Pocock, *Political Thought and History*, viii.

37. The Parisian origins of the work are discussed in Buccini, *The Americas in Italian Literature*, 173. Gianotti, "Botta, la Francia e gli Stati Uniti d'America," 36. Buttà, "Carlo Botta's History of the War of Independence of the United States of America," 68. On Botta's relationship to Sig.a Beccaria, see also Scipione Botta, *Vita Privata di Carlo Botta: Ragguagli domestici ed aneddotici raccolti dal suo maggior figlio Scipione* (Florence: Barbèra, 1877), 14.

38. Bessler, *The Birth of American Law*, in particular chpt. 2, A first English translation, including Voltaire's commentary, appeared in London in 1767. On Beccaria's early influence in the United States, see also Castiglioni, *Viaggio negli Stati Uniti dell'America settentrionale*, vol. 2, 23ff.

39. Maturi, *Interpretazioni del Risorgimento*, 37.

40. Fiorentino, "Il dibattito su Botta e la Storia della guerra dell'indipendenza tra Italia e Stati Uniti nel XIX secolo," 174.

41. Barbiera, *La principessa Belgiojoso*, 199. Meriggi describes Amari as an example of the new administrative elite: "Società, Istituzioni e ceti dirigenti," 148. On Amari also Romeo, *Il Risorgimento in Sicilia*, 295f.

42. Michele Amari, *Un periodo delle istorie siciliane del secolo XIII* (Palermo, 1842).

43. Giuseppe Montanelli, *Memorie sull'Italia e specialmente sulla Toscana dal 1814 al 1850* (Turin: Società Editrice Italiana, 1853), vol. 2, 181. Italian 1848ers frequently referred to this book. See, for instance, [Un cittadino palermitano], *Palermo e l'esercito regio o i 24 giorni di guerra dal 12 gennaio al 4 febbraro 1848: Relazione storica* ([Palermo, 1848?]), 47ff. (BL: Italian tracts 1848, 1440 G23). On the book's political impact, see also Brancato, "Il concetto di autonomia nella storiografia siciliana," 518. See also Recupero, "La Sicilia all'opposizione," 41.

44. See, for instance, Giovanni Battista Niccolini's tragedy *Giovanni da Procida* (first performance 1830). It formed the basis for Giuseppe Poniatowski's opera of the same title, performed in Florence in 1838 and in Lucca in 1840, and also for that of Verdi's *Les vêpres siciliennes* (1855), adapted by Scribe on the basis of an earlier libretto set in Flanders. See also Sorba, *Il melodramma della nazione*, 139. Banti, "Sacrality and the Aesthetics of Politics: Mazzini's Concept of the Nation," 68ff. I am grateful to Valeria Luccentini for information regarding Poniatowski's work.

45. Martino Galleano, "La vittoria del popolo siciliano" (Genoa: Casamara, [1848]) (BL: Miscellanee politiche genovesi. 804.k.13.149).

46. Michele Amari, *La guerra del vespro siciliano o un periodo delle istorie siciliane* (seconda edizione, accresciuta e corretta dall' autore e corredata di nuovi documenti), 2 vols. (Paris, 1843; and Florence, 1851). Amari, *History of the War of the Sicilian Vespers* (translated by Anne B. I. Percy, edited, with an introduction and notes, by the Earl of Ellesmere; London: Richard Bentley, 1850).

47. *L'Italia musicale* (20/6/1855). Scribe's claims are not very convincing, considering that he was usually eager to prove his scholarly credentials by adding to his libretti references to his sources: Hibberd, "Auber's Gustave III: History as Opera," 161.

48. Michele Amari, "Prefazione," in Carlo Botta, *Storia della guerra dell'indipendenza degli Stati Uniti d'America* (Florence: Le Monnier, 1856), vol. 1, i–lxii, i.

49. Banti, *La nazione del Risorgimento*, 27ff.

50. Amari, "Prefazione," i f.

51. Ibid., iv. Amari's assertion is easily challenged. Botta wrote most of the book on the basis of historical documents. Moreover, the second volume (libro sesto) of the 1809 edition includes translated extracts of the Declaration of Independence: Botta, *Storia della guerra dell'indipendenza* (1809), vol. 2, 350ff. For Botta's translation of particular constitutional terms, also see Bonazzi, "Tradurre/Tradire: The Declaration of Independence in the Italian Context," 1355ff. In addition to multiple French studies readily available at the time, also Castiglioni's two-volume work of 1790 included a commented translation of the American Constitution as well as detailed descriptions of each member state.

52. Amari, "Prefazione," xli.

53. Paul W. Schroeder, "Did the Vienna Settlement Rest on a Balance of Power?," in *Systems, Stability and Statecraft: Essays on the International History of Modern Europe* (New York: Palgrave, 2004), 37–58.

54. Jessie White Mario, *The Birth of Modern Italy* (London: T. Fisher Unwin, 1909), 137. Not surprisingly, especially American commentators liked this association: Gemme, *Domesticating Foreign Struggles*, 20.

55. Quoted in della Peruta, *Milano nel Risorgimento*, 132.

56. Without reference to Botta, Mazzini compares the situation in Milan in January 1848 with that of America before the War of Independence: Giuseppe Mazzini, "Al Signor Guizot, presidente del consiglio," *Edizione nazionale*, vol. 36, 245–60, 248. A similar allegory in Mazzini, "Agli italiani" (1848), *Edizione nazionale*, vol. 38, 213–20, 216. It is important to point to the differences between Botta and Mazzini: Sarti, "Giuseppe Mazzini and Young Europe," 281.

57. Sicily, Camera dei Comuni, 5/4/1848, Fuccio Leonardo Vigo, *Le Assemblee del Risorgimento*, vol. 12, 113. Comments on the Italian war of independence often used similar wordings, but it is not clear whether they constitute conscious references to Franklin's famous quote. See, for instance, Istituto Mazziniano, Genoa, AIM 001328: Un Italiano, *Nuova disposizione di guerra* (Genoa: Tip. Dagnino, s.d. [1848]).

58. Montanelli, *Memorie sull'Italia*, vol. 2, 125.

59. On the Tsar's interest, see Botta, *Vita Privata di Carlo Botta*, 43.

60. Carlo Botta, *Storia d'Italia dal 1789–1814* (Italia, 1826), vol. 4, 502.

61. Sicily, Camera dei Comuni, 14/4/1848, Angelo Marocco, *Le Assemblee del Risorgimento*, vol. 12, 192.

62. Botta, *Storia d'Italia*, vol. 3, 437. On the tradition in political thought of contrasting the American and French Revolutions, see Whatmore, "The French and North American Revolutions in Comparative Perspective."

63. Botta, *Storia d'Italia*, vol. 1, 60.

64. Amari, "Prefazione,"xlvii f.

65. Ibid., lv.

66. Carlo Dionisotti, *Vita di Carlo Botta* (Turin: Favale, 1867), 138.

67. For instance, the same passage is quoted without further discussion by Gianotti, "Botta, la Francia e gli Stati Uniti d'America," 36.

68. Buccini, *The Americas in Italian Literature*, 174.

69. Fiorentino, "Il dibattito su Botta e la Storia della guerra dell'indipendenza tra Italia e Stati Uniti nel XIX secolo," 173.

70. Carlo Cattaneo, "Prefazione," in *Il Politecnico*, 8 (1860), 5–9.

71. Lacaita, Gobbo, Turiel, eds., *La biblioteca di Carlo Cattaneo*, 159f.

72. Maturi, *Interpretazioni del Risorgimento*, 39. On the Romantic interest in a heroic past, see Lyttelton, "The Hero and the People."

73. Maturi, *Interpretazioni del Risorgimento*, 39f. On Botta's portrait of Washington, see Alberto Jori and Raffaele M. Mattei, "La figura di George Washington nella Storia della guerre dell'independenza degli Stati Uniti d'America di Botta."

74. Pocock, *Barbarism and Religion*, vol. 2, 5, also 8ff.

75. Sorba, *Il melodramma della nazione*, 131. The same technique was used by Rousseau: Thom, *Republics, Nations and Tribes*, 60.

76. Botta, *Storia della Guerra dell'Indipendenza* (1809), vol. 1, i–iv.

77. Maturi, *Interpretazioni del Risorgimento*, 41. Ugo Cardinale, "Botta, un giacobino dalle vedute atlantiche," 25.

78. Benedetto Croce recognized a trend of epic historiography during the Risorgimento but did not approve of Botta's use of it: *Teoria e storia della storiografia*, 44.

79. Botta to Count Littardi, 27/9/1822, quoted in Maturi, *Interpretazioni del Risorgimento*, 40.

80. Schiller, "Was heisst und zu welchem Ende studiert man Universalgeschichte? Eine akademische Antrittsrede," *Sämtliche Werke*, vol. 4, 749–67. The use of the term here is closer to Hannah Arendt's "animal laborans" than to Richard Sennett's "craftsman": Sennett, *The Craftsman*, prologue.

81. Pavesio, *Carlo Botta e le sue opere storiche*, 37.

82. Burrow, *A History of Histories*, 442.

83. Sontag, "Against Interpretation" (1964), *Against Interpretation and Other Essays*, 3–15, 14.

84. White, *Metahistory*.

85. Procacci speaks of an "accentuato disinteresse per il contenuto politico . . . ; la rivoluzione americana viene pertanto ridotta a fatto prevalentemente militare": "Rivoluzione Americana e storiografia italiana," 567.

86. One of the few references to civic traditions is the mentioning of debates in coffee houses and schools: Botta, *Storia della Guerra dell'Indipendenza* (1809), vol. 1, 64.

87. For Rousseau's influence on Botta, see San Mauro, ed., *Un opera inedita di Carlo Botta*, 29–35. Rota Ghibaudi, *La fortuna di Rousseau in Italia*, 239–42. Botta refers to Rousseau also in "Proposizione ai Lombardi di una maniera di governo libero," in Saitta, ed., *Alle origini del Risorgimento*, vol. 1, 3–171.

88. Quoted in Curnis, "Varianti d'autore e vicende editoriali della Storia della guerra dell'indipendenza degli Stati Uniti d'America," 159.

89. Fruttuoso Becchi, "Elogio di Carlo Botta," in *Florilegio di eloquenza italiana*, vol. 1 (Pistoia: Cino, 1839), 405–35, 415. Botta had been a corresponding member of the Accademia since 1824.

90. Banti, *La nazione del Risorgimento*, 76.

91. Giandomenico Romagnosi, "Della poesia considerata rispetto alle diverse età delle nazioni," *Scritti filosofici*, vol. 2, 5–11, 7.

92. Quoted in Albertoni, *La vita degli stati e l'incivilmento dei popoli nel pensiero politico di Gian Domenico Romagnosi*, 65. Mazzini also considered Romagnosi's influence harmful.

93. Quoted in Galante Garrone, *L'Albero della Libertà*, 206 n. See also Ragusa, "Italy, Romantico—Romanticismo," 298.

94. Botta, "Proposizione ai Lombardi di una maniera di governo libero." See also Botta, *Pensieri politici* (Italy, 1840).

95. Botta, *Pensieri politici*, 15f. Canfora and Cardinale, eds., *Il giacobino pentito*.

96. Buttà, "Carlo Botta's History of the War of Independence," 71.

97. Jori and Mattei, "La figura di George Washington nella Storia della guerra dell'independenza degli Stati Uniti d'America di Botta," 155.

98. Botta, *Pensieri politici*, 20.

99. On the bibliographic background, see Saitta, ed., *Alle origini del Risorgimento*, vol. 1, xviii, 5; on the original competition, see also Duggan, *The Force of Destiny*, 9ff. Gianotti, "Botta, la Francia e gli Stati Uniti d'America," 30f.

100. Botta, "Proposizione ai Lombardi di una maniera di governo libero," 49. See also the discussion in Dionisotti, *Vita di Carlo Botta*, 42f.

101. Carlo Botta, *De l'équilibre du pouvoir en Europe* (Carla San Mauro, ed.). Rome: Istituto Storico Italiano, 2008.

102. Ibid., 216.

103. Ibid., 188.

104. Ibid., 197.

105. M. Leoni, "Della storia della guerra dell'indipendenza degli stati uniti d'America, scritta da Carlo Botta (estratto dal *North American Review*)," in *Antologia*, 6 (1822), 201–33. *North American Review*, 13, 32 (July 1821), 169–200. On the American historiographical context of Botta's work, see Deconde, "Historians, the War of American Independence, and the Persistence of the Exceptionalist Ideal," 408. On Vieusseux's relationship with the publishers of the *North American Review*, see Bagnoli, *La politica delle idee*, 32f. Baker, *The Fortunate Pilgrims*, 59. Whereas French periodicals were easily accessible to most eductaed Italians, it was one of the *Antologia*'s aims to translate extracts from English and German periodicals: Spadolini, *Fra Vieusseux e Ricasoli*, 52.

106. The issue does not mention an author, but according to Fiorentino it was Edward Everett, later president of Harvard University and an American secretary of state under Millard Fillmore: "Il dibattito su Botta e la Storia della guerra dell'indipendenza tra Italia e Stati Uniti nel XIX secolo," 174. Walker Read claims F. C. Cray to be the author, "a gentleman from Boston devoted to literary pursuits": "The American Reception of Botta's Storia della guerra dell' Independenza degli Stati Uniti d'America," 7. On Everett's contacts with Italian exiles, see Garosci, *Antonio Gallenga*, vol. 1, 76.

107. [Michele Leoni], "Opinioni intorno la Musica di Gioacchino Rossini di Pesaro," *Antologia*, no. 10 (October 1821), 40–58. See also Steffan, ed., *Rossiniana*, 33–50. Similar to Verri, the piece argues against a transnational aesthetic.

108. Turchi, "Un collaboratore di Gianpietro Vieusseux: Michele Leoni." Fellheimer, "Michele Leoni's Venezia Salvata, the First Italian Translation of Otway's Tragedy." Ciampini, *Gian Pietro Vieusseux*, 193. On the periodical's suspension Coppini, *Il Granducato di Toscana*, 255.

109. Leoni, "Della storia della guerra dell'indipendenza degli stati uniti d'America," 208. The review describes the American events in a language that is easily applied to Risorgimento nationalism, praising "il congiunto sforzo di tutto un popolo, come dell'individuo, per la rivendicazione de' proprj diritti" (209).

110. Gemme, *Domesticating Foreign Struggles.*

111. Leoni, "Della storia della guerra dell'indipendenza degli stati uniti d'America," 212.

112. Conway, *War, State and Society,* 248, 252.

113. John Adams, quoted in Read, "The American Reception of Botta's Storia della guerra dell' Independenza," 7.

114. Turchi, "Un collaboratore di Gianpietro Vieusseux: Michele Leoni," 76f.

115. Botta, *History of the War of Independence* (transl. Otis), vol. 2, 161.

116. Read, "The American Reception of Botta's Storia della guerra dell' Independenza," 5, 8.

117. "Compagnoni's America," *North American Review,* 27, 60 (July 1828), 30–42

118. Londonio, *Storia delle colonie inglesi.* The preface to volume 1 as well as the bibliographic overview at the end of volume 3 give a useful indication of the works Londonio had read.

119. Carlo Giuseppe Londonio to Carlo Cattaneo, 4/9/1824, *Carteggi di Carlo Cattaneo,* serie 2, vol. 1, 5–7.

120. Marica Roda, "Londonio, Carlo Giuseppe,"*Dizionario Biografico degli Italiani,* vol. 65 (2005), http://www.treccani.it/enciclopedia/carlo-giuseppe-londonio_(Dizionario _Biografico)/ (accessed 20/1/2015).

121. Londonio, *Storia delle colonie inglesi,* vol. 1, 106. This description of religious life contrasts with Botta. See for instance Botta, *History of the War of Independence* (transl. Otis), vol. 1, 24.

122. Londonio, *Storia delle colonie inglesi,* vol. 1, 124.

123. Volume 1 includes a detailed appendix on the natural life of the colonies with a long, but not very sympathetic section on the Native population. Londonio, *Storia delle colonie inglesi,* t. 1, 255ff. For the quote, see vol. 2, 188. While some Italian authors demonstrated sympathy for the fate of Native Americans, during the early period of colonization the Italians' treatment of the Native population even appalled the Spanish: Taylor, *American Colonies,* 37. On the French descriptions of Natives, see Thom, *Republics, Nations and Tribes,* 137ff.

124. [Burke], *Storia degli stabilimenti europei in America,* vol. 1, 180f, 102

125. Compagnoni, *Storia dell'America,* vol. 27, 13f. See also his detailed overview of indigenous populations after independence: ibid., vol. 28, chpt. 6, 126ff.

126. Botta, *History of the War of Independence* (transl. Otis), vol. 2, 553.

127. Wilson, *The Earth Shall Weep,* 128f. Calloway, *The American Revolution in Indian Country,* 108ff.

128. In these words Compagnoni concluded a chapter on the massacres against the indigenous population of Pennsylvania: *Storia dell'America,* vol. 25, 149.

129. Londonio, *Storia delle colonie inglesi,* vol. 1, 270f.

130. Ibid., vol. 1, 272f.

131. Ibid., vol. 1, 283ff.

132. Ibid., vol. 1, 244f.

133. Ibid., vol. 2, 55.

134. Ibid., vol. 2, 58.

135. See, for instance, ibid., vol. 2, 88, 137, 141, 153. For descriptions of the War of Independence as civil war, see also Castiglioni, *Viaggio negli Stati Uniti dell'America Settentrionale,* vol. 2, 113. Otherwise this perception of the war as civil war was mostly common in England: Wood, *The American Revolution,* 76. See also Mason, "The American Loyalist Problem of Identity in the Revolutionary Atlantic World."

136. Londonio, *Storia delle colonie inglesi*, vol. 2, 96.

137. Ibid., vol. 3, 76f.

138. See for instance Osterhammel's description of Frederick Jackson Turner's frontier thesis as an influential topos informing narratives of European expansion: *Die Verwandlung der Welt*, 468–72.

139. Londonio, *Storia delle colonie inglesi*, vol. 2, 168. Londonio presents similar accounts of Americans destroying their own settlements throughout the book. See, for instance, vol. 3, 41.

140. Ibid., vol. 3, 9.

141. Ibid., vol. 3, 74f.

142. See, for instance, Taylor, *American Colonies*. Also Conway, *The War of American Independence*, emphasizes the war's international dimension.

143. Londonio, *Storia delle colonie inglesi*, vol. 3, 310f. Londonio's history finishes with a translation of the constitution and concludes with an outline of the tensions between federalists and antifederalists: "la controversia si agita ancora fra i due partiti e si agiterà forse finchè esisterà la Repubblica." Ibid., vol. 3, 167f.

144. Giuseppe Compagnoni, *Storia dell'America in continuazione del* "Compendio della storia universale" *del sig. Conte di Segur: Opera originale italiana*. Milan: Fusi, Stella, 1820–23. The series started as Louis-Philippe Comte de Ségur, *Abrégé de l'histoire universelle, ancienne et moderne à l'usage de la jeunesse*, 15 vols. (Paris: Eymery, 1817–19). The work was to grow to over one hundred volumes, of which Ségur completed less than a third. For a contemporary discussion of the project, see Franco Splitz, *Rivista generale de' libri usciti in luce nel Regno Lombardo nell'anno scolastico 1826* (Milan: Torchj D'Omobono Manini, 1827), 254ff.

145. Compagnoni, *Storia dell'America*, vol. 25, 6.

146. Apt, *Louis-Philippe de Ségur*, 121f.

147. Compagnoni, *Storia dell'America*, vol. 23, Indice generale (Milan: Tipografia di Commercio, 1823), ix.

148. On this particular reading, see Morandi, "Giuseppe Compagnoni e la 'Storia dell'America,'" 255f.

149. On Compagnoni, see Savini, "Profilo biografico."

150. On Compagnoni's years in Bologna, see Giacomelli, "La Bologna tardo illumnistica e prerivoluzionaria di Giuseppe Compagnoni."

151. Compagnoni, *Storia dell'America*, vol. 27, 6. Berengo, "Introduzione," lx. Giacomelli, "La Bologna tardo illuministica e prerivoluzionaria di Giuseppe Compagnoni," 39.

152. Infelise, "Gazzette e lettori nella Repubblica Veneta dopo l'ottantanove," 313, 315. See also Marino Berengo, "Introduzione," lix.

153. Savini, "Profilo biografico," 14. On the *Notizie del mondo*, see Berengo, "Introduzione," lviiif.

154. Infelise, "Gazzette e lettori nella Repubblica Veneta dopo l'ottantanove," 311f.

155. Giuseppe Compagnoni, *Saggio sugli ebrei, e sui greci* (Venice: Giacomo Storti, 1792). This edition was a reprint of a version first published in 1790. Romagnoli, "Le 'lettere piacevoli' e il 'Saggio sugli ebrei' di Giuseppe Compagnoni." Segre, *La storia degli ebrei in Italia*, 67f. Caffiero, *Storia degli ebrei nell'Italia moderna*, 179f. On the government response to the publication, see Balsamo, "Gli ebrei nell'editoria e nel commercio librario in Italia nel '600 e '700," 65. The saggio is not mentioned in the important study by Attilio Milano, *Storia degli ebrei in Italia* (1963) (Turin: Einaudi, 1992).

156. Savini, *Un abate "libertino,"* 17, 22f.

157. Savini, "Profilo biografico," 16.

158. Savini, *Un abate "libertino,"* 20, 23.

159. Compagnoni, *Storia dell'America*, vol. 28, 169ff.

160. Giuseppe Compagnoni, *Elementi di diritto costituzionale democratico ossia principj di giuspubblico universale* (Venice: Giustino Pasquali Qu. Mario, 1797), 221.

161. Quoted in Marcello Savini, "Le lettere di Giuseppe Compagnoni a Valentino Rossi," in Sante Medri, ed., *Giuseppe Compagnoni: Un intellecttuale tra giacobinismo e restaurazione* (Bologna: Edizioni Analisi, 1993), 23–32, 27.

162. Giuseppe Compagnoni to Luigi Stella, 23/12/1820, in Compagnoni, *Cinquantotto lettere e una supplica*, 81.

163. Morandi, "Giuseppe Compagnoni e la 'Storia dell'America,'" 257.

164. Compagnoni, *Storia dell'America*, vol. 28, 265.

165. Thom, *Republics, Nations and Tribes*, 1f. On Locke's observations on Native Americans in his *Two Treatises of Government*, see also Arneil, *John Locke and the American Indian*.

166. *North American Review*, 27, 60 (July 1828), 30–42, 31.

167. *Antologia*, 34 (April–June 1829), 76–83. See also, *Il Nuovo ricoglitore ossia Archivi d'ogni letteratura antica e moderna*, 5, 2 (July 1829), 540–47. See also the comment on Botta's and Compagnoni's reception in E. Mayer, "Pubblica Educazione negli Stati Uniti d'America," in *Antologia*. 45, 133 (January 1832), 3–19, 4.

168. [Giuseppe Compagnoni], *Storia universale antica e moderna del Conte di Ségur e i suoi continuatori. Storia Moderna*, t. lxxxiv (*Storia dell'America*, vol. 1; Naples: Iride, 1842).

169. See, for instance, Compagnoni's description of General Wilkinson's expedition of 1791 or that of Harrison in 1811: Compagnoni, *Storia dell'America*, vol. 28, 95f.; also chpt. 6, 126ff.

170. Ibid., vol. 28, 153.

171. Apt, *Louis-Philippe de Ségur*, 17, 41.

172. Ibid., 30.

173. Quoted in ibid., 42.

174. See Louis-Philippe Comte de Ségur, *Procès-verbal de la cérémonie du sacre et du couronnement de LL MM l'Empereur Napoléon et l'Impératrice Joséphine*. Paris: Imprimerie Impériale, 1805.

175. Apt, *Louis-Philippe de Ségur*, 126.

176. See, for instance, the bibliographic review by Splita, *Riviota gonoralc*, 155.

177. Compagnoni to Carlo Filoni, 16/3/1824, in Giuseppe Compagnoni, *Lettere varie (1776–1832)* (Marcello Savini, ed.; Ravenna: Longo, 2001), 195–97. As a matter of fact, in announcements of the work his name was often suppressed in favor of Ségur's. See, for instance, *Antologia*, vol. 12, 34 (October–December 1823), 212.

178. Savini, *Un abate "libertino,"* 467–76.

179. Compagnoni, *Storia dell'America*, vol. 28, 6.

180. Ibid., vol. 28, chpt. 2.

181. Giuseppe Compagnoni, "Prospetto politico dell'anno 1790," *Notizie del mondo* (1791), in Berengo, ed., *Giornali veneziani del settecento*, vol. 5, 519–47, 521. His argument against the despotism of George III he takes up again in Compagnoni, *Storia dell'America*, vol. 27, 6ff.

182. Compagnoni, "Prospetto politico dell'anno 1790," 521.

183. Compagnoni, *Storia dell'America*, vol. 28, 180ff.

184. Castiglioni, *Viaggio negli Stati Uniti dell'America settentrionale*, vol. 2, 98; also vol. 1, 92.

185. Compagnoni, *Storia dell'America*, vol. 28, chpt. 8.

186. Ibid., vol. 28, 196f.

187. Compagnoni to Gian Pietro Vieusseux, 1/3/1832, in Compagnoni, *Lettere varie*, 204f. For an appreciation, see "Necrologia—Giuseppe Compagnoni," in *Biblioteca italiana ossia Giornale di letteratura scienze ed arte* (vol. 74, 1834, 1).

188. Tullio Dandolo, "In Morte del Cavaliere Compagnoni," in *Ricoglitore italiano e straniero: Rivista mensile europea di scienze, lettere, belle arti*, 1, 1 (1834), 74–78, 75f.

189. On Balbo's political thought in European context, see Isabella, "Aristocratic Liberalism and Risorgimento"; Romani, "Reluctant Revolutionaries." See also Kroll, *Die Revolte*, 2f. On the "antithetic" meanings of Italian liberalism, see Meriggi, "Liberali/Liberalismo."

190. On Balbo as historian, see Fubini Leuzzi, "Introduzione," in particular 23ff.

191. Fubini Leuzzi, "Introduzione," 17.

192. Cesare Balbo, *Della monarchia rappresentativa in Italia, saggi politici di Cesare Balbo: Della politica nella presente civiltà, abbozzi, del medesimo autore* (Florence: Le Monnier, 1857), 11.

193. Sorba, *Il melodramma della nazione*, 129.

194. Balbo, *Della monarchia rappresentativa in Italia*, 11.

195. Compagnoni, *Storia dell'America*, vol. 26, 130.

196. Cesare Balbo, "La Vita di Cesare Balbo," in A. D'Ancona, ed., *Autobiografie* (Florence: Barbèra, 1859), 361–481. Balbo's assessment of Botta is not free of criticism, in particular regarding his works on Italian history. See Scaglia, *Cesare Balbo*, 394f.

197. Cesare Balbo, *Meditazioni storiche* (edizione seconda; Florence: Le Monnier, 1854), 531.

198. Balbo, *Della monarchia rappresentativa in Italia*, 7.

199. Rosmini to Balbo, 22/11/1846, quoted in de Rosa, "Introduzione: Cesare Balbo e il cattolicesimo liberale," 3.

200. Balbo, *Della Monarchia Rappresentativa*, 72ff.

201. Jaume, *Tocqueville*, 356. Aliberti, "Cesare Balbo: Il Federalismo," 151f.

202. Amari, "Prefazione," xliv.

203. Gioacchino Ventura, *La questione Sicula nel 1848 sciolta nel vero interesse della Sicilia, di Napoli e dell'Italia* (Rome: Zampi, 1848), 27.

204. Isabella has argued that "tension between liberty and nationality constituted a distinctive features of Italian post-revolutionary political culture": "Nationality before Liberty?," 507.

205. Romani, "Political Thought in Action: The Moderates in 1859"; for the quote, see 593.

206. Bagnoli, *La politica delle idee*, 69.

207. Montanelli (1851) quoted in Bagnoli, *La politica delle idee*, 69f. For Montanelli's critique of the fixation with independence in the political thought of Gioberti, Balbo, and D'Azeglio, see Montanelli, *Memorie sull'Italia*, vol. 1, 228ff.

208. Ferrari (1851) quoted in Bagnoli, *La politica delle idee*, 69f.

209. Bagnoli, *La politica delle idee*, 74. With regard to Risorgimento socialism, also Carlo Pisacane played an important role.

Chapter Two. Concepts in the Language of Politics

1. Editori del Politecnico, "Manifesto della Seconda Serie," *Il Politecnico*, 8 (1860), 5–9, 6.

2. Tortarolo, *Illuminismo e rivoluzioni*, 55f., 161f.

3. Giuseppe Mazzini, "Fede e avvenire" (1835), in *Edizione nazionale*, vol. 6, 291–358, 348f. (n.). See also Rossi, *The Image of America*, 5. Sarti, "Giuseppe Mazzini e la tradizione repubblicana," 60. On the materialism that Mazzini saw taking roots in France, see Ignace, "Il mito di Mazzini in Francia," 48. On French *Américomanie*, see also Thier, "A World Apart, a Race Apart?"

4. Haddock, "State and Nation in Mazzini's Political Thought," 335f.

5. Taylor, *Mary Wollstonecraft*, 174.

6. Quoted in Noether, "The Constitution in Action: The Young Republic in the Observations of Early Italian Commentators (1770s–1830s)," 90.

7. Ibid., 90f. Morelli, "The United States Constitution Viewed by Nineteenth-Century Italian Democrats," 108. Stefani, *I prigionieri dello Spielberg*, 38–76. On Confaloniere, see also Greenfield, *Economics and Liberalism in the Risorgimento*, 199f.

8. Stendhal (Henri Beyle), *La Chartreuse de Parme* (Paris: Hetzel, 1846), 166. In his appreciation of Stendhal's novel Balzac talks of "canaillocratie."

9. For Italian discussions of *Domestic Manners*, see "Costumi degli americani negli Stati Uniti," in *La Voce della ragione: Giornale filosofico, teologico, politico, istorico, letterario*, 31, 6 (1833), 181–93. George Hamilton, *Gli uomini ed i costumi agli Stati-Uniti d'America* (prima versione italiana di Luigi Ferreri; Milan: Pirotta, 1835), vol. 2, 66f. *La Moda*, 5/11/1838.

10. Pocock, "The History of Political Thought: A Methodological Inquiry" (1962), in Pocock, *Political Thought and History*, 3–19, 5, 9.

11. While Pocock and Skinner rely on the classical texts of great thinkers, Koselleck widens the range of sources, examining how conceptual change is reflected in legal and scientific language as well as in public discourse. For an exemplification of this approach, see his collected articles in Koselleck, *Begriffsgeschichten*.

12. Gemme, *Domesticating Foreign Struggles*.

13. Podlech, "Repräsentation," 509, 520ff.

14. *Programma: Una proposizione qualunque da svilupparsi* (Palermo, 1848) (BL: 8007.cc.33).

15. Tortarolo, *Illuminismo e rivoluzioni*, 121.

16. Francovich, "La rivoluzione americana e il progetto di costituzione del Granduca Pietro Leopoldo." Zimmermann, *Das Verfassungsprojekt des Grossherzogs Peter Leopold von Toscana*, 44f., 86ff. Palmer, *The Age of Democratic Revolution*, vol. 1, 386. The Virginia Declaration became the model for the American Bill of Rights of 1789.

17. The Livorno folio edition of the *Encyclopédie* was published under the duke's protection, remarkable considering the international efforts to suppress the work. Darnton, *The Business of Enlightenment*, 19, 35. On the political context, see also Israel, *Democratic Enlightenment*, 56 sq, 332ff. On its impact in Italy, see also Venturi, *Settecento riformatore. Da Muratori a Beccaria*, 567.

18. Conway, *Britain, Ireland, and Continental Europe in the Eighteenth Century*, 159.

19. Gianni wrote one of the first detailed commentaries on Leopold's legal, economic, and civic reforms, including the project for the constitution: Francesco Maria Gianni, "Memorie sulla costituzione di governo immaginata dal Granduca Pietro Leopoldo das servire all'istoria del suo regno in Toscana," in Francesco Maria Gianni, *Scritti di pubblica economia storico-economici e storico-politici del senatore Francesco Maria Gianni*, vol. 1 (Florence: Luigi Niccolai, 1848), 297–327, in particular 316ff. On Gianni, see Venturi, *Illuministi italiani*, vol. 3, 981–90. On Neri, see ibid., 945–50.

20. Zimmermann, *Das Verfassungsprojekt*, 34ff. and 78.

21. Tortarolo, *Illuminismo e rivoluzioni*. For a short introduction, see Mazzei, *Researches on the United States*, xi–xvii.

22. Tortarolo, *Illuminismo e rivoluzioni*, 43.

23. Filippo Mazzei, *Recherches historiques et politiques sur les États-Unis de l'Amérique Septentrionale par un citoyen de Virginie* (Paris: Froullé, 1788). For a detailed discussion, see Tortarolo, *Illuminismo e rivoluzioni*, 119ff.

24. Mazzei, *Recherches historiques*, vol. 1, xv.

25. Ibid., 123f., 158.

26. Ibid., 133ff.

27. There are a few references to ancient Rome and the Italian city-republics. References to modern Tuscany regard his viticultural experiments: Mazzei, *Recherches historiques*, vol. 3, 95.

28. Gianni refers to *monarchia temperata* in his "Memorie sulla costituzione di governo," 301ff.

29. Francovich, "La rivoluzione americana," 372f. See also Procacci, "Rivoluzione americana e storiografia italiana," 565. Pace, *Benjamin Franklin and Italy*, 106f.

30. See, for instance, *Gazzetta universale* 61, 30/7/1782, 492. See also the references quoted in Venturi, *The End of the Old Regime in Europe*, part 1, 173.

31. Polzonetti, *Italian Opera in the Age of the American Revolution*, 28.

32. His religious policies similarly met with resistance: Chadwick, *The Popes and European Revolution*, 418ff.

33. Francovich, "La rivoluzione americana," 376.

34. Montanelli, *Memorie sull'Italia*, vol. 1, 2f., 20f.

35. On the relationship between Jefferson and Mazzei, see Hayes, *The Road to Monticello*.

36. Bernstein, *Thomas Jefferson*, 120. Ibid., 83.

37. Hayes, *The Road to Monticello*, 430.

38. La Piana, *La cultura americana e l'Italia*, 6of.

39. Bernstein, *Thomas Jefferson*, 121.

40. Iermano, *Il giacobinismo e il Risorgimento italiano*, 44.

41. Criscuolo, *Albori di democrazia nell'Italia in rivoluzione*, 103ff. For a Milanese perspective, see della Peruta, *Milano nel Risorgimento*, 14. On the role of classical republicanism in Italian political thought, see Lenci, "From Republic to Representative Democracy: Some Observations on ohe Use of the Word 'Democracy' in Italian Political Thought between 1750–1861," 23.

42. Antonio Capece-Minutolo, Principe di Canosa, *In confutazione degli errori storici e politici da Luigi Angeloni Esposti contro Sua Maestà l'arciduchessa Maria Carolina d'Austria, defunta regina di Napoli: Epistola di un amico della verità* (Marseille, 1831), 6. On p. 97 the pamphlet refers briefly to Angeloni's Americanism.

43. Iermano, *Il giacobinismo*, 22. Galante Garrone, "L'emigrazione politica italiana del Risorgimento," 228.

44. Iermano, *Il giacobinismo*, 23f.

45. The pamphlet was published under the title *Sopra l'ordinamento che aver dovrebbono i governi d'Italia—ragionamenti*. See Luigi Angeloni, *Dell'Italia, uscente il settembre del 1818, ragionamenti IV* (Paris: Apresso l'autore, 1818), vol. 1, iv f.

46. Iermano, *Il giacobinismo*, 28f. Many Italian patriots were familiar with Jeremy Bentham's pro-Russian feelings as a basis for a new system of international relations. Conway, "Bentham versus Pitt: Jeremy Bentham and British Foreign Policy 1789." Meanwhile, the Risorgimento remained overwhelmingly critical toward Russia: Valle, "'Ombre russe': Considerazioni su Mazzini, Bakunin e la russofobia."

47. Iermano, *Il giacobinismo*, 30.

48. Ibid., 89f.

49. Luigi Angeloni, *Della forza nelle cose politiche* (London: Appresso l'autore, 1826), vol. 2, 114. Luigi Angeloni, *Esortazioni patrie* (London: Appresso l'autore, 1837), 699. Angeloni's evaluation of Alexander is documented in Iermano, *Il giacobinismo*, 30f.

50. Angeloni, *Dell'Italia*, vol. 2, 3. See also Isabella, "Mazzini's Internationalism in Context," 48. Morelli, "The United States Constitution," 100f.

51. Angeloni, *Dell'Italia*, vol. 1, 239.

52. Ibid., vol. 2, 13f.

53. Ibid., vol. 2, 34.

54. Ibid., vol. 1, 239.

55. Ibid., vol. 2, 178. On the Risorgimento's cult of Washington, see Lyttelton, "The Hero and the People," 43.

56. Iermano, *Il giacobinismo*, 50. See also Mazzini's obituary for the *Apostolato popolare*, 15/4/1842, *Edizione nazionale*, vol. 25, 103–6.

57. Galante Garrone, *L'Albero della Libertà*, 15.

58. Richard Cobden, Genoa, 16/1/1847, in *The European Diaries of Richard Cobden, 1846–1849*, 89.

59. Ibid., 19.

60. For its role in Italian political thought, see Antonio Chiavistelli, "Rappresentanza," in Banti et al., eds., *Atlante culturale*, 341–58, 349.

61. For a discussion of the relationship between representation and democracy, see Philp and Lenci, "Introduction."

62. Scirocco, *L'Italia del Risorgimento*, 77.

63. White Mario, *The Birth of Modern Italy*, 115. For Milan, see also della Peruta, *Milano nel Risorgimento*, 111.

64. de Pascale, *Filosofia e politica nel pensiero italiano fra sette e ottocento*, 149.

65. De Francesco, "Ideologie e movimenti politici," 254f. Also Cuoco lamented "the tendency to adopt slavishly foreign constitutional models": Biagini, "Citizenship and Religion," 213.

66. de Pascale, *Filosofia e politica*, 18, 72, 84f.

67. de Pascale, *Filosofia e politica*, 123, 172.

68. For Romagnosi's concept of civile filosofia, see Moravia, "Introduzione," 49f.; see also Albertoni, *La vita degli stati e l'incivilmento dei popoli*, 27.

69. Romagnosi, "Alcuni pensieri sopra un'atra metafisica filosofia della storia" (1832), in *Scritti filosofici*, vol. 2, 61–76. See also Moravia, "Introduzione," 21f., 39, 44f.; Albertoni, *La vita degli stati*, 27ff., 50f. On Kant, see Romagnosi, "Esposizione storico-critica del Kantismo e delle consecutive dottrine" (1828), in *Opere*, vol. 1, no. 1, 575–605. Romagnosi's most comprehensive critique of Vico was published in 1822: "Osservazioni su la Scienza Nuova di Vico," in Romagnosi, *Scritti filosofici*, vol. 2, 19–49.

70. Moravia describes Romagnosi as a "vichiano critico": "Introduzione," 45.

71. Giandomenico Romagnosi, "Delle leggi dell'incivilmento: Parte I" (1831), in *Scritti filosofici*, vol. 2, 84–183. For his 1827 article on ancient Mexico, see Albertoni, "La vita degli stati," 38. For his reflections on Robertson, see Guglielmo Robertson, *Ricerche storiche sull'India antica: Con note, supplementi ed illustrazioni di Gian Domenico Romagnosi* (1827) (Florence: Piatti, 1835).

72. Giandomenico Romagnosi, *La scienza delle costituzioni* (Bastia: Canfari, 1848), 446, 463. There are more (mostly statistical) references in Romagnosi's writings on political economy: Romagnosi, *Opere*, vol. 6, no. 1.

73. Mazzini to Carlo Bini, 20/7/1838, *Edizione nazionale*, App. vol. 2, 133–39, 135. J.C.L. de Sismondi to Santorre di Santarosa, 12/12/1835, in Santorre di Santarosa, *Memorie e lettere inedite con appendice di Gian Carlo Sismondi* (Nicomede Bianchi, ed.; Turin: Bocca, 1877), 134–35.

74. Woolf underestimates Romagnosi's role when he mistakes him for a "*uomo più noto e stimato che letto*": *Dal primo settecento all'Unità*, 266. Galasso recognized the remarkable European resonance of Romagnosi's ideas: *Da Mazzini a Salvemini*, 17.

75. Angeloni, *Dell'Italia*, vol. 1, 240.

76. On his international resonance, see, for instance, Clemens, "Torino e il Piemonte visti dalla Prussia," 628. His ideas are reflective of the broader association of liberalism with the political legacies of the Enlightenment. For this context, see Freeden and Stears, "Liberalism," 330f.

77. Raynal, *The Revolution of America*, 96.

78. Balbo, *Della monarchia rappresentativa*, 136f.

79. Ibid., 73f.

80. Ibid., 8.

81. Ibid., 73.

82. Scaglia, *Balbo*, 519ff. Ghisalberti, "La monarchia rappresentativa nel pensiero di Cesare Balbo," 121ff. On the aristocratic understanding of representation see Capra, "Nobiltà/Borghesia," 140.

83. Balbo, *Della monarchia rappresentativa*, 74.

84. Ibid., 76. Balbo refers here explicitly to 1793.

85. Jaume, *Tocqueville*, 30. This was in line with the principles of the French Revolution: Jennings, *Revolution and the Republic*, 30.

86. Balbo, *Della monarchia rappresentativa*, 11. On the changing concept of public opinion in Italy, see Meriggi, "Opinione pubblica," in particular 150, 158. Raynal had explained that "opinion is the property most dear to man, dearer even than his life": Raynal, *The Revolution of America*, 9.

87. Balbo, *Della monarchia rappresentativa*, 81f.; also 112f., 122f.

88. François Pierre Guillaume Guizot, *Democracy in Modern Communities* (London: C. and H. Senior, 1838). The English translation appeared in several editions. On the political context, see Jardin, *Histoire du Libéralisme Politique*, 257.

89. On Guizot's concept of constitutional monarchy, see Pasquino, "Sur la théorie constitutionelle de la monarchie de Juillet."

90. Rosanvallon, *Le Moment Guizot*, 93.

91. On Guizot and Tocqueville, see Rosanvallon, *Le Moment Guizot*, 54. Craiutu, *Liberalism under Siege*, 94–96, 100f., 113f. On political and theoretical differences between Guizot and Tocqueville, see Jaume, *Tocqueville*, 338ff. Manent, "Guizot et Tocqueville." For Guizot's understanding of representative government, see Lefort, "Guizot théoricien du pouvoir," 103ff.

92. Palmer, *The Age of Democratic Revolution*, vol. 1, 248. Filangieri, *La Scienza della Legislazione*/Constant, *Comento sulla Scienza della Legislazione*, vol. 1, 243. For further discussion, see Berti, "Modello brittanico, modello americano e antidispotismo."

93. Cattaneo, "Dell'economia Nazionale di Frederico List," in *Scritti economici*, vol. 2, 355–424, 382. First published in *Il Politecnico*, 1843. Here he might have been influenced by Londonio, whose book was included in his library: Lacaita et al., eds., *La biblioteca di Carlo Cattaneo*, 245.

94. François Guizot, *Du Gouvernement représentatif et de l'état actuel de la France* (Paris: Maradan, 1816), 1.

95. Giuseppe Mazzini, "'Sulla Democrazia' del Guizot" (1839), *Edizione nazionale*, vol. 22, 327–71. See also "In Defense of Democracy: A Reply to Mr Guizot," in Mazzini, *A Cosmopolitanism of Nations*, 66–79. For Mazzini's influence on democratic thought prior to 1848, see Mastellone, *Mazzini and Marx*.

96. Galante Garrone, *L'Albero della libertà*, 192, 202–6. On the impact of French concepts of progress in Italy, see Sofia, "Progresso/Incivilmento," and for Mazzini, see 28ff. Cousin in particular influenced the Italian exiles. See, for instance, Angelo Degubernatis, *Santorre di Santa Rosa* (Turin: Unione Tipografico-Editrice, 1860), 50ff.

97. Giuseppe Mazzini, "In Defense of Democracy: A Reply to Mr Guizot," 72.

98. Ibid. On Mazzini's attitude to English parliamentary conventions, see also Morelli, *L'Inghilterra di Mazzini*, 22ff.

99. Lenci, "From Republic to Representative Democracy," 54.

100. Giuseppe Montanelli, *Introduzione ad alcuni appunti storici sulla rivoluzione d'Italia* (Turin: Tip. Subalpina, 1851), 75f., 86. For his references to Guizot, see ibid., 5, 67. On England's view of the future of Italy, see also Giuseppe Montanelli, *L'impero, il papato e la democrazia in Italia: Studio politico* (Florence: Le Monnier, 1859), 11.

101. Montanelli, *Introduzione ad alcuni appunti storici*, 86f., 137.

102. Iermano, *Il giacobinismo*, 45. Like other foreign observers, the situation in Ireland particularly preoccupied Angeloni.

103. Constant, *Comento sulla Scienza della Legislazione*, vol. 1, 145. In other respects Constant was more positive of British society: Jennings, *Revolution and the Republic*, 160, 163.

104. Mazzini to Nicola Fabrizi, 15/2/1844, *Edizione nazionale*, vol. 26, 63–68, 66. See also Tóth, *An Exiled Generation*, 199.

105. Filangieri, *La Scienza della Legislazione*, vol. 2, 217. See also Israel, *Democratic Enlightenment*, 369.

106. Foscolo, *Lettere scritte dall'Inghilterra*, 37ff. They were composed during his first year in London. Foscolo lived vastly over his means and died in humiliating poverty in Turnham Green.

107. Lyttelton, "The Hero and the People," 41. For a short overview in English, see Duggan, *The Force of Destiny*, 13ff. For a recent discussion of British policy toward the Ionian Islands, see Paschalidi, *Constructing Ionian Identities*. On the tensions over Greece, see also Rosen, *Bentham, Byron and Greece*.

108. Foscolo's principal writings on the subject are collected in in *Edizione Nazionale delle opere di Ugo Foscolo*, vol. 13. On the conflict over Parga, see also Isabella, *Risorgimento in Exile*, 70ff. In this context also Niccolò Tommaseo is of interest: Dominique Reill, "The Risorgimento: A Multinational Movement."

109. Ugo Foscolo, "Stato politico delle Isole Jonie" (1817), in *Edizione Nazionale delle opere di Ugo Foscolo*, vol. 13, 3–37, 28ff. Similar ideas praising colonial emancipation were held up by Romagnosi during the 1830s: Isabella, "Liberalism and Empires in the Mediterranean," 243f. During the later Risorgimento the international outrange against England over the Ionian Islands was revived: *Die Folgen der Verschwörung von Plombiers: Oder Enthüllungen der hinterlistigen Anschläge unserer Feinde zum Raubanfalle gegen Oesterreich in Italien und Ungarn,—und einige sehr interessante Blicke in die Vergangenheit, Gegenwart und Zukunft* (Vienna: Mechitaristen-Buchhandlung, 1861), 23f.

110. Ventura, *La questione Sicula nel 1848*, 28. For the reference to slavery, see ibid., 30.

111. Pisacane, *Saggi storici-politici-militari sull'Italia*, 60.

112. Marco Minghetti, "Intorno alla tendenza agli interessi materiali che è nel secolo presente" (1841), in *Scritti vari*, 21–47, 34. Minghetti, "Nuove osservazioni intorno alla tendenza agli interessi materiali che è nel secolo presente in risposta alla lettera del sig. A. Pizzoli" (1841), ibid., 49–109, 104.

113. Gioberti, *Del rinnovamento civile d'Italia*, vol. 1, 57; see also 130. This description of Guizot is especially interesting in the context of Gioberti's views of Italian national character: Patriarca, *Italian Vices*, 24ff.

114. Patriarca, *Italian Vices*, 25. Gemme, *Domesticating Foreign Struggles*, 44f. Although the two had friendly exchanges in the early 1840s, Gioberti's tirade against Guizot was a direct critique of Balbo's Anglophilia. On the idea of a "feminine people," see also Riall, "Men at War: Masculinity and Military Ideals in the Risorgimento."

115. Pecchio, "Un'elezione di membri del parlamento in Inghilterra" (1826) in *Scritti politici*, 225–75, 229. On Pecchio's transnational liberal networks, see Isabella, *Risorgimento in Exile*, 35.

116. Giuseppe Pecchio, *Osservazioni semi-serie di un esule sull'Inghilterra* (Lugano: Ruggia, 1831), 258.

117. Pecchio, "L'anno mille ottocento ventisei dell'Inghilterra" (1827), *Scritti politici*, 277–354, 293. Santorre di Santarosa, who met Pecchio in London, mentions similar concern about the cost of maintaining the poor: *Ricordi 1818–1824*, 105. On Santarosa's experience of exile also Ginsborg, "Romanticismo e Risorgimento," 30f.

118. Pecchio, *Osservazioni semi-serie*, 2.

119. Marco Minghetti, *I miei ricordi*, vol. 3, 228. On liberal concepts of empire in Risorgimento political thought, see Isabella, "Liberalism and Empires in the Mediterranean," 235–41.

120. Sabetti, "Cattaneo e il modello americano," 354.

121. Pécout, "Cavour visto dagli Stati Uniti." See also Ridolfi, "La Démocratie en Amérique di Tocqueville," 134.

122. Pasquale Mancini, 6/12/1861, in *La politica estera dell'Italia negli atti, documenti e discussioni parlamentari dal 1861 al 1914* (Giacomo Petricone, ed.), vol. 1, Rome: Grafica editrice romana, 1971, 98. For the debate on the separation of church and state, see also Francesco Ferrara, "La chiesa e lo stato agli Stati-Uniti di America," in *Nuova antologia*, 2, 3 (March 1867), 562–82.

123. "Il liberalismo e gli Stati Uniti di America," in *Civiltà cattolica*, ser. 9, vol. 9, *January 1876*, 272–86, 284. The book under review was a critique of Tocqueville, revising his enthusiastic account of civil institutions in the United States.

124. Camillo Cavour, 26/2/1861, in *La politica estera dell'Italia* (Petricone, ed.), vol. 1, 15.

125. Istituto Mazziniano, Genoa: 2322 Cart. 19: Canale, Michele Giuseppe, *Osservazioni critiche ad alcune disposizioni dello Statuto* [1848].

126. *Discorsi parlamentari di Marco Minghetti*, vol. 1, 465–69, 466f.

127. Cesare Beccaria, *Dei delitti e delle pene: Contro le ingiustizie della giustizia* (1764) (Milan: Rizzoli, 1994) (§26), 113f. On Beccaria and Rousseau, see Venturi, *Settecento riformatore: Da Muratori a Beccaria*, 678ff. See also Israel, *Democratic Enlightenment*, 338. Lenci, "From Republic to Representative Democracy."

128. Cesare Beccaria, *On Crimes and Punishments* (transl. Graeme R. Newman and Pietro Marongiu); New Brunswick/London: Transactions, 2009) (§26), 66.

129. Isabella, *Risorgimento in Exile*, 93f.

130. Jean Charles Léonard Simonde de Sismondi, *Études sur les constitutions des peuples libres* (Paris: Treutetel et Würtz, 1836), 407–15. This was an argument Sismondi had presented before, for instance in his influential *History of the Italian Republics*.

131. Giovanni Antonio Ranza, "Soluzione del quesito proposto dall'amministrazione generale della Lombardia: Quale dei governi liberi meglio convenga alla felicità dell'Italia?" See also Thom, *Republics, Nations and Tribes*, 182. On the broader context of post-1796 constitutions in Italy, see Biagini, "Citizenship and Religion in the Italian Constitutions."

132. Ranza, "Soluzione del quesito proposto dall'amministrazione generale della Lombardia," 191.

133. Criscuolo, *Albori di democrazia*, 104ff.

134. See in particular the fourth edition of this pamphlet: Ranza, "Soluzione del quesito proposto dall'amministrazione generale della Lombardia," 195.

135. Ibid., 196. Ranza disagreed on this point with Botta, for whom financial independence presented one of Washington's qualities: Jori and Mattei, "La figura di George Washington nella Storia della guerre dell'independenza degli Stati Uniti d'America di Botta," 145.

136. Criscuolo, *Albori di democrazia*, 111.

137. The most detail we find in the following paragraphs of Balbo, *Della monarchia rappresentativa*, 80–83.

138. Balbo, "La vita di Cesare Balbo," 364f. On Balbo's understanding of Gioberti, see Aliberti, "Cesare Balbo: Il federalismo," 135f. Some historians have questioned Balbo's commitment to federalism: Clemens, *Sanctus amor patriae*, 265.

139. For an overview of his philosophical writings and an introduction, see Vincenzo Gioberti, *Scritti scelti di Vincenzo Gioberti*. On his Paris contacts, see Barbiera, *La principessa Belgiojoso*, 132ff.

140. Vincenzo Gioberti, *Del primato morale e civile degli Italiani* (Brussels: Meline, Cans, 1843), vol. 2, 57, 174, 498. In more detail, see also Gioberti, *Del rinnovamento*, vol. 1, 169ff. Although the relationship between the two philosophers needs further clarification, for Gioberti, Hegel's ideas and the spiritual transformation taking place in Germany after 1815 were directly related. For Hegel's influence on Gioberti, see also Guzzo, "Introduzione," 52.

141. Gioberti, *Del primato morale*, vol. 1, 19, 42; vol. 2, 399.

142. Ibid., vol. 1, 20; vol. 2, 166.

143. Apart from occasional allusions to Columbus's genius, *Del primato* mentions the United States only once, very briefly, toward the end of volume 2. Gioberti, *Del primato morale*, vol. 2, 445.

144. Candeloro, *Storia dell'Italia moderna*, vol. 2, 362. For a comprehensive summary, see Scirocco, *L'Italia del Risorgimento*, 223.

145. Gioberti, *Del primato*, vol. 1, 95f.

146. Casini, *L'antica sapienza italica*.

147. See in this respect the article by Manfredi, "Risorgimento e tradizioni municipali: Il viaggio di propaganda di Vincenzo Gioberti nell'Italia del 1848."

148. Gioberti, *Del rinnovamento civile*, vol. 1, *Proemio*.

149. On Gioberti's relationship to Balbo and other moderates, see Candeloro, *Storia dell'Italia moderna*, vol. 2, 378f.; Isabella, "Aristocratic Liberalism." Romani, "Reluctant Revolutionaries," 56f.

150. Gioberti, *Del rinnovamento civile*, vol. 1, 201f.

151. Ibid., vol. 1, 201; on England, Sicily, and Italy, see 276.

152. Ibid., vol. 1, 5.

153. Gioberti, *Del primato*, vol. 1, 119. If Gioberti's program includes a space for non-Christians, it is because Italo-Catholic civilization is able to offer "*libertà della coscienza*." For instance, "Israeliti italiani potranno partecipare ai diritti civili degli altri cittadini," but this is exactly because he sees Italy as the unquestioned center of civil progress, which unlike other nations enables the country to offer tolerance. Gioberti, *Del primato*, vol. 1, 378f.; vol. 2, 130f.

154. For Carducci's reference to Mazzini, see Carducci, *Lo studio bolognese*, 24. Drake, *Byzantium for Rome*, 6. Gentile, *La Grande Italia*, 46ff.

155. Montanelli, *Memorie sull'Italia*, vol. 1, 73f. On his relationship to liberal Catholicism, see ibid., 82f.

156. For Cattaneo's review of Balbo's *Vita di Dante*, see della Peruta, *Milano nel Risorgimento*, 54.

157. Pellegrino and Muratore, eds., *Stato unitario e federalismo nel pensiero cattolico del Risorgimento*.

158. Antonio Rosmini-Serbati, *La costituzione secondo la giustizia sociale con un appendice sull'Unità d'Italia* (Naples: C. Batelli, 1848), 64.

159. Rosmini-Serbati, *La costituzione secondo la giustizia sociale*, 64. His reasoning reflects the role Giacomo Durando accorded to the railways in overcoming the barrier of the Apenine and leading to the country's material unification. Scirocco, *L'Italia del Risorgimento*, 233.

160. Rosmini-Serbati, *La costituzione secondo la giustizia sociale*, 66.

161. On different aspects of their relationship, see the chapters in Beschin and Cristellon, eds., *Rosmini e Gioberti*. On conflicts, see also Traniello, *Società religiosa e società civile in Rosmini*, 169–84. For a more recent study, see Intini, *La controversia fra Rosmini e Gioberti*.

162. As Tesini was able to show, Tocqueville is the author most frequently quoted in Rosmini's *Filosopfia della politica*: "Rosmini lettore di Tocqueville," 266. Rosmini's personal archive contains a handwritten booklet of excerpts from Tocqueville's writings. See also Cassina, "Opening 'a New Path': Notes on the Constitutional Project of Antonio Rosmini." On the reception of Tocqueville in Italy, see Noto, *Un mancato incontro*.

163. Tesini, "Rosmini lettore di Tocqueville," 275f.

164. For a recent account of Rosmini's activities during the Revolution, see Botto, *Modernità in questione*, 79ff. Traniello, *Società religiosa*, 283ff.

165. Rosmini-Serbati, *La costituzione secondo la giustizia sociale*, 63. For a comprehensive discussion of this work, see D'Addio, "Progetti costituzionali di Antonio Rosmini."

166. Rosmini-Serbati, *La costituzione secondo la giustizia sociale*, 64.

167. Ibid., 68f.

168. Ibid., 7. On Rosmini's concept of natural rigts, see Traniello, "Letture rosminiane della Rivoluzione francese," 155.

169. Rosmini-Serbati, *La costituzione secondo la giustizia sociale*, 4. See also 67.

170. Rosmini, *Filosofia della politica*.

171. Rosmini, *Filosofia della politica*, 302.

172. Rosmini-Serbati, *La costituzione secondo la giustizia sociale*, 5.

173. Rosmini, *Filosofia della politica*, 303, 346.

174. Ibid., 199, 220. All these examples are based on Tocqueville.

175. Rosmini, *Filosofia della politica*, 346, footnote 135.

176. Rosmini-Serbati, *La costituzione secondo la giustizia sociale*, 71.

177. D'Addio, "Progetti costituzionali di Antonio Rosmini," 97. D'Addio, "Introduzione," in Rosmini, *Filosofia della politica*, 11–37, 28f.

178. Michele Dossi, *Antonio Rosmini: Ein philosophisches Profil* (Stuttgart: Kohlhammer, 2003), 265–74.

179. Traniello, *Società religiosa e società civile*, 294, 312.

180. Traniello, "Letture rosminiane della Rivoluzione francese," 157. For Rosmini, the future had to result in an organization in which "l'umanità ridiverrà una sola famiglia, un solo alveare": Rosmini-Serbati, *La costituzione secondo la giustizia sociale*, 71.

181. Rosmini, *Delle cinque piaghe della Santa Chiesa*. For a short outline of Rosmini's critique, see Zolo, "Governo temporale e 'senso ecclesiastico.'"

182. Botto, *Modernità in questione*, 85f.

183. Rosmini-Serbati, *La Costituzione secondo la giustizia sociale*, 5.

184. Ibid., 4.

185. D'Addio, "Introduzione," 17f. For the controversies between Cattaneo and Rosmini, see Francesco Lampato to Carlo Cattaneo, 24/10/1836, *Carteggi di Carlo Cattaneo* vol. 1 (1820–40), 55–56.

186. For the strong anti-Jesuit sentiment of 1848, see, for instance, "Dialogo fra due Gesuiti e il diavolo" ([Genoa]: Dagnino, [1848]); "Agonia dei Gesuiti" ([Genoa], Dagnino, [1848]) (BL: Miscellanee politiche genovesi. 804.k.13.37.15 and 17). The collection contains numerous leaflets directed against the Jesuits.

187. Giovanni Antonio Grassi, *Notizie varie sullo stato presente della repubblica degli Stati Uniti dell'America settentrionale* (Rome: Salvioni, 1818). The book saw two more editions before 1822. On his role in the US Jesuit community, see McKevitt, *Brokers of Culture*, 44f.

188. Dossi, *Antonio Rosmini*, 81ff.

189. Mazzini to Giuseppe Montanelli, 16/7/1847, *Edizione nazionale*, vol. 32, 220–26, 221.

190. Dal Lago, *William Lloyd Garrison and Giuseppe Mazzini*, 145.

191. On Carrel and America see Jennings, *Revolution and the Republic*, 219f. See also Thier, "A World Apart, a Race Apart?"

192. Mazzini, "Dell'unità italiana," *Edizione nazionale*, vol. 3, 261–335, 277. Mazzini to Lisette Mandrot, 29/10/1840, ibid., vol. 19, 419–36, 435. Guglielmo Pepe, *Memoirs: Comprising the Principal Military and Political Events of Modern Italy* (London: Bentley, 1846), vol. 3, 267f. This edition was followed by an Italian translation.

193. Mazzini to Jessie White Mario, 25/4/1860, *Edizione nazionale*, vol. 67, 245–50, 250.

194. Rossi, *The Image of America*, 7. See also Sarti, "Giuseppe Mazzini e la tradizione repubblicana," 60.

195. Mazzini to Melegari, 2/7/1838, *Edizione nazionale*, vol. 15, 53–57, 57. See also MackSmith, *Italy: A Modern History*, 13f. Sarti, "La democrazia radicale," 139, 147.

196. Sarti, "Giuseppe Mazzini and Young Europe," 286f.

197. Mazzini to Gioberti, Lausanne, 15/9/1834, *Edizione nazionale*, vol. 10, 62–77. Biagini, "Mazzini and Anticlericalism: The English in Exile." On Gioberti's concepts of a reorganization of the church, see Marangoni, "La riforma della chiesa in Gioberti." Levis Sullam has pointed out that the term most frequently used in Mazzini's *Doveri dell'uomo* (1860) is *"dio"*: *L'apostolo a brandelli*, 6. However, in this case there is no reason to understand these religious references as antiliberal.

198. Mazzini, "Agli italiani" (1853), *Edizione nazionale*, vol. 51, 17–84, 42.

199. Ibid., 39.

200. Ibid., 40. In 1868 he makes a similar argument in a letter to the director of *Courrier Français*: 2/2/1868, *Edizione nazionale*, vol. 85, 334–36, 335.

201. Mazzini to his mother, 13/10/1834, *Edizione nazionale*, vol. 10, 149–52, 151. Mazzini, "Dell'unità italiana," *Edizione nazionale*, vol. 3, 261–335, 277, 288. On the aristocratic elements Mazzini differs from Tocqueville: Jennings, *Revolution and the Republic*, 90.

202. Mazzini, "Dell'unità italiana," *Edizione nazionale*, vol. 3, 261–335.

203. Ibid., 291f. Occasionally Mazzini himself drew on direct comparisons. See, for instance, an article of September 1843 for the *Apostolato popolare*: "Simbolo politico della Giovine Italia," *Edizione nazionale*, vol. 25, 257–64, 262.

204. Mazzini to Nicola Fabrizi, 1/3/1844, *Edizione nazionale*, vol. 26, 85–89, 87.

205. Mazzini to Giuseppe Montanelli, 16/7/1847, *Edizione nazionale*, vol. 32, 220–26, 221.

206. Sismondi, *Études sur les constitutions*, 415.

207. Mazzini to Matilda Biggs, November 1862, *Edizione nazionale*, vol. 73, 179–85, 183.

208. Mazzini, "To Our friends in the United States" (1865), in Mazzini, *A Cosmopolitanism of Nations*, 222f. See also *Edizione nazionale*, vol. 83, 187–89. For Mazzni's postbellum reassessment of the United States, see also "Ai nemici" (1868), *Edizione nazionale*, vol. 86, 203–16, 205.

209. Lenci, "From Republic to Representative Democracy," 55. Instead of trying to emulate the United States, many Italian republicans took the emerging German labor movement as a model: Ridolfi, *Dalla setta al partito*, 92f.

210. Pisacane, *Saggi storici-politici-militari sull'Italia: Terzo saggio*, 78. For brief and unrelated references to the United States, see ibid., 62, 73. A longer passage on Washington serves to point out differences between the Italian and the American revolutions. Ibid., 147f. Contemporaries were keen to compare Pisacane to abolitionists in the United States: Dal Lago, *The Age of Lincoln and Cavour*, 39f.

211. Criscuolo, *Albori di democrazia*, 105. De Francesco, "Ideologie e movimenti politici," 287f. On the divisions between Buonarroti and Mazzini, and Young Europe in particular, see also Sarti, "Giuseppe Mazzini and Young Europe," 276, 286.

212. Quoted in Morelli, "The United States Constitution," 104. On the potential weakness of federal states, see also Criscuolo, *Albori di democrazia*, 109.

213. Botta, "Proposizione ai Lombardi di una maniera di governo libero," 49.

214. Morelli, "The United States Constitution," 109. Mazzini, "Agli italiani" (1853), *Edizione nazionale*, vol. 51, 17–84, 41.

215. Dal Lago, *William Lloyd Garrison and Giuseppe Mazzini*, 43. See also Mack Smith, *Mazzini*, 12. Scirocco, *L'Italia del Risorgimento*, 180, 184. Riall, "The Politics of Italian Romanticism: Mazzini and the Making of a Nationalist Culture," 172.

216. See, for instance, Capellini, *Ricordi di un viaggio scientifico*, 157, 161. *Almanacco Repubblicano 1872*. Pubblicazione del Giornale La Plebe (Enrico Bignami, ed.; Lodi: Società Cooperativo-Tipografica, 1871). See also Italian press coverage on American journalism: *L'Universo illustrato*, 1, 16/1/1867 and 19/2/1867. By 1840 the United States had 138 daily newspapers, by 1850, 254, with an average circulation rising to around three thousand: Rydell and Kroes, *Buffalo Bill in Bologna*, 17.

217. Meriggi, "Opinione pubblica," 159.

218. Duggan, "Giuseppe Mazzini in Britain and Italy: Divergent Legacies, 1837–1915," 194ff., 200.

219. Engels, "Das Auftreten Mazzinis gegen die Internationale," *Il Libero pensiero*, 31/8/1871. See also Galante Garrone, *I radicali in Italia*, 26ff.

220. For a general overview of these debates, see Schiera, "Centralismo e federalismo nell'unificazione statal-nazionale italiana e tedesca"; Meriggi, "Centralismo e federalismo in Italia. Le aspettative preunitarie." Also Ragionieri, *Politica e amministrazione nella storia dell'Italia unita*, 97. Doyle, *Nations Divided*, 29. On the Americas and Italian federalism, see also Isabella, *Risorgimento in Exile*, 60ff. In the context of these debates the Italian reception of Tocqueville is obviously important: Ridolfi, "La Démocratie en Amérique."

221. Carlo Cattaneo to Giuseppe Ferrari [1851], *Epistolario di Carlo Cattaneo*, vol. 2, 105–7, 106. On Mazzini's relationship with Cattaneo, see della Peruta, *Milano nel Risorgimento*, 95ff.

222. See in this context also the monarchical-federal pamphlet by Alessandro Luigi Bargani, *Progetto di costituzione dei Regni Uniti d'Italia offerto ai circoli politici e federativi degli stati italiani da un cittadino degli Stati Uniti d'America* (Turin, 1848).

223. Ridolfi, "Visions of Republicanism in the Writings of Giuseppe Mazzini," 473. Ridolfi, *Il Partito della Repubblica*, 278–87. Colombo, "Monarchia/Repubblica," 321.

224. Quoted in Urbinati, "The Legacy of Kant: Giuseppe Mazzini's Cosmopolitanism of Nations," 16.

225. Mill, "Considerations on Representative Government," 390, 395.

226. Ibid., 399. Urbinati, *Mill on Democracy*, 19. See also Thompson, *John Stuart Mill and Representative Government*, chpt. 3.

227. Minghetti, "Centralità o discentramento amministrativo," 8/6/1860, in *Discorsi parlamentari*, vol. 1, 45ff. See also Berselli, "Primi decenni dopo l'Unità," 258ff.

228. Romeo, *Vita di Cavour*, 503. Romanelli, "Le Regole del gioco: Note sull'impianto del sistema elettorale in Italia (1848–1895)," 685. Romanelli, *L'Italia liberale*, 43. Ragionieri, *Politica e amministrazione nella storia dell'Italia unita*, 93, 96f. See also Porciani, "Identità locale—identità nazionale: La costruzione di una doppia appartenenza," 168.

229. Alberto Mario, "Mazzini" (1873), in *La repubblica e l'ideale*, 76. See also Mattarelli, "Repubblicani senza la repubblica," 5ff. Conti, *L'Italia dei democratici*, 47.

230. Alberto Mario, "L'impotenza della sinistra e la repubblica federale" (*Preludio*, Cremona, 31/3/1877), in *Scritti politici di Alberto Mario*, vol. 1, 159–66, 165. See also his work on Cattaneo, ibid., 181–308, 282f. On the role of the United States for later generations of Italian Republicans, see, for instance, *Almanacco repubblicano: 1871*.

231. Mario, "L'impotenza della sinistra," 165.

Chapter Three. A Model Republic?
The United States in the Italian Revolutions of 1848

1. Montanelli, *Introduzione ad alcuni appunti storici sulla rivoluzione*, 1f. For a modern edition of his works, see Montanelli, *Opere politiche* (Paolo Bagnoli, ed.).

2. Bargani, *Progetto di costituzione dei Regni Uniti d'Italia*.

3. Quoted in Marraro, *American Opinion on the Unification of Italy*, 37.

4. Antonelli, "'E questo che fa la mia America': Il giornalismo di Margaret Fuller," 148.

5. Pascual Sastre, "La circolazione di miti politici tra Spagnia e Italia," 799–805.

6. Ferris, "A Model Republic," 54. For a more detailed overview see Ferris, *Imagining "America" in Late Nineteenth-Century Spain*.

7. Venturi, "Spanish and Italian Economists and Reformers in the Eighteenth Century," *Italy and the Enlightenment*, 265–91. Davis, *Naples and Napoleon*, 267.

8. Pepe, *Memoirs*, vol. 3, 110f. His main focus here is the king's role in the military command.

9. Ibid., vol. 3, 270, 273.

10. On the 1812 constitution in the Revolutions of 1820–21, see Späth, *Revolution in Europea 1820–23*. See also John A. Davis, "The Spanish Constitution of 1812 and the Mediterranean Revolutions (1820–1825)." On the transnational dimension of the Triennio Liberale, see also Isabella, *Risorgimento in Exile*, 32ff. Spini, *Mito e realtà della Spagna nelle rivoluzioni italiane 1820–21*. Biagini, "Citizenship and Religion," 213. Galante Garrone, "L'emigrazione politica italiana del Risorgimento," 233. Renda, "La rivoluzione del 1812 e l'autonomia siciliana." Colombo, "Una Corona per una nazione: Considerazioni sul ruolo della monarchia costituzionale nella costruzione dell'identità italiana," 22.

11. He was Ferdinando IV of Naples and Ferdinando III of Sicily, and in 1816 he became Ferdinand I of the Kingdom of the Two Sicilies. For an overview of the debates on the Sicilian constitution that is still crucial, see Rosselli, *Lord William Bentinck and the British Occupation of Sicily*. Here also are references to the relevant works published during the first half of the twentieth century. For aspects of the occupation's diplomatic and military history, see Gregory, *Sicily, the Insecure Base*.

12. Pepe, *Memoirs*, vol. 2, 321f.

13. Ugo Foscolo, quoted in Sciacca, *Riflessi del costituzionalismo europeo in Sicilia*, 9. On Bentinck's ambition to annex Sicily to the British Empire, see Ganci, *Storia antologica dell'autonomia siciliana*, vol. 1, 77ff. On the claims of a shared Norman heritage, see Charles Mac Farlane, *Sicily: Her Constitutions, and Viscount Palmerston's Sicilian Blue-Book* (London: Smith, 1849).

14. Sciacca, *Riflessi del costituzionalismo europeo in Sicilia*, 10.

15. Quoted in Fiume, *La crisi sociale del 1848 in Sicilia*, 193. See also the contemporary views of Charles Mac Farlane, *Sicily*, 42f.

16. Rosselli, *Lord William Bentinck and the British Occupation of Sicily*. On the social consequences of Sicily's escape of Napoleonic reforms, see Iachello and Signorelli, "Borghesie urbane dell'Ottocento," 95. See also Finley, MackSmith, and Duggan, *A History of Sicily*, 143ff.

17. De Francesco, "Ideologie e movimenti politici," 252f.

18. Giacinto Galanti, *La voce della verita' in sostegno della causa pubblica* (Naples, 1848), 5, 12.

19. Falzone, *La Sicilia nella politica mediterranea delle grandi potenze*, 75f.

20. Candeloro, *Storia dell'Italia moderna*, vol. 2, 86.

21. Against the allegedly "passive" attitude of southerners in these political processes, see Davis, *Naples and Napoleon*, 10.

22. Ferris, "A Model Republic."

23. Körner, "Die Julirevolution von 1830."

24. Carlo Pepoli's notes give excellent insights to the constitutional debates in 1831: *L'Archivio dei governi provvisori di Bologna e delle Provincie Unite del 1831* (Studi e Testi, 189; Lajos Pásztor, Pietro Pirri, eds.; Città del Vaticano: Biblioteca Apostolica Vaticana, 1956). "Sunto di memorie, Noterelle biografiche C. Carlo Pepoli," Forlí, Biblioteca Comunale Aurelio Saffi, Collezione Piancastelli, Autografi 19 sec., busta 151, Carlo Pepoli. It was in 1848 that the British model assumed importance in Pepoli's thought: University of Southampton, Hartley Library, Palmerston Papers, PP/GC/PE/50 Conte Carlo Pepoli.

25. Candeloro, *Storia dell'Italia moderna*, vol. 2, 194, 201, 210.

26. Mazzini, "Istruzione generale per gli affratellati della Giovine Italia," *Edizione nazionale*, vol. 2, 49.

27. A.R., "Canto dei popoli italiani" ([Genoa]: Frugoni, [1848]) (BL: Miscellanee politiche genovesi. 804.k.13.7).

28. Giuseppe Gazzino, "L'Italia e la lega: Canto popolare" (Genoa: Casamara, [1848]) (BL: Miscellanee politiche genovesi. 804.k.13.1).

29. "La Lega italiana: Canzone" ([Genoa]: Dagnino, [1848]) (BL: Miscellanee politiche genovesi. 804.k.13.5).

30. "Canto delle Donne Italiane: Sul Risorgimento d'Italia; Inno nazionale" (Genoa: Delle piane, [1848]) (BL: Miscellanee politiche genovesi. 804.k.13.4).

31. Un italiano, "L'avvenire d'Italia" Canzone" ([Genoa]: Dagnino, [1848]) (BL: Miscellanee politiche genovesi. 804.k.13.6).

32. For connections between the Roman Republic and the United States, see in particular Antonelli, Fiorentino, and Monsagrati, eds., *Gli americani e la Repubblica Romana*. Fiorentino, *Gli Stati Uniti e il Risorgimento d'Italia*, 69–97.

33. A useful first step in this direction is Biagini, "Citizenship and Religion," 214ff.

34. Quoted in della Peruta, *Milano nel Risorgimento*, 132. For an Austrian perspective on the event, see Rapport, *1848*, 43.

35. della Peruta, *Milano nel Risorgimento*, 146. Sked, *The Survival of the Habsburg Empire*, 106–12. Macartney, *The Habsburg Empire 1790–1918*, 319.

36. For a brief discussion of Cattaneo's position, see della Peruta, *Milano nel Risorgimento*, 133f.

37. Sabetti, *Civilization and Self-Government*, 35f. For an introduction, see Thom, "Unity and Confederation in the Italian Risorgimento: The Case of Carlo Cattaneo." Steinberg, "Carlo Cattaneo and the Swiss Idea of Liberty."

38. Marraro, *American Opinion on the Unification of Italy*, 38ff.

39. Meriggi, *Il Regno Lombardo-Veneto*, discusses 1848 within the political framework of the Austrian Regno Lombardo-Veneto. This presents a welcome exception to a historiographical tradition, which has tended to discuss the Revolution almost exclusively from the point of view of the Italian national movement, in the perspective of a future Italian nation-state.

40. Laven, *Venice and Venetia under the Habsburgs*. See also Tonetti, *Governo austriaco e notabili sudditi: Congregazioni e municipi nel Veneto della restaurazione, 1813–1848*.

41. See in this context especially Thom, "Europa, libertà e nazioni: Cattaneo e Mazzini nel Risorgimento," 354f.

42. Greenfield, *Economics and Liberalism in the Risorgimento*, 35ff. For a recent discussion of Greenfield, see Davis, "A Missing Encounter: Rosario Romeo's Place in International Historiography," 21f.

43. Mazohl-Wallnig, *Österreichischer Verwaltungsstaat und administrative Eliten im Königreich Lombardo-Venetien*, 93; on the concept of monarchy, see 311ff. Meriggi, *Gli*

stati italiani prima dell'Unità, 157. More critical as to claims of autonomy is Raponi, *Politica e amministrazione in Lombardia agli esordi dell'Unità*, 19ff.

44. Meriggi, *Il Regno Lombardo-Veneto*, 326.

45. Laven, "The Age of Restoration," 59. See also Laven, *Venice and Venetia under the Habsburgs, 1815–1835*; and Laven and Parker, "Foreign Rule? Transnational, National and Local Perspectives on Venice and Venetia within the 'Multinational' Empire." For a different viewpoint of the Restoration regime, see Ginsborg, *Daniele Manin and the Venetian Revolution*, 2–83. The "black legend" argument goes bak to Berengo, "Le origini del Lombardo-Veneto." On this controversy, see also Riall, *Il Risorgimento*, 51

46. della Peruta, *Milano nel Risorgimento*, 108f., 122f., 141. Meriggi, *Il Regno Lombardo-Veneto*, 328–32. On the involvement of women, see Soldani, "Donne e nazione nella rivoluzione italiana del 1848."

47. della Peruta, *Milano nel Risorgimento*, 156ff. On the impact of events in Lombardy on the rest of the monarchy, see Rumpler, *Eine Chance für Mitteleuropa*, 289f.

48. For a brief account of Radetzky's role, see Sked, *Radetzky*, 133–48.

49. On these tensions, see Meriggi, *Il Regno Lombardo-Veneto*, 332ff.

50. Dipper, "Revolutionäre Bewegungen auf dem Lande: Deutschland, Frankreich, Italien," 576. Sked, *The Survival of the Habsburg Empire*, 176–95, especially 187.

51. *Le Assemblee del Risorgimento*, vol. 1, 119–266.

52. Ibid., 133–88. For references to the French tradition, see ibid., 153–59, 177, 180.

53. *Giornale ufficiale*, 21/5/1848, quoted in *Le assemblee del Risorgimento*, vol. 1, 200–202.

54. Armani, *Carlo Cattaneo*, 84f.

55. Thom, "Unity and Confederation in the Italian Risorgimento," 71.

56. Sestan, *La Firenze di Vieusseux e di Caponi*, 19.

57. Bobbio, "Introduzione," 20.

58. Armani, *Carlo Cattaneo*, 42; see also 23, 42–46, 60.

59. Cattaneo, "Il Numero e la Volontà," *Stati Uniti d'Italia*, 141-61, 149, 159ff. Sabetti, *Civilization and Self-Government*, 129.

60. Quoted in Moe, *The View from Vesuvius*, 104.

61. Mazzini, "Pamphlet on the Affairs of Italy," quoted in Mastellone, "I prodromi del 1848: Mazzini e il dibattito sul tipo di rivoluzione (1843–1847)," 64.

62. Moe, *The View from Vesuvius*, 105, 107. On the construction of this myth, see Petrusewicz, *Come il Meridione divenne una Questione*.

63. Cattaneo, "Dell'insurrezione di Milano nel 1848 e della successiva guera: Memorie," 20, also 38.

64. Ventura, *La questione Sicula nel 1848*, 37. On Ventura, see Guccione, "Il costituzionalismo in Sicilia nel 1848," 186ff.

65. Quoted in Raponi, *Politica e amministrazione in Lombardia*, 36f. Based on the works of Valsecchi and Capra, Dipper argues for the crucial role of Viennese administrators in the interaction between Lombard Enlightenment and administrative reforms: Dipper, "Die Mailänder Aufklärung und der Reformstaat: Ein Beitrag zur Berichtigung der Urteile des Publikums über das Verhältnis der politischen Theorie zum administrativen Handeln."

66. Cattaneo, "Agli Esuli Italiani in Londra," *Stati Uniti d'Italia*, 163-74, 167.

67. Carlo Pisacane, *Guerra combattuta in Italia negli anni 1848–49: Narrazione* (Genoa: Pavesi Editore, 1851), 184. Rosselli, *Carlo Pisacane nel Risorgimento italiano*, 53.

68. *Corriere mercantile*, supplemento al N.117, Genoa, 20/5/1848.

69. Giuseppe Ferrari, "La révolution et les réformes en Italie," in *Revue indépendante*, 13 (10/1/1848), 85–119. Several years earlier, in an article for the *Revue des deux mondes*, he

had used similar terms to target Piedmont's aristocratic liberalism, which he considered a reactionary ideology: See Candeloro, *Storia dell'Italia moderna*, vol. 2, 385.

70. Gioberti, *Del rinnovamento civile d'Italia*, vol. 1, 482. In 1848 Gioberti supported the union of the Lombard-Venetian Kingdom with Piedmont: Vincenzo Gioberti, *Sull'unione del Lombardo-Veneto col Piemonte* (Genoa: Frugoni, 1848). On the context of Ferrari's dismissal, see Bruch, *Italien auf dem Weg zum Nationalstaat*, 41–46.

71. Cattaneo, "Dell'insurrezione di Milano," 282.

72. Overhoff, "Benjamin Franklin, Student of the Holy Roman Empire." Gottfried Achenwall later produced a published report about the conversations with Franklin: *Einige Anmerkungen über Nord-Amerika und über dasige Grosbrittannische Colonien: Aus mündlichen Nachrichten des Herrn D. Franklins*. Helmstedt: Kühnlin, 1777.

73. Overhoff, "Benjamin Franklin, Student of the Holy Roman Empire," 282.

74. Ibid., 283. For a recent overview of the empire's legal framework, see Stollberg-Rilinger, *Das Heilige Römische Reich Deutscher Nation*.

75. de la Croix, *Constitutions des principaux états de l'Europe et des États-Unis de l'Amérique*, vol. 1, 89. His work appeared in several editions and translations.

76. On Salfi, see Morelli, "The United States Constitution Viewed by Nineteenth-Century Italian Democrats," 101.

77. The piece was to form part of the program for a new newspaper, *Il Cisalpino*. Della Peruta, *Milano nel Risorgimento*, 167. See also Thom, "Unity and Confederation in the Italian Risorgimento," 71f. Gili, *Carlo Cattaneo*, 81. On the wider context of these debates just prior to the Revolution, see Romanelli, "Nazione e costituzione nell'opinione liberale italiana prima del '48."

78. Armani, *Carlo Cattaneo*, 133f. On Cattaneo's differences with Mazzini, see also Sabetti, *Civilization and Self-Government*, 6.

79. Armani, *Carlo Cattaneo*, 140–45, 173.

80. Cattaneo, "Dell'insurrezione di Milano," 24f., also 27. On Cattaneo's view of Britain, see in particular Thom, "Great Britain and Ireland in the Thought of Carlo Cattaneo," 389, also 405f.

81. Lyttelton, "Sismondi, the Republic and Liberty: Between Italy and England, the City and the Nation"; Rao, "Republicanism in Italy from the Eighteenth Century to the Early Risorgimento."

82. Cattaneo, "Dell'insurrezione di Milano," 103f.

83. Ibid., 144.

84. Ibid., 281.

85. Quoted in Armani, *Carlo Cattaneo*, 172.

86. Cattaneo, "Dell'insurrezione di Milano," 103f.

87. Cattaneo, "Militarismo e centralizzazione in Francia."

88. Sabetti, "Cattaneo e il modello Americano," 350f.

89. Cattaneo, "Il numero e la volontà," in *Stati Uniti d'Italia*, 141–61, 149, 159ff.

90. Armani, *Carlo Cattaneo*, 70f.

91. Cattaneo, "Considerazioni sul principio della filosofia," *Scritti filosofici*, vol. 1, 143–70, 157. Cattaneo developed this idea as a direct response to Ferrari's critique of the philosophy of history.

92. Cattaneo, "Dell'insurrezione di Milano," 271f.

93. Cattaneo, "Notizia sulla questione delle tariffe daziarie negli Stati Uniti d'America desunta da documenti officiali" (1833), *Scritti economici*, vol. 1, 11–55, 14.

94. Ibid., 52f. Cattaneo was not the only Italian who commented on this crisis. Amari concluded his introduction to the new edition of Botta with a reference to the same conflict. Amari, "Prefazione," li.

95. Cattaneo, "Notizia sulla questione delle tariffe daziarie," 38.
96. Cattaneo, "Dell'insurrezione di Milano," 271f. The reference to Machiavelli appears also in Cattaneo, "Il numero e la volontà," *Stati Uniti d'Italia*, 141–61, 149.
97. Cattaneo, "Dell'insurrezione di Milano," 198.
98. The context explains Cattaneo's later request for a national army based on conscription, following the Swiss or American models: Carlo Cattaneo, "Prefazione," in *Il Politecnico: Repertorio mensile di studj applicati alla prosperità e coltura sociale*, 9 (1860), 5–24, 7f.
99. Bobbio, "Introduzione," 49, 89.
100. Sabetti, "Cattaneo e il modello americano," 346, also 350f.
101. Carlo Cattaneo to Agostino Bertani, 5/12/1859, *Epistolario di Carlo Cattaneo*, vol. 3, 230–31, 231.
102. Thom, "Great Britain and Ireland in the Thought of Carlo Cattaneo," 394.
103. Richard Cobden, Milan, 4/6/1847, *The European Diaries of Richard Cobden*, 137.
104. In addition to the last chapter, also see Grew, "One Nation Barely Visible: The United States as Seen by Nineteenth-Century Italy's Liberal Leaders," 130.
105. Ridolfi, "La Démocratie en Amérique di Tocqueville e la sua ricezione nell'Italia del Risorgimento," 137. Colucci, "Carlo Cattaneo e il Regno Lombardo-Veneto."
106. For a list of references to Tocqueville in Cattaneo's work, see Sabetti, *Civilization and Self-Government*, 16.
107. Lacaita, Gobbo, and Turiel, eds., *La biblioteca di Carlo Cattaneo*, 52, 328. Rosmini also ignored volume 2.
108. Ridolfi, "La Démocratie en Amérique di Tocqueville e la sua ricezione nell'Italia del Risorgimento," 135.
109. Quoted in Tesini, "Rosmini lettore di Tocqueville," 266.
110. Sabetti, "Cattaneo e il modello americano," 354. Ridolfi, "La Démocratie en Amérique di Tocqueville," 137f. Mazzini largely abstained from more detailed discussions of Tocqueville: Mastellone, *Il progetto politico di Mazzini*, 214.
111. Rossi, *The Image of America*, 64–71.
112. Armani, *Carlo Cattaneo*, 13, 28, 30. Moos, "Cattaneo e il modello elvetico."
113. Walter, *Histoire de la Suissse*, vol. 4, 37f.
114. Sabetti, *Civilization and Self-Government*, 158. On Cattaneo's Swiss connections, see in particular Gili, *Carlo Cattaneo*. Armani, *Carlo Cattaneo*, 128.
115. Bruch, "Munizipale Identität und bürgerliche Kultur im Risorgimento: Die Bedeutung der Stadt für Carlo Cattaneos föderal-demokratische Konzeption." Bobbio, "Introduzione," 37. Thom, "City, Region and Nation: Carlo Cattaneo and the Making of Italy."
116. *La Lega italiana: Giornale politico, economico, scientifico e letterario* (Genoa: Tip. Ferrando). Anno 1, 15, 14/2/1848.
117. Kostka, *Schiller in Italy*, 27.
118. Thom, "Unity and Confederation in the Italian Risorgimento," 73f.
119. Botta, "Proposizione ai Lombardi di una maniera di governo libero," 71.
120. Armani, *Carlo Cattaneo*, 56. On the railway debate, see Bernadello, *La prima ferrovia fra Venezia e Milano*. See also Ginsborg, *Daniele Manin*, 51–58.
121. Cattaneo, "Di alcuni stati moderni" (1842), *Scritti storici e geografici*, vol. 1, 255–301.
122. Ibid., 283.
123. Carlo Cattaneo, "Il poeta americano Longfellow," *Scritti letterari*, vol. 1, 461–73.
124. Mario, "La Nostra Via" (1872), *La repubblica e l'ideale*, 85–87, 86.
125. Mario, "Cattaneo," *La repubblica e l'ideale*, 87–101, 87f.
126. Mario, "Mazzini and Cattaneo" (1880), *La repubblica e l'ideale*, 76–79, 77.

127. Mario, "Cattaneo," 87f.

128. Quoted in Lyttelton, "The Hero and the People," 45.

129. Franzina, "L'America," 332f.

130. Coppini, *Il Granducato di Toscana*, 172f., on Leopold II's reforms, see ibid., 247ff. Chiavistelli, *Dallo stato alla nazione*, 55ff. Volpi, "Contaminazioni fra diritto commerciale e tematiche economiche," 45. See also Barsanti, "Giuseppe Montanelli 'idolo della scolaresca pisana,'" 67.

131. See, for instance, Giuseppe Gazzino, "L'Italia e la Lega: Canto Popolare" ([Genoa]: Casamara, [1848]); A.R., "Canto dei popoli italiani" ([Genoa]: Frugoni, [1848]); Giulio Guerrieri, "Il perdono e l'abbraccio fra i fratelli Genovesi e Pisani. Inno" (Genoa: Pellas, 1847); "Catechismo Nazionale" ([Genoa, 1848]) (BL: Miscellanee politiche genovesi. 804.k.13.1, 7, 89, 190).

132. "Inno nazionale" ([Genoa]: Delle Piane, [1848]) (BL: Miscellanee politiche genovesi. 804.k.13.301).

133. On the role of municipal traditions in Tuscany's constitutional debates, see Chiavistelli, *Dallo stato alla nazione*, 221ff.

134. Luigi Calamai, quoted in Ronchi, *I democratici fiorentini nella rivoluzione*, 7. For the wider process, see also Bagnoli, "Lo statuto del granducato di Toscana."

135. Ronchi, *I democratici fiorentini*, 12.

136. Coppini, *Il Granducato*, 347. Chiavistelli, *Dallo stato alla nazione*, 203.

137. Cooper, *Gleanings in Europe*, 38–44, 79f.

138. Baker, *The Fortunate Pilgrims*, 54.

139. Coppini, *Il Granducato*, 237ff. See also Spadolini, *Fra Vieusseux e Ricasoli*, 13f. Chiavistelli, *Dallo stato alla nazione*, 84f., 120ff., 153ff.

140. Ronchi, *I democratici fiorentini*, 57 n.

141. Francia, "Il pane e la politica: Moti annonari e opinione pubblica in Toscana alla vigilia del 1848," 135ff.

142. Kroll, *Die Revolte des Patriziats*, 260.

143. Ibid., 263, 266, 278.

144. Coppini, *Il Granducato*, 379f. For a detailed discussion of the constitutional debate in early 1848, see Chiavistelli, *Dallo stato alla nazione*, 239ff., 249ff.

145. Candeloro, *Storia dell'Italia moderna*, vol. 3, 206. Kroll, *Die Revolte*, 267, 277.

146. For the biographical background, see Luseroni, *Giuseppe Montanelli e il Risorgimento*, 38ff. For his socialisation in Pisa, see also Coppini, "Giuseppe Montanelli e il Risorgimento," 20ff.

147. Benvenuto, "L'Italia di Giuseppe Montanelli: Cattolicesimo, democrazia e repubblica." Cherubini, "Giuseppe Montanelli e gli altri docenti pisani e senesi dall'Antologia." Breccia, "Dalla 'pubblica opinione' alla 'opinione democratica.'"

148. For Montanelli's federal thought it seems important to note that he had broken with Mazzini's association early in the 1830s. Later he was influenced by Gioberti, partly for his stance against the Jesuits, but his appreciation remained ambiguous. Luseroni, *Giuseppe Montanelli*, 100, 167. Scirocco, "Montanelli e Mazzini." Giuseppe Montanelli, *Lettere inedite* (Florence: Rivista Europea [estratto dalla], [1875]), 8. See also the documents published in Spadolini, *Un dissidente del Risorgimento*, 89–99.

149. On Montanelli's attempt to reconcile monarchy and democracy, see Benvenuto, "The Suicide of Power and the Birth of Democracy: Buonarroti, Mazzini and Montanelli," 183ff.

150. Kroll, *Die Revolte*, 310f.

151. See, for instance, Francesco Domenico Guerrazzi, "Parole di F. D. Guerrazzi lette sopra il campo di battaglia della Cavinana nella festa del 10 ottobre 1847," in *Un serto*

all'Italia ossia Raccolta dei migliori discorsi politici composti dalle piu valenti penne italiane (Livorno: [Antonelli?], 1849), 5–10, 7f.

152. On Montanelli's role in the libretto, see Walker, "Verdi, Giuseppe Montanelli and the Libretto of *Simon Boccanegra*." Springer, *Giuseppe Verdi: "Simon Boccanegra,"* 241–52. See also Budden, *The Operas of Verdi*, vol. 2, 247f.

153. This included French and Italian editions of Montanelli's tragedy *Cassandra* as well as his *Medée*. I am grateful to Anselm Gerhard for this information.

154. Both Antonio García Gutiérrez (on whose play Piave's libretto was based) and Montanelli might have known Schiller's tragedy. Verdi himself saw the work in Cologne before he completed the revised version of his opera. See Gerhard, "Verdi, Hiller und Schiller in Köln—Ein unbeachtetes Albumblatt und die Frage möglicher Beziehungen zwischen 'Die Verschwörung des Fiesko zu Genua' und 'Simon Boccanegra.'" See also Springer, *Giuseppe Verdi*, 368f. It seems irrelevant here that Filippo Filippi, after Boito's revisions to Verdi's opera in 1881, played down the importance of the plot's historical context: Filippo Filippi, "Review of the Simon Boccanegra Revision," in *Verdi's Otello and Simon Boccanegra* (Busch, ed.), vol. 2, 666–72, 666. (Eduard Hanslick seemed more interested in this context: ibid., 673f.).

155. I am grateful to Anselm Gerhard for this information.

156. Unfer Lukoschik, *Friedrich Schiller in Italien*, 253. See also Gerhard, "Verdi, Hiller and Schiller in Köln," 89.

157. *La congiura del Fiesco: Tragedia di Federico Schiller; Traduzione del Cavaliere Andrea Maffei* (Milan: Pirola, 1853). On Schiller and A. W. Schlegel in Italy, see Kostka, *Schiller in Italy*, chpts. 1 and 2. For Montanelli's and his wife's interest in Schiller, see del Vivo, ed., *In esilio e sulla scena: Lettere di Lauretta Cipriani Parra e Adelaide Ristori*, 130. Luseroni, *Giuseppe Montanelli*, 45f., 104. On Montanelli and the Schlegels, see Rosselli, "Giuseppe Montanelli," *Saggi sul Risorgimento e altri scritti*, 87–216, 101. Gherardini's translation of Schlegel was based on Madame de Staël's French version: Ragusa, "Italy, Romantico—Romanticismo," 296. In 1838 *Il Subalpino* featured several poems by Montanelli alongside the Italian translation of an essay by Schlegel, as well as several other articles on the role of Schlegel and Schiller in European literature: *Il Subalpino: Giornale di scienze, lettere ed arti*, 2, 2 (1838). For Montanelli's poetry, see ibid., 234–39. The fact that Schlegel was himself rather critical of Schiller was not necessarily understood in Italy.

158. Budden, *The Operas of Verdi*, vol. 2, 326. See also Phillips-Matz, *Verdi*, 234f.

159. Walker, "Verdi, Giuseppe Montanelli and the Libretto of Simon Boccanegra," 1380.

160. Montanelli, *Introduzione*, 146.

161. Bagnoli, *Democrazia e stato nel pensiero politico di Giuseppe Montanelli*, 85. For Montanelli's relationship with Tuscany, see in particular the colourful account by Rosselli, "Giuseppe Montanelli," *Saggi sul Risorgimento e altri scritti*, 87–216. On Rosselli, see Morgan, "Antifascist Historians and History in 'Justice and Liberty.'" For Montanelli's project of the *costituente*, see Montanelli, *Memorie sull'Italia*, vol. 2, 403. On the legal framework of the costituente and differences betwen Mazzini and Montanelli, see Morelli, "L'idea di costituente."

162. Bagnoli, *Democrazia e stato*, 23f. On his encounter with Protestantism, see also Montanelli, *Memorie*, vol. 1, 87ff.

163. Ibid., vol. 2, 26. For two rather unspecific references to Washington, see ibid., vol. 2, 408f., 422.

164. Coppini, "Giuseppe Montanelli," 21.

165. Montanelli, *Introduzione*, 8f. On his literary contacts in Paris, see Russi, "Montanelli e Pisacane," 69.

166. Bagnoli, *Democrazia e stato*, 64f. On his understanding of the American model, see also Rota Ghibaudi, "La Politica secondo Giuseppe Montanelli," 94ff. In addition to chapter 7 of Montanelli, *Introduzione*, Tocqueville is mentioned in Giuseppe Montanelli, *Dello ordinamento nazionale* (Florence: Tip. Garibaldi, 1862). See also Bagnoli, *Democrazia e stato*, 213–99, in particular 231, 235f., 249f.; also his discussion of the American municipality seems directly informed by Tocqueville. Ibid., 280f. As for Montanelli's reading of Guizot, see Montanelli, *Introduzione*, 5, 67, 92ff.

167. Montanelli, *Introduzione*, 23–25.

168. Ibid., 35. Montanelli, *Memorie*, vol. 2, 99ff. On Italy's lack of civil society, see also ibid., vol. 1, xvi. On the problem of papal power, see also Montanelli, *L'impero, il papato e la democrazia in Italia*, 31ff.

169. Montanelli, *Introduzione*, 6. See also Bagnoli, *Democrazia e stato*, 83ff.

170. Montanelli, *Introduzione*, 69. On the antiquity of this concept and the Etrusco-American analogy, see Montanelli, *Memorie*, vol. 1, 2, and vol. 2, 207; and Montanelli, *L'impero*, 13f. On Cattaneo's view of the Etruscan origins of municipal federations, see Sabetti, *Civilization and Self-Government*, 95. Thom, "City, Region and Nation," 199.

171. Montanelli, *Introduzione*, 64, 145.

172. Ibid., 95. On the contrast between French administration and Italian civic tradition, also see Montanelli, *Memorie*, vol. 1, 4f. and vol. 2, 207.

173. Montanelli's contacts with Minghetti go back to the years before the Revolution: Rotondi, "Giuseppe Montanelli e 'l'Italia,'" 206, 229ff. Bagnoli, *Democrazia e Stato*, 224, 275.

174. This was partly an issue of international security: See, for instance, an article in Montanelli's newspaper *L'Italia* of August 1848, quoted in Rotondi, "Giuseppe Montanelli e 'L'Italia,'" 225.

175. Montanelli, *Memorie*, vol. 2, 26. Montanelli, *L'impero*, 60.

176. Spadolini, *Un dissidente del Risorgimento*, 33, 39f.

177. Romeo, *Il Risorgimento in Sicilia*, 273.

178. Gaetano Somma, *La Sicilia e il resto d'Italia* (Palermo, 1848), 4f.

179. For a detailed bibliographical overview on Sicily in 1848, see Bottari, "Fuori e dentro la storia: Percorsi storiografici sulla Sicilia moderna prima e dopo Romeo." Still a useful account is Salvatore Francesco Romano, "Il 48," *Momenti del Risorgimento in Sicilia* (Messina/Florence: G. D'Anna, 1952), 71–107. On the constitutional debates in Naples, see Feola, "Costituzione e Parlamento a Napoli in 1848."

180. Galasso, *Il regno di Napoli*, 644.

181. This emphasis is clearly visible from the convocation of the Sicilian parliament in February: "Convocazione del Generale Parlamento di Sicilia," 24/2/1848, *Le Assemblee del Risorgimento*, vol. 12, 22ff.

182. Petrusewicz, *Come il Meridione divenne una questione*, 9. For a multidisciplinary approach to the issue, see Schneider, ed., *Italy's "Southern Question."*

183. Davis, *Naples and Napoleon*, 161ff. On the wider context of Napoleonic legacies in the peninsula, see Meriggi, "State and Society in Post-Napoleonic Italy."

184. See the observations in Filippo Minolfi, *Intorno ai giornali e alla odierna culura siciliana* (Palermo: Meli, 1837).

185. Palazzolo, *Intelletuali e giornalismo nella Sicilia preunitaria*, 21.

186. Galasso, *Il regno di Napoli*, 14f., 43f. Riall, *Sicily and the Unification of Italy*, 35.

187. For the consequences of the decline of wheat exports, see Schneider and Schneider, *Culture and Political Economy in Western Sicily*, 113ff. For a detailed study of commercial development on the mainland, see Storchi, "Grani, prezzi e mercati nel Regno di Napoli (1806–1852)."

188. Petrusewicz, *Come il Meridione divenne una questione*, 9.

189. Schneider and Schneider, *Culture and Political Economy in Western Sicily*, 6. For a more cautious evaluation of European connections, see Romeo, *Il Risorgimento in Sicilia*, 33ff.

190. Berti, "Socialismo utopistico in Sicilia prima del'48."

191. Baker, *The Fortunate Pilgrims*, 73f. On the implications of Sicily's island status, see Giarrizzo, *Mezzogiorno senza meridionalismo*, 37.

192. Falzone, *Il problema della Sicilia nel 1848 attraverso nuove fonti inedite*, 1f.

193. Antonio Arioti, *Cenno storico delle gloriose 25 giornate della rivoluzione di Palermo del 1848* ([Palermo, 1848]), 35 (BL: Italian Tracts 1440 C15).

194. See, for instance, "Conferma del fatto. . . ." (Genoa: Ferrando, 1848); "Indirizzo di Antonio Gaglia Ferro" (Genoa: Ferrando, 1848) (BL: Miscellanee politiche genovesi. 804.k.13.32 and 34).

195. Richard Cobden, Naples, 6/3/1847 and 12/3/1847, in *The European Diaries of Richard Cobden*, 109f. On the Neapolitan diplomatic response to demands for independence, see Moscati, *Ferdinando II di Borbone nei documenti diplomatici austriaci*, 87.

196. Rosselli, "Italia e Inghilterra nel Risorgimento," in *Saggi sul Risorgimento*, 3–68, 18. For a more recent account of British interests in Sicily, see Spagnoletti, *Storia del Regno delle Due Sicilie*, 265ff., and from a different perspective, see Riall, *Under the Volcano*.

197. Falzone, *La Sicilia nella politica mediterranea delle grandi potenze*, 87f. For the British perspective, see also Scherer, *Lord John Russell*, 196f. Fiume, *La crisi sociale del 1848 in Sicilia*, 69. David Laven has argued that Vienna's main concern was not revolution but French influence in the region: "Austria's Italian Policy Reconsidered: Revolution and Reform in Restoration Italy."

198. Valsecchi, "L'inghilterra e il problema italiano nella politica europea del 1848," 19f. For the debates in the liberal press, see Fiume, *La Crisi sociale del 1848 in Sicilia*, 41ff.

199. Guccione, "Il costituzionalismo in Sicilia nel 1848," 180.

200. [Luigi Settembrini], *Protesta del popolo delle Due Sicilie* ([Naples, 1847?]), 13 (BL: 1250.a.37).

201. Pagano, "Sicilia e Stati Uniti di America nel Risorgimento."

202. Sicily, Camera dei Pari, Seduta 14/7/1848, *Le Assemblee del Risorgimento*, vol. 15, 7. Marraro, "Il Risorgimento in Sicilia," 447f. (wherein Marraro delivers almost a caricature of Bourbon rule). See also Pagano, "Sicilia e Stati Uniti di America nel Risorgimento," 489f.

203. Guccione, "Il costituzionalismo in Sicilia nel 1848," 180f., 186. Writing after the Revolution from his exile in London, the autonomist Calvi strongly criticized the policies followed by the Sicilian Moderates during the Revolution.

204. [Michele Amari], "Catechismo politico siciliano" (1839, 1848), in Ganci, *Storia antologica*, vol. 1, 177–83, 180. Palmieri had been a victim of the cholera outbreak of 1837, for which the 1848ers blamed the invasion of Bourbon troops: [Un Siracusano], *La scoverta del cholera in Siracusa ossia il racconto fedele degli originali fatti ivi avvenuti nel luglio 1837* (Palermo, 1848). For the symbolic power of the cholera epidemic in 1848, see also [Un cittadino palermitano], *Palermo e l'esercito regio o i 24 giorni di gueraa dal 12 gennaio al 4 febbraio 1848: Relazione storica* ([Palermo?, 1848]), 32 (BL: Italian tracts 1848, 1440 G23).

205. Guccione, "Il costituzionalismo in Sicilia nel 1848," 188f.

206. For the Moderates' program, see Ventura, *La questione Sicula nel 1848 sciolta nel vero interesse della Sicilia, di Napoli e dell'Italia*. See also Ganci, *Storia antologica*, vol. 1, 201–21.

207. Cingari, *Mezzogiorno e Risorgimento*, 75ff. Moscati, *Ferdinando II di Borbone*, 74ff. and 83–87f.

208. Moscati, *Ferdinando II di Borbone*, 124.

209. Valsecchi, "L'Inghilterra e il problema italiano nella politica europea del 1848," 20. For a detailed analysis of the Sicilian constitution of 1812, see Renda, *La Sicilia nel 1812.* Sciacca, *Riflessi del costituzionalismo europeo in Sicilia.*

210. Romeo, *Il Risorgimento in Sicilia,* 286f.

211. Pisacane, *Guerra combattuta in Italia negli anni 1848–49,* 254.

212. Quoted in Romeo, *Il Risorgimento in Sicilia,* 289.

213. Gioberti, *Del rinnovamento,* vol. 1, 279f.

214. Romeo, *Il Risorgimento in Sicilia,* 303. See also Ganci, *Storia antologica,* vol. 1, 171ff. As a consequence of his contacts with Mazzini, Amari moved away from his former federalist positions, to adhere in 1859 to the unitary policies of Cavour and the Moderates.

215. Candeloro, *Storia dell'Italia moderna,* vol. 3, 231. However, in the debate of the Sicilian parliament of 13/4/1848 La Farina pronounced himself against Leopoldo: Ganci, *Storia antologica,* vol. 1, 297. For the enthusiasm surrounding the Duke of Genoa, see "L'Elezione di Ferdinando di Savoja Duca di Genova a Re della Sicilia" (Genoa: Carniglia, [1848]) (BL: Miscellanee politiche genovesi. 804.k.13.35).

216. Spagnoletti, *Storia delle Due Sicilie,* 294ff.

217. This argument follows Romeo's analysis of the Revolution's failure. For a critical evaluation in light of later research, see Riall, "Rosario Romeo and the Risorgimento in Sicily, 1848–1860," 209ff.

218. Recupero, "La Sicilia all'opposizione."

219. Sicily, Camera dei Comuni, Seduta inaugurale, 25/3/1848, Discorso del presidente del Comitato Generale, *Le assemblee del Risorgimento,* vol. 12, 37–43, 38f. See also Camillo Montalcino's introduction, ibid., ix.

220. Sicily, Camera dei Pari, 8/6/1848, sacerdote Filippo Evola, *Le assemblee del Risorgimento,* vol. 14, 611.

221. For a critical discussion of the constitution, see Rosselli, *Lord William Bentinck,* 76–81.

222. Finley, Mack Smith, and Duggan, *A History of Sicily,* 149

223. Riall, *Sicily and the Unification of Italy,* 47f.

224. Sicily, Camera dei Comuni, Seduta 30/3/1848, *Le assemblee del Risorgimento,* vol. 12, 73. On the adaptation of the 1812 constitution, see also the debate of 8/6/1848, ibid., 805ff.

225. Paolo Balsano, *Sulla istoria moderna del Regno di Sicilia: Memorie segrete* (Palermo, [1848]).

226. See, for instance, *Costituzione di Sicilia stabilita nel generale parlamento del 1812* (Palermo: Gaudiano, 1848).

227. Ventura, *La questione Sicula nel 1848,* 5f.

228. Isabella, *Risorgimento in Exile,* 5.

229. For instance, when an American fleet requested access to the port in Syracuse: Sicily, Camera dei Pari, Seduta 30/5/1848, *Le Assemblee del Risorgimento,* vol. 14, 563.

230. Sicily, Camera dei Comuni, Seduta 29/4/1848, *Le assemblee del Risorgimento,* vol. 12, 328. He formed part of the commission to reform the constitution of 1812, and in February 1849 he joined the Sicilian government. Luther, ed., *Documenti costituzionali di Italia e Malta, 1787–1850,* parte 2, 310.

231. Sicily, Camera dei Comuni, 30/10/1848: Programma per la Istruzione Secondaria, *Le assemblee del Risorgimento,* vol. 13, 630f.

232. The formation of National Guards was a major issue for all Italian states, including moderate supporters of the revolutions, but there were enough reference points to discuss the matter without recurring to foreign examples. See, for instance, Pietro Sterbini, *Ultimi avvenimenti di Roma* ([Rome, 1848]), 13 (BL: Italian Tracts 1440 C15). [Un cittadino palermitano], *Palermo e l'esercito regio,* 41.

233. Sicily, Camera dei Comuni, 17/6/1848, Francesco Paolo Perez, *Le assemblee del Risorgimento*, vol. 12, 938.

234. Sicily, Camera dei Comuni, Seduta 4/5/1848, *Le assemblee del Risorgimento*, vol. 12, 397.

235. Sicily, Camera dei Comuni, Seduta 29/5/1848, Stefano Napolitano, *Le assemblee del Risorgimento*, vol. 12, 724. He replied to the previous speaker, who had mentioned the English rule of habeas corpus.

236. Sicily, Camera dei Comuni, 17/6/48, Michele Bertolami, *Le assemblee del Risorgimento*, vol. 12, 945. He makes a very similar argument in a letter to Mazzini: Bertolami to Mazzini, 15/3/1848, in Ganci, *Storia antologica*, vol. 1, 243-47, 245.

237. Sicily, Camera dei Comuni, 24/6/48, Giuseppe Natoli, *Le assemblee del Risorgimento*, vol. 12, 1006.

238. Sicily, Camera dei Comuni, 3/7/48, Giuseppe Natoli, *Le assemblee del Risorgimento*, vol. 12, 1073. See the similar case of Vito D'Ondes Reggio: Sicily, Camera dei Comuni, 21/6/48, *Le assemblee del Risorgimento*, vol. 12, 983.

239. Sicily, Camera dei Comuni, 4/7/1848, Filippo Cordova, *Le assemblee del Risorgimento*, vol. 12, 1099f.

240. Sicily, Camera dei Pari, Seduta 21/6/1848, Marchese Vincenzo Mortillaro, *Le assemblee del Risorgimento*, vol. 14, 725.

241. See, for instance, Istituto Mazziniano, Genoa: 00457 La presente Camera (indirizzo ai deputati del popolo Ligure-Piemontese-Sardo), Genoa: Tip. Moretti, 1848.

242. Pagano, "Sicilia e Stati Uniti di America nel Risorgimento," 484. Lanza, Principe di Scordia, di Trabia e di Butera, belonged to Sicily's old nobility. He made the statement in the periodical *La Ruota*.

243. Sicily, Camera dei Comuni, 17/6/1848, Francesco Ventura, *Le assemblee del Risorgimento*, vol. 12, 930; see also ibid., Benedetto Venturelli e Baldanza, 940. For Ventura's position, see also his pamphlet "De' diritti delle Sicilia alla sua nazionale indipendenza," in Ganci, *Storia antologica*, vol. 1, 192–99.

244. Sicily, Camera dei Comuni, 12/6/1848, Giuseppe Natoli, *Le assemblee del Risorgimento*, vol. 12, 869.

245. Sicily, Camera dei Comuni, 16/6/1848, Giuseppe Natoli, *Le assemblee del Risorgimento*, vol. 12, 909.

246. Sicily, Camera dei Comuni, 16/6/1848, Giovanni Interdonato, *Le assemblee del Risorgimento*, vol. 12, 924.

247. Sicily, Camera dei Comuni, 16/6/1848, Gaetano La Rosa, *Le assemblee del Risorgimento*, vol. 12, 913.

248. Sicily, Camera dei Comuni, 1/4/1848, Francesco Ferrara; and 6/4/1848, *Le assemblee del Risorgimento*, vol. 12, 87, 118. On Ferrara's political ideas in 1848, see Lazzarino Del Grosso, "Gli Stati Uniti d'America nell'opera di Francesco Ferrara," *Francesco Ferrara e il suo tempo*, 558–61.

249. Sicily, Camera dei Comuni, 10/6/1848, *Le assemblee del Risorgimento*, vol. 12, 838-48.

250. Lazzarino Del Grosso, "Gli Stati Uniti d'America nell'opera di Francesco Ferrara," 563. Sicily, Camera dei Comuni, 8/6/1848, Vito D'Ondes Reggio, *Le assemblee del Risorgimento*, vol. 12, 817.

251. Sicily, Camera dei Comuni, 9/6/1848, Ignazio Romeo, *Le assemblee del Risorgimento*, vol. 12, 821.

252. Sicily, Camera dei Comuni, 8/6/1848, Vito D'Ondes Reggio, *Le assemblee del Risorgimento*, vol. 12, 818.

253. Sicily, Camera dei Comuni, 12/6/1848, Filippo Cordova, *Le assemblee del Risorgimento*, vol. 12, 867.

254. Giuseppe Ferrari, *Filosofia della Rivoluzione.* London, 1851, vol. 2, 347.

255. Sicily, Camera dei Comuni, 12/6/1848, Giuseppe Natoli, *Le assemblee del Risorgimento,* vol. 12, 869.

256. Romano, "Il 48," 76.

257. Giuseppe La Farina, *Storia della rivoluzione siciliana e delle sue relazioni coi governi italiani e stranieri 1848-49* (Milan: Brigola, 1860), 131.

258. "Rapporto della commissione sul lavoro preparatorio per la convocazione del parlamento," in Ganci, *Storia antologica,* vol. 1, 266–75, 270. On America as a model of a bicameral system, also, see *Programma: Una proposizione qualunque da svilupparsi, etc.* ([Palermo, 1848?]) (BL: Political Tracts, 8007 cc 33).

259. Sicily, Camera dei Pari, 8/6/1848, Roccaforte, *Le assemblee del Risorgimento,* vol. 14, 605.

260. Sicily, Camera dei Pari, 8/6/1848, Francesco Marletta, *Le assemblee del Risorgimento,* vol. 114, 604.

261. Sicily, Camera dei Pari, 10/6/1848, Marchese Vincnezo Mortillaro, *Le assemblee del Risorgimento,* vol. 14, 640.

262. Sicily, Camera dei Comuni, 19/6/48, Vito D'Ondes Reggio, *Le assemblee del Risorgimento,* vol. 12, 954.

263. Sicily, Camera dei Comuni, 8/5/48, Giuseppe Natoli, *Le assemblee del Risorgimento,* vol. 12, 450.

264. Sicily, Camera dei Comuni, 5/5/1848, Filippo Cordova, *Le assemblee del Risorgimento,* vol. 12, 414.

265. Sicily, Camera dei Comuni, 9/6/1848, Vito D'Ondes Reggio, *Le assemblee del Risorgimento,* vol. 12, 835.

266. Sicily, Camera dei Comuni, 5/5/1848, Francesco Paolo Perez, *Le assemblee del Risorgimento,* vol. 12, 411f.

267. Sicily, Camera dei Comuni, 5/5/1848, Filippo Cordova, *Le assemblee del Risorgimento,* vol. 12, 414.

268. Sicily, Camera dei Pari, Seduta 30/5/1848, Vincenzo Calafato Barone di Canalotti, *Le assemblee del Risorgimento,* vol. 14, 565.

269. Sicily, Camera dei Comuni, 9/6/1848, *Le assemblee del Risorgimento,* vol. 12, 833.

270. Sicily, Camera dei Pari, 21/8/1848, *Le assemblee del Risorgimento,* vol. 15, 209ff. The United States is mentioned only briefly.

271. Sicily, Camera dei Pari, 18/10/1848 and 19/12/1848, *Le assemblee del Risorgimento,* vol. 15, 435, 619.

272. For the focus of the debates on events elsewhere in Europe, see in particular 28/10/1848 and 18/12/1848: Sicily, Camera dei Comuni, *Le assemblee del Risorgimento,* vol. 13, 606f., 836f.

273. Sicily, Camera dei Pari, 26/2/1849, Giuseppe Poulet, ministro della guerra, *Le assemblee del Risorgimento,* vol. 15, 871.

274. Arioti, *Cenno storico.*

275. [Un cittadino palermitano], *Palermo e l'esercito regio,* 49.

276. Sicily, Camera dei Comuni, 17/2/1849, Michele Bertolami, *Le assemblee del Risorgimento,* vol. 14, 79f. Meanwhile, Sicilians had a strong aversion to patronizing foreign attempts explaining their failures. See, for instance, the reaction to the popular romantic writer Charles-Victor Prévost d'Arlincourt, who in 1850 published his account of the Risorgimento, *L'Italie rouge*: Vito D'Ondes Reggio, *Contro il sig. Visconte D'Arlincourt* (Turin: Voix de l'Italie, 1850). The author had been a member of Sicily's government.

277. Quoted in Bagnoli, *L'Idea dell'Italia,* 267.

278. Bagnoli, *L'Idea dell'Italia,* 269. Bobbio, "G. B. Tuveri nel primo centenario della morte," 35. Contu, *G. B. Tuveri: Vita e Opere,* 32.

279. Bagnoli, *L'Idea dell'Italia*, 270.

280. Giovanni Battista Tuveri, *Sofismi politici* (Naples: Rinaldi e Sellitto, 1883), 68. This is the last book published by Tuveri, containing very few references to the United States.

281. Bagnoli, *La politica delle idee*, 67ff. Bruch, *Italien*, 85f. On Ferrari and Mazzini, see also Livorsi, "Libertà e stato nel 1848–49 europeo: Note e riflessioni," 40ff.

282. Giuseppe Ferrari, "La Rivoluzione e le riforme in Italia" (January 1848), *Scritti politici*, 3–55, 10f.

283. Ibid., 14. On Ferrari's concept of federal democracy in particular, see Bruch, *Italien*, 106ff.

284. Lovett, *Giuseppe Ferrari and the Italian Revolution*, 37. Rota Ghibaudi, *Giuseppe Ferrari*, 148f.

285. Quoted in Lovett, *Giuseppe Ferrari*, 171.

286. Angelo Mazzoleni, *Giuseppe Ferrari: I suoi tempi e le sue opere* (Milan: TEI, 1877), 18. Sabetti, "Cattaneo e il modello americano," 356f. Lovett, *Giuseppe Ferrari*, 84. On the relationship with Cattaneo also della Peruta, *Carlo Cattaneo Politico*, 101ff. Galasso, "Cattaneo interprete della storia d'Italia."

287. della Peruta, *Carlo Cattaneo*, 101–4.

288. Lovett, *Giuseppe Ferrari*, 55. Bruch, *Italien*, 111ff.

289. Giuseppe Mazzini, "To Our Friends in the United States" (1865), *A Cosmopolitanism of Nations*, 222–23.

290. On the relation between the two works, see Rota Ghibaudi, *Giuseppe Ferrari*, 213ff.

291. Lovett, *Giuseppe Ferrari*, 187.

292. Ridolfi, "Visions of Republicanism in the Writings of Giuseppe Mazzini," 473.

293. Ibid., 474. See also Mauro Macchi, *Le armi e le idee* (Turin: Tip. Subalpina, 1855).

294. Sabetti, *Civilization and Self-Government*, 156. On Ferrara's ideas of both free government and laissez-faire economy, see also Romani, "Reluctant Revolutionaries: Moderate Liberalism in the Kingdom of Sardinia, 1849–1859," 51ff.

295. On the role of American political institutions in his political thought, see Lazzarino Del Grosso, "Gli Stati Uniti d'America nell'opera di Francesco Ferrara."

296. Agostino Bertani, "Contro le leggi eccezionali per la Sicilia" (1863), *Scritti e discorsi di Agostino Bertani*, 34–45, 37.

Chapter Four. Unveiling Modernity: Verdi's America and the Unification of Italy

1. References to the opera are based on Giuseppe Verdi, *Un ballo in maschera*. Melodramma in tre atti, libretto di Antonio Somma, partitura (nuova edizione riveduta e corretta) (Milan: Ricordi, 1966).

2. Grempler, "Hauptstadt des italienischen Königreichs: Die römische Theaterlandschaft vor dem Hintergrund der politischen und urbanen Veränderungen im 19. Jahrhundert," 168.

3. The manuscript version of the libretto refers to the eighteenth century. Rosen, "La disposizione scenica per il Un ballo in maschera di Verdi: Studio critico," 46.

4. For instance, in a letter to his friend Clarina Maffei of 23 June 1859, Verdi promises to adore Napoleon III "as I have adored *Vasington*" for the role the emperor played in the liberation of Italy. Quoted in: Walker, "Verdi, Giuseppe Montanelli and the Libretto of *Simon Boccanegra*," 1388f. During the rehearsals for the production of *Un ballo* in Bologna, in October 1860, Verdi repeatedly pressed the conductor Angelo Mariani for news on the war in Romagna: Giuseppe Verdi a Angelo Mariani, 1/10/1860, in Verdi, *Le*

lettere genovesi, 78. On the atmosphere during the war, see Marwil, *Visiting Modern War in Risorgimento Italy*.

5. For a specific case study, see Körner, "The Theatre of Social Change: Opera and Society in Bologna after Italian Unification."

6. See, for instance, *Un ballo in maschera: Pezzi per canto, con accompto di pianoforte* (Paris: Léon Escudier, [1859]). *Favourite Airs from Verdi's Opera Un ballo in maschera Arranged for the Piano as a Duet with Ad Lib: Accompt; For flute* (London: William H. Hallcott, [1859]). Joseph Ascher, *Nocturne cantible sur Un ballo in maschera* (London: Ascher, [1859]). Joseph Rummel, *Fantasia on Airs in Verdi's Opera Un ballo in maschera* (London: Rummel, [1859]). For brass arrangements, see Leydi, "Diffusione e volgarizzazione," 344.

7. John Brown, *The Northern Courts of the Sovereigns of Sweden and Denmark since 1766, Including the Extraordinary Vicissitudes in the Lives of the Grand-Children of George the Second*, vol. 2 (London: Archibald Constable, 1818). On Scribe's construction of the libretto, see Schneider, "Scribe and Auber: Constructing Grand Opéra," 181.

8. *Gustave ou Le bal masqué*. Paroles de M. Scribe. Musique de D.F.E. Auber. Opéra historique en cinq Actes, presenté pour la première fois sur le Theâtre de l'Academie Royale de Musique le 27 Février 1833 (Paris: Troupenas, 1833). [Saverio Mercadante], *Il reggente: Tragedia lirica in tre atti da rappresentarsi nel Teatro Nuovo di padova per la fiera del Santo 1843* (Padova: Penada [1843]). The original edition of the libretto lists the cast but does not mention author or composer. For the relationship between historical events and operatic plot in Auber's version, see Hibberd, "Auber's Gustave III: History as Opera." See also Hibberd, *French Grand Opera and the Historical Imagination* (Cambridge: Cambridge University Press, 2009), 57ff. For a comparison of the libretto's different adaptations see D'Amico, "Il ballo in maschera prima di Verdi." More recently, see also Sala, "Un ballo in maschera e il carnevale," 246.

9. Lippmann, *Vincenzo Bellini und die italienische Opera Seria seiner Zeit*, 38.

10. Budden, *The Operas of Verdi*, vol. 2, 372. See also Filippo Filippi in *Gazzetta musicale di Milano (GMM)*, 12/1/1862, supplement.

11. Romeo, *Vita di Cavour*, 371f. In December 1863 three Italians had been charged with the attempted assassination of Napoleon III, covered in detail by the Italian press. See, for instance, *Monitore di Bologna (MdB)*, 28/2/1864. Minghetti, *Miei ricordi*, vol. 3, 210. Calore, *Bologna a teatro*, 81f.

12. Rossi, *The Image of America*, 96.

13. Bacchin, "Felice Orsini and the Construction of the Pro-Italian Narrative in Britain," 102.

14. I am grateful to Anselm Gerhard and Alessandra A. Jones for encouraging me to emphasize this context.

15. Pospíšil, "Österreichische Opernzensur in Prag: *Gustave III und La Juive*," 123.

16. For a short recent overview of the state of debate on the role of the censors, see Jacobshagen, "Un ballo in maschera."

17. For an overview of Verdi's growing media perception, see Capra, *Verdi in prima pagina*, 2014.

18. *GMM*, 10/4/1859.

19. Toelle, "Zielpunkt: Austro-Italiens moralische Hegemonie," 185ff. Vella, "Verdi and Politics (c. 1859–61)." Numerous publications prepared public opinion in Europe for the upcoming war. See, for instance, *Der Kriegsschauplatz in Italien in drei Karten, nebst einer Uebersicht der Lage und Größe jedes Staates, der Staatsverfassung (etc.)*. Pest/Wien: Hartleben,1859. For similar references, see Marwil, *Visiting Modern War*.

20. For this debate, see the articles in *Opera and Nation in Nineteenth-Century Italy*, special issue of *Journal of Modern Italian Studies* (Axel Körner, ed.), 17, 4 (September

2012). Parker, *"Arpa d'or dei fatidici vati."* Smart, "Liberty On (and Off) the Barricades: Verdi's Risorgimento Fantasies." See also Davis, "Opera and Absolutism in Restoration Italy, 1815–1860," 570ff., 577. For the traditional view of Verdi as the bard of the Risorgimento, see Martin, "Verdi and the Risorgimento." The subtitle of one of the songs discussed in chapter 3 made a reference to the historical character of Nabucco, but without any apparent hint at Verdi's opera: L. Zattera, "La lega de' tre principi: Contro l'editto di Nabucco" ([Genoa]: Vaniola [1848]) (BL: Miscellanee politiche genovesi. 804.k.13.11).

21. See the editor's introduction to *Re Lear e Ballo in maschera: Lettere di Giuseppe Verdi ad Antonio Somma* (Alessandro Pascolato, ed.; Città di Castello: Lapi, 1913), 7. Pascolato, "Della vita e degli scritti di Antonio Somma." Somma died at age fifty-four, two years before the Veneto was liberated in consequence of the Austro-Prussian War. For a short biography, see Narici, "Somma, Antonio," 410.

22. This is evident even in the earliest correspondence about the project. See Somma to Verdi, 13/10/1857, in *Carteggio Verdi-Somma*, 183. Interesting in this context, commentators do not seem to explore the opera's plot as a narrative about the American people's resentment against (foreign) British rule. Contrasting with works such as *Les vêpres siciliennes* or *Don Carlos*, *Un ballo* is not a revolutionary opera denouncing foreign oppression.

23. *L'Armonia*, 26/2/1859.

24. Buccini, *The Americas in Italian Literature and Culture*, 51.

25. Raimondo Fidanza, *Colombo, ossia La scoperta del Nuovo Mondo* (Genoa, 1802). Cohen, "Feme di Gelosia! Italian Ballet Librettos, 1766–1865," 558. *Colombo all'isola di Cuba*, azione mimica di mezzo carattere in quattro parti di Antonio Monticini, represented at La Scala in Milan during the autumn 1832 and again at the Regio in Turin in 1838: New York Public Library (NYPL), Walter Toscanini Collection (WTC), Libretti da Ballo (LdB), 332 and 431.

26. Within this genre Carl Heinrich Graun's opera *Montezuma* (1755), based on a libretto by the king of Prussia Friedrich II, is of particular interest. While Friedrich abstains from presenting Native Americans as "noble savages," he condemns the (ignoble) barbarity of the Spaniards and of Christian religion. Polzonetti, *Italian Opera in the Age of the American Revolution*, 107–32.

27. Ibid., 10f.

28. Ibid., 20. Different versions of the title exist: *Gli napolitani, li napolitani,* etc.

29. Ibid., chpt. 8.

30. del Negro, *Il mito americano*, 469f., 483. On the wider debate on eighteenth-century female Quakers and agency, see Mack, "Religion, Feminism, and the Problem of Agency: Reflections on Eighteenth-Century Quakerism."

31. Pecchio, *Osservazioni semi-serie*, 317.

32. Fohlen, *Benjamin Franklin*, 126ff.

33. See Beghelli, ed., *L'equivoco stravagante*. In this context, see also the changing role of the soprano: Jacobshagen, *Gioachino Rossini und seine Zeit*, 183f.

34. Maione and Seller, "Cristoforo Colombo o sia la scoperta dell'America di Donizetti." For operas on the discovery of the New World, see Heck, "Toward a Bibliography of Operas on Columbus." Maione and Seller, "The Operatic Christopher Columbus: Three Hundred Years of Musical Mythology." For a general overview, see Maehder, "The Representation of the Discovery on the Opera Stage."

35. NYPL, WTC, LdB, n. 819. Along with *Colombo* and his celebrated ballet *Brahma*, Ippolito Monplaisir created *L'Isola degli Amori*, a *ballo fantastico* about Vasco da Gama, performed in 1861 at La Scala in Milan as well as the Teatro Apollo in Rome: NYPL, WTC, LdB, n. 785 and 793.

36. Franchetti's *Cristoforo Colombo* was premiered under Mancinelli in 1892, followed by presentations in Treviso and at Bologna's Comunale under Toscanini. For recent

bibliography on Franchetti, see Giorgi and Erkens, eds., *Alberto Franchetti: L'uomo, il compositore, l'artista.* The interest in Columbus was also expressed in contemporary pictorial representations: see, for instance, Palagio Palagi's Columbus scenes in Poppi, ed., *L'ombra di core: Disegni dal fondo Palagi della Biblioteca dell'Archiginasio,* 37ff.; probably more influential was the monument by Vincenzo Vela "Colombo e l'America" for the Paris World Exhibition of 1867, presenting Columbus generously protecting a female Native American nude; see illustration in *L'Universo illustrato,* 2, 8 (November 1867), 129f.

37. For Verdi's fortunes in Vienna, see Kreuzer, *Verdi and the Germans,* 54.

38. *GMM,* 6/3/1859. The conductor was Emilio Angelini. For the following overview of performances, see Kaufman, *Verdi and His Major Contemporaries,* 466ff.

39. *Teatri, arte, letteratura,* 10/3/1859.

40. *GMM,* 25/2/1859 and 27/2/1859.

41. *Les artistes contemporaines: Adelina Patti, Fraschini, Par Léo* (Paris: Montidier, 1865), 18, 25. Fraschini had also been the first Zamoro in Verdi's *Alzira* (1845): *Carteggio Verdi-Ricordi, 1882–1885,* 114.

42. Cited in Conati, *Interviews and Encounters with Verdi,* 51.

43. Poriss, "Julienne Dejean, Eugenia," 228.

44. *GMM,* 13/3/1859.

45. Arturo Pougin, *Giuseppe Verdi: Vita anneddotica* (Milan: Ricordi, 1881), 84.

46. *GMM,* 7/10/60.

47. Both performances were criticized by the periodical press. See in particular *GMM,* 12/1/1862; *La Fama,* 11/3/1862. *La Fama* also criticized the work itself, which it regarded as "inferior to the Verdi of *Boccanegra* and *Vespri.*" See also the *appendice* in *La Fama,* 14/1/1862. In 1866 Franco Faccio's career as conductor was launched with a performance of *Un ballo* in Venice: *Carteggio Verdi-Ricordi, 1880–1881,* 5. The following year Faccio conducted *Un ballo,* together with other works by Verdi, in Berlin: *Verdi's Otello and Simon Boccanegra in Letters and Documents,* vol. 2, 828.

48. The performance of *Un ballo* in Palermo in 1874 marked the beginning of the legendary career of tenor Francesco Tamagno in the role of Riccardo. See *Verdi's Otello and Simon Boccanegra in Letters and Documents,* vol. 2, 858.

49. Giuseppe Verdi, *Le lettere genovesi,* 40.

50. On the globalization of Italian opera, see Toelle, "Der Duft der großen weiten Welt: Ideen zum weltweiten Siegeszug der italienischen Oper im 19. Jahrhundert." Walton, "Italian Operatic Fantasies in Latin America." Cetrangolo, *Ópera, barcos y banderas.*

51. Most musical periodicals were full of praise for Verdi's new opera and for the productions in Florence and Bologna in particular: *L'Arpa,* 5/10/1860. Less enthusiastic was the correspondent from Bologna for the periodical *Il Trovatore,* 10/10/1860. See also Budden, *The Operas of Verdi,* vol. 2, 374.

52. Appendice, *La Fama,* 14/1/1862. On the impact of grand opera on Verdi, see Gerhard, *The Urbanization of Opera,* 11f.

53. *MdB,* 5/10/1860.

54. For Bottrigari's comments on Verdi, see Enrico Bottrigari, *Cronaca di Bologna 1845–1871* (Aldo Berselli, ed.; Bologna: Zanichelli, 1960–63), vol. 3, 116.

55. Martin, *Verdi in America,* 52f., 347ff.

56. See, for instance, the reports on Naples's first performance of *Un ballo* in 1862: *GMM,* 19/1/1862.

57. Abramo Basevi, *Studio sulle opere di Giuseppe Verdi* (Florence: Tofani, 1859). On Basevi, see Parker, "'Insolite forme,' or Basevi's Garden Path." For other works on music criticism, see also Della Seta, "Gli esordi della critica Verdiana: A proposito di Alberto Mazzucato."

58. For further discussion of this methodological issue, see Körner, "The Risorgimento's Literary Canon and the Aesthetics of Reception."

59. Rosen, "La disposizione scenica," 21ff. On the role of Verdi's production books, see Parker, "Reading the *Livrets*, or The Chimera of 'Authentic' Staging," in *Leonora's Last Act: Essays in Verdian Discourse*, 126–48. On the origins of Verdi's *disposizioni*, Viale Ferrero, "Luogo teatrale e spazio scenico," 98ff. See also *Verdi's Otello and Simon Boccanegra in Letters and Documents* (Busch, ed.), vol. 2, 423.

60. The Verdis' copies of Botta's *History of the American War of Independence* included the Amari edition of 1856, discussed in detail in chapter 1, as well as an earlier Italian edition of 1844. They also owned copies of Botta's Italian histories. Their specialized interest in Botta is also confirmed by a rare 1797 edition of his *Proposizione ai Lombardi*. I am grateful to Anselm Gerhard for access to this information.

61. Roccatagliati, "The Italian Theatre of Verdi's Day," 18.

62. della Seta, "New Currents in the Libretto," 69.

63. della Seta, *Italia e Francia nell'ottocento*, 216.

64. For a detailed analysis of the debate, see Elizabeth Hudson, "Masking Music: A Reconsideration of Light and Shade in Un ballo in maschera." Verdi's contemporaries noticed the use of contrasts in the opera: GMM, 6/3/1859 and 12/1/1862, supplement. Basevi commented on Verdi's use of chiaroscuro even before he knew *Un ballo*; see Basevi, *Studio sulle opere di Giuseppe Verdi*, 9, 12.

65. Budden, *The Operas of Verdi*, vol. 2, 376.

66. See in particular Hudson, "Masking Music," 262. Writing before *Un ballo* came out, Basevi noted in 1859 how audiences remarked on such contrasts in Verdi's work: Basevi, *Studio sulle opere di Giuseppe Verdi*, 12f.

67. On this aspect of Riccardo's character, see Senici, "'Teco io sto': Strategies of Seduction in Act II of 'Un ballo in maschera.'"

68. Hexter, "Masked Balls." For Botta, see his introduction to book 1; see also Buccini, *The Americas in Italian Literature and Culture*, 177.

69. One of the issues here is the question whether Oscar reveals Riccardo's identity out of jealousy. For details on Oscar, see the *disposizione scenica*: Rosen, "La disposizione scenica," 34.

70. Brown, *The Northern Court*, vol. 1, 30–36, 308; for the quotes, see 311, 317.

71. In this respect *Un ballo* also relates to traditions of *romantismo* in Italian music theater. For this context, see Jahrmärker, *Themen, Motive und Bilder des Romantischen*.

72. Gerhard, *The Urbanization of Opera*, 74.

73. Hibberd, "Auber's *Gustave III*," 160.

74. Everett, "Love or Money: What Isn't in 'The Merry Wives of Windsor.'" On this aspect of Verdi's understanding of Shakespeare, see also Mariani, "Scenografia Verdiana."

75. See, for instance, the case of Schiller's Don Karlos: Oellers, *Schiller*, 178.

76. Tyrell, *Transnational Nation*, 4f. Schiavi, "Moby-Dick in Italia." On Melville's own understanding of Italy, see Berthold, *American Risorgmento*.

77. Botta, *Storia della guerra dell'indipendenza degli Stati Uniti d'America* (1809), vol. 1, 2.

78. Several works were known to Italian readers in French translations as well as in *riduzioni*, abbreviated forms. Ruggieri Punzo, *Walter Scott in Italia*, 19ff.

79. Budden, *The Operas of Verdi*, vol. 2, 375.

80. Ruggieri Punzo, *Walter Scott in Italia*, 36f.

81. Gerhard has pointed to connections between *I puritani* and *Un ballo*: see *The Urbanization of Opera*, 434. For Pepoli's political role and the libretto, see Körner, "Carlo Pepoli."

82. Filippo Filippi, *GMM*, 12/1/1862, supplement.

83. Botta, *Storia della guerra dell'indipendenza degli Stati Uniti d'America* (1809), vol. 1, 1–105; for the description of Boston, see Botta, vol. 2, 1ff., 355f. Boston was relatively well known to Italian readers. Already *Il Gazzettiere americano* of 1763 included a long entry on the city: *Il Gazzettiere americano*, vol. 1, 42.

84. Amari, "Prefazione," xxivf.

85. Smart, *Mimomania*, 150f. For a detailed analysis of act 2, see Powers, "*La dama velata*: Act II of Un ballo in maschera."

86. *GMM*, 12/1/1862, supplement.

87. Balzano, *I confini del sole*.

88. Rosen, "La disposizione scenica."

89. Gerbi, *The Dispute of the New World*, 182.

90. Earle describes the symbolism behind the encounter between Spanish conquistadors and Indian women: "Argentina, the offspring of this encounter, was a *criolla*, a beautiful creole woman." Earle, *The Return of the Native*, 97. Commentators differentiated between a general term describing racial mixing, *mestizaje*, and the more specific union between European and indigenous blood. On the European obsession with racial classification, see also Bennett, *Colonial Blackness*, 185 n.

91. Bennett, *Colonial Blackness*, 86.

92. Pares, *Yankees and Creoles*.

93. Midlo Hall, *Africans in Colonial Louisiana*.

94. Sullivan, *New World Symphonies*, 195f. In 1872 Filippi compared Verdi's *Aida* directly to the music of Gottschalk.

95. Carlo Cattaneo, "Esplorazione dell'Istmo Messicano" (1845), in *Scritti storici e geografici*, vol. 2, 3–16, 13. The book under review is a report on an expedition led by Gaetano Moro: *Reconociemento del istmo de Tehuantepec con el objeto de una comunicación océanica* (London: Ackermann, 1844). On Cattaneo's own understanding of South American civilizations since the conquest, see also Sabetti, *Civilization and Self-Government*, 116.

96. Linati also created an important lithographic collection depicting local customs and people. On Linati, see, in particular, *Memorie parmensi per la storia del Risorgimento*, vol. 4, *Claudio Linati*.

97. Botta, *History of the War of Independence* (transl. Otis 1820), vol. 2, 553. Compagnoni, *Storia dell'America*, vol. 28, 74f. On Brant, see Calloway, *The American Revolution in Indian Country*, 60. The Calatrava family in Verdi's opera *La forza del destino* (1862) would play on very similar prejudices against the opera's main character, the mulatto Don Alvaro, son of a viceroy of Peru.

98. Earle, *The Return of the Native*, 2. Isabella, *Risorgimento in Exile*, 47f.

99. Gerbi, *The Dispute of the New World*, 183. Banti, *La nazione del Risorgimento*. By the 1840s Latin American intellectuals started themselves to dismiss the idea of the nations' roots in the pre-Columbian past. The historian and future president of Argentina Domingo Faustino Sarmiento claimed that "our fathers" were the conquistadors, not the Indians. Earle, *The Return of the Native*, 5, 93f.

100. Carlo Cattaneo, "Frammenti d'istoria universal," in *Scritti storici e geografici*, vol. 2, 97–122, 101.

101. Goethe wrote his poem in 1827. A generation later the influential Austrian journalist Ferdinand Kürnberger contrasted this image of the happy continent with his widely read novel *Der Amerika-Müde*. Liberal intellectuals struggled to relate the idea of political freedom to specific models of democratic government. See Fluck, "Die deutsche Kultur als Prüfstein amerikanischer Demokratie: Ferdinand Kürnbergers Roman *Der Amerika-Müde*."

102. *GMM*, 12/1/1862, supplement.

103. Gerhard, "Vergil in Nordamerika: Höllensprache und Kassandra-Rufe in Sommas Libretto für Verdi," 17f. On the cultural significance of Foscolo's poem within the Risorgimento, see Duggan, *The Force of Destiny*, 34f.

104. Jahrmärker, *Themen, Motive und Bilder des Romantischen*, 31–122. On the relationship between *couleur locale* and supernaturalism, see also Dahlhaus, "Drammaturgia dell'opera italiana," 85.

105. Ruggieri Punzo, *Walter Scott in Italia*, 29.

106. Brown, *The Northern Courts*, vol. 2, 213.

107. For an analysis of the relationship between the world of magic and historical consciousness, see Ernesto de Martino, *Il mondo magico*.

108. For an account of the different versions and negotiations with censors, in addition to the works previously cited, see Rosen, "A Tale of Five Cities." Gossett, *Divas and Scholars*, 491ff. Not convincing is Czaika, *Gustav III und Verdis Maskenball*.

109. Gerhard, *The Urbanization of Opera*, 415.

110. della Seta, *Not without Madness*, 135–39. On Verdi's understanding of Shakespeare, see also Gerhard, *The Urbanization of Opera*, 412ff.

111. See, for instance, the reactions in Bologna to *La battaglia* in 1860—"a private story about love and jealousy," deprived of its historical significance: *MdB*, 28/12/1860. See also Smart, "Verdi, Italian Romanticism and the Risorgimento," 31, 39.

112. For a more detailed discussion of those aspects of the opera, see Körner, "Masked Faces: Verdi, Uncle Tom and the Unification of Italy." See also Sala, "Un ballo in maschera e il carnevale," 237, also 253.

113. Conway, *War, State and Society*, 230, 248.

114. See, for instance, Gerhard, "Liebesduette in flagranti: *Suspense* und *pacing* in der Oper des 19. Jahrhunderts," 78. Pauls, *Giuseppe Verdi und das Risorgimento*, 231. On the criteria generally employed by the censors in the Kingdom of Naples, see di Stefano, *La censura teatrale in Italia*, 51f. Meanwhile, Giger argues that criteria of censorship were not applied consistently and that *Civiltà cattolica* criticized Verdi for his "bad examples of taste in matters of politics, religion, or morality": Giger, "Social Control and the Censorship of Giuseppe Verdi's Operas in Rome (1844–1859)," 233.

115. Giger, "Social Control and the Censorship," 260. Rosen, "La disposizione scenica," 14.

116. See, on censorship in particular, Davis, "Italy," and Palazzolo, *La perniciosa lettura*.

117. Venturi, *L'Italia in un mondo tra riforme e rivoluzioni*, 225ff. Venturi's observations are based on a detailed analysis of Italian press coverage of Swedish political and constitutional developments.

118. Barton, *Scandinavia in the Revolutionary Era, 1760–1815*, 202. North, *Geschichte der Ostsee*, 179, 210. On cultural life at the court and Gustav's own artistic ambition, see ibid., 199, and Gerste, *Der Zauberkönig*, 85ff.

119. Barton, *Scandinavia in the Revolutionary Era*, 77, 112. Members of the state church were still forbidden to leave it.

120. Gerste, *Der Zauberkönig*, 120. On the reforming spirit in Rome at the time of Pius VI, see Franco Venturi, "The Enlightenment in the Papal States," in *Italy and the Enlightenment: Studies in a Cosmopolitan Century*, 225–64, 242ff. On Gustav III and the Pio-Clementino, see also Howard, "An Antiquarian Handlist and Beginnings of the Pio-Clementino."

121. Sandström, "Bénigne Gagneraux e la Svezia." The original of Gagneraux's painting is today in the National Museum in Stockholm, the copy in the Sternberk Palais in Prague, part of the National Gallery.

122. *Il Trovatore*, 31/10/1860.

123. Between June 1847 and January 1857 Verdi spent a total of four and a half years in Paris, but during this long period Auber's opera was never on schedule. Rosen, "La disposizione scenica," 25.

124. After 1848–49 these works were performed as *Viscardello, Violetta, Gugliemo Wellingrode*, and *Giovanna di Guzman*. Roccatagliati, "The Italian Theatre of Verdi's Day," 21.

125. See, for instance, *Il Trovatore*, 10/10/1860. The periodical was published in Milan, but unlike the *GMM* it did not belong to the Ricordi company.

126. Verdi to the manager of the San Carlo in Naples Torelli, 14/10/1857, in Weaver, *Verdi*, 199.

127. Verdi to Somma, 8/7/1858, in *Carteggio Verdi-Somma*, 91.

128. Brown, *The Northern Courts*, vol. 2, 212.

129. For Verdi's discussion of the historical framework, see Verdi to Somma, 26/11/1857, in *Carteggio Verdi-Somma*, 243f. (That day Verdi wrote several letters to Somma.)

130. [Burke], *Storia degli stabilimenti europei in America*, vol. 2, 179ff.

131. della Seta, *Italia e Francia nell'ottocento*, 209, 228.

132. See, for instance, Gustavo Sangiorgio, *L'Arpa*, 5/10/1860. *GMM*, 12/1/1862, supplement.

133. For a comprehensive acount of the sibylline prophecies, see Momigliano, "Sibylline Oracles," in *Ottavo contributo alla storia degli studi classici e del mondo antico*, 349–54. On the reference to Virgil in Verdi, see Gerhard, "Vergil in Nordamerika."

134. See Auber, *Gustave III, ou le bal masqué* (1847), act 1, scène 3, 5. Mercadante, *Il Reggente*, atto 1, scena 5, 6. Also Scribe's main source speaks of a "Sibyl," in whom Gustav III allegedly confided: Brown, *The Northern Courts*, vol. 2, 212.

135. Antonio Somma, *Cassandra*. Tragedia (Venice: Cecchini, 1859). Somma's *Cassandra* is also included in *Opere scelte di Antonio Somma* (Alessandro Pascolato, ed.), 281–403.

136. For an analysis of Cassandra's role in a source that was available to Somma and Verdi, see August Wilhelm von Schlegel, *Vorlesungen über Dramatische Kunst und Literatur* (Bonn and Leipzig: Schroeder, 1923), vol. 1, 67–70.

137. Williams, "The Sixth Book of the Aeneid." For a list of early Christian interpretations of Virgil's *Fourth Eclogue*, see Bourne, "The Messianic Prophecy in Vergil's *Fourth Eclogue*."

138. On the Christian interpretation of the ancient promises, see Lauster, *Die Verzauberung der Welt*, 285. Osterhammel points to the persisting role of the *Aeneid* in modern history: *Die Verwandlung der Welt*, 199. For modern Italian references, see, for instance, Carli, *Delle lettere americane*, vol. 1, 172. Rosmini wrote one of his first theological treaties on the Sibylline oracles: Dossi, *Antonio Rosmini*, 57. Filangieri is full of references to Plato, to Neoplatonists, and to Virgil: Filangieri, *La Scienza della Legislazione*, vol. 2, 5f. See also Romagnosi's review of Giuseppe Micali, *Esame della storia degli antichi popoli italiani* (1833): Romagnosi, *Opere*, vol. 2, no. 1, 438–514.

139. Vance, *The Victorians and Ancient Rome*, 5, 29–33, 133ff.

140. Ferdinand Lassalle, *Der italienische Krieg und die Aufgabe Preußens* (Berlin: Duncker, 1859).

141. Virgil, *The Eclogues* (4, 5), 56.

142. Verdi to Torelli, 14/11/1857, quoted in Budden, *The Operas of Verdi*, vol. 2, 368.

143. Verdi to Somma, 11/9/1858, in *Carteggio Verdi-Somma*, 285. The evidence here seems to speak against Gossett, who argued that Verdi accepted the Boston setting only in order "to have the work performed at all": *Divas and Scholars*, 159.

144. Verdi's wife maintained that he never completely discarded the King Lear project: Giuseppina Verdi to Giuseppina Negroni Prati Morosini, 18/12/1879, in *Verdi's Otello and Simon Boccanegra in Letters and Documents* (Busch, ed.), vol. 1, 14.

145. Budden, *The Operas of Verdi*, vol. 2, 363.

146. Siehe Jahrmärker, "Scribe—Erfolgsautor und Reformator im Pariser Theaterleben," 15. Yon, *Eugène Scribe*, 84 sq, 277ff.

147. On this issue, also, see the reception of Verdi in Germany: Kreuzer, *Verdi and the Germans*, 151.

148. *Gazetta musicale di Napoli*, 16/3/1862.

149. Appendice, *La Fama*, 14/1/1862.

150. Filippo Filippi, *GMM*, 12/1/1862, supplement.

151. *GMM*, 12/1/1862, supplement.

152. *GMM*, 10/4/1859 and reprint 12/1/1862, supplement. He continues, "Verdi non è un maestro che cerchi d'innestare forzatamente o pezzi nel melodramma, a risico d'introdurre una superfluità, di arrestare il cammino veloce dell'azione, di costringere i personaggi a parlare più che vogliano o che non debbano, a scapito della verità e dell'interesse."

153. Filippo Filippi, *GMM*, 12/1/1862, supplement.

154. For a detailed documentation, see Luzio, ed., *Carteggi verdiani*, vol. 1, 241ff.

155. Owing to its fourteenth-century context, the new version did not feature a masked ball, but the ball itself can't have been the reason why the censors rejected the original: masked balls existed in other operas that had passed the censors. In 1857 two Neapolitan theaters had staged the Italian version of *Les vêpres siciliennes* under the title *Batilde di Turenna*, with a great masked ball in act 3. Pauls, *Giuseppe Verdi*, 224, 233.

156. Pauls, *Giuseppe Verdi*, 231.

157. della Seta, "New Currents in the Libretto," 74.

158. Pauls, *Giuseppe Verdi*, 246.

159. At the time the Roman censors were considered to be stricter than their Neapolitan colleagues, but in their negotiations with Verdi they were apparently not overly demanding. For a comparison of censorship rules in Naples and Rome, see di Stefano, *La censura teatrale*, 49–59.

160. Giger, "Social Control and the Censorship," 246, 248ff.

161. Ibid., 253.

162. Ibid., 260. Rosen, "La disposizione scenica," 14.

163. *New York Times* (*NYT*), 21/2/1861. On Lincoln's reception at the theater, see also Holzer, *Lincoln President-Elect*, 365f.

164. *NYT*, 4/2/1861.

165. *Brooklyn Eagle*, 20/2/1861. On the American response, see also *NYT*, 9/4/1861 and 18/10/1861.

166. *Brooklyn Eagle*, 18/2/1861.

167. *NYT*, 21/2/1861.

168. Edward Rothstein, "When honest Abe met this querulous metropolis," *NYT*, 8/10/2009.

169. Virgil, *Eclogues* (4, 13), 56.

170. For the symbolic repercussions of Cavour's sudden death, see Duggan, *The Force of Destiny*, xvi.

171. Sullivan, *New World Symphonies*.

172. James Fenimore Cooper, *The Pathfinder* (Paris: Galignani, 1840). James Fenimore Cooper, *The Spy: A Tale of the Neutral Ground*, with the portrait of the author (Leipzig, B. Tauchnitz, 1842). I am grateful to Anselm Gerhard for this information.

173. Minghelli Vaini to Verdi, 9/1/61, in Verdi, *I copialettere di Giuseppe Verdi*, 587. According to Anselm Gerhard, the couple held the following copies in their library: Harriet Beecher Stowe, *Le père Tom, ou vie des nègres en Amérique* (trad. La Bédouillère; Geneva: Librarie Européenne, 1853); Harriet Beecher Stowe, *Uncle Tom's Cabin* (with Italian notes by John Millhouse; Milan: Millhouse, Florence: Molini; Naples: Marghieri

1853). Minghelli-Vaini had competed against Verdi for a seat in parliament but remained on friendly terms with the family: Walker, *The Man Verdi*, 232, 236.

174. *L'Armonia*, 26/2/1859.

Chapter Five. A War for Uncle Tom:
Slavery and the American Civil War in Italy

1. Simonde de Sismondi, *Études sur les constitutions des peuples libres*, 11.

2. Mazzini to the editors of *Il Dovere*, 18/8/1863, *Edizione nazionale*, vol. 76, 32–34, 33. Garibaldi's address "Ad Abramo Lincoln emancipatore degli schiavi nella repubblica americana" was published on 6/8/1865 in the periodical *Il Diritto*.

3. Some versions of the libretto speak about "*dell'abbietto sangue de' negri*": Verdi, *Un ballo in maschera*, vol. 1, 4. On the different versions of the libretto, see Rosen, "La disposizione scenica," 19ff. In the original version by Scribe and Auber the witch's main offence was her alleged pact with the devil: "elle est de concert avec Lucifer."

4. Giuseppe Rota, *Bianchi e negri*, Azione coreografica di G. Rota, Musica di Paolo Giorza ed altri autori (Milan: F. Lucca, [1853]). For the libro da ballo, see Giuseppe Rota (music by Paolo Giorza), *Bianchi e Neri* (Milan: Teatro alla Scala, 1853). New York Public Library (NYPL), Walter Toscanini Collection (WTC), Libretti da Ballo (LdB), n. 809 and 939. The ballet was also performed under the titles *La capanna di Tom* (Bologna) or *I bianchi e i negri* (Turin). For a detailed study of the ballet's choreography and its various editions, see Butkas Ertz, *Nineteenth-Century Italian Ballet Music before National Unification*, 421ff.

5. See, for instance, Michele Leoni, "Viaggio agli stati uniti d'America: Od Osservazioni su la società, i costumi e'l governo di quella ontrada; Di Miss Wright; Londra 1821," *Antologia*, 7, July–September 1822, 390–410, 397f. Italian exiles picked up related debates from the English language press: See, for instance, Santorre di Santarosa, commenting on an article from the *Morning Chronicle* on 2/9/1824: *Ricordi*, 106f.

6. Sismondi, *Études sur les constitutions*, 118. Interesting in this context is Mazzini's review, rejecting a possible reading of Sismondi that sees slavery as a natural consequence of popular sovereignty: Giuseppe Mazzini, "Studi politici ed economici di Sismondi," in *Scritti editi ed inediti* (1863), 18–52, 32.

7. Polasky, *Revolutions without borders*, 78.

8. [Burke], *Storia degli stabilimenti europei in America*, vol. 2, 137ff., in particular 146.

9. Foscolo, "Della servitù dell'Italia," *Edizione nazionale*, vol. 8, 149–250, 199.

10. Rossi, *Cours d'économie politique*, vol. 2, 342, also 366–71. He further discusses slavery in his *Cours de droit constitutionnel*, mostly in the context of French colonization: vol. 1, 283ff. Important in this context are the physiocrats' arguments against slavery: Dorigny, "The Question of Slavery in the Physiocratic Texts: A Rereading of an Old Debate."

11. Filangieri, *La scienza della legislazione*/Constant, *Comento sulla scienza della legislazione*, vol. 1, 60, 306ff. On Constant's abolitionism, see Pitts, "Constant's Thought on Slavery and Empire."

12. Ferrari, *Filosofia della rivoluzione*, vol. 2, 173ff.

13. Botta, *Storia della guerra dell'indipendenza degli Stati Uniti* (1809), vol. 1, 16. The idea was picked up by other Italian commentators, too. See, for instance, Dandolo, *Il settentrione dell'Europa e dell'America nel secolo passato sin 1789*, 189. For a more detailed analysis, see also Jackson, "Bota sulla schiavitù in America," 117.

14. For a detailed discussion of this relationship, see Arena, *Libertas and the Practice of Politics in the Late Roman Republic*, 14.

15. For instance Castiglioni, *Viaggio negli Stati Uniti dell'America settentrionale*, vol. 1, 181ff., 315f., 373ff.

16. Compagnoni, *Storia dell'America*, vol. 25, 57; vol. 28, 167.

17. Francesco Apostoli, quoted in Del Negro, *Il mito americano nella Venezia del settencento*, 614. See also the former Jesuit G. B. Roberti, ibid., 613.

18. Rosmini, *Filosofia della politica*, 510f.

19. Hamilton, *Gli uomini ed i costumi agli Stati-Uniti d'America*, vol. 2, 85ff.

20. Draper, *The Price of Emancipation*, 139.

21. Cattaneo, "Compenso ai coloni britannici per la liberazione dei Negri," *Scritti economici*, vol. 1, 60–65. The article was originally published in the *Bollettino di notizie statistiche ed economiche*.

22. Cattaneo, "Notizia sulla questione delle tariffe daziarie negli Stati Uniti d'America desunta da documenti officiali" (1833), *Scritti economici*, vol. 1, 11–55, 30. The article, mentioned earlier in chapter 1, was first published in the Milanese *Annali universali di statistica*. Another reflection on slavery is Cattaneo's passionate review of poems by Henry Wadsworth Longfellow (1807–82), including "The Slave's Dream," "The Quadron Girl," and other poems on slavery: Carlo Cattaneo, "Il poeta americano Longfellow," *Scritti letterari*, vol. 1, 461–73, 462.

23. Cattaneo, "Notizia sulla questione delle tariffe daziarie negli Stati Uniti d'America," 13.

24. Ibid., 38.

25. Cattaneo, "Africa Liberia," in *Scritti politici*, vol. 1, 47.

26. Carlo Cattaneo, "Di alcuni stati moderni" (1842), *Scritti storici e geografici*, vol. 1, 255–301, 275.

27. For Genovesi, see Venturi, *Settecento riformatore: Da Muratori a Beccaria*, 615. Cattaneo, "Di alcuni stati moderni," 274.

28. Cattaneo, "Primo programma di un giornale libero," *Il 1848 in Italia*, 3–7, 4.

29. Mazzini, "I repubblicani e l'Italia," *Edizione nazionale*, vol. 66, 83–93, 86. Mazzini, "Dei doveri dell'uomo," vol. 69, 3–145, 73. See also Mazzini, "In torno alla questione dei negri in America" (1865), *Edizione nazionale*, vol. 83, 163–65. Mazzini to Francesco Dall'Ongaro, 9/2/1855, *Edizione nazionale*, vol. 53, 341–42, 342.

30. See Mazzini's "Prière a Dieu pour les planteurs par un exilé": Ramanzini, *Una lettera di Garibaldi ad Abramo Lincoln*, 10. Dal Lago, *William Lloyd Garrison and Giuseppe Mazzini*, 131. In a 1838 review of Sismondi's work for the *Edinburgh Magazine* he had pointed to the fact that in America slavery coexists with democratic institutions; Mazzini, "Sismondi's Studies of Free Constitutions," *Edizione nazionale*, vol. 17, 221–92, 249.

31. *La Nazione*, 24/11/1860. Under its entry "Abolizione della schiavitù dei negri," the highly derivative *Nuova enciclopedia popolare* used the same expression "*vergognosa piaga della schiavitù*" to describe slavery especially in the United States, presenting British abolitionism as a model. Hippolyte Roux-Fernand, *Storia dei progressi dell'incivilmento in Europa* (Venice: Tomasso Fontana, 1843), used the same expression to refer to slavery in the ancient world. I am grateful to David Laven for pointing me to these references.

32. Paolo Taglioni, *Theu o la fata dei fiori*: NYPL, WTC, LdB, n. 868. Pasquale Borri, *Nephte o il figliol prodigo*, ibid., n. 883 (Turin, 1869), n. 923 (Milan, 1873). Giuseppe Rota, *Elda e Dielma*, "azione mimica-danzante," ibid., n. 787. The ballet featured slaves in India. Thematically related, in 1862 Rota presented a Chinese ballet at the Pergola in Florence, *Lo spirito maligno*, ibid., n. 799. See also Antonio Pallerini's *L'Anello infernale ossia Folgore. Ballo fantastico in sei parti*, set in Cadiz during the 16th century and performed at La Scala during the autumn of 1862, ibid., n. 795.

33. *La Fama del 1853: Rassegna di scienze, lettere, arti, industria e teatri*, 14/11/1853.

34. Cattaneo, "Notizia sulla questione delle tariffe daziarie negli Stati Uniti d'America," 18.

35. Cattaneo, "La città considerata come principio ideale delle istorie italiane," *Scritti storici e geografici*, vol. 2, 383–437, 425.

36. *La Fama del 1853*, 14/11/1853.

37. *L'Italia musicale*, 12/11/1853.

38. Cattaneo, "Di alcuni stati moderni," 282.

39. Vollaro, "Lincoln, Stowe, and the 'Little Woman/Great War' Story: The Making, and Breaking, of a Great American Anecdote."

40. Carlo Cattaneo, "Tipi del genere umano" (1862), *Scritti storici e geografici*, vol. 3, 214–47, 245f. The article discusses several works of biological anthropology and was first published in *Il Politecnico*.

41. *Gazzetta musicale di Napoli*, 7/12/1862.

42. On the role of ballet in Italian theaters, see Sasportes, "La parola contro il corpo ovvero il melodramma nemico del ballo." The origins of the modern *coreodramma* go back to Salvatore Viganò, at the turn of the eighteenth to the nineteenth century. For an overview of Viganò's work, see Raimondi, ed., *Il sogno del coreodramma*.

43. NYPL, WTC, LdB, no. 432. There is a short reference to the ballo in Gatti, *Il Teatro alla Scala nella storia e nell'arte (1778–1963)*, 117. See also the introduction by Roger Parker in *The Works of Giuseppe Verdi*, Series 1, Operas, vol. 3 (Giuseppe Verdi, *Nabucodonosor: Dramma lirico in Four Parts*), ed. Roger Parker (Chicago/Milan: University of Chicago Press/G. Ricordi, 1987), xi–xxvi.

44. *Gazzetta musicale di Napoli*, 16/11/1862 and 23/11/1862. *La Fama*, 25/11/1862. On negative responses to Verdi, see Körner, "*Music of the Future*: Italian Theatres and the European Experience of Modernity between Unification and World War One."

45. *La capanna dello zio Tomaso o la schiavitù: Nuovissimo romanzo di Enrichetta Beecher Stowe* (4vols.); Milan: Borroni e Scotti, 1852).

46. Wilson, *Crusader in Crinoline*, 329.

47. Rossi, "Uncle Tom's Cabin and Protestantism in Italy," 418, 421f. On the reaction of *Civiltà cattolica*, see Gennaro Lerda, "La schiavitù e la guerra civile nelle pagine della *Civiltà cattolica*," 233–50, 238.

48. *La capanna dello zio Tommaso ossia La vita dei negri in America* (Lugano: Chiusi, 1853). *La capanna dello zio Tom: Racconto di Enrichetta Beecher Stowe; Nuova Versione* (Milan: Pagnoni, [1898]).

49. For a survey of the work's international circulation, see MacKay, "The First Years of Uncle Tom's Cabin in Russia," 69. Tolstoy read a German translation in 1854: Bartlett, *Tolstoy*, 109. On the novel's impact in Spain, see Surwillo, *Monsters by Trade*, 38, 40ff.

50. *L'Italia musicale*, 4/1/1858.

51. Kohn, Meer, and Todd, "Reading Stowe as a Transatlantic Writer," in Kohn, Meer, and Todd, eds., *Transatlantic Stowe*, xi–xxxi, xi.

52. For an assessment of press reactions to the novel, see Jackson, "Uncle Tom's Cabin in Italy," and Rossi, "Uncle Tom's Cabin and Protestantism in Italy," 419. Long after the novel's first publication the Italian press continued to write about Stowe. See, for instance, *L'Universo illustrato*, 1 (23/3/1867), 303. For references to Stowe in various treaties on slavery, see Luigi Cibrario, *Della schiavitù e del servaggio e specialmente dei servi agricoltori* (Milan: Civelli, 1868), vol. 1, 326. Carlo Bianchetti, *L'Antischiavismo alla fine del secolo XIX* (Turin: Tipografia subalpina, 1893), 270f.

53. Cattaneo, "Il poeta americano Longfellow," 461f.

54. Robbins, *The Cambridge Introduction to Harriet Beecher Stowe*, 76. An exception would be her play *Christian Slave*.

55. Stowe's other abolitionist and more radical novel, *Dred*, was also dramatized: Newman, "Staging Black Insurrection: Dred on Stage." Most scholars have treated Uncle Tom as an American phenomenon, neglecting the novel's transatlantic dimension.

56. Birdoff, *The World's Greatest Hit*, 24–28. Robbins, *The Cambridge Introduction to Harriet Beecher Stowe*, 78f. For an Italian equivalent of the Uncle Tom shows, see the periodical publication *Il teatro drammatico Napolitano di Luigi de Lise*, which starting in 1855 issued every month a short piece of theater. In February 1856 appeared the *fascicolo* 8, *La famiglia dello zio Tom*.

57. Birdoff, *The World's Greatest Hit*, 6.

58. Rossi, "Uncle Tom's Cabin and Protestantism in Italy," 418.

59. Quoted in Williams, *Playing the Race Card*, 45.

60. Cohen, "Feme di Gelosia!," 556. For the historian, ballet libretti constitute an interesting source, because they offer a commented synopsis of all scenes, unlike opera libretti, which consist mainly of dialogues.

61. *Il Trovatore*, 6/1/1858.

62. On the Italian *mimo-drama* (historical themes performed in several acts), see Binney, "Sixty Years of Italian Dance Prints," 17.

63. Au, "Augusta Maywood"; Celi, "Giuseppe Rota." "Maywood, Augusta," in Clarke and Vaughan, eds., *The Encyclopedia of Dance and Ballet*, 231. Guest, "Balli presentati tra il 1845 e il 1854," 23.

64. The score mentions additional pieces by other composers. On the music for the ballet, see Butkas Ertz, *Nineteenth-Century Italian Ballet Music*, chpt. 7.

65. Basso, *Storia del Teatro Regio di Torino*, vol. 2, 295. Viale Ferrero, *Storia del Teatro Regio di Torino*, vol. 3, 418.

66. Valebona, *Il Teatro Carlo Felice*, 348–57. The number of performances usually depended on the work's success. For the continuing appreciation of the audience in Genoa, see *Il Trovatore*, 21/5/1856.

67. Gatti, *Il Teatro alla Scala nella storia e nell'arte*, 195, 200. Marinelli Roscioni, ed., *Il Teatro di San Carlo*, vol. 2, 361. The fact that smaller theaters in medium-sized cities did not stage the piece had to do with the huge cast, requiring several hundred participants. This made the staging too expensive for smaller houses. Even at the San Carlo the role of ballet diminished during the second half of the century, and, as a consequence, most productions were retakes from successful productions at La Scala: Sasportes, "La Danza, 1737–1900," 395.

68. On the financial constraints, see Körner, *Politics of Culture*, 66ff. Rota and Giorza continued their collaboration, including the ballets *La maschera o Le notti di Venezia* and *Cleopatra*, both presented at La Scala in 1865: NYPL, WTC, LdB, n. 849 and 850.

69. See in particular *La Fama*, 14/11/1853. The importance accorded to the literary source in this genre of ballet goes back to the eighteenth century and was not uncontroversial: Sasportes, "La parola contro il corpo," 22.

70. Cohen, "Feme di Gelosia!," 555–64.

71. Note by Walter Toscanini in NYPL, WTC, LdB, n. 809. The bibliophile, collector, and ballet scholar Walter Toscanini was the son of the conductor Arturo Toscanini and husband of the famous dancer Cia Fornaroli. Eames, *When All the World Was Dancing*.

72. This summary is based on the following version of the libretto: *I bianchi ed i negri. Azione storica-allegorica in tre quadri e sette scene del coreografo Giuseppe Rota. Riprodotta dal Coreografo Ferdinando Pratesi nel Regio Teatro della Scala nell'autunno 1863*, Milan: Luigi di Giacomo Pirola (NYPL, WTC, LdB, n. 809). The original version presented in Milan in 1853 is similar to the one presented in Bologna in 1858 and in Milan in 1863. The versions produced in Rome in 1858 and in Turin in 1875 include further variations. As was the case for opera, it was common that individual theaters changed parts of a work according to the disposition and the requests of local artists. See, for instance, *L'Arpa*, 18/10/1858.

73. On the role of prefaces and introductions, see Parfait, *The Publishing History of Uncle Tom's Cabin*, 65f.

74. Social sciences and historical writing were particularly relevant here: O'Brian, "Catharine Macaulay's Histories of England: A Female Perspective on the History of Liberty." For an Italian perspective, see Porciani, "Disciplinamento nazionale e modelli domestici," 118ff.

75. Harriet Beecher Stowe, *La chiave della capanna dello zio Tomaso contenente i fatti e i documenti originali sopra cui è fonadato il romanzo colle note giustificative* (Milan: Borroni e Scotti, 1853).

76. Harriet Beecher Stowe, *La capanna dello zio Tomaso o la schiavitù* (1852), vol. 4, 192. (Quoted after the American edition of Stowe, *Uncle Tom's Cabin*, 506.)

77. Ibid., 197f. (American edition, 509).

78. *La Fama*, 14/11/1853. *L'Italia musicale*, 4/1/1858, opined that the literary source did not adapt itself to ballet. Much more positive is *Il Trovatore*, 6/1/1858. The caricatures reproduced in the issue of 20/1/1858 do not seem to criticize Rota's ballet, but the management of Turin's Teatro Regio and the simultaneous performance of *Rigoletto*.

79. See in particular *L'Arpa*, 18/10/1858. The more critical reviews had less to do with the ballet's content than with the performance of individual dancers.

80. Quoted in Wyck Brooks, *The Dream of Arcadia*, 129. On her visit to Italy, see also Wright, *American Novelists in Italy*, 87ff.

81. Giuseppe Regaldi, *Canti* (Turin: Franco 1858), 245.

82. Gemme, *Domesticating Foreign Struggles*, 121.

83. *La Nazione*, 30/3/1862.

84. *L'Amico di Casa: Almanacco popolare illustrato; 1863* (Turin: Stamperia dell'Unione Tipografico-Editrice), 1862.

85. Roberts, "The Relevance of Giuseppe Mazzini's Ideas of Insurgency to the American Slavery Crisis of the 1850s," 319f.

86. Marwil, *Visiting Modern War in Risorgimento Italy*, 177, 184.

87. Wright, *American Novelists in Italy*, 88f.

88. The novel was written in the winter of 1859–60 during her second visit to Italy. During the trip she went to Florence, Rome, and Naples, as well as to Como, Milan, Verona, and Venice. Vance, *America's Rome*, vol. 2, 22. Wright, *American Novelists in Italy*, 88, 90–103. On the Catholic reaction to *Uncle Tom*, see Rossi, "Uncle Tom's Cabin and Protestantism in Italy."

89. Philip Trauth, *Italo-American Diplomatic Relations*, xv. See also Lowenthal, *George Perkins Marsh: Versatile Vermonter*. Today he is mostly remembered as an early environmentalist. He published his pioneering *Man and Nature* in 1864, at the height of the American Civil War.

90. Williams, *Playing the Race Card*, 47.

91. On the concept of the "oriental despot" in the discourse of the European Enlightenment, see Venturi, *Italy and the Enlightenment*, 41–51. For Gilroy slavery was at the center of the Enlightenment debates on the concept of modernity: *The Black Atlantic*.

92. Davis, *The Problem of Slavery in Western Culture* (1966), 14f. See also the discussion in the introduction to this book.

93. *La Fama*, 29/9/1863.

94. Ibid.

95. *La Nazione*, 10/1/1861. See for similar campaigns Riall, *Garibaldi*, 296

96. Fiorentino, *Gli Stati Uniti e il Risorgimento d'Italia*, 189.

97. Riall, *Sicily and the Unification of Italy*.

98. Fiorentino, *Gli Stati Uniti e il Risorgimento d'Italia*, 128.

99. dal Lago, "Radicalism and Nationalism: Northern 'Liberators' and Southern Labourers in the USA and Italy, 1830–60," 197. Sarti, "La democrazia radicale," 145–48. Ramanzini, *Una lettera di Garibaldi ad Abramo Lincoln*. See also Richards, *Italian American*, 118.

100. In particular dal Lago, *William Lloyd Garrison and Giuseppe Mazzini*. For a few biographical sketches, see Mancini, "Corrispondenti americani del Mazzini."

101. dal Lago, *William Lloyd Garrison and Giuseppe Mazzini*, 107. Fiorentino, *Gli Stati Uniti e il Risorgimento d'Italia*, 43f. dal Lago, "Il governo degli Stati Uniti e la Repubblica Romana del 1849," 95. Rossi, *The Image of America*, 105. White Mario was introduced to the Beechers and Stowes by Mazzini: Mazzini to Jessie White Mario, 8/7/1858, *Edizione nazionale*, vol. 61, 65–66.

102. Mazzini to Jessie White Mario, 11/9/1861 and 15/9/1861, *Edizione nazionale*, vol. 71, 382–83, 393–95. A small minority of fighters in the Union's Garibaldi Guard were Italians. On foreign legions and the outcomes of the offer to Garibaldi, see Doyle, *The Cause of All Nations*, 158–81, 229–39.

103. Trauth, *Italo-American Diplomatic Relations*, 8–34. See also Belfiglio, "Italians and the American Civil War." For lists of Italians fighting in different units, see Cassani, *Italiani nella guerra civile americana*.

104. Rossi, *The Image of America*, 129.

105. Trauth, *Italo-American Diplomatic Relations*, 1.

106. For the Catholic church's ambiguous position, see "Il concetto morale della schiavitù," in *Civiltà cattolica*, 6th ser., 16, 1, vol. 1, *February 1865*, 427–45. For a wider context, see Jordan and Pratt, *Europe and the American Civil War*, 194. Martina, *Pio IX*, 485ff. Later the Papal States fully collaborated with the prosecution of one of the alleged accomplices of Lincoln's assassination: Trauth, *Italo-American Diplomatic Relations*, 36. For a recent study of the problem, see Sanfilippo, *L'affermazione del cattolicesimo nel Nord America*, 97ff.

107. For the Catholic church's ambiguous position, see "Il concetto morale della schiavitù," in *Civiltà cattolica*, 6th ser., 16, 1, vol. 1, *February 1865*, 427–45, 431.

108. Quoted in Noether, "The Constitution in Action," 88.

109. Gennaro Lerda, "La schiavitù e la guerra civile nelle pagine della *Civiltà cattolica*," 234.

110. "La Disunione negli Stati Uniti," in *Civiltà cattolica*, February 1861, 312–24, 312.

111. Ibid., 322. For a detailed analysis of the church's position in the American Civil War, see Sanfilippo, *L'affermazione del cattolicesimo nel Nord America*, 97–126.

112. Carlo Cattaneo had discussed the organization of the armed forces in "Di alcuni stati moderni," 280.

113. *La Nazione*, 13/10/1862.

114. *La Nazione*, 30/3/1862.

115. Capellini, *Ricordi di un viaggio scientifico*, 72, 144.

116. Ibid., 147.

117. Ibid., 148, 231.

118. "Cronaca Contemporanea," in *Civiltà cattolica*, 5th ser., 15, 11, July 1864, 243–56.

119. *La Nazione*, 11/11/1861. In some parts of Italy, 11 November is the opening of Carnival, which might explain the article's overall tone.

120. *La Nazione*, 11/5/1861 and 13/10/1862.

121. Quoted in Boritt, Neely Jr., and Holzer, "The European Image of Abraham Lincoln," 153.

122. "Cronaca Contemporanea," in *Civiltà cattolica*, October 1861, 249–56. For the Catholics' antiunionist propaganda, see also "Cronaca Contemporanea," *Civiltà cattolica*, July 1864, 243–56.

123. *MdB*, 28/4/1865.

124. *GdR*, 12/3/1865.

125. Quoted in Grew, "One Nation Barely Visible," 121.

126. See, for instance, the review of *Histoire de la guerre civile en Amérique*, par M. le. Comte de Paris, in *Nuova antologia*, Bollettino bibliografico, March 1876, 703–4. For a much more positive evaluation of the United States after the Civil War, see Aurelio Saffi, "Lezioni d'oltre l'Atlantico" (1865), *Ricordi e scritti di Aurelio Saffi*, vol. 3, 213–302.

127. Mazzini, "To Our Friends in the United States" (1865), *A Cosmopolitanism of Nations*, 222f.

128. Mazzini, "Letter to Moncure Daniel Conway, 30 October 1865," in *A Cosmopolitanism of Nations*, 219–21.

129. "Rassegna Politica," in *Nuova antologia*, August 1867, 820–42, 840.

130. Marco Minghetti, *I partiti politici e la ingerenza loro nella giustizia e nell'amministrazione* (Bologna: Zanichelli, 1881). Quoted after Minghetti, *Scritti politici*, 655.

131. Ibid., 656.

132. "Rassegna politica," in *Nuova antologia*, August 1867, 820–42, 840. The article partly follows Mazzini's argument that it was for geographical differences that the American federal model was not applicable to Italy. Just a year before the same periodical had offered a much more positive prospect of the United States' future: "Rassegna politica," *Nuova antologia*, January 1866, 187–201, 200f. For a more nuanced assessment, see Leonida Carpi, "Rivista politica," in *Rivista bolognese di scienze, lettere, arti e scuole*, 1, 3, 15/3/1867, 344–48.

133. Armani, *Carlo Cattaneo*, 23.

134. *Almanacco repubblicano: 1871* (Enrico Bignami, ed.; Lodi: Società Cooperativo-Tipografica, 1870). "Rassegna politica," *Nuova antologia*, January 1866, 187–201, 200f. See also "Rassegna Politica," *Nuova antologia*, June 1868, 421–40, 433f.

135. *Civiltà cattolica*, August 1868, 498–512, 502. See also *L'Universo illustrato*, 3, 2, October 1868, 20.

136. "Rassegna politica," *Nuova antologia*, December 1866, 840–49, 846. *Civiltà cattolica*, August 1868, 498–512.

137. Brock, *An American Crisis*, 4f., 15.

138. Ibid., 168.

139. On the parallels between these two histories, see also Daniele Fiorentino, *Gli Stati Uniti e il Risorgimento d'Italia*, 31 and 187ff.

140. See *La politica estera dell'Italia negli atti, documenti e discussioni parlamentari dal 1861 al 1914*, vol. 1, 179.

141. Recchia and Urbinati, "Introduction: Giuseppe Mazzini's International Political Thought," 20.

142. Pasquale Mancini, on 24/11/1873, in *La politica estera dell'Italia negli atti, documenti e discussioni parlamentari dal 1861 al 1914*, vol. 1, 553ff.

143. Cammarano, *Storia politica dell'Italia liberale, 1861–1901*, 16.

144. Pasquale Mancini, on 24/11/1873, in *La politica estera dell'Italia*, vol. 1, 555.

145. Visconti-Venosta, on 24/11/1873, in *La politica estera dell'Italia*, vol. 1, 567.

146. *Bollettino della Società antischiavista d'Italia*, 1867ff. On the wider context of this movement, see Laqua, "The Tensions of Internationalism: Transnational Anti-slavery in the 1880s and 1890s."

147. See, for instance, the praise for the Holy Siege and in particular for Leopoldo II in Bianchetti, *L'Antischiavismo alla fine del secolo XIX*.

148. As argued, for instance, by Giovanni Boglietti, "Repubblicani e Democratici negli Stati-Uniti d'America," in *Nuova antologia*, August 1868, 766–88.

149. Bianchetti, *L'Antischiavismo alla fine del secolo XIX*, 273.

150. Enrico Nencioni, "Il poeta della Guerra Americana."

151. Ibid., 207f.

152. For an overview of the thematic range of this field, see Ben-Ghiat and Fuller, eds., *Italian Colonialism*.

153. Croce, *History of Europe in the Nineteenth Century*, 146f., 152f.

154. Banti, *La nazione del Risorgimento*. See on this particular aspect also Capellini, *Ricordi di un viaggio*, 148.

Conclusions

1. Drehle, "The Way We Weren't."

2. In addition to the works cited in the introduction, this is the approach taken by Doyle, *Nations Divided*.

3. *GdR*, 28/4/65.

4. *GdR*, 29/4/65. For Mazzini's immediate reaction, see Mazzini to Matilda Biggs, 29/4/1865, *Edizione nazionale*, vol. 80, 221–28, 224. Mazzini to Clementia Taylor, 1/5/1865, *Edizione nazionale*, vol. 80, 230–32.

5. Philip Trauth, *Italo-American Diplomatic Relations*, 35f. For the wider context of international public responses see Doyle, *The Cause of all Nations*, 1–11.

6. Fiorentino, *Gli Stati Uniti e il Risorgimento d'Italia*, 223. Vance, *America's Rome*, vol. 2, 34.

7. Bottrigari, *Cronaca di Bologna*, vol. 3, 379.

8. Luzzatto, *La mummia della repubblica*, 35f. For a contextual analysis, see Körner, "Lokale und transnationale Dimensionen sakralisierter Politik." For a recent study of Lincoln's funeral, see Wightman Fox, *Lincoln's Body*, chpt. 5.

9. Luzzatto, *La mummia*, 35f.

10. Quoted in Wightman Fox, *Lincoln's Body*, 96.

11. Luzzatto, *La mummia*, 17.

12. On commemorations for Mazzini, see Ridolfi, "Feste civili e religione politiche nel 'laboratorio' della nazione italiana (1860–1859)," 89. Mengozzi, "Obseques laiques et mouvement ouvrier en Italie."

13. Luzzatto, *La mummia*, 20f. On this process, see also Finelli, " 'È divenuto un Dio': Santità, patria e rivoluzione nel culto di Mazzini (1872–1905)."

14. On the Risorgimento's martyr cult, see, in particular, Riall, "Martyr Cults in Nineteenth-Century Italy."

15. *Sommario di statistiche storiche dell'Italia, 1861–1975*. Rome: Istituto Centrale di Statistica, 1976, 34f.

16. Franzia, *Dall'Arcadia in America*, 69.

17. Quoted in Margariti, *America! America!*, 5.

18. La Sorte, *Images of Italian Greenhorn Experience*, 195. Rolle, *The Italian Americans*, 29. Friedman, "Beyond 'Voting with Their Feet': Toward a Conceptual History of 'America' in European Migrant Sending Communities, 1860s to 1914," 562.

19. Franzina, *L'immaginario degli emigranti*, 30 sq, 81.

20. Tacitus, *On Britain and Germany*, 102.

21. Pocock, *Barbarism and Religion*, vol. 4, 12.

22. Elliott, *The Old World and the New*, 104.

23. Botta, *Pensieri politici*, 12.

24. Ibid.

25. Cattaneo, "Ricerche economiche sulle interdizioni imposte dalla legge civile agli israeliti," *Scritti economici*, vol. 1, 178–342, 182.

26. Giuseppe Ferrari produced an important edition of Vico's writings, and in 1839 he published in Paris his study *Vico et l'Italie*, reviewed by Cattaneo for his journal *Politecnico*.

27. On Cattaneo's understanding of Vico, see Cattaneo, "Ideologia," *Scritti filosofici*, vol. 2, 279–379, 307f.

28. Mali, *The Rehabilitation of Myth*, 78ff.

29. Peruta, *Cattaneo politico*, 10.

30. Mali, *The Rehabilitation of Myth*, 82.

31. Vico, *The New Science of Giambattista Vico*, 424.

32. Pocock, *Barbarism and Religion*, vol. 1, 2, 6.

33. Cattaneo, "Dell'evo antico" (1840), *Scritti storici e geografici*, vol. 1, 125–87, 187. Cattaneo's mentioning of shepherds and ruins can be read as a reference to the "shepherd barbarian" of Edward Gibbon and William Robertson. See Pocock, *Barbarism and Religion*, vol. 4, 3, 157.

BIBLIOGRAPHY

Primary Sources

ARCHIVES

Forlí, Biblioteca Comunale "Aurelio Saffi":
  Collezione Piancastelli, Autografi XIX sec., busta 151, Carlo Pepoli
Genoa, Istituto Mazziniano
London, British Library (BL):
  Miscellanee politiche genovesi, 804.k.13
  Italian tracts 1848, 1440
  Layard Papers, vol. 138
New York, New York Public Library of the Arts (NYPL):
  Walter Toscanini Collection (WTC), Libretti da Ballo (LdB)
Paris, Archives Nationales, LH/302/49 (Botta, Charles)
Southampton, University of Southampton, Hartley Library:
  Palmerston Papers, PP/GC/PE/50 Conte Carlo Pepoli
Vienna, Österreiches Staatsarchiv, Allgemeines Verwaltungsarchiv:
  Ministerium des Innern, Akten I, Landesfürstliche Behörden: Lombardei-Venetien

PERIODICALS

Antologia: Giornale di scienze, lettere e arti
L'Armonia
L'Arpa (Bologna)
Biblioteca italiana ossia Giornale di letteratura scienze ed arte
Bollettino della società antischiavista d'Italia
Brooklyn Eagle
Civiltà cattolica
Corriere mercantile
La Fama: Rassegna di scienze, lettere, arti, industria e teatri (Milan)
Gazzetta delle Romagne (*GdR*)
Gazzetta musicale di Milano (*GMM*)
Gazzetta musicale di Napoli
Gazzetta universale
Giornale di Sicilia
L'Italia musicale (Milan)
La Lega italiana: Giornale politico, economico, scientifico e letterario
La Moda
Monitore di Bologna (*MdB*)
La Nazione (Florence)
New York Times (*NYT*)
North American Review
Nuova antologia
Il nuovo ricoglitore ossia Archivi d'ogni letteratura antica e moderna
Il politecnico: Repertorio mensile di studj applicati alla prosperità e coltura sociale

Revue Indépendante

Ricoglitore italiano e straniero: Rivista mensile europea di scienze, lettere, belle arti

Rivista bolognese di scienze, lettere, arti e scuole

Il Subalpino: Giornale di scienze, lettere ed arti

Teatri, Arte, Letteratura

Il Teatro drammatico napolitano di Luigi de Lise

Il Trovatore: Giornale letterario, artistico, teatrale con illustrazioni (Turin)

L'Universo illustrato

La Voce della ragione: Giornale filosofico, teologico, politico, istorico, letterario

Printed and Published Primary Sources

Achenwall, Gottfried, *Einige Anmerkungen über Nord-Amerika und über dasige Grosbrittannische Colonien: Aus mündlichen Nachrichten des Herrn D. Franklins*. Helmstedt: Kühnlin, 1777.

Almanacco repubblicano 1872. Pubblicazione del giornale La Plebe (Enrico Bignami, ed.). Lodi: Società Cooperativo-Tipografica, 1871.

Amari, Michele, *La guerra del vespro siciliano o un periodo delle istorie siciliane* (seconda edizione, accresciuta e corretta dall' autore e corredata di nuovi documenti). 2 vols. Paris, 1843 and Florence, 1851.

Amari, Michele, *History of the War of the Sicilian Vespers*. Translated by Anne B. I. Percy. Edited, with an introduction and notes, by the Earl of Ellesmere. London: Richard Bentley, 1850.

Amari, Michele, *Un periodo delle istorie siciliane del secolo XIII*. Palermo, 1842.

Amari, Michele, "Prefazione," in Carlo Botta, *Storia della Guerra dell'Indipendenza degli Stati Uniti d'America*. Florence: Le Monnier, 1856, vol. 1, i–lxii.

The American Gazetteer Containing a Distinct Account of All the Parts of the New World. London: Millar and Tonson, 1762.

L'Amico di casa: Almanacco popolare illustrato; 1863. Turin: Stamperia dell'Unione Tipografico-Editrice, 1862.

Angeloni, Luigi, *Della forza nelle cose politiche*. London: Appresso l'autore, 1826.

Angeloni, Luigi, *Dell'Italia, uscente il settembre del 1818, Ragionamenti IV*. Paris: Apresso l'autore, 1818.

Angeloni, Luigi, *Esortazioni patrie*. London: Appresso l'autore, 1837.

L'Archivio dei Governi Provvisori di Bologna e delle Provincie Unite del 1831 (Studi e Testi, 189. Lajos Pásztor, Pietro Pirri, eds.). Città del Vaticano: Biblioteca Apostolica Vaticana, 1956.

Arioti, Antonio, *Cenno storico delle gloriose 25 giornate della rivoluzione di Palermo del 1848*. [Palermo, 1848].

Les artistes contemporaines: Adelina Patti, Fraschini, Par Léo. Paris: Montidier, 1865.

Ascher, Joseph, *Nocturne cantible [sic] sur Un ballo in maschera*. London: Ascher, [1859].

Le Assemblee del Risorgimento: Atti raccolti e pubblicati per deliberazione della Camera dei Deputati. Rome: Tipografia della Camera dei Deputati, 1911.

Auber, Daniel François Esprit, *Gustave ou Le Bal masqué*. Paroles de M. Scribe. Musique de D.F.E. Auber. Opéra historique en cinq Actes, presenté pour la première fois sur le Théâtre de l'Academie Royale de Musique le 27 Février 1833. Paris: Troupenas, 1833.

Auber, Daniel François Esprit, *Gustave III, ou Le Bal masqué*. Opéra historique en cinq actes, paroles de M. Scribe, musique de M. Auber (La France dramatique au dix-neuvième siècle, choix de Pièces Modernes). Paris: Tresse, 1847.

Auber, Daniel François, *Gustave ou Le Bal masqué*. Libretto by Eugène Scribe (Early Romantic Opera, Philip Gossett and Charles Rosen, eds.). New York: Garland, 1980.

Balbo, Cesare, *Meditazioni storiche*. Edizione seconda. Florence: Le Monnier, 1854.

Balbo, Cesare, *Della Monarchia rappresentativa in Italia, saggi politici di Cesare Balbo: Della Politica nella presente civiltà, abbozzi, del medesimo autore*. Florence: Le Monnier, 1857.

Balbo, Cesare, *Storia d'Italia e altri scritti editi e inediti*. Turin: UTET, 1984.

Balbo, Cesare, "La Vita di Cesare Balbo," in A. D'Ancona, ed., *Autobiografie*. Florence: Barbèra, 1859, 361–481.

Balsano, Paolo, *Sulla istoria moderna del Regno di Sicilia: Memorie segrete*. Palermo, [1848].

Bargani, Alessandro Luigi, *Progetto di costituzione dei Regni Uniti d'Italia offerto ai circoli politici e federativi degli Stati italiani da un cittadino degli Stati Uniti d'America*. Turin, 1848.

Basevi, Abramo, *Studio sulle opere di Giuseppe Verdi*. Florence: Tofani, 1859.

Beausobre, Louis de, *Introduzione generale allo studio della politica, delle finanze, e del commercio: Opera riveduta dall' autore, ed accresciuta e corretta in più luoghi dal traduttore*. Yverdon, 1771.

Beccaria, Cesare, *Dei delitti e delle pene: Contro le ingiustizie della giustizia* (1764). Milan: Rizzoli, 1994.

Beccaria, Cesare, *On Crimes and Punishments* (transl. Graeme R. Newman and Pietro Marongiu). New Brunswick and London: Transactions, 2009.

Beecher Stowe, Harriet, *La capanna dello zio Tomaso o la schiavitù*. Nuovissimo romanzo di Enrichetta Beecher Stowe (4 vols.). Milan: Borroni e Scotti, 1852.

Beecher Stowe, Harriet, *La capanna dello zio Tommaso ossia La vita dei negri in America*. Lugano: Chiusi, 1853.

Beecher Stowe, Harriet, *La capanna dello zio Tom: Racconto di Enrichetta Beecher Stowe; Nuova Versione*. Milan: Pagnoni, [1898].

Beecher Stowe, Harriet, *La chiave della capanna dello zio Tomaso contenente i fatti e i documenti originali sopra cui è fonadato il romanzo colle note giustificative*. Milan: Borroni e Scotti, 1853.

Beecher Stowe, Harriet, *Le père Tom, ou vie des nègres en Amérique* (trad. La Bédouillère). Geneva: Librarie Européenne, 1853.

Beecher Stowe, Harriet, *Uncle Tom's Cabin*. New York: Barnes and Noble, 2003.

Beecher Stowe, Harriet, *Uncle Tom's Cabin*, with Italian notes by John Millhouse. Milan: Millhouse, Florence: Molini, Naples: Marghieri 1853.

Bertani, Agostino, *Scritti e discorsi di Agostino Bertani* (Jessie White Mario, ed.). Florence: Barbèra, 1890.

Bertolini, Francesco, *Garibaldi e la nuova Italia*. Naples: Detken, 1882.

Bianchetti, Carlo, *L'Antischiavismo alla fine del secolo XIX*. Turin: Tipografia subalpina, 1893.

Botero, Giovanni, *Relationi universali di G. B. Divise in quattro parti*. Venice: Bertani, 1659.

Botero, Giovanni, *Relations, of the Most Famous Kingdoms and Commonweales thorough the World*. London: Iohn Iaggard, 1616.

Botta, Carlo, *De l'equilibre du pouvoir en Europe* (Carla San Mauro, ed.). Rome: Istituto Storico Italiano, 2008.

Botta, Carlo, *History of the War of Independence of the United States of America by Charles Botta*, translated from the Italian by George Alexander Otis. New Haven, CT: Brainard, 1840.

Botta, Carlo, *Pensieri politici*. Italy, 1840.

Botta, Carlo, "Proposizione ai Lombardi di una maniera di Governo Libero," in Saitta, ed., *Alle Origini del Risorgimento*, vol. 1, 3–171.

Botta, Carlo, *Storia della guerra dell'indipendenza degli Stati Uniti d'America*. Florence: Le Monnier, 1856.

Botta, Carlo, *Storia della guerra dell'indipendenza degli Stati Uniti d'America scritta da.* 4 vols. Paris: D. Colas, 1809.

Botta, Carlo, *Storia d'Italia dal 1789-1814.* Italia, 1826.

Botta, Scipione, *Vita privata di Carlo Botta: Ragguagli domestici ed aneddotici raccolti dal suo maggior figlio Scipione.* Florence: Barbèra, 1877.

Bottrigari, Enrico, *Cronaca di Bologna 1845-1871* (Aldo Berselli, ed.). Bologna: Zanichelli, 1960–63.

Brown, John, *The Northern Courts of the Sovereigns of Sweden and Denmark since 1766, Including the Extraordinary Vicissitudes in the Lives of the Grand-Children of George the Second.* Two volumes. London: Archibald Constable, 1818.

[Burke], *An Account of the European Settlements in America: In Six Parts.* London: Dodsley, 1757.

[Burke], *Storia degli stabilimenti europei in America divisa in sei parti.* Venice: Antonio Graziosi, 1763.

Caccia, Antonio, *Europa ed America: Scene della vita dal 1848 al 1850.* Monaco, 1850.

Il Caffè: 1764-1766 (Gianni Francioni and Sergio Romagnoli, eds.). Turin: Bollati Boringhieri, 1993.

Capece-Minutolo, Antonio, Principe di Canosa, *In Confutazione degli errori storici e politici da Luigi Angeloni Esposti contro Sua Maestà l'arciduchessa Maria Carolina d'Austria, defunta regina di Napoli; Epistola di un amico della verità.* Marseille, 1831.

Capellini, Giovanni, *Ricordi di un viaggio scientifico nell'America settentrionale nel 1863.* Bologna: Vitali, 1867.

Carducci, Giosuè, *Lo studio bolognese* (1888). Bologna: Clueb, 1988.

[Carli, Gianrinaldo], *Delle lettere americane.* 2 vols. [Florence]: Cosmopoli, 1780.

Carteggio Verdi-Ricordi, 1880-1881 (Pierluigi Petrobelli, ed.). Parma: Istituto di Studi Verdiani, 1988.

Carteggio Verdi-Ricordi, 1882-1885 (Franca Cella, Madina Ricordi, and Marisa di Gregorio Casati, eds.). Parma: Istituto Nazionale di Studi Verdiani, 1994.

Carteggio Verdi-Somma (Simonetta Ricciardi, ed.). Parma: Istituto Nazionale di Studi Verdiani, 2003.

Castiglioni, Luigi, *Viaggio negli Stati Uniti dell'America settentrionale fatto negli anni 1758, 1786, e 1787.* Milan: Marelli, 1790.

Cattaneo, Carlo, *Carteggi di Carlo Cattaneo.* Serie 2: Lettere dei correspondenti, vol. 1: *1820-40* (Carlo Agliati, ed). Florence: Le Monnier, 2001.

Cattaneo, Carlo, *Il 1848 in Italia.* Turin: Einaudi, 1972.

Cattaneo, Carlo, *Epistolario di Carlo Cattaneo* (Rinaldo Caddeo, ed.). Florence: Barbèra, 1952.

Cattaneo, Carlo, "Dell'insurrezione di Milano nel 1848 e della successiva guera. Memorie," in *Il 1848 in Italia,* 11–283.

Cattaneo, Carlo, "Militarismo e centralizzazione in Francia," in *Il 1848 in Italia,* 8–10.

Cattaneo, Carlo, *Scritti economici* (Alberto Bertolini, ed.). Florence: Le Monnier, 1956.

Cattaneo, Carlo, *Scritti filosofici* (Norberto Bobbio, ed.). Florence: Le Monnier, 1960.

Cattaneo, Carlo, *Scritti letterari* (Piero Treves, ed.). Florence: Le Monnier, 1981.

Cattaneo, Carlo, *Scritti storici e geografici* (Gaetano Salvemini and Ernesto Sestan, eds.). Florence: Le Monnier, 1957.

Cattaneo, Carlo, *Stati Uniti d'Italia.* Turin: Chiantore, 1945.

Cibrario, Luigi, *Della Schiavitù e del servaggio e specialmente dei servi agricoltori.* Milan: Civelli, 1868.

Cobden, Richard, *The European Diaries of Richard Cobden, 1846-1849* (Miles Taylor, ed.). Aldershot: Scholar Press, 1994.

Compagnoni, Giuseppe, *Un abate "libertino": Le "Memorie autobiografiche" e altri scritti di Giuseppe Compagnoni* (Marcello Savini, ed.). Castelmaggiore: Banca del Monte di Lugo, 1988.

Compagnoni, Giuseppe, *Cinquantotto lettere e una supplica*. Ravenna: Longo, 1996.

Compagnoni, Giuseppe, *Elementi di diritto costituzionale democratico ossia principj di giuspubblico universale*. Venice: Giustino Pasquali Qu. Mario, 1797.

Compagnoni, Giuseppe, *Lettere varie (1776–1832)* (Marcello Savini, ed.) Ravenna: Longo, 2001.

Compagnoni, Giuseppe, "Prospetto politico dell'anno 1790," *Notizie del Mondo* (1791), in Berengo, ed., *Giornali veneziani del settecento*, vol. 5, 519–47.

Compagnoni, Giuseppe, *Saggio sugli Ebrei, e sui Greci*. Venice: Giacomo Storti, 1792.

Compagnoni, Giuseppe, *Storia dell'America in continuazione del "Compendio della storia universale" del sig. Conte di Segur: Opera originale italiana*. Milan: Fusi, Stella, 1820–23.

[Compagnoni, Giuseppe], *Storia universale antica e moderna del Conte di Ségur e i suoi continuatori*. Storia Moderna, vol. 84 (*Storia dell'America*, vol. 1). Naples: Iride, 1842.

Condorcet, Jean-Antoine-Nicolas Caritat Marquis de, *Political Writings* (Steven Lukes and Nadia Urbinati, eds.). Cambridge: Cambridge University Press, 2012.

Constant, Benjamin, *Comento sulla Scienza della Legislazione*. See: Filangieri, Gaetano, *La Scienza della Legislazione*/Constant, Benjamin, *Comento sulla Scienza della Legislazione* (Vittorio Frosini, ed.). Rome: Istituto Poligrafico e Zecca dello Stato, 1984.

Cooper, James Fenimore, *Gleanings in Europe: Italy* (1838). Albany: State University of New York Press, 1981.

Cooper, James Fenimore, *The Last of the Mohicans: A Narrative of 1757 by the Author of The Spy*. London: J. Miller, 1826.

Cooper, James Fenimore, *The Pathfinder*. Paris: Galignani, 1840.

Cooper, James Fenimore, *La spia: Romanzo storico relativo ai tempi della guerra americana*. Livorno: Sardi e Bertani, 1828.

Cooper, James Fenimore, *The Spy: A Tale of the Neutral Ground*, with the portrait of the author. Leipzig, B. Tauchnitz, 1842.

Cooper, James Fenimore, *L'ultimo dei Mohicani: Romanzo storico relativo ai tempi delle guerre americane*. Livorno: Vignozzi, 1828.

Costituzione di Sicilia stabilita nel generale parlamento del 1812. Palermo: Gaudiano, 1848.

Dandolo, Tullio, *Il settentrione dell'Europa e dell'America nel secolo passato sin 1789: L'Inghilterra e l'America*. Milan: Boniardi-Pogliani, 1853.

Da Ponte, Lorenzo, *Memorie di Lorenzo da Ponte da Ceneda in tre volumi scritti da esso* (2nd. ampl. ed.). New York: Gray and Bunce, 1829–30.

Da Ponte, Lorenzo, *Memoirs*. New York: New York Review of Books, 2000.

Degubernatis, Angelo, *Santorre di Santa Rosa*. Turin: Unione Tipografico-Editrice, 1860.

De la Croix [Delacroix], Jacques-Vincent, *Constitutions des principaux états de l'Europe et des États-Unis de l'Amérique*. Paris: Buisson, 1791.

Dionisotti, Carlo, *Vita di Carlo Botta*. Turin: Favale, 1867.

D'Ondes Reggio, Vito, *Contro il sig. Visconte D'Arlincourt*. Turin: Voix de l'Italie, 1850.

Engels, Friedrich, "Das Auftreten Mazzinis gegen die Internationale," *Il Libero pensiero*, 31 August 1871, in *Marx-Engels-Werke*, vol. 17, Berlin: Dietz, 1962, 390–92.

Ferrari, Giuseppe *Filosofia della rivoluzione*. London, 1851.

Ferrari, Giuseppe, *Scritti politici* (Ernesto Sestan, ed.). Turin: Einaudi, 1977.

Filangieri, Gaetano, *La scienza della legislazion*/Constant, Benjamin, *Comento sulla scienza della legislazione* (Vittorio Frosini, ed.). Rome: Istituto Poligrafico e Zecca dello Stato, 1984.

Florilegio di eloquenza italiana. Vol. 1. Pistoia: Cino, 1839.

Die Folgen der Verschwörung von Plombiers: Oder Enthüllungen der hinterlistigen Anschläge unserer Feinde zum Raubanfalle gegen Oesterreich in Italien und Ungarn,—und einige sehr interessante Blicke in die Vergangenheit, Gegenwart und Zukunft. Vienna: Mechitaristen-Buchhandlung, 1861.

Foscolo, Ugo, *Edizione nazionale delle opere di Ugo Foscolo.* Vol. 8: *Prose politiche e letterarie dal 1811 al 1816* (Luigi, Fassò, ed.). Florence: Le Monnier, 1933.

Foscolo, Ugo, *Edizione nazionale delle opere di Ugo Foscolo.* Vol. 13: *Prose politiche e apologetiche, 1817–1827* (Giovanni Gambarin, ed.). Florence: Le Monnier, 1964.

Foscolo, Ugo, *Lettere scritte dall'Inghilterra (Gazzettino del bel mondo)* (Edoardo Sanguineti, ed.). Milan: Mursia, 1978.

Galanti, Giacinto, *La voce della verita' in sostegno della causa pubblica.* Naples, 1848.

Ganci, Massimo, ed., *Storia antologica dell'autonomia siciliana.* Palermo: Flaccovio, 1980.

Garibaldi, Giuseppe, *Memorie autobiografiche.* Florence: Barbèra, 1888.

Il Gazzettiere americano (Silvia Di Batte, ed.). Livorno: Debatte Editore, 2003.

Il Gazzettiere americano contenente un distinto ragguaglio di tutte le parti del Nuovo Mondo. 3 vols. Livorno: Marco Coltellini, 1763.

Genovesi, Antonio, *Scritti* (Franco Venturi, ed.). Turin: Einaudi, 1977.

Gianni, Francesco Maria, *Scritti di pubblica economia storico-economici e storico-politici del senatore Francesco Maria Gianni.* Florence: Luigi Niccolai, 1848.

Gioberti, Vincenzo, *Del primato morale e civile degli italiani.* Brussels: Meline, Cans, 1843.

Gioberti, Vincenzo, *Del rinnovamento civile d'Italia.* Paris and Turin: Giuseppe Bocca, 1851.

Gioberti, Vincenzo, *Scritti scelti di Vincenzo Gioberti* (Augusto Guzzo, ed.). Turin: UTET, 1974.

Gioberti, Vincenzo, *Sull'unione del Lombardo-Veneto col Piemonte.* Genoa: Frugoni, 1848.

Goethe, Johann Wolfgang von, *Goethes Werke in zwölf Bänden* (Bibliothek Deutscher Klassiker). Berlin and Weimar: Aufbau, 1988.

Grassi, Giovanni Antonio, *Notizie varie sullo stato presente della Repubblica degli Stati Uniti dell'America settentrionale.* Rome: Salvioni, 1818.

Grimaldi, Domenico, *Saggio di economia campestre per la Calabria ultra.* Naples: Orsini, 1770.

Guerrazzi, Francesco Domenico, "Parole di F.D. Guerrazzi lette sopra il campo di battaglia della Cavinana nella festa del 10 ottobre 1847," in *Un serto all'Italia ossia Raccolta dei migliori discorsi politici composti dalle piu valenti penne italiane.* Livorno: [Antonelli?], 1849, 5–10.

Guizot, François, *Du Gouvernement représentatif et de l'état actuel de la France.* Paris: Maradan, 1816.

Guizot, François, *The History of the Origins of Representative Government in Europe* (transl. Andrew R. Scoble. Introduction and Notes by Aurelian Craiutu). Indianapolis: Liberty Fund, 2002.

Guizot, François Pierre Guillaume, *Democracy in Modern Communities.* London: C. and H. Senior, 1838.

Hamilton, George, *Gli uomini ed i costumi agli Stati-Uniti d'America.* Prima versione italiana di Luigi Ferreri. Milan: Pirotta, 1835.

Der Kriegsschauplatz in Italien in drei Karten, nebst einer Uebersicht der Lage und Größe jeden Staates, der Staatsverfassung (etc.). Pest/Wien: Hartleben,1859.

La Farina, Giuseppe, *Storia della Rivoluzione siciliana e delle sue relazioni coi governi italiani e stranieri 1848–49.* Milan: Brigola, 1860.

Lassalle, Ferdinand, *Der italienische Krieg und die Aufgabe Preußens.* Berlin: Duncker, 1859.

Leopardi, Giacomo, *Zibaldone: The Notebooks of Leopardi* (Michael Caesar and Franco D'Intino, eds.). London: Penguin, 2013.

Londonio, Carlo Giuseppe, *Storia delle colonie inglesi in America dalla loro fondazione, fino allo stabilmento della loro indipendenza*. Milan: Destefanis, 1812–13.

Luther, Jörg, ed., *Documenti costituzionali di Italia e Malta, 1787–1850*. Parte 2 (Constitutions of the World, Horst Dippel, ed.). Berlin and New York: De Gruyter, 2010.

Macchi, Mauro, *Le armi e le idee*. Turin: Tip. Subalpina, 1855.

Mac Farlane, Charles, *Sicily: Her Constitutions, and Viscount Palmerston's Sicilian Blue-Book*. London: Smith, 1849.

Maistre, Joseph de, *The Works of Joseph de Maistre* (Jack Lively, ed.) London: Allen and Unwin, 1965.

Mario, Alberto, *La Repubblica e l'ideale: Antologia degli scritti* (Pier Luigi Bagatin, ed.) Lendinara: Tipografia Litografia Lendinarese, 1984.

Mario, Alberto, *Scritti politici di Alberto Mario* (Giosue Carducci, ed.). Vol. 1. Bologna: Zanichelli, 1901.

Martinelli, Vincenzo, *Storia del governo d'Inghilterra e delle sue colonie*. London, 1776.

Mazzei, Filippo, *Recherches historiques et politiques sur les États-Unis de l'Amérique Septentrionale . . . par un citoyen de Virginie*. Paris: Froullé, 1788.

Mazzei, Philip, *Researches on the United States*. Translated and edited by Constance D. Sherman. Charlottesville: University Press of Virginia, 1976.

Mazzini, Giuseppe, *A Cosmopolitanism of Nations: Giuseppe Mazzini's Writings on Democracy, Nation Building, and International Relations* (Stefano Recchia and Nadia Urbinati, eds.). Princeton, NJ, and Oxford: Princeton University Press, 2009.

Mazzini, Giuseppe, *Edizione nazionale: Scritti editi ed inediti di Giuseppe Mazzini* (Mario Menghini, ed.), vols. 1–106. Imola: Galeati, 1906–43.

Mazzini, Giuseppe, *Scritti editi ed inediti di Giuseppe Mazzini: Edizione diretta dall'autore*. Milan: Daelli, 1863.

Mazzoleni, Angelo, *Giuseppe Ferrari: I suoi tempi e le sue opere*. Milan: TEI, 1877.

[Mercadante, Saverio], *Il Reggente: Tragedia lirica in tre atti da rappresentarsi nel Teatro Nuovo di padova per la fiera del Santo 1843*. Padua: Penada [1843].

Mill, John Stuart, "Considerations on Representative Government," in *Three Essays*. Oxford: Oxford University Press, 1975, 389–401.

Minghetti, Marco, *Discorsi parlamentari di Marco Minghetti, raccolti e pubblicati per deliberazione della camera dei deputati*. Rome: Fibreno, 1888.

Minghetti, Marco, *Miei ricordi*. Turin: L. Roux, 1888–90.

Minghetti, Marco, *I partiti politici e la ingerenza loro nella giustizia e nell'amministrazione*. Bologna: Zanichelli, 1881.

Minghetti, Marco, *Scritti politici* (Raffaella Gherardi, ed.). Rome: Presidenza del Consiglio dei Ministri, 1986.

Minghetti, Marco, *Scritti vari, raccolti e pubblicati da Alberto Dallolio*. Bologna: Zanichelli, 1896.

Minolfi, Filippo, *Intorno ai giornali e alla odierna culura siciliana*. Palermo: Meli, 1837.

Montanelli, Giuseppe, *Dello ordinamento nazionale*. Florence: Tip. Garibaldi, 1862.

Montanelli, Giuseppe, *L'impero, il papato e la democrazia in Italia: Studio politico*. Florence: Le Monnier, 1859.

Montanelli, Giuseppe, *Introduzione ad alcuni appunti storici sulla rivoluzione d'Italia*. Turin: Tip. Subalpina, 1851.

Montanelli, Giuseppe, *Lettere inedite*. Florence: Rivista europea [estratto dalla], [1875].

Montanelli, Giuseppe, *Memorie sull'Italia e specialmente sulla Toscana dal 1814 al 1850*. Turin: Società Editrice Italiana, 1853.

Montanelli, Giuseppe, *Opere politiche, 1847–1862* (Paolo Bagnoli, ed.). 3 vols. Florence: Polistampa, 1998.

Moro, Gaetano, *Reconocimiento del istmo de Tehuantepec con el objeto de una comuni-cación océanica*. London: Ackermann, 1844.

Nencioni, Enrico, *Saggi critici di letteratura inglese*. Florence, 1897.

Nuova enciclopedia popolare. Turin: Giuseppe Pomba, 1841.

Palermo e l'esercito regio o i 24 giorni di guerra dal 12 gennaio al 4 febbraro 1848: Relazione storica. [Palermo, 1848?].

Pavesio, Paolo, *Carlo Botta e le sue opere storiche*. Florence: Tipografia dell'Associazione, 1874.

Pisacane, Carlo, *Guerra combattuta in Italia negli anni 1848–49: Narrazione*. Genoa: Pavesi Editore, 1851.

Pisacane, Carlo, *Saggi storici-politici-militari sull'Italia: Terzo saggio; La rivoluzione*. Genoa: Stabilmento Tipografico Nazionale, 1858.

Pecchio, Giuseppe, *Osservazioni semi-serie di un esule sull'Inghilterra*. Lugano: Ruggia, 1831.

Pecchio, Giuseppe, *Scritti politici* (Paolo Bernadelli, ed.). Rome: Istituto per la Storia del Risorgimento Italiano, 1978.

Pepe, Guglielmo, *Memoirs: Comprising the Principal Military and Political Events of Modern Italy*. London: Bentley, 1846.

La politica estera dell'Italia negli atti, documenti e discussioni parlamentari dal 1861 al 1914 (Giacomo Petricone, ed.). Rome: Grafica editrice romana, 1971.

Pougin, Arturo, *Giuseppe Verdi: Vita anneddotica*. Milan: Ricordi, 1881.

Programma: Una proposizione qualunque da svilupparsi. [Palermo, 1848].

Ranza, Giovanni Antonio, "Soluzione del Quesito proposto dall'amministrazione generale della Lombardia: Quale dei governi liberi meglio convenga alla felicità dell'Italia?," in Saitta, ed., *Alle origini del Risorgimento*, vol. 2, 181–99.

Regaldi, Giuseppe, *Canti*. Turin: Franco, 1858.

Raynal, Guillaume-Thomas, *Histoire philosophique et politique des établissements et du commerce des Européens dans les deux Indes*. Geneva: Pellet, 1780.

Raynal, Guillaume Thomas François, *The Revolution of America*. London: Lockyer Davis, 1781.

Robertson, Guglielmo, *Ricerche storiche sull'India antica: Con note, supplementi ed illust-razioni di Gian Domenico Romagnosi* (1827). Florence: Piatti, 1835.

Robertson, William, *The History of America*. Dublin: Whitestone, etc., 1777.

Romagnosi, Gian Domenico, *Opere* (Alessandro de Giorgi, ed.). Milan: Perelli e Mariani, 1848.

Romagnosi, Giandomenico, *La scienza delle costituzioni*. Bastia: Canfari, 1848.

Romagnosi, Giandomenico, *Scritti filosofici* (Sergio Moravia, ed.). Milan: Ceschina, 1974.

Rosmini, Antonio, *Delle cinque piaghe della Santa Chiesa* (A. Valle, ed., *Opere edite ed inedite di Antonio Rosmini*, vol. 56), Rome: Città Nuova Editrice, 1998.

Rosmini, Antonio, *Filosofia della politica* (Mario d'Addio, ed. Opere edite ed inedite di Antonio Rosmini, 33). Rome: Città Nuova, 1997.

Rosmini-Serbati, Antonio, *La Costituzione secondo la giustizia sociale con un appendice sull'unità d'Italia*. Naples: C. Batelli, 1848.

Rossi, Pellegrino, *Cours d'économie politique*, 4th ed. Paris: Guillaumin, 1865.

Rossi, Pellegrino, *Cours de droit constitutionnel*. Paris, Guillaumin, 1866.

Rossi, Pellegrino, *Traité de droit pénal*. 3rd ed. (Faustin Hélie, ed.). Paris: Guillaumin, 1863.

Rota, Giuseppe, *I bianchi ed i negri*. Azione storica-allegorica in tre quadri e sette scene del coreografo Giuseppe Rota. Riprodotta dal Coreografo Ferdinando Pratesi nel Regio Teatro della Scala nell'autunno 1863. Milan: Luigi di Giacomo Pirola, [1863].

Rota, Giuseppe, *Bianchi e negri*. Azione coreografica di G. Rota. Musica di Paolo Giorza ed altri autori. Milan: F. Lucca, [1853].

Rota, Giuseppe, *Bianchi e neri* [Libro da ballo] (music by Paolo Giorza). Milan: Teatro alla Scala, 1853.

Roux-Fernand, Hippolyte, *Storia dei progressi dell'incivilmento in Europa*. Venice: Tomasso Fontana, 1843.

Rummel, Joseph, *Fantasia on airs in Verdi's opera Un ballo in maschera*. London: Rummel, [1859].

Saffi, Aurelio, *Ricordi e scritti di Aurelio Saffi* (Municipio di Forlì, ed.). Florence: Barbèra, 1902.

Saitta, Armando, ed., *Alle origini del Risorgimento: I testi di un celebre concorso*. Rome: Istituto Storico Italiano, 1964.

Santa Rosa [Santarosa], Santorre di, *Memorie e lettere inedite con appendice di Gian Carlo Sismondi* (Nicomedc Bianchi, ed.). Turin: Bocca, 1877.

Santa Rosa [Santarosa], Santorre di, *Ricordi 1818-1824 (Torino, Svizzera, Parigi, Londra)*. Florence: Olschki, 1998.

Savary des Brûlons, Jacques, *Dizionario di commercio, accresciuto di vari importantissimi articoli, tratti dall'enciclopedia e dalle memorie dell'accuratissimo Mr. Carcin, ecc. ed. prima italiana*. Venice: G. Pasquale, 1770-71.

Schiller, Friedrich, *La Congiura del Fiesco: Tragedia di Federico Schiller; traduzione del Cavaliere Andrea Maffei*. Milan: Pirola, 1853.

Schiller, Friedrich, *Sämtliche Werke*. Munich: Deutscher Taschenbuch Verlag, 2004.

Schlegel, August Wilhelm von, *Vorlesungen über dramatische Kunst und Literatur*. Bonn and Leipzig: Schroeder, 1923.

Ségur, Louis-Philippe Comte de, *Abrégé de l'histoire universelle, ancienne et moderne à l'usage de la jeunesse*. 15 vols. Paris: Eymery, 1817-19.

Ségur, Louis-Philippe Comte de, *Procès-verbal de la cérémonie du sacre et du couronnement de LL MM l'Empereur Napoléon et l'Impératrice Joséphine*. Paris: Imprimerie Impériale, 1805.

Un serto all'Italia ossia Raccolta dei migliori discorsi politici composti dalle piu valenti penne italiane. Livorno: [Antonelli?], 1849.

[Settembrini, Luigi], *Protesta del popolo delle Due Sicilie*. [Naples, 1847?].

Simonde de Sismondi, Jean Charles Léonard, *Études sur les constitutions des peuples libres*. Paris: Treutetel et Würtz, 1836.

Smith, Adam, *The Theory of Moral Sentiments* (D. D. Raphael and A. L. Macfie, eds.). Oxford: Clarendon, 1976.

Somma, Antonio, *Cassandra. Tragedia*. Venice: Cecchini, 1859.

Somma, Antonio, *Opere scelte di Antonio Somma* (Alessandro Pascolato, ed.). Venice: Antonelli, 1868.

Somma, Gaetano, *La Sicilia e il resto d'Italia*. Palermo, 1848.

Sommario di statistiche storiche dell'Italia, 1861-1975. Rome: Istituto Centrale di Statistica, 1976.

Splitz, Franco, *Rivista generale de'libri usciti in luce nel Regno Lombardo nell'anno scolastico 1826*. Milan: Torchj D'Omobono Manini, 1827.

Stendhal (Henri Beyle), *La Chartreuse de Parme*. Paris: Hetzel, 1846.

Sterbini, Pietro, *Ultimi avvenimenti di Roma*. [Rome, 1848].

Strafforello, Gustavo, *Letteratura americana* (Manuali Hoepli). Milan: Hoepli, 1884.

Tacitus, Publius Cornelius, *On Britain and Germany* (transl. H. Mattingly). London: Penguin, 1951.

Tocqueville, Alexis de, *De la démocratie en Amérique*. Paris: Vrin, 1990

Todeschi, Claudio, *Saggi di agricoltura, manifatture, e commercio, coll'applicazione di essi al vantaggio del dominio pontificio*. Rome: Stamperia di A. Casaletti, 1770.

Tuveri, Giovanni Battista, *Sofismi politici*. Naples: Rinaldi e Sellitto, 1883.

Ventura, Gioacchino, *La questione Sicula nel 1848 sciolta nel vero interesse della Sicilia, di Napoli e dell'Italia*. Rome: Zampi, 1848.

Verdi, Giuseppe, *Un ballo in maschera*. Melodramma in tre atti. Libretto di Antonio Somma. Partitura (nuova edizione riveduta e corretta). Milan: Ricordi, 1966.

Verdi, Giuseppe, *Un ballo in maschera: Melodramma tragico in tre atti*. Riduzione per canto e pianoforte di Luigi ed Alessandro Truzzi. Milan: Ricordi, [1860].

Verdi, Giuseppe, *Un ballo in maschera: Pezzi per canto, con accompto di pianoforte*. Paris: Léon Escudier, [1859].

Verdi, Giuseppe, *Carteggio*. See *Carteggio*.

Verdi, Giuseppe, *I copialettere di Giuseppe Verdi* (Gaetano Cesari and Alessandro Luzio, eds.). Milan: Stucchi Ceretti, 1913.

Verdi, Giuseppe, *Favourite airs from Verdi's opera Un ballo in maschera arranged for the piano as a duet with ad lib: Accompt. for flute*. London: William H. Hallcott, [1859].

Verdi, Giuseppe, *Le lettere genovesi* (Roberto Iovino and Raffaella Ponte, eds., Quaderni dell'Istituto nazionale di studi verdiani 7). Parma: Istituto di studi verdiani, 2013.

Verdi, Giuseppe, *Re Lear e Ballo in maschera: Lettere di Giuseppe Verdi ad Antonio Somma* (Alessandro Pascolato, ed.). Città di Castello: Lapi, 1913.

Verdi's Otello and Simon Boccanegra in Letters and Documents (Hans Busch, ed.). Oxford: Clarendon, 1988.

Vico, Giambattista, *The New Science of Giambattista Vico*. Unabridged Translation of the Third Edition (1744) with the addition of "Practice of the New Science" (transl. Thomas Goddard Bergin and Max Harold Fisch). Ithaca, NY, and London: Cornell University Press, 1948/1968.

Virgil, [Publius Vergilius Maro], *Eclogues. Georgics. Aeneid 1-6 and 7-12* (Loeb Classical Library. Transl. H. Rushton Fairclough, rev. ed. G. P. Goold). 2 vols. Cambridge, MA: Harvard University Press, 1999/2001.

Virgil, [Publius Vergilius Maro], *The Eclogues* (Latin text with a verse translation and brief notes by Guy Lee). London: Penguin, 1984.

White Mario, Jessie, *The Birth of Modern Italy* (Posthumous Papers of Jessie White Mario, edited by the Duke Litta-Visconti-Arese). London: T. Fisher Unwin, 1909.

White Mario, Jessie, *Garibaldi e i suoi tempi*. Milan: Treves, 1884.

Secondary Sources

Ajello, Raffaele, et al., eds., *Il Teatro di San Carlo*. Naples: Guida, 1988.

Albertone, Manuela, and de Francesco, Antonino, eds., *Rethinking the Atlantic World: Europe and America in the Age of Revolutions*. London: Palgrave Macmillan, 2009.

Albertoni, Ettore A., *La vita degli stati e l'incivilmento dei popoli nel pensiero politico di Gian Domenico Romagnosi*. Milan: Giuffrè, 1979.

Aliberti, Giovanni, "Cesare Balbo: Il federalismo," in de Rosa and Traniello, ed., *Cesare Balbo alle origini del Cattolicesimo liberale*, 135–53.

Alpers, Svetlana and Baxandall, Michael, *Tiepolo and the Pictorial Intelligence*. New Haven, CT, and London: Yale University Press, 1994.

Antonelli, Sara, "'E questo che fa la mia America': Il giornalismo di Margaret Fuller," in Antonelli, Fiorentino, and Monsagrati, eds., *Gli Americani e la Repubblica Romana*, 131–58.

Antonelli, Sara, Fiorentino, Daniele, and Monsagrati, Giuseppe, eds., *Gli americani e la Repubblica Romana del 1849*. Rome: Gangemi, 2000.

Apt, Leon, *Louis-Philippe de Ségur: An intellectual in a revolutionary age*. The Hague: Martinus Nijhoff, 1969.

Arena, Valentina, *Libertas and the Practice of Politics in the Late Roman Republic*. Cambridge: Cambridge University Press, 2012.

Armani, Giuseppe, *Carlo Cattaneo: Il padre del federalismo italiano*. Milan: Garzanti, 1997.

Armitage, David, *The Declaration of Independence: A Global History*. Cambridge, MA: Harvard University Press, 2007.

Armitage, David, *Foundations of Modern Political Thought*. Cambridge: Cambridge University Press, 2013.

Armitage, David, and Subrahmanyam, Sanjay, eds., *The Age of Revolutions in Global Context, c. 1760–1840*. London: Palgrave Macmillan, 2010.

Armitage, David, and Subrahmanyam, Sanjay, "Introduction: The Age of Revolutions, c. 1760–1840—Global Causation, Connection, and Comparison," in Armitage and Subrahmanyam, eds., *The Age of Revolutions in Global Context*, xii–xxxii.

Arneil, Morag Barbara, *John Locke and the American Indian*. PhD diss., University College London, 1992.

Atti del I Congresso Internazionale di Storia Americana: Italia e Stati Uniti dall'indipendenza americana ad oggi (1776/1976). Genoa: Tilgher, 1978.

Au, Susan, "Augusta Maywood," in *International Encyclopedia of Dance*, vol. 4, 338–39.

Aymard, Maurice, and Giarrizzo, Giuseppe, eds., *La Sicilia (Storia d'Italia. Le regioni dall'Unità a oggi)*. Turin: Einaudi, 1987.

Bacchin, Elena, "Felice Orsini and the Construction of the Pro-Italian Narrative in Britain," in Carter, ed., *Britain, Ireland and the Italian Risorgimento*, 80–103.

Badinter, Elisabeth, and Badinter, Robert, *Condorcet: Un intellectuel en politique*. Paris: Fayard, 1988.

Bagnoli, Paolo, *Democrazia e stato nel pensiero politico di Giuseppe Montanelli*. Florence: Olschki, 1989.

Bagnoli, Paolo, ed., *Giuseppe Montanelli: Unità e democrazia nel Risorgimento*. Florence: Olschki, 1990.

Bagnoli, Paolo, *L'Idea dell'Italia*. Reggio Emilia: Diabas, 2007.

Bagnoli, Paolo, *La politica delle idee: Giovan Pietro Vieusseux e Giuseppe Montanelli nella Toscana preunitaria*. Florence: EPF, 1995.

Bagnoli, Paolo, "Lo statuto del granducato di Toscana," in Livorsi, ed., *Libertà e stato nel 1848-49*, 293–304.

Baker, Paul R., *The Fortunate Pilgrims: Americans in Italy*. Cambridge, MA: Harvard University Press, 1964.

Balsamo, Luigi, "Gli ebrei nell'editoria e nel commercio librario in Italia nel '600 e '700," in *Italia Judaica: Gli ebrei in Italia dalla segregazione alla prima emancipazione; Atti del III Convegno internazionale*, 49–65.

Balthazar, Scott L., ed., *The Cambridge Companion to Verdi*. Cambridge: Cambridge University Press, 2004.

Balzano, Marco, *I confini del sole: Leopardi e il Nuovo Mondo*. Venice: Marsilio, 2008.

Bannister, Jerry, and Riordan, Liam, eds., *The Loyal Atlantic: Remaking the British Atlantic in the Revolutionary Era*. Toronto; Buffalo, NY; London: University of Toronto Press, 2012.

Banti, Alberto M., *La nazione del Risorgimento: Parentela, santità e onore alle origini dell'Italia unita*. Turin: Einaudi, 2000.

Banti, Alberto M., *L'onore della nazione: Identità sessuali e violenza nel nazionalismo europeo dal XVIII secolo alla Grande Guerra*. Turin: Einaudi, 2005.

Banti, Alberto M., *Il Risorgimento italiano*. Rome and Bari: Laterza, 2004.

Banti, Alberto M., "Sacrality and the Aesthetics of Politics: Mazzini's Concept of the Nation," in Bayly and Biagini, eds., *Giuseppe Mazzini and the Globalisation of Democratic Nationalism*, 59–74.

Banti Alberto M., et al., eds., *Atlante culturale del Risorgimento: Lessico del linguaggio politico dal settecento all'Unità*. Rome and Bari: Laterza, 2011.

Banti Alberto M., and Ginsborg, Paul, eds., *Storia d'Italia*. Annali 22: *Il Risorgimento*. Turin, Einaudi, 2007.

Barbiera, Raffaello, *La principessa Belgiojoso: I suoi amici—il suo tempo*. Milan: Treves, 1902.

Barsanti, Danilo, "Giuseppe Montanelli 'idolo della scolaresca pisana,'" in Rogari, ed., *Giuseppe Montanelli fra storia e storiografia a 150 anni della scomparsa*, 60–80.

Bartlett, Rosamund, *Tolstoy: A Russian Life*. London: Profile, 2010.

Barton, H. Arnold, *Scandinavia in the Revolutionary Era, 1760–1815*. Minneapolis: University of Minnesota Press, 1986.

Basso, Alberto, *Storia del Teatro Regio di Torino*. Vol. 2: *Il teatro della città*. Turin: Cassa di Risparmio, 1976.

Bayly, Christopher A., *The Birth of the Modern World*. Oxford: Blackwell, 2004.

Bayly, Christopher A., and Biagini, Eugenio F., eds., *Giuseppe Mazzini and the Globalisation of Democratic Nationalism 1830–1920* (Proceedings of the British Academy, 152). Oxford: Oxford University Press, 2008.

Beales, Derek, *Joseph II*. Vol. 2. Cambridge: Cambridge University Press, 2009.

Beales, Derek, and Biagini, Eugenio F., *The Risorgimento and the Unification of Italy*. Harlow: Pearson, 2002.

Beghelli, Marco, ed., *L'equivoco stravagante* (I libretti di Rossini, 20). Pesaro: Fondazione Rossini, 2014.

Belfiglio, Valentino J., "Italians and the American Civil War," *Italian Americana*, 4, 2 (Spring/Summer 1978), 163–75.

Bender, Thomas, *A Nation among Nations: America's Place in World History*. New York: Hill and Wang, 2006.

Ben-Ghiat, Ruth, and Fuller, Mia, eds., *Italian Colonialism*. New York: Palgrave Macmillan, 2005.

Benigne Gagneraux: Un pittore francese nella Roma di Pio VI (Accademia di Francia a Roma, ed.). Rome: De Luca, 1983.

Bennett, Herman, *Colonial Blackness: A History of Afro-Mexico*. Bloomington: Indiana University Press, 2009.

Benvenuto, Paolo, "L'Italia di Giuseppe Montanelli: Cattolicesimo, democrazia e repubblica," *Rassegna storica toscana*, 7 (2011), 173–200.

Benvenuto, Paolo, "The Suicide of Power and the Birth of Democracy: Buonarrotti, Mazzini and Montanelli," in Lenci and Calabrò, eds., *Democracy and Risorgimento*, 173–87.

Berger, Karol, *Bach's Cycle, Mozart's Arrow: An Essay on the Origins of Musical Modernity*. Berkeley: University of California Press, 2007.

Berengo, Marino, ed., *Giornali veneziani del settecento*, Milan: Feltrinelli, 1962.

Berengo, Marino, "Introduzione," in Berengo, ed., *Giornali veneziani del settecento*, vol. 5, ix–lxiv.

Berengo, Marino, "Le origini del Lombardo-Veneto," *Rivista storica italiana*, 83 (1971), 524–44.

Bergamini, Giovanni, "*Spoliis Orientis onustus*. Paul-Emile Botta et la découverte de la civilisation assyrienne," in Fontan, ed., *De Khorsabad à Paris*, 68–85.

Berger, Stefan, Donovan, Mark, and Passmore, Kevin, eds., *Writing National Histories: Western Europe since 1800*. London: Routledge, 1999.

Bernadello, Adolfo, *La prima ferrovia fra Venezia e Milano: Storia della imperial-regia privilegiata strada ferrata Ferdinandea Lombardo-Veneta (1835–1852)*. Venice: Istituto veneto di scienze, lettere ed arti, 1996.

Bernstein, R. B., *Thomas Jefferson*. New York and Oxford: Oxford University Press, 2003.

Berselli, Aldo, "Primi decenni dopo l'Unità," in Berselli, *Storia della Emilia Romagna*, vol. 3, 257–304.

Berselli, Aldo, ed. *Storia della Emilia Romagna*. Imola: Santerno, 1976–80.

Berthold, Dennis, *American Risorgimento: Herman Melville and the Cultural Politics of Italy*. Columbus: Ohio State University Press, 2009.

Berti, Francesco, "Modello brittanico, modello americano e antidispotismo," in Trampus, ed., *Diritti e costituzione*, 19–60.

Berti, Giuseppe, "Socialismo utopistico in Sicilia prima del'48," in *La Sicilia e l'unità d'Italia*, vol. 2, 349–56.

Beschin, Giuseppe, and Cristellon, Luca, eds., *Rosmini e Gioberti: Pensatori europei*. Brescia: Morcelliana, 2003.

Bessler, Karl, *The Birth of American Law: An Italian Philosopher and the American Revolution*. Durham, NC: Carolina Academic Press, 2014.

Bevilacqua, Piero, de Clementi, Andreina, and Franzina, Emilio, eds., *Storia dell'emigrazione italiana*. Vol. 1: *Partenze*. Rome: Donzelli, 2001.

Biagini, Eugenio F., "Citizenship and Religion in the Italian Constitutions, 1789–1849," *History of European Ideas*, 37, 2 (2011), 211–17.

Biagini, Eugenio F., "Mazzini and Anticlericalism: The English in Exile," in Bayly and Biagini, eds., *Giuseppe Mazzini and the Globalisation of Democratic Nationalism 1830–1920*, 145–66.

Bianconi, Lorenzo, and Pestelli, Giorgio, eds., *Storia dell'opera italiana*, 1988.

Billias, George Athan, ed., *American Constitutionalism Abroad: Selected Essays in Comparative Constitutional History*. New York: Greenwood, 1990.

Billias, George Athan, "American Constitutionalism and Europe, 1776–1848," in Billias, ed., *American Constitutionalism Abroad*, 13–39.

Binney, Edwin, "Sixty Years of Italian Dance Prints," *Dance Perspectives* 53, Spring 1973, 8–60.

Birdoff, Harry, *The World's Greatest Hit: Uncle Tom's Cabin*. New York: Vanni, 1947.

Bitterli, Urs, *Die "Wilden" und die "Zivilisierten": Grundzüge einer Geistes- und Kulturgeschichte der europäisch-überseeischen Begegnung*. München: Beck, 1976.

Bizzocchi, Roberto, "Una nuova morale per la donna e la famiglia," in Banti and Ginsborg, eds., *Storia d'Italia*, 69–96.

Bobbio, Norberto, "G. B. Tuveri nel primo centenario della morte," in *G. B. Tuveri e i suoi tempi*, 25–44.

Bobbio, Norberto, "Introduzione," in Cattaneo, *Stati Uniti d'Italia*, 7–126.

Bonazzi, Tiziano, "La nazione americana negli anni del primo Risorgimento," in Antonelli, Fiorentino, and Monsagrati, eds., *Gli americani e la Repubblica Romana*, 11–20.

Bonazzi, Tiziano, "Tradurre/Tradire: The Declaration of Independence in the Italian Context," *Journal of American History*, 85, 4 (March 1999), 1350–61.

Boni, Giacomo, "Studi danteschi in America," *Rivista d'Italia*, 1, 6 (June 1898), 292–316.

Boritt, Gabor S., Neely Jr., Mark E., and Holzer, Harold, "The European Image of Abraham Lincoln," *Winterthur Portfolio*, 21, 2/3 (Summer–Autumn 1986), 153–83.

Borré, Matteo, *Un rivoluzionario durante l'antico regime: Jacques-Vincent Delacroix (1766–1789)*. PhD diss., Università degli Studi di Milano, 2012–13.

Bottari, Salvatore, "Fuori e dentro la storia: Percorsi storiografici sulla Sicilia moderna prima e dopo Romeo," in Bottari, ed., *Rosario Romeo e Il Risorgimento in Sicilia*, 25–115.

Bottari, Salvatore, ed., *Rosario Romeo e Il Risorgimento in Sicilia: Bilancio storiografico e prospettive di ricerca*. Soveria Mannelli: Rubbettino, 2002.

Botto, Evandro, *Modernità in questione: Studi su Rosmini*. Milan: Franco Angeli, 1999.

Bourke, Richard, *Empire and Revolution: The Political Life of Edmund Burke*. Princeton, NJ, and Woodstock: Princeton University Press, 2015.

Bourne, Ella, "The Messianic Prophecy in Vergil's *Fourth Eclogue*," *Classical Journal*, 11, 7 (April 1916), 390–400.

Bracewell, Wendy, and Drace-Francis, Alex, eds., *Under Eastern Eyes: A Comparative Introduction to East European Travel Writing on Europe*. Budapest: Central European University Press, 2008.

Brading, David *The First America*. Cambridge: Cambridge University Press, 1993.

Brancato, Francesco, "Il concetto di autonomia nella storiografia siciliana," in *La Sicilia e l'unità d'Italia: Atti del Congresso Internazionale di Studi Storici sul Risorgimento italiano*, vol. 2, 512–22.

Breccia, Alessandro, "Dalla 'pubblica opinione' alla 'opinione democratica': Note su Giuseppe Montanelli giornalista," in Rogari, ed., *Giuseppe Montanelli fra storia e storiografia a 150 anni della scomparsa*, 169–95.

Brock, W. R., *An American Crisis: Congress and Reconstruction, 1865–1867*. London: Macmillan, 1963.

Bruch, Anne, *Italien auf dem Weg zum Nationalstaat: Giuseppe Ferraris Vorstellungen einer föderal-demokratischen Ordnung*. Hamburg: Krämer, 2005.

Bruch, Anne, "Munizipale Identität und bürgerliche Kultur im Risorgimento: Die Bedeutung der Stadt für Carlo Cattaneos föderal-demokratische Konzeption," *Jahrbuch zur Liberalismus-Forschung*, 22 (2010), 165–79.

Brunner, Otto, Conze, Werner, and Koselleck, Reinhart, eds., *Geschichtliche Grundbegriffe: Historisches Lexikon zur politisch-sozialen Sprache in Deutschland*. Stuttgart: Klett-Cotta, 1984.

Buccini, Stefania, *The Americas in Italian Literature and Culture: 1700–1825*. Philadelphia: Pennsylvania State University Press, 1997.

Budden, Julian, *The Operas of Verdi*. Vol. 2. Oxford: Clarendon, 1992.

Buonomo, Leonardo, *Backward Glances: Exploring Italy, Reinterpreting America (1831–1866)*. Teaneck: Fairleigh Dickinson University Press, 1996.

Burk, Kathleen, *Old World, New World: The Story of Britain and America*. London: Little, Brown, 2007.

Burrow, John, *A History of Histories: Epics, Chronicles, Romances and Inquiries from Herodotus and Thucydides to the Twentieth Century*. London: Penguin, 2009.

Butkas Ertz, Matilda Ann, *Nineteenth-Century Italian Ballet Music before National Unification: Sources, Style, and Context*. PhD diss., University of Oregon, 2010.

Buttà, Giuseppe, "Carlo Botta's History of the War of Independence of the United States of America," in Noether, ed., *The American Constitution*, 68–79.

Caesar, James W., *Reconstructing America: The Symbol of America in Modern Thought*. New Haven, CT, and London: Yale University Press, 1997.

Caffiero, Marina, *Storia degli ebrei nell'Italia moderna: Dal Rinascimento alla Restaurazione*. Rome: Carocci, 2014.

Calloway, Colin, *The American Revolution in Indian Country: Crisis and Diversity in Native American Communities*. Cambridge: Cambridge University Press, 1995.

Calore, Marina, *Bologna a teatro: L'Ottocento*. Bologna: Giudicini e Rosa, 1982.

Cammarano, Fulvio, *Storia politica dell'Italia liberale, 1861–1901*. Rome: Laterza, 2004.

Campanini, Giorgio, and Traniello, Francesco, eds., *Filosofia e politica: Rosmini e la cultura della restaurazione*. Brescia: Morcelliana, 1993.

Candeloro, Giorgio, *Storia dell'Italia moderna*, Milan: Feltrinelli, 1956–86.

Canfora, Luciano, and Cardinale, Ugo, eds., *Il giacobino pentito: Carlo Botta fra Napoleone e Washington*. Rome and Bari: Laterza, 2010.

Canizares-Esguerra, Jorge, *How to Write the History of the New World*. Stanford, CA: Stanford University Press, 2000.

Capra, Carlo, "Nobiltà/Borghesia," in Banti et al., eds., *Atlante culturale*, 134–48.

Capra, Marco, *Verdi in prima pagina: Nascita, sviluppo e affermazione della figura di Verdi nella stampa italiana dal XIX al XXI secolo*. Lucca: Libreria musicale italiana, 2014.

Cardinale, Ugo, "Botta, un giacobino dalle vedute atlantiche," in Canfora and Cardinale, eds., *Il giacobino pentito*, 21–29.

Carlini, Antonio, ed., *Fuori dal teatro: Modi e percorsi della divulgazione di Verdi*. Venice: Marsilio, 2015.

Carter, Nick, ed., *Britain, Ireland and the Italian Risorgimento*. New York: Palgrave Macmillan, 2015.

Casini, Paolo, *L'antica sapienza italica: Cronistoria di un mito*. Bologna: il Mulino, 1998.

Cassani, Emanuele, *Italiani nella guerra civile americana, 1861–1865*. Civitavecchia: Prospettivaeditrice, 2006.

Cassina, Cristina, "Opening 'a New Path': Notes on the Constitutional Project of Antonio Rosmini," in Lenci and Calabrò, eds., *Democracy and Risorgimento*, 135–50.

Castronovo, Valerio, and Tranfaglia, Nicola, eds., *Storia della stampa italiana*. Rome: Laterza, 1979.

Celi, Claudia, "Giuseppe Rota," in *International Encyclopedia of Dance*, vol. 5, 408–9.

Certeau, Michel de, *L'écriture de l'histoire*. Paris: Gallimard, 1975.

Cetrangolo, Aníbal E., *Ópera, barcos y banderas: El melodrama y la migración en Argentina (1880–1920)*. Madrid: Biblioteca nueva, 2015.

Chadwick, Owen, *The Popes and European Revolution*. Oxford: Clarendon, 1981.

Charlton, David, ed., *The Cambridge Companion to Grand Opéra*. Cambridge: Cambridge University Press, 2003.

Cherubini, Donatella, "Giuseppe Montanelli e gli altri docenti pisani e senesi dall'Antologia," in Rogari, ed., *Giuseppe Montanelli fra storia e storiografia a 150 anni della scomparsa*, 97–112.

Chiapelli, Fred, ed., *First Images of America: The Impact of the New World on the Old*. Berkeley: University of California Press, 1976.

Chiavistelli, Antonio, *Dallo stato alla nazione: Costituzione e sfera pubblica in Toscana dal 1814 al 1849*. Rome: Carocci, 2006.

Chiavistelli, Antonio, "Rappresentanza," in Banti et al., eds., *Atlante culturale*, 341–58.

Chickering, Roger, "Introduction: A Tale of Two Tales; Grand Narratives of War in the Age of Revolution," in Chickering and Stig Förster, eds., *War in an Age of Revolution*, 1–17.

Chickering, Roger, and Förster, Stig, eds., *War in an Age of Revolution, 1775–1815*. New York: Cambridge University Press, 2010.

Chorley, Patrick, *Oil, Silk and Enlightenment: Economic Problems in XVIIIth-Century Naples*. Naples: Istituto Italiano per gli Studi Storici in Napoli, 1965.

Chusid, Martin, ed., *Verdi's Middle Period, 1849–1859: Source Studies, Analysis, and Performance Practice*. Chicago: University of Chicago Press, 1997.

Ciampini, Raffaele, *Gian Pietro Vieusseux: I suoi viaggi, i suoi giornali, i suoi amici*. Turin: Einaudi, 1953.

Cingari, Gaetano, *Mezzogiorno e Risorgimento: La restaurazione a Napoli dal 1821 al 1830*. Bari: Laterza, 1970.

Clarke, Mary, and Vaughan, David, eds., *The Encyclopedia of Dance and Ballet*. London: Pitman, 1977.

Clemens, Gabriele B., *Sanctus amor patriae: Eine vergleichende Studie zu deutschen und italienischen Geschichtsvereinen im 19. Jahrhundert*. Tübingen: Niemeyer, 2004.

Clemens, Gabriele B., "Torino e il Piemonte visti dalla Prussia," in Leva, ed., *Il Piemonte alle soglie del 1848*, 623–41.

Cohen, Selma Jeanne, "Feme di Gelosia! Italian Ballet Librettos, 1766–1865," in *Bulletin of the New York Public Library*, 67 (November 1963), 555–64.

Colombo, Paolo, "Una corona per una nazione: Considerazioni sul ruolo della monarchia costituzionale nella costruzione dell'identità italiana," in Tesoro, ed., *Monarchia, tradizione, identità nazionale*, 21–33.

Colombo, Paolo, "Monarchia/Repubblica," in Banti et al., eds., *Atlante culturale*, 315–29.

Colucci, Lauretta, "Carlo Cattaneo e il Regno Lombardo-Veneto," in Livorsi, ed., *Libertà e stato nel 1848–49*, 199–210.

Conati, Marcello, *Interviews and Encounters with Verdi*. London: Gollancz, 1984.

Connell, William J., "Darker Aspects of Italian American Prehistory," in Connell and Gardaphé, eds., *Anti-Italianism*, 11–22.

Connell, William J., and Gardaphé, Fred, eds., *Anti-Italianism: Essays on a Prejudice*. New York: Palgrave Macmillan, 2010.

Conti, Fulvio, *L'Italia dei democratici: Sinistra risorgimentale, massoneria e associazionismo fra Otto e Novecento*. Milan: Angeli, 2000.

Contu, Gianfranco, *G. B. Tuveri: Vita e opere*. Cagliari: Editrice democratica sarda, 1973.

Conway, Stephen, "Bentham versus Pitt: Jeremy Bentham and British Foreign Policy 1789," *Historical Journal*, 30, 4 (1987), 791–809.

Conway, Stephen, *Britain, Ireland, and Continental Europe in the Eighteenth Century: Similarities, Connections, Identities*. Oxford: Oxford University Press, 2011.

Conway, Stephen, *The War of American Independence, 1775–1783*. London: Arnold, 1995.

Conway, Stephen, *War, State And Society in Mid-Eighteenth-Century Britain and Ireland*. Oxford: Oxford University Press, 2006.

Coppini, Romano Paolo, "Giuseppe Montanelli e il Risorgimento," in Rogari, ed., *Giuseppe Montanelli fra storia e storiografia a 150 anni della scomparsa*, 17–29.

Coppini, Romano Paolo, *Il Granducato di Toscana: Dagli "anni francesi" all'Unità (Storia d'Italia*, Giuseppe Galasso, ed., vol. 13, 3). Turin: UTET, 1993.

Corti, Paola, and Sanfilippo, Matteo, eds., *Storia d'Italia*. Annali 24: *Migrazioni*. Turin: Einaudi, 2009.

Craiutu, Aurelian, *Liberalism under Siege: The Political Thought of the French Doctrinaires*. Lanham: Lexington Books, 2003.

Craiutu, Aurelian, and Isaacs, Jeff, eds., *America through European Eyes*. Philadelphia: Pennsylvania State University Press, 2009.

Criscuolo, Vittorio, *Albori di democrazia nell'Italia in rivoluzione (1792–1802)*. Milan: Franco Angeli, 2006.

Croce, Benedetto, *History of Europe in the Nineteenth Century*. London: Allen and Unwin, 1934.

Croce, Benedetto, *Teoria e storia della storiografia* (1915). Milan: Adelphi, 2001.

Curnis, Michele, "Varianti d'autore e vicende editoriali della *Storia della guerra dell'indipendenza degli Stati Uniti d'America*," in Canfora and Cardinale, eds., *Il giacobino pentito*, 158–68.

Czaika, Ingrid, *Gustav III und Verdis Maskenball*. Vienna and Berlin: Lit, 2008.

D'Addio, Mario, "Progetti costituzionali di Antonio Rosmini," in Livorsi, ed., *Libertà e stato nel 1848–49*, 89–117.

Dahlhaus, Carl, "Drammaturgia dell'opera italiana," in Bianconi and Pestelli, eds., *Storia dell'opera italiana*, vol. 6, 77–162.

dal Lago, Enrico *The Age of Lincoln and Cavour: Comparative Perspectives on Nineteenth-Century American and Italian Nation-Building*. New York: Palgrave, 2015.

dal Lago, Enrico, "Radicalism and Nationalism: Northern 'Liberators' and Southern Labourers in the USA and Italy, 1830–60," in dal Lago and Halpern, eds., *The American South and the Italian Mezzogiorno*, 197–214.

dal Lago, Enrico, *William Lloyd Garrison and Giuseppe Mazzini: Abolition, Democracy and Radical Reform*. Baton Rouge: Lousiana State University, 2013.

dal Lago, Enrico, and Rick Halpern, eds., *The American South and the Italian Mezzogiorno: Essays in Comparative History*. Basingstoke: Palgrave, 2002.

dall'Osso, Claudia, *Voglia d'America: Il mito americano in Italia tra otto e novecento*. Rome: Donizelli, 2007.

D'Amico, Fedele, "Il ballo in maschera prima di Verdi," *Bollettino quadrimestrale dell'Istituto di studi verdiani*, 1, 3 (1960), 1251–328.

Darnton, Robert, *The Business of Enlightenment: A Publishing History of the Encyclopédie*. Cambridge, MA: Harvard University Press, 1979.

Darnton, Robert, *George Washington's False Teeth: An Unconventional Guide to the Eighteenth Century*. New York: Norton, 2003.

Davis, David Brion, *The Problem of Slavery in Western Culture* (1966). New York and Oxford: Oxford University Press, 1988.

Davis, John A., "Italy," in Goldstein, ed., *The Frightful Stage*, 190–227.

Davis, John A., ed., *Italy in the Nineteenth Century, 1796–1900* (Short Oxford History of Italy). Oxford: Oxford University Press, 2000.

Davis, John A., "A Missing Encounter: Rosario Romeo's Place in International Historiography," in Bottari, ed., *Rosario Romeo e Il Risorgimento in Sicilia: Bilancio storiografico e prospettive di ricerca*, 15–24.

Davis, John A., *Naples and Napoleon: Southern Italy and the European Revolutions (1780–1860)*. Oxford: Oxford University Press, 2006.

Davis, John A., "Opera and Absolutism in Restoration Italy, 1815–1860," *Journal of Interdisciplinary History*, 36, 4 (2006), 569–94.

Davis, John A., "The Spanish Constitution of 1812 and the Mediterranean Revolutions (1820–1825)," *Bulletin for Spanish and Portuguese Historical Studies*, 37, 2 (2012), http://digitalcommons.asphs.net/bsphs/vol37/iss2/7.

de Angelis, Marcello, *Le carte dell'impresario: Melodrama e costume teatrale nell'ottocento*. Florence: Sassoni, 1982.

Deconde, Alexander, "Historians, the War of American Independence, and the Persistence of the Exceptionalist Ideal," *International History Review*, 5, 3 (August 1983), 399–430.

de Francesco, Antonio, "Ideologie e movimenti politici," in Sabbatucci and Vidotto, eds., *Storia d'Italia*, vol. 1, 229–336.

della Peruta, Franco, *Carlo Cattaneo politico*. Milan: Franco Angeli, 2001.

della Peruta, Franco, *Milano nel Risorgimento: Dall'età napoleonica alle cinque giornate*. Milan: Edizioni Comune di Milano, 1998.

della Seta, Fabrizio, "Gli esordi della critica Verdiana: A proposito di Alberto Mazzucato," in Döhring and Osthoff, eds., *Verdi-Studien: Pierluigi Petrobelli zum 60. Geburtstag*, 59–74.

della Seta, Fabrizio, *Italia e Francia nell'ottocento* (*Storia della musica*, vol. 9). Turin: EDT, 1993.

della Seta, Fabrizio, "New Currents in the Libretto," in Balthazar, ed., *The Cambridge Companion to Verdi*, 69–87.

della Seta, Fabrizio, *Not without Madness: Perspectives on Opera*. Chicago and London: University of Chicago Press, 2013.

del Vivo, Caterina, ed., *In esilio e sulla scena: Lettere di Lauretta Cipriani Parra e Adelaide Ristori*. Florence: Florence University Press, 2014.

de Martino, Ernesto, *Il mondo magico: Prolegomeni a una storia del magismo* (1948). Turin: Boringhieri, 1967.

de Pascale, Carla, *Filosofia e politica nel pensiero italiano fra sette e ottocento: Francesco Mario Pagano e Gian Domenico Romagnosi*. Naples: Guida, 2007.

de Rosa, Gabriele, "Introduzione: Cesare Balbo e il cattolicesimo liberale," in de Rosa and Traniello, eds., *Cesare Balbo alle origini del cattolicesimo liberale*, 3–12.

de Rosa, Gabriele, and Traniello, Francesco, eds., *Cesare Balbo alle origini del cattolicesimo liberale*. Rome: Laterza, 1996.

Deschamps, Bénédict, "Dal fiele al miele: La stampa esule italiana di New York e il Regno di Sardegna (1849–1861)," *Annali della Fondazione Luigi Einaudi*, 42 (2008), 82–98.

Dipper, Christof, "Die Mailänder Aufklärung und der Reformstaat: Ein Beitrag zur Berichtigung der Urteile des Publikums über das Verhältnis der politischen Theorie zum administrativen Handeln," in Jung and Kroll, eds., *Italien in Europa*, 15–36.

Dipper, Christof, "Revolutionäre Bewegungen auf dem Lande: Deutschland, Frankreich, Italien," in Dowe, Haupt, and Langewiesche, eds., *Europa 1848*, 555–85.

di Stefano, Carlo, *La censura teatrale in Italia*. Rocca San Casciano: Cappelli, 1964.

Döhring Sieghart, and Osthoff, Wolfgang, eds., *Verdi-Studien: Pierluigi Petrobelli zum 60. Geburtstag*. Munich: Ricordi, 2000.

Dorigny, Marcel, "The Question of Slavery in the Physiocratic Texts: A Rereading of an Old Debate," in Albertone and de Francesco, eds., *Rethinking the Atlantic World*, 147–62.

Dossi, Michele, *Antonio Rosmini: Ein philosophisches Profil*. Stuttgart: Kohlhammer, 2003.

Dowe, Dieter, Haupt, Heinz-Gerhard, and Langewiesche, Dieter, eds., *Europa 1848: Revolution und Reform*. Bonn: Dietz, 1998.

Doyle, Don H., *The Cause of all Nations: An International History of the American Civil War*. New York: Basic Books, 2015.

Doyle, Don H., *Nations Divided: America, Italy, and the Southern Question*. Athens: University of Georgia Press, 2002.

Drake, Richard, *Byzantium for Rome: The Politics of Nostalgia in Umbertian Italy, 1878–1900*. Chapell Hill: University of North Carolina Press, 1980.

Draper, Nicholas, *The Price of Emancipation: Slave-Ownership, Compensation and British Society at the End of Slavery*. Cambridge: Cambridge University Press, 2010.

Drehle, David von, "The Way We Weren't: North and South Shared the Burden of Slavery, and after the War, They Shared Forgetting about It; But 150 Years Later, It's Time to Tell the Truth," *Time*, 18 April, 2011, 40–51.

Ducci, Lucia, Luconi, Stefano, and Pretelli, Matteo, *Le relazioni tra Italia e Stati Uniti: Dal Risorgimento alle conseguenze dell'11 settembre*. Rome: Carocci, 2012.

Duggan, Christopher, *The Force of Destiny: A History of Italy since 1796*. London: Allen Lane, 2007.

Duggan, Christopher, "Giuseppe Mazzini in Britain and Italy: Divergent Legacies, 1837–1915," in Bayly and Biagini, eds., *Giuseppe Mazzini*, 187–207.

Dwan, David, and Insole, Christopher J., eds., *The Cambridge Companion to Edmund Burke*. Cambridge: Cambridge University Press, 2012.

Eames, Marian, *When All the World Was Dancing: Rare and Curious Books from the Cia Fornaroli Collection*. New York: New York Public Library, 1957.

Earle, Rebecca, *The Return of the Native: Indians and Myth-Making in Spanish America, 1810–1930*. Durham, NC, and London: Duke University Press, 2007.

Eichner, Hans, *"Romantic" and Its Cognates: The European History of a Word*. Manchester: Manchester University Press, 1972.

Elliott, John H., *The Old World and the New, 1492–1650*. Cambridge: Cambridge University Press, 1970.

Etges, Andreas, ed., *Europa trifft Amerika: Vergleichende und transnationale Perspektiven.* Berlin: Lit, 2008.

Everett, Barbara, "Love or Money: What Isn't in 'The Merry Wives of Windsor,'" in *Times Literary Supplement*, no. 5742 (19 April 2013), 13–15.

Falzone, Gaetano, *Il problema della Sicilia nel 1848 attraverso nuove fonti inedite: Indipendenza e autonomia nel giuoco della politica internazionale.* Palermo: Priulla, 1951.

Falzone, Gaetano, *La Sicilia nella politica mediterranea delle grandi potenze: Indipendenza o autonomia nei documenti inediti del Quai d'Orsay.* Palermo: Flaccovio, 1974.

Fauser, Annegret, and Everist, Mark, eds., *Music, Theatre, and Cultural Transfer.* Chicago and London: University of Chicago Press, 2009.

Fellheimer, Jeannette, "Michele Leoni's Venezia Salvata, the First Italian Translation of Otway's Tragedy," *Italica*, 22, 1 (March 1945), 1–13.

Feola, Raffaele, "Costituzione e Parlamento a Napoli in 1848," in Livorsi, ed., *Libertà e Stato nel 1848-49*, 141–78.

Fernández Armesto, Felipe, *The Americas: The History of a Hemisphere.* London: Weidenfeld and Nicolson, 2003.

Ferris, Kate, "A Model Republic," in Körner et al., eds., *America Imagined*, 51–79.

Ferris, Kate, *Imagining "America" in Late Nineteenth-Century Spain.* London: Palgrave, 2016.

Fisher, Herbert A. L., *The Republican Tradition in Europe.* London: Methuen, 1911.

Finelli, Pietro, "'È divenuto un Dio': Santità, patria e rivoluzione nel culto di Mazzini (1872–1905)," in Banti and Ginsborg, eds., *Storia d'Italia*, 665–95.

Finley, Moses I., Mack Smith, Denis, and Duggan, Christopher, *A History of Sicily.* London: Chatto and Windus, 1986.

Fiorentino, Daniele, "Il dibattito su Botta e la *Storia della guerra dell'indipendenza* tra Italia e Stati Uniti nel XIX secolo," in Canfora and Cardinale, eds., *Il giacobino pentito*, 169–76.

Fiorentino, Daniele, "Il governo degli Stati Uniti e la Repubblica Romana del 1849," in Antonelli, Fiorentino, Monsagrati, eds., *Gli americani e la Repubblica Romana del 1849*, 89–130.

Fiorentino, Daniele, *Gli Stati Uniti e il Risorgimento d'Italia, 1848-1901.* Rome: Gangemi, 2013.

Fiorentino, Daniele, "La politica estera degli Stati Uniti e l'unità d'Italia," in Fiorentino and Sanfilippo, eds., *Gli Stati Uniti e l'unità d'Italia*, 45–81.

Fiorentino, Daniele, and Sanfilippo, Matteo, eds., *Gli Stati Uniti e l'unità d'Italia.* Rome: Gangemi, 2004.

Fiume, Giovanna, *La Crisi sociale del 1848 in Sicilia.* Messina: Sfameni, 1982.

Fluck, Winfried, "Die deutsche Kultur als Prüfstein amerikanischer Demokratie: Ferdinand Kürnbergers Roman *Der Amerika-Müde*," in Etges, ed., *Europa trifft Amerika*, 12–46.

Fohlen, Claude, *Benjamin Franklin: L'Américain des Lumières.* Paris: Payot, 2000.

Fontan, Elisabeth, ed., *De Khorsabad à Paris: La découverte des Assyiriens.* Paris: Réunion des musées nationaux, 1994.

Francesco Ferrara e il suo tempo. Atti del congresso, Palermo 27–30 ottobre 1988 (Pier Francesco Asso, Piero Barucci, and Massimo Ganci, eds.). Palermo: Bancaria Editrice, 1990.

Francia, Enrico, "Il pane e la politica: Moti annonari e opinione pubblica in Toscana alla vigilia del 1848," *Passato e Presente*, 17, 46 (1999), 129–55.

Francovich, Carlo, "La rivoluzione americana e il progetto di costituzione del Granduca Pietro Leopoldo," *Rassegna storica del Risorgimento*, 41, 2/3 (April/September 1954), 371–77.

Franzina, Emilio, "L'America," in Isnenghi, ed., *I luoghi della memoria: Simboli e miti dell'Italia unita*, 329–60.

Franzina, Emilio, *Dall'Arcadia in America: Attività letteraria ed emigrazione transoceanica in Italia*. Turin: Fondazione Agnelli, 1996.

Franzina, Emilio, *L'immaginario degli emigranti: Miti e raffigurazioni dell'esperienza italiana all'estero fra due secoli*. Paese: PAGUS, 1992.

Freeden, Michael, and Stears, Marc, "Liberalism," in Freeden, Michael, Tower Sargent, Lyman, and Stears, Marc, *The Oxford Handbook of Political Ideologies*. Oxford: Oxford University Press, 2013, 329–47.

Friedman, Max Paul, "Beyond 'Voting with Their Feet': Toward a Conceptual History of 'America' in European Migrant Sending Communities, 1860s to 1914," *Journal of Social History* 40, 3 (Spring 2007), 557–75.

Frosini, Vittorio, "Introduzone," in Filangieri, *La Scienza della Legislazione*/Constant, *Comento sulla Scienza della Legislazione* (Vittorio Frosini, ed.), vol. 1, vii–xxiv.

Fubini Leuzzi, Maria, "Introduzione," in Balbo, *Storia d'Italia e altri scritti editi e inediti*, 9–66.

Gabaccia, Donna R., *Foreign Relations: American Immigration in Global Perspective*. Princeton, NJ: Princeton University Press, 2012.

Gadamer, Hans-Georg, *Wahrheit und Methode*. Tübingen, 1960.

Galante Garrone, Alessandro, *L'Albero della libertà: Dai giacobini a Garibaldi*. Florence: Le Monnier, 1987.

Galante Garrone, Alessandro, "L'emigrazione politica italiana del Risorgimento," *Rassegna storica del Risorgimento*, 41, 2/3 (April/September 1954), 223–42.

Galante Garrone, Alessandro, "I giornali della Restaurazione 1815–1847," in Castronovo and Tranfaglia, eds., *Storia della stampa italiana*, vol. 2, 1–246.

Galante Garrone, Alessandro, *I radicali in Italia (1849–1925)*. Milan: Garzanti, 1973.

Galante Garrone, Alessandro, *La stampa periodica italiana dal 1815 al 1847: Corso di storia del Risorgimento*. Turin: Giappichelli, 1976.

Galasso, Giuseppe, "Cattaneo interprete della storia d'Italia," in Colombo, della Peruta, and Lacaito, eds., *Carlo Cattaneo*, 457–68.

Galasso, Giuseppe, *Da Mazzini a Salvemini: Il pensiero democratico nell'Italia moderna*. Florence: Le Monnier, 1974.

Galasso, Giuseppe, *Il regno di Napoli: Il mezzogiorno borbonico e risorgimentale (1815–1860)* (*Storia d'Italia*, Giuseppe Galasso, ed., vol. 15, 5). Turin: Utet, 2007.

Ganci, Massimo, ed., *Storia antologica dell'autonomia siciliana*. Palermo: Flaccovio, 1980.

Garosci, Aldo, *Antonio Gallenga: Vita avventurioso di un emigrato dell'ottocento*. Turin: Centro Studi Piemontesi, 1979.

Gatti, Carlo, *Il Teatro alla Scala nella storia e nell'arte (1778–1963)*. Milan: Ricordi, 1964.

G. B. Tuveri e i suoi tempi (Archivio Sardo del Movimento Operaio contadino e autonomistico, ed.). Cagliari: Editrice Sardegna, 1979.

Gemme, Paola, *Domesticating Foreign Struggles: The Italian Risorgimento and Antebellum American Identity*. Athens and London: University of Georgia Press, 2005.

Gennaro Lerda, Valeria, "La schiavitù e la guerra civile nelle pagine della *Civiltà cattolica*," in Spini et al., eds., *Italia e America*, 233–50.

Gentile, Emilio, *La Grande Italia: Ascesa e declino del mito della nazione nel ventesimo secolo*. Milan: Mondadori, 1997.

Gerbi, Antonello, *The Dispute of the New World: The History of a Polemic, 1750–1900* (1955). Pittsburgh: University of Pittsburgh Press, 1973.

Gerhard, Anselm, "Liebesduette in flagranti. *Suspense* und *pacing* in der Oper des 19. Jahrhunderts" in Mungen, ed., *Mitten im Leben*, 51–81.

Gerhard, Anselm, *The Urbanization of Opera: Music Theater in Paris in the Nineteenth Century*. Chicago and London: University of Chicago Press, 1998.

Gerhard, Anselm, "Verdi, Hiller und Schiller in Köln—Ein unbeachtetes Albumblatt und die Frage möglicher Beziehungen zwischen 'Die Verschwörung des Fiesko zu Genua' und 'Simon Boccanegra,'" *VerdiPerspektiven*, 1 (2016), 65–91.

Gerhard, Anselm, "Vergil in Nordamerika. Höllensprache und Kassandra-Rufe in Sommas Libretto für Verdi," *Programmheft Un ballo in maschera*. Cologne: Oper Köln, 2007, 13–20.

Gerhard, Anselm, and Schweikert, Uwe, eds., *Verdi Handbuch* (2nd ed.). Stuttgart: Metzler, 2013.

Gerste, Ronald D., *Der Zauberkönig: Gustav III und Schwedens Goldene Zeit*. Göttingen: Steidl, 1996.

Ghisalberti, Carlo, "La monarchia rappresentativa nel pensiero di Cesare Balbo," in De Rosa and Traniello, ed., *Cesare Balbo alle origini del cattolicesimo liberale*, 117–34.

Giacomelli, Alfeo, "La Bologna tardo illuministica e prerivoluzionaria di Giuseppe Compagnoni," in Medri, ed., *Giuseppe Compagnoni*, 33–83.

Gianotti, Gian Franco, "Botta, la Francia e gli Stati Uniti d'America," in Canfora and Cardinale, eds., *Il giacobino pentito*, 30–46.

Giarrizzo, Giuseppe, *Mezzogiorno senza meridionalismo: La Sicilia, lo sviluppo, il potere*. Venice: Marsiglio, 1992.

Giger, Andreas, "Social Control and the Censorship of Giuseppe Verdi's Operas in Rome (1844–1859)," *Cambridge Opera Journal*, 11, 3 (1999), 233–66.

Gili, Antonio, *Carlo Cattaneo (1801–1869): Un "italiano svizzero."* Castagnola: Casa Carlo Cattaneo, 2001.

Gilroy, Paul, *The Black Atlantic: Modernity and Double Consciousness*. Cambridge, MA: Harvard University Press, 1993.

Ginsborg, Paul, *Daniele Manin and the Venetian Revolution, 1848–49*. Cambridge: Cambridge University Press, 1979.

Ginsborg, Paul, "Romanticismo e Risorgimento: L'io, l'amore e la nazione," in Banti and Ginsborg, eds., *Storia d'Italia*, 5–67.

Giorgi, Paolo, and Erkens, Richard, eds., *Alberto Franchetti: L'uomo, il compositore, l'artista*. Lucca: Libreria musicale italiana, 2015.

Giura, Vincenzo, *Russia, Stati Uniti d'America e Regno di Napoli nell'età del Risorgimento*. Naples: Edizioni Scientifiche Italiane, 1967.

Gli Italiani negli Stati Uniti: L'emigrazione e l'opera degli italiani negli Stati Uniti d'America. Atti del III Symposium di Studi Americani, Firenze, 27–29 Maggio 1969. Florence: Istituto di Studi Americani, 1972.

Goldstein, Robert Justin, ed., *The Frightful Stage: Political Censorship of the Theatre in Nineteenth-Century Europe*. New York and Oxford: Berghahn Books, 2009.

Golini, Antonio, and Amato, Flavia, "Uno sguardo a un secolo e mezzo di emigrazione italiana," in Bevilacqua, de Clementi, and Franzina, eds., *Storia dell'emigrazione italiana*, vol. 1, 45–60.

Gossett, Philip, *Divas and Scholars: Performing Italian Opera*. Chicago University Press, 2006.

Grab, Alexander, "The Italian Enlightenment and the American Revolution," in Noether, ed., *The American Constitution*, 35–53.

Greenblatt, Stephen, *Marvelous Possessions: The Wonder of the New World*. Chicago: University of Chicago Press, 1991.

Greenfield, Kent R., *Economics and Liberalism in the Risorgimento: A Study of Nationalism in Lombardy, 1814–1848*. Baltimore: Johns Hopkins University Press, 1964.

Gregory, Desmond, *Sicily, the Insecure Base: A History of the British Occuation of Sicily, 1806–1815*. London and Toronto: Associated University Press, 1988.

Grempler, Martina, "Hauptstadt des italienischen Königreichs: Die römische Theater-landschaft vor dem Hintergrund der politischen und urbanen Veränderungen im 19. Jahrhundert," in Müller, Ther, Toelle, and zur Nieden, eds., *Die Oper im Wandel der Gesellschaft: Kulturtransfers und Netzwerke des Musiktheaters in Europa*. Vienna: Böhlau, 2010, 157–72.

Grew, Raymond, "One Nation Barely Visible: The United States as Seen by Nineteenth-Century Italy's Liberal Leaders," in Noether, ed., *The American Constitution*, 119–34.

Guccione, Eugenio, "Il costituzionalismo in Sicilia nel 1848," in Livorsi, ed., *Libertà e stato nel 1848–49*, 179–98.

Guest, Ivor, "Balli presentati tra il 1845 e il 1854," *La danza italiana*, 8–9 (Winter 1990), 17–26.

Guida, Francesco, ed., *Dalla Giovine Europa alla Grande Europa*. Rome: Carocci, 2007.

Guzzo, Augusto, "Introduzione," in Vincenzo Gioberti, *Scritti scelti di Vincenzo Gioberti*, 9–78.

Haddock, Bruce, "State and Nation in Mazzini's Political Thought," *History of Political Thought*, 20, 2 (1999), 313–36.

Hagemann, Karen, Mettele, Gisela, and Rendall, Jane, eds., *Gender, War and Politics: Trans-atlantic Perspectives, 1775–1830*. London: Palgrave Macmillan, 2010.

Hayes, Kevin J., *The Road to Monticello: The Life and Mind of Thomas Jefferson*. Oxford and New York: Oxford University Press, 2008.

Heck, Thomas F., "Toward a Bibliography of Operas on Columbus," *Notes*, 49, 2 (December 1992), 474–97.

Heck, Thomas F., "The Operatic Christopher Columbus: Three Hundred Years of Musical Mythology," *Annali d'italianistica*, 10, 1992, 236–78.

Helmberger, Werner, and Staschull, Matthias, *Tiepolo's World: The Ceiling Fresco in the Staircase Hall of the Würzburg Residence*. Munich: Bayerische Verwaltung der Staatli-chen Schlösser, 2008.

Hexter, Ralph, "Masked Balls," *Cambridge Opera Journal*, 14, 1/2 (March 2002), 93–108.

Hibberd, Sarah, "Auber's Gustave III: History as Opera," in Fauser and Everist, eds., *Music, Theatre, and Cultural Transfer*, 157–75.

Hibberd, Sarah, *French Grand Opera and the Historical Imagination*. Cambridge: Cam-bridge University Press, 2009.

Hodges, Sheila, *Lorenzo Da Ponte: The Life and Times of Mozart's Librettist*. London: Granada, 1985.

Holzer, Harold, *Lincoln President-Elect: Abraham Lincoln and the Great Secession Winter 1860–1861*. New York: Simon and Schuster, 2008.

Honour, Hugh, *The New Golden Land: European Images of America from the Discoveries to the Present Time*. London: Allen Lane, 1976.

Howard, Seymour, "An Antiquarian Handlist and Beginnings of the Pio-Clementino," *Eighteenth-Century Studies*, 7, 1 (Autumn 1973), 40–61.

Hudson, Elizabeth, "Masking Music: A Reconsideration of Light and Shade in *Un ballo in maschera*," in Chusid, ed., *Verdi's Middle Period*, 257–72.

Hufton, Olwen, *The Prospect before Her: A History of Women in Western Europe*. London: Fontana, 1997.

Hughes, H. Stuart, *The United States and Italy*. Cambridge, MA: Harvard University Press, 1979.

Hunt, Lynn, Jacob, Margaret C., and Mijnhardt, Wijnand, *The Book That Changed Europe: Picart's and Bernard's Religious Ceremonies of the World*. Cambridge, MA: Harvard University Press, 2010.

Iachello, Enrico, and Signorelli, Alfio, "Borghesie urbane dell'ottocento," in Aymard and Giarrizzo, eds., *La Sicilia*, 89–155.

Iermano, Toni, *Il giacobinismo e il Risorgimento italiano: Luigi Angeloni e la teoria della forza*. Naples: Società Editrice Napoletana, 1983.

Ignace, Anne-Claire, "Il mito di Mazzini in Francia," in Guida, ed., *Dalla Giovine Europa alla Grande Europa*, 45–56.

Infelise, Mario, "Gazzette e lettori nella Repubblica Veneta dopo l'ottantanove," in Zorzi, ed., *L'eredità dell'ottantanove e l'Italia*, 307–50.

International Encyclopedia of Dance, Oxford University Press, 1998.

Intini, Domenico, *La controversia fra Rosmini e Gioberti*. Stresa: Edizioni Rosminiane Sodalitas, 2002.

Isabella, Maurizio, "Aristocratic Liberalism and Risorgimento: Cesare Balbo and Piedmontese Political Thought after 1848," *History of European Ideas*, 39, 6 (2013), 835–57.

Isabella, Maurizio, "Liberalism and Empires in the Mediterranean: The View-Point of the Risorgimento," in Patriarca and Riall, eds., *The Risorgimento Revisited*, 232–54.

Isabella, Maurizio, "Mazzini's Internationalism in Context: From the Cosmopolitan Patriotism of the Italian Carbonari to Mazzini's Europe of the Nations," in Bayly and Biagini, eds., *Giuseppe Mazzini and the Globalisation of Democratic Nationalism 1830-1920*, 37–58.

Isabella, Maurizio, "Nationality before Liberty? Risorgimento Political Thought in Transnational Context," *Journal of Modern Italian Studies*, 17, 5 (2012), 507–15.

Isabella, Maurizio, *Risorgimento in Exile: Italian Émigrés and the Liberal International in the Post-Napoleonic Era*. Oxford: Oxford University Press, 2009.

Isnenghi, Mario, *L'Italia in piazza: I luoghi della vita pubblica dal 1848 ai giorni nostri*. Bologna: il Mulino, 2004.

Isnenghi, Mario, ed., *I luoghi della memoria: Simboli e miti dell'Italia unita*. Rome and Bari: Laterza, 1998.

Israel, Jonathan, *Democratic Enlightenment: Philosophy, Revolution, and Human Rights 1750-1790*. Oxford: Oxford University Press, 2011.

Israel, Jonathan, *Revolutionary Ideas: An intellectual History of the French Revolution from The Rights of Man to Robespierre*. London and Princeton, NJ: Princeton University Press, 2014.

Italia Judaica: Gli ebrei in Italia dalla segregazione alla prima emancipazione; Atti del III Convegno internazionale, Tel Aviv 15-20 giugno 1986. Rome: Ministero per i Beni culturali e ambientali, 1989.

Jackson, Frederick H., "Uncle Tom's Cabin in Italy," *Symposium*, 7 (1953), 323–32.

Jackson, Maurice, "Botta sulla schiavitù in America," in Canfora and Cardinale, eds., *Il giacobino pentito*, 117–21.

Jacobshagen, Arnold, "Un ballo in maschera," in Gerhard and Schweikert, eds., *Verdi Handbuch* (2nd ed.), 486–93.

Jacobshagen, Arnold, *Gioachino Rossini und seine Zeit*. Laaber: Laaber, 2015.

Jahrmärker, Manuela, "Scribe—Erfolgsautor und Reformator im Pariser Theaterleben," in Werr, ed., *Eugène Scribe und das europäische Musiktheater*, 8–19.

Jahrmärker, Manuela, *Themen, Motive und Bilder des Romantischen: Zum italienischen Musiktheater des 19. Jahrhunderts*. Berlin: LIT, 2006.

Janz, Oliver, Schiera, Pierangelo, and Siegrist, Hannes, eds., *Centralismo e federalismo tra Otto e Novecento: Italia e Germania a confronto*. Bologna: il Mulino, 1997.

Jardin, André, *Histoire du Libéralisme Politique: De la crise de l'absolutisme à la constitution de 1875*. Paris: Hachette, 1985.

Jaume, Lucien, *Tocqueville: Les sources aristocratiques de la liberté*. Paris: Fayard, 2008.

Jennings, Jeremy, *Revolution and the Republic: A History of Political Thought in France since the Eighteenth Century*. Oxford: Oxford University Press, 2010.

Johnson, Claudia L., ed., *The Cambridge Companion to Mary Wollstonecraft*. Cambridge: Cambridge University Press, 2002.

Jones, Chris, "Mary Wollstonecraft's *Vindications* and Their Political Tradition," in Johnson, ed., *The Cambridge Companion to Mary Wollstonecraft*, 42–58.

Jones, Colin, and Wahrman, Dror, eds., *The Age of Cultural Revolutions: Britain and France, 1750–1820*. Berkeley: University of California Press, 2002.

Jones, Colin, and Wahrman, Dror, "Introduction: An Age of Cultural Revolutions?," in Jones and Wahrman, eds., *The Age of Cultural Revolutions*, 1–16.

Jordan, Donaldson, and Pratt, Edwin J., *Europe and the American Civil War*. Boston and New York: Houghton Mifflin, 1931.

Jori, Alberto, and Mattei, Raffaele M., "La figura di George Washington nella *Storia della guerre dell'independenza degli Stati Uniti d'America* di Botta," in Canfora and Cardinale, eds., *Il giacobino pentito*, 141–57.

Jung, Frank, and Kroll, Thomas, eds., *Italien in Europa: Die Zirkulation der Ideen im Zeitalter der Aufklärung*. Paderborn: Fink, 2014.

Kaplan, Benjamin J., *Divided by Faith: Religious Conflict and the Practice of Toleration in Early Modern Europe*. Cambridge, MA: Harvard University Press, 2007.

Kaufman, Thomas G., *Verdi and His Major Contemporaries: A Selected Chronology of Performances and Casts*. New York: Garland, 1990.

Knott, Sarah, and Taylor, Barbara, eds., *Women, Gender and Enlightenment*. Basingstoke: Palgrave Macmillan, 2007.

Kohn, Denise, Meer, Sarah, and Todd, Emily B., "Reading Stowe as a Transatlantic Writer," in Kohn, Meer, and Todd, eds., *Transatlantic Stowe*, xi–xxxi.

Kohn, Denise, Meer, Sarah, Todd, Emily B., eds., *Transatlantic Stowe: Harriet Beecher Stowe and European Culture*. Iowa City: University of Iowa Press, 2006.

Körner, Axel, "Barbarous America," in Körner, Miller, Smith, eds., *America Imagined*, 125–59.

Körner, Axel, "Carlo Pepoli," in *Dizionario Biografico degli Italiani*. Vol. 82. Rome: Istituto della Enciclopedia Italiana, 2015, 261–66.

Körner, Axel, "Introduction," in Körner, Miller, Smith, eds., *America Imagined*, 1–18.

Körner, Axel, "Die Julirevolution von 1830: Frankreich und Europa," in Peter Wende, ed., *Grosse Revolutionen der Geschichte*. Munich: Beck, 2000, 138–57.

Körner, Axel, "Lokale und transnationale Dimensionen sakralisierter Politik. Nationale Bewegung und Zivilgesellschaft im liberalen Italien," *Historische Zeitschrift*, 300, 3 (June 2015), 698–719.

Körner, Axel, "Masked Faces: Verdi, Uncle Tom and the Unification of Italy," *Journal of Modern Italian Studies*, 18, 2 (March 2013), 176–89.

Körner, Axel, "*Music of the Future*: Italian Theatres and the European Experience of Modernity between Unification and World War One," *European History Quarterly*, 41, 2 (April 2011), 189–212.

Körner, Axel, *Politics of Culture in Liberal Italy: From Unification to Fascism*. New York: Routledge, 2009.

Körner, Axel, "The Risorgimento's Literary Canon and the Aesthetics of Reception: Some Methodological Considerations," *Nations and Nationalism*, 15, 3 (July 2009), 410–18.

Körner, Axel, "The Theatre of Social Change: Opera and Society in Bologna after Italian Unification," *Journal of Modern Italian Studies*, 8, 3 (Fall 2003), 341–69.

Körner, Axel, "Uncle Tom on the Ballet Stage: Italy's Barbarous America, 1850–1900," *Journal of Modern History*, 83, 4 (December 2011), 721–52.

Körner, Axel, Miller, Nicola, and Smith, Adam I. P., eds., *America Imagined: Explaining the United States in Nineteenth-Century Europe and Latin America*. New York: Palgrave Macmillan, 2012.

Koselleck, Reinhart, *Begriffsgeschichten: Studien zur Semantik und Pragmatik der politischen und sozialen Sprache*. Frankfurt/M.: Suhrkamp, 2006.

Kostka, Edmund, *Schiller in Italy: Schiller's Reception in Italy: 19th and 20th Centuries*. New York: Peter Lang, 1997.

Kreuzer, Gundula, *Verdi and the Germans: From Unification to the Third Reich*. Cambridge: Cambridge University Press, 2010.

Kroll, Thomas, *Die Revolte des Patriziats: Der toskanische Adelsliberalismus im Risorgimento*. Tübingen: Niemeyer, 1999.

Krückmann, Peter O., *Heaven on Earth: Tiepolo; Masterpieces of the Würzburg Years*. Munich and New York: Prestel, 1996.

Lacaita, Carlo G., Colombo, Arturo, and Della Peruta, Franco, eds., *Carlo Cattaneo: I temi e le sfide*. Milan: Casagrande, 2004.

Lacaita, Carlo G., Gobbo, Raffaella, and Turiel, Alfredo, eds., *La biblioteca di Carlo Cattaneo*. Bellinzona: Ed. Casagrande, 2003.

La Piana, Angelina, *La cultura americana e l'Italia*. Turin: Einaudi, 1938.

Laqua, Daniel, "The Tensions of Internationalism: Transnational Anti-slavery in the 1880s and 1890s," *International History Review*, 33, 4 (2011), 705–26.

Larsen, Mogens Trolle, *The Conquest of Assyria: Excavations in an Antique Land, 1840–1860*. London: Routledge, 1994.

La Sorte, Michael, *Images of Italian Greenhorn Experience*. Philadelphia: Temple University Press, 1985.

Lauster, Jörg, *Die Verzauberung der Welt: Eine Kulturgeschichte des Christentums*. Munich: Beck, 2014.

Laven, David, "The Age of Restoration," in Davis, ed., *Italy in the Nineteenth Century*, 51–73.

Laven, David, "Austria's Italian Policy Reconsidered: Revolution and Reform in Restoration Italy," *Modern Italy*, 2, 1 (1997), 3–33.

Laven, David, *Venice and Venetia under the Habsburgs: 1815–1835*. Oxford: Oxford University Press, 2002.

Laven, David, and Parker, Laura, "Foreign Rule? Transnational, National and Local Perspectives on Venice and Venetia within the 'Multinational' Empire," *Modern Italy*, 19, 1 (2014), 5–19.

Laven, David, and Riall, Lucy, eds., *Napoleon's Legacy: Problems of Government in Restoration Europe*. Oxford and New York: Berg, 2000.

Lazzarino Del Grosso, Anna Maria, "Gli Stati Uniti d'America nell'opera di Francesco Ferrara," in *Francesco Ferrara e il suo tempo*, 551–72.

Lefort, Claude, "Guizot théoricien du pouvoir," in Valensise, ed., *François Guizot et la culture politique de son temps*, 95–110.

Lenci, Mauro, "From Republic to Representative Democracy: Some Observations on the Use of the Word 'Democracy' in Italian Political Thought between 1750–1861," in Lenci and Calabrò, eds., *Democracy and Risorgimento*, 21–58.

Lenci, Mauro, and Calabrò, Carmelo, eds., *Democracy and Risorgimento*. Pisa: ETS, 2011.

Lerg, Charlotte A., *Amerika als Argument: Die deutsche Amerika-Forschung im Vormärz und ihre politische Deutung in der Revolution von 1848/49*. Bielefeld: transcript Verlag, 2011.

Leva, Umberto, ed., *Il Piemonte alle soglie del 1848*. Turin: Comitato di Torino dell'Istituto per la storia del Risorgimento italiano, 1999.

Levis Sullam, Simon, *L'apostolo a brandelli: L'eredità di Mazzini tra Risorgimento e fascismo*. Rome and Bari: Laterza, 2010.

Leydi, Roberto, "Diffusione e volgarizzazione," in Bianconi and Pestelli, eds., *Storia dell'opera italiana*, vol. 6, 301–92.

Liburdi, Enrico, "Le memorie autobiografiche di Pasqule Papiri e i suoi viaggi in America," *Rassegna storica del Risorgimento*, 41, 2/3 (April/September 1954), 391–97.

Lippmann, Friedrich, *Vincenzo Bellini und die italienische Opera Seria seiner Zeit: Studien über Libretto, Arienform und Melodik* (Analecta Musicologica. Veröffentlichungen der Musikabteilung des Deutschen Historischen Instituts in Rom, vol. 6). Köln: Böhlau, 1969.

Livingstone, Arthur, "Introduction," in Da Ponte, *Memoirs*, xv–xxxii.

Livorsi, Franco, "Libertà e stato nel 1848–49 europeo. Note e riflessioni," in Livorsi, ed., *Libertà e stato nel 1848–49*, 22–56.

Livorsi, Franco, ed., *Libertà e stato nel 1848–49: Idee politiche e costituzionali*. Milan: Giuffrè, 2001.

Lock, F. P., *Edmund Burke*. Vol. 1: *1730–84*. Oxford: Clarendon, 1998

Lo Iacono, Concetta, "Manzotti e Marenco: Il diritto di due autori," *Nuova rivista musicale Italiana*, 3 (July–September 1987), 421–46.

Lombardo, Agostino, *La ricerca del vero: Saggi sulla tradizione letteraria americana*. Rome: Edizioni di Storia e Letteratura, 1961.

Lovett, Clara M., *Giuseppe Ferrari and the Italian Revolution*. Chapel Hill: University of North Carolina Press, 1979.

Lowenthal, David, *George Perkins Marsh: Versatile Vermonter*. New York: Columbia University Press, 1958.

Lumley, Robert, and Morris, Jonathan, eds., *The New History of the Italian South: The Mezzogiorno Revisited*. Exeter: University of Exeter Press, 1997.

Luseroni, Giovanni, *Giuseppe Montanelli e il Risorgimento: La formazione e l'impegno civile e politico prima del'48*. Milan: Franco Angeli, 1996.

Luzio, Alessandro, ed., *Carteggi Verdiani: Reale Accademia d'Italia; Studi e Documenti 4*. Rome: Reale Accademia d'Italia, 1935.

Luzzatto, Sergio, *La mummia della repubblica: Storia di Mazzini imbalsamato, 1872–1946*. Milan: Rizzoli, 2001.

Lyttelton, Adrian, "The Hero and the People," in Patriarca and Riall, eds., *The Risorgimento Revisited*, 37–55.

Lyttelton, Adrian, "Sismondi, the Republic and Liberty: Between Italy and England, the City and the Nation," *Journal of Modern Italian Studies* 17, 2 (2012), 167–82.

Macartney, C. A., *The Habsburg Empire 1790–1918*. London: Weidenfeld and Nicolson, 1971.

Maciag, Dew, *Edmund Burke in America: The Contested Career of the Father of Modern Conservatism*. Ithaca, NY, and London: Cornell University Press, 2013.

Mack, Phyllis, "Religion, Feminism, and the Problem of Agency: Reflections on Eighteenth-Century Quakerism," in Knott and Taylor, eds., *Women, Gender and Enlightenment*, 434–59.

MacKay, John, "The First Years of Uncle Tom's Cabin in Russia," in Kohn, Meer, and Todd, eds., *Transatlantic Stowe*, 67–88.

MackSmith, Dennis, *Garibaldi*. London, 1957.

MackSmith, Dennis, *Italy: A Modern History*. New edition. Ann Arbor: University of Michigan Press, 1969.

MackSmith, Dennis, *Mazzini*. New Haven, CT, and London: Yale University Press, 1994

Macry, Paolo, "The Southern Metropolis. Redistributive Circuits in Nineteenth-Century Naples," in Lumley and Morris, eds., *The New History of the Italian South*, 59–82.

Madsen, Deborah, ed., *Visions of America since 1492*. London: Leicester University Press, 1994.

Maehder, Jürgen, "The Representation of the Discovery on the Opera Stage," in Robertson, ed., *Musical Repercussions of 1492*, 257–83.

Maione, Paologiovanni, and Seller, Francesca, "Cristoforo Colombo o sia la scoperta dell'America di Donizetti," *Studi Musicali*, 34, 2 (2005), 421–49.

Mali, Joseph, *The Rehabilitation of Myth: Vico's New Science*. Cambridge: Cambridge University Press, 1992.

Mancall, Peter C., *Valley of Opportunity: Economic Culture along the Upper Susquehanan, 1700–1800*. Ithaca, NY, and New York: Cornell University Press, 1991.

Mancini, Augusto, "Corrispondenti Americani del Mazzini," *Rassegna storica del Risorgimento*, 41, 2/3 (April/September 1954), 421–25.

Manent, Pierre "Guizot et Tocqueville," in Valensise, ed., *François Guizot et la culture politique de son temps*, 147–59.

Manfredi, Marco, "Risorgimento e tradizioni municipali: Il viaggio di propaganda di Vincenzo Gioberti nell'Italia del 1848," *Memoria e Ricerca*, 44 (September–December 2013), 6–23.

Marangoni, Paolo, "La riforma della chiesa in Gioberti," in Beschin and Cristellon, eds., *Rosmini e Gioberti*, 343–59.

Marchesan, Angelo, *Della vita e delle opere di Lorenzo da Ponte: Con la giunta della famosa poetica per la quale dovette esulare da Venezia e altri versi inediti*. Treviso: Turazza, 1900.

Margariti, Antonio, *America! America!*, Salerno: Galzerano, 1980.

Margavio, Anthony V., "The Reaction of the Press to the Italian-American in New Orleans, 1880–1920," *Italian Americana*, 4, 1 (Fall/Winter 1978), 72–83.

Mariani, Valerio, "Scenografia Verdiana," *Giuseppe Verdi nel cinquantenario della morte*. Accademia Nazionale dei Lincei, 369 (1952), no. 26, 3–13.

Mariano, Marco, "Da Genova a New York? Il Regno di Sardegna e gli Stati Uniti tra restaurazione e integrazione nel mondo atlantico." *Annali della Fondazione Luigi Einaudi*, 42 (2008), 23–38.

Marinelli Roscioni, Carlo, ed., *Il Teatro di San Carlo*. Naples: Guida, 1988.

Marraro, Howard R., *American Opinion on the Unification of Italy: 1846–1861*. New York: Columbia University Press, 1932.

Marraro, Howard R., ed., *L'unificazione italiana vista dai diplomatici statunitensi*, 3 vols., Rome: Istituto per la Storia del Risorgimento Italiano, 1963–66.

Martellone, Anna Maria, "Italian Mass Emigration to the United States, 1876–1930: A Historical Survey," *Perspectives in American History*, 1, 1984, 379–423.

Martin, George W., "Verdi and the Risorgimento," in Weaver and Chusid, eds., *The Verdi Companion*, 13–41.

Martin, George W., *Verdi in America: "Oberto" through "Rigoletto."* Rochester, NY: University of Rochester Press, 2011.

Martin, Robert K., and Person, Leland S., eds., *Roman Holidays: American Writers and Artists in Nineteenth-Century Italy*. Iowa: University of Iowa Press, 2002.

Martina, Giacomo, *Pio IX*. Rome: Pontificia Università Gregoriana, 1986.

Marwil, Jonathan, *Visiting Modern War in Risorgimento Italy*. New York: Palgrave Macmillan, 2010.

Mason, Keith, "The American Loyalist Problem of Identity in the Revolutionary Atlantic World," in Bannister and Riordan, eds., *The Loyal Atlantic*, 39–74.

Massafra, Angelo, ed., *Il mezzogiorno preunitario: Economia, società e istituzioni*. Bari: Dedalo, 1988.

Mastellone, Salvo, *Mazzini and Marx: Thoughts upon Democracy in Europe*. Westport and London: Praeger, 2005.

Mastellone, Salvo, "I prodromi del 1848: Mazzini e il dibattito sul tipo di rivoluzione (1843–1847)," in Livorsi, ed., *Libertà e stato nel 1848–49*, 57–69.

Mastellone, Salvo, *Il progetto politico di Mazzini*. Florence: Olschki, 1994.

Mattarelli, Sauro, "Repubblicani senza la Repubblica," in Ridolfi, ed., *Almanacco della Repubblicca*, 3–18.

Maturi, Walter, *Interpretazioni del Risorgimento: Lezioni di storia della storiografia*. Turin: Einaudi, 1962.

Mayer, Holly A., "Bearing Arms, Bearing Burdens: Women Warriors, Camp Followers and Home-Front Heroines of the American Revolution," in Hagemann, Mettele, and Rendall, eds., *Gender, War and Politics*, 169–87.

Mazohl-Wallnig, Brigitte, *Österreichischer Verwaltungsstaat und Administrative Eliten im Königreich Lombardo-Venetien, 1815–1859*. Mainz: von Zabern, 1993.

McKevitt, Gerald, *Brokers of Culture: Italian Jesuits in the American West, 1848–1919*. Stanford, CA: Stanford University Press, 2007.

Medri, Sante, ed., *Giuseppe Compagnoni: Un intellettuale tra giacobinismo e restaurazione*. Bologna: Edizioni Analisi, 1993.

Memorie Parmensi per la Storia del Risorgimento. Vol. 4: *Claudio Linati*. Parma: Tipografia già cooperativa, 1935.

Mengozzi, Dino, "Obseques laiques et mouvement ouvrier en Italie," in Unfried, ed., *Riten, Mythen und Symbole*, 231–48.

Meriggi, Marco, "Centralismo e federalismo in Italia. Le aspettative preunitarie," in Janz, Schiera, Siegrist, eds., *Centralismo e federalismo tra Otto e Novecento*, 21–46.

Meriggi, Marco, *Gli stati italiani prima dell'Unità*. Bologna: il Mulino, 2011.

Meriggi, Marco, "Liberali/Liberalismo," in Banti et al., eds., *Atlante culturale del Risorgimento*, 101–14.

Meriggi, Marco, "Opinione pubblica," in Banti et al., eds., *Atlante culturale*, 149–62.

Meriggi, Marco, *Il Regno Lombardo-Veneto* (*Storia d'Italia* 18, 2, Giuseppe Galasso ed.). Turin: UTET, 1987.

Meriggi, Marco, "Società, Istituzioni e ceti dirigenti," in Sabbatucci and Vidotto, eds., *Storia d'Italia*, vol. 1, 119–228.

Meriggi, Marco, "State and Society in Post-Napoleonic Italy," in Laven and Riall, eds., *Napoleon's Legacy: Problems of Government in Restoration Europe*, 49–63.

Midlo Hall, Gwendolyn, *Africans in Colonial Louisiana: The Development of Afro-Creole Culture in the Eighteenth Century*. Baton Rouge: Louisiana State University Press, 1992.

Milano, Attilio, *Storia degli ebrei in Italia* (1963). Turin: Einaudi, 1992.

Miller, Nicola, "Liberty, Lipstick, and Lobsters," in Körner et al., eds., *America Imagined*, 81–117.

Moe, Nelson, *The View from Vesuvius: Italian Culture and the Southern Question*. Berkeley: University of California Press, 2002.

Momigliano, Arnaldo, *Ottavo contributo alla storia degli studi classici e del mondo antico*. Rome: Edizioni di Storia e letteratura, 1987.

Monsagrati, Giuseppe, "Gli intellettuali americani e il processo di unificazione italiana," in Fiorentini and Sanfilippo, eds., *Gli Stati Uniti e l'Unità d'Italia*, 17–44.

Montemorra Marvin, Roberta, ed., *The Cambridge Verdi Encyclopedia*. Cambridge: Cambridge University Press, 2013.

Montini, Renzo U., "Vita Americana di Pietro Borsieri," in *Rassegna storica del Risorgimento*, 41, 2/3 (April/September 1954), 467–76.

Moos, Carlo, "Cattaneo e il modello elvetico," in Colombo, della Peruta, and Lacaita, eds., *Carlo Cattaneo: I temi e le sfide*, 325–44.

Morandi, Carlo, "Giuseppe Compagnoni e la 'Storia dell'America,'" *Annali della R. Scuola Normale Superiore di Pisa: Lettere, storia e filosofia*, 2nd ser., 8 (1939), 252–61.

Moravia, Sergio, "Introduzione," in Romagnosi, *Scritti filosofici*, vol. 1, 5–52.

Morelli, Emilia, "L'idea di costituente," in Bagnoli, ed., *Giuseppe Montanelli: Unità e democrazia nel Risorgimento*, 57–63.

Morelli, Emilia, "Gli esuli italiani e la società inglese nella prima metà dell'ottocento," *Rassegna storica del Risorgimento*, 66, 1 (1979), 3–13.

Morelli, Emilia, *L'Inghilterra di Mazzini*. Rome: Istituto per la Storia del Risorgmento Italiano, 1965.

Morelli, Emilia, "The United States Constitution viewed by Nineteenth-Century Italian Democrats," in Noether, ed., *The American Constitution*, 99–118.

Morgan, Philip, "Antifascist Historians and History in 'Justice and Liberty,'" in Berger, Donovan, and Passmore, eds., *Writing National Histories*, 150–59.

Moscati, Ruggero, *Ferdinando II di Borbone nei documenti diplomatici austriaci*. Naples: Edizioni scientifiche Italiane, 1947.

Moyn, Samuel, *Human Rights and the Uses of History*. London: Verso, 2014.

Müller, Sven Oliver, Ther, Philipp, Toelle, Jutta, and zur Nieden, Gesa, eds., *Die Oper im Wandel der Gesellschaft: Kulturtransfers und Netzwerke des Musiktheaters in Europa*. Wien: Böhlau, 2010.

Mungen, Anno, ed., *Mitten im Leben: Musiktheater von der Oper zur Everyday Performance* (*Thurnauer Schriften zum Musiktheater* 23), Würzburg: Königshausen und Neumann, 2011.

Narici, Ilaria, "Somma, Antonio," in Montemorra Marvin, ed., *The Cambridge Verdi Encyclopedia*, 410.

Nash, Gary B., "Sparks from the Altar of '76: International Repercussions and Reconsiderations of the American Revolution," in Armitage and Subrahmanyam, eds., *The Age of Revolutions in Global Context*, 1–19.

Negro, Piero del, *Il mito americano nella Venezia del settecento*. Rome: Accademia Nazionale dei Lincei, 1975.

Newman, Judie, "Staging Black Insurrection: Dred on Stage," in Weinstein, ed., *The Cambridge Companion to Harriet Beecher Stowe*, 113–30.

Noether, Emiliana P., ed., *The American Constitution as a Symbol and Reality for Italy*. Lewitson: Edwin Mellen, 1989.

Noether, Emiliana P., "The Constitution in Action: The Young Republic in the Observations of Early Italian Commentators (1770s–1830s)," in Noether, ed., *The American Constitution*, 81–98.

Noether, Emiliana P., "Introduction," in Noether, ed., *The American Constitution*, vi–xii.

North, Michael, *Geschichte der Ostsee: Handel und Kulturen*. Munich: Beck, 2011, 179.

Noto, Adolfo, *Un mancato incontro: L'italia e il pensiero politico di Alexis de Tocqueville*. Rome: LeN, 1996.

O'Brian, Karen, "Catharine Macaulay's Histories of England: A Female Perspective on the History of Liberty," in Knott and Taylor, eds., *Women, Gender and Enlightenment*, 523–37.

O'Connor, Maura, *The Romance of Italy and the English Imagination*. Basingstoke and London: Macmillan, 1998.

Oellers, Norbert, *Schiller: Elend der Geschichte, Glanz der Kunst*. Stuttgart: Reclam, 2005.

O'Gorman, Edmundo, *The Invention of America*. Indianapolis: Indiana University Press, 1961.

Opera and Nation in Nineteenth-Century Italy. Special issue of *Journal of Modern Italian Studies* (Axel Körner, ed.), 17, 4 (September 2012).

Osterhammel, Jürgen, *Die Verwandlung der Welt: Eine Geschichte des 19. Jahrhunderts*. Munich: Beck, 2011.

Overhoff, Jürgen, "Benjamin Franklin, Student of the Holy Roman Empire: His Summer Journey to Germany in 1766 and His Interest in the Empire's Federal Constitution," *German Studies Review*, 34, 2 (May 2011), 277–86.

Pace, Antonio, *Benjamin Franklin and Italy*. Philadelphia: American Philosophical Society, 1985.

Pacini, Monica, "Ospiti stranieri di casa Vieusseux nella Firenze di metà ottocento," *Memoria e Ricerca*, 46 (May–August 2014), 47–62.

Pagano, Luigi Antonio, "Sicilia e Stati Uniti di America nel Risorgimento," *Rassegna storica del Risorgimento*, 41, 2/3 (April/September 1954), 484–93.

Pagden, Anthony, *European Encounters with the New World: From Renaissance to Romanticism*. New Haven, CT: Yale University Press, 1993.

Pagden, Anthony, *The Fall of Natural Man*. Cambridge: Cambridge University Press, 1982.

Palazzolo, Maria Iolanda, *Intelletuali e giornalismo nella Sicilia preunitaria*. Catania: Società di storia patria per la Sicilia Orientale, 1975.

Palazzolo, Maria Iolanda, *La perniciosa lettura: La chiesa e la libertà di stampa nell'Italia liberale*. Rome: Viella, 2010.

Palmer, R. R., *The Age of Democratic Revolution: A Political History of Europe and America, 1760–1800*. Princeton, NJ: Princeton University Press, 1959.

Pares, Richard, *Yankees and Creoles: The Trade between North America and the West Indies before the American Revolution*. London: Longmans, 1956.

Parfait, Claire, *The Publishing History of Uncle Tom's Cabin, 1852–2002*. Aldershot: Ashgate, 2007.

Parker, Roger, *"Arpa d'or dei fatidici vati": The Verdian Patriotic Chorus in the 1840s*. Parma: Istituto Nazionale di Studi Verdiani, 1997.

Parker, Roger, *Leonora's Last Act: Essays in Verdian Discourse*. Princeton, NJ: Princeton University Press, 1997.

Parker, Roger, "'Insolite forme,' or Basevi's Garden Path," in Chusid, ed., *Verdi's Middle Period*, 129–46.

Parker, Roger, "Introduction," in *The Works of Giuseppe Verdi*. Series 1, Operas, vol. 3 (Giuseppe Verdi, *Nabucodonosor: Dramma lirico in Four Parts*, ed. by Roger Parker). Chicago and Milan: University of Chicago Press/G. Ricordi, 1987.

Paschalidi, Maria, *Constructing Ionian identities: The Ionian Islands in British Official Discourses, 1815–1864*. PhD diss. University College London, 2010.

Pascolato, Alessandro, "Della vita e degli scritti di Antonio Somma," in Antonio Somma, *Opere scelte di Antonio Somma*, vii–xxxii.

Pascual Sastre, Isabel María, "La circolazione di miti politici tra Spagnia e Italia," in Banti and Ginsborg, eds., *Storia d'Italia*, 797–824.

Pasquino, Pasquale, "Sur la théorie constitutionnelle de la monarchie de Juillet," in Valensise, ed., *François Guizot et la culture politique de son temps*, 111–28.

Patriarca, Silvana, *Italian Vices: Nation and Character from the Risorgimento to the Republic*. Cambridge: Cambridge University Press, 2010.

Patriarca, Silvana, and Riall, Lucy, eds., *The Risorgimento Revisited: Nationalism and Culture in Nineteenth-Century Italy*. New York: Palgrave Macmillan, 2012.

Pauls, Birgit, *Giuseppe Verdi und das Risorgimento: Ein politischer Mythos im Prozeß der Nationsbildung*. Berlin: Akademie, 1996.

Pécout, Gilles, "Cavour visto dagli Stati Uniti," in Fiorentini and Sanfilippo, eds., *Gli Stati Uniti e l'Unità d'Italia*, 125–32.

Pellegrino, Giuseppe, and Muratore, Umberto, eds., *Stato unitario e federalismo nel pensiero cattolico del Risorgimento*. Stresa-Milazzo: Sodalitas-Spes, 1994.

Pellegrino Suttcliffe, Marcella, *Victorian Radicals and Italian Democrats* (Royal Historical Society: Studies in History). Woodbridge: Boydell, 2014.

Perosa, Sergio, ed., *Le traduzioni italiane di Herman Melville e Gertrude Stein*. Venice: Istituto Veneto di Scienze, Lettere ed Arti, 1997.

Petrusewicz, Marta, *Come il Meridione divenne una Questione: Rappresentazione del Sud prima e dopo il Quarantotto*. Soveria Mannelli: Rubbettino, 1998.

Petrusewicz, Marta, Schneider, Jane, and Schneider, Peter, eds., *Il Sud: Conoscere, capire, cambiare*. Bologna: il Mulino, 2009.

Phillips-Matz, Mary Jane, *Verdi: A Biography*. Oxford: Oxford University Press, 1993.

Philp, Mark, and Lenci, Mauro, "Introduction," in Lenci and Calabrò, eds., *Democracy and Risorgimento*, 7–18.

Philip Trauth, Mary, *Italo-American Diplomatic Relations, 1861-1882: The Mission of George Perkins Marsh, First American Minister to the Kingdom of Italy*. Washington: Catholic University of America, 1958.

Pierattini, Maria Giovanna, *"Vien via, si va in America, si parte": Un secolo di emigrazione pistoiese; Storia e storie, itinerari e mestieri*. Pistoia: CRT, 2002.

Pitts, Jennifer, "Constant's Thought on Slavery and Empire," in Rosenblatt, *The Cambridge Companion to Constant*, 115–45.

Pocock, John G. A., *Barbarism and Religion*. Vol. 1: *The Enlightenments of Edward Gibbon, 1737-1764*. Cambridge: Cambridge University Press, 1999.

Pocock, John G. A., *Barbarism and Religion*. Vol. 2: *Narratives of Civil Government*. Cambridge: Cambridge University Press, 1999.

Pocock, John G. A., *Barbarism and Religion*. Vol. 4: *Barbarians, Savages and Empires*. Cambridge: Cambridge University Press, 2005.

Pocock, John G. A., *The Machiavellian Moment: Florentine Political Thought and the Atlantic Republican Tradition* (1975). Princeton, NJ: Princeton University Press, 2003.

Pocock, John G. A., *Political Thought and History: Essays on Theory and Method*. Cambridge: Cambridge University Press, 2009.

Podlech, Adalbert, "Repräsentation," in Brunner, Conze, Koselleck, eds., *Geschichtliche Grundbegriffe*, vol. 5, 509–47.

Polasky, Janet, *Revolutions without Borders: The Call to Liberty in the Atlantic World*. New Haven, CT, and London: Yale University Press, 2015.

Polzonetti, Pierpaolo, *Italian Opera in the Age of the American Revolution*. Cambridge: Cambridge University Press, 2011.

Poppi, Claudio, ed., *L'ombra di core: Disegni dal fondo Palagi della Biblioteca dell'Archiginasio*. Bologna: Grafis, 1989.

Porcella, Marco, "Premesse dell'emigrazione di massa in età prestatistica (1800–1850)," in Bevilacqua, de Clementi, and Franzina, eds., *Storia dell'emigrazione italiana*, vol. 1, 17–44.

Porciani, Ilaria, "Disciplinamento nazionale e modelli domestici nel lungo ottocento: Germania e Italia a confronto," Banti and Ginsborg, eds., *Storia d'Italia*, 97–125.

Porciani, Ilaria, "Identita' locale—identita' nazionale: La costruzione di una doppia appartenenza," in Janz, Schiera, Siegrist, eds., *Centralismo e federalismo*, 141–84.

Poriss, Hilary, "Julienne Dejean, Eugenia," in Montemorra Marvin, ed., *The Cambridge Verdi Encyclopedia*, 228.

Pospíšil, Milan, "Österreichische Opernzensur in Prag: *Gustave III* und *La Juive*," in Werr, ed., *Eugène Scribe und das europäische Musiktheater*, 122–52.

Powers, Harold, *"La dama velata*: Act II of *Un ballo in maschera*," in Chusid, ed., *Verdi's Middle Period*, 273–336.

Preti, Alberto, ed., *Un democratico del Risorgimento: Quirico Filopanti*. Bologna: Il Mulino, 1997.

Procacci, Giuliano, "Rivoluzione americana e storiografia italiana," *Rassegna storica del Risorgimento*, 41, 2/3 (April/September 1954), 565–71.

Ragionieri, Ernesto, *Politica e amministrazione nella storia dell'Italia unita*. Rome: Editori Riuniti, 1979.

Ragusa, Olga, "Italy, Romantico—Romanticismo," in Eichner, *"Romantic" and Its Cognates*, 293–340.

Raimondi, Ezio, ed., *Il sogno del coreodramma: Salvatore Viganò, poeta muto*. Bologna: il Mulino, 1984.

Ramanzini, Leopoldo, *Una lettera di Garibaldi ad Abramo Lincoln*. Vincenza: Neri Pozza, 1970.

Rao, Anna Maria, "Republicanism in Italy from the Eighteenth Century to the Early Risorgimento," *Journal of Modern Italian Studies* 17, 2 (2012), 149–67.

Raponi, Nicola, *Politica e amministrazione in Lombardia agli esordi dell'Unità: Il programma dei moderati*. Milan: Giuffrè, 1967.

Rapport, Mike, *1848: Year of Revolution*. London: Little, Brown, 2008.

Read, Allen Walker, "The American Reception of Botta's *Storia della guerra dell' Independenza degli Stati Uniti d'America*," *Italica*, 14, 1 (March 1937), 5–8.

Recchia, Stefano, and Urbinati, Nadia, "Introduction. Giuseppe Mazzini's International Political Thought," in Mazzini, *A Cosmopolitanism of Nations*, 1–29.

Recupero, Antonino, "La Sicilia all'opposizione," in Aymard and Giarrizzo, eds., *La Sicilia*, 39–85.

Reill, Dominique, "The Risorgimento: A Multinational Movement," in Patriarca and Riall, eds., *The Risorgimento Revisited*, 255–69.

Renda, Francesco, "La rivoluzione del 1812 e l'autonomia siciliana," in *La Sicilia e l'unità d'Italia*, vol. 2, 523–32.

Renda, Francesco, *La Sicilia nel 1812*. Rome: Salvatore Sciascia, 1963.

Riall, Lucy, *Garibaldi: Invention of a Hero*. New Haven, CT: Yale University Press, 2007.

Riall, Lucy, "Martyr Cults in Nineteenth-Century Italy," *Journal of Modern History* 82 (June 2010), 255–87.

Riall, Lucy, "Men at War: Masculinity and Military Ideals in the Risorgimento," in Patriarca and Riall, eds., *The Risorgimento Revisited*, 152–70.

Riall, Lucy, "The Politics of Italian Romanticism: Mazzini and the Making of a Nationalist Culture," in Bayly and Biagini, eds., *Giuseppe Mazzini*, 167–86.

Riall, Lucy, *Il Risorgimento: Storia e interpretazioni*. Rome: Donzelli, 1997.

Riall, Lucy, "Rosario Romeo and the Risorgimento in Sicily, 1848–1860," in Bottari, ed., *Rosario Romeo e Il Risorgimento in Sicilia*, 207–16.

Riall, Lucy, *Sicily and the Unification of Italy*. Oxford: Clarendon, 1998.

Riall, Lucy, *Under the Volcano: Revolution in a Sicilian Town*. Oxford: Oxford University Press, 2013.

Richards, David A. J., *Italian American: The Racializing of an Ethnic Identity*. New York: New York University Press, 1999.

Ridolfi, Maurizio, ed., *Almanacco della Republicca: Storia d'Italia attraverso le tradizioni, le istituzioni e le simbologie repubblicane*. Milan: Mondadori, 2003.

Ridolfi, Maurizio, *Dalla setta al partito: Il caso dei repubblicani cesenati dagli anni risorgimentali alla crisi di fine secolo*. Rimini: Maggioli, 1988.

Ridolfi, Maurizio, "La Démocratie en Amérique di Tocqueville e la sua ricezione nell'Italia del Risorgimento," in Fiorentini and Sanfilippo, eds., *Gli Stati Uniti e l'Unità d'Italia*, 133–39.

Ridolfi, Maurizio, ed., *La democrazia radicale nell'ottocento europeo* (Annali Fondazione Giangiacomo Feltrinelli, 39). Milan: Feltrinelli, 2005.

Ridolfi, Maurizio, "Feste civili e religione politiche nel 'laboratorio' della nazione italiana (1860–1859)," *Memora e Ricerca*, 3 (July 1995), 83–108.

Ridolfi, Maurizio, *Il Partito della Repubblica: I repubblicani in Romagna e le origini del PRI nell'Italia liberale (1872–1895)*. Milan: Franco Angeli, 1989.

Ridolfi, Maurizio, "Visions of Republicanism in the Writings of Giuseppe Mazzini," *Journal of Modern Italian Studies*, 13, 4, 2008, 468–79.

Robbins, Sarah, *The Cambridge Introduction to Harriet Beecher Stowe*. Cambridge: Cambridge University Press, 2007.

Roberts, Timothy M., "The Relevance of Giuseppe Mazzini's Ideas of Insurgency to the American Slavery Crisis of the 1850s," in Bayly and Biagini, eds., *Giuseppe Mazzini and the Globalisation of Democratic Nationalism*, 311–22.

Robertson, Carol E., ed., *Musical Repercussions of 1492*. Washington: Smithsonian Institution Press, 1992.

Robertson, John, *The Case for the Enlightenment: Scotland and Naples 1680–1760*. Cambridge: Cambridge University Press, 2005.

Roccatagliati, Alessandro, "The Italian Theatre of Verdi's Day," in Balthazar, ed., *The Cambridge Companion to Verdi*, 15–28.

Rogari, Sandro, ed., *Giuseppe Montanelli fra storia e storiografia a 150 anni della scomparsa* (Atti del convegno di studi, Fucecchio, 6 ottobre 2012). Florence: Polistampa, 2013.

Roger, Philippe, *The American Enemy: A Story of French Anti-Americanism* (2002). Chicago: University of Chicago Press, 2005.

Roger, Philippe, "Aufklärer gegen Amerika," in von Thadden and Escudier, eds., *Amerika und Europa*, 16–34.

Rolle, Andrew, *The Immigrant Upraised: Italian Adventurers and Colonists in an Expanding America*. Oklahoma: University of Oklahoma Press, 1968.

Rolle, Andrew, *The Italian Americans: Troubled Root*. New York: Free Press, 1980.

Romagnoli, Sergio, "Le 'lettere piacevoli' e il 'Saggio sugli ebrei' di Giuseppe Compagnoni," *La rassegna della letteratura italiana*, 97, 1/2 (January–August 1993), 38–58.

Romanelli, Raffaele, *L'Italia liberale: 1861–1900*. Bologna: il Mulino, 1979.

Romanelli, Raffaele, "Nazione e costituzione nell'opinione liberale italiana prima del '48," *Passato e Presente*, 46 (January–April 1999), 157–71.

Romanelli, Raffaele, "Le Regole del Gioco: Note sull'impianto del sistema elettorale in Italia (1848–1895)," *Quaderni storici*, 69, 3 (1988), 685–725.

Romani, Roberto, "Political Thought in Action: The Moderates in 1859," *Journal of Modern Italian Studies*, 17, 5 (2012), 593–607.

Romani, Roberto, "Reluctant Revolutionaries: Moderate Liberalism in the Kingdom of Sardinia, 1849–1859," *Historical Journal*, 55, 1 (2012), 45–73.

Romano, Salvatore Francesco, *Momenti del Risorgimento in Sicilia*. Messina and Florence: G. D'Anna, 1952.

Romeo, Rosario, *Il Risorgimento in Sicilia* (1950). Rome and Bari: Laterza, 1982.

Romeo, Rosario, *Vita di Cavour*. Rome and Bari: Laterza, 1990.

Ronchi, Carla, *I democratici fiorentini nella rivoluzione del '48–'49*. Florence: Barbèra, 1962.

Rosanvallon, Pierre, *Le Moment Guizot*. Paris: Gallimard, 1985.

Rosen, David, "La disposizione scenica per il Un ballo in maschera di Verdi: Studio critico," in Rosen and Pigozzi, eds., *Un ballo in maschera di Giuseppe Verdi*, 5–119.

Rosen, David, "A Tale of Five Cities: The Peregrinations of Somma's and Verdi's *Gustavo III* (and *Una vendetta in dominò* and *Un ballo in maschera*) at the Hands of the Neapolitan and Roman Censorship," *Verdi Forum*, 26–27 (1999), 53–66.

Rosen, David, and Pigozzi, Marinella, eds., *Un ballo in maschera di Giuseppe Verdi: Collana di Disposizioni sceniche*. Rome: Ricordi, 2002.

Rosen, Frederick, *Bentham, Byron and Greece: Constitutionalism, Nationalism, and the Early Liberal Political Thought*. Oxford: Oxford University Press, 1992.

Rosenblatt, Helena, *The Cambridge Companion to Constant*. Cambridge: Cambridge University Press, 2009.

Rosselli, John, *Lord William Bentinck and the British Occupation of Sicily, 1811–1814*. Cambridge: Cambridge University Press, 1956.

Rosselli, John, "The Opera Business and the Italian Immigrant Community in Latin America 1820–1930: The Example of Buenos Aires," *Past and Present*, 127, 1 (1990), 155–82.

Rosselli, John, *The Opera Industry in Italy from Cimarosa to Verdi: The Role of the Impresario*. Cambridge: Cambridge Paperback Library, 1987.

Rosselli, John, *Music and Musicians in 19th Century Italy*. London: Batsford, 1991.

Rosselli, Nello, *Carlo Pisacane nel Risorgimento Italiano*. Turin: Einaudi, 1977.

Rosselli, Nello, "Giuseppe Montanelli," in *Saggi sul Risorgimento e altri scritti*, 87–216.

Rosselli, Nello, *Saggi sul Risorgimento e altri scritti*. Turin: Einaudi, 1946.

Rossi, Joseph, *The Image of America in Mazzini's Writings*. Madison: University of Wisconsin Press, 1954.

Rossi, Joseph, "Uncle Tom's Cabin and Protestantism in Italy," *American Quarterly*, 11, 3 (Autumn 1959), 416–24.

Rota Ghibaudi, Silvia, *La fortuna di Rousseau in Italia (1750-1815)*. Turin: Giappichelli, 1961.

Rota Ghibaudi, Silvia, *Giuseppe Ferrari: L'evoluzione del suo pensiero (1838-1860)*. Florence: Olschki, 1969.

Rota Ghibaudi, Silvia, "La Politica secondo Giuseppe Montanelli," in Bagnoli, ed., *Giuseppe Montanelli*, 89–113.

Rotondi, Clementina, "Giuseppe Montanelli e 'l'Italia,'" in Bagnoli, ed., *Giuseppe Montanelli*, 195–232.

Ruggieri Punzo, Franca, *Walter Scott in Italia, 1821–1971*. Bari: Adriatrice Editrice, 1975.

Rumpler, Helmut, *Eine Chance für Mitteleuropa: Bürgerliche Emanzipation und Staatsverfall in der Habsburgermonarchie* (Österreichische Geschichte, 1804–1914). Vienna: Ueberreuter, 2005.

Russell Ascoli, Albert, and von Henneberg, Krystyna, eds., *Making and Remaking Italy: The Cultivation of National Identity around the Risorgimento*. Oxford: Berg, 2001.

Russi, Luciano, "Montanelli e Pisacane," in Bagnoli, ed., *Giuseppe Montanelli*, 65–88.

Rydell, Robert W., and Kroes, Rob, *Buffalo Bill in Bologna: The Americanization of the World, 1869–1922*. Chicago and London: University of Chicago Press, 2005.

Sabbatucci, Giovanni, and Vidotto, Vittorio, eds., *Storia d'Italia*. Rome and Bari: Laterza, 1994.

Sabetti, Filippo, "Cattaneo e il modello americano: Per una scienza politica nuova," in Lacaita, Colombo, and Della Peruta, eds., *Carlo Cattaneo: I temi e le sfide*, 345–66.

Sabetti, Filippo, *Civilization and Self-Government: The Political Thought of Carlo Cattaneo*. Lanham: Lexington Books, 2010.

Sala, Emilio, "Un ballo in maschera e il carnevale," in Olga Jesurum, ed., *Verdi e Roma* (Accademia Nazionale dei Lincei). Rome: Gangemi, 2015, 233–55.

Sandström, Brigitta, "Bénigne Gagneraux e la Svezia," in *Benigne Gagneraux: Un pittore francese nella Roma di Pio VI*, 35–39.

Sanfilippo, Matteo, *L'affermazione del cattolicesimo nel Nord America: Elite, emigranti e chiesa cattolica negli Stati Uniti e in Canada, 1750–1920*. Viterbo: Sette Città, 2003.

San Mauro, Carla, ed., *Un opera inedita di Carlo Botta: De L'Equilibre du Pouvoir en Europe*. Rome: Istituto Storico Italiano, 2008.

Sarti, Roland, "La democrazia radicale: Uno sguardo reciproco tra Stati Uniti e Italia," in Ridolfi, ed., *La democrazia radicale nell'ottocento europeo*, 133–57.

Sarti, Roland, "Giuseppe Mazzini and Young Europe," in Bayly and Biagini, eds., *Giuseppe Mazzini and the Globalisation of Democratic Nationalism*, 275–97.

Sarti, Roland, "Giuseppe Mazzini e la tradizione repubblicana," in Ridolfi, ed., *Almanacco della Republicca*, 56–67.

Sasportes, José, "La Danza, 1737–1900," in Ajello et al., eds., *Il Teatro di San Carlo*, vol. 1, 365–96.

Sasportes, José, "La parola contro il corpo ovvero il melodramma nemico del ballo," *La Danza Italiana*, 1 (Fall 1984), 21–42.

Savini, Marcello, *Un abate "libertino": Le "Memorie autobiografiche" e altri scritti di Giuseppe Compagnoni*. Castelmaggiore: Banca del Monte di Lugo, 1988.

Savini, Marcello, "Le lettere di Giuseppe Compagnoni a Valentino Rossi," in Medri, ed., *Giuseppe Compagnoni*, 23–32.

Savini, Marcello, "Profilo biografico," in Giuseppe Compagnoni, *Cinquantotto lettere e una supplica*. Ravenna: Longo, 1996, 11–20.

Scaglia, Giovanni Battista, *Cesare Balbo: Il Risorgimento nella prospettiva storica del progresso cristiano*. Rome: Vita Nova, 1975.

Scherer, Paul, *Lord John Russell: A Biography*. Cranbury, NJ: Associated Press, 1999.

Schneider, Herbert, "Scribe and Auber: Constructing Grand Opéra," in Charlton, ed., *The Cambridge Companion to Grand Opéra*, 168–88.

Schneider, Jane, ed., *Italy's "Southern Question": Orientalism in One Country*. Oxford: Berg, 1998.

Schneider, Jane, and Schneider, Peter, *Culture and Political Economy in Western Sicily*. New York: Academic Press, 1976.

Schneider, Jane, and Schneider, Peter, "Gli Stati Uniti e la Sicilia: Ripercussioni di un rapport nord-sud," in Petrusewicz, Schneider, Schneider, ed., *Il Sud: Conoscere, capire, cambiare*, 201–26.

Schiavi, Giuliana, "Moby-Dick in Italia," in Perosa, ed., *Le traduzioni italiane di Herman Melville e Gertrude Stein*, 43–75.

Schiera, Pierangelo, "Centralismo e federalismo nell'unificazione statal-nazionale italiana e tedesca," in Janz, Schiera, Siegrist, eds., *Centralismo e federalismo tra Otto e Novecento: Italia e Germania a confronto*, 21–46.

Schroeder, Paul W., *Systems, Stability and Statecraft: Essays on the International History of Modern Europe*. New York: Palgrave, 2004.

Sciacca, Enzo, *Riflessi del Costituzionalismo Europeo in Sicilia (1812–1815)*. Catania: Bonanno, 1966.

Scirocco, Alfonso, *Garibaldi: Citizen of the World*. Princeton, NJ: Princeton University Press, 2007.

Scirocco, Alfonso, *L'Italia del Risorgimento: 1800–1871*. Bologna: il Mulino, 1993.

Scirocco, Alfonso, "Montanelli e Mazzini," in Bagnoli, ed., *Giuseppe Montanelli*, 23–55.

Sebald, W. G., *Vertigo*. London: Vintage, 2002.

Segre, Bruno, *La storia degli ebrei in Italia*. Milan: Fenice, 1993

Senici, Emanuele, "'Teco io sto': Strategies of Seduction in Act II of 'Un ballo in maschera,'" *Cambridge Opera Journal*, 14, 1/2 (March 2002), 79–92.

Sennett, Richard, *The Craftsman*. London: Penguin, 2009.

Sestan, Ernesto, *La Firenze di Vieusseux e di Caponi*. Florence: Olschki, 1986.

Shannon, Timothy J., "The Native American Way of War in the Age of Revolution," in Chickering and Förster, eds., *War in an Age of Revolution*, 137–57.

La Sicilia e l'unità d'Italia: Atti del Congresso Internazionale di Studi Storici sul Risorgimento italiano (Palermo 15–20 aprile 1961, Salvatore Massimo Ganci and Rosa Guccione Scaglione, eds.). Milan: Feltrinelli, 1962.

Sioli, Marco, "Se non c'è il conquibus si muore come cani: Luigi Tinelli a New York (1851–1873)," in Fiorentini and Sanfilippo, eds., *Gli Stati Uniti e l'Unità d'Italia*, 141–50.

Sked, Alan, *Radetzky: Imperial Victor and Military Genius*. London: I. B. Tauris, 2011.

Sked, Alan, *The Survival of the Habsburg Empire: Radetzky, the Imperial Army and the Class War, 1848*. London: Longman, 1979.

Smart, Mary Ann, "Liberty On (and Off) the Barricades: Verdi's Risorgimento Fantasies," in Russell Ascoli and von Henneberg, eds., *Making and Remaking Italy*, 103–18.

Smart, Mary Ann, *Mimomania: Music and Gesture in Nineteenth-Century Opera*. Berkeley: University of California Press, 2004.

Smart, Mary Ann, "'Proud, Indomitable, Irascible': Allegories of Nation in *Attila* and *Les Vêpres siciliennes*," in Chusid, ed., *Verdi's Middle Period*, 227–56.

Smart, Mary Ann, "Verdi, Italian Romanticism and the Risorgimento," in Balthazar, ed., *The Cambridge Companion to Verdi*, 29–45.

Sofia, Francesca, "Progresso/Incivilmento," in Banti et al., eds., *Atlante culturale*, 19–32.

Soldani, Simonetta, "Donne e nazione nella rivoluzione italiana del 1848," *Passato e Presente*, 46 (January–April 1999), 75–102.

Soldani, Simonetta, "Il Risorgimento delle donne," in Banti and Ginsborg, eds., *Storia d'Italia*, 183–224.

Solé, Jacques, *Les Révolutions de la fin du XVIIIe siècle aux Amériques et en Europe*. Paris: Seuil, 2005.

Sontag, Susan, *Against Interpretation and Other Essays* (1964). London: New York: Penguin, 2009.

Sorba, Carlotta, *Il melodramma della nazione: Politica e sentimenti nell'età del Risorgimento*. Rome and Bari: Laterza, 2015.

Sorba, Carlotta, *Teatri: L'Italia del Melodramma nell'eta' del Risorgimento*. Bologna: il Mulino, 2001.

Spadolini, Giovanni, *Un dissidente del Risorgimento: Giuseppe Montanelli, con documenti inediti*. Florence: Le Monnier, 1962.

Spadolini, Giovanni, *Fra Vieusseux e Ricasoli: Dalla vecchia alla "Nuova Antologia."* Florence: Cassa di Risparmio, 1982.

Spagnoletti, Angelantonio, *Storia del Regno delle Due Sicilie*. Bologna: il Mulino, 1997.

Späth, Jens, *Revolution in Europea 1820-23: Verfassung und Verfassungskultur in den Königreichen Spanien, beider Sizilien und Sardinien-Piedmont*. Cologne: SH-Verlag, 2012.

Spini, Giorgio, *Mito e realtà della Spagna nelle rivoluzioni italiane 1820–21*. Rome: Perrella, 1950.

Spini, Giorgio, *Risorgimento e Protestanti*. Naples: ESI, 1956.

Spini, Giorgio, et al., eds., *Italia e America dal settecento all'età dell'imperialismo*. Milan: Marsilio, 1976.

Springer, Christian, *Giuseppe Verdi: "Simon Boccanegra"; Dokumente—Materialien—Texte zur Entstehung und Rezeption der beiden Fassungen*. Vienna: Praesens, 2008.

Stefani, Giuseppe, *I prigionieri dello Spielberg sulla via dell'esilio*. Udine: De Bianco, 1963.

Steffan, Carlida, ed., *Rossiniana: Antologia della critica nella prima metà dell'Ottocento*. Pordenone: Studio Tesi, 1992.

Steinberg, Jonathan, "Carlo Cattaneo and the Swiss Idea of Liberty," in Bayly and Biagini, eds., *Giuseppe Mazzini*, 211–35.

Stollberg-Rilinger, Barbara, *Das Heilige Römische Reich Deutscher Nation: Vom Ende des Mittelalters bis 1806*. Munich: Beck, 2013.

Storchi, Mario R., "Grani, prezzi e mercati nel Regno di Napoli (1806–1852)," in Massafra, ed., *Il mezzogiorno preunitario*, 133–47.

Sullivan, Jack, *New World Symphonies: How American Culture Changed European Music*. New Haven, CT, and London: Yale University Press, 1999.

Surwillo, Lisa, *Monsters by Trade: Slave Traffickers in Modern Spanish Literature and Culture*. Stanford, CA: Stanford University Press, 2014.

Tarozzi, Fiorenza, "Filopanti professore universitario e insegnante popolare," in Preti, ed., *Un democratico del Risorgimento*, 93–119.

Taylor, Alan, *American Colonies*. New York and London: Penguin, 2001.

Taylor, Barbara, *Mary Wollstonecraft and the Feminist Imagination*. Cambridge: Cambridge University Press, 2003.

Tesini, Mario, "Rosmini lettore di Tocqueville," *Rivista rosminiana di filosofia e di cultura*, 81 (1987), 265–87.

Tesoro, Marina, ed., *Monarchia, tradizione, identità nazionale: Germania, Giappone e Italia tra ottocento e novecento*. Milan: Mondadori, 2004.

Thadden, Rudolf von, and Escudier, Alexandre, eds., *Amerika und Europa—Mars und Venus? Das Bild Amerikas in Europa*. Göttingen: Wallstein, 2004.

Ther, Philipp, ed., *Kulturpolitik und Theater: Die kontinentalen Imperien in Europa im Vergleich*. Vienna: Böhlau, 2012.

Thier, Maike, "A World Apart, a Race Apart?," in Körner et al., eds., *America Imagined*, 161–89.

Thom, Martin, "City, Region and Nation: Carlo Cattaneo and the Making of Italy," *Citizenship Studies*, 3, 2 (1999), 187–201.

Thom, Martin, "Europa, libertà e nazioni: Cattaneo e Mazzini nel Risorgimento," in Banti and Ginsborg, eds., *Storia d'Italia*, 331–78.

Thom, Martin, "Great Britain and Ireland in the Thought of Carlo Cattaneo," in Colombo, della Peruta, and Lacaita, eds., *Carlo Cattaneo*, 387–429.

Thom, Martin, "The 'hermite des Apennins': Leopardi and the *Antologia* in 1824–26," *Journal of Modern Italian Studies*, 17, 5 (2012), 532–46.

Thom, Martin, *Republics, Nations and Tribes*. London: Verso, 1995.

Thom, Martin, "Unity and Confederation in the Italian Risorgimento: The Case of Carlo Cattaneo," in Berger, Donovan, and Passmore, eds., *Writing National Histories*, 69–81.

Thompson, Dennis F., *John Stuart Mill and Representative Government*. Princeton, NJ: University Press, 1976.

Todorov, Tzvetan, *La Conquête de Amérique: La question de l'autre*. Paris: Seuil, 1982.

Toelle, Jutta, "Der Duft der großen weiten Welt: Ideen zum weltweiten Siegeszug der italienischen Oper im 19. Jahrhundert," in Müller, Ther, Toelle, and zur Nieden, eds., *Die Oper im Wandel der Gesellschaft: Kulturtransfers und Netzwerke des Musiktheaters in Europa*, 251–61.

Toelle, Jutta, "Zielpunkt: Austro-Italiens moralische Hegemonie," in Ther, ed., *Kulturpolitik und Theater*, 175–90.

Tonetti, Eurigio, *Governo austriaco e notabili sudditi: Congregazioni e municipi nel Veneto della restaurazione, 1813–1848*. Venice: Istituto Veneto di scienze, lettere ed arti, 1997.

Tortarolo, Edoardo, *Illuminismo e Rivoluzioni: Biografia politica di Filippo Mazzei*. Milan: Franco Angeli, 1986.

Tóth, Heléna, *An Exiled Generation: German and Hungarian Refugees of Revolution, 1848–1871*. Cambridge: Cambridge University Press, 2014.

Trampus, Antonio, ed., *Diritti e costituzione: L'opera di Gaetano Filangieri e la sua fortuna europea*. Bologna, 2005.

Trampus, Antonio, "Verfassung und Recht: Filangieri und die europäische Rezeption der *Scienza della legislazione*," in Jung and Kroll, eds., *Italien in Europa*, 119–41.

Traniello, Francesco, "Letture rosminiane della rivoluzione francese," in Campanini and Traniello, eds., *Filosofia e politica*, 147–58.

Traniello, Francesco, *Società religiosa e società civile in Rosmini*. Bologna: il Mulino, 1966.

Turchi, Roberta, "Un collaboratore di Gianpietro Vieusseux: Michele Leoni," *La Rassegna della letteratura italiana*, 97, 1/2 (January–August 1993), 59–80.

Turgeon, Laurier, Delâge, Denys, and Ouellet, Réal, eds., *Transferts culturels et métissages: Amérique—Europe XVIe–XXe siècle*. Paris: L'Harmattan, 1996.

Tyrrell, Ian, *Transnational Nation: United States History in Global Perspective since 1789*. New York: Palgrave Macmillan, 2007.

Unfer Lukoschik, Rita, *Friedrich Schiller in Italien (1785–1861): Eine quellengeschichtliche Studie*. Berlin: Duncker und Humblot, 2004.

Unfried, Berthold, ed., *Riten, Mythen und Symbole—Die Arbeiterbewegung zwischen "Zivilreligion" und Volkskultur*. Vienna: Akademische Verlagsanstalt, 1999.

Urbinati, Nadia, "The Legacy of Kant: Giuseppe Mazzini's Cosmopolitanism of Nations," in Bayly and Biagini, eds., *Giuseppe Mazzini*, 11–35.

Urbinati, Nadia, *Mill on Democracy: From the Athenian Polis to Representative Government*. Chicago: University of Chicago Press, 2002.

Valebona, G. B., *Il Teatro Carlo Felice: Cronistoria di un secolo, 1828-1928*. Genoa: Cooperativa Fascista Poligrafici, 1928.

Valensise, Marina, ed., *François Guizot et la culture politique de son temps*. Paris: Gallimard, 1991.

Valle, Roberto, "'Ombre russe': Considerazioni su Mazzini, Bakunin e la russofobia," in Guida, ed., *Dalla Giovine Europa alla Grande Europa*, 163–203.

Valsecchi, Franco, "L'inghilterra e il problema italiano nella politica europea del 1848," *Rassegna storica del Risorgimento*, 66, 1 (January–March 1979), 14–24.

Vance, Norman, *The Victorians and Ancient Rome*. Oxford: Blackwell, 1997.

Vance, William L., *America's Rome*. Vol. 2: *Catholic and Contemporary Rome*. New Haven, CT, and London: Yale University Press, 1989.

Vangelista, Chiara, and Reginato, Mauro, "L'emigrazione valdese," in Corti and Sanfilippo, eds., *Storia d'Italia*. Annali 24, 161–82.

Vella, Francesca, "Verdi and Politics (c. 1859–1861)," *Studi Verdiani* 24 (2014), 79–120.

Venturi, Franco, *The End of the Old Regime in Europe, 1776–1789*. Part 1: *The Great States of the West*. Princeton, NJ: Princeton University Press, 1991.

Venturi, Franco, *Illuministi italiani*. Vol. 3: *Riformatori Lombardi, piemontesi e toscani*. Milan and Naples: Riccardo Ricciardi, 1958.

Venturi, Franco, *L'Italia in un mondo tra riforme e rivoluzioni*. Turin: Tirenia, 1978.

Venturi, Franco, *Italy and the Enlightenment: Studies in a Cosmopolitan Century*. New York: New York University Press, 1972.

Venturi, Franco, *Settecento riformatore: Da Muratori a Beccaria*. Turin: Einaudi, 1969.

Venturi, Franco, *Settecento riformatore: La Caduta dell'Antico Regime (1776–1789)*. Turin: Einaudi, 1984.

Viale Ferrero, Mercedes, "Luogo teatrale e spazio scenico," in Bianconi and Pestelli, eds., *Storia dell'opera italiana*, vol. 5, 1–122.

Viale Ferrero, Mercedes, *Storia del Teatro Regio di Torino*. Vol. 3: *La scenografia*. Turin: Cassa di Risparmio, 1980.

Vollaro, Daniel R., "Lincoln, Stowe, and the 'Little Woman/Great War' Story: The Making, and Breaking, of a Great American Anecdote," *Journal of the Abraham Lincoln Association*, 30, 1 (Winter 2009), 18–34.

Volpi, Alessandro, "Contaminazioni fra diritto commerciale e tematiche economiche," in Rogari, ed., *Giuseppe Montanelli fra storia e storiografia a 150 anni della scomparsa*, 43–57.

Walker, Frank, *The Man Verdi*. London: Dent, 1962.

Walker, Frank, "Verdi, Giuseppe Montanelli and the Libretto of *Simon Boccanegra*," *Bollettino dell'Istituto di Studi Verdiani*, 1, 3 (1960), 1373–90.

Walter, François, *Histoire de la Suissse*. Vol. 4: *La création de la Suisse moderne (1830-1930)*. Neuchâtel: Alphil-Presses universitaires suisses, 2011.

Walton, Benjamin, "Operatic Fantasies in Latin America," *Journal of Modern Italian Studies*. Special issue of *Opera and Nation in Nineteenth-Century Italy* (Axel Körner, ed.), 17, 4 (September 2012), 460–71.

Weaver, William, *Verdi: A Documentary Study*. London: Thames and Hudson, 1977.

Weaver, William, and Chusid, Martin, eds., *The Verdi Companion*. New York: Norton, 1979.

Wehler, Hans-Ulrich, *Der Aufstieg des amerikanischen Imperialismus: Studien zur Entwicklung des Imperium Americanum 1865-1900*. Göttingen: Vandenhoeck und Ruprecht, 1974.

Weinstein, Cindy, ed., *The Cambridge Companion to Harriet Beecher Stowe*. Cambridge: Cambridge University Press, 2004.

Werr, Sebastian, ed., *Eugène Scribe und das europäische Musiktheater*. Berlin: LIT, 2007.

White, Hayden, *Metahistory: The Historical Imagination in Nineteenth-Century Europe*. Baltimore: Johns Hopkins University Press, 1973.

Wightman Fox, Richard, *Lincoln's Body: A Cultural History*. New York: Norton, 2015.

Williams, David, *Condorcet and Modernity*. Cambridge: Cambridge University Press, 2004.

Williams, Linda, *Playing the Race Card: Melodramas of Black and White from Uncle Tom to O. J. Simpson*. Princeton, NJ: Princeton University Press, 2001.

Williams, R. D., "The Sixth Book of the Aeneid," *Greece and Rome*, 2nd ser., 11, 1 (March 1964), 48–63.

Wilson, Forrest, *Crusader in Crinoline: The Life of Harriet Beecher Stowe* (1941). Westport: Greenwood, 1972.

Wilson, James, *The Earth Shall Weep: A History of Native America*. New York: Grove, 1998.

Whatmore, Richard, "Burke on Political Economy," in Dwan and Insole, eds., *The Cambridge Companion to Edmund Burke*, 80–91.

Whatmore, Richard, "The French and North American Revolutions in Comparative Perspective," in Albertone and de Francesco, eds., *Rethinking the Atlantic World*, 219–38.

Wood, Gordon S., *The American Revolution: A History*. London: Phoenix, 2005.

Woolf, Stuart, *Dal primo settecento all'Unità* (*Storia d'Italia*, vol. 3, *La storia politica e sociale*). Turin: Einaudi, 1973.

Wright, Nathalia, *American Novelists in Italy: The Discoverers; Allston to James*. Philadelphia: University of Pennsylvania Press, 1965.

Wyck Brooks, Van, *The Dream of Arcadia: American Writers and Artists in Italy, 1760–1915*. New York: Dutton, 1958.

Yon, Jean-Claude, *Eugène Scribe: La fortune et la liberté*. Saint-Genouph: Nizet, 2000.

Zimmermann, Joachim, *Das Verfassungsprojekt des Grossherzogs Peter Leopold von Toscana*. Heidelberg: Carl Winter, 1901.

Zingarelli, Luciana, "Teatri nuovi e nuova domanda," in Massafra, ed., *Il mezzogiorno preunitario*, 945–64.

Zolo, Danilo, "Governo temporale e 'senso ecclesiastico,'" in Campanini and Traniello, eds., *Filosofia e politica*, 191–99.

Zorzi, Renzo, ed., *L'eredità dell'ottantanove e l'Italia*. Florence: Olschki, 1992.

Lessing, Gotthold Ephraim, 63
Levi, Carlo, 228
liberalism, 15, 24, 35, 38, 40, 48, 61, 79,
    94–98, 100, 108, 115–16, 127, 130–31,
    148–49, 152, 204, 219–21, 252n189,
    256n76, 280n101. *See also* Moderates
Liberals (Italian). *See* liberalism
Liberia, 204
liberty, concepts of, 11–12, 18, 22, 31–32,
    34, 48–49, 54–55, 60, 65, 75–79, 81,
    84–87, 90–93, 96–98, 105–6, 108, 110,
    122, 124, 127–28, 130, 132–33, 135,
    145, 153–54, 157, 159–62, 200–202,
    205, 214, 230, 252n204
Liguria, 118–19, 139, 144. *See also* Genoa
Lima, 174–75
Linati, Claudio, 183, 280n96
Lincoln, Abraham, 160, 195–96, 199–200,
    206, 216–20, 225–27
Lisbon, 174
literacy, 7, 32, 41, 151, 204
Littardi, Tommaso, 57
Livorno, 32, 81; Revolution of 1848, 129,
    141
Livy (Titus Livius), 57
Lloyd Garrison, William, 108
Locke, John, 68, 251n165
Lombardy, 24, 33–34, 41, 46, 50, 59, 65,
    98, 100, 124–25, 135–37, 140, 147, 166,
    168, 176, 229; Revolution of 1848, 6,
    38, 119–134, 137, 140–41, 147, 160
London, 15, 33, 47, 81, 85, 87, 94–96,
    129, 166, 172–74, 180, 201, 216, 220,
    239n123
Londonio, Carlo Giuseppe, 6, 9, 43–45,
    62–66, 69, 72, 180
Longfellow, Henry Wadsworth, 26–27,
    137, 197, 207, 285n22
Louis XV (of France), 69
Louis XVI (of France), 54
Louis Bonaparte. *See* Napoleon III
Louis-Philippe (King of the French), 54,
    75, 87, 94
Lucania, 228
Lucca (Italian city), 86, 136
Lucca (publishing house), 209
Lugano, 126, 136
Lugo di Romagna, 67
Luzzatto, Sergio, 226
Lyon, 117
Lyttelton, Adrian, 130

Mably, Gabriel Bonnot de, 82
Macchi, Mauro, 112, 162
Machiavelli, Niccolò, 22–23, 85, 130, 133
Madison, James, 106, 129
Madrid, 174
Maffei, Andrea, 144
Mafia, 220. *See also* crime
magic, 179, 184–85, 190–91, 281nn104
    and 107, 284n3
Mainz, 128
Malet, Claude François de, 85
Mali, Joseph, 230
Malta, 174
Malvica, Ferdinando, 116
Mancinelli, Luigi, 277n36
Mancini, Pasquale Stanislao, 222
Manin, Daniele, 114
Manzoni, Alessandro, 50, 58–59, 136, 144
Marburg, 128
Mariani, Angelo, 173, 275n4
Maria Theresia (of Austria), 81, 127,
    236n51
Marie-Louise (of Parma), 62
Mario, Alberto, 113, 135, 138
Marletta, Francesco, 158
Marraro, Howard, 19, 237n88
Martineau, Harriet, 12, 236n48
Martinelli, Vincenzo, 33
Marx, Karl, 39, 157
Maryland, 26
Massachusetts, 157, 180–81, 186
materialism, 11, 30, 79, 94, 109–11, 252n3
May, Karl, 28
Maywood, Augusta, 209
Mazzci, Filippo, 11–12, 79, 81–85, 99
Mazzini, Giuseppe, 6, 11, 14–16, 25, 27,
    39–40, 43, 59, 79–80, 87, 89, 93–95,
    102, 108–13, 115, 117, 119, 126–29, 135,
    138, 141, 143, 150, 152, 160–62, 166,
    192, 195, 199, 204, 215–17, 220–21,
    226–28, 238n103, 240n146, 246n56,
    248n92, 284n6
Mazzoni, Giuseppe, 140
Mediterranean, 2, 25, 63, 88, 95–96, 116,
    149, 223, 229, 236n57
Mediterraneo, Il, 207
Melegari, Luigi Amedeo, 110
Melville, Herman, 27, 180, 197
Mercadante, Saverio, 165–66, 191
Mercier, Louis-Sébastien, 12
Messina, 147, 155

St. Petersburg, 174
Straet, Jan van der, 1–2, 233n1
Strafforello, Gustavo, 239n134
Strassburg, 3, 161
Stravinsky, Igor, 197
Stuttgart, 174
Subrahmanyam, Sanjay, 19
superstition, 181. *See also* magic
suffrage, 20, 93, 96, 115, 141–42, 144, 151, 155–56, 220
Sullivan, Jack, 197
Sweden, 2, 165–66, 178, 180, 182, 187–191, 281n117
Switzerland, xi–xii, 7, 15–16, 20, 46, 55, 74, 79, 81, 87, 98–99, 110, 128–29, 135–6, 138, 150, 159–60, 207, 227, 267n98

Tacitus, Publius Cornelius, 57, 229
Taglioni, Paolo, 205
Tamagno, Francesco, 278n48
Tedaldi, Giuseppe, 155
Tell, Wilhelm, 74, 136
Texas, 114
theater, 3–4, 6, 26, 28–30, 40–41, 80, 163, 166, 169, 179, 198, 205, 208–9, 225, 241n155. *See also* opera
Thierry, Auguste, 136
Thom, Martin, 136
Thornton, Robert, 192
Thucydides, 57
Tiepolo, Giovanni Battista, xv, 2–5, 169, 233n7
Time (periodical), 225
time, semantics of, 9, 11, 16, 21, 23, 27, 31–32, 44, 53–54, 60, 68, 73, 80, 89, 100, 102, 107, 179–80, 186, 191–94, 228–31
Tinelli, Luigi, 240n142
Toaldo, Giuseppe, 13
Tocqueville, Alexis de, 12, 22–23, 40, 51, 58, 91–92, 96, 104–7, 110–11, 130–31, 134–35, 140, 145, 162, 201–3, 207, 220, 258n123, 260nn162 and 174, 262n220
Tolstoy, Leo, 286n49
Tommaseo, Niccolò, 257n108
Torelli, Vincenzo, 186, 193
Toscanini, Arturo, 277n36
Toscanini, Walter, 287n71

trade. *See* America: economic life
travel, 9, 11, 15–16, 21–25, 27–28, 33, 40, 89, 128, 139, 148, 165, 177, 188, 202–3
travel writing. *See* travel
Treviso, 29, 277n36
Trier, 128
Trieste, 168, 172
Trollope, Frances, 80, 115. *See also* America: domestic manners
Trovatore, Il (periodical), 174, 189, 209
Turin, 46, 87, 141, 160, 207, 209–10; Teatro Regio, 205, 210
Turkey. *See* Ottoman Empire
Turner, Frederick Jackson, 250n138
Tuscany, 12, 30–33, 41, 67, 81, 87, 100, 147, 160, 214; Revolution of 1848, 6, 38, 81, 119–20, 129, 138–146, 152–53, 183
Tuveri, Giovanni Battista, 121, 160
Twain, Mark, 27

Uncle Tom Shows, 206, 208–9
United Provinces. *See* Netherlands, the
United States of America: agriculture (*see* economic life *this entry*); Bill of Rights, 19, 253n17; Civil War, 5–7, 28, 40–41, 111, 113, 132, 138, 146, 167, 174, 196–97, 200, 204–30; Confederacy, 215, 217–21; Constitution of, xi–xii, 5, 12, 14–23, 34–36, 41, 50, 53, 55, 59–60, 62, 69, 71–72, 81, 86–92, 94–97, 103–5, 108–9, 115, 118–19, 128–34, 138, 145, 150–59, 212, 217, 220–21, 246n51; Declaration of Independence, 19, 202, 238n94, 246n5 (*see also* Revolution: American; War of Independence *this entry*); Democratic Party, 14, 166, 216; demographic development, 8, 34–35, 72, 137; economic life, 12–13, 32–35, 38–39, 43, 48, 55, 64, 66, 69, 72, 79, 82, 88, 132–33, 137, 152, 162, 170, 201–5, 218, 224, 236n57, 240n148 (*see also* slavery); education, 32, 82, 108–9, 220; Emancipation Declaration, 216; expansion of, 14, 60; Founding Fathers, 20, 23, 50; in literature (*see* America: in literature); Pilgrim Fathers, 22, 157; political institutions, xi, 6, 12–16, 19, 22, 33–34, 38–40, 48, 51, 55, 65, 69, 79–84, 89–93, 97, 103, 110, 118–24, 127–33, 139, 144, 151–52,

A NOTE ON THE TYPE

{≈≈≈⊚w⊙≈≈≈}

THIS BOOK has been composed in Miller, a Scotch Roman typeface designed by Matthew Carter and first released by Font Bureau in 1997. It resembles Monticello, the typeface developed for The Papers of Thomas Jefferson in the 1940s by C. H. Griffith and P. J. Conkwright and reinterpreted in digital form by Carter in 2003.

Pleasant Jefferson ("P. J.") Conkwright (1905–1986) was Typographer at Princeton University Press from 1939 to 1970. He was an acclaimed book designer and AIGA Medalist.

The ornament used throughout this book was designed by Pierre Simon Fournier (1712–1768) and was a favorite of Conkwright's, used in his design of the *Princeton University Library Chronicle.*